Level One   Scott, Foresman French Program

Son et Sens

Teacher's Annotated Edition

New Edition

Albert Valdman
Guy MacMillin
Marcel LaVergne
Simon Belasco

Scott, Foresman and Company • Glenview, Illinois

Dallas, Tex. • Oakland, N.J. • Palo Alto, Cal. • Tucker, Ga.

ISBN: 0-673-13014-2

345678910-KPK-8584838281807978

Contents

PART I

SON ET SENS: The Balanced-Skills Approach

Language is basically a complex system of symbols whereby thoughts are transmitted from one person to another through the medium of sound. Thus language is both sound and meaning—*son et sens*. The Scott, Foresman French Program gives appropriate emphasis to both. In addition, sounds have their own written representations, so the spoken and written word are treated interdependently in a balanced-skills approach.

SON ET SENS is audio-lingual inasmuch as we cultivate the listening and speaking skills and stress the importance of proper pronunciation. We provide dictations and listening comprehension exercises, pronunciation drill, and throughout the book offer abundant opportunity for oral practice. Most of the exercises and questionnaires can be handled orally, and in the sections entitled *Lecture et Conversation* (under the headings *Parlons de vous* and *A propos. . .*), we ask the students to talk about themselves, their interests, feelings, and activities.

SON ET SENS is cognitive. At each step of the way the student must understand what he or she is doing. There are explanations and generalizations, presented always in simple, clear language directed to the student, who is never asked to work with material that has not been explained. We discourage useless memorization and suggest no mindless repetition. The exercises are designed to lead to a conscious control of the language system. We have at all times striven to make the learning activities meaningful to the student.

But SON ET SENS is more than audio-lingual or cognitive or a mere combination of the two. It is predicated on the belief that no one or two of the language skills should be emphasized to the neglect of the others. We believe the four skills to be interdependent. Accordingly, the New Edition of the Scott, Foresman French Program retains as its goal student acquisition of *balanced skills*. Each of the skills is given careful treatment in and of itself, but all are consistently intermingled. Our *Lectures* are on tape so that the student can listen and read simultaneously. Similarly, in certain of the listening comprehension exercises, the student reads and listens. Even in our *Dictées,* there is a certain amount of reading and copying. The review sections at the end of each lesson (*Révision et Thème*) are meant to be written, but the comic strip that is the *Thème* lends itself to oral review as well. These are but a few examples of the ways in which SON ET SENS takes into account the interdependence of skills, allowing each to interact with and reinforce the others.

In addition, we use many visuals to help students acquire vocabulary in as real a context as possible and with minimal dependence on English. These drawings are then used as cues or visual stimuli for vocabulary and grammar exercises. This approach is designed to permit students, at a very early point in their study, immediately to associate the French word with the object without first falling back on their native language to arrive at the French equivalent.

Consistent with our position, we do not have separate "culture sections." There is nothing more basic to any culture than the language itself. Thus the French way of life, French attitudes and customs are central to the book, pervading the dialogues, the readings, the line drawings and photographs, and many of the exercises. In this teacher's edition we have included a Cultural Supplement, which may be used to point out the less obvious or otherwise unnoted cultural aspects of each lesson, as well as the photographs and *documents*.

Above all, our efforts have been directed toward the students. We do not pretend that every moment will be fun. We ask them to work; we require them to understand. But the many different types of activities, the varied exercises, the numerous sections and topics within a given lesson afford little opportunity for tedium or indifference. The cartoonlike drawings will amuse as they teach. The *Parlons de vous* and *A propos . . .* will provide opportunities for students to use the language in a personal context. When done in conjunction with the carefully structured *Révisions,* the *Thèmes* will offer that vital sense of accomplishment at the end of each lesson. The brief self-tests *(Vérifiez vos progrès)* that follow each *Explications* section will allow students to make sure they understand the target structure or structures before they move ahead. The longer, end-of-lesson *Auto-Tests* will serve as review for the end-of-lesson tests. (Answers to both types of self-tests appear in the back of the student book.) The varied techniques that we employ have been developed in an effort to reach all students, with their differing interests and differing levels of ability, and to make language-learning a very real and enjoyable activity.

PART II

Components of the Program

The student textbook, SON ET SENS, consists of eighteen lessons illustrated with visuals for presenting vocabulary and for cueing exercises and review. It also includes a unit with full-color photographs of life in France and in certain regions of the French-speaking world, an appendix containing answers to the two types of self-tests found in each lesson, French-English and English-French vocabularies, and a grammatical index.

The combination workbook and tape manual includes additional exercises and learning activities. There are twenty-two lessons in the workbook—one to supplement each lesson in the student book, plus special sections covering Lessons 1–5, 6–9, 10–13, and 14–18. The latter serve as review for the four major tests in the testing program. The tape manual portion contains all of the material necessary to do the special taped exercises.

The tape set contains eighteen tapes, one per lesson, plus teacher's script for all nonbook exercises.

The testing program on duplicating masters provides the teacher with guidelines for evaluating student mastery of structure and vocabulary. There are twenty-two tests—one per lesson, plus major tests covering Lessons 1–5, 6–9, 10–13, and 14–18.

The teacher's annotated edition reproduces the student textbook with overprinted answers and teaching suggestions. It also contains the Cultural Supplement with lesson-by-lesson notes, sample lesson plans and teaching suggestions, a section on how to adapt SON ET SENS for individualized and small-group instruction, and an answer key for the *Révisions* and *Thèmes*.

The second- and third-level texts, SCÈNES ET SÉJOURS and PROMENADES ET PERSPECTIVES, have formats almost identical to that of SON ET SENS. In each case, a smooth transition between levels is effected through early lessons that incorporate important structural review in a fresh context. SCÈNES ET SÉJOURS consists of eighteen lessons; PROMENADES ET PERSPECTIVES, fifteen lessons plus a section of carefully chosen readings.

PART III

The Balancing of Skills

On the left are listed the components of each lesson in SON ET SENS. The shadings on the right indicate the emphasis that the corresponding section places on each of the four language skills:

(dark shading)	great emphasis
(medium shading)	some emphasis

Thus while some sections are designed to strengthen all four skills, others concentrate heavily on only one or two. Together they provide the integrated experience necessary to an ability to understand, speak, read, and write French.

	LISTENING	SPEAKING	READING	WRITING
DIALOGUE / QUESTIONNAIRE	great	great	great	some
PRONONCIATION	great	great		
MOTS NOUVEAUX / EXERCICES	great	great	some	some
EXPLICATIONS / EXERCICES	great	great	great	great
VÉRIFIEZ VOS PROGRÈS			great	great
CONVERSATION ET LECTURE				
PARLONS DE VOUS	great	great		
LECTURE	some	some	great	
A PROPOS . . .	great	great	some	some
RÉVISION			great	great
THÈME			some	great
AUTO-TEST			great	great
PROVERBE		some	some	
POÈME	some	some	great	

Nevertheless, no method, goal, or set of techniques is imposed upon teachers who use the program, and they are free to assign relative weight to particular skills. See Part 5 of this manual, "Flexibility," Part 6, "Sample Lesson Plans," and Part 7, "Individualizing a Lesson."

It goes without saying that the tape program emphasizes listening and speaking; the workbook, reading and writing. However, even here there is a balancing of the skills. We would point particularly to the dictation and listening comprehension exercises:

	LISTENING	SPEAKING	READING	WRITING
DICTÉE	███		▒▒	███
ÉCOUTONS	███		▒▒	

The testing program, available on duplicating masters, includes a pronunciation check for every lesson, as well as a dictation and/or listening comprehension section on every test.

PART IV

Description of a Lesson

DIALOGUE

Each lesson begins with a teen-oriented *Dialogue* that serves as an introduction to the material that follows. The *Dialogues* are idiomatic and culturally authentic. Each is followed by a fully colloquial English version. Beginning with Lesson 3, there is also a brief *Questionnaire,* which, though designed for oral practice, can also be assigned as written homework. Lesson-by-lesson notes in the Cultural Supplement (Part 9 of this manual) point out the cultural aspects of each *Dialogue.*

PRONONCIATION

This section isolates one or more French sounds, offers help in forming them, and provides pertinent drills.

The sounds are first practiced in isolated words, then, where appropriate, in minimal pairs *(vous/vu; sous/su),* and finally in complete sentences, where the student develops an awareness of French rhythm and intonation.

In the interests of pedagogical simplicity and in accord with statistical studies of prevailing speech patterns among educated native speakers of French, where two differing acceptable pronunciations may exist, we offer only one. Thus for the spelling *a* or *â* we use only [a], and not, in addition, [ɑ]. And for such words as *c'est, plaît,* and *maison,* we use only [e], and not, in addition, [ɛ].

Description
of a Lesson

T7

MOTS NOUVEAUX

Each lesson has two *Mots Nouveaux* sections, where new active vocabulary is introduced either in visuals or in a written context—or both. Where possible, the contextual presentations are in the form of mini-dialogues, so that students can have additional exposure to communication models.

Each *Mots Nouveaux* section has its own set of *Exercices de vocabulaire* designed to lighten the task of vocabulary acquisition. Numerous types of exercises are used: visual, question-answer, which word best fits the context?, which is the logical response?, etc. Special care is given throughout the book to regular re-entry of the vocabulary presented in the *Mots Nouveaux*.

EXPLICATIONS

Every lesson has two *Explications* sections, each of which presents one or more grammatical points. In the *Explications,* the various aspects of a given grammar topic are presented in a series of numbered subpoints, with clear examples and in language directed to the student. The explanations are followed by abundant and varied exercises, arranged in order of difficulty and generally following the sequence of the subpoints.

From time to time a brief *Vocabulaire* is presented at the beginning of an *Explications* section. These are new words that were held back from the *Mots Nouveaux* because students would not have been able to use them appropriately at that point in the lesson. For example, several -*er* verbs are presented in a *Vocabulaire,* followed immediately by an explanation of their structural implications. The lexical items in the *Vocabulaires,* together with those in the *Mots Nouveaux,* constitute the active vocabulary of SON ET SENS.

Vérifiez vos progrès, a brief self-test, follows each of the *Explications* sections. Here the students check their own understanding of the grammatical material just presented and practiced. Answers appear in the back of the student book.

CONVERSATION ET LECTURE

This section, which comes between *Explications I* and *II,* has, in most instances, three parts:

Description
of a Lesson

1. *Parlons de vous* Beginning in Lesson 4, we offer questions that allow students to talk about themselves—their families, their daily lives, their interests, opinions, plans, and ambitions. This section re-enters known vocabulary and structure in such a way that students can readily see that French, like their native language, is a tool for self-expression.
2. *Lecture* In all lessons there is a reading in which previously learned vocabulary and structures are recombined in a new context. Some new—passive—vocabulary also appears in each reading.
3. *A propos . . .* These questionnaires, which check student comprehension of the reading, are a constant element after Lesson 1. In addition, beginning in Lesson 5, they end in a series of personalized questions that are designed to bring about stronger individual participation in the reading and to re-emphasize the conversational aspects of the *Conversation et Lecture* section.

RÉVISION ET THÈME

This section consists of a two-part summary and review of the vocabulary and structures presented in the lesson:
1. *Révision* Here the student is given a French sentence. Beneath it are English phrases or sentences that are to be put into French. When correctly completed, the student will have formed two sentences that are in every way structurally identical to the model. There are a series of four, five, or six such models in every *Révision,* each designed to review one or more specific grammar points.
2. *Thème* This is a cartoon strip of four, five, or six panels. Each panel has an English sentence beneath it which represents the dialogue or describes the scene. The sentences in the cartoon strip are structurally identical to the model sentences in the *Révision.* Upon rendering them into French in paragraph form, the student will have written a unified French *Thème.*

AUTO-TEST

This is an end-of-lesson self-test, which covers the vocabulary and grammar topics of the lesson. Just as the *Révision et Thème* will help the student review for doing the *Auto-Test,* so the latter will help the student prepare for the end-of-lesson classroom test offered on duplicating masters. Answers appear in the back of the student book.

PROVERBE / POÈME

Beginning in Lesson 7, each lesson ends with a French proverb accompanied by a cartoon visual.

The following poems by Jacques Prévert appear in the book: "Refrains enfantins," "Mea Culpa," "Page d'écriture," and "Déjeuner du matin." In addition, the words to the popular French songs "Au clair de la lune" and "Sur le pont d'Avignon" are included.

These two sections have been included purely for enjoyment. Students should be able to read and understand them independently, but they may also enjoy reading them aloud and discussing them in class.

PART V

Flexibility

The materials in this program are carefully designed to provide a balanced approach to French language-learning skills. We emphasize no one of the skills to the neglect of the others. This balanced-skills orientation is illustrated by the charts on pages 6–7.

In accord with its balanced-skills framework and as a corollary to it, SON ET SENS is flexible. No methods, goals, or sets of techniques are imposed. The design of the materials leaves the teacher free to use them in a way that best corresponds to the needs, abilities, and interests of the class, and to the course objectives set out in the curriculum for level-one French in each school.

Thus SON ET SENS is adaptable to

. . . Individualized or small-group instruction. (See Part 7 of this supplement.)

. . . A variety of modes of presentation and practice. Some suggestions for classroom procedures follow.

DIALOGUE

Play tape, asking students to listen then repeat (books closed)

or: Play tape, asking students to listen then repeat (books open)

You may want

to interrupt the tape to ask simple factual questions

to assign roles and let students read parts aloud

to return to the *Dialogue* from time to time as warm-up for class period

The English equivalent of the *Dialogue* may be introduced first to familiarize students with new vocabulary or it may be left solely for student reference. If the latter, students should be forewarned not to look for one-to-one correspondences. Both the French and the English are in the natural, idiomatic language of today.

QUESTIONNAIRE

Handle orally in class after student preparation at home

or: Handle orally without previous preparation (this will be more successful in later lessons)

or: Handle as written homework to be gone over in class

You may want
> to expand upon the questions by asking for fuller, more informative answers than are absolutely necessary (*quand? comment? pourquoi?*)

PRONONCIATION

Play tape, asking students to listen then repeat (books open)
or: Play tape, asking students to listen then repeat (books closed)

You may want
> to use the section over several days, doing one exercise per day
> to handle pronunciation chorally and/or individually
> to ask students to turn to the *Dialogue* to find examples of a given sound
> to ask students to give other examples from previously learned vocabulary of words that contain a given sound
> to interrupt the tape to ask students to deduce how a given sound is spelled
> to write unknown words containing the target sound on the board, asking students to pronounce them
> to ask students to write words on the board as they hear them spoken on the tape or by you (this can work particularly well with minimal pairs)
> to use the section primarily as a lab assignment

MOTS NOUVEAUX

For new words presented visually
> Use synonyms, related words, gestures, or act out the new words (books closed)
or: Use the visuals in the book, asking students to repeat the words after you

For new words not presented visually
> Write the sentences from the book on the board, acting out or using gestures, etc., to teach meaning
or: Read sentences from the book aloud, asking students to cover the English equivalents

or: Read sentences aloud, allowing students to refer to the English
or: Use the sentences to create mini-dialogues

You may want
> to ask questions using the words just introduced
> to ask students to use all forms of a new adjective in brief sentences
> to ask students to use a new verb in all its forms if it follows a previously learned conjugation
> to have frequent reviews and occasional vocabulary quizzes

Exercices, see p. 12.

EXPLICATIONS (VERBS)

Introduce verbs orally (books open)
or: Introduce orally (books closed, perhaps with the paradigm on the board)

You may want
> to teach those forms that sound alike first
> to make some use of the verb explanations or leave them for student reference only
> to drill verbs orally, using simple substitution, before doing the exercises in the book

Exercices, see p. 12.

EXPLICATIONS (OTHER THAN VERBS)

Introduce orally (books closed), writing examples on the board
or: Introduce orally (books open)
or: Ask students to study the section first as homework

You may want
> to give examples in addition to those in the book
> to ask students to explain the grammar point in their own words
> to ask students to give further examples, once they have grasped the concept
> to use any simple drills that you have found successful before doing the exercises in the book
> to intersperse grammar presentation with exercises (sidenotes in the teacher's edition point out when exercises can be done)

Exercices, see p. 12.
Vérifiez vos progrès, see *Auto-Test,* p. 11.

Flexibility

CONVERSATION ET LECTURE

Handle the *Parlons de vous* orally in class (books closed)

or: Handle orally in class (books open or after student preparation at home)

Play tape of the *Lecture* while students read silently

or: Play tape while students listen (books closed)

You may want

to interrupt the tape to ask simple factual questions

to give students in advance a few questions that they will have to answer after listening to the tape (this will give focus to their listening)

to ask students to cover the glossed words and try to figure out their meaning from context or derivation

to go over glossed words in advance

to assign roles and ask students to read aloud after listening to the tape

to assign the reading as homework or lab work (this will be more successful in later lessons)

to handle the *A propos . . .* orally in class after preparation at home or without preparation

to handle the *A propos . . .* as written homework to be gone over in class

to intersperse personalized questions throughout the lesson

to use visuals to stimulate conversation

to elaborate on any questions that particularly interest students

to use the *Parlons de vous* and *A propos . . .* as a basis for creating personalized questions tailored to your particular class (only questions whose answers are within the lexical and grammatical competence of the student are asked in the book)

RÉVISION ET THÈME

Assign the *Révision* as homework to be gone over in class

or: Do the *Révision* orally in class

Assign the *Thème* as homework

or: Handle it in class, with students writing one sentence at a time on the board

You may want

to create further substitutions based on the models to give additional practice and review

to use items in the *Révision* for quizzing the class on particular grammar points

to emphasize (1) that the *Révision* is review, and thus students should ask questions on points they don't understand, and (2) that it is also preparation for the *Thème*

to use the comic strip as a stimulus for conversation or class discussion

AUTO-TEST

These self-tests, along with the *Vérifiez vos progrès* following each *Explications* section, are designed to be done by the students so that they may assess their own progress. With the single exception of Exercise A, page 183, the answers to all self-test exercises appear in the back of the student book.

You may want to emphasize the importance *to the students* of the *Vérifiez* and *Auto-Tests* and, at times, to devote a couple of minutes of class time to explaining any unusual exercise procedures.

Vérifiez vos progrès: You might assign these in lieu of, or in addition to, a regular homework assignment or specifically as preparation for a quiz. Encourage students to bring to class any questions they might have concerning the correct answers. (A quiz might occasionally be given that is very closely based on the particular *Vérifiez*. This can help students recognize that an acceptance of responsibility for one's own progress can bring a very real sense of achievement.)

Auto-Tests: We would recommend that these be assigned as homework two evenings before the end-of-lesson test (available on duplicating masters) is to be administered. This will give students an opportunity to identify any areas of uncertainty and to bring their questions to class the day before the test.

Though we do not recommend that you assign the *Vérifiez* or *Auto-Tests* as homework that "must" be done, or that you devote valuable class time to working through material for which the answers are already provided, we nonetheless urge you to express your availability to help with any problems and to answer any questions that may arise.

PROVERBE

Point the proverbs out

or: Allow students to discover these on their own

You may want

to use these as the basis for conversation in French, with students explaining what is happening in the cartoon or, if they are able, giving further examples or visual illustrations of the proverbs

POÈME

Read aloud in class

or: Play tape (books open)

or: Allow students to discover these on their own

You may want

to discuss the poems in English if the class expresses any desire to do so

EXERCICES

Most of the exercises in SON ET SENS are designed to be used either orally or in writing—or both.

It is a good idea to make certain that students understand the mechanics and the object of a given exercise when assigning it as written homework. The exercises have been developed to give students practice toward mastery. Getting them off to a good start by making sure that they know what to do will help make that practice effective.

It is advisable to check homework, the sooner the better. This can be done by providing answer sheets for student self-correction; by letting students exchange papers and correct each other as you read aloud the correct answers; by asking students to write their answers on the board and letting the class correct them, which allows you to circulate and to make certain that students are correcting their work; and, occasionally, by collecting papers and checking student progress yourself. In all instances it is worth taking the time to help students understand their errors.

PART VI

Sample Lesson Plans

Several lesson plans are presented here as representative. They illustrate the variety of ways in which the lesson elements can be handled.

Lessons 2 and 17, according to the following plans, take eight days; Lesson 7, nine days; Lesson 13, ten days. There is, however, no magic figure for the number of days *any* lesson should take, no "average" number of days prescribed. The adaptability of the program

to differing course goals, abilities and interests of students, and modes of teacher presentation and practice preclude the establishment of a rigid set of guidelines.

Note that the order "go over—present—do" has been followed for clarity of presentation only. It is not intended that such an ordering necessarily be followed within the class period. On the contrary, a certain amount of variety in your presentation can help maintain interest and enthusiasm.

In each lesson plan we have arranged for class days with lighter loads. On those days you might use the taped *Dictées* and *Ecoutons* (listening comprehension exercises) or certain of the vocabulary and structure exercises that are unique to the tape program.

LEVEL I		ONE-YEAR PROGRAM		LESSON 2
DAY	GO OVER	PRESENT	DO	ASSIGN
1	Test on Lesson 1	Dialogue, p. 13 Mots Nouveaux I, pp. 16–17	Ex. A, p. 18	Mots Nouveaux I, pp. 16–17 Write Ex. B, p. 18 Study Ex. C, p. 18
2	Homework Dialogue	Les Accents, p. 15 Mots Nouveaux II, p. 19	Prononciation, Ex. A, p. 14 Ex. C, p. 18	Write Ex. B, p. 20
3	Homework Mots Nouveaux II Dialogue	Les pronoms et le verbe *aller*, pp. 21–22	Ex. A, p. 20 Practice imperative (see Sidenote, p. 22)	Write Ex. A, p. 22 Read Lecture, p. 23
4	Homework	Lecture, p. 23	Prononciation, Ex. B, p. 14 Ex. B, p. 22 A propos . . . , p. 23	Vérifiez, pp. 22–23, in preparation for quiz on vo- cabulary & *aller*
5	Answer questions arising from the Vérifiez Lecture	10-minute quiz Le pluriel des noms, pp. 23–24	Ex., p. 24 (items 2–3)	Write Ex., p. 24 Study *De* possessif, p. 25
6	Quiz Homework *De* possessif		Ex., p. 25 Prononciation, Ex. C, p. 14 Drill on Les accents	Vérifiez, p. 26 Write Révision, p. 26
7	Answer questions arising from the Vérifiez Révision		Thème, p. 26	Auto-Test, p. 27
8	Answer questions arising from the Auto-Test Thème		Expand Révision for further review Redo & expand Ex. C, p. 18	Prepare for test on Lesson 2
9	*Test on Lesson 2			

*You may want to give a test of your own, a test from the SON ET SENS testing program, or no test at all. If a shorter test is given, the remainder of the class period may be devoted to personalized questions, to learning a song or playing a game, or to a presentation of the *Dialogue* from the next lesson.

LEVEL I	ONE-YEAR PROGRAM		LESSON 7
DAY	**GO OVER**	**PRESENT**	**DO**	**ASSIGN**
---	---	---	---	---
1	Test on Lesson 6	Dialogue, p. 97 Mots Nouveaux I, p. 99	Prononciation, Ex. A, p. 98	Write Ex. A, p. 100 Study Questionnaire, p. 98 Study Ex. B, p. 100
2	Homework Dialogue	Mots Nouveaux II, p. 101	Questionnaire, p. 98 Ex. B, p. 100 Ex. A, p. 102	Write Exs. B – C, p. 102
3	Homework	Les verbes en -ir/ -iss-. p. 103	Ex. D, p. 102 A pattern drill on -ir/-iss- verbs	Write Ex., p. 104 Study Les nombres 21 – 69, p. 104
4	Homework Les nombres 21 – 69	5-minute quiz on Mots Nouveaux	Ex. B, p. 105 Parlons de vous, p. 106	Write Ex. A, p. 105 Read Lecture, p. 106 Study A propos . . . , p. 107
5	Homework	Lecture, p. 106	Prononciation, Ex. B, p. 98 A propos . . . , p. 107	Vérifiez, p. 105, in preparation for dictée
6	Answer questions arising from the Vérifiez	5-minute dictée Les déterminants indéfinis, p. 108 (points 1 – 3)	Correct dictée Ex. A, p. 109 Révision, p. 112 (items 1 – 3)	Write Exs. C – D, p. 110
7	Homework Révision (items 1 – 3)	Les déterminants indéfinis, p. 108 (point 4)	Exs. B & E, pp. 109 – 110 Révision, p. 112 (items 4 – 6)	Vérifiez, p. 111 Write Thème, p. 112
8	Answer questions arising from the Vérifiez Thème			Auto-Test, p. 113
9	Answer questions arising from the Auto-Test		Conversation based on art & photos, pp. 96, 102, 112	Prepare for test on Lesson 7
10	Test on Lesson 7			

LEVEL I		ONE-YEAR PROGRAM		LESSON 13
DAY	**GO OVER**	**PRESENT**	**DO**	**ASSIGN**
1	Test on Lesson 12	Dialogue, p. 205 Mots Nouveaux I, p. 207		Write Questionnaire, p. 206 Write Ex., p. 208
2	Homework Dialogue	Mots Nouveaux II, pp. 208–209	Prononciation, Exs. A–C, p. 206	Write Ex. B, p. 210
3	Homework	Les verbes *voir* et *croire*, p. 211 Proverbe, p. 223 *A qui, à quoi*, p. 212	Ex. A, p. 210 Exs. A–B, pp. 211– 212	Write Ex. A, p. 211 (items 7–9) Write Ex. B, p. 212 Write Ex. on *à qui, à quoi*, p. 212
4	Homework	Les adjectifs pluriels placés avant le nom, p. 213	Exs. A–B, p. 213	Vérifiez, p. 214, in preparation for quiz
5	Answer questions arising from the Vérifiez	10-minute quiz Lecture, pp. 214–216	Parlons de vous, p. 214	Read Lecture Write A propos . . . , p. 216 (ques- tions 1–6)
6	Quiz Lecture	Les pronoms complé- ments d'objet direct, pp. 216– 217 (points 1–3)	A propos . . . , p. 216	Study Les pronoms compléments (points 1–3) Write Ex. A, p. 217
7	Homework Dialogue	Les pronoms complé- ments, p. 217 (points 4–6)	Exs. C–E, pp. 217– 218	Write Ex. B, p. 217 Write Ex. F, p. 218
8	Homework	Les nombres et les dates, p. 219	Prononciation, Ex. D, p. 206 Ex. B, p. 220 Révision, p. 221 (items 1–3)	Prepare to do Ex. A, p. 219, in class Vérifiez, p. 220
9	Answer questions arising from the Vérifiez		Ex. A, p. 219 Révision (items 4–5) Thème, p. 221	Auto-Test, p. 222
10	Answer questions arising from the Auto-Test	Poème, p. 223	Review through dis- cussion of art, pp. 207–209	Prepare for test on Lesson 13
11	Test on Lesson 13			

LEVEL I		ONE-YEAR PROGRAM		LESSON 17
DAY	GO OVER	PRESENT	DO	ASSIGN
1	Test on Lesson 16	Dialogue, p. 279 Mots Nouveaux I, p. 281	Ex., p. 281	Write Questionnaire, p. 280 Study Mots Nou- veaux I
2	Dialogue Homework	Mots Nouveaux II, pp. 282–283	Prononciation, Exs. A–B, p. 280	Write Ex., p. 284
3	Homework	Le verbe *venir*, pp. 284–285 Au clair de la lune, p. 294	Ex. A, p. 285	Write Ex. C, p. 286
4	Homework	Le passé composé avec *être*, pp. 286–287	Ex. B, p. 285 Ex. A, p. 287	Write Exs. B & D, pp. 287–288
5	Collect homework	Lecture, pp. 289– 290	Prononciation, Ex. C, p. 280 Exs. C–D, p. 288 Parlons de vous, p. 289	Write A propos . . . , p. 291 (ques- tions 1–6) Vérifiez, p. 288, in preparation for quiz
6	Answer questions arising from the Vérifiez Lecture	5-minute quiz Continents, pays et villes, p. 291	A propos . . . , p. 291 Révision, p. 293 (items 4–6)	Write Ex. A, p. 292 Vérifiez, p. 292
7	Homework Answer questions arising from the Vérifiez	Sur le pont d'Avi- gnon, p. 295	Exs. B–C, p. 292 Révision, p. 293 (items 1–3)	Auto-Test, p. 294 *or* Thème, p. 293
8	Answer questions arising from the Auto-Test		Thème, p. 293 Discuss Proverbe, p. 295	Prepare for test on Lesson 17
9	Test on Lesson 17			

The chart that follows takes Lesson 7 as an example to show how a lesson might be organized for classes that spread Level One over two years. Again, there is no prescribed average number of days for each lesson.

LEVEL I		TWO-YEAR PROGRAM		LESSON 7
DAY	GO OVER	PRESENT	DO	ASSIGN
1	Test on Lesson 6	Dialogue, p. 97		Study Questionnaire, p. 98
2	Dialogue		Questionnaire, p. 98 Prononciation, Ex. A, p. 98	Write Questionnaire, p. 98
3	Dialogue Prononciation, Ex. A	Mots Nouveaux I, p. 99	Ex. A, p. 100	Write Ex. A, p. 100 Study Ex. B, p. 100
4	Homework	Mots Nouveaux II, p. 101	Ex. B, p. 100	Write Ex. A, p. 102
5	Homework	Les verbes en -ir/ -iss-, p. 103	Exs. B–C, p. 102	Write Ex., p. 104
6	Homework	Les nombres 21–69, p. 104	Ex. D, p. 102	Write Ex. A, p. 105 Study Ex. B, p. 105
7	Homework Mots Nouveaux I–II		Prononciation, Ex. B, p. 98 Ex. B, p. 105	Vérifiez, p. 105, in preparation for quiz
8	Answer questions arising from the Vérifiez	10-minute quiz		Study Parlons de vous, p. 106
9	Quiz	Lecture, p. 106	Parlons de vous, p. 106	Read Lecture, p. 106 Write A propos . . . , p. 107 (ques- tions 1–8)
10	Lecture	Les déterminants indéfinis, p. 108 (points 1–3)	A propos . . . , p. 107	Write Exs. C–D, p. 110
11	Homework	Les déterminants indéfinis, p. 108 (point 4)	Exs. A–B, pp. 109– 110	Write Ex. E, p. 110
12	Homework Lecture		Révision, p. 112 (items 1–3)	Vérifiez, p. 111

(continued)

(Continued)

	LEVEL I	TWO-YEAR PROGRAM		LESSON 7
DAY	GO OVER	PRESENT	DO	ASSIGN
13	Answer questions arising from the Vérifiez Les nombres 21–69		Révision, p. 112 (items 4–6)	Write Thème, p. 112
14	Thème			Auto-Test, p. 113 Exs. A–B
15	Answer questions arising from the Auto-Test	Proverbe	Expand Révision for further review	Auto-Test, p. 113, Ex. C
16	Answer questions arising from the Auto-Test		Conversation based on art & photos, pp. 96, 102, 112	Prepare for test on Lesson 7
17	Test on Lesson 7			

PART VII

Individualizing a Lesson

by Florence Steiner[1]

The following plan is one of many possible models for adapting a lesson to individualized learning.

Since in a program of individualized instruction, the student works largely on his own, he must be provided with certain introductory information and guidelines. He must know what he will have to work with, together with the conditions under which he will be asked to perform, and the minimum standard of performance expected of him. He must, therefore, be provided with:

1. A set of performance objectives, clearly stating the goals to be achieved and the maximum number of errors he can make and still maintain a satisfactory level of achievement.

2. A suggested plan of study.

3. Tapes, or access to tapes.

4. Self-tests so that he can assess his own progress.

5. A key for checking self-tests and text and tape exercises.

6. A schedule or calendar listing group sessions, hours when the teacher is available to meet with individual students, and test days.

Using Lesson 13 as an example, we have created some possible performance objectives, a student study-plan, and sample self-tests. In regard to the study plan, you may want to encourage the student to discover what works well for him and to adapt the study plan to his own needs.

Though much of the material in SON ET SENS can be easily handled outside of class, sections like *Mots Nouveaux, Parlons de vous,* and the *Questionnaires* are designed for group interaction and are so designated in the study plan.

---

[1]This section, written by Dr. Steiner for the first edition, has been altered only where necessary to reflect changes made in the new edition. Lesson 13, on which the section is based, is equivalent to Lesson 10 in the first edition.

STUDENT PLAN (Sample for Lesson 13)

PERFORMANCE OBJECTIVES	PROCEDURES
DIALOGUE / QUESTIONNAIRE	
The student shall be able to:	The student should:
1. Read aloud the *Dialogue* in French with pronunciation acceptable to the teacher. Maximum: 2 errors. 2. Answer orally in French, with correct structure and acceptable pronunciation, 4 questions from the *Questionnaire*. Maximum: 2 errors of structure, vocabulary, or pronunciation.	1. Look at the French *Dialogue*, p. 205, and, if necessary, check the English verson for meaning. 2. Listen to the *Dialogue* on the tape while following the French in the text. 3. Repeat the *Dialogue* in the pauses provided. 4. Write out answers to the *Questionnaire*, p. 206. Check with the Key. 5. Attend class or group session for oral practice on the *Dialogue* and *Questionnaire*. 6. Do Self-Test 1. Check with the Key.[1] You are now ready to be tested on Performance Objectives 1 – 2.
PRONONCIATION	
3. Pronounce acceptably 10 words chosen from *Prononciation*. Maximum: 2 errors of pronunciation.	1. Do *Prononciation* and Exs. A – C, p. 206, with the tape. 2. Read to your teacher (or an aide) the words in Exs. A – C, p. 206, to check your pronunciation. 3. Do Ex. D, p. 206, with the tape. You are now ready to be tested on Performance Objective 3.

[1]See pages 24 – 25 for examples of Self-Tests. Ideally the teacher would prepare two forms of each Self-Test so that the student who makes mistakes on Form A may study the material again and retest himself.

PERFORMANCE OBJECTIVES	PROCEDURES

MOTS NOUVEAUX

The student shall be able to:	The student should:
4. Give orally with acceptable pronunciation the French equivalent of 10 words from *Mots Nouveaux I* and *II* in response to visuals or English cues. Maximum: 2 errors of meaning or pronunciation. 5. Write correctly the French equivalent of 10 words from *Mots Nouveaux I* and *II* in response to visuals or English cues. Maximum: 2 errors of meaning or spelling.	1. Attend class or group session where *Mots Nouveaux I*, p. 207, are pronounced and practiced. 2. Write Ex., p. 208. Check with the Key. 3. Do Self-Test 2. Check with the Key. 4. Attend class or group session where *Mots Nouveaux II*, pp. 208–209, are pronounced and practiced. 5. Write Exs. A–B, p. 210. Check with the Key. 6. Do Self-Test 3. Check with the Key. You are now ready to be tested on Performance Objectives 4–5.

VOIR, CROIRE

6. Pronounce and write correctly the present tense of *voir* and *croire*. Maximum: 1 error of pronunciation and 1 error of spelling. 7. Answer orally with correct structure and pronunciation 5 questions using *voir* and *croire*. Maximum: 2 errors of structure, vocabulary, or pronunciation.	1. Pronounce the present tense forms of the verbs *voir* and *croire*, p. 211, with your teacher. Note the spelling. 2. Write Exs. A–B, pp. 211–212. Check with the Key. 3. Do Self-Test 4. Check with the Key. You are now ready to be tested on Performance Objectives 6–7.

À QUI, À QUOI

8. Change 6 statements to written questions using *à qui* and *à quoi*. Maximum: 2 errors of structure or spelling. 9. Answer orally in French 6 questions in which *à qui* and *à quoi* are used. Maximum: 2 errors of structure or vocabulary.	1. Study explanation under *à qui* and *à quoi*, p. 212. Summarize it in your own words. Review *Mots Nouveaux I* and *II*. 2. Write Ex., p. 212. Check with the Key. 3. Do Self-Test 5. Check with the Key. You are now ready to be tested on Performance Objectives 8–9.

PERFORMANCE OBJECTIVES	PROCEDURES
LES ADJECTIFS PLURIELS	
The student shall be able to:	The student should:
10. Read aloud in French with correct liaisons 8 sentences containing plural adjectives coming before the noun. Maximum: 1 liaison error.	1. Read aloud the model sentences in point 1, *Les adjectifs pluriels,* p. 213. Note all the liaisons. Summarize the explanations in your own words. 2. Write Exs. A – B, p. 213, marking the liaisons. 3. Attend class or group session for oral practice on Exs. A – B, p. 213. 4. Write the *Vérifiez vos progrès,* p. 214. You are now ready to be tested on Performance Objective 10.
CONVERSATION ET LECTURE	
11. Answer orally in French 5 questions from *Parlons de vous* or other similar questions. Maximum: 2 errors of structure or vocabulary. 12. Read aloud with correct pronunciation the opening paragraph of the *Lecture.* Maximum: 1 error of pronunciation. 13. Answer orally in French, with open book, 5 questions from the *A propos . . .* Maximum: 2 errors of structure, vocabulary, or pronunciation.	1. Practice with a classmate the questions in *Parlons de vous,* p. 214. 2. Attend class or group session and participate in the conversation. 3. Listen to the tape while following the *Lecture,* pp. 214–216. 4. Reread the *Lecture* without the tape. 5. Listen to the tape again. 6. Reread the *Lecture* silently and make note of any part you do not understand; attend class or group session or see your teacher and ask questions. 7. Write answers to the questions in the *A propos . . . ,* p. 216. Check with the Key. 8. Attend a class or group session for oral practice on the *A propos . . .* You are now ready to be tested on Performance Objectives 11–13.

PERFORMANCE OBJECTIVES	PROCEDURES
PRONOMS COMPLÉMENTS D'OBJET DIRECT	
The student shall be able to:	The student should:
14. Rewrite 10 French sentences (negative or affirmative) that contain a direct object, substituting the correct form of the object pronoun and placing it correctly in the sentence. Maximum: 2 pronoun or structure errors.	1. Study explanations 1–3 under *Les pronoms compléments d'objet direct*, pp. 216–217. Summarize them in your own words.
	2. Copy the sentences in the first column of point 1, underlining the noun direct objects. Compare them with the direct object pronouns in the second column.
	3. Copy sentences in Exs. A, C, and E, pp. 217–218, underlining the direct object. Next to each sentence, write the object pronoun to be substituted. Rewrite the sentence, substituting the object pronoun for the noun. Check with the Key.
	4. Study point 4; write Exs. B and D, pp. 217–218. Check with the Key.
	5. Study point 5; write Ex. F, p. 218. Check with the Key.
	6. Do Self-Test 6. Check with the Key.
	You are now ready to be tested on Performance Objective 14.
LES NOMBRES ET LES DATES	
15. Count in French from 70–100. Maximum: 2 errors in counting or pronunciation.	1. Attend class or group sessions for pronunciation and oral work on *Les nombres*, p. 219.
16. Give the solutions in arabic numerals to 10 arithmetic problems written in French. Maximum: 1 arithmetical error.	2. Do Exs. A–B, pp. 219–220, orally with your teacher.
	3. Count orally from 1–100 by 10's.
17. Read aloud in French with correct pronunciation 3 dates given in English, such as: July 14, 1789, your birth date, today's date. Maximum: 3 errors in numbers or pronunciation.	4. Write the *Vérifiez vos progrès*, p. 220.
	You are now ready to be tested on Performance Objectives 15–17.

PERFORMANCE OBJECTIVES	PROCEDURES

RÉVISION ET THÈME

The student shall be able to:	The student should:
18. Given a three-line segment from the *Révision,* put the English cues into written French. Time limit: 3 minutes. Maximum: 2 errors of spelling; 1 error of vocabulary; no errors of structure. 19. Write the *Thème.* Maximum: 5 errors of structure or spelling.	1. Prepare the *Révision,* p. 221, in writing. Check with the Key. If you have questions, write them in your notebook and ask your teacher. 2. Write the *Thème.* Check with the Key. You are now ready to be tested on Performance Objectives 18–19.

SELF-TESTS

General Directions for all Self-Tests: Do the test. Check answers with the Key. If you made errors, review the material and do Form B[1] of the test before continuing to the next section on the Student Plan.

(Samples of typical exercises)

SELF-TEST 1
Dialogue (p. 205)

A. Complete the *Dialogue* by writing the missing words:
Hamidou va travailler pour Air Mali. *(He is training for six months)* à Boston pour apprendre l'anglais. Un jour, après ses cours, *(he runs into)* Thierry, un autre jeune Noir.

HAMIDOU *(You're making progress)* en anglais!

B. Answer in French:
1. Que fait Hamidou à Boston?
2. Qui est-ce qu'il rencontre?

———————

[1]Ideally the Self-Tests would be available in two forms.

SELF-TEST 2
Mots Nouveaux I (p. 207)

A. Write the French equivalent for the following:
1. job
2. work
3. engineer

B. Write the definite determiner for each of the words below. If the word begins with a vowel or mute *h,* indicate the gender:
1. _____ boutique
2. _____ avocate
3. _____ juge

SELF-TEST 3
Mots Nouveaux II (pp. 208–209)

A. Complete the following sentences:
1. Le _____ est dans l'armée ("army").
2. Dans ce théâtre on va jouer une _____.
3. Une _____ inconnue va jouer le _____ principal.
4. Un _____ travaille à la poste.

B. Answer the following questions in French:
1. Qui travaille chez elle?
2. Qui travaille dans une usine?
3. Où travaille une femme d'affaires?

A. Write the correct form of *voir* or *croire:*
1. Nous _____ des marins avec ces soldats.
2. Ils _____ que la pharmacie est loin d'ici.
3. Tu _____ le petit chien gris?

B. Answer the following questions:
1. Qu'est-ce que vous voyez? (le cochon)
2. Qui voit l'infirmière? (nous)
3. Qui croit que la réponse est correcte?
   (le professeur et l'étudiant)

C. Write the correct form of the verb:
1. Est-ce que vous *(voir)* cette boutique?
2. Je *(croire)* que ce sont des vendeurs.
3. Nous *(croire)* que la ferme est près d'ici.

SELF-TEST 5
A qui, à quoi   (p. 212)

A. Answer the questions using the cues in parentheses:
   Model: 1. A qui est-ce que tu penses? (l'hôtesse
   de l'air) *Je pense à l'hôtesse de l'air.*

2. A qui est-ce que vous pensez? (le pharmacien)
3. A quoi est-ce qu'elle joue? (les cartes)
4. A quoi est-ce qu'il pense? (la lettre)

B. Look at each statement below and write a question
   using the verb *penser* and the appropriate expression
   à qui or *à quoi:*
   Model: 1. L'avocat pense au juge. *A qui est-ce que
   l'avocat pense?*

2. Les étudiants pensent aux examens de
   maths.
3. L'acteur pense à son rôle.

SELF-TEST 6   (pp. 216–217)
Pronoms compléments d'objet direct

Rewrite the following sentences replacing all under-
lined words with pronouns:
1. Je ne vois pas les employés.
2. Elles apprennent leurs rôles par cœur.
3. Il faut voir le médecin.
4. Tu ne vas pas regarder la télé?

PART VIII

Techniques for Teaching Certain Key Concepts

by Florence Steiner[1]

We have chosen to use verbs, direct object pronouns,
and the partitive construction in order to offer some
ideas on how to present material graphically using the
overhead projector. The techniques exemplified here
can be adapted to a broad range of presentation and
practice situations in teaching SON ET SENS.

[1]This section, written by Dr. Steiner for the first edition, has
been altered only where necessary to reflect changes made in
the new edition.

TEACHING VERBS

Try to avoid letting students feel overwhelmed with verbs. Let verbs develop systematically, but simply and naturally. The following considerations may be helpful.

1. Does the student know the MEANING of the verb? Teach the infinitive meaning as a vocabulary item before using the inflections. A good way to do this is by using the verb as a completing infinitive in questions:

> Qui aime **chanter?**
> Qui aime **danser?**

2. Does the student understand the various PERSONS of the verb?
Students who have never studied a second language need help with *tu* and *vous, ils* and *elles,* and *on.*

3. Does the student understand the FORMATION OF THE TENSE being studied?
The presentation of a tense poses the problem of the differences between the spoken and written forms.

 It is easier to begin with the spoken forms. In this way teacher and student can communicate easily, using a number of the forms along with familiar vocabulary.

Tu vois le tableau?	Oui, **je vois** le tableau.
Il voit le tableau?	Oui, **il voit** le tableau.
Et elle?	**Elle voit** le tableau aussi.
Qui voit le pilote?	Les hôtesses de l'air **voient** le pilote.

4. Does the student know the ENGLISH EQUIVALENT of the tense being studied?

5. Does the student recognize the IRREGULARITY in an irregular verb?
Introduce the irregular verb orally, as mentioned above, so that the student can first hear the spoken forms that vary. When you present the written form, they will then see the forms that vary in writing. Point out that an irregular verb doesn't usually mean six new forms to memorize.

THE FORMATION OF TENSES: PASSÉ COMPOSÉ   Lesson 11

The basic questions posed above apply also to the formation of tenses. Before presenting a new tense:

1. Drill the meanings of the verbs you expect to use so that the student will know at all times what he is saying.

2. Limit the number of verbs you use.

3. Decide how much you think it wise to develop at one time; you may want to limit the initial presentation to one or two steps.

4. Review any earlier material that may have bearing on the presentation.

5. Keep the presentation as simple as possible.

A. Oral presentation

What is the passé composé? With minimal explanation let students see the French and English equivalents by writing an example on the board.

J'ai étudié la leçon.	{ I **have studied** the lesson. I **studied** the lesson.

Then give several oral examples, such as *J'ai demandé les billets; J'ai regardé la télé; J'ai parlé français.* ASK: From what verb does *j'ai* come? Can you give the other forms? Then give practice with a simple substitution drill.

J'ai demandé les billets. (elle)	**Elle a demandé** les billets.
J'ai regardé la télé. (tu)	**Tu as regardé** la télé.
J'ai parlé français. (nous)	**Nous avons parlé** français.

B. Preparation of written presentation

At this point, reinforce the presentation with the written forms. An overhead projector is very effective for this purpose, because it focuses complete attention on the problem at hand.

1. *Transparency 1: -er* verbs. Print or use large type, and space as shown, so that the negative forms can be added later. Note the order: first give two rounds of pronouns in the expected order, then change the order; finally use noun subjects:

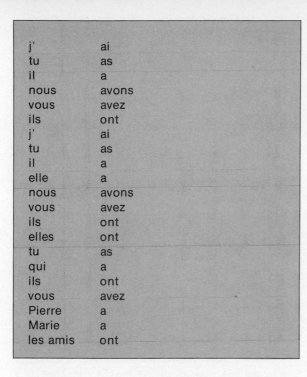

j'	ai	
tu	as	
il	a	
nous	avons	
vous	avez	
ils	ont	
j'	ai	
tu	as	
il	a	
elle	a	
nous	avons	
vous	avez	
ils	ont	
elles	ont	
tu	as	
qui	a	
ils	ont	
vous	avez	
Pierre	a	
Marie	a	
les amis	ont	

2. *Transparency 2: -er* verbs. Choose examples equal to the number of pronouns listed on Transparency 1. Use familiar vocabulary for teaching a new point of grammar, then substitute the new vocabulary:

> regardé la télé
> demandé les billets
> parlé français
> étudié la leçon

3. *Transparency 3:* Space as shown to match Transparency 1:

> n'   pas
> n'   pas
> n'   pas

4. *Transparency 4: -ir, -ir/-iss-* verbs. List a few examples of verbs students know:

> dormi hier soir
> choisi un livre
> fini la leçon

5. *Transparency 5: -re* verbs. List examples of verbs students know:

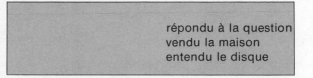

> répondu à la question
> vendu la maison
> entendu le disque

6. *Transparency 6:* List further examples of *-er, -ir, -ir/-iss-,* and *-re* verbs, using the infinitive as the cue:

> (préparer) le dîner
> (vendre) la maison
> (choisir) un livre

C. Teaching procedures

1. Place *Transparency 1* on the projector and put *Transparency 2* over it. The results will be:

j'	ai	regardé la télé
tu	as	demandé les billets
il	a	parlé français
etc.		

Ask students what conclusions might be drawn about the formation of the passé composé with *-er* verbs. Give further practice.

2. Do Ex. B, p. 176.

3. Now you are ready to teach the negative with the passé composé. Put *Transparencies 1, 2,* and *3* on the projector. Don't forget to change *j'* to *je:*

je	n'	ai	pas regardé la télé
tu	n'	as	pas demandé les billets

Point out the position of *ne* and *pas.* Give further practice.

4. Do Ex. C, p. 176.

5. Using *Transparencies 1* and *4*, present the *-ir* and *-ir/-iss-* verbs as you did the *-er* verbs.

6. Using *Transparencies 1, 3,* and *4,* review the negative passé composé.

7. Do Ex. A, p. 180.

8. Using *Transparencies 1* and *5*, present the *-re* verbs as you did the others.

9. Do Ex. B, p. 180.

10. Using *Transparencies 1* and *6,* give further practice with the three verb groups, using the infinitive as a cue:

j'	ai	(préparer) le dîner
tu	as	(vendre) la maison

11. Do Ex. C, p. 181.

12. Use personalized questions so that the students can see that this tense is a very usable one in French:

> Tu as préparé les exercices?
> Ton voisin a étudié les verbes?
> Qui a regardé la télé hier soir?

TEACHING DIRECT OBJECT PRONOUNS   Lesson 13

The teaching of direct object pronouns centers on three problems: which pronoun to use, where to place it, and when to use elision and liaison.[1]

A. Oral presentation

1. Tell the student to associate the definite determiner

---

[1] The further pronunciation question of the retention or dropping of mute *e*'s should be avoided at this stage. However, the pronunciation section on mute *e* (page 226) lends itself to presentation with transparencies.

(*le, la, les*) with the pronoun to be used. Start with a feminine noun, since the determiner *la* is easier to recognize orally as well as in the written form. WRITE OR SAY: Je vois **la** maison. Je **la** vois.

2. Give further practice, using the same verb, but changing the noun. Have students respond with the pronoun form:

Je vois **la** ferme.	Je **la** vois.
Je vois **la** boutique.	Je **la** vois.
Je vois **la** pharmacie.	Je **la** vois.
Je vois **la** poste.	Je **la** vois.

3. Now substitute the masculine nouns:

Il voit **le** pilote.	Il **le** voit.
Il voit **le** facteur.	Il **le** voit.
Il voit **le** médecin.	Il **le** voit.
Il voit **le** soldat.	Il **le** voit.

Since these are teaching patterns, the sentences should be kept very simple. If students have questions, answer them as you go along.

4. Using the same verb in each sentence, mix masculine and feminine singular nouns. Avoid words that might create pronunciation problems:

Nous voyons **la** vache.	Nous **la** voyons.
Nous voyons **le** cheval.	Nous **le** voyons.
Nous voyons **la** poule.	Nous **la** voyons.
Nous voyons **le** cochon.	Nous **le** voyons.

5. Now mix both verbs and nouns, but keep the vocabulary simple. Avoid elision by using only verbs that begin with a consonant sound:

Il regarde **le** pilote.	Il **le** regarde.
Il voit **le** chat.	Il **le** voit.
Il prend **la** lettre.	Il **la** prend.

B. Preparation for written presentation

At this point, reinforce the learning with writing if you have not already done so.

1. *Transparency 1:* Print or use large type, and space as follows:

je	vois
je	vois
je	vois
je	vois
je	vois
je	vois
il	voit
il	voit
il	voit
il	voit
je	regarde
je	cherche
je	prends
je	trouve

2. *Transparency 2:* Print and space as shown:

la maison
la voiture
la leçon
la lettre
la plage
la chaise

le pilote
le billet
le soldat
le facteur

le mouton
la boutique
la fleur
le théâtre

3. *Transparency 3:* Print and space as shown:

la	(	)
la	(	)
la	(	)
la	(	)
la	(	)
la	(	)
le	(	)
le	(	)
le	(	)
le	(	)
le	(	)
la	(	)
la	(	)
le	(	)

4. *Transparency 4:* Print and space as shown:

ne	pas
ne	pas
ne	pas
ne	pas
ne	pas
ne	pas
ne	pas
ne	pas
ne	pas
ne	pas
ne	pas
ne	pas
ne	pas
ne	pas

C. Teaching procedures

1. Place *Transparency 1* on the projector and put *Transparency 2* over it. The results will be:

```
je          vois        la maison
je          vois        la voiture
etc.
```

Have the students read the sentences aloud.

2. Now put *Transparency 3* over *Transparencies 1* and *2;* the sentences will look like this:

```
je          la vois     (la maison)
je          la vois     (la voiture)
etc.
```

Point out that the French equivalent of the English object pronoun "it" is *la* when "it" refers to a feminine noun.

3. Do Exs. A and C, p. 217.

4. Now give practice using verbs that begin with a vowel or mute *h:*

Il aime la ferme.	Il l'aime.
Il aime le film.	Il l'aime.
Il habite la maison.	Il l'habite.

5. Continue, this time using plural nouns:

Il regarde les nuages.	Il les regarde.
Il regarde les montagnes.	Il les regarde.
Il aime les bandes.	Il les aime.
Il aime les films.	Il les aime.

6. Do Ex. E, p. 218.

7. To show the negative word order, put *Transparencies 1, 2,* and *4* on the projector:

```
je      ne  vois    pas la maison
je      ne  vois    pas la voiture
etc.
```

8. Now add *Transparency 3,* showing the use of the pronoun with *ne* and *pas:*

```
je      ne  la vois  pas (la maison)
je      ne  la vois  pas (la voiture)
etc.
```

9. Do Exs. B and D, pp. 217–218.

Note: Remember that if you want to focus on only one sentence at a time, you can do this by covering the rest of the sentences on the transparency with a paper. Lowering the paper to show each new sentence provides an element of surprise.

TEACHING THE PARTITIVE CONSTRUCTION   Lesson 15

A. Oral presentation

Select the nouns you are going to use in presenting the partitive and give practice in using them first in a general sense. Using visual cues, ask:

Qu'est-ce que tu aimes?   J'aime la salade.
   (*salad*)
Qu'est-ce que tu aimes?   J'aime les pommes frites.
  (*French fries*)

Concentrate first on words of one gender, then mix the genders.

B. Preparation and written presentation

To master the partitive the student must first know:
. . . The use of the definite determiner with nouns.
. . . The formation of the partitive and the difference in meaning between it and the noun used with the definite determiner.
. . . The use of *de* after a negative.

1. The definite determiner with nouns. Show *Transparency 1:*

> j'aime les hors-d'œuvre
> les haricots verts
> les œufs
>
> j'aime le rôti de porc
> le riz
> le poisson
>
> j'aime la salade
> la tarte aux pommes
> la confiture

Ask the student what the difference is between the French meaning of these sentences and the English equivalent. If he doesn't know, explain that when the French speak of something in general, they always use the definite determiner. We never do. Do Ex. A, p. 248.

2. The partitive versus the noun used in a general sense. Show *Transparency 2:*

> je voudrais des hors-d'œuvre
> des haricots verts
> des petits pois
> des œufs
>
> je voudrais du rôti de porc
> du riz
> du poisson
>
> je voudrais de la salade
> de la tarte aux pommes
> de la confiture

Point out the difference in meaning of the sentences when *des, du,* and *de la* are used to mean "some."

a. At this point, the *Dialogue,* p. 243, is a starting point for further practice in the use of the partitive. Using simple substitution, say for example:

Pour commencer, messieurs-dames, de la soupe?
de la salade?

Et pour madame? Du jambon?
Du gigot?
Du rôti de porc?

Et comme dessert? De la tarte?
De la mousse au chocolat?

b. Do Exs. B–C, p. 248. Provide further practice by holding up a picture. Have the student give the noun and the proper form of the partitive.

Picture of:	*Student says:*
le coq au vin	du coq au vin
la confiture	de la confiture
les haricots verts	des haricots verts

c. Do Exs. A–D, F, pp. 251–252.

3. Use of *de* after a negative.
a. Remind the student that he saw these sentences before (Lesson 7, p. 108):

Est-ce qu'il y a un hôtel près d'ici?	Non, il n'y a pas d'hôtel près d'ici.
Est-ce qu'il a une sœur?	Non, il n'a pas de sœur.
Est-ce qu'elle regarde des dessins animés?	Non, elle ne regarde pas de dessins animés.

In case he has forgotten, remind him that after a negative, the indefinite determiner *un, une,* or *des* becomes *de.*

b. Show *Transparency 3:*

> je ne veux pas de sucre
> de confiture
> de crème
> de poisson
> de petits pois
>
> tu ne prends pas de salade
> de fromage
> de pommes frites
> de jambon
> de gigot
>
> tu n' aimes pas le lait
> la soupe
> le pain
> les escargots

Techniques for Teaching
Certain Key Concepts

Tell the students that in a negative sentence the partitive forms *du, de la,* and *des* become *de.*

Explain that the definite determiner *le, la,* or *les* is used in the last group because the nouns are used in a general sense. This is always true, even when the sentence is negative.

c. Do Ex. E, p. 252.

PART IX

Cultural Supplement

Language is at the very core of a people's culture and is in turn a vital expression of that culture. It is thus essential for a meaningful approach to the study of French that the students understand and appreciate how the language they are learning expresses and reflects French culture.

Accordingly, taking the language and the situations of the *Dialogues,* the *Lectures,* the *Mots Nouveaux,* and certain exercises as points of departure, this Cultural Supplement offers pertinent cultural facts that you may want to share with—and enlarge upon for—your students. In addition, it offers captions for photographs and documents, which have been omitted from the student text for three reasons:

(1) The simple identification type of caption is basically acultural—the history, the attitudes toward and emotions evoked by a given monument, for example, can in no way be conveyed by such a caption.

(2) The longer type of caption, an "essay caption," that we would want to offer, and which we can offer to a limited extent in this supplement, would be cumbersome in the student text. It could also lead the students to a sense of separation of language study and cultural appreciation—French culture would become an additional "assignment."

(3) Experiences differ and cultures change. For five teachers, each of whom has studied or lived for a time in a different region (Strasbourg, Grenoble, Bordeaux, Rennes, Paris), the concept of *ce qui est français* might be quite different. We feel it important to give you room to take exception to our general cultural statements and to expand upon them based on your own experience. Similarly, as some of the more clearcut aspects of the culture change—and change so quickly—you can keep up-to-date without statements that are suddenly erroneous being made in the student book. For example, a very few years ago, French students had Thursdays off; today, Wednesdays. The August vacation, the long lunch hour—neither is as certain today as it was yesterday. As the high rise goes up, the concierge begins to disappear. *La chaisière,* who once rented you a seat in the Paris park, is no longer a definite part of the scene. Subscriptions to one or more French newspapers or magazines will help you keep abreast of changes, both abrupt and gradual, and will offer access to current news and opinion.

French, of course, is not only the language of France, but is also the official language in more than a dozen African nations and in Haiti. It is spoken, too, by significant percentages of the population of Belgium, Switzerland, and Canada, as well as Polynesia and the Far East. Thus French is the language of a variety of cultures, and this point should not be neglected.

Nor is French entirely a foreign language in the U.S., where varieties of it are spoken in the home by hundreds of thousands of Americans in New England and Louisiana, as well as in isolated spots in the East and Midwest. In New York City alone there are nearly

Cultural
Supplement

T32

250,000 Haitians who speak French and Creole. Our French heritage—from Marquette, Joliet, and La Salle to the existence today in our country of large communities of speakers of some variety of French—should be emphasized.

COVER

Henri Matisse (1869–1954) had an unusually long and productive life as an artist. Only Picasso and Chagall among twentieth-century artists are his rivals in public esteem. Though best-known for his paintings and for the brilliantly colored cut-out designs that he produced toward the end of his life (for such diverse purposes as tiles, wallpaper, and clerical vestments), he also designed stained glass windows and stage sets for the ballet, and illustrated deluxe editions of several books.

The painting reproduced on the cover, entitled *The Open Window,* was painted in 1905. It was in that same year, at the Salon d'Automne, that Matisse first gained renown as one of the leaders of what became known as the *fauvist* movement. What is recognized today as a logical development from impressionism was seen at the time as the work of charlatans and madmen, whom one of the leading art critics of the day called *les fauves,* "wild beasts." In reality, the fauvists (including also Vlaminck, Derain, and later Braque and Dufy) were advocating nothing more than the primacy of color. There was no one fauvist style and no real "movement." The fauvists nonetheless had an enormous impact on twentieth-century art. In his "Notes d'un peintre" in *La Grande Revue* (1908), Matisse wrote thus about his attitude toward color:

> J'ai à peindre un intérieur; j'ai devant moi une armoire, elle me donne une sensation de rouge bien vivant, et je pose un rouge qui me satisfait. Un rapport s'établit entre ce rouge et le blanc de la toile. Que je pose à côté un vert, que je rende le parquet par un jaune, et il y aura encore, entre ce vert ou ce jaune et le blanc de la toile, des rapports qui me satisferont. Mais ces différents tons se diminuent mutuellement. Il faut que les signes divers que j'emploie soient équilibrés de telle sorte qu'ils ne se détruisent pas les uns les autres. Pour cela, je dois mettre de l'ordre dans mes idées: la relation entre les tons s'établira de telle sorte qu'elle les soutiendra au lieu de les abattre.

COLOR SECTION: OPENING PAGE

View of la Tour Eiffel from le Pont Alexandre III. La Tour Eiffel was built for the Exposition of 1889. At 300 meters (a little under 1000 feet), it was then the tallest structure in the world, and Parisians were at first aghast at what they considered to be an ugly skeleton towering over the city. Though the recent building of the enormous business and residential complex known as La Défense—sometimes derogatorily called "Manhattan-sur-Seine"—has lessened the impact of the tower, it nonetheless remains the proud symbol of the city. Designed by the architectural engineer Gustave Eiffel, it was constructed entirely of steel, including 2,500,000 steel rivets. There are restaurants at the first and second levels and an observation platform near the top. The tower now also serves as a radio and television transmitter.

Le Pont Alexandre III was named for the Tsar of Russia (1845–1894), a friend and ally of France. It is one of the most beautiful bridges in Paris and is particularly notable for its elegantly ornamented lampposts. At one end of the bridge is the Quai d'Orsay and l'Hôtel des Invalides, the large veterans' hospital in whose chapel, l'Eglise du Dôme, one finds the tomb of Napoléon. The opposite end of the bridge leads onto l'avenue Winston Churchill and into the Champs-Elysées. (For a note on the naming of streets and bridges, see CS* Color Section: *Paris.*)

COLOR SECTION: TRANSPORTS

Left page: (a) La Gare Saint-Lazare (see CS Lesson 2, p. 16: *la Gare*). You might want to post a reproduction of one of Monet's paintings of this station.

(b) The entrance to the Métro at la Place Pigalle in Montmartre. Point out the map that one finds at the entrance to the Métro. Inside many of the stations there is a special map, called *un plan-indicateur,* on which, when one pushes a button indicating the desired destination, the route lights up, showing which line to take and where to transfer if necessary. A given Métro line

*CS = Cultural Supplement.

is known by its two end stops. For example, the first line to open in July 1900, was *la ligne Porte de Vincennes-Porte Maillot* (since extended to become *Château de Vincennes-Pont de Neuilly*), which cuts across the city with stops at such points as la Gare de Lyon, la Place de la Bastille, le Louvre, les Tuileries, and l'Etoile. The Pigalle stop is on *la ligne numéro 2: Porte Dauphine-Nation.*

La Place Pigalle is on le boulevard de Clichy, which is the central nightclub area of the city (see CS Color Section: *Paris*).

(c) A tour bus in Versailles. Guides are, of course, multilingual, and such tours are usually conducted in French, English, and German.

(d) An Air France clerk at Kennedy International Airport, New York.

(e) The railroad station in Fontainebleau, a town of 20,000 inhabitants 22 kilometers southeast of Paris. The town is the site of the beautiful château built in the early sixteenth century for François Ier on the site of a royal hunting lodge dating back to the eleventh century. It was at Fontainebleau that on April 20, 1814, Napoléon Ier abdicated the throne. One wing of the building now houses a museum of American arts.

Right page: La Polynésie française, comprising les Iles de la Société (including Tahiti, Moorea, Huahine, and Bora Bora), les Marquises, les Tuamoto, les Tubuaï (or les Australes) and les Gambier, has a total population of 120,000. The islands were discovered during the mid-eighteenth century, largely by British and Dutch expeditions, and the first French missionaries landed in 1834. The various island chains became French protectorates during the 1840's, were annexed during the 1880's, and the entire group of 130 islands was established as *un territoire français d'outre-mer* in 1946, with the seat of government in Papeete, Tahiti. It is ruled by an elected assembly and a governor appointed by the French Government.

The photos of Polynesia in the Color Section are from les Iles de la Société, the largest and most important of the island groups that make up la Polynésie française. Named after the Royal Society which sponsored Capt. James Cook's expeditions in the 1760's,

they comprise 40% of the land area and 80% of the population. The islands are of two types: a few are coral atolls, but most are the tips of underwater volcanos. Tahiti, for example, consists of two volcanic cones rising to 7,333 feet above sea level. The population is centered in the coastal area and the lowlands, with the steep, mountainous region being uninhabited. The area, which once exported large quantities of copra, vanilla, and mother-of-pearl, now depends largely on tourism. There is a large airport (*l'aérodrome de Faaa*) in Papeete, and small aircraft or boat transportation among the other islands.

(a) A girl on a motorbike on the island of Bora Bora. On most of the islands, roads range from poor to nonexistent.

(b) Known as *les trucks,* these are the buses of Papeete. On top there is room for parcels or provisions. Passengers sit on two benches that run the length of the bus.

(c) One of the supply ships that go regularly from island to island. Few of the islands are fully self-sufficient. A typical village consists of a church, a school, a shop, and a few homes. The supply ships bring food, medical supplies, and manufactured goods.

COLOR SECTION: LOISIRS

Left page: (a) Boys and girls skateboarding near la Tour Eiffel. Students might enjoy the following vocabulary: skateboard, *la patinette;* to skate, *patiner;* to roller-skate, *faire du patin à roulettes;* skate, *le patin (à roulettes).*

(b) Temps Futurs, a store specializing in science fiction (see CS Lesson 12, p. 195: *la Science-Fiction*).

(c) Playing with the pigeons in front of Notre-Dame, la cathédrale de Paris. Between the doors and the famous rose window (*la rose*), which serves as a halo for the statue of Notre-Dame in the center, is *la Galerie des rois,* with statues of the kings of Judah and Israel. In 1793, the Commune, led by Danton, Robespierre, and Marat, thought these to be statues of the kings of France and ordered their heads removed. They were later restored. The three portals are of irregular size and shape. In the Middle Ages, lack of symmetry was considered important in breaking the monotony of a large façade. It took sixty years (1190–1250) to construct the façade of Notre-Dame.

The cathedral is on l'Ile de la Cité, one of the two small islands in the center of the city. It was on this island, then called Lutèce, that the Gallic tribe known as the Parisii settled. The island remained the administrative center of the city until Charles V moved to the Louvre in the fourteenth century. The smaller island, l'Ile Saint-Louis, has always been a quiet residential quarter. Today it remains a creation of the seventeenth century, the era when most of its homes and churches were built. It is a fashionable and expensive place to live and has many elegant restaurants.

Right page: (a) Playing *belote,* a popular card game in France.

(b) Young man playing the guitar on the island of Huahine. Polynesians are a tall, large-boned people with light to medium brown skin. They are sometimes considered to be a separate race.

(c) One of the coral atolls near the island of Moorea. Note the lively decoration on the boat and the outrigger—*un outrigger* [awtrigœr]—which balances the boat.

The traditional Polynesian costume is known as *un paréo.* It is a beautifully colored print cloth that is wrapped around, draped, and then tucked or tied in any one of several ways.

COLOR SECTION: PARCS

Left page: (a) Late afternoon in the Bois de Boulogne. This enormous woods was originally a royal hunting ground surrounded by a wall. After the fall of Napoléon Ier, British and Russian troops camped there and almost totally destroyed the area. It was then replanted with chestnut trees, sycamores, and acacias in place of the dense oaks that had formerly been there. In 1852, Napoléon III gave the woods to the city of Paris and it was transformed into a public park on the model of Hyde Park in London. Few parks on earth can offer the beauty and variety of the Bois de Boulogne, with its gardens, lakes, waterfalls, restaurants, a Shakespeare Garden, open-air Shakespeare theater, restaurants, kiosks, l'Hippodrome de Longchamp (the fashionable race course where the Grand Prix is held each year), le champ de courses d'Auteuil (racing over hurdles), a zoo, polo fields, bicycle paths, bridle paths, etc.

(b) Toy sailboat rental in les Tuileries. Originally the private gardens of Catherine de Médicis (1519–1589),

les Tuileries were given their present form in the mid-seventeenth century, when they became a public garden. At that time they were redesigned by the great landscape artist André Le Nôtre, who also designed the gardens at Versailles. He created here a small, but magnificent combination of greenery, pools, terraces, stairways, and statuary.

(c) On the Left Bank, le jardin du Luxembourg is a particularly popular spot among children and students. Its proximity to the schools of le Quartier Latin accounts for the latter; the presence of le Guignol to some extent accounts for the number of children to be seen there on a nice day. (See also CS Lesson 4, pp. 44–45.)

Right page: (a) The entrance to the Botanical Gardens in Tahiti. On the grounds one finds le musée Gauguin, where reproductions of the artist's work are exhibited.

You might want to post some reproductions of Gauguin's paintings and tell the class a bit about him. Paul Gauguin (1848–1903) was the son of a liberal journalist who fled France when Napoléon III came to power. The family went to Peru, where Gaugin's mother's family lived, returning to France when Paul was seven. As a young man, after a six-year stint in the merchant marine and the French navy, he went to work as a stockbroker. He devoted his free time to painting and, by 1883, encouraged by Camille Pissarro and other Impressionists, he gave up his successful business to devote himself full-time to art. He gradually fled from his middle-class life and surroundings—and from his family. He worked for varying periods in Paris, Brittany, and Arles, traveled in Panama and Martinique, and in 1891 moved to Tahiti, where he learned the language and adopted a totally new way of life. With the exception of a one-year return to Brittany, Gauguin spent the last twelve years of his life in Polynesia.

(b) Another scene in le jardin du Luxembourg. (See also CS Lesson 4, pp. 44–45.)

COLOR SECTION: PARIS

Left page: (a) L'avenue Franklin D. Roosevelt, which begins at le Pont des Invalides, is one of the major avenues that intersect at le Rond-Point des Champs-Elysées. The French often name streets after both their own great men and women and those of other nations as well. For example: rue Franklin and l'avenue du Président-Wilson near le Palais de Chaillot and l'avenue du Président-Kennedy on the Seine between le Pont de Bir-Hakeim and le Pont de Grenelle.

(b) Le Moulin Rouge on le boulevard de Clichy. This former music hall was made famous by the works of Henri de Toulouse-Lautrec (1864–1901). You might want to post some of his works for the class to enjoy. Note the three *deux-chevaux* (see footnote and sidenote, p. 279).

(c) Note the posters for Jean-Jacques Debout at l'Olympia (see right page), for a show of the art or music perhaps of La Belle Epoque (the poster done in the style of Toulouse-Lautrec, who is himself shown in the lower right-hand corner), and for a concert by Little Richard. You might want to point out that American entertainers have long been extremely popular in France. There was, for example, a statue of Louis Armstrong in Nice before there was one in New Orleans (see also Lesson 14, p. 235).

(d) Billboards atop a painted wall. Another ad for le Cirque Bouglione appears on p. 203.

(e) A small butcher shop. Paris is filled with small shops such as this.

(f) You might want to point out that wrought-iron grillwork adorns many of the buildings of Paris; that paper and writing supplies are sold at *une papeterie;* that *une moquette* is a carpet and *le papier peint,* wallpaper.

(g) A tourist office. You might want to point out the sign in the lower left-hand corner offering the prize of a trip to Forest Hills. Students might be interested to know that tennis is a modern version of the very old French game, *le jeu de paume.* The name itself comes from the French *tenez,* which one called out upon serving the ball.

(h) Menu outside a restaurant. Menus are very often posted in restaurant windows so that before entering one knows that the selection—and price—are right.

Right page: (a) Outside the Saint-Lazare entrance to the Métro (see CS Color Section: *Transports*).

(b) A bookstore near Notre-Dame. Point out that French students must go to a store to buy their books. The signs here, for example, are pointing out school books, technical books, and books for *les Grandes Ecoles* (see footnote, p. 215, and CS Lesson 5, p. 63: *le Lycée*).

(c) An open-air food stand. Point out the *Buvez Coca-Cola* sign. Note that the specialty is *croque-monsieur* (see footnote, p. 245).

(d) L'Olympia, the Parisian music hall, which has long been to French entertainers what the Palace Theater in New York once was to American entertainers.

(e) Window display featuring the game of chess. Note the translation of Bobby Fischer's book, *Les Echecs.*

(f) An advertisement for chocolate.

(g) A laundress sitting outside her establishment. Students might be interested in some of the many very specific terms associated with laundry: to do the laundry, *laver le linge;* the dirty clothes themselves, *le linge;* a commercial laundry, *une blanchisserie;* the person who does the laundry, *le blanchisseur* or *la blanchisseuse;* a laundromat, *une laverie;* a laundry room in a building, *une buanderie;* a washing machine, *une machine à laver;* detergent, *la lessive;* to iron, *repasser;* an iron, *un fer (à repasser).* (The adjective *blanc* is taught in Lesson 6. See also the hotel laundry list, p. 204, where the terms *marque de·buanderie* and *le linge* are used.)

(h) The flea market. Students might enjoy the sign that reads to the effect that "we buy furniture, bronze, objets d'art—stuff cleared out of cellars and attics." You might point out the window with its hinged shutters *(les persiennes),* which can be closed to keep the sun and rain out, but which allow some light to come in. Stationary, decorative shutters—i.e., shutters that cannot be shut—are uncommon in France.

COLOR SECTION: ARTS

Left page: (a) La Victoire de Samothrace, one of the treasures of the Louvre, was discovered on the island of Samothrace in 1863. Because of its resemblance to the Nikes found on the prows of ancient ships, the statue is believed to have been created to celebrate a great naval victory.

(b) One of the most popular paintings in the Louvre is *La Liberté guidant le peuple* by Eugène Delacroix (1798–1863). Painted in 1831, this work lends a mythological aspect to the Revolution of 1830 which brought Louis-Philippe to the throne of France. Delacroix, one of the major artists of the Romantic school, is known for his numerous works on mythological subjects and for his murals in the Louvre, la Chambre des Députés, and l'église Saint-Sulpice. He was remarkable above all for his use of color. Charles Baudelaire, poet and esthetician, was a strong supporter of the art of Delacroix and wrote of him in 1855:

> D'abord il faut remarquer, et c'est très important, que, vu à une distance trop grande pour analyser ou même comprendre le sujet, un tableau de Delacroix a déjà produit sur l'âme une impression riche, heureuse ou mélancolique. On dirait que cette peinture, comme les sorciers et les magnétiseurs, projette sa pensée à distance. Ce singulier phénomène tient à la puissance du coloriste, à l'accord parfait des tons, et à l'harmonie . . . entre la couleur et le sujet. Il semble que cette couleur . . . pense par elle-même, indépendamment des objets qu'elle habille.

Right page: (a,b) Painters mastering their art by copying the great works. This is a common sight in the Louvre, and visitors are often as interested in watching this as in seeing the great works themselves.

In the photo on the right, the woman is copying *Officier de chasseurs de la Garde impériale chargeant* by Théodore Géricault (1791–1824), the first of the great Romantic painters. This painting, done when the artist was 20, was exhibited at the Salon of 1812. He died young and left behind few paintings. He had, however, a profound influence on those who came after him—particularly the young Delacroix.

(c) A sidewalk portrait painter in Montmartre (see CS Lesson 7, p. 96).

COLOR SECTION: PLAGES

Left page: (a) *Une colonie de vacances* on la Côte d'Azur. Such vacations for children began in the days before a one-month paid vacation was guaranteed by law to all French workers. Similar to our summer camps, they are subsidized by various groups and are directed by specially trained *moniteurs* and *monitrices.* This group, for example, consists of the sons of postal employees.

(b) The beach at Nice. There are many such pebble beaches *(plages de galets),* though this is one of the most beautiful and popular ones. You might point out that, bounded as it is by four major bodies of water *(la Méditerranée, l'Atlantique, la Manche, la Mer du Nord),* France has an extensive coastline with many beaches and resort areas. (See also CS Lesson 15, p. 243: *Nice.*)

Right page: (a) A pedal boat *(un pédalo)* near the beach at Saint-Tropez. Students might enjoy learning the term *aller en pédalo* (after Lesson 4) or the more common *faire du pédalo* (after Lesson 8).

(b) The coastline of Martinique. The island lies 270 miles north of Venezuela. Its population is 340,000; its capital, Fort-de-France. First visited by Columbus in 1504, it has been occupied by French-speaking people since a group of 80 settlers landed there in 1635. Since then, with the exception of three brief periods when it was under English rule (1762–63, 1794–1802, 1809–14), it has been recognized as part of France, first as a colony and, since 1946, as one of the *départements d'outre-mer.* Sugar cane was introduced from Brazil in 1654, Arabian coffee in 1723. Other products are pineapples and rum. There is now an oil refinery on the island. La Compagnie du Sénégal, founded in 1664, brought black slaves to Martinique. After the abolition of slavery there in 1848, laborers came from China and India. There is thus a vigorous ethnic diversity to be found there. The literacy rate is close to 100%, and many of the young people pursue their higher education in continental France.

The island has three large mountain masses, with numerous rivers and forests and abundant, varied vegetation. Today it is an extremely popular tourist spot.

(c) The bay of Cannes (see CS Lesson 5, p. 61: *Cannes/La Côte d'Azur*).

COLOR SECTION: PROVISIONS

Left page: (a) Buying melons on a street in Paris. Such open-air markets are very common in France (see CS Lesson 9, p. 137: *le Marché*).

(b) *Une boulangerie* with numerous types and shapes of bread.

(c) A produce market in Paris. Note that where the produce came from is considered important *(tomates de Perpignan, haricots verts d'Italie)*. Perpignan, once capital of the province of Roussillon, is a city of 100,000 located in the Pyrénées near the Mediterranean and the Spanish border. It is noted for its fine fruits, vegetables, and vineyards. Students might enjoy knowing that *sans fil* means "stringless."

(d) A far wider selection of seafood is usually available in a French fish market than in an American one. Some of the seafood shown here are: sole, *la sole;* gilthead, *la daurade* (common in the Mediterranean); limander, *la limande* (a type of flounder); gurnard or grunt, *le grondin* (a member of the snapper family); red mullet, *le rouget barbet;* prawn, *la langoustine;* porpoise or seahog, *le cochon de mer* or *le marsouin* (the sign here reads *mercochons*); sardine, *la sardine;* gray mullet, *la lisette. Filets frais* are of course "fresh fillets."

(e) The fruit section of a market. The esthetic appeal of food is important to the French, whether at the table or in the market. Note the attractive arrangement of the strawberries and peaches, with the lemons and foliage to add color. Students might enjoy learning the terms *les fraises, les pêches, les citrons,* and *les ananas.*

(f) *Une boucherie* featuring certain meats that are very popular in France but which are rare or unknown in the U.S.: a cut of lamb for sautéeing, *le sauté-agneau;* boneless turkey and chicken breast, *une escalope de dinde (de poulet);* rabbit back, *le râble de lapin;* rabbit parts, *le lapin coupé;* calf's head, *la tête (de veau),* and on the top row: *la dinde, le pigeon, la brochette* (meat and vegetables for skishkebab), *le lapin,* and *le coq au vin.*

You might want to point out that poultry is often sold with head and feet still attached; the rabbit fur is left on the feet. Heads and feet are used to flavor soups

and sauces; the fur is left on the rabbit as a very old form of consumer protection, a guarantee that one is buying rabbit and not another animal of similar size and shape.

Right page: (a,b) Market day in Marigot on the island of Saint-Martin in the Antilles. The island is half-French, half-Dutch. Market day is Saturday, and food is bought for the entire week.

(c) Tahitian fishermen bringing home their catch.

(d) A small food shop on the island of Martinique.

COLOR SECTION: ÎLES

(a) The town square on the island of Terre de Haut, one of les Iles des Saintes, which, along with Marie-Galante, Saint-Barthélemy, and the northern half of Saint-Martin, are dependencies of Guadeloupe (see CS Lesson 13, p. 205: *la Guadeloupe*). The tree is *un flamboyant.* The building on the far right is *la gendarmerie.*

(b) Traveler's palm in the harbor at Martinique.

(c) Young children on the island of Huahine in French Polynesia. The wreath of flowers worn in the hair is called a *hei* and is worn as a decoration or given as a token of friendship, much like the *lei* on the Hawaiian Islands. Note that *le chewing gum* [ʃwiŋɔm] *à bulles* is found the world over.

(d) A small mission church on the island of Bora Bora. The picture is straight; the church has settled at an angle.

LESSON 1

Page 2

(a) L'Eglise Saint-Germain-des-Prés, located near the Seine, is the oldest church in Paris. The building was completed in 1021. Today only the church and the abbot's palace remain of what was originally a large complex of buildings that made up l'abbaye de Saint-Germain-des-Prés.

(b) Outdoor market in Sarlat, a picturesque old town of 8,000 inhabitants in Dordogne in the Périgord region. Its principal products are wine, brandy, and the truffles for which Périgord is famous. You might want to point out the chicken which the woman on the left is carrying (see also CS Lesson 12, p. 196).

(c) A group of young people, guitars in hand, outside the church in Vallauris. A town of 11,000 on la Côte d'Azur, Vallauris is noted as a center of the French pottery and ceramics industry. The many ceramics designed by Pablo Picasso were made there in the studio of Mme Ramié.

(d) Outside a pastry shop on la Côte d'Azur. Note the long loaves of bread (*les baguettes*) and the copies of *Nice-Matin* on the newspaper rack.

Page 3

Les Salutations: You may wish to point out that *bonjour*, despite its literal meaning "good day," can be used at any time of the day or night and is equivalent to "hello." The same is not true, of course, for *bonsoir* or *bonne nuit*, which you may wish to introduce later.

Despite its widespread usage, *ça va* is still considered to be informal. You may also want to teach *Comment ça va?* or the more formal *Comment allez-vous? (Comment vas-tu?)* either now or with the verb *aller* (Lesson 2). In general, *ça va* is said only to someone with whom one would use the *tu* form. Because the French tend to be more formal than Americans, it is better not to initiate the greeting until fairly close ties have been established.

You may wish to tell the students that handshaking consists of a firm, but gentle, pump rather than a continued shaking.

Another very common way of greeting a good friend or relative is by embracing and kissing on both cheeks (although the number of kisses varies regionally, a single kiss is rare and two or three is the most frequent number). This form of greeting has become increasingly popular among young people.

Page 5

Le Cahier: Pages in a *cahier* are usually ruled somewhat like graph paper, with both vertical and horizontal lines. This is meant to encourage neat, straight writing. In addition to taking notes in a *cahier*, students may also do homework assignments in them and turn in the entire notebook for corrections.

La Fenêtre: You may wish to ask students if they are familiar with the term "French windows." Point out that windows in France are usually hinged, and open inward from the center. They have several small,

square panes. Like doors, they may have movable handles.

La Porte: In France, especially in older buildings, door handles may be very ornate and are frequently made of porcelain.

Le Professeur: You may wish to tell your students about the more formal relationship which exists between students and teachers in France. In some schools, students are still expected to rise when the teacher enters the classroom. French textbooks are largely factual, and the teacher explains or interprets the facts. Students are expected to accept and digest both the facts and the interpretation.

Le Rouge et le Noir: Point out that this is a famous novel by Stendhal (1830). Should the question arise, you might mention that the red stands for the military and the black for the Church, two major forces in European political history.

Le Stylo: Though this is the generic term for a pen, the French usually distinguish between a ballpoint (*un stylo à bille*) and a fountain pen (*un stylo*). Fountain pens are still very common in France and are considered a necessity for formal correspondence. In such cases, a typewritten letter would appear too cold and impersonal, while one written in ballpoint pen would be considered too informal. It is only in the recent past that school children have been allowed to use ballpoints rather than fountain pens both in school and for their homework.

Page 6

Photo: A coed school (*un lycée mixte*) in Paris. You might point out that coeducation is a recent, postwar development in France, and large numbers of students still attend *lycées de jeunes filles* or *lycées de garçons*. Note the desks at which students sit two abreast.

Page 7

Merci: Used alone, the word often means "no thank you." A word like *bien* or *beaucoup* will usually be added to give a positive response. In addressing someone with whom one would not use *tu*, the words *monsieur*, *madame*, or *mademoiselle* are essential. Point out, too, that *merci* is not usually used to acknowledge a compliment. The French will shrug or say something on the order of *Vous le croyez?* In such an instance, *merci* would imply agreement that the compliment was deserved.

Page 10

Le Thème: This exercise refers to the translation of a text from one's own language to another; translating from a foreign language to one's own is called *une version. Une composition* is always an original composition.

Page 11

Photo: Windows on a building on la Côte d'Azur. Note the wrought-iron railings, the shutters, and the flower pots. The French love flowers, which are a common sight on apartment building window sills. (See also CS Lesson 4, pp. 48–49: *le Jardin*).

LESSON 2

Page 12

Three scenes on la Côte d'Azur. Should students show interest, you might want to teach the term *jouer de l'harmonica.* The expressions *jouer du piano* and *jouer de la guitare* are taught in Lesson 14, but you may want to introduce them and other common instruments orally at any point.

Page 13

La Plage: See CS Color Section: *Plages.*

Chez: Remind students that this word is frequently used in the U.S. with names of restaurants, beauty parlors, etc. They will be able to see that it means more than "at (to) the home of."

Page 15

Les Accents: You might wish to tell students a little bit about the history of accent marks in French. They first appeared during the Renaissance. Greek texts were held in the highest esteem and French scribes used the Greek accent marks to "elevate" their transcriptions of French texts. For a long time, usage was inconsistent. The playwright Pierre Corneille (1606–1684), father of the classic French theater, was the first to use accent

marks specifically to distinguish between open *(aigu)* and closed *(grave)* e sounds.

La cédille was originally a small *s* written underneath a *c* to indicate that it was pronounced [s]. You might want to compare the *ss* in *lesson* with the *ç* in *la leçon.*

Le circonflexe usually indicates than an *s* has been dropped from a word. It originally indicated as well that the vowel was to be slightly elongated to compensate for the missing *s.* Your students might enjoy figuring out the English meanings of such words as *bête, fête,* and *côte.*

La Martinique: See CS Color Section: *Plages.* Students should be able to understand the billboard with no difficulty. You should, however, introduce orally the terms *vingt-cinq* and *cinquante-deux* so that students can read it perfectly.

Pages 16–17*

L'Appartement: Explain that this means only the apartment itself. An apartment building is *un immeuble.*

La Banque: See CS Lesson 8, p. 121.

La Poste: The letters P.T.T. *(Postes, Télégraphes et Téléphones)* indicate the post office. More recent ones are marked simply P. et T. *(Postes et Télécommunications).* You may wish to explain that the postal and telephone services are directed by one government agency. Due to a chronic shortage of telephone equipment, there is often a very long waiting list for telephone service. Thus many French families do not have a telephone at home. People go to *la poste,* therefore, not only to purchase stamps and send parcels, but also to make telephone calls or to send telegrams.

L'Eglise: For the French, the word *église* identifies only a Catholic church. Protestants worship in *le temple;* Jews, in *la synagogue.*

La Gare: French trains are noted for their efficiency, and because of heavy passenger traffic, the stations are usually bustling with activity. (See also CS Lesson 4, pp. 48–49: *le Train.*) Paris alone has six major stations (Gare du Nord, Gare de l'Est, Gare de Lyon, Gare d'Austerlitz, Gare Montparnasse, Gare Saint-Lazare) and four stations providing exclusively suburban ser-

*In the first printing, the note "See Cultural Supplement" appears by accident in the student text. Should students ask, you might want to tell them that it refers to the Color Section: *Plages.*

vice (Gare de la Bastille, Gare Saint-Michel, Gare d'Orsay, Gare des Invalides). Each of the major stations, in addition to some suburban service, handles traffic to and from a specific region. La Gare du Nord, la Gare de l'Est, and la Gare de Lyon, for example, serve the northern, eastern, and southeastern (Côte d'Azur) sections of France, respectively. La Gare Montparnasse provides most of the service to the west and la Gare d'Austerlitz serves the southwest. La Gare Saint-Lazare serves the northwest and the port of Le Havre. The major stations are also linked into the Métro, so that one can easily get to any point in the city from the stations. The larger French railroad stations also have nice shops, cafés, and sometimes very good restaurants.

You may want to bring in reproductions of Claude Monet's studies of la Gare Saint-Lazare.

Page 18

Photo: Children at la Gare Saint-Lazare. You might point out that the term *la grande banlieue* refers to the more distant suburbs of Paris (twenty to thirty kilometers away).

Page 19

La Carte: Point out that France is smaller than the State of Texas. If students question the letter "O" where they would expect to see "W," let them look up the word "west" in the English-French Vocabulary. The sooner they learn how to use the end vocabulary, the better.

You may want to point out French names of towns and cities in the U.S. (St. Louis, Terre Haute, Des Moines, etc.). Also point out Québec Province and other French-speaking regions and countries.

Le Drapeau: Le tricolore is the flag of France: blue, white, red. Mention also, as symbols of France, the royal *fleur de lis* and *le coq gaulois*. Ask students what they think of as symbols of France (e.g., la Tour Eiffel, Toulouse-Lautrec posters, the chef, etc.).

The Canadian flag is red and white with a maple leaf. The flag of Québec Province is pale blue and white with a *fleur de lis*.

Le Calendrier: See CS Lesson 7, p. 101: *les Jours de la semaine.*

Page 21

Tu/vous: You might want to tell students that should they find themselves in a situation where they are not sure of the appropriateness of using *tu*, it is preferable to use *vous*. It should be left to the French person to

suggest switching to *tu*. Though *vous* is always used with older people and almost always with people one does not know, French students do call each other *tu*, even if they do not know each other. This is true at both the university and high-school levels. The same is true in French-speaking Canada. In such instances, it indicates a kind of camaraderie or solidarity.

Photo: The photo shows a school in Bergheim, Alsace. The word is plural because the building houses both *une école de jeunes filles* and *une école de garçons*.

The area that comprises Haut-Rhin and Bas-Rhin was formerly the province of Alsace. It was first joined to France by the Treaty of Westphalia in 1648. Though ceded to Germany in 1871 following the Franco-Prussian War, it retained its strong French ties, and again became a part of France following World War I. It was, of course, occupied by the Germans from 1940 to 1945 and was the scene of fierce fighting at the time of its liberation. The majority of towns bear German names, and the architecture and atmosphere of the region are decidedly Rhenish. It is neither "typically German" nor "typically French." Though highly industrial, Alsace remains a very beautiful area.

Page 24

Photo: L'hôtel de Dame Carcas in the ancient walled city of Carcassonne in the south of France. The wall consists of a double line of ramparts, the earliest of which was built in 485 A.D. Though the town has built up around them, more than 1000 people still live within the walls. Carcassonne is the best-preserved walled city in Europe.

LESSON 3

Page 28

Scenes on la Côte d'Azur. Note *la plage de sable* (top right) and *la plage de galets* (bottom). (See also CS Color Section: *Plages.*)

Page 29

Le Chapeau: Note that this is not a generic term in French. Though it may be made of any material, such as felt or straw, a *chapeau* always has a brim. A cap is *une casquette;* a stocking cap is *un bonnet;* a military hat is *un képi.* Generic terms for "hat" are *le couvre-chef* or *la coiffure.* (See also CS Lesson 4, p. 53: *le Béret.*)

Page 30

Children at a summer camp on l'Ile de Ré, an island of 10,000 inhabitants in the Atlantic Ocean, due west of La Rochelle and part of le département de la Charente-Maritime. The island is a popular tourist spot in the summer, especially for those who enjoy fishing.

Page 31

La Famille: Family and home life are central to the French way of life. Respect for tradition further reinforces the familial bond. Because families are so closely knit, social life and family life are often synonymous in France, and family activities are far more common than in the U.S. Teen-agers participate in them well past the age when their activities are more or less autonomous in the U.S. Grandparents are often present and are treated with respect, and cousins see each other frequently. (You may wish to point this out when going over the Dialogue, p. 29.)

Children are expected to behave, and good manners are taught at home. The frequency of the compliment *bien élevé* testifies to the importance of teaching children proper behavior. Children tend to sit quietly when in the presence of adults, and usually enter into a conversation only when they have been spoken to first. With friends their own age, they are not so reserved. This behavior pattern applies to teen-agers as well as to small children.

Because of the strong emphasis on the family, outsiders are not readily invited into a French home. Relationships tend to be more formal in France than in the U.S., so that an invitation to a home in France should be considered a great compliment. Social or business acquaintances are far less often invited into the home for a drink or a meal than in the U.S.

Though the M.L.F. *(le Mouvement pour la libération de la femme)* is well-known and very active, the issue of women's liberation does not yet seem to have the widespread appeal in France that it does in the U.S. In part, this is because men and women have always been considered to be necessary complements to one another; though their roles may be different, each is, and always has been, highly respected. Nevertheless, more and more women do work outside the home. Day-care fa-

cilities *(les crèches)* — often run by companies for their employees or by the government — are excellent. The father is still generally considered to be the figure of authority, although women play an active, if sometimes subtle, role in the decision-making process within the home. (See also CS Lesson 14, p. 235: *les Femmes.*)

Included in the Social Security system are *les allocations familiales,* monthly payments given to heads-of-households. The amount of these payments varies according to the number of children in the family. Originally a way of increasing the birth rate to make up for the population lost during World War II, it is now an established fact of life.

Increased industrialization and its companion effects have, of course, modified some of the fundamental aspects of French family life. Nonetheless, young people still support and attempt to uphold the basic tradition of the closely knit family. (See also CS Lesson 6, p. 89: *la Famille.*)

Page 35

Photo: L'autobus numéro 95, Gare Montparnasse.

Page 37

Photo: Outside one of the banks in the Crédit Lyonnais chain, one of the largest, most respected banking firms in the world. Note the large number of bicycles parked outside and the woman on the left riding one (see CS Lesson 4, pp. 48–49: *le Vélo*).

Le Jean: See CS Lesson 4, p. 47.

Page 38

Photo: See CS Lesson 4, pp. 48–49: *le Jardin.*

Page 43

Photo: Near the Rambuteau stop on the Métro, near les Archives Nationales. Note that the grandfather is carrying his lunch; his grandson, a briefcase. One often sees very young school children carrying bookbags or briefcases — sometimes quite heavy — on the way to and from school. (See also CS Lesson 5, p. 63: *le Lycée.*)

LESSON 4

Pages 44–45

Point out that the French use their parks a great deal. They may be large wooded areas, like the famous Bois de Boulogne in Paris, or smaller oases of green where one can find a few moments of relaxation. Parks are frequently located in business districts of Paris, and since Parisians especially are great *flâneurs,* they often stroll through them, watching the people or looking at the gardens.

Although there are benches in many parks, sometimes there are folding chairs set up in front of the gardens and ponds. The chairs are stored indoors overnight and brought out in the morning. Before 1972, if one sat down on these, a government-employed woman—usually quite elderly—called *la chaisière* would approach, charge a small fee for the rental of the chair, and issue a receipt. The rental price was fixed by the government. *Les chaisières* are now a thing of the past in Paris, though they are still to be found *en province*.

When the weather permits, the Guignol is a favorite amusement for young and old alike. A bell is rung before a performance to summon spectators, and then a series of knocks is given as the curtain is about to rise. Guignol himself does not appear until the audience has chanted "Guignol, Guignol, Guignol" for a short time. One of the most popular Parisian Guignols is in le jardin du Luxembourg, located in le Quartier Latin. (See also CS Color Section: *Parcs*.)

Page 46

Photo: You might want to point out that one is as apt to see a woman as a man riding *une moto*. (See also CS, pp. 48–49: *la Moto*.)

Page 47

Le Jean: Jeans are as popular in France as they are in the U.S. Students might enjoy knowing that the word "denim" comes from the blue serge cloth which was manufactured in Nîmes, a city in southwestern France, and which was known as *la serge de Nîmes*. When Levi Strauss first began manufacturing jeans, he ordered the material from Nîmes.

Pages 48–49

L'Avion: France has played a large role in the history of aviation, beginning with the brothers Joseph and Etienne Montgolfier. By trapping heated air in a paper bag, they caused it to float upward. This led to their development of the balloon (*la montgolfière*), which in 1783 first carried humans into flight. That first flight spanned six miles and took 25 minutes. In 1789, the French army organized a balloon corps to serve as military observers, and as late as 1870, during the Franco-Prussian War, balloons were used to evacuate personnel and carry mail out of the city of Paris. Other landmarks in French aviation history are Clément Ader's steam airplane, which in 1897 "flew" a distance of 300 meters (roughly the length of three football fields), Louis Blériot's first flight over the English Channel in 1909; and, more recently, le Concorde, the supersonic trans-

port plane co-produced with the British. (See also CS Lesson 5, p. 63: *l'Aéroport,* and Lesson 13, p. 219.)

Le Garage: Though country homes in France frequently have garages, in cities there are few garages attached to houses or apartment buildings. After 7:00 P.M., on-the-street parking is usually allowed. Between the hours of 9:00 A.M. and 7:00 P.M., parking is allowed only in certain areas called *les zones bleues*. Instead of putting a coin in a parking meter (*un parc-mètre),* one places a plastic or cardboard *disque* on the windshield. This is a square card with a rotating circular piece that has hours marked on it; the hours, indicating the time of arrival and the required time of departure, are visible through two square windows. The areas are patrolled regularly, and if a car is in the zone longer than the allotted time—usually a maximum of one and a half hours—a ticket (*une contravention)* is issued. The driver must then pay a fine (*une amende)* by going to a *tabac* and purchasing a special stamp (its cost based on the violation), which is affixed to the ticket and mailed to the police station. Parking meters are, however, becoming more common. There are also parking lots, called *le parking,* which are under municipal control.

Le Jardin: Gardening is considered an art in France, and gardens differ from those in the U.S. The French prefer many beds, laid out in perfect geometric designs and surrounded by neatly pebbled paths. Even trees and shrubs in parks are trimmed and clipped to blend into the complex patterns.

In cities, one often sees plants and flowers adorning window sills or in pots anchored to shutters (see photo Lesson 3, p. 38). Every city has public gardens. Among the most beautiful in Paris are les Tuileries, near the Louvre, and le jardin du Luxembourg, both of which were designed during the Renaissance. La Roseraie in Lyon is also a well-known garden, filled with a wide variety of roses which bloom nearly all year round.

Fresh-cut flowers are readily available in markets, and there is almost always a small vase of flowers on the dinner table in a French home.

Le Train: The French railroad is controlled by a government agency, the S.N.C.F., *la Société Nationale des Chemins de Fer Français.* Trains are noted for their punctuality and comfort. More and more lines are being operated by electricity. Some coaches are marked first and second class, *fumeurs* and *non-fumeurs*. First-class compartments seat six persons; second-class, eight. Newer coaches are designed more like U.S. trains, with an aisle between paired seats. In peak travel times, it is difficult to find a place unless reservations have been made.

The government provides many economical travel plans for families. People in the Western Hemisphere can take advantage of the Eurailpass, which permits unlimited first-class travel in thirteen Western European countries for periods ranging from three weeks to three months. These passes cannot be purchased in Europe.

Most families prefer to take their baggage with them into their compartment. Frequently, in such cases, one person will board the train and the others will pass the suitcases through the window. They are then placed on large racks above the seats.

Sleeping cars require the purchase of a *wagon-lit* ticket. If the train is going to cross into another country during the night, the porter will often collect passports and papers so that travelers need not be wakened by the customs officer.

Meals are served in two sittings, and passengers make meal reservations with the conductor. The menu is usually limited to three or four courses, but the food is quite good, as is the food served in the railroad stations. But many French families bring their own food and drinks, enough to last throughout the trip. When a train pulls into a station, vendors go by pushing carts loaded with sandwiches, fruit, candy, and beverages. One need only roll down the train window to make a purchase. When travelers reach their destination, they must show their tickets to the agent at the gate before they can go into the station.

French trains are now being used on certain runs in the U.S., where Amtrak has purchased turboliners from the S.N.C.F. The turboliner was first introduced on the Chicago-St. Louis run, and the initials of the French agency were imprinted on the ashtrays and other accessories. Roadbeds, however, will have to be vastly improved if these trains are to achieve anything like the speed and efficiency for which they are known in France. (See also photos, p. 296, and CS Lesson 2, pp. 16–17: *la Gare.*)

Le Vélo/La Moto: Explain that, to most Europeans, bikes and motorbikes are primarily a means of transportation. Bikes are not "toys" and are used by people of all ages, including the very elderly. French mothers do not usually drive their children places. If young people want to go somewhere, they take their bike or motorbike. Girls ride motorbikes in France almost as frequently as boys do. Young people traveling in groups either walk or take the bus or Métro.

Cycling (*le cyclisme*) is an extremely popular sport in France and attracts large crowds at the *vélodromes*. Professional cyclists are well-paid sports heroes who can be compared to the best-known professional athletes in the U.S. Le Tour de France, an annual 21-day 3000-kilometer race, is a major sporting event. In towns throughout France, cheering crowds line the streets as the cyclists pass through. The race takes place in July, and the route takes the cyclists through the rugged mountains of the Alps and the Pyrénées. Some of your students might enjoy preparing a report on le Tour de France and on some of the better-known racers, such as Jacques Anquetil, Eddy Merckx, Raymond Poulidor, and Bernard Thévenet.

In recent years, there has been a growing interest in motorcycling. Despite the fact that France is not considered to be a "motorcycling country," an estimated 500,000 people own motorcycles, most in the under-20 age group. French motorcyclists seem to share a certain spirit and solidarity. In Paris, for example, as many as 500 cyclists gather at la Place de la Bastille each Friday night to share experiences and to discuss such topics as equipment and safety.

La Voiture: Small cars are practical and are therefore popular in France, where most streets are very narrow and where the price of gas is more than twice that in the U.S. The French have traditionally built cars that get forty miles to the gallon. The number of cars in France has increased greatly during the past few years, and the majority of French families now own one.

Pages 53–54

Le Mardi Gras: This is the last day before the forty meatless days of Lent—in other words, the last day when one can *manger gras.* Beginning on Ash Wednesday, one must *manger maigre.*

The largest and best-known Mardi Gras celebrations are held in New Orleans, Nice, and Rio de Janeiro. The parades are generally spectacular, the costumes elaborate, and the amusements joyous and varied.

Le Béret: The béret is not the common sight that it once was in France. This type of hat is now most commonly worn by elderly members of the working class.

Le Clown: In January 1973, the French government instituted a policy whereby English words would be banned in government documents and in radio and television broadcasts. Private companies, as well as the general public, were encouraged to follow suit. The attempt has not been very successful. Such words as *le camping, le standing, le snob, le hobby,* and *le weekend* are now very much a part of the French language.

Photos: Floats at the Mardi Gras parade in Nice.

Page 56

Photos: Four standard European traffic signs: *arrêt à l'intersection; interdit aux camions,* and, in the background, *fin de section d'autoroute; virage à gauche interdit* and *stationnement interdit* at a tow-away zone. Many of these international signs are now in use in the U.S. Point out that the amount of international travel within Europe makes such a purely visual system of signs important for travelers who do not speak the language of a particular country.

Page 57

Photo: You might point out the brick street, of which there are a number in Paris. They are often laid out in patterns, as in the photo on p. 59.

LESSON 5

Page 60

(a) A policeman in Paris

(b) The rooftops of Cannes.

(c) A policeman giving a young woman directions in front of le cinéma Champs-Elysées. Paris police are usually exceptionally well informed and very helpful in giving directions. You might want to point out the white gloves that the traffic policeman wears so that his gestures will be readily noticeable (see also photos, pp. 71 and 85).

Page 61

Cannes/La Côte d'Azur: Point out this resort city on a map.

The full name of the convention hall is Le Palais des Festivals et des Congrès. As the footnote mentions, it is the site of the annual Cannes Film Festival, held in late spring. Motion pictures from all over the world are shown and judged by an international jury which awards prizes, the most coveted of which is the Grand Prix. Unlike the Academy Awards, *le festival du film* is truly an international event.

Students might be interested to learn that the process of cinematography was invented in 1895 by two French brothers, Auguste and Louis Lumière. Students may know the names of such internationally famous French film directors as Claude Chabrol, Jean-Luc Godard, and François Truffaut, or of such stars as Brigitte Bardot, Catherine Deneuve, Jeanne Moreau, Simone Signoret, Jean-Paul Belmondo, Alain Delon, Yves Montand, and Jean-Louis Trintignant.

Another popular event in Cannes is *la Bataille des fleurs.* It takes place at the height of the summer flower season and is celebrated with parades and floats from which girls throw blossoms to the crowd.

Point out that flowers are abundant in the south of France, which is why the town of Grasse, near Cannes, is the center of the French perfume industry.

La Côte d'Azur stretches from east of Marseille to the Italian-French border. The region is one of France's most popular vacation and resort areas. Other important cities on la Côte d'Azur are Antibes, Nice, Saint-Raphaël, and Saint-Tropez. (See also photos, pp. 12 and 28, and CS Color Section: *Plages.*)

Page 62

Photo: L'hôtel Carlton, a very elegant hotel in Cannes.

Page 63

L'Aéroport: Orly, located south of Paris, is a large, modern international airport capable of handling all the largest, most advanced intercontinental aircraft. Le Bourget, northeast of Paris, which handles short flights and smaller planes, is best known to us as the field where Charles Lindbergh landed in 1927.

Paris's newest airport is located northeast of Paris in the town of Roissy-en-France. Though officially named after Charles de Gaulle, the airport is often referred to as Roissy. It is predicted that by 1985, Roissy will handle 45 to 50 million passengers a year. The airport is noted for its architectural design. The main building is eleven stories high and is connected by tunnels to seven "satellites," where planes are boarded and unloaded.

Le Café: In French cities, the cafés, with their tables spread over the sidewalk *(la terrasse)*, are very much a part of daily life. This is equally true in small towns, where the cafés are not always sidewalk cafés. In many small towns in France, it is common for retired men to gather with their friends and pass the time of day. Like the nineteenth-century general store in rural America and the drive-in for many of today's teen-agers, the café is a hub of social life, a living room away from home. The pace is unhurried and one drink guarantees your table for as long as you want, though in principle one is expected to reorder every hour or so. One can read or write, chat with friends, or simply watch the world go by. (See also CS Lesson 10, p. 150.)

Le Château: There are châteaux throughout France, but many of the best known and most beautiful are in the Loire valley. Among the most famous are Amboise, whose large turret shelters the spiraling road that permitted messengers and royal carriages to climb to the castle high above the Loire; Chenonceaux, which straddles the Cher River; Blois, with its beautifully carved exterior staircase; and Chambord, the largest, with 365 rooms. Nearer to Paris is, of course, the famous château de Versailles, the magnificent palace of Louis XIV. You may want to post photos of some of these châteaux.

Le Lycée: In the French educational system, all students must attend *une école primaire* followed by four years in *un collège d'enseignement secondaire* (C.E.S.). The first year is known as *sixième;* the second year, *cinquième,* etc. After *troisième,* students receive *un brevet.* They may then terminate their schooling, go to a commercial school, or attend *un lycée.* The three years of *lycée* education are known as *seconde, première,* and *terminale.* The final year is spent in careful preparation for the college entrance exam — *le baccalauréat.*

In terms of difficulty and amount of material to be mastered, *le lycée* is roughly equivalent to a good U.S. high school plus junior college. A private or parochial school is generally called *un collège privé.*

There are both public and private schools in France, but since education is centralized, all students must take the same examinations to receive a diploma recognized by the state. In most cases, the French student is in school from 8:00 until 5:00, with two hours off for lunch. Classes are held five days a week, with Wednesday (not Saturday) and Sunday free. French children must attend school until the age of sixteen. Education in Europe is still based primarily on the acquisition of facts, and seminar-type discussions play only a small part in the educational process.

Although modern *lycées* are being built, many very old ones are still in use. In French schools, the teacher's desk is usually on a raised platform and student desks (often double) are usually arranged in long rows. Today the trend is toward coeducation *(lycées mixtes),* though there remain many schools reserved for boys or girls.

French children tend to be very serious about school, since later their education — and eventually their career — will depend upon their performance on competitive examinations. They tend to have far more homework than students in the U.S. and carry many books home with them. For this reason, even a very small child may carry a large briefcase *(un cartable),* which is often strapped on the back.

Le Musée: Though the average Parisian comes into daily contact with art in the parks and streets of the city, at the Louvre one is able to see masterpieces collected from all parts of the world. Located on the right bank of the Seine, the Louvre, once the palace of the kings of France, is the largest museum in the world and has one of the most distinguished collections to be found anywhere.

Some other major museums in Paris are le Musée du Jeu de Paume, on la Place de la Concorde, which houses the Louvre's large collection of Impressionist paintings; le Musée Rodin near les Invalides; le Musée National d'Art Moderne, situated on the Seine between l'avenue de New-York and l'avenue du Président-Wilson; and le Musée Cluny, in le Quartier Latin, which is devoted to treasures from the Middle Ages.

Le Restaurant: The French are noted for their excellent cuisine, and there are many fine restaurants in France. Within the last few years, self-service restaurants have sprung up here and there, including a number of Mac-Donald's. For the most part, however, restaurants pride themselves on serving good — and complete — meals. Although families tend to eat at home, it is very common for friends or business associates to meet for lunch or dinner in a restaurant. (See also CS Lesson 3, p. 31: *la Famille.*) Explain that the gratuity is figured into the cost of the meal *(service compris)* or automatically added to the bill before the customer receives it *(service non compris).* However, one may often add a small tip to the amount that is figured in. (See also Lesson 15.)

Each year, culinary specialists from the publishers of *le Guide Michelin* travel throughout France and rate restaurants. To earn a star in *le Guide Michelin* is truly an honor. Two- and three-star awards are given very sparingly.

Le Théâtre: The French love for the theater dates back to the Middle Ages, when the mystery and miracle plays were performed, first in the churches and then in the churchyard. Some companies subsidized by the state play only the classics, and it is not uncommon for a French person to have seen certain plays by Racine, Corneille, or Molière three or four times. The price of admission is not prohibitive; one can get a balcony seat for less than two dollars. Among the best-known repertory companies in France are la Comédie Française and le T.N.P. (Théâtre National Populaire). Le Théâtre de la Huchette presents modern plays in repertory. It specializes in Ionesco and is one of the few theaters that remains open all summer. Popular musical shows are presented at le Bobino and l'Olympia. You may wish to point out that one is seated in a theater by *une ouvreuse* and that if one wants a program it must be bought. Ushers are tipped in many theaters, although tipping is prohibited at certain others, including the Comédie Française (see CS Lesson 9, p. 143: *le Cinéma*).

Page 70

La Cantine: In the past, students always went home for lunch. Today, however, more and more students eat their lunch at school, and a hot meal is usually served.

Your students may be interested in learning the names of other schoolrooms. *Une salle de permanence* is a supervised study hall. It is not located in a library, as in many U.S. schools, but is simply a room where students go when they have a free period. A school library is called *une salle de documentation* and contains mainly reference works, newspapers, magazines, and journals. The teacher's lounge is *la salle des professeurs;* the principal's office in a C.E.S., *le bureau du directeur (ou de la directrice)* and in a *lycée, le bureau du proviseur (ou de la directrice);* the gym, *le gymnase;* the language lab, *le laboratoire de langues.*

Le Football: The term is frequently shortened to *le foot.* Your students might be interested in learning certain soccer terms in French: a team (in any contest) is *une équipe;* the positions on a soccer team are: forward, *l'avant;* wing, *l'ailier;* halfback, *le demi;* fullback, *l'arrière;* goalie, *le gardien (de but).* To shoot is *shooter;* a goal is *un but;* the referee is *l'arbitre.* You might point out that many sports terms in French are taken from English because many of the games originated in Great Britain.

Soccer is to Europeans what major-league baseball or professional football is in the U.S. or hockey is in Canada. Most large towns have teams that compete in professional leagues, and the rivalry between certain teams often exceeds anything we know here. There is also major international competition.

Page 73

(a) The young boy is looking at a sign advertising the appearance in Nice of the British Royal Air Force Red Arrows. The sign reads: *Parade aérienne de la patrouille acrobatique de la Royal Air Force.*

On the sign underneath, you might want to point out that *le stationnement* means "parking," and *le parking* means "parking lot" or "parking area."

(b) Sign on l'autoroute pointing toward the seaside route to Nice and to the Nice airport.

LESSON 6

Page 76

(a) Class in a *lycée mixte* in Paris.

(b, d) Doing one's homework. Note that the boy is using ink. Though ballpoint pens are now widely accepted, some French schools still insist that liquid ink be used. Penmanship and neatness are considered very important in French schools. (See also CS Lesson 1, p. 5: *le Stylo.*)

(c) Outside le lycée Chaptal in Paris.

Page 77

Les Devoirs: As noted earlier (see CS Lesson 5, p. 63: *le Lycée*), French students tend to be quite serious about their school work. A great deal of homework is assigned daily. Students are expected to complete the assignments in a *cahier,* one of which is kept for each class.

Les Sports: Although there are no competitive athletic events between schools, sports do play an important part in French life. In general, however, the French tend to prefer individual to team sports. One of the biggest events of the year is le Tour de France, which attracts participants from both France and abroad. It is the equal of the World Series or the Super Bowl in terms of the excitement it creates. (See also CS Lesson 4, pp. 48–49: *le Vélo.*)

Other than soccer, *le rugby* is by far the most popular game in France, particularly in the Southwest. Other popular team sports are basketball and volleyball. Tennis, too, has long been popular in France. One of the oldest French games, and a favorite among older men, is *boules.* This game resembles bowling, but the balls, which are made of metal, are smaller, and the game is played outdoors. There are regional versions; in the South, for example it is called *la pétanque.* (See footnote, p. 214, and photo, p. 215.)

The French also enjoy swimming *(la natation),* skiing *(le ski),* walking *(les promenades),* fishing *(la pêche),* hunting *(la chasse),* boating *(les promenades en bateau),* and card-playing *(les jeux de cartes).*

Page 78

Photo: A balloon man on la Côte d'Azur. You might want to point out that baseball is very rarely played in Europe.

Page 79

Les Films: Point out that the French are avid and knowledgeable moviegoers. Poor reviews are apt to kindle interest rather than to discourage moviegoers. There is very much an attitude of seeing for oneself. Many young people belong to *ciné-clubs,* associations that present the best films, old and new, from all over the world, with a discussion period after. American films are quite popular in Europe. Since most of these are dubbed, certain individuals have made a career of dubbing the voice of a particular American movie star. American musicals, however, are shown in English. (See also CS Lesson 9, p. 132, and photos, p. 144.)

Westerns are particularly popular among the French, whose interest in American Indians *(les Peaux-Rouges)* goes back to the early days of French romanticism, when, after his travels in America, Chateaubriand wrote his praise of the "noble savage" in *Atala* (1801). (See also CS Lesson 5, p. 61: *Cannes.*)

Jouer aux cartes: Point out *le roi, la dame, le valet.* Should students ask, the joker is *le joker* [ʒɔkɛr], the ace is *l'as* [as], and the four suits are *trèfles* (clubs), *carreaux* (dia-

monds), *coeurs* (hearts), and *piques* (spades). Trump is *atout;* no trump, *sans atout.*

A very popular card game in France is called *la belote.* It may be played by two, three, or four players, but uses only thirty-two cards. (See CS Color Section: *Loisirs.*) Bridge is *le bridge.* Other popular games include *le jeu de dames* (checkers), *le trictrac* (backgammon), *les dominos.*

Le Journal: The French are avid newspaper readers, and some people will read several newspapers in order to get a broad range of opinions. *Le Figaro* and *Le Monde* are probably those best known outside of France.

La Télé: French TV is supervised by government agencies, although there are slight regional differences in broadcasts, especially with respect to newscasts. In many sections of France, people are able to receive French-language broadcasts from Monaco, Luxembourg, Belgium, and Switzerland.

You might wish to teach *ouvrir,* "to turn on," and *fermer,* "to turn off," as additional meanings of these verbs. Should students ask, *la chaîne* is the word for a TV channel.

Page 81

Le Petit Déjeuner: The French (continental) breakfast usually consists of *café au lait* (very strong coffee served with an equal amount of hot milk), bread, butter, and jam. In many homes, the *café au lait* is served in bowls. If convenient, a parent or older child will often go to the bakery early in the morning to get fresh-baked bread for breakfast. In hotels and restaurants, *croissants* (flaky, crescent-shaped rolls) or *brioches* (small, round rolls made with a leavened dough) may replace the bread (see photo, p. 82, and footnote, p. 265).

Le Déjeuner: Lunch is usually a full meal, though it may have fewer courses than the evening meal. Many working people still return home for the midday meal. You may wish to point out the full family at table in the art on p. 81. Note, too, that wine is customarily served at lunch as well as at dinner. Milk is not served, and children may sometimes have a bit of wine heavily diluted with bottled water.

Le Dîner: Despite the social and economic changes that tend more and more to infringe on the family unit, the traditional family dinner still retains its role. Until recently, the noon meal was the largest, since working parents and school-age children were able to return home during the two-hour midday break. Due to transportation difficulties, however, the French are beginning to have their main meal in the evening. Since dinner is served late—no earlier than 7:00—people will often have a snack *(un goûter)* around 4:00. Dinner consists of several courses and is never rushed. It is savored, along with the wine and conversation. (See also CS Lesson 15, p. 243: *le Déjeuner, le dîner.*)

Les Manières de table: Just as ideas of what constitutes good food differ from culture to culture, so too do ideas concerning good table manners. For example, in France, both hands should always be above the table (it is considered impolite for one hand to be held in the lap); the fork is not switched from hand to hand in cutting and eating meat; a piece of bread is used to help push vegetables onto the fork; soup is taken into the mouth from the front of the spoon, not the side; at the table, nothing but bread is eaten with the hands (even fresh fruit is carefully sliced then eaten with a fork). Even very small children are expected to sit properly at the dinner table.

Page 85
Photo: See CS Lesson 5, p. 60.

Page 88
Photo: Magician-mime outside a sidewalk café in Montréal.

Page 89
Photo: Mail delivery to a home in Paris.

La Famille: Despite the traditional solidarity of the French family, it is becoming increasingly common for young people to live and work away from home. This is more than anything the result of a changing economic structure. Before World War II, this type of dispersion was extremely rare, and it was quite common for young people to follow in their parents' footsteps. It was assumed that the child of a farmer would be a farmer, that the child of a porcelain-maker would very likely be a porcelain-maker, etc.

Page 93
Photo: Three professors from the University of Strasbourg. A meal without interesting conversation would be considered incomplete.

Page 95
Photo: A window in a home in Paris. Note the wrought-iron railing and the detailed work on the building itself.

LESSON 7

Page 96
(a) A flower vendor *(un fleuriste)* on la rue de Seine in Paris. (See CS Lesson 4, pp. 48–49: *le Jardin.*)

(b) A rainy day on le Champs-Elysées.

(c) Winter in Montmartre. The highest natural point in Paris, Montmartre has long been known for its bohemian atmosphere. Numerous artists and writers have lived in the quarter, and one still sees many sidewalk artists working and selling their pictures there (see also CS Color Section: *Arts*). Montmartre is also a center of night life; many of the best-known cabarets in Paris are there (le Moulin de la Galette, le Lapin Agile, le Moulin Rouge). The area derives its name *(le Mont des Martyrs)* from the tradition that St. Denis, the first bishop of Paris, and others were executed there around the year 250.

Page 97
Le Temps: Though moderate, the climate of France has many characteristics of a maritime region. This is because the country is bounded on three sides by water and has extensive interior waterways. Rain is abundant and falls throughout the year. The one major exception to this is the climate in the Mediterranean region, where it is usually mild all winter and where the summer months may be quite dry. Even there, however, one may encounter the Mistral, a cold, violent wind that sometimes sweeps down from the Alps and through the Rhône valley to the sea. It is strongest and most likely to occur in the winter and spring. The winds may continue for several days, reaching a velocity of 100 kilometers or more. (The name *Le Mistral* was given to the train that links Paris-Lyon-Marseille-Nice because it is one of the fastest trains in the world.)

Page 99
Les Saisons: Spring and summer are usually considered to be the nicest seasons in France. Winters tend to be relatively mild, with rain falling more often than snow, though in eastern France and in the mountainous areas near Spain and Switzerland, the winters are cold and quite snowy. August is usually the hottest and driest month, and because pleasant weather is most likely to

occur then, it is the traditional time for the four-week vacation guaranteed to all workers by law.

La Température: For those who are not completely familiar with the metric system, the following conversion rates may be of help:

°C = ⁵⁄₉ (°F − 32) or °F = ⁹⁄₅ (°C + 32)

Other equivalences are:

1 meter = 39.37 inches
1 kilometer = 0.62 miles
1 liter = 1.057 quarts
1 kilogram = 2.2 pounds

Page 100

Photo: Exercise period at *une école primaire* in Paris. School playgrounds are not common in France. Schools are often built around a small courtyard (*une cour*), however, where students take exercise. At most one usually finds only a small amount of equipment, such as a basketball hoop or jungle gym.

Page 101

Photo: A lottery ticket window on le boulevard des Italiens in Paris, where a special lottery is being advertised for Friday the thirteenth. One can buy *un dixième*, one-tenth of a ticket, for only three francs. Note the lucky horseshoe (*le fer à cheval*) and the pot of ivy (*le lierre*) to bring a touch of natural greenery to an otherwise very urban situation.

Les Jours de la semaine: Point out that Monday is the first day of the calendar week. The names for the days of the week in France stem from Roman mythology and from the Bible. Students may be interested in the derivations of the names. The *di* common to all of them comes from the Latin word for day, *dies.*

lundi: jour de la lune
mardi: jour de Mars
mercredi: jour de Mercure
jeudi: jour de Jupiter
vendredi: jour de Vénus
samedi: jour du Sabbat (Sabbat = Sambatum)
dimanche: jour du Seigneur (du Seigneur = Dominicus).

The English names for the days are quite different: Sunday (Sun's Day) and Monday (Moon's Day) stem from Anglo-Saxon sources, and Tuesday through Friday from the names of Norse gods (Tiw's day, Woden's day, Donar's [Thonar's] day, and Fria's day). Only Saturday is of Latin origin (Saturn's day).

Page 103

Photo: A sidewalk artist in Québec.

Page 105

Les Plaques d'immatriculation: The last two digits indicate the *département* in which the owner has registered the vehicle. (There are presently 100 *départements,* or administrative districts, numbered 1-95. There is none numbered 96, but Finistère Nord and Finistère Sud are 29N and 29S respectively. The four *départements d'outre-mer* are: 971, Guadeloupe; 972, Martinique; 973, Guyane Française; 974, Réunion. In France, license plates serve as an identification number for the car, not the owner. Thus when a car is sold, the license plate is not changed unless it is sold to someone living in another *département.*

Page 106

La Fête foraine: Usually lasting about a week, these fairs often come into a town as part of the celebration of local, regional, national, or religious holidays. The number and size of the attractions vary from fair to fair, but usually consist of rides, games, amusements, and refreshments. In a large city like Paris, one can find neighborhood fairs going on at different times throughout the year.

The most important fair in Paris is *la Foire du Trône,* which lasts for a month each April-May. Though it now takes place near the entrance to le Bois de Vincennes, its name derives from its earlier location at la Place de la Nation (originally known as la Place du Trône, because an enormous royal throne had been erected there in August 1660 for the entrance into Paris of Louis XIV and his bride, Marie-Thérèse, the Infanta of Spain. It became known as la Place du Trône renversé when, in 1793, the guillotine was moved there after the residents of la rue Saint-Honoré grew tired of watching the condemned driven by on their way to what is now la Place de la Concorde.). The fair itself dates to Easter week, 957, when the disciples of St. Antoine distributed bread and honey to the poor in remembrance of their patron's having spent five years in the desert living only on milk and honey 700 years earlier.

Page 107

Photo: Scene in Vallauris, near Cannes (see CS Lesson 1, p. 2). You might want to post reproductions of works by Fernand Léger (1881–1955), one of the major cubist painters.

Page 111

Photo: Scene on le boulevard Saint-Michel (le Boul' Mich'), one of the major shopping streets in Paris.

Page 113

Photo: Restaurant on la Côte d'Azur. You might want to point out that *bar-restaurant* means that the establishment has a separate bar.

Les Numéros de téléphone: Most phone numbers in France are now all digits. Telephones in the provinces usually consist of six numbers, though in small towns there may be even fewer. In the area of Paris, where the population is dense, phone numbers have seven digits, as in the U.S. Parisian phone numbers formerly consisted of a three letter exchange and four digits; occasionally, one still sees the old system. There are also area codes (*les indicatifs régionaux*). (See also CS Lesson 9, p. 133: *le Téléphone.*)

LESSON 8

Page 114

(a) Mont Tremblant lodge.

(b) Le Château Frontenac in Québec. This magnificent hotel was named for Louis de Buade, comte de Frontenac (1620–1698), who was governor of la Nouvelle-France from 1672 to 1682 and from 1689 until his death.

Québec City was founded by Samuel de Champlain (1567–1635), who visited la Nouvelle-France in 1603 and in 1608 convinced Henri IV to create a colony there. The original walled city has been extremely well preserved and is a major tourist attraction. Today the city is a business and industrial center with a population of 167,000. Built on an escarpment overlooking the confluence of the St. Lawrence (*le Saint-Laurent*) and St. Charles Rivers (the former *un fleuve;* the latter, *une rivière*), Québec commands a beautiful view.

(c) A café in Montréal.

Page 115

Le Canada: Québec is the only province in Canada where the population is predominantly French. Other French-speaking groups live in Nova Scotia and southern New Brunswick (where the inhabitants are descendants of the founders of the French colony of Acadia), as well as in certain areas of northern Ontario and the Ottawa Valley.

The roots of la Nouvelle-France date back to 1534 and the voyages of Jacques Cartier (1491–1557). From the earliest days, fur trading was a major enterprise in the French colony. (The name of the family in the dialogue, Pelletier, means "trapper" and is a very common French Canadian name.) Missionary activity was also extremely important. Indeed, the discoverer of the Mississippi River was the great Jesuit missionary, le père Jacques Marquette (1637–1675).

From the earliest times, tensions and strains existed between Canada's French and British rulers. In a certain sense, therefore, the origins of the separatist movement in Canada date back several centuries. Since World War II, the movement has rapidly gained in support and popularity among many Québécois. As a political issue, separatism is likely to remain a vital force in Québec. Your students might enjoy following current events in this province, as well as doing research into French Canada's early history, in order to gain a fuller understanding of this vital facet of French culture in North America.

Sherbrooke: This city is located at the confluence of the Magog and St. Francis Rivers, about 45 kilometers north of the Vermont border. Originally Sherbrooke was a fur-trading post. In addition to being an administrative center, it is now a commercial and industrial center. L'université de Sherbrooke, a French-language Roman Catholic university, was founded in 1954.

Les Laurentides: The Laurentian Mountains are one of the world's oldest, though not highest, ranges. The peaks were greatly worn down during the Ice Age. The area is heavily wooded and rich in minerals, and there are numerous lakes and rivers. For these reasons, the main industries in the area are lumbering, paper-milling, and year-round tourism.

Page 116

Photos: Here are a café sign and a painted wall in Montréal, which, like Paris, is a major center for artists. The city was founded in 1642 under the name Ville-Marie, by Paul de Chomedey de Maisonneuve (1612–1676). Today, with a population of approximately a million and a quarter, it is the largest city in Canada. It is one of the world's truly bicultural cities; forty percent of the population speaks both French and English. The city is the home of four major universities—two French (l'université de Montréal and l'université de Québec) and two English (McGill and Sir George Williams Universities)—and of numerous fine restaurants, art galleries, museums, and both English and French theaters. Below the city is the St. Lawrence River; overlooking the city at its highest point, le Mont Royal.

Page 120

L'Auto-stop: Hitchhiking does not have the stigma attached to it in France that it does in many places in the U.S. Young people frequently hitchhike, both short and long distances. (See photo, p. 285.)

Page 121

Document: A deposit slip from la Banque de Montréal. Students might like to know some of the following terms: bank account, *le compte en banque;* checking account, *le compte courant;* savings account, *le compte d'épargne;* savings bank, *la caisse d'épargne;* passbook savings account, *le compte sur livret;* coins, *la monnaie;* currency, *les billets;* coins and currency, *les espèces;* dividends from government bonds, *les coupons;* deposit, *le dépôt;* teller or cashier, *le caissier, la caissière;* to deposit, *déposer* or *verser.*

Page 122

Chamonix: Located near the French-Swiss border, at the foot of Mont Blanc, Chamonix is an extremely popular tourist and winter sports area. It is also the site of France's Ecole Nationale de Ski et d'Alpinisme. Point out that the *x* is not usually pronounced.

Page 123

Photo: La Porte Saint-Jean, one of the gates to the old walled city of Québec.

Page 124

Langue et langage: Through a number of legislative acts, such as the Official Languages Act of 1969, bilingualism has been encouraged throughout Canada. The French spoken in the province of Québec and, by minorities, in the other Canadian provinces, differs from that spoken in metropolitan France mainly in terms of pronunciation and vocabulary rather than of grammatical

structure. Educated Québécois are able to shift from local varieties to a form of French almost indistinguishable from that of France. Because of constant contact with English, some words have been borrowed. However, most differences between the vocabulary of Québécois French and that of France reflect either expressions stemming from a different way of life or the preservation of words that were at one time common in France but which have now been lost. For example, *être vite sur ses patins* (literally, "to be quick on one's skates"), which means "to be lively," is a quite logical expression to have arisen among people accustomed to snow, ice, and skating. On the other hand, the verb *magasiner,* "to shop," has been preserved in Canada; in France the verb is no longer used, and one must resort to a less specific expression, such as *faire des courses, faire des emplettes, faire des achats,* or even the anglicism *faire du shopping.*

To help your students realize that languages always borrow from one another, you might ask them to think of common English words borrowed from the French, such as café, chef, façade, foulard, hors d'œuvre, cul-de-sac, faux pas, rendez-vous, laissez-faire, filet mignon, and so on. They might also be interested in thinking of words borrowed from other languages: rodeo, patio, plaza, and poncho from Spanish; gesundheit, blitzkrieg, torte from German, etc.

Page 125

(a) Sleigh ride in the Laurentians.

(b) Ice sculpture outside a home in the old walled city during le Carnaval de Québec, an annual Mardi Gras-type winter carnival.

(c) Le bonhomme Carnaval reigns over the carnival from the gigantic ice palace that is the center of the festivities.

Page 126

Photo: A hockey match, one of the many events taking place during the carnival. Hockey is the national sport of Canada.

Page 128

Document: Portions of two pages from the Montréal phone directory (*l'annuaire*). You might want particularly to point out the 24-hour clock in the top right-hand corner. You might also want to use this for practicing numbers. You would need to introduce a bit of vocabulary (*un appel, coûter*), but students might find it an enjoyable exercise. For example: *Un appel de trois minutes de Montréal à Sainte-Agathe coûte 68 cents. Le dimanche, après 6 h. du soir, ça coûte . . . (34 cents).*

Page 131

Jacques Prévert: The early writing of Prévert (b. 1900) was mostly for the movies, of which his best known is *Les Enfants du paradis* (1943). His reputation was established with the publication of the book of poems entitled *Paroles* (1946), in which he revealed a highly sensitive and imaginative approach to the most ordinary things in life. Other collections are *Histoires* (1946) and *Spectacle* (1951). Prévert's very simple verse makes his poems ideally suited to beginning students of French.

LESSON 9

Page 132

(a) An ad for two Marx Brothers movies. Point out that comedians such as Chaplin, Buster Keaton, and the Marx Brothers are as widely appreciated in France as in the U.S. Some, such as Jerry Lewis, are cult figures in France. Note the terms *la réalisation,* meaning "direction," and *l'interprétation,* which in this context means "cast."

(b) The ticket is from le cinéma Saint-Michel in Paris.

(c) The lists of films and of special events are from l'université de Sherbrooke. You might want to point out the 24-hour time system and the meaning of the term *s[ous] titré.*

Page 133

Le Téléphone: The French telephone system is operated by the government, and not all homes have one. The demand for new service far exceeds the availability of equipment, and it is not unusual to have to wait several years for a phone. As a result, many people use pay telephones, and public phone booths are quite numerous.

Pay phones are located in many cafés and all post offices. Sometimes one must buy a special token *(un jeton)* in order to use the phones. This is particularly true in cafés. There is a button on the phone which is pushed after the party on the other end answers. (If it is pushed before that and no one answers, the token is not returned.) If the button is not pushed at all, the party cannot hear the caller speak.

Some terms students might want to know are: phone call, *le coup de téléphone:* phone booth, *la cabine*

téléphonique; phone book, *l'annuaire;* to dial, *composer le numéro;* to pick up the receiver, *décrocher;* to hang up, *raccrocher.* Many French people answer the phone by saying, *Allô, j'écoute* or *Allô, oui. Ne quittez pas* is equivalent to "just a moment please." A common question is *Qui est à l'appareil?* ("Who's calling?"); similarly, many callers identify themselves as X *à l'appareil* rather than *Ici X.* If your students are interested in learning these terms, it might be fun to have "telephone conversations" in French to practice simple dialogues and to review numbers. (See also CS Lesson 7, p. 113: *les Numéros de téléphone.*)

Epernay, Reims: These two cities are the major commercial centers for the production and sale of champagne. Epernay has a population of about 30,000, and most people who live there are, in one way or another, directly involved in the champagne industry. Reims, with a population of approximately 160,000, is also the site of a large university and is the largest city in the old province of Champagne. (You may want to point out that the wine is *le champagne,* but the region is *la Champagne.*)

During the First World War, the Champagne region was the site of the fierce Battles of the Marne. The French troops were led by le maréchal Joseph Joffre (1852–1931). Early in the war, in September 1914, the French were able to halt the advance of the German troops. In subsequent battles, however, the area was overrun by the German army. Under the leadership of le maréchal Ferdinand Foch (1851–1929), the region was recaptured by the French in July 1918.

Page 135

Documents: Three ads for a Chinese, a Japanese, and an Italian restaurant. You may want to point out that the numbers in the addresses *Paris 10, boulevard Saint-Michel 5e,* and *rue de Montparnasse (14e)* represent the *arrondissement.* Paris is divided into twenty such administrative districts, which were first established by Napoléon I er in 1800. The number of the *arrondissement* is more than merely a part of the address; it is very meaningful to Parisians, who think of and describe places as being located in such and such an *arrondissement.*

Page 137

Les Trois Mousquetaires: Students may well have read this historical novel by Alexandre Dumas *père* (1844), the story of d'Artagnan and the three musketeers (Athos, Porthos, and Aramis), who set out to defend the honor of Queen Anne of Austria. Students may be interested to know that following a person's name *père* is the equivalent of "Sr." and *fils* of "Jr."

Le Lac: This poem by Alphonse de Lamartine appeared in the collection *Méditations poétiques* (1820). Lamartine was the first in a long succession of great romantic poets. Like many other celebrated French writers, he was deeply involved in the life and politics of his time. First elected to the *chambre des députés* in 1833, he was later to be minister of foreign affairs and head of the provisionary government in 1848. Among many notable examples of such *engagement* have been Montaigne, mayor of Bordeaux; Montesquieu, president of the Parlement of Bordeaux; André Chenier, who died on the scaffold (1794) after his protestations against the Reign of Terror; Chateaubriand, ambassador to London, minister of foreign affairs; Victor Hugo, elected *député* in 1848, who lived nearly twenty years as a political exile in England (1851–1870); Emile Zola, with his strong protestations against government action in the Dreyfus Affair; and more recently, Paul Claudel, ambassador to Japan the U.S., and Belgium, and André Malraux, minister of cultural affairs.

Le Petit Chaperon rouge: One of the fairy tales from *Histoires du temps passé: Contes de ma mère l'oie* (1697) written by Charles Perrault. Among his other still-popular tales are *Le Chat botté, Cendrillon,* and *Barbe-Bleue.*

Le Marché: The market remains an important part of French life. Two or three times a week, and daily in certain areas of Paris, open-air markets are set up where all kinds of fresh meat, fish, fruit, vegetables, and flowers can be purchased.

The most famous French market, *les Halles,* was called by Emile Zola *le ventre de Paris.* Dating back to the Middle Ages, these huge covered markets occupied the center of Paris. From midnight on, trucks loaded with produce rolled in from the provinces. Between 5:00 and 8:00 A.M. the market was in full operation, with wholesale merchants purchasing foods for the neighborhood street markets. By noon, all was cleaned up and closed. It was a popular spot for late-night snacks, particularly for the onion soup served at some of the cafés there. Because of the congestion caused by the narrow streets in the vicinity of *les Halles,* the central market of Paris has been moved to Rungis, near Orly Airport.

Le Supermarché: This large store, which offers a wide variety of products, is much like the American supermarket. Comparatively new to France, it is becoming increasingly popular.

Le Grand Magasin: There are many department stores in France. Some of the best known are those in Paris: Les Galeries Lafayette, Au Bon Marché, Au Printemps, La Samaritaine, Le Bazar de l'Hôtel de Ville. Throughout France, there are branches of the popular Prisunic and Monoprix, which are self-service stores selling clothing, housewares, cosmetics, etc. There are also *hypermarchés,* usually found in shopping centers, that are very like our large discount chains, carrying everything from food to auto supplies.

Page 140

Photo: Au Printemps, on le boulevard Haussmann, one of the major department stores in Paris.

Page 142

Photo: One of the many large kiosks in Paris, where newspapers, magazines, paperback books, and tobacco products are sold.

Page 143

Le Cinéma: The concept of tipping a movie usher may be quite surprising to your students. Similarly, the fact that mixed in with documentaries and newsreels there are often many commercial advertisements. Where tipping is expected, the tips and the money from the sale of candy and ice cream bars represent the only payment the ushers receive.

Page 149

Photo: You might want to tell students that a supermarket cart is called *un chariot.* You might also want to tell them about *le filet,* the net shopping bag that market patrons use to carry home their purchases.

LESSON 10

Page 150

(a) Le Café de Flore on le boulevard Saint-Germain. Along with le Café des Deux-Magots, two doors away, this is one of the best-known cafés in Paris. Jean-Paul Sartre, Simone de Beauvoir, and others often met and sometimes actually wrote their works here.

(b) A sidewalk café in Saint-Jean-de-Luz, in the Pyrénées. A town of 11,000 on the Atlantic Coast, it is known for its sardine and tuna fishing and as a popular bathing resort. It was here that Louis XIV and Marie Thérèse, the Infanta of Spain, were married in 1660 (see CS Lesson 7, p. 106: *la Fête foraine*).

(c) Another sidewalk café in Paris.

It is quite common for people to frequent a certain café. It is an especially popular spot for a breakfast of *café au lait* and perhaps *une tartine beurrée* (bread and butter) or *croissants*. Pinball machines and other games, such as darts, attract young people and are extremely popular. Students may even meet in cafés before classes to play a few rounds (see also *lecture,* p. 160).

In addition to beer and wine, there are many favorite nonalcoholic drinks, such as Coke and grenadine. There is also a variety of noncarbonated fruit drinks made from thick syrup, and the popular *citron pressé* (see art and footnote, p. 153). Note that *une limonade* is a carbonated soft drink with a lemon base.

After lunch, French people may stop by a café for a cup of strong coffee, called *un filtre* or *un express,* which is made by filtering hot water through freshly ground coffee. One can also order mineral water — either a noncarbonated one, such as Evian, or a carbonated one, such as Vichy. Mineral water is very popular throughout Europe.

Page 151

La Terrasse d'un café: The *terrasse* is that section of a café where tables and chairs are set up outside. This is very common in larger towns and cities. *La terrasse* is usually enclosed and heated in the winter.

Georges Simenon: This well-known Belgian writer was born in Liège in 1903. One of the most prolific writers of fiction, he has at times written as many as a dozen books a year. Having used 17 different pseudonyms, his output thus far consists of approximately 1500 short stories and 500 novels. He is best known for his detective series, which features the pipe-smoking Parisian police inspector, *le commissaire Maigret,* a character who first appeared in 1930. Simenon's works are noted for their keen psychological insight and accurate portrayal of day-to-day police functions.

Page 154

Photo: Soft-drink stand at a picnic area in Paris.

Page 155

Les Langues: Remind students that French teen-agers frequently study several languages. In *sixième,* at age eleven, students must begin the study of a modern language; a second is begun in *quatrième.* (One can also begin to study Latin or Greek at that time.) In *seconde,* the first year of *lycée,* one may begin the study of yet a third modern language. Sometimes parents send their children to another country for the summer so that they can learn still another language or master one they are studying.

Point out that for centuries French was the universal diplomatic language, as well as the language of the Russian and German royal courts. Explain that l'Académie Française, composed always of forty *Immortels,* was created by Richelieu in 1635 to standardize the French language and to maintain its purity. French is today one of the five official languages of the U.N., as well as the international language of many airlines. (You might mention *défense de fumer; attachez vos ceintures.*)

In regions of France where there exists a strong feeling of local cultural autonomy and a local language that is not a dialect of French (Brittany: Breton, a Celtic language; the Basque country: Basque, a language of mysterious origin not related to any European language; the Midi: varieties of Occitan — Gascon, Limousin, Languedocien, Provençal, Nisart, Catalan), the local language may be studied where *lycée* instruction is available. (See CS Lesson 16, p. 261: *Provence.*) Alsace is the only officially bilingual region of France. Standard German is used in newspapers there, and in daily speech, the local German dialect — Alsacien — is widely used.

You may want to point out that English, Flemish, German, Dutch, and certain of the Scandinavian languages are termed Germanic and have common root words. Contrast these with French, Spanish, Italian, Portuguese, and Rumanian, which are Romance languages, derived from a form of Latin spoken by the Roman people. Because of the Norman conquest in 1066, roughly a quarter of our English words are derived from Latin (see CS Lesson 13, p. 214: *la Normandie*).

Page 157

Photo: An ice cream wagon on la Côte d'Azur.

Pages 158–159

Photo/Document: A Colonel Sanders stand in Montréal, and the front of a menu flyer from there.

Page 160

L'Avenue de la République: Located in the 11th *arrondissement*, this avenue flows into la Place de la République designed by Baron Georges Haussmann (1809–1891) in the middle of the nineteenth century. Hausmann was a city planner, appointed during the Second Empire to redesign the streets of Paris to make them more difficult to barricade and easier for the Army to enter in case of another popular uprising. He changed the atmosphere from that of a large town with myriad small, narrow streets into a modern city of long, wide boulevards. He developed the large parks (le Bois de Boulogne, le Bois de Vincennes), built l'Opéra and the magnificent iron and glass buildings in Les Halles—now gone. He opened a vital new system of water supply and drainage. Though he did destroy buildings of historic value and many charming areas of the city, he also turned Paris into a modern city of beautiful thoroughfares with pleasant vistas and much greenery. (In this context, it is of note that a Frenchman, Pierre L'Enfant (1754–1825), laid the plans for the capital city of Washington.)

La Machine à sous: You might want to point out that *un sou* is a coin that no longer exists. It equalled one-twentieth of a franc, or five centimes. It now refers to money in general and is used largely in set expressions: *compter ses sous. être près de ses sous (= être avare),* etc. The photo shows a teen-ager playing a pinball machine in Paris.

Page 161

Photo: A café called Café des Sports in a small town in le département de la Vienne, the eastern section of the old province of Poitou, southwest of Paris. The area has suffered from emigration in recent years and is now largely poor and rural. Industry is centered in the city of Poitiers, famous as the site of the battle in 732 where Charles Martel, father of Pépin le Bref and grandfather of Charlemagne, defeated the Arabs and assured the dominance of Christianity in Europe.

Page 163

Document: You might want to point out that the prices are in francs and centimes (3 Fr., 3 Fr. 50, etc.). Should students ask, *à la pression* means "on tap" or "from a fountain."

LESSON 11

Page 166

(a,b) Two bookstores in le Quartier Latin. This area on the left bank is the site of many well-known schools—among them la Sorbonne, l'Ecole Polytechnique, l'Ecole Normale Supérieure. The area is called le Quartier Latin because in the Middle Ages, the Church ran the schools and Latin was the language used. Since students must find and buy their own books, the many bookstores are often quite crowded and busy. Le Boul' Mich', the main street of the quarter, is lined with stores and theaters that cater to the tastes of the students attending the nearby schools. (See photo, p. 111, noting the signs "Pub Latin" and "Librairie Picart.")

(c) Billboard advertising a reduced price on razors for Father's Day.

Page 167

La Fête des Pères: In recent years, there have been attempts to promote Mother's Day and Father's Day in France. Such holidays are not, however, as popular as in the U.S. Some greeting cards are available for these occasions—as well as for birthdays, etc.—but they are still produced on a comparatively small scale (see CS, p. 177).

Page 170

Photo: An English class in a French Canadian school in Montréal.

Page 171

Les Cours: Other courses available to French students are *les sciences naturelles, l'éducation musicale, le dessin* ("art"), *l'éducation physique et sportive* (abbreviated EPS; "phys. ed."), *les travaux manuels éducatifs* (abbreviated TME; "shop"), *l'instruction civique* ("civics"), *la comptabilité* ("accounting"), *la botanique, les sciences économiques, les arts ménagers* ("home economics"), *la technologie* ("mechanics"), *les sciences politiques, la psychologie, la sociologie, la couture* ("sewing"), and *la dactylographie.* "Driver ed." is *la conduite automobile.* It is not taught in French schools, because in order to obtain a driver's license one must take a course from a certified driving school, *une auto-école.*

Pages 174–175
Photos: The library *(la salle de documentation)* and a classroom in a *collège* in Québec. Almost all of the books in the library are in French. The painting on the wall of the classroom was done by the students.

Page 176
Document: Une carte d'identité for a student at a parochial school in Sherbrooke, Canada.

Page 177
Document: A typical, very plain French greeting card.

Page 178
Les Papiers: Upon reaching the age of 18, all French people must obtain *une carte nationale d'identité.* The card, with the owner's photograph, is issued by a local police station upon presentation of a birth certificate. Other papers often carried by French people are voter's registration, *une carte d'électeur,* and a driver's license, *un permis de conduire.* University students carry *une carte d'étudiant(e).*

Le Gangster: Gangster films have always been quite popular in France, perhaps even more so than in the U.S. The Humphrey Bogart cult, for example, is of very long standing there.

Page 179
Document/Photo: Note that in France many informational signs and brochures are written in French, English, and German. The building in the photo is *la préfecture de police,* police headquarters for the city of Paris. Located on le Quai des Orfèvres on l'Île de la Cité, it is the site of a fascinating museum of crime and criminology. A precinct police station is *un commissariat.*

Page 183
Document: Une carte d'identité for a student at *un collège mixte* in Gournay-en-Bray, a town of 6000 inhabitants in le département de la Seine-Maritime, not far from Rouen. This area in the former province of Normandy is particularly noted for its dairy farms (see CS Lesson 13, p. 214: *la Normandie*).

LESSON 12

Page 184
Scenes from the south of France. Students might be interested in some of the following words: knob, *le bouton;* handle, *la poignée;* knocker, *le heurtoir;* bell, *la sonnette;* to ring the bell, *appuyer sur la sonnette.* You might mention that it is considered rude to knock hard or often on a person's door. One should give two or three gentle, but firm raps. To the French, one's home is truly one's castle, and loud or insistent banging or ringing is an invasion of privacy.

You might also want to tell students that a large door, as in a church or public building, is *un portail;* the door of a car or train is *une portière.*

Page 185
Le/La Concierge: Your students may be interested in some expressions that have resulted from the stereotypical view of concierges: *bavarde comme une concierge* and *c'est une vraie concierge,* for example, both referring to someone whom we might call a "chatterbox" or who is otherwise indiscreet. In general, however, the concierge is expected to keep a close watch on those entering and leaving the building. Usually, the concierge's apartment is on the ground floor, near the entrance, and it is often the concierge who lets people in. Many apartment buildings have a buzzer that one rings from the outside, while pushing the door. Though the buzzer opens the door, the concierge is thus alerted and can check on those entering. In high rises, the concierge is called *un(e) gardien(ne).*

In the situation given in the Dialogue, it would not be unusual for the concierge to ask the children in to wait for their grandfather, especially if it were likely that he would return soon.

Page 195
Clermont-Ferrand: This city is located in le département de Puy-de-Dôme in le Massif Central, the mountain range that extends through the Auvergne and Limousin regions of central France. It has a population of approximately 155,000. Clermont-Ferrand is a major industrial city, noted especially as the center of the large French tire industry (Michelin et Cie is located there).

La Science-Fiction: This literary genre developed along with the advancements made in science and scientific research. In general, scientific discoveries serve as a point of departure for fictional speculation, so the works have always been a curious mixture of fact and imagination.

George Orwell is the pseudonym of Eric Arthur Blair (1903–1950). While fighting in the Spanish Civil War, Orwell became a staunch anti-Communist, and many have suggested that *Animal Farm* (1945) is fundamentally an anti-Stalinist work. *Nineteen Eighty-Four* (1949), a satire on modern politics, points to what "will" occur if wars and dictatorships continue. Students have long had a special fondness for Orwell's works.

Jules Verne (1828–1905) has often been called the father of science fiction, and his novels continue to be extremely popular. Your students may enjoy learning the original French titles of some of Verne's best-known works: *From the Earth to the Moon (De la terre à la lune,* 1865), *Twenty Thousand Leagues Under the Sea (Vingt Mille Lieues sous les mers,* 1870), *Around the World in Eighty Days (Le Tour du monde en quatre-vingts jours,* 1873), *Mysterious Island (L'Ile mystérieuse,* 1874).* Of particular interest is the fact that Verne foresaw the development of a number of scientific achievements, including submarines, aqualungs, television, and space travel.

Savinien Cyrano de Bergerac (1619–1655) is another French author who should be mentioned. His works of science-fantasy inspired later writers. Though he advanced the acceptance of scientific theories, it was also his hope to satirize—and eventually dispel—those aspects of religious thought that he believed to be arbitrary and tyrannical. His two best-known works are *l'Histoire comique des états et empires de la lune* and *l'Histoire comique des états et empires du soleil,* known in English under the combined title, *A Voyage to the Moon with Some Account of the Solar World.*

Page 196

(a) Temps Futurs, a science-fiction bookstore in Paris.

(b) Farmer's market in Sarlat. (See CS Lesson 1, p. 2.) You may want to point out that pigs are important to the Périgord region because, leashed, they are used to uncover the rare, edible black fungi called truffles *(les truffes)* that are one of the major industries of the area around Sarlat. Truffles grow underground on the roots of certain types of oak trees *(les chênes truffiers).* They are prized for their delicate flavor and are an important ingredient in French cuisine.

Page 199

Photo: A farm in le département des Alpes-Maritimes. This area, of which Nice is the major city, includes both la Côte d'Azur and the beautiful mountain country near the Italian border.

Page 203

Document: An ad for a circus. The modern, traveling circus as we know it began in England toward the end of the eighteenth century. It is an enormously popular form of entertainment throughout Europe, and there are numerous small troupes that travel from town to town as well as larger, better-known ones that go from country to country.

Poème: You might want to point out that the phrase *mea culpa* is part of the *confiteor,* the Catholic prayer of confession and supplication said toward the beginning of the Mass. Traditionally, one beats one's breast while saying these words.

LESSON 13

Page 204

(a) Sidewalk souvenir stand in Paris.

(b) Hotel receipt from l'hôtel le Relais des Gourmets in Caen. You might point out the European method of giving dates as day-month-year. (Any such *document* is ideal for reviewing numbers and vocabulary.)

The city of Caen—[kã] as opposed to Cannes [kan]—is in le département du Calvados in the former province of Normandy. It has a population of roughly 114,000. Calvados and the neighboring département de la Manche were the site of the Allied landings led by General Eisenhower in June 1944. Omaha Beach is in Calvados; Utah Beach, in Manche. Caen is an industrial city (iron and electronics) that like much of France successfully combines the very old and very new. Portions of its Abbaye Saint-Etienne and Eglise Saint-Pierre date to the eleventh century; l'université de Caen is extremely modern. (See also CS, p. 214: *la Normandie.*)

(c) Laundry list from l'hôtel Windsor in Paris. (See CS Color Section: *Paris*.)

Page 205

Le Mali: Known as French Sudan before its independence, la République du Mali is located on the west coast of Africa. Its population is approximately 5,260,000; its capital, Bamako. Much of the country is desert. Mali gained its independence from France in 1958 and, after a brief union with Sénégal as la Fédération du Mali, became a separate republic in 1960.

You might point out other former French African territories on a map—*le Maroc, l'Algérie, la Tunisie, la Mauritanie, la Guinée, la Côte d'Ivoire, la Haute-Volta, le Togo, le Bénin* (formerly *le Dahomey), le Niger, le Tchad, le Cameroun, la République Centrafricaine, le Gabon, le Congo-Brazzaville, le Malagasy* (Madagascar). The one remaining French African possession is *le Territoire Français des Afars et des Issas* (formerly French Somaliland), which is located in East Africa on the Gulf of Aden. Its capital is Djibouti.

La Guadeloupe: In addition to Grande-Terre and Basse-Terre, there are several island dependencies: la Désirade, les Iles des Saintes, Marie-Galante, Saint-Barthélemy, and the northern part of Saint-Martin. The group of islands was first visited by Columbus in 1493 and consecrated to Our Lady of Guadeloupe in Spain. A French colony was established in 1635 and quickly prospered. Except for three brief periods of British occupation (1759–1763; 1794; 1810–1816), the territory has been French ever since. Guadeloupe became a *département* in 1946. Its population is largely creole (black or mulatto) and white, many of the latter descended from the original Norman and Breton settlers. Its main industries are sugar, bananas, and tourism; its population, about 325,000. (See also CS Color Section: *Iles*.)

Page 206

Document: Stamp commemorating the first anniversary of Malian independence. Note that the emphasis is on education and literacy.

Page 207

L'Infirmier: Male nurses are quite common in France. Though they often perform paramedical functions, they may also do the work more traditionally performed by female nurses. This is particularly true in hospital clinics and emergency rooms.

L'Ingénieur: Engineering is one of the most important and popular occupations in France. Some students may be interested in learning the names for certain areas of engineering: agricultural engineer, *l'ingénieur agronome;* chemical engineer, *l'ingénieur chimiste;* civil engineer, *l'ingénieur civil;* electrical engineer, *l'ingénieur électricien;* mechanical engineer, *l'ingénieur mécanicien.* Because *l'ingénieur* is always masculine, one may sometimes use the term *une femme ingénieur,* just as one may speak of *une femme médecin,* etc.

Page 211

Documents: Malian stamps showing chess pieces—a fourteenth-century European bishop and an eighteenth-century Indian knight. The stamps were issued to commemorate the 1972 world chess championship match in Reykjavik.

Page 213

Photo: Two *pharmaciennes* in a Parisian pharmacy. The French drugstore remains a pharmacy, where the sole business is compounding and selling medicines and drugs. American-style drugstores are, however, beginning to appear.

Page 214

La Normandie: This region, located in the northwest of France along the English Channel *(la Manche),* was invaded and settled in the tenth century by Scandinavian tribes who intermarried with the French population. Descendants of these first settlers, led by William the Conqueror *(Guillaume le Conquérant),* invaded England in 1066. From this conquest and occupation, one can trace the abundance of words of French origin in the English language. Normandy was an English fiefdom from 1106 until 1204 and was a cause of long-standing enmity between France and England. Since 1468 it has been an undisputed part of France.

The Norman area is noted for its dairy products and iron industry. The largest inland Norman cities are Rouen and Caen, and there are major ports at Cherbourg, Le Havre, and Dieppe. The coastline is dotted with popular beach areas.

Les Boules: There are two versions of this game: *les boules* (played on a special playing field with carefully marked boundaries) and *la pétanque* (a less formal game played without a special playing field and without strict boundaries). The former is popular in northern and central France; the latter is played mainly in southern France. Almost every city, town, and village has at least one *terrain de boules.*

Le Sénégal: Sénégal, on the west coast of Africa, is not far from the Sahara Desert, and the climate ranges from very dry to rainy. The capital, Dakar, is a modern city of 581,000 inhabitants. La République du Sénégal gained its independence from France in 1958 and, after a brief union with Mali, became a separate republic in 1960.

 The first president of Sénégal, Léopold Sédar Senghor (b. 1906), is a world-renowned poet who writes in French. Among his collections are *Chants d'ombre* (1945), *Hosties noires* (1948), *Ethiopiques* (1956), and *Nocturnes* (1961). Senghor has been instrumental in promoting the works of other African writers and his *Anthologie,* first published in 1948, a collection of poems by sixteen Black Africans writing in French, is considered a landmark in the history of African literature of French expression. It alerted the European world to the vital literary force flourishing in French-speaking Africa.

Page 215
(a) A game of *boules* in the shadow of the Eiffel Tower.

(b) A scene on le boulevard Saint-Michel. You might point out that a traffic light is called *un feu (rouge, vert)* and that *un piéton* is a pedestrian.

Page 216
Document: L'université de Dakar is noted for its college (*faculté*) of medecine and pharmacy.

Page 218
Photo: A young *avocate* outside le Palais de Justice on l'Ile de la Cité.

Page 219
Documents: Malian stamps offering a three-part "history" of French contributions to aviation. (See CS Lesson 4, pp. 48–49: *l'Avion.*) Although Capt. F. Ferber, whose glider No. 5 is depicted here, is not associated

with any major event in the history of aviation, he was one of many Frenchmen at the turn of the century who designed and developed planes. He negotiated with the Wright brothers for production rights to their plane. The latter were lionized in France well before the importance of their feat was widely understood in the U.S. The French army very early and fervently supported developments in aviation.

LESSON 14

Page 224
(a) Salespeople in la boutique Ted Lapidus, an exclusive shop on le boulevard Saint-Germain.

(b) The window of a men's store in Paris. You might want to tell students that a store window is *une vitrine;* to window shop, *faire du lèche-vitrines.*

Page 225
La Surprise-party: Your students may enjoy learning the term *une boum,* which is slang for *une surprise-party. Une fête* is a more formal, planned party.

Page 229
Photo: La boutique Bruno-Laurent, one of many very elegant shops in Montréal.

Page 230
Photo: A music class in a *collège* in Québec. This is an elective course, and instruments are lent to students free of charge.

Page 232
Photo: Elysées Soieries, a men's shop on le Champs-Elysées. The sign on the door to the left says *air conditionné.* You might want to point out that *les soieries* are "silk goods."

Page 235
Documents: Malian stamps honoring American jazz artists. (See CS Color Section: *Paris.*)

Les Langues et les Professions: Because the U.S. has been a strongly monolingual country, the importance of language training has often been forgotten. With the recent influx of Spanish speakers, however, there is a growing awareness of the benefits that the knowledge of a second language can bring. Many high schools and colleges have organized conferences to inform students of the diverse ways in which foreign languages can be useful. Whatever the means, it is helpful to provide students with information concerning the advantages of knowing a second language. It is essential that they understand that it is not necessary to major in a language for it to be "relevant" or "useful." Contact with people involved in any type of international operation—commercial, technical, educational, scientific, religious, military— will illustrate the ways in which second-language training can complement other talents and professions. (See also CS Lesson 10, p. 155: *les Langues.*)

Les Femmes: As in the U.S. and Canada, many women in France pursue active professional careers. As of 1976, there were five women in the Cabinet, Simone Veil and Françoise Giroud being the best known. Veil, who was appointed *secrétaire d'Etat pour la santé* in 1974, was the first woman to occupy a ministerial post in France. Giroud, as *secrétaire d'Etat à la condition féminine*, was instrumental in the enactment of legislation guaranteeing the equality of women in France. Simone de Beauvoir has long been one of the most widely known and respected advocates of women's rights. Your students might enjoy reading magazine and newspaper articles about these and other well-known Frenchwomen. You might also suggest some research projects in this area. (See also CS Lesson 3, p. 31: *la Famille.*)

Page 236
Document: Front of a brochure put out by les P.T.T. You might remind students that les P.T.T. includes not only the postal service, but also la Caisse nationale d'épargne and what in the U.S. would be the telephone industry. This is, then, a career in government, business, or banking as opposed to being a postal inspector as the term *inspecteur* might imply.

Page 237
Document: From Canada, a bilingual ad for Master Charge. You might want to help students translate so that they can see that the message in French, though similar, is quite different from the English. In such an ad one can see how the use of language is a reflection of the culture. In the French there is no bold assumption that one will join (as there is in the English "Welcome"); there is an appeal to thought; the card is spoken of as the most "recognized." All in all, it is a much less hard-sell approach.

LESSON 15

Page 242
(a) Outdoor sign for a *bar-restaurant* in Paris. Note that meals cost only up to 16 Fr. 50 (about $3.65); drinks and tip extra. You might point out that *en sus* means *non compris.*

(b) Bill from *une brasserie* in Paris. *Une brasserie* (literally, "brewery") is more than a café, less than a restaurant. Meals are served, but with less than the full attention to detail and usually with fewer courses than in a restaurant.

(c) Quatrilingual page from a menu. You might want to call attention to *la salade niçoise.*

Page 243
Nice: A port on the Mediterranean with a population of 325,000, Nice is one of France's most popular resort cities. It was a part of Italy until 1860, and Italian influence remains strong in the culture, cuisine, and architecture. Giuseppe Garibaldi, who led the fight for the unification of Italy, was born in Nice.

Le Déjeuner, le Dîner: The more formal the occasion— luncheon or dinner—the more courses there are in a French meal. (See also CS Lesson 6, p. 81.) A complete meal might consist of:

  hors-d'oeuvre variés (raw carrots, celery, beets, sardines, etc.); *salade de tomates (de concombres, niçoise)*, dressed with oil and vinegar *(sauce vinaigrette); soupe* (which has meat, vegetables, or bread in it), *potage* (with strained vegetables), or *bouillon* (clear broth).
  entrée: omelette (aux champignons, aux fines herbes) or *poisson.* (These can be served as either a first or main course. You might alert students to the fact that in the U.S. we use the term *entrée* to mean "main course." In France, it is a first course or "entrance" to the meal.)
  plat principal (or *plat de résistance*): meat, usually served very rare. Most meat dishes are served with potatoes and/or a vegetable.
  salade: usually a lettuce salad (see CS, p. 254).
  fromage: Cheeses are served on a tray, and one may take a small portion of as many kinds as one wishes, though usually only one is selected. (If more than one cheese is taken, one usually eats the mildest first and the strongest last, in order to enjoy the full flavor of each.) Some common French cheeses are *brie, roquefort, gruyère, camembert, chèvre* (made from goat's milk), *port salut*, and *cantal.*

dessert: fresh fruit, pastry, ice cream, *mousse, crème caramel.*

boissons: Wine (sometimes mineral water) is usually served with lunch and dinner. Tea or strong black coffee is served after the meal.

Page 249
Photo: The wall of a building in Québec.

Page 253
La Suisse: This is one of the smallest and most mountainous countries in Europe—60 percent of its surface is in the Alps, 11 percent in the Jura Mountains.

Four languages are officially recognized in Switzerland: German, French, Italian, and Romansch. The latter, consisting of a closely related group of dialects derived from Latin, is spoken in relatively isolated valleys in the eastern and central part of the country. Two forms of German are used: a local variety in speech and standard German in writing. German is spoken by 74 percent of the population, French by 20 percent, Italian by 4 percent, Romansch by 2 percent.

Switzerland is a federation of *cantons.* Each is a sovereign political entity, even more so than our states. While educated Swiss usually know several languages, individual cantons are not officially multilingual: French is spoken in the French-speaking cantons *(la Suisse romande),* German in the German-speaking cantons, etc. Romansch speakers are usually bilingual in German or Italian.

Page 254
La Salade Niçoise/La Salade Verte: In the Dialogue (p. 243), M. Valjean ordered *une salade niçoise* as a main course. Here Laurent orders *une salade verte* to be served after the main course. *Une salade verte* (or *une salade de laitue,* which is made of whiter types of lettuce rather than the dark green leaves) is considered a means of freshening the palate after the heavy *plat principal* and before the sharp cheeses and/or sweet desserts. Other types of salads—with tomatoes or fresh vegetables—are generally served as a first course.

Photo: Two cooks from the town of Jougne in le département du Doubs. The town, with a population of only 800, is in a major ski resort area close to the Swiss border.

Page 257
Photo: Young man sitting in the window of a small restaurant specializing in pastries and ice cream. Note the posted menu.

Document: Note that the tip of 75 centimes is already added into the total. The bottom line states that the tips are received directly by the waiters. This is to reassure those who might doubt that the waiters actually do receive the money withheld.

Page 259
Photo: Salad, fruit, bread, a bottle of wine, a plate of cheese and yogurt. *Le yogourt* (or *yaourt*) has long been very popular in France.

LESSON 16

Page 260
(a) A fishmonger *(une poissonnière)* on la Côte d'Azur. (See also CS Color Section: *Provisions.*)

(b,c) Fishing on the banks of the Seine in Paris and in a pond in the west of France. Students might want to know the following terms: fishing, *la pêche (à la ligne);* to fish, *pêcher.* You might want to alert them to the importance of the accent mark by telling them that *pécher* means "to sin."

Page 261
La Bouillabaisse: Many kinds of seafood are used in making *bouillabaisse.* In preparing the dish, ingredients are placed in a large pot: tomatoes, onions, garlic, fennel, parsley, thyme, bay leaf, and dried orange peel. To these are added first the shellfish and the firmer fish, together with olive oil, salt, pepper, and saffron. After these have boiled for a short time, the more delicate fish, heads included, are added.

Most foods associated with Provence are heavily seasoned with garlic and spices grown in the area—thyme, basil, oregano, parsley, laurel—and with olive oil, which is also produced there. Other well-known *provençal* dishes are *la ratatouille,* made with green pepper, eggplant, tomatoes, onions, and zucchini, flavored with *fines herbes,* garlic, and olive oil, and *le pistou,* a thick vegetable soup containing oil, garlic, and spices. A popular sandwich is *le pan bagnat (provençal* for *pain baigné),* which is olive-oil-soaked bread with tuna, ripe olives, and onions.

Marseille: This is France's second largest city (900,000 people) and the Mediterranean's largest commercial seaport. Le Vieux Port—the original harbor—dates to 600 B.C., when Phoenician mariners settled there. The port district was badly damaged by German mines in 1944, and postwar reconstruction has given much of the area a very modern appearance architecturally. However, the fish markets of le Vieux Port are still lively and active.

The French national anthem, though written in Strasbourg in 1792 by Claude Rouget de Lisle for the Army of the Rhine, is known as *La Marseillaise* because it was quickly adopted by the ardent federalist revolutionaries of Marseille. Its original title was *Chant de guerre pour l'armée du Rhin.*

Provence: This region, once a Roman province, is on the Mediterranean coast between the Alps and the Rhône River. It is well-known for its cultural and linguistic traditions. There are many reminders of Roman days, including arenas in Arles and Nîmes.

The term *provençal* is sometimes used to refer to the language spoken in southern France, *la langue d'oc.* The name derives from an earlier distinction between the word for "yes" in northern France *(oïl* now *oui)* and southern France *(oc).* Both words are from Latin, *hoc ille.* Today, throughout southern France, closely related dialects are used which their speakers refer to as *l'occitan.* It is estimated that nearly 6,000,000 people speak some variety of Occitan.

Occitan-speaking France *(l'Occitanie* or *le Midi)* includes la Gascogne, le Languedoc, le Limousin, l'Auvergne, and la Provence. In the twelfth and thirteenth centuries, before the conquest of Occitania by the lords of northern France, a literary form of Occitan *(le limousin),* spread by *les troubadours,* enjoyed the highest prestige in western Europe. Dante, the great Italian poet, debated whether he should write his *Divine Comedy* in Occitan or in the Florentine dialect of Italian. Frédéric Mistral attempted a literary revival of Occitan at the end of the nineteenth century, and there is today a strong movement to revalorize all varieties of the language. (See also CS Lesson 10, p. 155: *les Langues.*)

Page 262

Photo: A Parisian fish market *(une poissonnerie)* specializing in the fish required for a proper *bouillabaisse marseillaise.*

Page 265

Document: From a bilingual tourist's handbook, a listing of late-night markets. You might want to call attention to the nonliteral translation, the 24-hour time system, the comma between the number and the street, the use of the *arrondissement* number.

Le Couvert: You might want to mention that the French place setting is somewhat different from ours. Spoons are placed bowl-down; forks, tines-down. To the right of the knife is *la cuillère à soupe.* Above the plate are *le couteau à fromage,* then *la cuillère à dessert.* Immediately above them are, to the left, *le verre à eau* and, to the right, *le verre à vin.*

Two other items often found on the dinner table in French homes are: the knife-rest *(le porte-couteau)* and the napkin ring *(le rond de serviette).* Though different spoons and forks are used for different courses, in a home, one knife may be used throughout the meal. It is placed on a knife-rest between courses. Linen napkins are still widely used, and each family member will use one napkin for several days. Between meals it is kept in a napkin ring, which is initialed or is in some way identifiable as belonging to that individual.

Le Café au lait: The French usually drink their *café au lait* from a bowl, not a cup, and the bread that accompanies the coffee is usually dunked in the bowl. French children drink coffee (in the form of *café au lait)* long before children in the U.S. do. As the child becomes older, the ratio of coffee to milk increases. Although milk is recognized as an important nutritional source, the French do not usually drink it plain. *Café au lait* or hot chocolate is served to provide nutrition and to disguise the taste of the milk.

Page 266

Photo: A French Canadian family at dinner.

Page 269

Photo: A French family at dinner. Though the wine is being poured, note the large bottle of Coke on the table.

Page 270

Photo: After dinner in a French home. Note the bottles of wine, carafes of water, bowl of fruit, and fruit knives on the plates.

Page 276

Photo: Un poissonnier in Cannes.

LESSON 17

Pages 278–279

Scenes at le Festival d'Avignon, an annual summer festival of modern and classical theater, street theater, art shows, and other cultural events. Here, for example, *une troupe de danseurs, un vendeur de poupées, un contorsionniste.*

Avignon, in le département de Vaucluse, is known as the site of le palais des Papes, where the popes took up residence in 1309 to escape unstable political conditions in Rome. At that time Avignon was not a part of France, but belonged to papal vassals. When Gregory XI returned to Rome in 1378, the cardinals elected a second pope—or antipope—to hold power in Avignon. The Great Schism was not resolved until 1417. The city belonged to the Church until 1791, when it became a part of France.

Medieval Avignon is extremely well preserved. The ramparts surrounding the city are largely intact. The city is floodlit at night, and when viewed from across the Rhône, the towers, churches, crenelated walls, and the famous twelfth-century bridge are a magnificent site. (See song and photo, p. 295.)

Avignon lies in an area some of whose place names might already be familiar to students (see map, p. 280): Arles, with its well-preserved Roman theater and arenas; les Baux (whence the word "bauxite"), with its medieval ruins, where the ramparts, homes, and château are made of the reddish native stone; Tarascon, known to readers of Daudet; Châteauneuf-du-Pape, where the world-famous wines are produced. You might want to post photos or *documents* from this fascinating region, or reproductions of some of Van Gogh's paintings done in Provence (in Arles or while hospitalized at Saint-Rémy-de-Provence).

La Deux-chevaux: See photo, p. 292. Note how the window opens.

Page 285

Photo: Two girls hitchhiking on la Côte d'Azur.

Page 286

Photo: In Paris, on the bank of the Seine. Students might enjoy learning the word for "back pack," *le sac au dos.*

Page 287

Louis Pasteur: A chemist and biologist, Pasteur developed treatment for rabies and anthrax. He discovered the bacilli that were killing the silkworm in France, thus saving the important silk industry. He also discovered the effects of bacteria in decay and fermentation. The process of pasteurizing milk to prevent fermentation was named in his honor.

Marie Curie: Marie Curie and her husband, Pierre, discovered the elements radium and polonium. The latter element was named after Poland, her native land. Together they were awarded the Nobel Prize for physics in 1903. After her husband's death, Mme Curie continued doing research, and in 1911 was awarded the Nobel Prize for chemistry in recognition of her further work on radium and its compounds. The Curies' daughter and son-in-law, Irène and Frédéric Joliot-Curie, were nuclear physicists and joint winners of the Nobel Prize for chemistry in 1935.

Page 289

Le Voyage: When traveling, the French rarely stay at luxury hotels. *Le camping* is very popular, and campers and colorful tents abound at camping sites throughout Europe.

Page 290

Document: Map from a brochure for a two-star campground near Bordeaux. Students might be interested in the equipment for the playground *(le terrain de jeux):* swing, *la balançoire;* sandbox, *la sablière;* slide, *le tobog(g)an;* merry-go-round, *le tourniquet.*

Page 291

Document: Trilingual shoeshine cloth *(un chiffon à chaussures)* from l'hôtel Sainte-Anne in Paris.

LESSON 18

Page 296

(a) Waving good-by as passengers lean out the window. (See CS Lesson 4, pp. 48–49: *le Train.*)

(b) Poster offering an SNCF mid-August weekend in Brittany.

(c) Second-class railway ticket between Paris and Amiens. Note that the metric distance between the cities is given on the ticket.

(d) An SNCF ad for trips to London (rail and boat) and Florence.

Page 297

Les Pyrénées: This mountain range, which stretches between the Mediterranean and the Bay of Biscay, forms a kind of natural wall between France and Spain. The area is rich in religious history, not only for the battles fought there during the Crusades, but also as the site of the major pilgrimage center of Lourdes. Earlier, Charlemagne had hoped to capture and convert Muslim Spain, and his defeat by the Basques at Roncevaux (Roncevalles) in 778 was immortalized in the twelfth-century *Chanson de Roland.*

On the western edge of the mountain range is the Basque country, an area rich in history and legends. The origin of the Basques is obscure, though it is thought that they are descendants of Roman tribes. Today, Basques speak French or Spanish in addition to their own language. *Le béret* and the game *la pelote* (jai alai) are Basque in origin.

Because of its natural beauty and favorable climate, the Pyrénées are an extremely popular vacation area. As far back as ancient times, the Romans were fond of the region for its abundance of springs and thermal baths, believed to be medicinal. Today, the baths, skiing, hiking, fishing, and mountain-climbing are among the area's attractions. There are also many fine camping facilities.

Page 298

Photo: Café in la Gare de Lyon. Like a supermarket cart, a baggage cart is called *un chariot.*

Page 300

Photo: A modern apartment building near Antibes on la Côte d'Azur.

Page 301

Photo: Departure board at Orly. Note the bilingual signs, the 24-hour clock, and the listing of international flights: Baghdad-Istanbul; Marseille-Ajaccio (Corse); Perpignan (in the Pyrénées); Rome-Tripoli-Benghazi (Libye); Lyon; Los Angeles; Amsterdam-Helsinki; Tunis; Frankfort; Athens-Tel Aviv.

Page 303

Document: Ticket for the shuttle bus between one of the Paris airports and the air terminal at les Invalides (l'Aérogare des Invalides).

Page 304

Photo: Departure board in a railroad station on la Côte d'Azur. North- and westbound are toward Marseille; south- and eastbound toward Vintimille (Italy).

Page 305

Photo: You might want to point out that *la sortie* means "exit" and that the word for "entrance" is *l'entrée.*

Page 306

Photo: An Air France desk at Orly.

La Louisiane: In 1682, the French explorer La Salle claimed for France all the land drained by the Mississippi River and named it Louisiana in honor of Louis XIV. Later, when the French settlers were driven from their homes in Acadia (Nova Scotia) in 1755, many of them made their way to Louisiana and were welcomed by the French people of that region. Their story is told by Longfellow in his poem *Evangeline.*

The town of Lafayette was first settled by exiled Acadians. Originally called Vermilionville after the Vermilion River on which it was built, the town was renamed for the Marquis de Lafayette in 1884. As a very young man, Lafayette (1757–1834) had come to fight with the colonists in their struggle for independence. He has ever since been a symbol of America's close ties to our first ally. Until Sir Winston Churchill was made an honorary citizen of the U.S. in the early 1960's, Lafayette had been the only foreigner so honored.

The older French culture is still evident in and around Lafayette. With the aid of the French government, the area has initiated a strong movement for the preservation of bilingualism, and young people from France, Belgium, and Québec come to teach French to school children in the state.

Haïti: This republic occupies the western third of the island of Hispaniola (the Dominican Republic occupies the rest). The island was discovered by Columbus, and the Haitian area was ceded to France in 1697 by the Treaty of Ryswick. Most of the land is mountainous, and the economy depends mainly on agriculture, with coffee and sugar being the major export crops.

In 1802, Pierre Toussaint L'Ouverture, a former slave, led a rebellion to end slavery. Imprisoned in

France, he died the following year. Jean-Jacques Dessalines, one of his generals, proclaimed the country's independence in 1804 and named it Haiti, the name the original inhabitants, the Arawak Indians, were believed to have given to the island (the French had called it Saint-Domingue). Dessalines was assassinated in 1806 and another of Toussaint's generals, Henri Christophe, became ruler. He declared himself king in 1811. Convinced that the French were going to try to retake the island, he built the magnificent Citadelle near Cap-Haïtien in the north. It was in large part Napoléon's concern with Haiti, as well as his precarious military position in Europe, that led him to sell Louisiana to the U.S. in 1804.

The history and culture of this island republic are unique. Students might enjoy doing research on its history or some of its more colorful traditions, such as voodoo *(le vaudou),* a mixture of Roman Catholicism and the religious practices of tribes from Bénin.

Page 307

Photo: The coffee section of a supermarket. Note that coffee is usually sold in bags, not cans.

Page 308

Photo: L'hôtel La Louisiane in Paris. Note the butcher shop with the sign for liver and heart for 6 Fr. 50. The chestnut vendor *(le marchand de marrons)* is a common sight in France. His foot is on the bellows to keep the roasted chestnuts warm. Chestnuts are very popular in France — preserved in syrup or glazed with sugar *(marrons glacés),* in turkey stuffing *(dinde aux marrons),* or simply roasted and eaten plain.

Page 309

Photo: A restaurant in Québec.

Page 311

Photo: Toronto International Airport. Note that, as throughout Canada, all signs are bilingual.

PART X

Answer Key for <u>Révisions et Thèmes</u>

LESSON 1, p. 10

1. C'est la corbeille. Et voici l'affiche. / C'est la fenêtre. Et voilà la porte. / C'est l'élève. Et voici le professeur.

2. Bonjour, Henri. Ça va? Très bien, merci, monsieur. / Bonjour, Henri. Ça va? Bien, merci, madame. / Bonjour, Henri. Ça va? Oui, très bien, merci.
3. Et toi, Jacqueline? Oui, ça va. / Et vous, monsieur? Comme ci, comme ça. / Et vous, Luc et Eric? Pas mal.

C'est la salle de classe. Et voici le professeur.
"Bonjour, Eve et Guy. Ça va?"
"Bien, merci, madame. Et vous?"
"Très bien, merci."

LESSON 2, p. 26

1. Voici M. Lenoir. Il va à la poste. / Voici les élèves. Ils (Elles) vont à la campagne. / Voici Mme Leblanc. Elle va à l'église.
2. Ce sont les bandes et les magnétophones de M. Lenoir. / Ce sont les cartes et les images de Suzanne. / Ce sont les drapeaux et les affiches d'Henri.
3. Voilà Jacques, l'ami d'Hélène et de Georges. / Voilà Jeanne et Raymond, les amis de Paul et de Guy. / Voilà Alice, l'amie d'André et de Brigitte.
4. Vous allez à la piscine. / Nous allons à l'usine. / Je vais a l'hôpital.

Voici Xavier et Sara. Ils vont à l'école. Ce sont les livres et les cahiers de Xavier et de Sara. Voilà Jacques, l'ami de Xavier et de Sara. Il va à la gare.

LESSON 3, p. 42

1. Nous sommes chez nous. / Je suis chez Martin. / Il est chez lui.
2. Monsieur et Mme Lafont sont mes cousins. Raymond est mon frère. / Monsieur et Mme Lafont sont ses grands-parents. Raymond est son père. / Monsieur et Mme Lafont sont ses amis. Raymond est son grand-père.
3. Je vais à la campagne avec ma sœur. / Je vais à l'église avec sa tante. / Je vais à la banque avec ta mère.
4. Je suis en jupe et en blouse. / Elle est en robe. / Les garçons sont en pantalon et en pull-over.

Nadine est chez elle. Monsieur et Mme Duclos sont ses parents. Denise est sa sœur. Nadine va à la plage avec sa famille. Les jeunes filles sont en maillot.

LESSON 4, p. 58

1. Notre oncle et notre tante sont devant leur garage. / Votre vélo et votre moto sont devant leur garage. / Leurs chaussures et leurs chemises sont devant leur garage.
2. Nous avons nos chapeaux. / Tu as tes bateaux. / Elles ont leurs bateaux à voiles.
3. Son camion n'est pas dans le garage. Il est dans le parc. / Ma voiture n'est pas dans le garage. Elle est sous l'arbre. / Nos vélos ne sont pas dans le garage. Ils sont sur l'herbe.
4. Il est là, derrière son jardin. / Il est là, devant sa maison. / Il est là, avec ses voisines.
5. Nous avons deux copines. / L'arbre a neuf feuilles. / J'ai cinq camions.
6. Ils vont à la campagne en avion avec mes parents. / Nous allons à l'église en autobus avec mes parents. / Je vais à la montagne par le train avec mes parents.

Marc et Chantal sont devant leur maison. Ils ont leurs vélos. Leur mère n'est pas dans la maison. Elle est dans le garage. Leur père est derrière la maison, dans son jardin. Il a quatre fleurs. Marc et Chantal vont à la poste avec leurs amis (copains).

LESSON 5, p. 74

1. Voilà le cinéma. Les élèves sont là, près du cinéma. / Voilà le théâtre. Les élèves sont ici, en face du théâtre. / Voici le musée. Les élèves sont là, à gauche du musée.
2. Le restaurant est à côté du musée. / L'hôtel est au coin de la rue. / Le stade est loin de l'aéroport.
3. Il y a cinq camions rouges devant l'hôtel. / Il y a trois vélos jaunes derrière l'arbre. / Il y a deux voitures bleues dans le garage.
4. Les motos sont à droite de l'autobus. / Les motos sont en face des usines. / Les motos sont à côté du cinéma.
5. Les quatre cousins vont au lycée près de la gare. / Les six amies (copines) vont au café à droite du lycée. / Les huit jeunes filles vont à la plage loin du port.

Voilà l'opéra. Les élèves sont là, en face de l'opéra. Le restaurant est au coin de la rue. Il y a deux voitures noires près du restaurant. Les élèves sont à gauche des voitures. Ils vont au café à droite de l'opéra.

LESSON 6, p. 94

1. Il est huit heures. Madame Lambert arrive à l'usine. / Il est six heures. Monsieur Lambert rentre du bureau. / Il est deux heures. Gigi et Paul Lambert entrent dans la maison.

2. Jean est paresseux. / Louise est heureuse. / Eric est triste.
3. Il regarde la télé pendant que sa sœur travaille. / Elle joue aux échecs pendant que son frère prépare le déjeuner. / Il révise la leçon pendant que ses amis (copains) jouent au football américain.
4. A quatre heures il prépare le goûter. / A midi ils déjeunent. / A sept heures nous dînons.
5. L'après-midi, j'aime jouer aux cartes. / L'après-midi, vous aimez regarder les journaux. / L'après-midi, tu aimes écouter la radio.

Il est cinq heures. Andrée rentre de l'école. Elle est énergique. Elle joue au tennis pendant que son frère écoute la radio. A sept heures sa famille dîne. Le soir, ils aiment regarder la télé.

LESSON 7, p. 112

1. C'est aujourd'hui vendredi le vingt-cinq septembre. / C'est aujourd'hui mardi le premier juillet. / C'est aujourd'hui jeudi le trente août.*
2. C'est l'automne. Il fait frais et il pleut. / C'est le printemps. Il fait du soleil mais il gèle. / C'est l'été. Il fait du vent et il fait froid.
3. Mathieu et Danielle regardent un film policier. / J'écoute une pièce. / Nous préparons des documentaires.
4. Parce que c'est lundi nous n'avons pas de match. / Parce que c'est samedi il n'y a pas de dessins animés. / Parce que c'est dimanche elle n'a pas de journal.
5. Quand je choisis mon livre, je rentre à la maison. / Quand nous finissons nos leçons, nous allons dehors. / Quand il finit son déjeuner, il reste à l'intérieur.
6. Tu aimes le vent. / Elle aime le soleil. / Vous aimez la pluie.

C'est aujourd'hui mercredi le vingt et un janvier.* C'est l'hiver. Il fait froid et il neige. Sophie et Didier préparent un goûter. Parce que c'est mercredi, ils n'ont pas de devoirs. Alors quand ils finissent leur goûter, ils vont dehors. Ils aiment la neige.

*In first printing only. In all subsequent printings, the *révision* answer will be *le trente et un août;* the *thème* will be *le vingt janvier.*

Answer Key for
Révisions et Thèmes

LESSON 8, p. 129

1. Elles sont à la plage. Il fait nuit. / Elles sont au lac. Il fait jour. / Elles sont près de la mer. Il fait du vent.
2. Il y a des étoiles, mais pas de lune. / Il y a des fleuves, mais pas de montagnes. / Il y a des lacs, mais pas de sable.
3. La terre est jaune et laide. / Le ciel est bleu et beau. / Les voitures sont vieilles et blanches.
4. Martin est à la maison, mais il n'a pas faim. / Nous sommes à l'intérieur, mais nous n'avons pas sommeil. / Je suis dehors, mais je n'ai pas peur.
5. Il fait ses achats. / Ils (Elles) font la vaisselle. / Nous faisons de l'auto-stop.

Nous sommes à la montagne. Il fait jour. Il y a des nuages, mais pas de soleil. La neige est belle et blanche. Huguette est dehors, mais elle n'a pas froid. Elle fait du ski.

LESSON 9, p. 148

1. Robert part du cinéma à quatre heures dix. / Je sors de la maison à neuf heures moins vingt-cinq. / Vous partez pour l'aéroport à onze heures cinq.
2. Il va jouer au basketball au gymnase. / Ils (Elles) vont faire des achats au supermarché. / Nous allons déjeuner dans le grand magasin.
3. Après le dîner, il faut finir l'histoire. / Après le dîner, il faut choisir un roman. / Après le dîner, il faut aller au concert.
4. On va jouer un western italien. / Tu vas servir un dîner allemand. / Ils (Elles) vont finir un poème espagnol.
5. Le fleuve n'est pas grand, mais il est très large. / Les histoires ne sont pas bonnes, mais elles sont très courtes. / La jeune fille n'est pas petite, mais elle est très grosse.
6. Maintenant il est midi vingt-cinq. Nous partons. / Maintenant il est neuf heures et quart. Ils (Elles) sortent. / Maintenant il est dix heures et demie. Tu dors.

Dominique et Madeleine sortent de la maison à sept heures et quart. Ils vont dîner au restaurant. Après le dîner, il faut aller au théâtre. On va jouer une pièce anglaise. La pièce n'est pas mauvaise, mais elle est très longue. Maintenant il est minuit moins le quart. Dominique et Madeleine dorment.

LESSON 10, p. 164

1. Ce soir, les Dufort vont à un petit théâtre espagnol à New York. / Cette semaine, les Dufort vont à un grand restaurant grec à New York. / Ce matin, les Dufort vont à une petite bibliothèque allemande à New York.
2. Cette maison est en face d'un château célèbre. / Ces fleurs sont sous un grand arbre. / Cet hôpital est près d'un joli parc.
3. Il écoute un long opéra français. / Il regarde le même western bête. / Il regarde un autre dessin animé.
4. Là, nous vendons les disques. / Là, elle entend le vent. / Là, tu attends la serveuse.
5. Je travaille lentement, et le professeur attend mes devoirs. / Il joue mal, et ils perdent le match. / Les boissons ne coûtent pas cher, et nous commandons un citron pressé et une bière.

Cet après-midi, les Ballard déjeunent à (dans) un petit café hollandais à Londres. Ce café est à côté d'un grand hôtel. Les Ballard choisissent la seule table libre près d'une fenêtre. Là, ils attendent le garçon. Le garçon arrive vite et ils commandent des Cocas.

LESSON 11, p. 182

1. Il n'a pas parlé aux étudiants la semaine dernière. / Tu n'as pas téléphoné à la librairie hier soir. / Nous n'avons pas joué au football le mois dernier.
2. Elle a perdu les photos à l'université. / Nous avons attendu les vendeuses à la terrasse d'un café. / Elles ont passé la soirée au gymnase.
3. Demain matin, il faut aller au cours de géométrie. / Ce soir, il faut trouver ces livres de poche. / Cet après-midi, il faut réviser la leçon d'histoire.
4. Mais je n'ai pas dormi et je ne veux pas regarder les journaux. / Mais ils n'ont pas fini et ils ne peuvent pas chercher les cadeaux. / Mais nous n'avons pas maigri et nous ne voulons pas commander des esquimaux.
5. Il est nul en biologie et il ne va pas vouloir faire de la physique. / Elle est forte en maths mais elle ne va pas pouvoir faire de l'algèbre. / Elles sont nulles en histoire et elles ne vont pas vouloir faire de la géographie.

Simone n'a pas assisté aux cours hier. Elle a passé la journée chez elle. Ce matin, il faut passer un examen de chimie. Mais elle n'a pas étudié et elle ne peut pas répondre aux questions. Elle est nulle en chimie, et elle ne va pas pouvoir réussir à l'examen.

LESSON 12, p. 201

1. Anne et son frère aîné sont au bord de la mer, avec leurs parents. / Anne et ses frères cadets sont au coin de la rue, à côté de la librairie. / Anne et son jeune mari sont au bord de la route, près de la ferme.
2. Nous demandons: "Quels cochons vendez-vous bientôt?" / Nous demandons: "Quel poème apprenez-vous enfin?" / Nous demandons: "Quelles langues comprennent-elles déjà?"
3. Tu réponds: "Il y a un vieux chien anglais." / Tu réponds: "Il y a une vieille vache hollandaise." / Tu réponds: "Il y a un vieil hippopotame sénégalais."
4. Vous demandez: "Où trouve-t-on ces léopards noirs?" / Vous demandez: "Pourquoi cherche-t-il cet agriculteur aimable?" / Vous demandez: "Quand apporte-t-elle ces souris blanches?"
5. Va regarder ce nouveau coq rouge là-bas! / Va regarder cette nouvelle poule blanche là-bas! / Va regarder ce nouvel éléphant gris là-bas!

Mathieu et sa sœur cadette sont au milieu du zoo, devant les singes. Elle demande: "Quels animaux veux-tu regarder maintenant?" Mathieu répond: "Il y a un nouvel ours russe." Elle demande: "Pourquoi aimes-tu ces animaux méchants? Allons regarder ce bel oiseau blanc là-bas!"

LESSON 13, p. 221

1. Monsieur Bertaud est pharmacien dans une nouvelle pharmacie. / Anne et Monique sont médecins dans un petit hôpital. / Adèle est employée de bureau dans un grand bureau de tourisme.
2. Je crois que le jean est laid, et je ne le porte pas. / Ils (Elles) croient que les chaussures sont chères (coûtent cher), et ils (elles) ne les prennent pas. / Nous croyons que les livres sont difficiles, et nous ne les aimons pas.
3. Un jour vous apprenez qu'on cherche de jeunes vendeurs. / Un jour ils (elles) apprennent qu'on

cherche de beaux acteurs. / Un jour tu apprends qu'on cherche de bons poètes.

4. Il y a déjà cent cinquante élèves qui veulent apprendre l'anglais. / Il y a déjà soixante-quinze ingénieurs qui veulent passer l'examen. / Il y a déjà quatre-vingts avocats qui veulent voir le juge.

5. Tu vois que tu ne vas pas faire de progrès. / Nous voyons que tu ne vas pas faire de progrès. / Ils (Elles) voient que tu ne vas pas faire de progrès.

Marion est vendeuse dans une petite boutique. Elle croit que le travail est facile, mais elle ne l'aime pas. Un jour elle apprend qu'on cherche de jeunes actrices inconnues. Mais il y a déjà quatre-vingt-onze jeunes filles qui veulent jouer le rôle principal. Elle voit qu'elle ne va pas réussir.

LESSON 14, p. 240

1. J'ai emprunté une enveloppe à Chantal. / Ils ont emprunté des cravates à papa. / Nous avons prêté des timbres à plusieurs ami(e)s (copains, copines.).

2. Nous voulons vous offrir un foulard. / Nous voulons lui offrir (donner) un portefeuille. / Nous voulons leur faire une visite.

3. Tu dis: Elle croit que j'écris des poèmes intéressants. / Nous disons: Nous croyons qu'ils (qu'elles) écrivent des chansons françaises. / Vous dites: Ils (Elles) croient que nous écrivons des histoires ennuyeuses.

4. Elle peut te montrer un complet. / Elle peut m'offrir (me donner) une veste. / Elle peut nous apporter un réveil.

5. Elle dit: Mais j'ai toujours besoin d'un manteau. / Ils (Elles) disent: Mais elle a vraiment besoin d'un imperméable. / Je dis: Mais ils (elles) ont toujours besoin de ceintures.

6. Alors, tu m'écris une lettre et une carte postale. / Alors, je leur offre (donne) un collier et une bague. / Alors, nous vous offrons (donnons) l'électrophone et le magnétophone.

Hier, Solange a prêté un parapluie à Maryse. Maintenant Maryse veut lui apporter un cadeau. Le frère de Maryse dit: "Je crois qu'elle aime les romans policiers. Tu peux lui offrir (donner) un livre." Maryse répond:

"Mais elle a surtout besoin d'un parapluie." "Alors, tu lui offres (donnes) un livre et son parapluie."

LESSON 15, p. 258

1. Les frères Legrand sont au régime cette semaine. / Les frères Legrand ont assisté à la pièce hier soir. / Les frères Legrand vont jouer aux cartes demain après-midi.

2. J'y rentre parce que c'est le dernier jour de mes vacances. / Nous y nageons parce que c'est la nouvelle piscine de nos voisin(e)s. / Nous y commençons parce que c'est la première leçon de notre livre.

3. Ils prennent des escargots comme hors-d'œuvre. / Nous prenons du vin comme boisson. / Je prends des fruits et du fromage comme dessert.

4. Je prends du coq au vin. Il n'aime pas le coq au vin. Alors, il n'en prend pas. / Je prends des haricots verts. Vous n'aimez pas les haricots verts. Alors, vous n'en prenez pas. / Je prends du pain et de la confiture. Ils (Elles) aiment le pain et la confiture. Alors, ils (elles) en veulent.

5. Ensuite je voudrais une omelette et de l'eau minérale. / Ensuite je voudrais un croque-monsieur et du lait. / Ensuite je voudrais une pâtisserie et du thé.

6. Les pommes coûtent peu, mais il ne mange pas de fruits. Les fruits sont bons! / Les petits pois coûtent peu, mais tu ne manges pas de légumes. Les pommes de terre sont bonnes! / Le bifteck coûte cher, alors nous ne mangeons pas de viande. Le poisson est bon.

La famille Laurent dîne au restaurant ce soir. Ils y sont parce que c'est l'anniversaire de Mme Laurent. Les deux enfants commandent des huîtres comme hors-d'œuvre. Leur mère prend de la soupe à l'oignon. Monsieur Laurent n'aime pas les oignons. Alors, il n'en prend pas. Ensuite tout le monde prend du gigot, du riz, des petits pois et une salade verte. Le dîner coûte cher, mais M. Laurent ne laisse pas de pourboire. Le service est compris.

LESSON 16, p. 275

1. Nous avons pu prononcer les mots. / J'ai pu commencer mon travail. / Elle a voulu mettre son imperméable.

2. Il l'a ouvert dans la salle à manger et il m'a dit "félicitations!" / Nous l'avons vue au cinéma et nous

lui avons dit "bon anniversaire!" / Elle les a données aux enfants et ils lui ont dit "merci."

3. Tu n'as pas apporté ton portefeuille, alors il faut faire de l'auto-stop. / Je n'ai pas mis le couvert, alors il faut faire le ménage. / Nous n'avons pas fait la cuisine, alors il faut faire la vaisselle.

4. Il a appris les chansons et il les a chantées à la surprise-party. / Elle a compris les réponses et elle les a écrites dans son cahier. / J'ai trouvé le sel et le poivre et je les ai mis dans (à) la cuisine.

5. "On y met les verres?" m'a demandé le garçon. / "Ils y mettent (ont mis) les couteaux," nous a dit le médecin. / "J'y mets (ai mis) les cuillères et les fourchettes," lui a répondu la ménagère.

6. Tu as vendu la cuisinière, n'est-ce pas? / Il a caché les serviettes et la nappe, n'est-ce pas? / Nous avons cassé la tasse et la soucoupe, n'est-ce pas?

Bruno et Diane ont voulu faire des achats. Leur père les a rencontrés à la porte et il leur a dit: "Ah, non! Vous n'avez pas préparé le repas, alors il faut débarrasser la table." Ils ont pris la vaisselle et ils l'ont mise dans l'évier. "Vous y laissez la vaisselle?" leur a demandé leur père. "Nous avons débarrassé la table, n'est-ce pas?" lui a répondu Bruno.

LESSON 17, p. 293

1. Nous venons d'arriver d'Espagne. / Ils viennent de rentrer des Pays-Bas. / Je viens de revenir de Norvège.

2. J'y ai fait du camping avec des copains. / Ils (Elles) y ont fait une visite à leurs grands-parents. / Elle y a visité les musées avec son frère.

3. Il est allé au Mexique il y a deux ans. Il aime le Mexique. / Elle est venue aux Etats-Unis il y a longtemps. Elle aime les Etats-Unis. / Elles sont arrivées en Suisse il y a quinze jours (deux semaines). Elles aiment la Suisse.

4. Il fait presque toujours du soleil au bord de la mer. / Il pleut toujours au sud de la ville. / Il neige trop au nord-ouest de l'état.

5. Je n'y ai pas plongé. / Nous n'en avons pas mangé. / Elle n'y a pas nagé.

6. Chaque matin je suis arrivé à la pharmacie à l'heure. / Chaque soir nous sommes montés dans l'autobus à l'heure. / Chaque année vous êtes parties en vacances en retard.

Albert et Yvette viennent de rentrer du Portugal. Ils y ont fait une visite à leurs cousins. Ils sont allés en Suède il y a un an. Ils aiment la Suède. Mais il fait souvent froid au nord-est du pays. Ils n'y ont pas nagé, par exemple. Mais au Portugal, chaque matin ils sont descendus à la plage de bonne heure.

LESSON 18, p. 312

1. Pourquoi est-ce qu'il n'y a que des clefs dans la boîte? / Pourquoi est-ce qu'il n'y a personne dans l'immeuble? / Pourquoi est-ce qu'il n'y a rien dans la malle?

2. Trop de gens sont arrivés sur la Côte d'Azur. / Tant d'étudiantes sont entrées dans la salle de classe. / Beaucoup d'ouvriers (d'ouvrières) sont sorti(e)s de la salle à manger.

3. Bien sûr, rien n'y est arrivé en hiver. / En effet, personne n'y est rentré (retourné) au printemps. / Alors personne n'y est descendu en automne.

4. Nous savons qu'il y a beaucoup de bruit là-bas aussi. / Ils savent qu'il y a assez d'horaires là-bas aussi. / Je sais qu'il y a trop de circulation là-bas aussi.

5. Cette année elle passe huit jours au Danemark. / Quelquefois nous passons la journée en ville. / Cette fois je passe tous les jours chez moi.

6. Je connais bien les renseignements. / Il connaît (sait) déjà la fin. / Elles connaissent (savent) vraiment le commencement.

Pourquoi est-ce qu'il n'y a que des touristes à Paris? Beaucoup de gens sont allés sur la Côte d'Azur. Cependant les Giraud n'y sont jamais allés en été. Ils savent qu'il y a trop de touristes là-bas aussi. D'habitude ils passent leurs vacances en Autriche. Ils connaissent bien le pays.

Son et Sens

TRANSPORTS

LOISIRS

PARCS

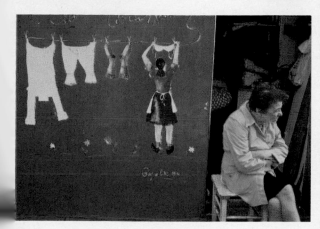

PARIS

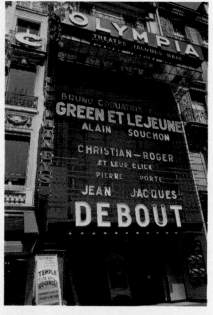

ARTS

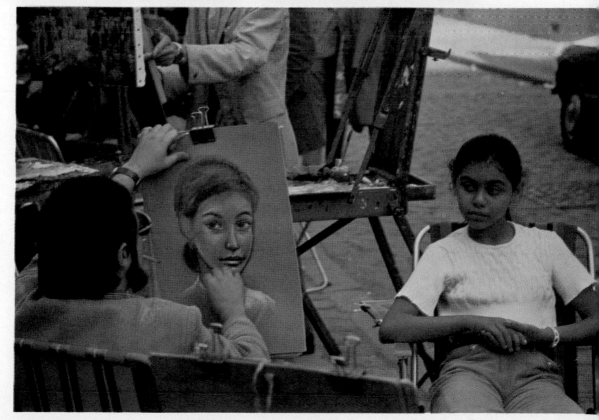

PLAGES

PROVISIONS

ÎLES

Level One   Scott, Foresman French Program

Son et Sens

New Edition

Albert Valdman
Guy MacMillin
Marcel LaVergne
Simon Belasco

Scott, Foresman and Company • Glenview, Illinois

Dallas, Tex. • Oakland, N.J. • Palo Alto, Cal. • Tucker, Ga.

*The authors and publisher wish to thank
the following teachers who have served
as consultants and critic readers:*

ESTELLA GAHALA Lyons Township High School, Ill.
NANCY CAPLAN MELLERSKI Binghamton, N.Y.
ALBIN J. POLZ Winnipeg, Manitoba, Canada
MARIE-PAUL TRICOT Gournay-en-Bray, France

*Their active participation in the preparation
and checking of manuscript and in field-testing
certain elements new to this edition
have been of invaluable assistance.*

"Page d'écriture" and "Déjeuner du matin" from *Paroles* by Jacques Prévert.
"Refrains enfantins" from *Spectacle* by Jacques Prévert.
"Mea Culpa" from *Histoires* by Jacques Prévert.
All © Editions Gallimard. Used by permission.

ISBN: 0-673-13014-2

A la mémoire de
FLORENCE STEINER
1925–1974

*ce livre est affectueusement dédié
par les auteurs et les éditeurs*

On est ordinairement le maître
de donner à ses enfants
ses connaissances;
on l'est encore plus
de leur donner
ses passions. —

MONTESQUIEU

Table des Matières

iv

*Preceded by Parlons de vous, beginning in Lesson 4;
  followed by questions (A propos . . .), beginning in Lesson 2.

v

Acknowledgments

COVER: Henri Matisse, *The Open Window* (1905). Private collection.

COLOR SECTION
Title Page   Bob Amft
Transports   Left page: *(top left)* Wayne Sorce; *(others)* Bob Amft
            Right page: Arlene Kickert
Loisirs   Left page: *(bottom left)* Wayne Sorce; *(others)* Bob Amft
            Right page: *(top right & bottom)* Arlene Kickert
Parcs   Left page: *(top left)* Nancy Caplan Mellerski; *(bottom)* Bob Amft
            Right page: *(top)* Arlene Kickert
Paris   Left page: *(top left & right. center right & bottom right)* Bob Amft; *(others)* Wayne Sorce
            Right page: *(top right & center top right)* Bob Amft; *(others)* Wayne Sorce
Arts   Left page: Bob Amft
            Right page: *(top left & right)* Bob Amft
Plages   Right page: *(top right)* Arlene Kickert
Provisions   Left page: *(top right & center left)* Bob Amft; *(others)* Wayne Sorce
            Right page: Arlene Kickert
Iles   Arlene Kickert

BLACK AND WHITE
Dorka Raynor: 2 *(top right & bottom left)*; 14; 18; 21; 30; 43; 44 *(right)*; 57; 60 *(top)*; 93; 96 *(top left)*; 101;
     107; 111; 150 *(top & bottom left)*; 154; 161; 166 *(top left)*; 184 *(top right)*; 187; 195; 196 *(right)*; 199;
     215; 218; 224 *(top)*; 254; 260 *(bottom left & right)*; 276; 278; 286; 308
Wayne Sorce: 35; 46; 134; 160; 166 *(bottom)*; 196; 204; 242; 257; 280; 292; 296 *(top left)*; 305
Bob Amft: 6; 44 *(bottom)*; 75; 76 *(top left & bottom left)*; 100; 140; 179; 181; 262; 298
Owen Franken/Stock, Boston: 88; 103; 114 *(top right & bottom)*; 116 *(bottom)*; 123; 158; 170; 249; 309
Paolo Koch/Photo Researchers: 174; 175; 230; 266; 311
Gouvernement du Québec, gracieuseté de la Direction Générale du Tourisme: 114 *(top left)*; 125 *(center)*;
     126
Nancy Caplan Mellerski: 54; 295
By courtesy of Canadian Government Office of Tourism: 125 *(bottom)*; 229
By courtesy of Canadian Government Travel Bureau: 116 *(top)*; 125 *(top)*
Jean-Pierre Ducatez: 96 *(bottom)*

Son et Sens

Première Leçon

Bonjour

ALICE	Bonjour, Philippe.[1]
PHILIPPE	Bonjour, Alice. Ça va?
ALICE	Oui, ça va. Et toi?
PHILIPPE	Pas mal.

[1]The French almost never say *bonjour* without adding the person's first name or *monsieur, madame,* or *mademoiselle.* These two young people would also probably be shaking hands. In France, even people who see each other every day usually shake hands when they meet. This is as true of teen-agers as of adults.

See Cultural Supplement in the Teacher's Section.

You might introduce yourself. using *je m'appelle.* By gestures. encourage students to introduce themselves. then let them perform the dialogue using their own names.

Hello

ALICE   Hello, Philippe.
PHILIPPE   Hi, Alice. How's it going?
ALICE   Okay. How about you?
PHILIPPE   Not bad.

PRONONCIATION

In pronouncing French vowel sounds, the jaw, lips, and tongue muscles are held more tense than in English. For that reason, French vowels sound more precise. For the [a] sound, as in the English word "pop," the lips are spread and held tense. Try saying *pas mal.* For the [i] sound, as in the English word "me," the lips are held in a smiling position. Smile and say *Philippe.* For the [u] sound, as in the English "do," the lips are rounded. Round your lips firmly and say *jour.*

Exercices

A. Listen carefully to the pronunciation of the following words, then say them aloud. Try to imitate what you hear, and don't worry about sounding funny. You won't. You may even sound like a French person.

[a] m<u>a</u>dame   ç<u>a</u> va   p<u>a</u>s m<u>a</u>l   Annie
[i] Phil<u>i</u>ppe   M<u>i</u>chel   Al<u>i</u>ce   Sylv<u>i</u>e
[u] <u>où</u>   v<u>ou</u>s   j<u>ou</u>r   bonj<u>ou</u>r

B. Listen to the following greetings, then say them aloud.

Bonj<u>ou</u>r, M<u>i</u>chel.   Bonj<u>ou</u>r, Mar<u>i</u>e.
Bonj<u>ou</u>r, Ph<u>i</u>lippe.   Bonj<u>ou</u>r, D<u>a</u>v<u>i</u>d.

C. Listen carefully, then repeat.

Ç<u>a</u> va, Mar<u>i</u>anne?   P<u>a</u>s m<u>a</u>l, Al<u>i</u>ce.
Bonj<u>ou</u>r, Ph<u>i</u>lippe. Ç<u>a</u> va?   P<u>a</u>s m<u>a</u>l, M<u>i</u>chel.

Colloquial language is used in all English versions of the dialogues. If necessary, point out that there is no one-to-one correlation between French and English here.

As students practice pronunciation, encourage them not to be self-conscious. Avoid expectations of perfection. You need not complete a pronunciation section at one time. Here, e.g., you might read aloud the introductory paragraph, then ask students to find examples of the [a], [i], and [u] sounds in the dialogue. Next day, re-read the paragraph and do Ex. A. On Day 3, do Exs. B–C. This will help students maintain awareness of pronunciation.

MOTS NOUVEAUX I

La Salle de Classe

la porte

l'affiche (f.)

la fenêtre

la corbeille

le professeur   le professeur

l'élève (f.)

l'élève (m.)

le livre   le cahier   le stylo   le crayon   la gomme   le papier

In French, nouns have gender; they are either masculine or feminine. There is a group of words called "determiners" that come before nouns. They usually indicate the gender.

1. What do the following have in common?

   la porte   la fenêtre   la corbeille

   They all have the determiner *la. La* is called a "definite determiner" and indicates a feminine noun. Its English equivalent is "the."

2. How can you tell that these are masculine nouns?

   le stylo   le cahier   le crayon

   They all have the definite determiner *le.* which indicates a masculine noun.

3. When a noun begins with a vowel sound, the determiner *l'* is used for both masculine and feminine nouns. *L'affiche* is a feminine noun; *l'élève* can be either masculine or feminine.

4. Note that *le professeur.* a masculine noun, is used to refer to both male and female teachers.

See Cultural Supplement.

If possible, bring a *cahier* to class.

The popular Bic pens are made by a French company. If your students have them, they will enjoy using the French pronunciation.
Now is a good time to display French posters. You might ask students interested in art to give brief reports on the life and/or work of one of the great poster artists (Toulouse-Lautrec, Alfons Mucha, Pierre Bonnard, Jean-Michel Folon, Sempé). Or you might assign reports on the subject matter of any posters that particularly interest students.

Lesson 1

5

Exercices de vocabulaire

A. Look at the pictures and tell what the objects are. Follow the models.

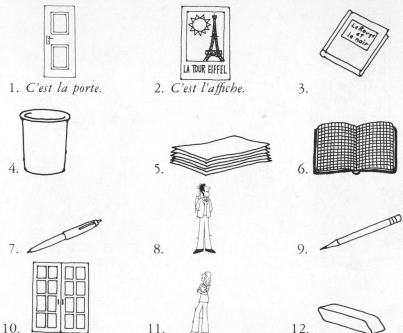

3. C'est le livre.
4. C'est la corbeille.
5. C'est le papier.
6. C'est le cahier.
7. C'est le stylo.
8. C'est le professeur.
9. C'est le crayon.
10. C'est la fenêtre.
11. C'est l'élève.
12. C'est la gomme.

1. *C'est la porte.*   2. *C'est l'affiche.*   3.

4.   5.   6.

7.   8.   9.

10.   11.   12.

B. *Où est* is the French equivalent of "where is." Your teacher will now ask where certain objects are. For example: *Où est la porte?* If the door is across the room, point to it and say:

Voilà la porte.   *There's the door.*

If it is near you, touch it and say:

Voici la porte.   *Here's the door.*

C. Now ask your neighbor where some of these objects are. For example, you ask: *Où est la porte?* Your neighbor will answer: *Voici la porte* or *Voilà la porte.*

MOTS NOUVEAUX II

C'est Michel?	*Is that Michel?*
Oui, c'est Michel.	*Yes, it's Michel.*
C'est Alice?	*Is that Alice?*
Non, c'est Sylvie.	*No, it's Sylvie.*
C'est Mme Lenoir.[1]	*That's Mrs. Lenoir.*
C'est M. Brel.	*That's Mr. Brel.*
C'est Mlle Caron.	*That's Miss Caron.*
Bonjour, Guy. Ça va?	*Hello, Guy. How are things?*
Oui, ça va.	*Okay.*
Pas mal.	*Not bad.*
Comme ci, comme ça.	*So-so.*
Bien, merci.[2]	*Fine, thanks.*
Très bien, merci.	*Very well, thank you.*
Eh bien, au revoir, Guy.	*Well, so long, Guy.*
Au revoir.	*Good-by.*

See Cultural Supplement.

monsieur: You may want to point out the pronunciation. [məsjø].

Here we use "How are things?" as the English equivalent of *Ça va?*; on p. 3, "How's it going?" Encourage students to see that *Ça va?* will serve as an equivalent for any informal greeting.

bien/eh bien: Point out that, depending on context, *bien* can have several English equivalents ("well," "good," "okay," "fine"). Help students see that many words in English can have multiple meanings, depending upon their function in the sentence and often, unlike French, upon intonation (e.g., "well . . . ," "well?" "well!").

You may want to take part in the exercise. If so, introduce the concept of *toi/vous* (p. 8) in advance.

Exercice de vocabulaire

Using the four-line dialogue on page 3 as a model, greet someone in the class. When you ask each other how things are going, use any of the appropriate responses from the list above. End the dialogue by saying good-by to each other.

---

[1]By themselves, *madame, monsieur,* and *mademoiselle* are like our polite forms of address: "ma'am," "sir," and "miss." Before a name they mean "Mrs.," "Mr.," and "Miss." When speaking directly to someone, the French rarely use the last name. Note that *M., Mme,* and *Mlle* are the abbreviations for *Monsieur, Madame,* and *Mademoiselle.* In general, if the abbreviation ends in the same letter as the complete word *(Madame→Mme),* the French do not put a period after it.

[2]Politeness is very important to French people. Though you might say *pas mal* or *comme ci, comme ça* to a friend, a more polite response to someone you don't know well is *bien, merci* or *ça va bien, merci.*

EXPLICATIONS I

Les pronoms <u>toi</u>, <u>vous</u>

The pronouns *toi* and *vous* both mean "you." In the three sets of sentences below, note how Alice uses them.

Bonjour, Alice. Ça va?   Bien merci, **Michel**. Et toi?
Bonjour, Alice. Ça va?   Bien merci, **madame**. Et vous?
Bonjour, Alice. Ça va?   Bien merci, **Guy et Lise**. Et vous?

Use *toi* when addressing a friend, a relative, a small child, or a pet. Use *vous* when addressing anyone else or more than one person. A good general rule is to use *toi* only with people whom you would call by their first names or by even more familiar names, such as "mom" or "dad."

Exercices

A. Reply using the appropriate pronoun. Follow the models.
   1. Bonjour, Guy. Ça va?   Oui, Michel. Et *toi?*
   2. Bonjour, Alice. Ça va?   Bien, merci, madame. Et *vous?*

   3. Bonjour, Philippe. Ça va?   Oui, Alice et Guy. Et . . . ?
   4. Bonjour, Michel. Ça va?   Oui, Marie. Et . . . ?
   5. Bonjour, Marie. Ça va?   Bien, merci, mademoiselle. Et . . . ?
   6. Bonjour, Anne. Ça va?   Oui, Sylvie et Michel. Et . . . ?

B. If the people in the list below were to say: *Bonjour. Ça va?*, how would you reply and ask how they were? Answer, using the cues given. Follow the models.

   1. a classmate/you feel "not bad"   *Pas mal. Et toi?*
   2. the postman/you feel fine   *Bien, merci, monsieur. Et vous?*

   3. your father/you feel so-so
   4. your teacher/you feel very well
   5. your grandmother's friend/you feel fine
   6. a gentleman you just met/you feel very well
   7. your cousin/you feel "not bad"
   8. two classmates/you feel fine

Vérifiez vos progrès

Throughout the book you will find exercises called *Vérifiez vos progrès*. These are for you to check your own progress. Pretend that you meet the people pictured below. Each asks, *Ça va?* and you answer by saying "Fine, thanks, and you?" Be sure to use the proper form of "you." Write the answers, then turn to the back of the book to make sure that your answers are correct.

1.   2.   3.   4.

LECTURE

La salle de classe

LE PROFESSEUR	Christiane, où est ton° stylo?	ton: *your*
CHRISTIANE	Voici mon° stylo, madame.	mon: *my*
LE PROFESSEUR	Bien.° Lise, où est ton papier?	bien: *(here) good*
LISE	Dans° mon cahier, madame.	dans: *in*
5 LE PROFESSEUR	Où est ton cahier, alors?°	alors: *then*
LISE	Chez moi.°	chez moi: *at my house*
LE PROFESSEUR	Chez toi?° Encore?!°	chez toi: *at your house*
		encore: *again*

EXPLICATIONS II

Je m'appelle

For "my name is," the French say *je m'appelle.*

Here is a list of common French names. If your name is not included, your teacher may know its closest equivalent in French. Or, if you like, here is your chance to choose your own name.

BOYS	Adam	Denis	Guy	Pascal
	Alain	Didier	Henri	Patrice
	Albert	Dominique	Hervé	Patrick
	Alexandre	Edouard	Hugues	Paul
	Alfred	Eric	Jacques	Philippe
	André	Etienne	Jean	Pierre
	Antoine	Eugène	Jérôme	Raoul
	Arnaud	Fabrice	Joseph	Raymond
	Arthur	François	Julien	Rémi
	Benoît	Frédéric	Laurent	René
	Bernard	Gaël	Léon	Richard
	Bertrand	Gauthier	Louis	Robert
	Bruno	Georges	Luc	Roger
	Charles	Gérard	Marc	Serge
	Christian	Gilbert	Marcel	Thierry
	Christophe	Gilles	Mathieu	Thomas
	Claude	Grégoire	Michel	Vincent
	Daniel	Guillaume	Nicolas	Xavier
	David	Gustave	Olivier	Yves

GIRLS	Adèle	Antoinette	Caroline	Claude
	Agnès	Aude	Catherine	Claudine
	Alice	Béatrice	Cécile	Colette
	Andrée	Bénédicte	Chantal	Danielle
	Anne	Bernadette	Christiane	Delphine
	Annick	Blanche	Christine	Denise
	Annie	Brigitte	Claire	Diane

See "Flexibility" in the Teacher's Section for suggestions on how to present the *lecture.* Beginning in Lesson 2, questions are asked. Here you may simply want to let the class read and enact the dialogue.

le professeur / madame: Remind students that the noun remains masculine even though the teacher is a woman.

For diagnostic purposes, you may want to listen for the students' pronunciation of the following sounds:

[a]: *salle, classe, Christiane, madame, papier, cahier, alors*
[i]: *Christiane, stylo, voici, Lise*
[j]: *Christiane, bien, papier, cahier*
[wa]: *voici, moi, toi*
[ɔr]: *alors, encore*

Let students select French names. In case of duplications, be prepared to effect a compromise or let them use hyphenated names. If they write their names on cards that can stand on their desks, it will help others learn the names more quickly.

You may want to let students know the French pronunciation of their last names. This can help them get a feel for sound-symbol correspondence in the new language.

The list reflects names now common among French teen-agers. Thus, once popular names (Armand, Emile, Germaine, Yvonne) have been omitted in favor of such currently popular names as Bruno, Fabrice, Gaël, Pascal, Xavier; Agnès, Aude, Lydie, Odile, Sabine, etc.

Lesson
1

9

Younger students might enjoy assuming the role of a famous French person. First ascertain each student's interests; if necessary, you can then assign an appropriate personage. Students can bring in pictures of the individuals and introduce themselves. The pictures can be kept, and as the students' knowledge of French increases, they can add new information. At the end of the year they can then have completed an "auto-biography," which they can present to the class. For example: *Je m'appelle X. Je suis roux. J'ai . . . ans., etc.*

Dominique	Huguette	Marlène	Renée
Dorothée	Isabelle	Marthe	Sabine
Edith	Jacqueline	Martine	Sara
Elisabeth	Jeanne	Maryse	Simone
Elise	Julie	Michèle	Solange
Emilie	Laure	Mireille	Sophie
Estelle	Lise	Monique	Suzanne
Eve	Lisette	Nadine	Suzette
Florence	Louise	Nathalie	Sylvie
France	Lydie	Nicole	Thérèse
Françoise	Madeleine	Odile	Véronique
Gabrielle	Marguerite	Pascale	Virginie
Geneviève	Marianne	Patricia	Viviane
Gisèle	Marie	Paule	Yolande
Hélène	Marion	Pauline	Yvette

Hyphenated first names are also very common in France. They are most often formed with Jean and Marie: Jean-Paul, Jean-Jacques, Jean-François; Marie-France, Jeanne-Marie, Marie-Thérèse.

Exercice

Having decided upon your French name, introduce yourself to your neighbor, and ask his or her name. Your neighbor will then answer. For example:

YOU	Je m'appelle Guy. Et toi?
YOUR NEIGHBOR	Je m'appelle Philippe.

RÉVISION ET THÈME

See Cultural Supplement.

See "Flexibility" in the Teacher's Section for suggestions on how to present the *révision* and *thème*. The Answer Key also appears in the Teacher's Section.

Review of:
1. *le, la, l'*
   voici / voilà
2. greetings
3. *toi / vous*
   greetings

Consult the model sentences, then put the English cues into French and use them to form new sentences based on the models.

1. C'est *la corbeille.* Et *voici l'affiche.*
   (the window)   (there's the door)
   (the student)   (here's the teacher)

2. Bonjour, Henri. Ça va? *Très bien merci, monsieur.*
   (Fine, thanks, ma'am.)
   (Yes, very well, thank you.)

3. Et *toi, Jacqueline?*   *Oui, ça va.*
   (you, sir)   *(So-so.)*
   (you, Luc and Eric)   *(Not bad.)*

Now that you have done the *Révision*, you are ready to write a composition. Put the English captions describing each cartoon panel into French to form a paragraph.

This is the classroom.

And here's the teacher.

"Hello, Eve and Guy. How are things?"

"Fine thanks, ma'am. And you?"

"Very well, thank you."

AUTO-TEST

At the end of every lesson you will find a self-test, called an *auto-test*. This is for you and will help you find out how well you have understood the lesson. Always write the answers on a sheet of paper. When you have finished, turn to the section entitled "Answers to *Auto-Tests*" in the back of the book to check your answers.

See "Description of a Lesson" for the purpose of these end-of-lesson self-tests and for suggestions on how you might help students with them.

A. Look at the pictures and tell what the objects are. Follow the model.

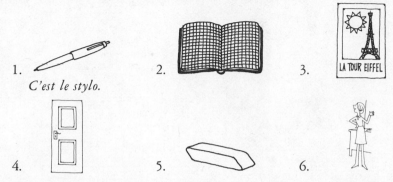

1. *C'est le stylo.*
2.
3.
4.
5.
6.

B. Look at the pictures and tell where the objects are. Remember to use *voici* to mean "here is" and *voilà* to mean "there is." Follow the model.

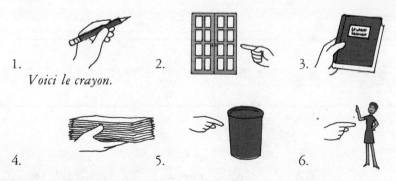

1. *Voici le crayon.*
2.
3.
4.
5.
6.

C. The people in the list below say *Bonjour. Ça va?* Answer according to the cues given and ask how they are. Follow the models.

1. a teacher/thank him and say you feel fine
   Bien merci, monsieur. Et vous?
2. your brother/you feel fine
   Bien. Et toi?

3. your aunt/you feel so-so
4. two friends/just say "yes, and you"
5. your grandfather/you feel fine
6. a woman visiting from another country/thank her and say you're feeling very well

Deuxième Leçon

On va à la plage?

MICHEL   Salut, Jean-Pierre. On va à la plage?
JEAN-PIERRE   Non, allons chez Suzanne.
MICHEL   Chez qui?
JEAN-PIERRE   Chez Suzanne, l'amie d'Annette.
MICHEL   Mais non, allons à la plage!

See Cultural Supplement.

You may want to point out that *salut* can be used in place of either *bonjour* or *au revoir*. It is a more familiar term, however, and would be used among friends.

Though *on* can replace any subject pronoun, we restrict it to its most common, 1 & 3 pl. usage. Help students realize that, unlike the English pronoun "one," *on* is very often used in French and, as the equivalent of *nous*, is not at all formal.

Are we going to the beach?

MICHEL   Hi, Jean-Pierre. Are we going to the beach?
JEAN-PIERRE No, let's go to Suzanne's house.
MICHEL   Whose house?
JEAN-PIERRE Suzanne's, Annette's friend.
MICHEL   No way. Let's go to the beach.

PRONONCIATION

French words of more than one syllable have a fairly even rhythm. All syllables are pronounced at the same pitch and with the same amount of stress. They sound like a series of short, sharp bursts.

voi-ci   bon-jour   al-lons   sa-lut

If you raise the pitch of your voice on the last syllable of a sentence, it turns a statement into a question.

STATEMENT Ça va, Michel.   QUESTION Ça va, Michel?
      On va à la plage.   On va à la plage?

Exercices

A. Listen carefully, then say the following words aloud.

madame   l'amie   papa   le papier
voici   Michel   merci   l'affiche

B. Say the following statements aloud, then change them to questions by raising the pitch of your voice on the last syllable.

C'est Philippe. Ça va bien.   Chez Suzanne.
Chez Michel.   C'est Jacqueline. C'est Sylvie.

C. Repeat the following questions aloud, then change them to statements.

Ça va bien?   Chez Philippe? C'est papa?
C'est le livre? C'est le cahier? C'est le professeur?

Les accents

See Cultural Supplement.

There are five marks that occur with letters in French. All are important for spelling; most are important for pronunciation.

1. *La cédille* (¸) appears only under the letter *c.* When the letter *c* comes before the vowel letters *a, o,* and *u,* it has the [k] sound, as in "car." The cedilla changes that sound to [s], as in "see." Compare: le c̲ahier, c̲a; la c̲orbeille, la leç̲on.

2. *L'accent aigu* (´) is used only over the letter *e:* am̲éricain, l'̲école, l'̲église.

3. *L'accent grave* (`) is used over the letters *a, e,* and *u:* voil̲à, l'̲élève, o̲ù.

4. *L'accent circonflexe* (^) may be used over any vowel: thé̲âtre, fen̲être, h̲ôtel.

5. *Le tréma* (¨) shows that two vowels next to each other are pronounced separately: No̲ël, na̲ïve.

6. An accent mark can also change the meaning of a word. For example, you know that the word *où* means "where." *Ou*—without the accent—means "or."

See Cultural Supplement.

MOTS NOUVEAUX I

la villa

la plage

l' hôtel (*m.*)

la piscine

l'appartement (*m.*)

la banque

l'école (*f.*)

l'autobus (*m.*)

Where possible, sentences in the *Mots nouveaux* are set up so that you can use them as brief substitution drills or mini-dialogues.

Salut, on va à la plage?
Mais non, allons à la montagne.
   à la campagne.
   à l'hôtel.[1]
   à l'église.
   à l'école.

Hi, are we going to the beach?
No, let's go to the mountains.
   to the country.
   to the hotel.
   to (the) church.
   to (the) school.

Deuxième
Leçon

16

[1]In French, an *h* at the beginning of a word is not pronounced, so the word *hôtel* begins with the vowel sound [o] and the determiner *l'* is used.

la campagne

la montagne

la gare

la maison

l' usine (_f._)

P.T.T.

la poste

l' église (_f._)

l' hôpital (_m._)

C'est **la maison** de Suzanne. **la villa**¹ d'Henri.	*That's Suzanne's **house.*** *Henri's **villa.***
Allons chez Suzanne.²	*Let's go to Suzanne's (house).*
Qui est Suzanne?	***Who's** Suzanne?*
C'est **l'amie** *(f.)* d'Henri.	*She's Henri's **friend.***
Qui est Henri?	***Who's** Henri?*
C'est **l'ami** *(m.)* de Suzanne.	*He's Suzanne's **friend.***

l'autobus: Point out the final pronounced consonant: [ɔtɔbys]. You may also want to point out that the word is often shortened to *le bus* and that it refers only to an intracity bus. *L'autocar (le car)* is an intercity bus.

¹A *villa* is any house in the suburbs or the country.
²*Chez* is used only with people; *à* is used with places.

Exercices de vocabulaire

A. Replace the words in italics with the cues in parentheses. Follow the model.

1. Allons à *la montagne.* (la campagne)
   Allons à la campagne.

2. Allons à *la poste.* (la banque)
3. Allons à *l'hôtel.* (l'appartement)
4. Allons à *la plage.* (la piscine)
5. Allons à *la maison.* (la villa)
6. Allons à *l'école.* (l'église)
7. Allons à *l'usine.* (l'hôpital)
8. Allons à *la gare.* (la porte)

2. Allons à la banque.
3. Allons à l'appartement.
4. Allons à la piscine.
5. Allons à la villa.
6. Allons à l'église.
7. Allons à l'hôpital.
8. Allons à la porte.

B. Answer the questions according to the pictures. Follow the model.

1. On va à la plage?
   Non, on va à la piscine.
2. On va à la poste?
3. On va à la plage?

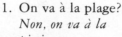

4. On va à la poste?
5. On va à l'église?
6. On va à l'école?

7. On va à la porte?
8. On va à l'usine?
9. On va à la campagne?

2. Non, on va à la gare.
3. Non, on va à la montagne.
4. Non, on va à la porte.
5. Non, on va à la poste.
6. Non, on va à la banque.
7. Non, on va à la fenêtre.
8. Non, on va à l'école.
9. Non, on va à la plage.

C. Using the first four lines of the dialogue on page 13 as a model, have a conversation with a classmate. Instead of Jean-Pierre, Suzanne, and Annette, use the names of other class members. And instead of *à la plage,* substitute another noun that you know. For example:

YOU	Salut, *Françoise.* On va *à la campagne?*
YOUR CLASSMATE	Non, allons chez *René.*
YOU	Chez qui?
YOUR CLASSMATE	Chez *René,* l'ami de *Pierre.*

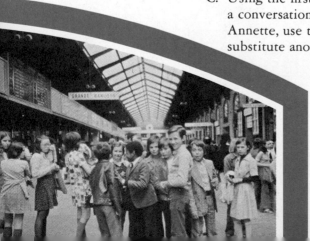

MOTS NOUVEAUX II

See Cultural Supplement.

You may want to point out that the French usually use a rag *(un chiffon)* or a sponge *(une éponge)* to erase the blackboard.

If possible, bring to class a French calendar and French and Canadian flags.

You might want to use a variation of Exs. B-C, p. 6.

la carte

Où est.. ?
Voici
Voilà

le tableau

le bureau

le magnétophone

la craie

la bande

SEPTEMBRE

L	M	M	J	V	S	D
			1	2	3	4	5
6	7	8	9	10	11	12
13	14	15	16	17	18	19
20	21	22	23	24	25	26
27	28	29	30			

le calendrier

le pupitre

la chaise

le drapeau français

le drapeau américain

la table

le drapeau canadien

la page

l' image (f.)

Exercices de vocabulaire

A. Answer the questions according to the pictures. Follow the models.

1. C'est la chaise?
   Oui, c'est la chaise.

2. C'est l'image?
   Non, c'est le calendrier.

3. C'est le magnétophone?

4. C'est la carte?

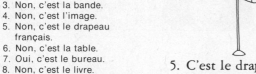

5. C'est le drapeau canadien?

6. C'est le tableau?

7. C'est le bureau?

8. C'est le cahier?

9. C'est le crayon?

10. C'est le pupitre?

11. C'est la page?

12. C'est la bande?

You may want to personalize, using classroom objects.
3. Non, c'est la bande.
4. Non, c'est l'image.
5. Non, c'est le drapeau français.
6. Non, c'est la table.
7. Oui, c'est le bureau.
8. Non, c'est le livre.
9. Non, c'est la craie.
10. Oui, c'est le pupitre.
11. Oui, c'est la page.
12. Non, c'est la carte.

To reinforce sound-symbol correspondence, use both orally and in writing.
2. la montagne / la campagne
3. la fenêtre / le pupitre
4. la maison / le crayon
5. la porte / la poste
6. le drapeau / le tableau
7. le cahier / le papier
8. l'usine / la piscine
9. la banque / la bande

Deuxième
Leçon

20

B. Give the French equivalents of the following pairs of English words. Say them aloud very distinctly. You will note that each pair has certain similarities of spelling and pronunciation. Follow the model.

1. page / beach   *la page / la plage*

2. mountain / countryside
3. window / student desk
4. house / pencil
5. door / post office
6. flag / blackboard
7. notebook / paper
8. factory / swimming pool
9. bank / tape

EXPLICATIONS I

Les pronoms et le verbe <u>aller</u>

See Cultural Supplement.

Look at the present tense of the verb *aller*. "to go":

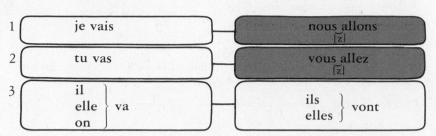

	SINGULAR	PLURAL
1	je vais	nous allons [z̃]
2	tu vas	vous allez [z̃]
3	il elle on } va	ils elles } vont

IMPERATIVE: va! allons! allez!

1. The subject pronouns are:

je	*I*	nous	*we*
tu	*you*	vous	*you*
il	*he, it*	ils	*they (m.)*
elle	*she, it*	elles	*they (f.)*
on	*we, they*		

2. Like *toi, tu* is used only in speaking to *one* member of your family, *one* person with whom you are on a first-name basis, *one* child, or *one* pet. *Vous* is used in all other instances.

3. *Nous* means "we." In informal conversation, *on* often means "we."

4. The *s* of *nous* and *vous* is usually not pronounced. However, when these words appear before a verb form beginning with a vowel sound, the *s* is pronounced [z].

5. Note the following:

Raymond et Léon vont à Paris.   **Ils** vont à Paris.
Caroline et Jacqueline vont à Paris.   **Elles** vont à Paris.
Léon et Jacqueline vont à Paris.   **Ils** vont à Paris.

Use *elles* when two or more girls are the subject. Use *ils* if boys—or a combination of girls and boys—are the subject.

6. In English we have different ways of expressing the present tense. In French, there is only one way. So, for example:

Je vais à la campagne.   {*I go* to the country.
                            {*I'm going* to the country.

7. When the second singular (2 sing.) and first and second plural (1 and 2 pl.) forms are used without the pronouns *tu*, *nous*, and *vous*, they are commands. In writing, the *s* is dropped from the word *vas* when it is a command. These are called imperative forms.

Va!	*Go!*
Allons!	*Let's go!*
Allez!	*Go!*

Exercices

A. Answer the questions using the cues in parentheses and the appropriate form of the verb *aller*. Follow the model.

1. Qui va à la plage? (vous)   *Vous allez à la plage.*

2. Qui va à la campagne? (ils)
3. Qui va à l'église? (nous)
4. Qui va à l'hôtel? (je)
5. Qui va à la poste? (Annie et Claire)
6. Qui va à la gare? (tu)
7. Qui va à l'hôpital? (vous)
8. Qui va à la piscine? (elle)

B. Restate the following sentences using pronouns instead of nouns as the subject. Follow the models.

1. Jacqueline va à la gare.   *Elle va à la gare.*
2. Annette et toi, vous allez à la poste?   *Vous allez à la poste?*

3. Raymond va à l'école.
4. Georges et Denis vont à la montagne.
5. Léon et Alice vont à l'usine.
6. Denise et Nicole vont à la banque.
7. Caroline et vous, vous allez à la villa?
8. Pierre, Paul et Marie vont à la plage.
9. Sylvie et Christine vont chez Suzanne.

Vérifiez vos progrès

Tell where each of the people mentioned is going. Write a complete sentence using the subject given, the appropriate form of the verb *aller*, and the place pictured. Follow the model.

1. tu
Tu vas à l'appartement.

2. vous

3. Raoul et Denis

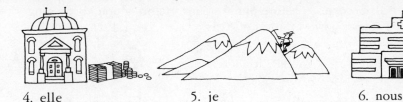

4. elle   5. je   6. nous

LECTURE

Trois° amis

Daniel et Joseph vont à la piscine. En route,° ils rencontrent° Sylvie. Elle va à la poste.

trois: *three*

en route: *on the way*
rencontrer:[1] *to meet*

SYLVIE	Bonjour, Daniel. Bonjour, Joseph.
DANIEL	Salut, Sylvie.
5 JOSEPH	Bonjour. Ça va?
SYLVIE	Bien. Et vous?
DANIEL	Très bien, merci.
JOSEPH	Ça va bien. Où est-ce que tu vas?[2]
SYLVIE	A la poste, et puis° je vais à la piscine.
10 JOSEPH	Nous aussi,° nous allons à la piscine.
SYLVIE	A bientôt alors.°

puis: *then*
aussi: *too*
à bientôt alors: *see you later then*

You might ask why Sylvie uses *vous* (l. 6), while Joseph uses *tu* (l. 8). Students may need help in recognizing *vous* both as a polite form and a plural form.

A propos ...

1. Où vont Daniel et Joseph?   2. Qui est-ce qu'ils rencontrent?   3. Où va Sylvie?   4. Et vous, vous allez à la plage? à la piscine?

Interrogatives are presented in Lessons 5-6. Though students should be able to "accept" the way the questions are formed here, you may want to introduce certain interrogative concepts orally now.

EXPLICATIONS II

Le pluriel des noms

VOCABULAIRE		
ce sont *these are, those are*		**où sont?** *where are?*

1. Look at the following:

le crayon	*pencil*	la table	*table*
les crayons	*pencils*	les tables	*tables*

There is no difference in pronunciation between the singular and plural forms of nouns. In speaking, the only difference is in the sound of the determiner, which becomes *les*.

---

[1]We will always give the infinitive, or dictionary, form of verbs.
[2]*Est-ce que* turns a statement into a question.

2. *Le, la,* and *l'* all become *les* before plural nouns. Before a noun beginning with a vowel sound, however, the *s* of *les* is pronounced [z]. This is called *liaison.* For example:

l'élève   les élèves   l'hôtel   les hôtels
        [z]   [z]

3. The plural of nouns is usually formed by adding *s* to the singular form. However, if the singular form ends in *s.* the singular and plural forms are the same:

l'autobu<u>s</u>   les autobu<u>s</u>

4. Singular nouns ending in *eu, au,* or *eau* form their plural by adding *x:*

le tabl<u>eau</u>   les tabl<u>eaux</u>

5. Singular nouns ending in *al* usually form their plural by changing the *al* to *aux:*

l'hôpi<u>tal</u>   les hôpi<u>taux</u>

6. Nouns that are made up of two separate nouns are called "compound nouns." Note how their plurals are formed:

la salle de classe   <u>les</u> salle<u>s</u> de classe

Exercice

For each pair of pictures, state that the first set of objects is nearby, ask where the second is, then say that both sets are nearby. Follow the model.

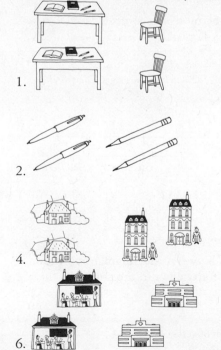

1.

Voici les tables.
Où sont les chaises?
Voici les tables et les chaises.

2.

3.

4.

5.

6.

7.

De possessif

Look at the following:

C'est la piscine de Raymond.   *It's Raymond's swimming pool.*
C'est l'amie de Jean et d'Hélène.   *It's Jean and Hélène's friend.*

The word *de* often indicates possession. When used before a noun beginning with a vowel sound, the *de* becomes *d'*. Note that the *de* (or *d'*) must be repeated if more than one person is mentioned as the possessor.

You may want to introduce the concept by using classroom objects belonging to students.

Exercice

Below each picture is the name of the person to whom the object or objects belong. Give complete sentences telling what the object is and to whom it belongs. Follow the model.

Personalize, using objects belonging to the students.
2. Ce sont les usines de M. Lenoir.
3. C'est la maison de Guillaume.
4. Ce sont les cahiers d'Eve et de Claude.
5. Ce sont les stylos d'Henri.
6. Ce sont les livres de Pierre et de Paul.
7. C'est la craie de Mlle Monet.
8. C'est le calendrier de Mme Labelle.

1. Marie
C'est la chaise de Marie.

2. M. Lenoir

3. Guillaume

4. Eve et Claude

5. Henri

6. Pierre et Paul

7. Mlle Monet

8. Mme Labelle

Vérifiez vos progrès

Put the sentences in the plural, adding the name of the person who owns the objects. Follow the model.

1. C'est l'image. (Antoinette)
   Ce sont les images d'Antoinette.

2. C'est le bureau. (Jean-Paul)
3. C'est la salle de classe. (Alice et Suzanne)
4. C'est la villa. (Mme Lebrun et Mme Lenoir)

RÉVISION ET THÈME

See Teacher's Section for answers to the *révision* and *thème*.

Review of:
1. *aller*
2. plural nouns possession with *de*
3. repetition of *de*
4. *aller*

Consult the model sentences, then put the English cues into French and use them to form new sentences based on the models.

1. Voici *M. Lenoir. Il va à la poste.*
   (the students) (They're going to the country.)
   (Mrs. Leblanc) (She's going to church.)

2. Ce sont *les bandes et les magnétophones de M. Lenoir.*
   (Suzanne's maps and pictures)
   (Henri's flags and posters)

3. Voilà *Jacques, l'ami d'Hélène et de Georges.*
   (Jeanne and Raymond, Paul and Guy's friends)
   (Alice, André and Brigitte's friend)

4. *Vous allez à la piscine.*
   (We're going to the factory.)
   (I'm going to the hospital.)

Now that you have done the *Révision,* you are ready to write a composition. Put the English captions describing each cartoon panel into French to form a paragraph.

Here are Xavier and Sara. They're going to school.

These are Xavier and Sara's books and notebooks.

There's Jacques, Xavier and Sara's friend.

He's going to the train station.

AUTO-TEST

A. Tell where each person is going, according to the pictures. Follow the model.

1. Denise
   Denise va à la fenêtre.

2. vous

3. nous

4. tu

5. Jean-Claude et Roger

6. je

B. Put the following questions into the plural.

1. Où est le drapeau?
2. Où est l'hôpital?
3. Où est le stylo?
4. Où est l'autobus?
5. Où est la salle de classe?
6. Où est la carte?

C. Below each picture is the name of the person to whom the object or objects belong. Give complete sentences telling what the object is and to whom it belongs. Follow the model.

1. Georges et Philippe
   Ce sont les pupitres de Georges et de Philippe.

2. M. Lenoir et Mme Dupont

3. Isabelle

4. Marie-Claire

5. Olivier et Hélène

6. Mme Thomas, Mlle Monet et M. Jeanson

Troisième Leçon

A la plage

Laure Broussard est à la plage avec son frère, sa sœur et ses cousins Raymond et Marie.[1]

See Cultural Supplement.

LAURE	Où est mon frère?
RAYMOND	Là-bas, avec Marie.
5 LAURE	Et qui sont les jeunes filles en chapeau?
RAYMOND	Jeanne et Colette Dumont, les amies de ma sœur.
LAURE	Alors, on va là-bas?
RAYMOND	D'accord.

---

[1]French teen-agers usually go out in groups, rather than on dates as couples. It is not uncommon for brothers, sisters, and cousins to go out together as part of a group.

At the beach

Laure Broussard is at the beach with her brother, her sister, and her cousins Raymond and Marie.

LAURE   Where's my brother?
RAYMOND   Over there, with Marie.
5 LAURE   And who are the girls in the hats?
RAYMOND   Jeanne and Colette Dumont, my sister's friends.
LAURE   Let's go over there then.
RAYMOND   Okay.

Compare the English equivalent of *on va* here with that in the dialogue of Lesson 2 (pp. 13–14).

Questionnaire

1. Où est Laure Broussard?   2. Qui est avec Laure?   3. Où est le frère de Laure?   4. Qui sont les jeunes filles en chapeau?

PRONONCIATION

The vowel sound [ɔ̃] is a nasal vowel. It is pronounced with the lips firmly rounded and, like all French vowels, with the jaws and lips held steady.

Exercices

A. Listen to the following words, then say them aloud.

on   mon   vont
Léon   crayon   maison

B. Listen carefully to the following sentences, then say them aloud. Remember to round your lips and to hold your jaws steady as you pronounce the [ɔ̃] sound.

Allons chez Léon.   Allons chez Raymond.
Où est mon crayon?   Où sont les crayons?

C. Listen carefully, then say the following questions and answers aloud.

On va chez Léon?   Non, allons chez Raymond.
On va à la maison?   Non, allons à la montagne.

Troisième
Leçon

30

Ma Famille

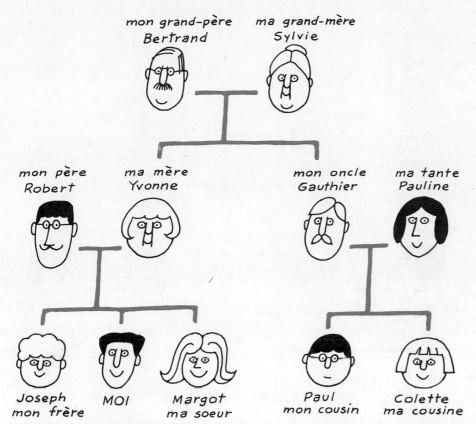

mon grand-père
Bertrand

ma grand-mère
Sylvie

mon père
Robert

ma mère
Yvonne

mon oncle
Gauthier

ma tante
Pauline

Joseph
mon frère

MOI

Margot
ma soeur

Paul
mon cousin

Colette
ma cousine

See Cultural Supplement.

fils: Point out the irregularity of the pronounced final *s:* [fis].

If necessary, remind students of the need to repeat *de* in the possessive construction.

Students have learned interrogative *qui.* Though the word serves a different grammatical function here, if treated purely lexically, it should pose no problems.

Point out the *s* on *grand* in *grands-parents.*

C'est **mon cousin** Paul, qui est **le fils** de **mon oncle** Gauthier et de **ma tante** Pauline. Alors, Paul est **le neveu** de **mes parents.**
Qui sont **les fils** de Robert et d'Yvonne et **les neveux** de Gauthier et de Pauline? Joseph et moi.
C'est **ma cousine** Colette, qui est **la fille** de mon oncle Gauthier et de ma tante Pauline. Alors, Colette est **la nièce** de mes parents.
Paul et Colette sont **les enfants** de mon oncle et de ma tante.
Ma mère et mon oncle sont les enfants de **mes grands-parents.**

l'enfant (*m.*)

Exercices de vocabulaire

A. According to the family tree, tell how each person is related to you. For example: 1. *Bertrand est mon grand-père.*

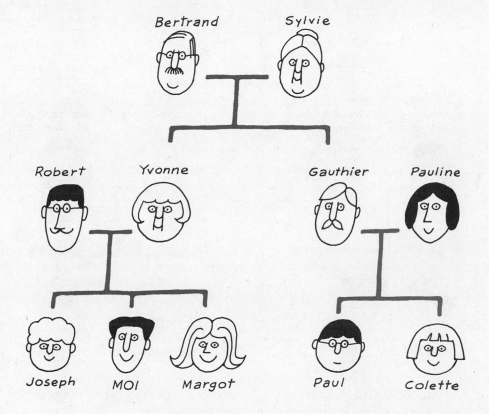

B. According to the family tree, choose the appropriate word to complete the sentences.

1. Colette est ____ de ma tante. (*la mère, la sœur, la fille*)
2. Gauthier est ____ de ma cousine. (*l'oncle, le père, le frère*)
3. Paul est ____ de ma tante. (*le fils, la fille, le frère*)
4. Gauthier est ____ de ma mère. (*l'oncle, le frère, le cousin*)
5. Margot est ____ de mon oncle. (*la fille, la cousine, la nièce*)
6. Paul est ____ de mon père. (*le fils, le neveu, le frère*)
7. Pauline est ____ de Paul. (*la mère, la sœur, la cousine*)
8. Colette est ____ de Paul. (*la tante, la mère, la sœur*)
9. Colette et Paul sont ____ de Gauthier et de Pauline. (*les parents, les grands-parents, les enfants*)
10. Ma grand-mère est ____ de mon oncle Gauthier et de ma mère. (*l'oncle, la mère, la tante*)

MOTS NOUVEAUX II

Les Habits (m.pl.)

la chemise
le chapeau
la chaussette
la chaussure
le maillot
le pantalon
la robe
le bas
la blouse
le maillot
le pull-over
la jupe
la chaussure

You may want to call attention to the following:

1. that *le pantalon* is a singular noun.

2. that because *le pull-over* was borrowed from English, the final *r* is pronounced: [pulɔver].

3. that after *en*, the French speak of articles of clothing in the singular. You may want to refer to the dialogue (l. 5).

4. that *à* can have several English equivalents, depending on context.

You might post clothing ads. Some students might be interested in writing a report on one of the great French couturiers—Dior, Chanel, Saint-Laurent, Cardin, etc.

Le garçon et **la jeune fille** sont **là-bas.**
Le garçon est **en pantalon,** mais la jeune fille est **en maillot.**[1]
Les jeunes filles sont **en pantalon** et **en pull-over.**
Les chapeaux de M. Martin sont **sur** la table. Les chaussures de Mme Martin sont **sous** la chaise.

Il va **à la plage avec toi.**
Il est **à la plage** avec sa sœur.

Il est **à l'école.**

The boy and girl are over there.
The boy's wearing pants, but the girl's in a swimsuit.
The girls are in slacks and sweaters.
Mr. Martin's hats are on the table. Mrs. Martin's shoes are under the chair.

He's going to the beach with you.
He's at the beach with his sister.
{ *He's in school.*
{ *He's at school.*

---

[1]Note that there is no determiner when *en* is used to describe what a person is wearing.

Exercices de vocabulaire

2. C'est le pantalon de M. Thomas.
3. Ce sont les chaussures de M. Thomas.
4. C'est le chapeau de M. Thomas.
5. C'est la robe de Mme Thomas.
6. Ce sont les chaussures de Mme Thomas.
7. Ce sont les bas de Mme Thomas.
8. C'est le maillot de Pierre.
9. C'est la jupe d'Hélène.
10. C'est le pull-over d'Hélène.
11. Ce sont les chaussettes d'Hélène.

A. Identify the articles of clothing. Use *c'est* or *ce sont* as needed. Follow the model.

1. *C'est la chemise de M. Thomas.*

M. Thomas   Pierre   Mme Thomas   Hélène

Ex. B
You may want to divide the class into two teams. Team 1 makes a sentence using *la bande* (1). If, within ten seconds, Team 2 can answer with a sentence using *le magnétophone* (e), they then offer a sentence using *le bas* (2), and Team 1 must answer using *la chaussure* (b). Correct answers—or correcting errors made by the other team—earn points. When students know the words well, they might do the column in random order, or make the lettered column the lead-off column, or cover one column and answer without benefit of the printed word.
1/e; 2/b; 3/g; 4/j; 5/h; 6/c; 7/i; 8/d; 9/a; 10/f

B. Choose one word from each list to make a pair.

1. la bande	a. la chaise
2. le bas	b. la chaussure
3. la chemise	c. la fille
4. la craie	d. la jeune fille
5. le crayon	e. le magnétophone
6. le fils	f. l'oncle
7. le frère	g. le pantalon
8. le garçon	h. le papier
9. la table	i. la sœur
10. la tante	j. le tableau

EXPLICATIONS I

Les pronoms

Review the list of subject pronouns on page 21. These pronouns are used only with verbs. There is another group of pronouns that you will need to know. They are called "disjunctive pronouns." Here is a list of the subject and disjunctive pronouns:

Review the list of subject pronouns on page 21.

SINGULAR				PLURAL			
je	moi	*I*	*me*	nous	nous	*we*	*us*
tu	toi	*you*	*you*	vous	vous	*you*	*you*
il	lui	*he*	*him*	ils	eux	*they*	*them (m.)*
elle	elle	*she*	*her*	elles	elles	*they*	*them (f.)*

1. Disjunctive pronouns are used after certain prepositions, such as *chez* and *avec:*

Il va **chez lui.**	*He's going **home.***
Je vais **chez lui.**	*I'm going **to his house.***
Je vais à la plage **avec lui.**	*I'm going to the beach **with him.***

2. Note how disjunctive pronouns are used in the following statements:

Lui, il va à l'hôtel.	***He's** going to the hotel.*
Moi, je m'appelle Michel.	***My** name is Michel.*
Tu vas à l'école, **toi?**	{ *Are **you** going to school?* { *Do **you** go to school?*
Ils vont chez Paul, **eux?**	*Are **they** going to Paul's?*

Individual words are not usually given stress in a French sentence. To emphasize the subject pronoun, the French add the disjunctive pronoun at the beginning or end of the sentence.

3. Note how disjunctive and subject pronouns are used together in the following statements:

Toi et moi, nous allons à la poste.	***You and I** are going to the post office.*
Claire et toi, vous allez à la banque.	***You and Claire** are going to the bank.*

Exercices

A. Form sentences, using *chez* and the pronoun that corresponds to the subject of the sentence. Follow the model.

1. Je vais . . .   *Je vais chez moi.*
2. Il va . . .
3. Tu vas . . .
4. Elles vont . . .
5. Nous allons . . .
6. Ils vont . . .
7. Vous allez . . .
8. Elle va . . .

Note that to avoid the concept of *soi,* we do not include *on* among the subject pronouns here.

We introduce disjunctive pronouns early so that the class can practice verb forms in a more natural way: *Nous allons à la plage. Et toi? Et elles?* You may want to use them in oral substitution drills before doing the verb exercises in the book, as well as for quick, routine review of verb forms.

2. Il va chez lui.
3. Tu vas chez toi.
4. Elles vont chez elles.
5. Nous allons chez nous.
6. Ils vont chez eux.
7. Vous allez chez vous.
8. Elle va chez elle.

Through gestures, help
students understand, e.g.,
that *Et Odile et toi?* (5)
leads to a *nous* response.
Whenever logical, accept
je or *nous* responses to
vous questions, *nous* or
vous responses to *nous*
questions.
2. Lui, il va à la piscine.
3. Elle, elle va à l'église.
4. Moi, je vais à la mon-
  tagne.
5. Nous, nous allons à
  l'appartement.
6. Elles, elles vont à
  l'hôpital.
7. Vous, vous allez à la
  gare.
8. Eux, ils vont à la
  banque.
9. Toi, tu vas à la maison.

B. Answer the questions, using the correct verb form and the appropriate pronouns. Follow the model.

1. Lui, il va à la maison. Et Jacqueline et moi? (à l'hôtel)
   Vous, vous allez à l'hôtel.

2. Moi, je vais à la plage. Et Jean? (à la piscine)
3. Nous, nous allons à l'école. Et Claire? (à l'église)
4. Vous, vous allez à la campagne. Et toi? (à la montagne)
5. Elle, elle va à la villa. Et Odile et toi? (à l'appartement)
6. Eux, ils vont à l'usine. Et Marie et Christine? (à l'hôpital)
7. Toi, tu vas à l'hôtel. Et Pierre et moi? (à la gare)
8. Lui, il va à la poste. Et Georges et Pauline? (à la banque)
9. Elles, elles vont à l'école. Et moi? (à la maison)

Le verbe <u>être</u>

	SINGULAR		PLURAL	
1	je **suis**	*I am*	nous **sommes**	*we are*
2	tu **es**	*you are*	vous **êtes** [z̆]	*you are*
3	il elle on [n̆] } **est**	*he is, it is* *she is, it is* *we are, they are*	ils elles } **sont**	*they are*

1. *Il* means both "he" and "it"; *elle* means both "she" and "it." Use *il* or *ils* in place of a masculine noun and *elle* or *elles* in place of a feminine noun:

   La corbeille est sous le bureau.   **Elle** est sous le bureau.
   Les crayons sont sur la table.   **Ils** sont sur la table.

   Use *ils* in place of a combination of masculine and feminine nouns:

   La blouse et le maillot sont là bas.   **Ils** sont là-bas.

We do not discuss the dis-
tinctions between *c'est*
and *il est*. For now you
may simply want to men-
tion that *c'est* and *ce sont*
are used to point some-
thing out or to refer to a
person or thing that has
already been mentioned.

2. *C'est* is used before singular nouns and *ce sont* before plural nouns:

   C'est la jupe de Marie.   *That's Marie's skirt.*
   Ce sont les habits de Marie.   *Those are Marie's clothes.*

   Sometimes *c'est* and *ce sont* are used to refer to people:

   C'est Henri?   *Is that Henri?*
   Mais non, **c'est** Guy.   *No. It's Guy.*

Exercices

A. Replace the words in italics with the appropriate pronoun. Follow the model.

1. *La chemise* est sur la chaise.   *Elle est sur la chaise.*

2. *Le garçon* est à l'hôpital.
3. *Les habits* sont à la maison.

2. Il est à l'hôpital.
3. Ils sont à la maison.

Troisième
Leçon

4. *Les parents de Jacques* vont à Nice.
5. *La tante de Marie* va chez elle.
6. *Les chaussettes et les chaussures* sont sous la table.
7. *Les grands-parents de Claire* sont chez eux.
8. *L'affiche* est sur le bureau.
9. *Jeanne et Georges* sont à la plage.

4. Ils vont à Nice.
5. Elle va chez elle.
6. Elles sont sous la table.
7. Ils sont chez eux.
8. Elle est sur le bureau.
9. Ils sont à la plage.

B. Review the pronoun section on page 35. Then answer the questions, using the pronouns given and the appropriate form of the verb *être*. Follow the model.

1. Je suis chez moi. Et lui?   *Il est chez lui.*

2. Et eux? (ils)
3. Et David? (il)
4. Et ma tante et ma cousine? (elles)
5. Et ma tante Louise? (elle)
6. Et nous? (vous)

7. Et toi et moi? (nous)
8. Et mon père et moi? (vous)
9. Et moi? (tu)
10. Et toi? (je)
11. Et Alice et lui? (ils)

2. Ils sont chez eux.
3. Il est chez lui.
4. Elles sont chez elles.
5. Elle est chez elle.
6. Vous êtes chez vous.
7. Nous sommes chez nous.
8. Vous êtes chez vous.
9. Tu es chez toi.
10. Je suis chez moi.
11. Ils sont chez eux.

Vérifiez vos progrès

In each case, write a sentence saying that the person is at home. Follow the model.

1. Elles . . .   *Elles sont chez elles.*
2. Tu . . .
3. Il . . .
4. Nous . . .
5. Je . . .
6. Vous . . .
7. Elle . . .
8. Ils . . .

LECTURE

Le chercheur d'or°

Julie est la nièce de Mme Deschamps. Aujourd'hui° elle va à la banque et elle rencontre° son ami Guy. Julie est en jupe et en pull-over. Guy est en jean.°

le chercheur d'or: *gold digger*
aujourd'hui: *today*
rencontrer: *to meet*
le jean: *jeans*

GUY	Bonjour, Julie. Ça va?
5 JULIE	Très bien, merci. Et toi?
GUY	Pas mal. Je vais à la gare avec Jean.
JULIE	Pourquoi?°
GUY	Sa° sœur arrive de° Paris.
JULIE	Moi, je vais à la banque.
10 GUY	Tu es riche,° hein?°
JULIE	Oh là là, non! C'est l'argent° de ma tante!
GUY	C'est dommage.° Au revoir, alors.
JULIE	Au revoir, chercheur d'or!

Point out that *le jean*, like *le pantalon*, is a singular noun. Note, too, its irregular (i.e., English) pronunciation: [dʒin].

pourquoi: *why*
sa: *(here) his*
arriver de: *to arrive from*
riche: *rich*
hein?: *huh?*
l'argent *(m.)*: *money*
dommage: *too bad*

Lesson
3

37

À propos ...

1. Qui est Julie?   2. Qui est Guy?   3. Julie est en pantalon aujourd'hui? Et Guy?   4. Où va Guy?   5. Sa sœur arrive aujourd'hui?   6. Où va Julie?   7. C'est l'argent de Julie?

EXPLICATIONS II

Les déterminants possessifs singuliers

1. Look at the following:

ma		*my*	
----		------	
ta	fenêtre	*your*	*window*
sa		*his, her, its*	

The words *ma, ta,* and *sa* are called "possessive determiners." Like the definite determiner *la,* they are used only with feminine nouns. Note that *sa* is equivalent to "his," "her," and "its":

C'est la piscine **d'Albert.**   C'est sa piscine. *(his)*
C'est la piscine **de Nancy.**   C'est sa piscine. *(her)*
C'est la piscine **de l'hôtel.**   C'est sa piscine. *(its)*

2. Now look at the following:

mon		*my*	
-----		------	
ton	drapeau	*your*	*flag*
son		*his, her, its*	

Mon, ton, and *son* are possessive determiners of masculine nouns.

3. Look at the following:

mon		mon	
-----		-----	
ton	ami	ton	amie
son		son	

The possessive determiners *mon, ton,* and *son* are used before both masculine and feminine nouns that begin with a vowel sound. Compare the pronunciation of the determiners in the following words:

mon crayon   mon hôtel   ton père   ton oncle
                  [n]   [n]

Hôtel and *oncle* begin with a vowel sound. Thus there is liaison, and the *n* of the possessive determiner is pronounced.

4. Like the plural definite determiner *(les),* plural possessive determiners do not have different feminine and masculine forms:

ma sœur	mes sœurs	
mon frère	mes frères	the letter *m* gives the meaning "my"

ta cousine	tes cousines	
ton cousin	tes cousins	the letter *t* gives the meaning "your"

You may want to present
Exs. A–B after covering
Point 2.

Ex. C can be presented
after covering Point 3.

Troisième
Leçon

sa nièce   ses nièces ⎫ the letter *s* gives the meaning "his,"
son neveu   ses neveux ⎭ "her," or "its"

5. Note when the *s* of the plural determiners is pronounced:

me*s* maillots   te*s* tantes   se*s* parents
mes habits   tes oncles   ses enfants
  [z]   [z]   [z]

When a plural determiner comes before a noun beginning with a vowel sound, there is liaison and the *s* is pronounced [z].

6. Note how these plurals are formed:

monsieur (mon + sieur)   messieurs (mes + sieurs)
madame (ma + dame)   mesdames (mes + dames)
mademoiselle (ma + demoiselle) mesdemoiselles (mes + demoiselles)

These words literally mean "my lord," "my lady," and "my damsel." The plurals are formed just as if they were still two separate words.

Exercices

A. Form questions and answers based on the pictures. Always use the appropriate form of the possessive determiner. Follow the models.

1. *C'est ton maillot?*
Oui, c'est mon maillot.

2. *C'est ta blouse?*
Oui, c'est ma blouse.

3.

4. 5. 6.

7. 8. 9.

10. 11. 12.

Exs. D-E can be presented after covering Point 5.

You may want to reinforce the concept of *sa* and *son* referring to the noun that follows rather than to the possessor by redoing Ex. A. p. 34, using 3 sing. possessive determiners instead of *de*.

3. C'est ton maillot? Oui, c'est mon maillot.
4. C'est ta chemise? Oui, c'est ma chemise.
5. C'est ta chaussure? Oui, c'est ma chaussure.
6. C'est ton pantalon? Oui, c'est mon pantalon.
7. C'est ta chaussure? Oui, c'est ma chaussure.
8. C'est ta chaussette? Oui, c'est ma chaussette.
9. C'est ton pull-over? Oui, c'est mon pull-over.
10. C'est ton chapeau? Oui, c'est mon chapeau.
11. C'est ta jupe? Oui, c'est ma jupe.
12. C'est ta robe? Oui, c'est ma robe.

B. Answer the questions, replacing the words in italics with the appropriate form of the possessive determiner *sa* or *son*. Follow the models.

> 1. C'est *la* grand-mère *de Philippe?*
>   *Oui, c'est sa grand-mère.*
> 2. C'est *le* neveu *de Mme Deschamps?*
>   *Oui, c'est son neveu.*

3. Oui, c'est sa nièce.
4. Oui, c'est son père.
5. Oui, c'est sa tante.
6. Oui, c'est son grand-père.
7. Oui, c'est son frère.
8. Oui, c'est sa fille.
9. Oui, c'est sa mère.
10. Oui, c'est son fils.
11. Oui, c'est sa cousine.
12. Oui, c'est sa sœur.

> 3. C'est *la* nièce *de Mme Dubonnet?*
> 4. C'est *le* père *d'Annick?*
> 5. C'est *la* tante *de Jérôme?*
> 6. C'est *le* grand-père *d'Isabelle?*
> 7. C'est *le* frère *de Marianne?*
> 8. C'est *la* fille *de Mme Thomas?*
> 9. C'est *la* mère *de ton ami?*
> 10. C'est *le* fils *de ton professeur?*
> 11. C'est *la* cousine *de ta grand-mère?*
> 12. C'est *la* sœur *de ton grand-père?*

C. Say the following sentences aloud, replacing the words in italics with the cues in parentheses. Remember to pronounce the *n* of the possessive determiner before a vowel sound. Follow the model.

> 1. Où est *le* cahier? (mon)
>   *Où est mon cahier?*

2. C'est ton hôtel?
3. C'est son oncle?
4. Voici mon maillot.
5. Où est ton pupitre?
6. C'est son enfant.
7. Voici mon appartement.
8. Où est ton stylo?
9. Où est son cousin?
10. C'est mon usine.
11. Voilà ton chapeau.
12. C'est son école.

> 2. C'est *l'*hôtel? (ton)
> 3. C'est *l'*oncle *de Paul?* (son)
> 4. Voici *le* maillot. (mon)
> 5. Où est *le* pupitre? (ton)
> 6. C'est *l'*enfant *de M. Dupont.* (son)
> 7. Voici *l'*appartement. (mon)
> 8. Où est *le* stylo? (ton)
> 9. Où est *le* cousin *de Diane?* (son)
> 10. C'est *l'*usine. (mon)
> 11. Voilà *le* chapeau. (ton)
> 12. C'est *l'*école *de Jean.* (son)

D. Say the following sentences aloud, then change them entirely to the plural. Remember to pronounce the *s* of the possessive determiner when it comes before a vowel sound. Follow the model.

> 1. Mon affiche est sur le bureau.
>   *Mes affiches sont sur les bureaux.*

2. Tes chaussures sont sous les chaises.
3. Ses images sont sur les tables.
4. Mes cousines sont chez elles.
5. Tes enfants sont là-bas.
6. Ce sont ses oncles.
7. Où sont mes chaussettes?
8. Tes amis sont chez eux.
9. Où sont ses sœurs?
10. Voilà mes amies.
11. Ce sont tes fils?

2. Ta chaussure est sous la chaise.
3. Son image est sur la table.
4. Ma cousine est chez elle.
5. Ton enfant est là-bas.
6. C'est son oncle.
7. Où est ma chaussette?
8. Ton ami est chez lui.
9. Où est sa sœur?
10. Voilà mon amie.
11. C'est ton fils?

E. Look at the pictures under the pronoun headings *moi, toi, lui/elle.* Then, using the form of the possessive determiner which corresponds to that pronoun, complete the sentences below. Follow the models.

MOI   TOI   LUI/ELLE

1. C'est *mon affiche.*   2. Ce sont *tes gommes.*   3. Où est _____?

4. Voilà _____.   5. C'est _____.   6. Il va à _____.

7. Voilà _____.   8. Où sont _____?   9. On va à _____.

10. Où est _____?   11. Voici _____.   12. Voilà _____.

13. Ce sont _____.   14. Où sont _____?   15. Ce sont _____.

3. Où est son drapeau (canadien)?
4. Voilà mes stylos.
5. C'est ta fenêtre.
6. Il va à son hôtel.
7. Voilà mon église.
8. Où sont tes cahiers?
9. On va à sa piscine.
10. Où est ma carte?
11. Voici ton image.
12. Voilà ses calendriers.
13. Ce sont mes habits.
14. Où sont tes enfants?
15. Ce sont ses usines.

For personalized practice, you might point to a student's desk (pencils). Ask: *C'est ton pupitre? (Ce sont tes crayons?)* Student A: *Oui, c'est mon pupitre. (Ce sont mes crayons.)* Ask another student: *C'est le pupitre de A? (Ce sont les crayons de A?)* Student B: *Oui, c'est son pupitre. (Oui, ce sont ses crayons.)*

Vérifiez vos progrès

Answer the questions by writing sentences telling how the people are related to *you.* Follow the model.

1. Brigitte est la sœur de ta mère?   *Oui, c'est ma tante.*
2. Paul et Marcel sont les frères de ta cousine?
3. Louis est le frère de ton père?
4. Anne est la nièce de ta mère?
5. Martine est la mère de ta mère?
6. Gérard est le fils de ton père?
7. Monsieur et Mme Dupont sont les parents de ton père?
8. Thomas et Claude sont les fils de ta sœur?

RÉVISION ET THÈME

See Teacher's Section for
answers to the *révision*
and *thème*.

Review of:
1. *être*
   chez
2. plural possessives
   son = his / her
3. singular possessives
4. *être*
   en + clothing

Consult the model sentences, then put the English cues into French and use
them to form new sentences based on the models.

1. *Nous sommes chez nous.*
   (I'm at Martin's house.)
   (He's at home.)

2. Monsieur et Mme Lafont sont *mes cousins.* Raymond est *mon frère.*
                   (her grandparents)   (her father)
                   (his friends)   (his grandfather)

3. Je vais *à la campagne* avec *ma sœur.*
         (to church)   (his aunt)
         (to the bank)   (your mother)

4. *Je suis en jupe et en blouse.*
   (She has a dress on.)
   (The boys are in pants and sweaters.)

Now that you have done the *Révision,* you are ready to write a composition.
Put the English captions describing each cartoon panel into French to form
a paragraph.

Nadine is at home.

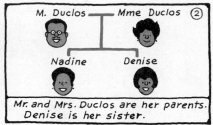

Mr. and Mrs. Duclos are her parents.
Denise is her sister.

Nadine is going to the beach with
her family.

The girls are in bathing suits.

AUTO-TEST

A. Write the answers to the following questions using the cues in parentheses. Follow the model.

1. Jean est à la banque. Et toi? (la poste)
   Moi, je suis à la poste.

2. Vous êtes à l'église. Et lui? (l'école)
3. Etienne est à l'hôtel. Et nous? (l'appartement)
4. Marie et Pierre sont à la piscine. Et elles? (la plage)
5. Je suis à la campagne. Et vous? (la montagne)
6. Tu es à l'usine. Et eux? (l'hôpital)
7. Paul est à la gare. Et elle? (la maison)

B. Identify the articles of clothing. Use *c'est* or *ce sont* and the possessive determiner *sa, son,* or *ses.* Follow the model.

1. *C'est sa blouse.*

C. Answer the following questions and then ask where the items mentioned in parentheses are. Be sure to use the appropriate form of the possessive determiner *ma, mon,* or *mes.* Follow the model.

1. C'est ton crayon? (les stylos)
   Oui, c'est mon crayon, mais où sont mes stylos?

2. C'est ton frère? (la sœur)
3. Ce sont tes gommes? (le cahier)
4. C'est ta robe? (les chaussures)
5. Ce sont tes bandes? (le magnétophone)
6. C'est ton oncle? (la tante)
7. C'est ton chapeau? (le pull-over)
8. C'est ta table? (les chaises)
9. C'est ton calendrier? (les livres)
10. Ce sont tes nièces? (les grands-parents)

Quatrième Leçon

Dans le parc

Trois copains—Antoine et sa sœur Nicole et leur amie Chantal—sont dans le parc.

CHANTAL	Vous n'avez pas vos vélos?
NICOLE	Non, nous sommes à pied. Pourquoi?
5 CHANTAL	Parce que moi, j'ai mon vélo là-bas, devant le Guignol.[1]
ANTOINE	Oh, c'est chouette, le Guignol.
NICOLE	Oui, allons-y!
CHANTAL	D'accord, mais vite!
(Pan! pan! pan!)[2]	

---

[1] *Le Guignol* is the traditional French equivalent of Punch and Judy shows. When the weather is nice, these puppet shows are performed in parks and attract great crowds. *Guignol* is the name of the main character.

[2] Any theatrical performance in France always begins with three loud knocks from backstage.

See Cultural Supplement.

le parc: Point out the final pronounced consonant: [park].

chouette: You may want to explain that this is a popular slang expression. (Though the form appears to be feminine. the adjective has only one form.)

allons-y!: For the moment. we present this purely lexically, as an emphatic form of *allons!* We offer two English equivalents: "let's go on over there" (p. 46) and "let's get going" (p. 47).

Students might enjoy the French words for other sounds. E.g., *dring, dring* = a phone ringing; *crac* = thud; *aie* = ouch; *atchoum* = sneezing; *toc, toc* = knock, knock; *tacatacatac* = ratatatat (a machine gun); *boum* = boom; *plouf* = plop.

In the park

Three friends—Antoine and his sister Nicole and their friend Chantal—are in the park.

CHANTAL   Don't you have your bikes?
NICOLE   No, we're on foot. Why?
5   CHANTAL   Because I've got my bike over there, in front of the Guignol.
ANTOINE   Gee, the Guignol is great.
NICOLE   Yeah, let's go on over there.
CHANTAL   Okay, but hurry!
(Boom, boom, boom)

Questionnaire

1. Où sont les trois amis?   2. Qui est Chantal?   3. Nicole et Antoine sont à pied?   4. Où est le vélo de Chantal?   5. Le Guignol est chouette?

PRONONCIATION

1. In French, a consonant at the very end of a word is usually not pronounced. Listen to the following words.

   je vai**s**   tu va**s**   il**s** von**t**
   che**z** nou**s**   che**z** vou**s**   che**z** Raymon**d**

2. Three consonants that very often are pronounced when they come at the end of a word are *c, l,* and *r.*

   ave<u>c</u>   par<u>c</u>   ma<u>l</u>   i<u>l</u>   bonjou<u>r</u>   professeu<u>r</u>

3. When certain very common words are followed by a word which begins with a vowel sound and with which they are closely linked, their final consonant is always pronounced. This is called "liaison."

   allon**s**!   nou**s**   nous allon**s**   allons-y!
                             [z]   [z]

   alle**z**!   vou**s**   vous alle**z**   allez-y!
                             [z]   [z]

4. When a word ends in the letter *e,* the consonant before it is always pronounced. Compare: Loui**s**, Loui<u>s</u>e; por**t**, por<u>t</u>e.

Exercice

Practice saying the final consonant sound in the following sentences.

Michè<u>l</u>e est ma cousi<u>n</u>e.   La car<u>t</u>e est dans la sa<u>ll</u>e de cla<u>ss</u>e.
Suza<u>nn</u>e est ma voisi<u>n</u>e.   Mada<u>m</u>e Lafontai<u>n</u>e va à la ban<u>qu</u>e.
Vous allez à la campa<u>gn</u>e?   Vi<u>t</u>e, Danie<u>l</u>! Voilà le Guigno<u>l</u>.
Nadi<u>n</u>e est ma voisi<u>n</u>e.   Nous allons dans le par<u>c</u> ave<u>c</u> Lu<u>c</u>.

You may want to give students the mnemonic CaReFuL, the four consonants of which are very often pronounced at the end of a word in French. You might mention *neuf* as an example ending in *f*.

MOTS NOUVEAUX I

Jean est en France
C'est le jean de ma voisine
C'est le cousin de mon voisin

Le bureau est **dans** la salle de classe.	*The desk is **in** the classroom.*
Le tableau est **derrière** le bureau.	*The blackboard is **behind** the desk.*
Le professeur est **devant** le bureau.	*The teacher is **in front of** the desk.*
Les crayons sont **sur** le bureau.	*The pencils are **on** the desk.*
La corbeille est **sous** le bureau.	*The wastebasket is **under** the desk.*
Le copain[1] de Marc **est en jean.**[2]	*Marc's **friend** (m.) **has jeans on.***
La copine de Marc est en jean aussi.	*Marc's **friend** (f.) is wearing jeans, too.*
Pourquoi? Parce que ses copains vont à la campagne.	*Why? Because his friends are going to the country.*
Le voisin de Bernadette est en maillot.	*Bernadette's **neighbor** (m.) is wearing a bathing suit.*
La voisine de Bernadette est en maillot aussi.	*Bernadette's **neighbor** (f.) has on a bathing suit, too.*
Pourquoi? Parce qu'ils vont à la plage.	*Why? Because they're going to the beach.*
Et toi et moi, nous allons à la plage aussi.	*And you and I are going to the beach, too.*
Chouette! Vite! Allons-y!	***Great! Hurry! Let's get going!***

See Cultural Supplement.

---

[1]In French, there are many words that are more or less equivalent to the English word "friend." *L'ami* and *l'amie* mean "friend" in general. *Le copain* and *la copine* are used to speak of someone with whom you spend a lot of time.

[2]*Le jean*, like *le pantalon*, is a singular noun.

Exercice de vocabulaire

Answer the questions according to the pictures. In your answers, use the appropriate preposition. Follow the model.

2. Non, elles sont sous la chaise.
3. Non, il est sur le pupitre.
4. Non, il est derrière son bureau.
5. Non, ils sont devant la banque.
6. Non, elle est derrière lui.
7. Non, il est sur la table.
8. Non, il est devant le tableau.
9. Non, il est sous la fenêtre.

1. Ton voisin est devant sa maison?
   Non, il est dans sa maison.

2. Les chaussures sont sur la chaise?

3. Le livre est sous le pupitre?

4. Le professeur est sur son bureau?

5. Les copains sont dans la banque?

6. Sa copine est devant lui?

7. Le chapeau est sous la table?

8. Le drapeau est derrière le tableau?

9. Ton vélo est derrière la fenêtre?

MOTS NOUVEAUX II

Nous allons à Paris	*We're going to Paris*
en avion	*by plane*
en voiture	*by car*
en bateau	*by boat*
en bateau à voiles	*by sailboat*
en autobus	*by bus*
en camion	*by truck*
en vélo	*by bike*
en moto	*by motorcycle*
	(or *motorbike*)
par le train	*by train*
à pied	*on foot*

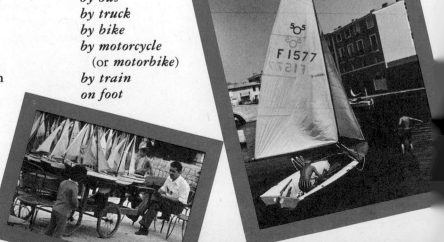

l'avion (m.)

la fleur

l'arbre (m.)

le bateau à voiles

l'herbe (f.)

la feuille

le garage

le bateau

le vélo

la moto

le camion

le parc

la voiture

le jardin

le train

Exercices de vocabulaire

A. Answer the questions according to the pictures. Follow the model.

 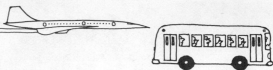

2. Non, je vais à Paris en avion.
3. Non, je vais à l'école en autobus.
4. Non, je vais à la campagne en vélo.
5. Non, je vais à la plage en voiture.
6. Non, je vais à Nice par le train.
7. Non, je vais à Cannes en moto.
8. Non, je vais à la villa en bateau.
9. Non, je vais chez moi à pied.

1. Tu vas à l'usine à pied?
   Non, je vais à l'usine en camion.

2. Tu vas à Paris par le train?

3. Tu vas à l'école à pied?

4. Tu vas à la campagne en avion?

5. Tu vas à la plage en autobus?

6. Tu vas à Nice en bateau?

 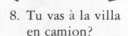

7. Tu vas à Cannes en bateau à voiles?

8. Tu vas à la villa en camion?

9. Tu vas chez toi en voiture?

B. Answer the questions according to the picture. Follow the model.

2. Le jardin est devant la maison.
3. L'arbre est derrière la maison.
4. Les feuilles sont sur l'herbe.
5. La jeune fille est dans la maison.
6. La voiture est dans le garage.
7. Le garçon est sous la voiture (dans le garage).

1. Où sont les fleurs?   *Les fleurs sont dans le jardin.*

2. Où est le jardin?
3. Où est l'arbre?
4. Où sont les feuilles?

5. Où est la jeune fille?
6. Où est la voiture?
7. Où est le garçon?

Quatrième
Leçon
_____

50

C. Answer the questions based on the picture on page 50. If your answer is negative, tell where the object is located. Follow the model.

1. La voiture est dans le parc?
   Non, la voiture est dans le garage.
2. Les feuilles sont sur l'arbre?
3. La moto est devant la maison?
4. Le jardin est devant la maison?
5. L'arbre est dans le jardin?
6. Le garçon est avec la jeune fille?
7. La jeune fille est dans la maison?
8. Les fleurs sont dans la maison aussi?

2. Non, les feuilles sont sur l'herbe.
3. Oui, la moto est devant la maison.
4. Oui, le jardin est devant la maison.
5. Non, l'arbre est derrière la maison.
6. Non, le garçon est dans le garage (sous la voiture).
7. Oui, la jeune fille est dans la maison.
8. Non, les fleurs sont dans le jardin.

EXPLICATIONS I

Les déterminants possessifs pluriels

1. Look at the following:

C'est **notre** frère.	Ce sont **nos** frères.
C'est **votre** sœur.	Ce sont **vos** sœurs.
C'est **leur** frère.	Ce sont **leurs** frères.
C'est **leur** sœur.	Ce sont **leurs** sœurs.

These are the possessive determiners equivalent to "our," "your," and "their." They have the same form before both masculine and feminine nouns.

2. The *e* of *notre* and *votre* is pronounced before a word beginning with a consonant sound, but not before a word beginning with a vowel sound:

notre tante   notr¢ oncle   votre maison   votr¢ appartement

3. When *nos, vos,* and *leurs* appear before a word beginning with a vowel sound, there is liaison and the *s* is pronounced [z]:

no$ copains   vo$ villas   leur$ cartes
but: nos_amis   vos_hôtels   leurs_images

You might personalize these forms by asking two students, *Ce sont vos cahiers?* When they answer, *Oui, ce sont nos cahiers,* ask a third student, *Ce sont leurs cahiers?* Encourage them to ask similar questions.

Exercices

A. Answer the questions using the appropriate form of the determiner *notre* or *nos.* Follow the models.

1. C'est votre voisin?   *Oui, c'est notre voisin.*
2. Ce sont vos bateaux?   *Oui, ce sont nos bateaux.*
3. C'est votre voiture?
4. Ce sont vos parents?
5. C'est votre appartement?
6. C'est votre ami?
7. Ce sont vos copines?
8. Ce sont vos images?
9. C'est votre jardin?
10. Ce sont vos habits?

3. Oui, c'est notre voiture.
4. Oui, ce sont nos parents.
5. Oui, c'est notre appartement.
6. Oui, c'est notre ami.
7. Oui, ce sont nos copines.
8. Oui, ce sont nos images.
9. Oui, c'est notre jardin.
10. Oui, ce sont nos habits.

B. Answer the questions using the cues in parentheses and the appropriate form of the determiner *votre* or *vos*. Follow the models.

1. Où sont nos chaussures? (dans la voiture)
   Vos chaussures sont dans la voiture.
2. Où est notre voiture? (dans le garage)
   Votre voiture est dans le garage.

3. Où est notre hôtel? (derrière l'église)
4. Où sont nos vélos? (devant la maison)
5. Où sont nos amis? (chez eux)
6. Où est notre professeur? (dans la salle de classe)
7. Où sont nos images? (dans le bureau)
8. Où vont nos parents? (à la plage)
9. Où va notre oncle? (à la campagne)

C. Replace the words in italics with the appropriate form of the determiner *leur* or *leurs*. Follow the models.

1. C'est *l'*appartement *de ses parents.*
   C'est leur appartement.
2. Ce sont *les* chapeaux *de Jean et de Guy.*
   Ce sont leurs chapeaux.

3. Voici *les* cahiers *de Sylvie et d'Yvette.*
4. Je vais à *la* villa *de M. Lafont et de sa sœur.*
5. Où est *l'*hôtel *d'Annie et de Marie-France?*
6. Où sont *les* affiches *de Serge et de Marie?*
7. Voilà *le* jardin *de mon oncle et de ma tante.*
8. Nous allons à *l'*usine *de M. Dupont et de son frère.*
9. Ce sont *les* habits *de Benoît et de Philippe.*

D. Look at the pictures under the pronoun headings *nous, vous, eux/elles.* Then, using the appropriate form of the possessive determiner which corresponds to that pronoun, complete the sentences.

NOUS   VOUS   EUX / ELLES

1. Allons à *notre* piscine.
2. Voilà *vos* bateaux.
3. Ils vont à . . .
4. Voilà . . .
5. C'est . . . ?
6. Ils sont derrière . . .

NOUS	VOUS	EUX/ELLES

7. Ce sont . . .

8. Où sont . . . ?

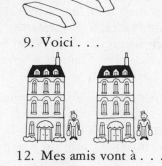

9. Voici . . .

10. Voilà . . .

11. Où sont . . . ?

12. Mes amis vont à . . .

7. Ce sont nos fleurs.
8. Où sont vos chemises?
9. Voici leurs gommes.
10. Voilà nos écoles.
11. Où sont vos affiches?
12. Mes amis vont à leurs hôtels.

Vérifiez vos progrès

Rewrite the following sentences, changing the italicized words to the plural. Follow the model.

1. *Notre vélo est* dans le garage.
   Nos vélos sont dans le garage.

2. *Votre cousine va* à la plage en autobus.
3. *Leur livre est* sous le pupitre.
4. *Votre copain est* chez nous.
5. *Notre crayon est* avec le cahier.
6. *Leur ami va* à la gare en moto.
7. *Notre chaise est* derrière la porte.
8. *Leur bateau à voiles est* à la plage.
9. *Votre sœur va* à l'église à pied.

You may want to prepare a chart—or ask students to prepare their own charts—of the personal pronouns and determiners presented thus far. E.g.:

je / moi   mon, ma, mes
tu / toi   ton, ta, tes

The chart can be expanded when students learn the object pronouns (Lesson 14).

CONVERSATION ET LECTURE

Parlons de vous

1. Vous allez à l'école en autobus?   2. Vos amis sont dans votre classe de français?   3. C'est chouette, votre classe?   4. Où sont vos livres?   5. Où est le bureau de votre prof?

Le mardi gras[1]

Ce soir° Etienne et Françoise Lemaire sont chez leurs amis Philippe et Christine Bonnel.

ce soir: *this evening*

See Cultural Supplement.

You may want to post photos of Mardi Gras and of *le Vieux Quartier* in New Orleans.

---

[1]*Le mardi gras* is the day before Ash Wednesday *(le mercredi des Cendres)*, which is the beginning of Lent. It is the last day of Carnival time, with parties, parades, and great feasts and festivities before the forty days of Lent begin.

Etienne est en béret. Il a° une° palette et un
pinceau.° Il a aussi un foulard° et une barbe.°

5　C'est un artiste? Mais non, c'est le mardi
gras et Etienne et sa sœur sont chez les Bonnel[1]
parce qu'il y a° un bal masqué° ce soir. Voilà
pourquoi Etienne a ses habits d'artiste. Les habits
de Françoise sont bizarres° aussi—elle a les

10　chaussures de son père et le pantalon de son
grand-père. Son nez° est rouge.° C'est le clown
Auguste.[2]

CHRISTINE	Voilà Etienne. C'est un artiste.
PHILIPPE	Oui, mais où est Françoise alors?
ETIENNE	Elle est là°—c'est notre Gugusse.
CHRISTINE	Ah! Ce n'est pas un garçon? Son déguisement° est chouette!
PHILIPPE	Elle est très drôle!°

il a: *he has*
un, une: *a, an*
le pinceau: *brush*
le foulard: *scarf*
la barbe: *beard*
il y a: *there is*
le bal masqué: *costume party*
bizarre: *strange*
le nez: *nose*
rouge: *red*

là: *there*

le déguisement: *costume*
drôle: *funny*

À propos ...

1. Où sont Etienne et Françoise?　2. Décrivez ("describe") le déguisement
d'Etienne.　3. Etienne est en habits d'artiste. Pourquoi?　4. Qui est le
clown Gugusse?　5. Décrivez son déguisement.　6. Les clowns sont drôles?

le clown: Point out the
pronunciation: [klun]. You
might point out that, like
le pull-over and *le jean*,
this is a word borrowed
from English. Help stu-
dents compile a list of
French words and expres-
sions that we use in Eng-
lish: façade, naïve, c'est
la vie, bon voyage, etc.
You might keep the list on
the board or on a poster
and let students add to it
during the year.

[1]The French do not add an *s* to make a family name plural. "The Bonnels" is *les Bonnel;* "the
Bonnels' villa" would be *la villa des Bonnel.*
[2]In France, *Auguste* is a common name for a clown. The nickname is *Gugusse.* The name is
funny because the word *auguste* means "dignified" or "solemn."

EXPLICATIONS II

Les nombres 1 à 20

In French, the numbers 1 to 20 are as follows:

1	un	11	onze
2	deux	12	douze
3	trois	13	treize
4	quatre	14	quatorze
5	cinq	15	quinze
6	six	16	seize
7	sept	17	dix-sept
8	huit	18	dix-huit
9	neuf	19	dix-neuf
10	dix	20	vingt

You might want to teach the terms for addition and subtraction (Lesson 8) and give students simple math problems.

Exercice

Determine the pattern in the following series of numbers, then continue them as far as you can.

1. un, trois, cinq, sept . . .
2. deux, quatre, six . . .
3. cinq, dix . . .
4. vingt, dix-neuf, dix-huit . . .

1. neuf, onze, treize, quinze, dix-sept, dix-neuf
2. huit, dix, douze, quatorze, seize, dix-huit, vingt
3. quinze, vingt
4. dix-sept, seize, quinze, quatorze, treize, douze, onze, dix, neuf, huit, sept, six, cinq, quatre, trois, deux, un

Le verbe avoir

	SINGULAR	PLURAL
1	j'ai	nous avons [z̃]
2	tu as	vous avez [z̃]
3	il elle on [ñ] } a	ils [z] elles [z] } ont

1. When *je* comes before a verb form beginning with a vowel sound, the *e* is dropped. This is called "elision." In spelling, an apostrophe is used in place of the *e*. Thus, *je + ai → j'ai.*

2. In all of the plural forms of *avoir*, there is liaison between the pronoun and the verb. Remember that liaison *s* is pronounced [z]. The *n* of *on* also represents a liaison consonant here: *on a.*

Exercice

Restate the sentences using the pronoun and the form of *avoir* that correspond to the determiner in italics. Follow the models.

1. Ce sont *leurs* bateaux à voiles.
   Ils ont leurs bateaux à voiles.
or: *Elles ont leurs bateaux à voiles.*
2. C'est *mon* maillot.
   J'ai mon maillot.

3. C'est *son* jean.
4. Ce sont *nos* bas.
5. C'est *votre* magnétophone.
6. C'est *ton* stylo.
7. Ce sont *mes* chaussettes.
8. Ce sont *vos* cahiers.
9. C'est *leur* livre.
10. Ce sont *ses* habits.
11. Ce sont *tes* crayons.
12. C'est *notre* craie.

Les phrases négatives

Look at the following:

Je suis dans le parc.   Je **ne** suis **pas** chez moi.
La voiture est dans le garage.   Elle **n'**est **pas** devant la maison.

To make a French sentence negative, put *ne* before the verb and *pas* after it. *Ne* becomes *n'* before a word beginning with a vowel sound.

Exercice

Answer the following questions in the negative. Follow the model.

1. Vos parents ont trois bateaux?
   Non, nos parents n'ont pas trois bateaux.

2. Thomas va à l'école à pied?
3. La moto est dans le garage?
4. Tu as cinq frères?
5. Nous allons à Montréal par le train?
6. J'ai son livre?
7. Il est dans le parc?
8. Claire et Jeanne sont en pantalon?
9. Ils vont à Cannes en moto?
10. Nous avons nos maillots?
11. Elles vont dans le jardin?
12. Tu vas à Paris en voiture?

Vérifiez vos progrès

Write negative answers to the following questions. Spell out the numbers in your answers. Follow the model.

1. Vous avez 3 frères?
   Non, je n'ai pas trois frères.

2. Elle a 17 livres?
3. Jean-Jacques a 5 calendriers?
4. Nous avons 8 fenêtres
   dans la salle de classe?
5. Elles ont 15 robes?
6. Vous avez 20 crayons?
7. Madame Lebeau a 13 chapeaux?
8. Tu as 14 cousins?
9. Ils ont 9 stylos?

RÉVISION ET THÈME

See Teacher's Section for answers to the *révision* and *thème*.

Review of:
1. repetition of possessive determiners
2. *avoir* possessives plurals in *-x*
3. possessives negative prepositions
4. prepositions possessives
5. *avoir* numbers
6. *aller* prepositions + modes of transportation

Consult the model sentences, then put the English cues into French and use them to form new sentences based on the models.

1. *Notre oncle et notre tante* sont devant leur garage.
   (*Your* (pl.) *bike and motorbike*)
   (*Their shoes and shirts*)

2. *Nous avons nos chapeaux.*
   (*You* (sing.) *have your boats.*)
   (*They* (f.) *have their sailboats.*)

3. *Son camion n'est pas* dans le garage. *Il est dans le parc.*
   (*My car isn't*)   (*It's under the tree.*)
   (*Our bikes aren't*)   (*They're on the grass.*)

4. Il est là, *derrière son jardin.*
   (*in front of his house*)
   (*with his neighbors* (f.))

5. *Nous avons deux copines.*
   (*The tree has nine leaves.*)
   (*I have five trucks.*)

6. *Ils vont à la campagne en avion* avec mes parents.
   (*We're going to church by bus*)
   (*I'm going to the mountains by train*)

Now that you have done the *Révision*, you are ready to write a composition. Put the English captions describing each cartoon panel into French to form a paragraph.

Marc and Chantal are in front of their house.

They have their bikes.

Their mother isn't in the house. She's in the garage.

Their father is behind the house, in his garden.

He has four flowers.

Marc and Chantal are going to the post office with their friends.

AUTO-TEST

A. Replace the words in italics with the cues in parentheses. Be sure to change the possessive determiner to agree with the cue. Follow the model.

1. Anne est avec *son frère.* (copines)
   Anne est avec ses copines.

2. Nous allons à Cannes avec *notre tante.* (oncles)
3. Vous avez *vos jupes.* (robe)
4. Tu vas à la gare avec *ton voisin?* (voisine)
5. Ils ont *leurs motos.* (voiture)
6. Nous sommes avec *notre ami.* (amies)
7. Vous avez *votre vélo.* (motos)
8. Voilà *leur garage.* (jardins)

B. Rewrite the sentences, spelling out each number.

1. Georges a 3 sœurs, 2 frères, 10 cousins, 13 cousines, 4 oncles et 5 tantes.
2. Dans la salle de classe, nous avons 19 élèves et 20 pupitres.
3. Monsieur Dupont a 16 crayons, 8 stylos, 3 gommes et 11 cahiers sur son bureau.

C. Write the sentences in the negative, using the correct form of the appropriate verb *aller, être,* or *avoir.* Follow the model.

1. Le drapeau . . . devant la poste.
   Le drapeau n'est pas devant la poste.

2. Vous . . . vos motos.
3. Je . . . à l'école à pied.
4. Nous . . . nos pull-overs.
5. Tu . . . à Nice en vélo.
6. Ce . . . mes cousines.
7. Tu . . . ma voiture.
8. Ils . . . à Paris par le train.
9. Elles . . . leurs bateaux à voiles.
10. Les feuilles . . . sur l'herbe.
11. Nous . . . en jean.
12. Vous . . . en pantalon et en blouse.

Cinquième Leçon

A Cannes

Michèle est à Cannes,[1] sur la Côte d'Azur, avec sa sœur Françoise. Elles vont au Palais des Festivals.[2] Maintenant elles sont au coin de la rue, près de l'hôtel Carlton.

MICHÈLE   Pardon, monsieur l'agent.[3] Le Palais des Festivals, s'il vous plaît?
5   Est-ce qu'il est loin d'ici?
L'AGENT   Pas du tout, mademoiselle. Il est là, en face de l'hôtel.
MICHÈLE   Merci beaucoup, monsieur.
L'AGENT   Je vous en prie, mademoiselle. A votre service.[4]

---

[1] Cannes is a resort city on the Mediterranean in southeastern France. The Mediterranean is warm, and the area is ideal for swimming and boating. The sea is noted for its color, a deep blue known as azure. The French name for the Riviera—la Côte d'Azur—means "the Azure Coast."

[2] The Palais des Festivals is a convention hall where, among other events, the Cannes Film Festival is held.

[3] The French never address someone simply as "officer" or "teacher." They always use the polite form: *monsieur l'agent, monsieur le professeur* (or *madame le professeur*), or simply *monsieur, madame,* or *mademoiselle.*

[4] Here *A* = *à*. When a letter that has an accent mark is capitalized, the accent mark is usually dropped.

See Cultural Supplement.

We do not repeat the terms of politeness in the *Mots Nouveaux.* Try to use them regularly and naturally in the classroom. You may also want to introduce *s'il te plaît* and *je t'en prie.*

le festival: You may want to point out the irregular plural.

In Cannes

Michèle is in Cannes, on the Riviera, with her sister Françoise. They are going to the Palais des Festivals. Right now they are on the corner, near the Hotel Carlton.

MICHÈLE   Excuse me, officer. Where's the Palais des Festivals, please? Is
5   it far from here?
POLICEMAN   Not at all, miss. It's there, opposite the hotel.
MICHÈLE   Thanks a lot.
POLICEMAN   Certainly, miss. At your service.

Questionnaire

1. Qui est avec Françoise?   2. Où sont Michèle et Françoise?   3. Où est-ce qu'elles vont?   4. Est-ce que le Palais des Festivals est loin ou ("or") près de l'hôtel?   5. Où est-ce qu'il est?

PRONONCIATION

You may want to review the numbers 1–20 orally before doing the *Prononciation*.

You have learned the numbers from 1 to 20. When some of these numbers appear with other words, their pronunciation changes. Pronounce the numbers 1 through 10 in the following examples:

1. un[1]   un frère   un oncle
                                        [n̄]

2. deux   deux camions   deux autobus
                                        [z̄]

3. trois   trois cartes   trois affiches
                                        [z̄]

4. quatre   { quatre lycées
               { or: quatre lycées   quatre écoles

5. cinq   cinq feuilles   cinq avions
                                        [k]

6. six   six fleurs   six arbres
                                        [z̄]

7. sept   sept copains   sept amis
                                        [t̄]

8. huit   huit copines   huit amies
                                        [t̄]

9. neuf   neuf maisons   neuf hôtels

10. dix   dix professeurs   dix élèves
                                        [z̄]

11–20. Most of the numbers from 11 through 20 have only one pronunciation. Two exceptions are *dix-huit*, which is like *huit*, and *vingt*:

          vingt gares   vingt aéroports
                                        [t̄]

[1]*Un* is used only with masculine nouns.

MOTS NOUVEAUX I

See Cultural Supplement.

l'aéroport: Point out that both the *a* and the *e* are pronounced: [aerɔpɔr].

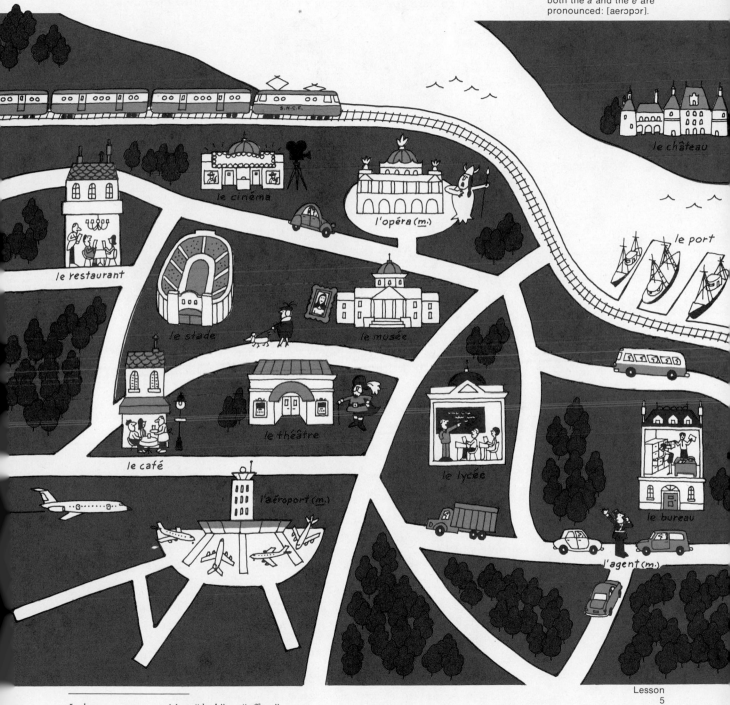

le château

le cinéma

l'opéra (m.)

le port

le restaurant

le stade

le musée

le théâtre

le lycée

le café

l'aéroport (m.)

le bureau

l'agent (m.)

Le bureau can mean either "desk" or "office."
L'école means "school" in general; *le lycée* is roughly equivalent to the American high school.

Exercice de Vocabulaire

Tell where you are going according to the pictures. Follow the model.

Though no transformations are required here, you may want to introduce Point 2, p. 71, before doing the exercise.

2. Nous allons au lycée.
3. Nous allons au stade.
4. Nous allons au musée.
5. Nous allons au port.
6. Nous allons au cinéma.
7. Nous allons au café.
8. Nous allons au restaurant.
9. Nous allons au théâtre.

1.
Nous allons au bureau.[1]

2.

3.

4.

5.

6.

7.

8.

9.

MOTS NOUVEAUX II

Qu'est-ce qui est au coin de la rue?	*What's on the corner?*
L'autobus est au coin de la rue.	*The bus is on the corner.*
La voiture est à côté de l'opéra.	*The car is next to the opera house.*
Elle est à gauche de l'opéra.	*It's to the left of the opera house.*
Qu'est-ce qui est loin de l'aéroport?	*What's far from the airport?*
Le bureau est loin de l'aéroport.	*The office is far from the airport.*
Le lycée est près de l'aéroport.	*The lycée is near the airport.*
Il est à droite de l'aéroport.	*It's to the right of the airport.*
Combien de camions est-ce qu'il y a?[2]	*How many trucks are there?*
Deux ou trois?	*Two or three?*
Il y a deux camions.	*There are two trucks.*
Il y a deux fleurs?	*Are there two flowers?*
Pas du tout. Il y a sept fleurs maintenant.	*Not at all. There are seven flowers now.*
Qui est là?	*Who's there?*
Moi, je suis là.	*I'm here.*
Moi, je suis ici et toi, tu es là.[3]	*I'm here and you're there.*

---

[1]*Au = à + le.*

[2]*Il y a* and *voilà* both mean "there is" and "there are." However, they are not interchangeable. Look at the following examples:

Voilà le camion.	*There's the truck.*
Il y a un camion dans le garage.	*There's one truck in the garage.*
Voilà tes chemises.	*There are your shirts.*
Il y a deux chemises sur la chaise.	*There are two shirts on the chair.*

Use *voilà* to point something out. Otherwise use *il y a* to mean "there is" or "there are."

[3]Though *ici* always means "here," *là* may mean either "here" or "there." *Là* always means "there" when it is used in a sentence with *ici*.

Exercices de vocabulaire

A. Answer the questions according to the picture. Follow the model.

1. Qu'est-ce qui est à gauche du théâtre?[1]
   Le restaurant est à gauche du théâtre.

2. Qu'est-ce qui est à côté du cinéma?
3. Qu'est-ce qui est en face du café?
4. Qu'est-ce qui est au coin de la rue?
5. Qu'est-ce qui est près de l'aéroport?
6. Qu'est-ce qui est à droite du bureau?
7. Qu'est-ce qui est loin du restaurant?
8. Qu'est-ce qui est en face du théâtre?
9. Qu'est-ce qui est près du stade?
10. Qu'est-ce qui est à gauche du lycée?

B. Choose the inappropriate word in each series, then make up a complete sentence using that word.

1. à gauche	à côté	à pied	à droite
2. en avion	en maillot	en voiture	en autobus
3. dix	dans	deux	douze
4. l'opéra	le théâtre	le cinéma	l'usine
5. le port	la gare	le garçon	l'aéroport
6. lui	eux	toi	trois
7. l'agent	la feuille	la fleur	l'arbre

[1]*Du = de + le.*

Though no transforma-
tions are required here,
you may want to introduce
Point 2, p. 71, before doing Ex. A.
2. Le théâtre est à côté
   du cinéma.
3. Le lycée est en face du
   café.
4. Le cinéma (le bureau)
   est au coin de la rue.
5. Le stade est près de
   l'aéroport.
6. Le lycée est à droite
   du bureau.
7. Le stade (l'aéroport /
   le bureau / le lycée /
   le café) est loin du
   restaurant.
8. Le musée est en face
   du théâtre.
9. L'aéroport est près du
   stade.
10. Le bureau est à
    gauche du lycée.

1. à pied
2. en maillot
3. dans
4. l'usine
5. le garçon
6. trois
7. l'agent

EXPLICATIONS I

Les phrases interrogatives

VOCABULAIRE

comment?	*how?*	n'est-ce pas?	*(see point 3)*

---

1. There are several ways of asking questions in French. As you know, one way is simply to raise the pitch of your voice on the last syllable of a sentence. Another common way of turning a statement into a question is by using *est-ce que* at the beginning of the sentence:

   Il est là.   *He's there.*
   Est-ce qu'il est là?   *Is he there?*

   Note that before a word beginning with a vowel sound, *est-ce que* becomes *est-ce qu'.*

2. Note how the question words are used:

   Alice va à Cannes.   { Où est-ce qu'elle va?
     { Où va Alice?

   Alice va à Cannes en avion.   Comment est-ce qu'elle va à Cannes?
   Elle va à Cannes avec Yves.   Avec qui est-ce qu'elle va à Cannes?
   Alice et Yves sont } à l'aéroport.   Qui est[1] } à l'aéroport?
   L'avion est }   Qu'est-ce qui est }
   Il y a trois aéroports et dix gares à Paris.   Combien d'aéroports et de gares est-ce qu'il y a à Paris?

3. *N'est-ce pas* is used at the end of a sentence and implies that a "yes" answer will be given. It has several English equivalents. For example:

   Elle va à l'école, n'est-ce pas?   { *She goes to school, **doesn't she?***
    { *She's going to school, **isn't she?***

   Tu vas à la plage, n'est-ce pas?   { *You go to the beach, **don't you?***
    { *You're going to the beach, **aren't you?***

4. One other question word that you know is *pourquoi*, "why":

   Pourquoi est-ce qu'elle va à Cannes?   **Parce que** sa famille est là.

Exercices

A. Change the statements into questions with *est-ce que.* Follow the model.

   1. Etienne et son frère vont au cinéma.
     Est-ce qu'Etienne et son frère vont au cinéma?

   2. La maison de leurs amis est près de la banque.

---

[1]Like "who," *qui* is followed by a singular form of the verb unless the people are mentioned:

   Qui est à l'aéroport?   ***Who's** at the airport?*
but: **Qui sont** Alice et Yves?   ***Who are** Alice and Yves?*

3. Les agents vont dans le parc.
4. Le camion est dans le garage.
5. Il y a deux restaurants au coin de la rue.
6. Votre bureau est en face de la gare.
7. Il y a deux arbres à côté de l'école.
8. Ses parents vont à Nice en bateau.

B. Redo the above exercise using *n'est-ce pas.* Follow the model.

1. Etienne et son frère vont au cinéma.
   Etienne et son frère vont au cinéma, n'est-ce pas?

C. Read the following statements, then ask as many questions as you can about each one. Follow the model.

1. Georges va à Nice en voiture avec ses trois sœurs.
   Est-ce que Georges va à Paris?
   Où va Georges?
   Qui va à Nice?
   Avec qui est-ce qu'il va à Nice?
   Comment est-ce qu'ils vont à Nice?
   Combien de sœurs est-ce qu'il a?

2. Le théâtre est au coin de la rue, en face de la banque.
3. Ils vont à la plage en autobus parce qu'ils n'ont pas leur voiture.
4. Ses amis vont à New York avec leurs deux enfants.
5. Le musée est à droite de l'hôtel et à gauche de l'église.

Les adjectifs comme <u>rouge</u>, <u>noir</u> et <u>joli</u>

VOCABULAIRE

de quelle couleur?	what color?	jeune	young
bleu, -e	blue	joli, -e	pretty
jaune	yellow	facile / difficile	easy / difficult
noir, -e	black	possible / impossible	possible / impossible
rouge	red	riche / pauvre	rich / poor

1. In French, adjectives have different forms and must agree with the person or thing they are describing. The forms are masculine and feminine, singular and plural. Look at the adjectives in the following sentences:

Le maillot est	rouge.	La robe est	rouge.
Les maillots sont	rouges.	Les robes sont	rouges.

An adjective whose masculine form ends in the letter *e* has identical masculine and feminine forms. In the plural, an *s* is added. All four forms are pronounced the same.

3. Est-ce que les agents vont dans le parc?
4. Est-ce que le camion est dans le garage?
5. Est-ce qu'il y a deux restaurants au coin de la rue?
6. Est-ce que votre bureau est en face de la gare?
7. Est-ce qu'il y a deux arbres à côté de l'école?
8. Est-ce que ses parents vont à Nice en bateau?

2. La maison de leurs amis est près de la banque, n'est-ce pas?
3. Les agents vont dans le parc, n'est-ce pas?
4. Le camion est dans le garage, n'est-ce pas?
5. Il y a deux restaurants au coin de la rue, n'est-ce pas?
6. Votre bureau est en face de la gare, n'est-ce pas?
7. Il y a deux arbres à côté de l'école, n'est-ce pas?
8. Ses parents vont à Nice en bateau, n'est-ce pas?

Ex. C
You might want to do this type of exercise from time to time. Students might also now ask each other questions about the introductory paragraph to the dialogue (p. 61).

2. Qu'est-ce qui est au coin de la rue (en face de la banque)?
   Où est le théâtre (la banque)?
3. Où est-ce qu'ils vont? Comment est-ce qu'ils vont à la plage? Pourquoi est-ce qu'ils vont à la plage en autobus (ne vont pas en voiture)?
4. Où vont ses amis? Avec qui est-ce qu'ils vont à New York? Combien d'enfants est-ce qu'ils ont?
5. Où est le musée (l'hôtel / l'église)? Qu'est-ce qui est à droite de l'hôtel (à gauche de l'église)?

Exs. A – B can be done after Point 1.

Exs. C–D can be done after Point 2.

2. Now look at the adjectives *noir* and *joli:*

Le maillot est	**noir.**	Le chapeau est	joli.
Les maillots sont	**noirs.**	Les chapeaux sont	jolis.
La robe est	**noire.**	La jupe est	jolie.
Les robes sont	**noires.**	Les jupes sont	jolies.

Certain adjectives that end in a pronounced consonant or in a vowel other than *e* also have only one pronunciation. But they have four different written forms.

Ex. E can be done after Point 3.

You might practice adjectives using classroom objects and articles of clothing.

3. Look at the following:

    Voilà ma robe bleue.   *There's my blue dress.*
but: Voilà ma jolie robe.   *There's my pretty dress.*

Most adjectives follow the noun. A few very common ones, such as *jeune* and *joli,* come before. For the moment, we will deal mostly with adjectives that follow the noun.

Exercices

A. Form sentences using the feminine cues in parentheses and the possessive determiner *sa.* Follow the model.

1. Le vélo de Jean est rouge. (la moto)
   Sa moto est rouge aussi.

2. Le fils de M. Lenoir est riche. (la fille)
3. Le crayon d'Hélène est jaune. (la gomme)
4. L'oncle de ma copine est jeune. (la tante)
5. Le maillot de mon amie est rouge. (la robe)
6. L'ami de Marie est pauvre. (la voisine)

2. Sa fille est riche aussi.
3. Sa gomme est jaune aussi.
4. Sa tante est jeune aussi.
5. Sa robe est rouge aussi.
6. Sa voisine est pauvre aussi.

B. Redo the above exercise in the plural. Follow the model.

1. Les vélos de Jean sont rouges. (les motos)
   Ses motos sont rouges aussi.

2. Ses filles sont riches aussi.
3. Ses gommes sont jaunes aussi.
4. Ses tantes sont jeunes aussi.
5. Ses robes sont rouges aussi.
6. Ses voisines sont pauvres aussi.

C. Answer the questions, using the feminine cues in parentheses and the possessive determiner *sa.* Follow the model.

1. Le chapeau de M. Lebeau est noir, n'est-ce pas? (la chemise)
   Oui, et sa chemise est noire aussi.

2. Le maillot de mon amie est joli, n'est-ce pas? (la jupe)
3. Le pull-over d'Hélène est bleu, n'est-ce pas? (la blouse)
4. Le vélo de ton voisin est noir, n'est-ce pas? (la moto)
5. Le bureau de leur grand-père est jaune, n'est-ce pas? (la chaise)
6. Le camion de votre frère est bleu, n'est-ce pas? (la voiture)

2. Oui, et sa jupe est jolie aussi.
3. Oui, et sa blouse est bleue aussi.
4. Oui, et sa moto est noire aussi.
5. Oui, et sa châise est jaune aussi.
6. Oui, et sa voiture est bleue aussi.

D. Answer the questions using the appropriate pronoun and the cues in parentheses. Be careful! Some of the nouns are masculine and others are feminine. Follow the model.

1. De quelle couleur sont les tableaux? (noir)
   Ils sont noirs, n'est-ce pas?

2. De quelle couleur sont les robes? (rouge)
3. De quelle couleur sont les bateaux? (jaune)
4. De quelle couleur sont les vélos? (noir)
5. De quelle couleur sont les feuilles? (rouge)
6. De quelle couleur sont les voitures? (bleu)
7. De quelle couleur sont les motos? (noir)
8. De quelle couleur sont les autobus? (bleu)

E. Combine the following pairs of sentences according to the model.

1. C'est mon maillot. Il est bleu.
   C'est mon maillot bleu.

2. Ce sont leurs chaussures. Elles sont noires.
3. C'est ma robe. Elle est rouge.
4. Voilà ma chemise. Elle est bleue.
5. C'est le livre. Il est difficile.
6. Voici ta jupe. Elle est noire.
7. Voilà les fleurs. Elles sont rouges.
8. Voilà les cahiers. Ils sont jaunes.

Vérifiez vos progrès

Write questions based on the statements, using the appropriate interrogative word *qu'est-ce qui. comment. combien.* or *de quelle couleur.* Follow the model.

1. L'arbre est à côté de la maison.
   Qu'est-ce qui est à côté de la maison?

2. Elle a cinq livres et trois cahiers.
3. Les chaussures sont noires.
4. Ils vont à Cannes par le train.
5. Le palais est en face de notre hôtel.
6. Le musée est à droite de l'opéra.
7. L'autobus est jaune et bleu.
8. Ils ont sept enfants.
9. Nous allons à l'aéroport en voiture.
10. Le théâtre est à gauche de l'église.

Because inversion after *de quelle couleur* corresponds to English, it should cause no problem.

2. Elles sont rouges, n'est-ce pas?
3. Ils sont jaunes, n'est-ce pas?
4. Ils sont noirs, n'est-ce pas?
5. Elles sont rouges, n'est-ce pas?
6. Elles sont bleues, n'est-ce pas?
7. Elles sont noires, n'est-ce pas?
8. Ils sont bleus, n'est-ce pas?

2. Ce sont leurs chaussures noires.
3. C'est ma robe rouge.
4. Voilà ma chemise bleue.
5. C'est le livre difficile.
6. Voici ta jupe noire.
7. Voilà les fleurs rouges.
8. Voilà les cahiers jaunes.

CONVERSATION ET LECTURE

Parlons de vous

See Cultural Supplement.

You may want to bring in sports magazines or newspapers, such as *l'Equipe*.

1. Comment est-ce que vous allez à l'école? à pied? en vélo? 2. Qu'est-ce qu'il y a dans votre salle de classe qui est jaune? noir? bleu? rouge? 3. Est-ce que votre maison ou appartement est loin de votre lycée? 4. Qu'est-ce qui est en face de votre maison? de votre lycée? 5. Est-ce que vous allez à la campagne? à la montagne? à la plage? 6. Comment est-ce que vous allez à la plage? Avec qui?

Le match° de football[1]

Dans un° coin de la cantine,° près de la fenêtre, il y a deux garçons. Le garçon à gauche porte° un pantalon noir et une chemise rouge. Il s'appelle° Marc. Le garçon à droite est en jean et il porte une jolie
5 chemise jaune et bleue. C'est Jean-Jacques. Devant eux, sur la table, il y a une revue° de football.

MARC	Je vais au cinéma samedi° avec Sara.
JEAN-JACQUES	Moi, je vais au match de football avec mon père.
10 MARC	Dis,° le stade est près du cinéma, n'est-ce pas?
JEAN-JACQUES	Oui, c'est à côté.°
MARC	Après° le match, allons ensemble° au café.
15 JEAN-JACQUES	Merci, mais c'est impossible. Après un match, mon père est toujours° fatigué.°
MARC	Fatigué? Pourquoi?
JEAN-JACQUES	Mon père est un vrai° fana de football[2] et il crie° beaucoup. . . .

le match: *game*

un, une: *a, an*
la cantine: *lunchroom*
porter: *to wear*
il s'appelle: *his name is*
la revue: *magazine*

samedi: *Saturday*

dis: *say!*

à côté: *(here) next door*
après: *after*
ensemble: *together*

toujours: *always*
fatigué, -e: *tired*

vrai, -e: *real*
crier: *to shout*

You may want to point out that *le / la fan(a)* is short for *fanatique*.

À propos ...

In addition to (or instead of) Questions 1–8, you might ask students to formulate a certain number of questions to ask their classmates. With stronger classes you might use this as a regular procedure.

1. Où sont les deux garçons? 2. Qui est le garçon en chemise rouge? 3. De quelle couleur sont les habits de Jean-Jacques? 4. Qu'est-ce qu'il y a sur la table? 5. Où vont Marc et son amie samedi? 6. Jean-Jacques va au cinéma avec eux? Pourquoi? 7. Où est le stade? 8. Jean-Jacques et son père vont au café après le match? Pourquoi? 9. Est-ce que vous allez aux[3] matchs de football ou de football américain de votre lycée? 10. Quand ("when") vous êtes à un match de football, est-ce que vous criez beaucoup?

---

[1]In France, what we call soccer is called *le football*. American football is *le football américain*.
[2]The French use *le* or *la fana* to speak of someone who enjoys a particular activity or thing: *un fana du cinéma, une fana des sports*. They use *le* or *la fan* to describe someone who is a fan of a particular performer or sports figure.
[3]*Aux = à + les.*

EXPLICATIONS II

À et de

1. The word *à* has several meanings:

Je vais à Paris.	*I'm going **to** Paris.*
Je suis à Paris.	*I'm **in** Paris.*
Je vais à la plage.	*I'm going **to** the beach.*
Je suis à la plage.	*I'm **at** the beach.*

The word *de* also has several meanings:

Anne est l'amie **de** ma cousine.	*Anne is my cousin's friend.*
Mon ami **de** New York est ici.	*My friend **from** New York is here.*

Both *à* and *de* are also part of many common expressions:

Ils vont à **pied.**	*They're going **on foot.***
Ils sont à **côté de** la porte.	*They're **next to** the door.*

Exs. A–C can be done after Point 2.

2. Look at the following:

Voilà Paris.	Je suis à Paris.	Je suis près de Paris.
Voilà **la** porte.	Je suis à **la** porte.	Je suis près **de la** porte.
Voilà l'hôtel.	Je suis à l'hôtel.	Je suis près **de** l'hôtel.
Voilà **le** café.	Je suis **au** café.	Je suis près **du** café.

The prepositions *à* and *de* combine with the masculine definite determiner *le* to become *au* and *du*.

Exs. D–E can be done after Point 3.

3. Look at the plural forms:

Voilà **les** portes.	Ils vont **aux** portes.	Ils sont près **des** portes.
Voilà **les** hôtels.	Ils vont **aux** hôtels.	Ils sont près **des** hôtels.
Voilà **les** cafés.	Ils vont **aux** cafés.	Ils sont près **des** cafés.

The prepositions *à* and *de* combine with the plural determiner *les* to become *aux* and *des*. Before a noun beginning with a vowel sound, the *x* and *s* are pronounced [z].

Exercices

A. Answer the questions according to the pictures. Follow the model.

Note that this also reviews *aller*.
2. Nous allons à l'hôtel.
3. Ils vont à la porte.

1. Où est-ce que tu vas?
   Je vais à la montagne.

2. Où est-ce que vous allez, mes amis?

3. Où est-ce qu'ils vont?

4. On va à la poste.
5. Elles vont à la piscine.
6. Je vais à l'église.
7. Il va à l'usine.
8. Vous allez (Nous allons) à l'appartement.
9. Je vais à l'aéroport.

4. Où est-ce qu'on va?

5. Où est-ce qu'elles vont?

6. Où est-ce que tu vas, Cécile?

7. Où est-ce qu'il va?

8. Où est-ce que nous allons?

9. Où est-ce que tu vas, Jean?

You might ask similar questions relating to the art on p. 63.
2. Ils vont au restaurant.
3. Je vais au jardin.
4. Je vais au lycée.
5. Elle est au cinéma.
6. Elles sont au musée.
7. Je suis au café.
8. Ils vont au parc.

B. Answer the questions using the cues in parentheses. Follow the model.

1. Où est-ce que vous allez, messieurs? (le bureau)
   Nous allons au bureau.

2. Où est-ce qu'ils vont? (le restaurant)
3. Où est-ce que vous allez, madame? (le jardin)
4. Où est-ce que tu vas, Léon? (le lycée)
5. Où est-ce qu'elle est? (le cinéma)
6. Où est-ce qu'elles sont? (le musée)
7. Où est-ce que tu es? (le café)
8. Où est-ce qu'ils vont? (le parc)

C. Combine the following pairs of sentences according to the models.

1. Voici l'élève. Ce sont ses livres.
   Ce sont les livres de l'élève.
2. Voilà le copain de Guy. C'est son vélo.
   C'est le vélo du copain de Guy.

3. Voici la jeune fille. Ce sont ses robes.
4. Voici le professeur. C'est sa voiture.
5. Voici l'enfant. C'est sa chemise.
6. Voici l'agent. C'est son bureau.
7. Voilà l'ami de Guy. Ce sont ses bateaux.
8. Voilà le neveu de Mme Lafont. C'est son pull-over.
9. Voilà le frère d'Alice. C'est son camion.
10. Voilà la cousine de Marie. C'est sa maison.

3. Ce sont les robes de la jeune fille.
4. C'est la voiture du professeur.
5. C'est la chemise de l'enfant.
6. C'est le bureau de l'agent.
7. Ce sont les bateaux de l'ami de Guy.
8. C'est le pull-over du neveu de Mme Lafont.
9. C'est le camion du frère d'Alice.
10. C'est la maison de la cousine de Marie.

Cinquième
Leçon

D. Each day five policemen make their rounds. Tell where each of them goes, using the appropriate form of *à* + determiner. Follow the model.

1. Monsieur Leclerc . . . (les écoles/la poste/le parc)
   Monsieur Leclerc va aux écoles, à la poste et au parc.

2. Monsieur Alphonse . . . (l'opéra/le théâtre/les cinémas)
3. Monsieur Dupont . . . (les banques/les cafés/le musée)
4. Monsieur Lenoir . . . (les jardins/le lycée/l'hôpital)
5. Monsieur Bernard . . . (l'aéroport/la gare/le stade)

2. Monsieur Alphonse va à l'opéra, au théâtre et aux cinémas.
3. Monsieur Dupont va aux banques, aux cafés et au musée.
4. Monsieur Lenoir va aux jardins, au lycée et à l'hôpital.
5. Monsieur Bernard va à l'aéroport, à la gare et au stade.

E. Answer the questions using the plural form of the cues in parentheses. Follow the model.

1. Où est le drapeau? (près de la fenêtre)
   Le drapeau est près des fenêtres.

2. Où est le musée? (en face du jardin)
3. Où est la moto? (à côté du vélo)
4. Où est le cahier? (à gauche du livre)
5. Où est le stade? (en face de l'usine)
6. Où est l'aéroport? (loin de l'hôtel)
7. Où est le bureau? (en face du pupitre)
8. Où est la carte? (à droite de l'affiche)

2. Le musée est en face des jardins.
3. La moto est à côté des vélos.
4. Le cahier est à gauche des livres.
5. Le stade est en face des usines.
6. L'aéroport est loin des hôtels.
7. Le bureau est en face des pupitres.
8. La carte est à droite des affiches.

Vérifiez vos progrès

Write complete sentences using the correct form of the words given. Follow the model.

1. Le café/être/en face de/le musée
   Le café est en face du musée.

2. La banque/être/à gauche de/la poste
3. Je/aller/à/le bureau
4. L'arbre/être/à côté de/le garage
5. Les enfants/aller/à/les lycées/en autobus
6. Nous/aller/à/le théâtre
7. Sa villa/être/près de/le port
8. Nous/être/loin de/l'aéroport
9. L'opéra/être/à droite de/les restaurants
10. Le cinéma/être/en face de/les jardins

REVISION ET THÈME

See Teacher's Section for answers to the *révision* and *thème*.

Review of:
1. *voici/voilà*
   ici/là
   prepositions with *de*
2. prepositions with *de*
3. numbers
   position and agreement
   of adjectives
   prepositions
4. prepositions with *de*
5. numbers
   forms of *à*
   prepositions with *de*

Consult the model sentences, then put the English cues into French and use them to form new sentences based on the models.

1. *Voilà le cinéma.* Les élèves sont *là, près du cinéma.*
   (*There's the theater.*)   (*here, across from the theater*)
   (*Here's the museum.*)   (*there, to the left of the museum*)

2. *Le restaurant* est *à côté du musée.*
   (*The hotel*)   (*on the corner*)
   (*The stadium*)   (*far from the airport*)

3. Il y a *cinq camions rouges devant l'hôtel.*
   (*three yellow bikes behind the tree*)
   (*two blue cars in the garage*)

4. Les motos sont *à droite de l'autobus.*
   (*across from the factories*)
   (*next to the movie theater*)

5. Les *quatre cousins* vont *au lycée près de la gare.*
   (*six girl friends*)   (*to the café to the right of the high school*)
   (*eight girls*)   (*to the beach far from the port*)

Now that you have done the *Révision,* you are ready to write a composition. Put the English captions describing each cartoon panel into French to form a paragraph.

① There's the opera house. The students are there, opposite the opera house.

② The restaurant is on the corner.

③ There are two black cars near the restaurant.

④ The students are to the left of the cars.

⑤ They're going to the café to the right of the opera house.

AUTO-TEST

A. Write questions based on the statements, using an appropriate interrogative. Sometimes you may be able to ask more than one question. Follow the model.

1. Marie-Thérèse est là.
   Qui est là? Où est Marie-Thérèse?

2. Il y a trois bateaux à voiles.
3. Leurs chaussettes sont bleues.
4. Thomas et Frédéric vont au restaurant.
5. Le cinéma est en face du café.
6. Nous allons à notre villa par le train.
7. Jean est à l'aéroport.
8. Ils ne vont pas à la piscine parce qu'ils n'ont pas leurs maillots.

B. Write answers to the questions using the cues in parentheses. Follow the model.

1. De quelle couleur sont tes chaussures? (noir)
   Mes chaussures sont noires.

2. De quelle couleur est ton pull-over? (rouge)
3. De quelle couleur est ta moto? (bleu)
4. De quelle couleur sont tes chemises? (jaune)
5. De quelle couleur sont tes livres? (noir)
6. De quelle couleur sont tes voitures? (bleu)

C. Write answers to the questions using the cues in parentheses. Follow the models.

1. Où est-ce que tu vas? (la poste/près de/le lycée)
   Je vais à la poste près du lycée.
2. Où est l'aéroport? (loin de/les maisons)
   L'aéroport est loin des maisons.

3. Où est-ce qu'il va avec son frère? (le café/à côté de/le cinéma)
4. Où est-ce que tu vas? (la plage/près de/le port)
5. Où est-ce que vous allez? (les jardins/en face de/le château)
6. Où sont les habits du garçon? (sur la chaise/à gauche de/la table)
7. Où est-ce qu'elles vont? (le restaurant/en face de/le bureau)
8. Où est l'école? (loin de/les hôtels)
9. Où est-ce qu'ils vont? (la banque/à droite de/les usines)
10. Où vont leurs amis? (les musées/près de/le parc)

Sixième Leçon

Au lycée

Il est huit heures. André Gallet entre dans la salle de classe. Il est triste.

See Cultural Supplement.

LE PROFESSEUR   Bonjour, André. Comment ça va?
ANDRÉ   Ça va mal, monsieur.
LE PROFESSEUR   Pourquoi?
5   ANDRÉ   Parce que chez moi, mon frère regarde toujours les sports
à la télé pendant que je révise mes leçons.
LE PROFESSEUR   Et alors?
ANDRÉ   Alors, j'aime étudier, mais j'aime aussi regarder les sports.
Et quand mon frère . . .
10   LE PROFESSEUR   André!
ANDRÉ   Oui, monsieur?
LE PROFESSEUR   Où sont vos devoirs?[1]
ANDRÉ   Euh . . .

Point out that *Comment ça va?* is the full form of the greeting taught in Lesson 1. You may also want to teach the formal *Comment allez-vous?*

You might want to remind students of the literal meaning of *mal* (l. 3) and explain that *pas mal* is short for *Ça ne va pas mal.*

---

[1]*Les devoirs* is a masculine noun that is used in the plural to mean written homework. Note that the teacher uses the *vous* form (*vos devoirs*). Usually, elementary-school teachers use *tu* when talking to students and secondary-school teachers use *vous.*

At school

It is eight o'clock. André Gallet comes into the classroom. He is sad.

TEACHER	Good morning, André. How are you?
ANDRÉ	Not very well, sir.
TEACHER	Why?
5 ANDRÉ	Because at home, my brother always watches sports on TV while I'm going over my lessons.
TEACHER	So?
ANDRÉ	Well, I like to study, but I like to look at sports, too. And when my brother . . .
10 TEACHER	André!
ANDRÉ	Yes, sir?
TEACHER	Where's your homework?
ANDRÉ	Er . . .

Questionnaire

1. Où est André? 2. Comment est-ce qu'il est? 3. Pourquoi est-ce que ça va mal? 4. Qu'est-ce qu'il y a (= qu'est-ce qui est) à la télé pendant qu'André étudie? 5. Est-ce que le frère d'André aime regarder les sports? Et André aussi? 6. Est-ce qu'André a ses devoirs?

PRONONCIATION

The vowel sound [e] is produced with the lips in a smiling position and the jaws held very steady.

Exercices

A. Listen to the following words, then say them aloud. Be sure to hold your jaws absolutely steady as you pronounce the [e] sound.

c'est   chez   les   le cahier   le papier
le café   l'école l'église la télé   le lycée

B. Carefully pronounce the [e] sound in the following words. Pronounce each syllable with equal stress.

aller   entrer   regarder   étudier   réviser

C. Listen to the following sentences, then say them aloud.

C'est le café.   J'aime regarder la télé.
Allez chez René.   Edith révise ses leçons.
Il est chez André.   Bénédicte aime étudier.

You may want to point out these common spellings of the [e] sound: é, er, es, ez. If necessary, remind students that because le pull-over is a borrowed word, it does not follow this pattern: [pulovɛr].

Sixième
Leçon

MOTS NOUVEAUX I

la radio

la télé

le disque

le journal télévisé

le documentaire

jouer au football américain

jouer au football

jouer au tennis

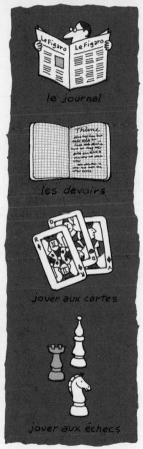

le journal

les devoirs

jouer aux cartes

la pièce

le dessin animé

le film policier

réviser ses leçons

jouer aux échecs

See Cultural Supplement.

animé: Help students see that this is an adjective and thus agrees with the noun *le(s) dessin(s).* Remind them of the plural *les jeunes filles.* Ask how they would form the plural of *le drapeau américain (canadien, français).*

réviser: Help students see that the *révision* at the end of each lesson is a "going over" or "review" of the lesson.

If possible, you might tape radio ads or a brief radio program from France or Canada.

Bring French newspapers, fan magazines, records, sheet music to class. Hand out song lyrics before playing records, and remind students of the pronouncing of mute *e* in songs.

Students will enjoy knowing the French titles of some of their favorite movies. A subscription to a weekly magazine, such as *L'Express,* can help you keep up to date on films, books, etc.

Qu'est-ce qu'il fait?	What's he doing?
Est-ce qu'il **regarde les dessins animés?**	Is he **watching cartoons?**
Non, il **écoute la radio.**	No, he's **listening to the radio.**
Est-ce qu'elle **joue au tennis?**	Is she **playing tennis?**
Non, elle regarde **le match de football.**	No, she's watching **the soccer match.**

Exercice de vocabulaire

Answer the questions according to the pictures. Follow the model.

1. Il joue aux cartes?
   Non, il ne joue pas aux cartes. Il joue aux échecs.

2. Elle écoute la radio?

3. Elle regarde le film policier?

4. Il joue au football?

5. Il joue au football américain?

6. Il regarde le journal?

7. Il regarde le documentaire?

8. Elle joue aux échecs?

9. Elle regarde le dessin animé?

2. Non, elle n'écoute pas la radio. Elle écoute le disque.
3. Non, elle ne regarde pas le film policier. Elle regarde le dessin animé.
4. Non, il ne joue pas au football. Il joue aux cartes.
5. Non, il ne joue pas au football américain. Il joue au football.
6. Non, il ne regarde pas le journal. Il regarde la télé.
7. Non, il ne regarde pas le documentaire. Il regarde le journal télévisé.
8. Non, elle ne joue pas aux échecs. Elle joue au tennis.
9. Non, elle ne regarde pas le dessin animé. Elle regarde la pièce.

MOTS NOUVEAUX II

Note that only the 3 sing. form of *faire* is introduced here. The full conjugation is taught in Lesson 8.

Qu'est-ce qu'elle fait?	*What's she doing?*
Où sont ses devoirs?	*Where's her homework?*
Pourquoi est-ce qu'elle n'étudie pas?	*Why isn't she studying?*
Elle ne révise pas la leçon?	*Isn't she reviewing the lesson?*
Elle n'aime pas réviser ses leçons.	*She doesn't like to go over her lessons.*
Elle aime mieux regarder les matchs de football américain à la télé.	*She prefers to watch football games on TV.*
On n'étudie pas pendant qu'on regarde la télé.	*We don't study while we're watching TV.*

Sixième Leçon

80

Quand est-ce que tu vas à l'école?
Je vais à l'école **le matin**.[1]
L'après-midi je joue au football.
Le soir je révise mes leçons.

When do you go to school?
*I go to school **in the morning**.*
In the afternoon I play soccer.
In the evening I go over my lessons.

See Cultural Supplement.

You may want to introduce *Quelle heure est-il?* (p. 92).

le matin

le petit déjeuner

l'après-midi (*m.*)

le déjeuner

l'après-midi (*m.*)

le goûter

le soir

le dîner

Je prépare **le petit déjeuner**.
      le déjeuner.
      le dîner.
      le goûter.[2]

*I'm making **breakfast**.*
      lunch.
      dinner.
      the snack.

---

[1]*Le matin* means both "the morning" and "in the morning"; *l'après-midi (m.)* means "the afternoon" and "in the afternoon"; *le soir* means "the evening" and "in the evening."

[2]*Le goûter* is an afternoon snack. It may be bread and butter or jam and perhaps a cup of hot chocolate. Another very common snack is a piece of chocolate eaten with bread.

Lesson
6

Maintenant je déjeune.   *Now I'm eating breakfast.*
           déjeune.   *eating lunch.*
           dîne.   *eating dinner.*

Le matin mon père va **toujours**   *My father **always** goes to his office*
   à son bureau.   *in the morning.*
Est-ce qu'il est **toujours** là?   *Is he **still** there?*
Non, **pas maintenant**.   *No, **not now**.*

Exercices de vocabulaire

A. Answer the questions by telling when the activity mentioned would most likely occur. Follow the model.

1. Est-ce que sa mère prépare le petit déjeuner l'après-midi?
   Pas du tout! Elle prépare le petit déjeuner le matin.

2. Est-ce que ses parents vont au théâtre le matin?
3. Est-ce qu'on prépare le goûter le soir?
4. Est-ce que nous allons au cinéma le matin?
5. Est-ce que Martine déjeune le soir?
6. Est-ce que sa cousine dîne l'après-midi?
7. Est-ce que Jean regarde les documentaires le matin?

B. Answer the questions according to the pictures. Follow the model.

1. Qu'est-ce qu'elle fait?
   Elle écoute le disque.

2. Qu'est-ce qu'elle fait?

3. Qu'est-ce qu'il fait?

4. Qu'est-ce qu'il fait?

5. Qu'est-ce qu'elle fait?

6. Qu'est-ce qu'elle fait?

7. Qu'est-ce qu'il fait?

8. Qu'est-ce qu'il fait?   9. Qu'est-ce qu'elle fait?

EXPLICATIONS I

Qu'est-ce qui / qu'est-ce que

1. Look at the following:

   La **télé** est sur la table.   Qu'est-ce qui est sur la table?

   Ma **mère** regarde **la télé**.   { Qu'est-ce que ta mère regarde?
                                        { Qu'est-ce qu'elle regarde?

   Qu'est-ce qui means "what" as the subject of a question ("What's on the table?"). *Qu'est-ce que* means "what" as the object of a question ("What's she watching?").

2. *Qu'est-ce qu'il y a* can be used in place of *qu'est-ce qui est*:

   Qu'est-ce qu'il y a sur la table?   ***What's on the table?***
   Qu'est-ce qu'il y a à la télé?   ***What's on TV?***

3. Another common use of *qu'est-ce que* is in the expression *Qu'est-ce que c'est?* ("What's that?").

Exercices

A. Based on the statements, ask questions using *qu'est-ce que*. Follow the model.

   1. Paul regarde le match de football à la télé.
      Qu'est-ce que Paul regarde à la télé?

   2. Son frère révise les trois leçons difficiles.
   3. Marie aime les documentaires.
   4. Roger écoute son disque.
   5. Elle aime les livres faciles.
   6. On joue les films policiers au cinéma.

B. Restate the questions using *qu'est-ce qu'il y a*. Follow the model.

   1. Qu'est-ce qui est sous la chaise?
      Qu'est-ce qu'il y a sous la chaise?

   2. Qu'est-ce qui est dans le parc?
   3. Qu'est-ce qui est au coin de la rue?
   4. Qu'est-ce qui est devant le camion?
   5. Qu'est-ce qui est derrière l'arbre?
   6. Qu'est-ce qui est en face du théâtre?

Les verbes réguliers en -er

VOCABULAIRE

apporter	*to bring*	ouvrir	*to open*
arriver	*to arrive*	parler	*to speak, to talk*
demander	*to ask, to ask for*	porter	*to wear*
donner	*to give*	rentrer { à	*to go back to*
entrer dans	*to go in, to come in*	rentrer { de	*to come back from*
fermer	*to close*	rester	*to stay, to remain*
habiter	*to live, to live in*	travailler	*to work*
montrer	*to show*		

Aller, avoir, and *être* are irregular verbs; that is, the six forms do not follow a pattern. Regular verbs do have a standard pattern. The most common class of regular verbs has infinitives ("to" forms) ending in *-er.* To get the present-tense forms, start with the "stem," which is the infinitive minus the *-er,* then add the appropriate ending *-e, -es, -e; -ons, -ez,* or *-ent:*

INFINITIVE: **regarder** *to look at, to watch*
STEM: **regard-**

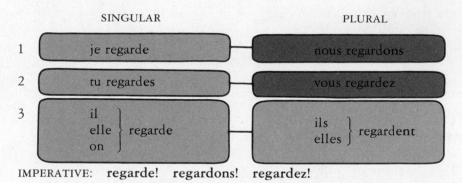

	SINGULAR	PLURAL
1	je regarde	nous regardons
2	tu regardes	vous regardez
3	il / elle / on } regarde	ils / elles } regardent

IMPERATIVE: **regarde! regardons! regardez!**

1. All three singular forms and the 3 pl. form are pronounced the same:

   je regarde   tu regardes   il regarde   ils regardent

2. As with *tu vas* "you're going" and *va!* "go!" the *s* of the 2 sing. form does not appear in the imperative.

3. When a verb begins with a vowel sound, elision and liaison occur: *j'écoute, on écoute, nous écoutons, vous écoutez, ils écoutent, elles écoutent.* Remember that liaison *s* is always pronounced [z].

4. Although *ouvrir,* "to open," is not an *-er* verb, in the present tense its forms are just like those of *aimer* or *écouter.* The stem of *ouvrir* is *ouvr-* (*j'ouvre, tu ouvres,* etc.).

5. Sometimes we use a preposition in English where the French do not:

J'**écoute** les disques.   *I'm listening **to** the records.*

Je **regarde** le professeur.   { *I'm looking **at** the teacher.*
                                        { *I'm watching the teacher.*

Je **demande** les cartes.   *I'm asking **for** the cards.*
J'**habite** l'hôtel.   *I live **in** the hotel.*

Similarly, the French sometimes use a preposition where we do not:

Je joue **au** tennis.   *I play tennis.*

J'entre **dans** le musée.   { *I'm entering the museum.*
                                      { *I'm going into the museum.*

Je montre[1] la voiture **à** Jean. { *I'm showing Jean the car.*
                                      { *I'm showing the car to Jean.*

Je demande les cartes **à** Jean.   *I'm asking Jean for the cards.*

Exercices

A. Answer the questions according to the pictures. Follow the model.

1. Qu'est-ce qu'elle ouvre?
Elle ouvre les fenêtres.

2. Qu'est-ce qu'elle porte?

3. Où est-ce qu'il habite?

4. Où est-ce qu'il travaille?

5. Où est-ce qu'elle arrive?

6. Qu'est-ce qu'il donne à Martine?

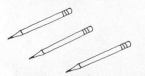 

7. Qu'est-ce qu'il apporte aux élèves?

8. Où est-ce qu'elle rentre?

9. Où est-ce qu'il entre?

To help students learn the meanings of the new verbs, Ex. A uses 3 sing. forms only.
2. Elle porte le (son) pantalon.
3. Il habite la maison.
4. Il travaille à l'usine.
5. Elle arrive à l'aéroport.
6. Il donne les livres à Martine.
7. Il apporte les crayons aux élèves.
8. Elle rentre à l'hôtel.
9. Il entre dans le lycée.

Lesson
6

---

[1]*Apporter* and *donner* also follow this pattern: *J'apporte le livre à Jean; Je donne le livre à Jean.*

LA TOUR EIFFEL

10. Elle demande l'affiche.
11. Elle regarde la télé.
12. Elle montre le journal à Jacques.

10. Qu'est-ce qu'elle demande?

11. Qu'est-ce qu'elle regarde?

12. Qu'est-ce qu'elle montre à Jacques?

B. Answer the questions according to the statements. In your answer, use the appropriate pronoun *ils* or *elles*. Follow the models.

1. Jacqueline et Anne portent leurs pull-overs noirs.
   (a) Qu'est-ce que les jeunes filles portent?
   Elles portent leurs pull-overs.
   (b) De quelle couleur sont les pull-overs?
   Ils sont noirs.

2. Tes cousins donnent les fleurs rouges aux jeunes filles.
   (a) Qu'est-ce que mes cousins donnent aux jeunes filles?
   (b) De quelle couleur sont les fleurs?

3. Maintenant Odile et Georges jouent aux échecs à la maison.
   (a) Odile et Georges jouent aux cartes maintenant?
   (b) Est-ce qu'Odile et Georges sont à l'hôtel?

4. Mes trois tantes arrivent toujours par le train.
   (a) Combien de tantes est-ce que tu as?
   (b) Comment est-ce que tes tantes arrivent?

5. Mes frères étudient pendant que mes sœurs écoutent leurs disques.
   (a) Est-ce que tes frères écoutent leurs disques?
   (b) Est-ce que tes sœurs étudient aussi?

6. Le soir ses neveux dînent toujours au restaurant.
   (a) Où est-ce qu'ils dînent?
   (b) Quand est-ce que ses neveux vont au restaurant?

7. Antoinette et Elise habitent la maison en face de la gare.
   (a) Où habitent les jeunes filles?
   (b) Leur maison est loin de la gare?

8. Barbara et Colette ont quatre frères qui aiment regarder les matchs de football.
   (a) Combien de frères ont Barbara et Colette?
   (b) Qu'est-ce que leurs frères aiment regarder?

C. Answer the questions using the cues in parentheses. Follow the models.

1. J'aime aller à la plage. Et toi, Brigitte? (jouer au tennis)
   Oui, mais j'aime mieux jouer au tennis.

2. Tu aimes aller à Paris. Et lui? (rester chez lui)
   Oui, mais il aime mieux rester chez lui.

3. Vous aimez travailler au bureau. Et elle? (rester à la maison)

4. Elle aime aller par le train. Et vous, monsieur? (aller en avion)

5. Nous aimons regarder la télé. Et eux? (écouter la radio)

6. Ils aiment habiter Paris. Et elles? (habiter la campagne)

To reinforce comprehension and encourage longer utterances, Ex. B uses the 3 pl. forms only. Note that this is also a review of interrogatives.

2. (a) Ils donnent les fleurs rouges aux jeunes filles.
   (b) Elles sont rouges.
3. (a) Non, ils jouent aux échecs.
   (b) Non, ils sont à la maison.
4. (a) J'ai trois tantes.
   (b) Elles arrivent (toujours) par le train.
5. (a) Non, ils étudient.
   (b) Non, elles écoutent leurs disques.
6. (a) Ils dînent (toujours) au restaurant.
   (b) Ils vont au restaurant le soir.
7. (a) Elles habitent la maison en face de la gare.
   (b) Non, elle est (très) près de (en face de) la gare.
8. (a) Elles ont quatre frères.
   (b) Ils aiment regarder les matchs de football.

3. Oui, mais elle aime mieux rester à la maison.
4. Oui, mais j'aime mieux aller en avion.
5. Oui, mais ils aiment mieux écouter la radio.
6. Oui, mais elles aiment mieux habiter la campagne.

7. Elle aime dîner au restaurant. Et toi? (dîner à la maison)
8. Tu aimes parler à tes amis après la classe. Et lui? (rentrer chez lui)
9. J'aime rentrer du stade en autobus. Et vous, mes amis? (rentrer à pied)
10. Vous aimez aller au cinéma. Et moi? (aller au théâtre)

D. Answer the questions using the cues in parentheses. Follow the models.

1. Qu'est-ce que votre grand-mère fait pendant que vous regardez le journal télévisé? (préparer le dîner)
   Elle prépare le dîner pendant que nous regardons le journal télévisé.
2. Qu'est-ce que ta sœur fait pendant que tu écoutes les disques? (jouer aux échecs)
   Elle joue aux échecs pendant que j'écoute les disques.

3. Qu'est-ce que son frère fait pendant que nous jouons au tennis? (préparer le goûter)
4. Qu'est-ce que votre oncle fait pendant que vous regardez la pièce? (rester à la maison)
5. Qu'est-ce que Catherine fait pendant que Jeanne et Denise parlent à Georges? (regarder les dessins animés)
6. Qu'est-ce qu'Adèle fait pendant que ses enfants sont au lycée? (travailler à Paris)
7. Qu'est-ce que David fait pendant que je ferme les fenêtres? (ouvrir la porte)
8. Qu'est-ce que votre mère fait pendant que vous étudiez? (jouer aux cartes)
9. Qu'est-ce que Bruno fait pendant que nous déjeunons? (arriver)
10. Qu'est-ce que son père fait pendant que vous dînez au restaurant? (rentrer à l'appartement)
11. Qu'est-ce que le professeur fait pendant que tu apportes les chaises? (regarder mes devoirs)
12. Qu'est-ce que Pierre fait pendant que je montre le jardin à Yvonne? (parler aux enfants)

Vérifiez vos progrès

Complete the sentences using the appropriate form of each verb in the correct slot. You will use each verb once.

1. Les Leclerc . . . quatre enfants maintenant. Ils . . . toujours Montréal, où M. Leclerc . . . à l'hôpital. (*travailler/habiter/avoir*)
2. L'après-midi les jeunes filles . . . au tennis. Le soir elles . . . leurs leçons pendant que tu . . . la télé. (*regarder/réviser/jouer*)
3. Notre mère . . . à la banque et nos grands-parents . . . à la maison avec nous. Le soir nous . . . chez nous ou au restaurant au coin de la rue. (*travailler/rester/dîner*)
4. Vous . . . la porte et Thomas . . . dans la maison. Il . . . son pull-over rouge et son jean. Il . . . du lycée. (*rentrer/porter/ouvrir/entrer*)

---

7. Oui, mais j'aime mieux dîner à la maison.
8. Oui, mais il aime mieux rentrer chez lui.
9. Oui, mais nous aimons mieux rentrer à pied.
10. Oui, mais tu aimes mieux aller au théâtre.

3. Il prépare le goûter pendant que vous jouez (nous jouons) au tennis.
4. Il reste à la maison pendant que nous regardons la pièce.
5. Elle regarde les dessins animés pendant que Jeanne et Denise (qu'elles) parlent à Georges.
6. Elle travaille à Paris pendant que ses enfants (qu'ils) sont au lycée.
7. Il ouvre la porte pendant que tu fermes les fenêtres.
8. Elle joue aux cartes pendant que nous étudions.
9. Il arrive pendant que vous déjeunez (nous déjeunons).
10. Il rentre à l'appartement pendant que nous dînons au restaurant.
11. Il regarde mes devoirs pendant que j'apporte les chaises.
12. Il parle aux enfants pendant que tu montres le jardin à Yvonne.

CONVERSATION ET LECTURE

Parlons de vous

1. Est-ce que vous aimez les sports? Est-ce que vous jouez au football? au football américain? 2. Est-ce que vous aimez jouer au tennis? aux cartes? aux échecs? 3. Avec qui est-ce que vous jouez? 4. Est-ce que vous aimez regarder la télé? Qu'est-ce que vous aimez regarder à la télé? le journal télévisé? les dessins animés? 5. Est-ce que vous aimez regarder le journal? les revues ("magazines") de sports? les revues de mode ("fashion")? 6. Est-ce que vous écoutez la radio? les disques? 7. Est-ce que vous habitez loin du lycée? 8. Est-ce que vous aimez rester chez vous le soir? Si ("if") non, où est-ce que vous aimez aller? au théâtre? au cinéma? au restaurant?

Le matin chez les Guichard

C'est aujourd'hui° mercredi° et Mme Guichard prépare le petit déjeuner pour° M. Guichard et leurs
deux filles, Viviane et Michèle.[1] Les Guichard ont
quatre enfants, mais les deux aînés° n'habitent pas
5   chez leurs parents. Alain est marié° et travaille
dans une° banque à Paris. Il y a aussi Marie qui
travaille à Radio-Canada à Montréal.

Pendant qu'ils déjeunent, le facteur° arrive. Il apporte une carte postale° de Marie. Madame Gui-
10 chard montre la carte à son mari° et à ses filles.
Regardons la carte avec eux:

"Ça va toujours très bien ici. Aujourd'hui on travaille de 8 h.° jusqu'à° 20 h.[3] Nous préparons un
documentaire sur les Esquimaux.° Le documentaire
15 n'est pas en français, mais en anglais. C'est toujours
très difficile pour moi et je suis très fatiguée."°

VIVIANE	Ecoute, Michèle! Ce n'est pas fa-cile pour elle! Elle est pares-seuse,° notre sœur!
20 MME GUICHARD	Mais non, ta sœur n'est pas pares-seuse! L'anglais est très difficile pour elle.
VIVIANE	Mais moi aussi, je travaille douze heures° par jour.° Je suis au lycée
25	de huit heures jusqu'à cinq heures. Et le soir je révise mes leçons.
MME GUICHARD	Pauvre Viviane!
VIVIANE	Oui! Et qui paie° les élèves
30	quand ils travaillent?

À propos ...

1. Qui prépare le petit déjeuner?   2. Combien d'enfants ont M. et Mme
Guichard?   3. Où habite Alain? Qu'est-ce qu'il fait?   4. Où habite Marie?
Qu'est-ce qu'elle fait?   5. Qui arrive pendant que les Guichard déjeunent?
6. Qu'est-ce qu'il apporte?   7. A qui est-ce que Mme Guichard montre la
carte?   8. Qu'est-ce que Marie prépare à Montréal?   9. Est-ce qu'elle tra-

---

[1]In most cases, French students are in school from 8:00 to 4:00, 5:00, or even 6:00, with two
hours off for lunch. There are no classes on Wednesday, but there are classes on Saturday until
noon. Students are expected to study on Wednesdays, but they also take the opportunity to
participate in sports or cultural activities, such as visiting museums.
[2]Radio-Canada is the French name of the Canadian Broadcasting Company.
[3]Note that the French often use a twenty-four-hour system to avoid confusion between morning
and evening. Train and plane schedules are always based on this system. In everyday conversation, however, the French usually speak in terms of a twelve-hour clock.

Sidebar glosses:

c'est aujourd'hui: *today is*
mercredi: *Wednesday*
pour: *for*
l'aîné, -e: *older child*
marié, -e: *married*
un, une: *a, an*

le facteur: *mailman*
la carte postale: *post card*
le mari: *husband*

h. = heures: *o'clock*
jusqu'à: *until*
l'Esquimau: *Eskimo*
fatigué, -e: *tired*

paresseux, -euse: *lazy*

l'heure (f.): (here) *hour*
par jour: *per day*

payer: *to pay*

See Cultural Supplement.

You might want to point out that *toujours* means "still" here.

To encourage conversa-
tion, you might ask *pourquoi* after students answer
Questions 11–12.

vaille beaucoup? Pourquoi?   10. Et Viviane, est-ce qu'elle travaille beaucoup?   11. Et vous, est-ce que vous travaillez beaucoup?   12. Est-ce que
vous aimez étudier?   13. Qu'est-ce que vous aimez mieux: écouter la radio
ou regarder la télé? les documentaires ou les films? les films ou les dessins
animés?   14. Est-ce que vous aimez mieux regarder les journaux ou le journal télévisé?

EXPLICATIONS II

Les adjectifs comme petit, heureux, blanc

VOCABULAIRE			
blanc, blanche	*white*	généreux, généreuse	*generous*
gris, grise	*gray*	avare	*stingy*
vert, verte	*green*		
		heureux, heureuse	*happy*
grand, grande	*big, large*	triste	*sad*
petit, petite	*little, small*		
		paresseux, paresseuse	*lazy*
		énergique	*energetic*

Read the examples aloud
as students listen.

Ask what the plural of *le
petit dejeuner* would be.

To help students learn the
meanings of the new ad-
jectives, you might use
them in true-life questions
(*Qu'est-ce qu'il y a dans
la salle de classe qui est
rouge? Est-ce que vous
êtes heureux? Pourquoi?
Est-ce que Wilt Chamber-
lain est grand ou petit?
Est-ce que Scrooge est
avare ou généreux?* etc.).

You might mention that
the French speak of the
colors of their flag from
left to right (*bleu, blanc,
rouge*) and that the
Canadian flag is *rouge et
blanc. La feuille (d'érable)
est rouge.*

1. Look at the adjective *petit* in the following sentences:
   Le camion est **petit**.   La voiture est **petite**.
   Les camions sont **petits**.   Les voitures sont **petites**.

   Most adjectives whose masculine form ends in a silent consonant have
   feminine forms ending in *e*.[1] Remember that a consonant followed by *e* is
   always pronounced:

   Le por~~t~~ est peti~~t~~.   *but:* La por~te~ est peti~te~.
   Les por~ts~ sont peti~ts~.   *but:* Les por~tes~ sont peti~tes~.

2. Adjectives like *heureux* and *blanc* also have masculine and feminine forms
   pronounced differently. In addition, they show special features of spelling:

   Son frère est **heureux**.   Sa sœur est **heureuse**.
   Ses frères sont **heureux**.   Ses sœurs sont **heureuses**.
   Le maillot est **blanc**.   La robe est **blanche**.
   Les maillots sont **blancs**.   Les robes sont **blanches**.

   Almost all adjectives whose masculine forms end in *eux* have feminine
   forms ending in *euse*. The masculine singular and plural forms are the
   same.[2]

   There are very few adjectives like *blanc*. It is the only one of its type
   that you will learn this year.

---

[1]Note, however, that there is no *e* on the word *grand* in *la grand-mère*. The plural forms are *les
grands-pères, les grands-mères,* and *les grands-parents.*
[2]A singular adjective or noun that ends in *x* or *s* does not add *s* to form the plural. For example:
l'autobus gris, les autobus gris; son fils paresseux, ses fils paresseux.

Exercices

A. Answer the questions using the feminine cues in parentheses and the possessive determiner *sa*. Follow the model.

1. Le fils de Mme Renoir est triste? (la fille)
   Non, mais sa fille est triste.

2. Le grand-père de Christian est avare? (la grand-mère)
3. Le copain de Guy est énergique? (la sœur)
4. Le chapeau d'Aude est joli? (la robe)
5. L'oncle de Jean est jeune? (la tante)
6. Le bureau du professeur est noir? (la chaise)
7. Le voisin d'Yvette est riche? (la voisine)

B. Put the words in italics into the plural. Follow the model.

1. Nos sœurs regardent *le bateau noir.*
   Nos sœurs regardent les bateaux noirs.

2. Les enfants habitent toujours *la maison rouge.*
3. Ma copine demande *son pull-over noir et rouge.*
4. Elles aiment *le chapeau jaune.*
5. Ils aiment *la leçon facile.*
6. Est-ce que vous avez *le cahier bleu?*
7. Est-ce que vous êtes toujours *triste, monsieur?*
8. *La jeune fille énergique joue.*

C. Answer the questions using the cues in parentheses and the appropriate possessive determiner *son* or *sa*. Follow the model.

1. La villa de M. Dupont est petite? (le jardin)
   Oui, et son jardin est petit aussi.

2. La blouse de Véronique est grise? (le pull-over)
3. Le bureau du professeur est grand? (la maison)
4. Le bateau du garçon est vert? (la moto)
5. La nièce de Mme Lejeune est paresseuse? (le neveu)
6. Le professeur de Julie est heureux? (la famille)
7. Le cousin de Thierry est généreux? (la cousine)
8. La chemise d'Hervé est blanche? (le pantalon)

D. Answer the questions using the adjective that means the opposite of the one given. Follow the models.

1. Est-ce que les vélos sont noirs?   *Mais non, ils sont blancs.*
   Et les motos?   *Elles sont blanches aussi.*

2. Est-ce que vos frères sont énergiques? Et vos sœurs?
3. Est-ce que les tableaux sont grands? Et les affiches?
4. Est-ce que les devoirs sont difficiles? Et les leçons?
5. Est-ce que vos grands-pères sont avares? Et vos grands-mères?
6. Est-ce que vos oncles sont tristes? Et vos cousines?

Exs. A–D should be done both orally and in writing.

2. Non, mais sa grand-mère est avare.
3. Non, mais sa sœur est énergique.
4. Non, mais sa robe est jolie.
5. Non, mais sa tante est jeune.
6. Non, mais sa chaise est noire.
7. Non, mais sa voisine est riche.

2. Les enfants habitent toujours les maisons rouges.
3. Ma copine demande ses pull-overs noirs et rouges.
4. Elles aiment les chapeaux jaunes.
5. Ils aiment les leçons faciles.
6. Est-ce que vous avez les cahiers bleus?
7. Est-ce que vous êtes toujours tristes, messieurs?
8. Les jeunes filles énergiques jouent.

2. Oui, et son pull over est gris aussi.
3. Oui, et sa maison est grande aussi.
4. Oui, et sa moto est verte aussi.
5. Oui, et son neveu est paresseux aussi.
6. Oui, et sa famille est heureuse aussi.
7. Oui, et sa cousine est généreuse aussi.
8. Oui, et son pantalon est blanc aussi.

2. Mais non, ils sont paresseux. Elles sont paresseuses aussi.
3. Mais non, ils sont petits. Elles sont petites aussi.
4. Mais non, ils sont faciles. Elles sont faciles aussi.
5. Mais non, ils sont généreux. Elles sont généreuses aussi.
6. Mais non, ils sont heureux. Elles sont heureuses aussi.

Lesson
6

Quelle heure est-il?

Il est une heure. Il est neuf heures.[1] Il est midi. Il est minuit.

A quelle heure est-ce que vous allez à l'école?   *What time do you go to school?*

Je vais à l'école à 9 h.[2]   *I go to school at 9:00.*
Je rentre chez moi à 1 h.   *I return home at 1:00.*

A quelle heure est-ce que tu arrives?   *What time are you arriving?*
J'arrive à 10 h. du matin.   *I'm arriving at 10:00 A.M.*
       à 2 h. de l'après-midi.   *at 2:00 P.M.*
       à 9 h. du soir.   *at 9:00 P.M.*

Exercice

1. Il est deux heures.
2. Il est cinq heures.
3. Il est sept heures.
4. Il est six heures.
5. Il est midi.
6. Il est onze heures.
7. Il est une heure.
8. Il est minuit.
9. Il est neuf heures.

Answer the question according to the pictures.

Quelle heure est-il?

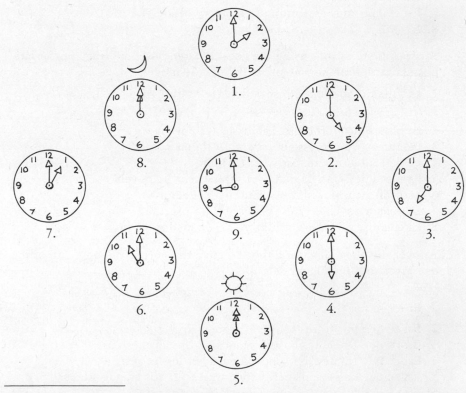

---

[1]When *neuf* comes before the word *heures*, the *f* is pronounced [v].
[2]The abbreviation for *heure* or *heures* is *h*.

Vérifiez vos progrès

Write answers to the questions, using the correct form of the adjective which means the opposite of the one given. Follow the model.

1. Est-ce que Virginie est triste?   *Non, elle est heureuse.*
2. Est-ce que les garçons sont énergiques?
3. Est-ce que leur maison est grande?
4. Est-ce que les jeunes filles sont avares?
5. Est-ce que ses chaussures sont noires?
6. Est-ce que Jean-Luc est petit?
7. Est-ce que Marie-France est paresseuse?
8. Est-ce que ses amis sont généreux?
9. Est-ce que son pull-over est blanc?
10. Est-ce que ses frères sont heureux?

RÉVISION ET THÈME

See Teacher's Section for answers to the *révision* and *thème*.

Review of:
1. telling time
   -er verbs
   prepositions
2. agreement of adjectives
3. -er verbs
   sa/son
4. telling time
   -er verbs
5. -er verbs + infinitive

Consult the model sentences, then put the English cues into French and use them to form new sentences based on the models.

1. Il est *huit heures. Madame Lambert arrive à l'usine.*
        (six o'clock) *(Mr. Lambert returns from the office.)*
        (two o'clock) *(Gigi and Paul Lambert go into the house.)*

2. *Jean est paresseux.*
   (Louise is happy.)
   (Eric is sad.)

3. *Il regarde la télé* pendant que *sa sœur travaille.*
   (She's playing chess)   *(her brother makes lunch)*
   (He's going over the lesson)   *(his friends play football)*

4. *A quatre heures il prépare le goûter.*
   (At noon they eat lunch.)
   (At seven o'clock we eat dinner.)

5. *L'après-midi, j'aime jouer aux cartes.*
        (you (pl.) *like to look at the newspapers)*
        (you (sing.) *like to listen to the radio)*

Now that you have done the *Révision*, you are ready to write a composition. Put the English captions describing each cartoon panel into French to form a paragraph.

It's 5:00. Andrée is returning from school.

She's energetic. She plays tennis while her brother listens to the radio.

At 7:00 her family eats dinner.

In the evening, they like to watch TV.

AUTO-TEST

A. Write answers to the questions using the cues in parentheses. Follow the model.

1. Quand il rentre de l'école, Georges aime jouer au football. Et toi? (aimer jouer au football américain)
   Moi, j'aime jouer au football américain.

2. Les garçons écoutent la radio. Et vous? (regarder la télé)
3. Guy et Luc jouent aux échecs. Et nous? (préparer le goûter)
4. Ses fils vont à l'école. Et ses filles? (travailler au bureau)
5. Maintenant nous dînons. Et vous? (regarder le journal télévisé)
6. Il aime déjeuner au café. Et moi? (aimer mieux rester ici)
7. Claude donne son livre à Marie. Et elle? (demander son cahier à Claude)
8. Grégoire et Christine montrent l'affiche à Henri. Et toi? (montrer les images à Cécile)

B. Write answers to the questions according to the pictures.

1. A quelle heure est-ce que tu vas à l'école?
   Je vais à l'école à huit heures.

2. A quelle heure est-ce que tu déjeunes?

3. A quelle heure est-ce que tu joues au tennis?

4. A quelle heure est-ce que tu rentres du bureau?

5. A quelle heure est-ce que tu dînes?

C. Rewrite the paragraphs using the proper form of each adjective.

1. Martin va toujours au lycée à 8 h. du matin. Il est *(grand)*. Il porte son pantalon *(bleu)*, sa chemise *(blanc)* et son pull-over *(rouge)*. Ses chaussettes sont *(bleu)* aussi, mais ses chaussures sont *(noir)*.
2. Françoise n'est pas du tout *(paresseux)*. Elle travaille à la banque. Aujourd'hui elle porte sa jupe *(vert)*, ses bas *(gris)* et sa blouse *(blanc)*. Ses chaussures sont *(gris)* et son chapeau est *(vert)*. Ses habits sont *(joli)*, n'est-ce pas?

Septième Leçon

Mercredi matin

Nous sommes mercredi, neuf heures du matin, le premier décembre. Catherine écoute la radio. Sa sœur, Annick, regarde par la fenêtre.

ANNICK	Oh zut! Il neige.
CATHERINE	Il neige?! Chic! Allons dans le jardin.[1]
ANNICK	Mais non. Il fait trop froid dehors.
CATHERINE	Bof. . . .[2] Tu es trop paresseuse.
ANNICK	Je ne suis pas paresseuse, moi. Mais quand il fait froid, j'aime mieux rester à l'intérieur.
CATHERINE	Toi, tu es toujours difficile.

(line 5 marks ANNICK "Mais non. Il fait trop froid dehors.")

---

[1] *Le jardin* is the area surrounding the house. A vegetable garden is *un jardin potager;* a flower garden is *un jardin de fleurs.*
[2] This expression is usually accompanied by a shrug, which to the French is a sign of annoyance or indifference.

See Cultural Supplement.

You might need to remind students that French schools are closed on Wednesdays. (See Cultural Supplement, Lesson 5.)

You might want to point out that the names of months and days of the week are never capitalized in French.

You might want to compare *le jardin* with the British use of the word "garden" to refer either to a carefully planted area or to what in the U.S. we call a "yard."

Wednesday morning

It's Wednesday, nine o'clock in the morning, December first. Catherine is listening to the radio. Her sister, Annick, looks out the window.

ANNICK	Oh darn, it's snowing.
CATHERINE	It's snowing?! Great! Let's go out in the yard.
5 ANNICK	No way. It's too cold out.
CATHERINE	Aw, you're too lazy.
ANNICK	I'm *not* lazy. But when it's cold, I'd rather stay inside.
CATHERINE	You're always a killjoy.

Questionnaire

1. Quelle heure est-il?   2. Quelle est la date?   3. Qu'est-ce que Catherine fait? Et sa sœur, qu'est-ce qu'elle fait?   4. Est-ce qu'Annick est heureuse quand il neige? Et Catherine?   5. Pourquoi est-ce qu'Annick n'aime pas aller dehors quand il neige?   6. Où est-ce qu'elle aime mieux rester?

PRONONCIATION

Liaison consonants join two words into a single pronunciation unit. The liaison consonants that you have learned are the plural markers *s* and *x*, which are pronounced [z], and the *n* in *on, mon, ton, son*, and *en*.

Exercices

A. Listen carefully, then say the following sentences aloud.

Nous apportons nos affiches.	Vous aimez vos amis.
Vous avez deux enfants.	Nous arrivons à trois heures.
On arrive en avion.	Mon oncle aime son appartement.

B. When *-er* verbs begin with a vowel sound, the [z] sound of the liaison *s* lets you know that the subject and verb are plural. Say the following singular and plural sentences aloud.

Elle écoute l'élève.	Elles écoutent les élèves.
Elle apporte l'image.	Elles apportent les images.
Il entre dans l'appartement.	Ils entrent dans les appartements.
Elle aime l'opéra.	Elles aiment les opéras.
Il arrive devant l'usine.	Ils arrivent devant les usines.
Il habite l'hôtel.	Ils habitent les hôtels.

Page 99

See Cultural Supplement.

If your students are not yet adept at handling the Celsius scale or the metric system, you might try to help them. For example:

Use daily temperature recordings from the newspaper and ask students to tell what the weather was the day before in a given city. It will have to be transposed to the present tense. E.g., *Nous sommes à New York. Il fait du vent et il fait frais aujourd'hui. La température est quinze degrés.* After students have covered Mots Nouveaux II, they can begin their weather report with the date.

Similarly with the metric system, use a regional highway map and ask students to tell the distance in kilometers between two towns. Since students will know numbers only to 69, make certain that the distances you ask them to calculate are no greater than 69 km (43 miles).

Septième
Leçon

MOTS NOUVEAUX I

Il fait chaud

Il fait froid

Il gèle

Quel temps fait-il?
Il pleut **aujourd'hui.**
Est-ce qu'il fait **souvent** mauvais?
Non, **quelquefois** il fait beau.
Est-ce qu'il gèle quelquefois?[1]
Pas souvent. Mais il pleut **beaucoup.**
   Et il fait toujours **trop** frais.
Toujours?
Non, **pas toujours.** Mais **presque**
   toujours.
Est-ce que tu aimes aller **dehors**
   quand il fait frais?
J'aime mieux rester **à l'intérieur.**

What's it like out?
*It's raining **today.***
*Is the weather **often** bad?*
*No, **sometimes** it's nice out.*
Does it freeze sometimes?
Not often. But it rains a lot.
*   And it's always too cool.*
Always?
*No, **not always.** But **almost**
   always.*
*Do you like to go **outside** when
   it's cool?*
*I prefer to stay **indoors.***

Il fait frais

En quelle saison est-ce qu'il fait
   beau?
Il fait beau **au printemps.**
Ecoute **le vent.**
Il fait chaud **en été.**
Regarde **le soleil.**
Il fait frais **en automne.**
Ecoute **la pluie.**
Il fait froid **en hiver.**
Regarde **la neige** et la glace.

*In what season is the weather
   nice?*
*It's nice out **in the spring.***
*Listen to **the wind.***
*It's hot **in the summer.***
*Look at **the sun.***
*It's cool **in the fall.***
*Listen to **the rain.***
*It's cold **in the winter.***
*Look at **the snow** and ice.*

Il neige

Il fait mauvais

Il pleut

Il fait du vent

Il fait beau
Il fait du soleil

[1]On the Celsius scale, 0° is freezing; 18–20° is comfortable room temperature.

Exercices de vocabulaire

A. Answer the questions according to the pictures. Follow the model.

1. Est-ce qu'il fait mauvais?

   Non, il fait beau.

2. Est-ce qu'il fait froid?

3. Est-ce qu'il fait chaud?

4. Est-ce qu'il fait du soleil?

5. Est-ce qu'il gèle?

6. Est-ce qu'il fait beau?

7. Est-ce qu'il neige?

8. Est-ce qu'il pleut?

9. Est-ce qu'il fait frais?

2. Non, il fait chaud.
3. Non, il fait frais.
4. Non, il fait du vent.
5. Non, il pleut.
6. Non, il fait mauvais.
7. Non, il fait beau.
8. Non, il neige.
9. Non, il fait froid.

B. Answer the following questions.

You may want to use this personalized exercise somewhat informally, with books closed. Such a procedure can also help to increase listening comprehension.

1. En quelle saison est-ce qu'on joue au football américain?
2. Est-ce qu'il pleut souvent chez vous? En quelle saison?
3. Est-ce qu'il neige beaucoup chez vous? En quelle saison?
4. Est-ce qu'il gèle en hiver chez vous? Presque toujours ou quelquefois?
5. Est-ce que vous aimez la neige et la glace? Est-ce que vous aimez aller dehors quand il fait froid?
6. En été est-ce qu'il fait toujours du soleil chez vous? Est-ce qu'il fait trop chaud?
7. Est-ce que vous aimez mieux le soleil ou la pluie?
8. En quelle saison est-ce que les feuilles sont jaunes et rouges?
9. Quel temps fait-il en automne chez vous? Est-ce qu'il fait quelquefois très chaud en automne chez vous?
10. Quel temps fait-il aujourd'hui?

MOTS NOUVEAUX II

See Cultural Supplement.

Point out that French calendars begin with Monday, not Sunday.

L	M	M	J	V	S	D
	1	2	3	4	5	6
7	8	9	10	11	12	13
14	15	16	17	18	19	20
21	22	23	24	25	26	27
28	29	30	31			

une semaine → (ligne 7–13)   un jour → (21)   } un mois

Il y a combien de **jours** dans **une semaine**? Il y a 7 jours dans une semaine.
de **mois**   une année?   12 mois   une année.
de **mois**   une saison?   3 mois   une saison.
de **saisons**   une année?   4 saisons   une année.

Les quatre saisons sont:
le printemps   l'été *(m.)*   l'automne *(m.)*   l'hiver *(m.)*

Les douze mois de l'année sont:

janvier février mars   avril   mai   juin
juillet août   septembre octobre novembre décembre

Les sept jours de la semaine sont:
lundi mardi mercredi jeudi vendredi samedi dimanche

Quel jour sommes-nous?	*What day is it?*
Nous sommes lundi (mardi, mercredi, etc.).	*It's Monday (Tuesday, Wednesday, etc.).*
Quelle est la date?	*What's the date?*
C'est aujourd'hui lundi, le **premier** janvier.	*It's Monday, January 1.*
C'est aujourd'hui mardi, **le deux** février.	*It's Tuesday, February 2.*

Après les **vacances** de Noël, quand est-ce qu'on rentre au lycée?[1]	*After Christmas vacation, when do you go back to school?*
On rentre au lycée	*We go back to school*
après le premier janvier.	*after the first of January.*
avant le dix janvier.	*before the tenth of January.*
vers le quatre ou le cinq janvier.	*around the fourth or fifth.*

You might want to make a practice of beginning class sessions by asking what the date is and what the weather is like.

You might want to point out that the definite determiner must be repeated when two dates are mentioned.

---

[1]*Les vacances* is a feminine noun that is always used in the plural.

Exercices de vocabulaire

1. Non, il fait froid.
2. Non, il neige.
3. Oui, il gèle.
4. Oui, ils sont à la montagne.
5. C'est le treize janvier.
6. C'est après les vacances de Noël.
7. C'est l'hiver.
8. Les mois de la saison sont décembre, janvier, février et mars.
9. Oui, il neige souvent en hiver.

---

1. Il fait beau (chaud / du soleil).
2. Non, il ne fait pas froid.
3. Oui, il fait du soleil.
4. Non, elles jouent au tennis (ne jouent pas aux cartes).
5. Non, elles sont dehors (ne sont pas à l'intérieur).
6. C'est le quinze juillet.
7. C'est l'été.
8. Les mois de la saison sont juin, juillet, août et septembre.

---

1. Il pleut (fait frais / fait mauvais).
2. Non, il fait mauvais (il ne fait pas beau).
3. Il y a un arbre et quatre fleurs.
4. C'est le vingt avril.
5. C'est le printemps.
6. Les mois de la saison sont mars, avril, mai et juin.
7. Oui, il pleut souvent au printemps.

---

1. Il fait du vent (fait frais).
2. Non, ils jouent au football américain.
3. C'est le dix-huit octobre. C'est l'automne.
4. Les mois de la saison sont septembre, octobre, novembre et décembre.
5. Les feuilles sont jaunes et rouges en automne.
6. Oui, il fait quelquefois très chaud en automne.

Septième
Leçon

102

A. Answer the questions according to the picture.

1. Est-ce qu'il fait chaud?
2. Est-ce qu'il pleut?
3. Est-ce qu'il gèle?
4. Ils sont à la montagne?
5. Quelle est la date?
6. C'est avant ou après les vacances de Noël?
7. Quelle est la saison?
8. Quels sont les mois de la saison?
9. Il neige souvent en hiver?

le 13 janvier

B. Answer the questions according to the picture.

1. Quel temps fait-il?
2. Est-ce qu'il fait froid?
3. Est-ce qu'il fait du soleil?
4. Elles jouent aux cartes?
5. Elles sont à l'intérieur?
6. Quelle est la date?
7. Quelle est la saison?
8. Quels sont les mois de la saison?

le 15 juillet

C. Answer the questions according to the picture.

1. Quel temps fait-il?
2. Est-ce qu'il fait beau?
3. Combien d'arbres et de fleurs est-ce qu'il y a?
4. Quelle est la date?
5. Quelle est la saison?
6. Quels sont les mois de la saison?
7. Il pleut souvent au printemps?

le 20 avril

D. Answer the questions according to the picture.

1. Quel temps fait-il?
2. Est-ce qu'ils jouent au tennis?
3. Quelle est la date? la saison?
4. Quels sont les mois de la saison?
5. De quelle couleur sont les feuilles en automne?
6. Est-ce qu'il fait quelquefois très chaud en automne?

le 18 octobre

EXPLICATIONS I

Les verbes en -ir/-iss-

VOCABULAIRE			
choisir	*to choose*	finir	*to finish*
grossir	*to gain weight*	jaunir	*to turn yellow*
maigrir	*to lose weight*	rougir	*to turn red, to blush*

Most verbs whose infinitive form ends in *-ir* follow this pattern in the present tense:

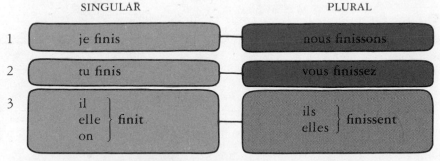

SINGULAR

1 je finis

2 tu finis

3 il
   elle } finit
   on

PLURAL

1 nous finissons

2 vous finissez

3 ils
   elles } finissent

IMPERATIVE: finis! finissons! finissez!

1. The plural forms have a stem ending in *iss* *(finiss-),* to which the plural endings *-ons, -ez, -ent* are added.

2. For the singular forms, the *ss* of the plural stem is dropped *(finiss- → fini-)* and the endings *-s, -s, -t* are added. All three singular forms are pronounced the same.

3. Remember that in the present tense, *ouvrir* follows the pattern of regular *-er* verbs.

Complete the sentences using the appropriate form of the verbs in parentheses.

1. Après les vacances, vers le premier octobre, les feuilles des arbres *(jaunir).*
2. Est-ce que tu *(choisir)* toujours tes habits? Presque toujours, mais quelquefois ma mère *(choisir)* mes habits.
3. Nous *(finir)* nos devoirs et après nous *(aller)* dehors. Quand nous *(jouer)* au tennis ou au football nous ne *(grossir)* pas.
4. Moi, je *(grossir).* Mais toi, tu *(maigrir)* parce que tu ne *(déjeuner)* pas.
5. Quand est-ce que vous *(rougir)?* Eh bien, nous *(rougir)* quand nous ne *(réviser)* pas nos leçons et quand le professeur *(demander)* pourquoi.
6. Le professeur *(entrer)* dans la salle de classe: "*(Ouvrir)* vos livres! *(Finir)* vos devoirs!" Les élèves *(ouvrir)* leurs livres et leurs cahiers et ils *(finir)* leurs devoirs avant onze heures.

Les nombres 21–69

VOCABULAIRE					
trente	*thirty*	**cinquante**	*fifty*	**zéro**	*zero*
quarante	*forty*	**soixante**	*sixty*		

1. Note how the numbers 21 through 29 are formed:

20	vingt	22	vingt-deux	25	vingt-cinq	28	vingt-huit
21	vingt et un	23	vingt-trois	26	vingt-six	29	vingt-neuf
		24	vingt-quatre	27	vingt-sept		

With the exception of *vingt et un,* these numbers follow a regular pattern.

When used before nouns, they follow the pronunciation pattern of the numbers 1 through 9. For example:

vingt et un garçons   *but:* vingt et un amis (vingt et une amies)
          [t]   [t]   [n]   [t]

vingt-deux fleurs   *but:* vingt-deux arbres
                                                [z]

2. The numbers 30 through 69 are formed in the same way:

trente, trente et un, trente-deux, trente-trois . . .
quarante, quarante et un, quarante-deux, quarante-trois . . .
cinquante, cinquante et un, cinquante-deux, cinquante-trois . . .
soixante, soixante et un, soixante-deux, soixante-trois . . .

You might first want to do a simple oral drill using disjunctives. E.g., *Je finis le livre maintenant. Et eux? (Eux, ils finissent le livre aussi.* or *Eux, ils ne finissent pas le livre.)*

1. jaunissent
2. choisis; choisit
3. finissons; allons; jouons; grossissons
4. grossis; maigris; déjeunes
5. rougissez; rougissons; révisons; demande
6. entre; ouvrez; finissez; ouvrent; finissent

vingt: Point out that though the *t* is not pronounced when the word occurs alone, it is always pronounced in the compound numbers 21 – 29: [vɛ̃tdø. vɛ̃ttrwɑ. . . .].

soixante: Point out that the letter *x* between two vowel sounds is pronounced [s]: [swasɑ̃t].

Septième
Leçon

Exercices

A. Look at a calendar for this year and write the dates in French for the occasions listed below. Include the day, the date, and the month. Then say them aloud. Follow the model.

See Cultural Supplement.

1. Memorial Day   *C'est lundi, le 25 mai.*

2. New Year's Day   6. Mother's Day   10. Halloween
3. Valentine's Day   7. Father's Day   11. Thanksgiving
4. St. Patrick's Day   8. Bastille Day   12. Christmas
5. April Fool's Day   9. Labor Day   13. Your birthday

B. French license plates are written like this: 4502 DD 53. They are said like this: *quarante-cinq zéro deux DD cinquante-trois.* Look at the following license plates and write them in French. Practice saying them aloud, too.

1. 1555 BC 33
2. 6729 DP 37
3. 4107 MW 28
4. 4014 DX 06
5. 2156 RR 59
6. 6224 NG 67

If you have not yet presented the alphabet, you should do so now. It is included on the tape that accompanies Lesson 1.

1. quinze cinquante-cinq BC trente-trois
2. soixante-sept vingt-neuf DP trente-sept
3. quarante et un zéro sept MW vingt-huit
4. quarante quatorze DX zéro six
5. vingt et un cinquante-six RR cinquante-neuf
6. soixante-deux vingt-quatre NG soixante-sept

You might want to post a map of the *départements* so that students can point to the areas these cars come from. The *départements* represented in Ex. B (and their major cities) are: 33: Gironde (Bordeaux); 37: Indre-et-Loire (Tours); 28: Eure-et-Loir (Chartres); 06: Alpes Maritimes (Nice); 59: Nord (Lille); 67: Bas Rhin (Strasbourg).

Vérifiez vos progrès

A. Answer the following questions, writing out the numbers in French.

1. Il y a combien de semaines dans une année?
2. Il y a combien de jours dans le mois de février?
3. Il y a combien de jours dans le mois de juillet?
4. Il y a combien d'heures dans deux jours?

B. Complete each sentence using the appropriate form of the verb in parentheses.

1. Quand il fait beau, nous ne *(finir)* pas toujours nos devoirs.
2. Quelquefois les feuilles ne *(jaunir)* pas en automne.
3. Je ne *(rougir)* pas souvent.
4. En été elle *(maigrir)* parce qu'elle joue au tennis.
5. En hiver tu *(grossir)* beaucoup parce que tu n'aimes pas aller dehors.
6. Quand il ne pleut pas, on *(ouvrir)* les fenêtres.
7. *(Choisir)* les affiches, mes enfants!

CONVERSATION ET LECTURE

Parlons de vous

1. En quelle saison est-ce que vous n'allez pas à l'école?   2. Est-ce que vous aimez les vacances? Est-ce que vous allez loin de chez vous?   3. En quelle saison est-ce que vous rentrez à l'école après les vacances? Vers quelle date?   4. Où est-ce que vous aimez aller quand il fait beau? quand il pleut? quand il neige?   5. Quel temps fait-il chez vous au printemps? en été? en hiver?   6. Quel jour sommes-nous aujourd'hui? Quelle est la date?

See Cultural Supplement.

La fête foraine[1]

la météo: You might want to point out that this is short for la *météorologie.*

Nous sommes dimanche matin vers dix heures. Il y a une° fête foraine à Paris. C'est l'automne et il fait frais dehors. René Gobert et sa cousine Monique écoutent la météo° à la radio:

5 "Dans le nord° il pleut des cordes[2] et il va pleuvoir° à Paris avant midi. Sur la Côte d'Azur, il fait du soleil mais le vent . . ."

René ferme° la radio.

RENÉ   Zut alors. Il pleut toujours quand il y a
10   une fête foraine!

MONIQUE   Mais ça, c'est le climat maritime[3] de la France. Voilà pourquoi j'aime beaucoup la Côte d'Azur. Là-bas il fait mauvais seulement° en hiver. Ce n'est pas com-
15   me° à Paris où il pleut souvent.

RENÉ   D'accord, d'accord, mais arrête° la classe de météo, je t'en prie![4] On va toujours à la fête foraine ou est-ce qu'on va au musée? ou quoi?°
20 MONIQUE   S'il° pleut on ne va pas à la fête foraine. Et dans les musées, il fait toujours un froid de canard[5] en automne. Alors, finissons notre déjeuner et allons chez

un, une: *a, an*

la météo: *weather report*
le nord: *north*
il va pleuvoir: *it's going to rain*
fermer: *(here) to turn off*

seulement: *only*
comme: *like*
arrêter: *to stop*

quoi: *what*
si (s'): *if*

---

[1]A *fête foraine* is like a small carnival, with rides, games, and other amusements. These carnivals often travel from town to town, especially on holidays. In smaller towns, they are eagerly awaited, and young and old take part in the festivities.

[2]The expression *pleuvoir des cordes* means "to rain ropes." It is equivalent to the English expression "to rain cats and dogs."

[3]Much of France has a maritime climate because it is bordered by water on three sides and because there are numerous rivers and streams in the middle sections of the country. As a result, in much of France it rains a great deal.

[4]*Je t'en prie* is used instead of *je vous en prie* when you are speaking to someone with whom you would use the *tu* form. In this context, it means "please" or "for goodness' sake."

[5]*Il fait un froid de canard* literally means "It's a duck's cold" or "It's for the ducks." It is equivalent to the English expression "It's freezing cold."

25

Anne-Marie. Il fait toujours chaud
dans son appartement et elle a beaucoup de° disques.

beaucoup de: *a lot of*

RENÉ   Ce n'est pas une mauvaise idée,° ça!

une mauvaise idée:
a bad idea

À propos ...

1. Nous sommes un samedi en automne? Qu'est-ce qu'il y a à Paris aujour-
d'hui?   2. Quel temps fait-il?   3. Qu'est-ce que René et Monique écoutent?   4. Où est-ce qu'il pleut des cordes? Est-ce qu'il pleut aussi à Paris?
sur la Côte d'Azur?   5. Pourquoi est-ce que René n'est pas heureux?
6. Pourquoi est-ce que Monique aime la Côte d'Azur?   7. D'après ("According to") Monique, où est-ce qu'il fait trop froid en automne?   8. Après
le déjeuner, où vont René et Monique? Pourquoi?   9. Et vous, est-ce que
vous écoutez souvent la météo à la radio ou à la télé?   10. Quel temps
fait-il chez vous maintenant?   11. Est-ce qu'il y a quelquefois des fêtes
foraines chez vous? En quelle saison? Est-ce que vous aimez les fêtes foraines?

EXPLICATIONS II

Les déterminants indéfinis <u>un</u>, <u>une</u>, <u>des</u>

1. *Un* means "one." It can also mean "a" or "an":

Il a **un** fils et deux filles.   *He has **one** son and two daughters.*
On joue **un** dessin animé.   *They're showing **a** cartoon.*
Elle a **un** oncle à Paris.   *She has **an** uncle in Paris.*
   [ñ]

Un is used only with masculine nouns. When it comes before a word beginning with a vowel sound, there is liaison.[1]

Ex. A can be presented after covering Point 2.

2. Before feminine nouns, an *e* is added: *une*. The feminine form is pronounced [yn]:

Il a **une** fille et deux fils.   *He has **a** daughter and two sons.*
Il est **une** heure.   *It's **one** o'clock.*
Elle a **une** tante à Paris.   *She has **an** aunt in Paris.*

Exs. B–D can be presented after covering Point 3.

3. Look at the following:

Est-ce qu'elle a **des** disques?   { *Does she have **any** records?*
                                       { *Does she have records?*

Ils ont **des** amis à Paris.   { *They have **some** friends in Paris.*
   [z]   { *They have friends in Paris.*

In these sentences, *des* is a plural indefinite determiner. Its English equivalent is "some" or "any." Though we can omit "some" or "any" in English, *des* cannot be omitted in French. As with all other plural determiners, the *s* is pronounced [z] before a vowel sound.

Ex. E can be presented after covering Point 4.

4. Note the following:

Est-ce qu'il y a **un** hôtel près   Non, il n'y a **pas** d'hôtel près
   d'ici?   d'ici.
Est-ce qu'il a **une** sœur?   Non, il n'a **pas** de sœur.
Est-ce qu'elle regarde **des** des-   Non, elle **ne** regarde **pas** de dessins animés?   sins animés.

After a negative, the indefinite determiners *(un, une, des)* often become *de* or, before a vowel sound, *d'*. Its English equivalent is "a," "an," or "any."

---

[1]In English, too, some determiners have a different spelling or pronunciation when they come before a vowel sound: "*a* book," but "*an* author." Pronounce these words: "the bee," "the ant," "the lip," "the ear." Before a vowel, the word "the" has a distinct [i] sound; before a consonant, it is pronounced somewhat like the vowel sound in the French word *le*.

Exercices

A. Answer the questions according to the pictures, using the appropriate indefinite determiner, *un* or *une*. Follow the model.

1. Qu'est-ce que tu portes, Paul?
   Je porte un pantalon.

2. Qu'est-ce que vous demandez à votre père?

3. Qu'est-ce qu'ils ouvrent?

4. Qu'est-ce qu'il demande?

5. Qu'est-ce qu'elles choisissent?

6. Qu'est-ce que vous regardez?

7. Qu'est-ce qu'elle donne à Pierre?

8. Qu'est-ce qu'on joue?

9. Qu'est-ce qu'ils écoutent?

10. Qu'est-ce que vous regardez, madame?

11. Qu'est-ce que tu donnes à ton père?

12. Qu'est-ce qu'elle choisit?

2. Nous demandons (je demande) une voiture à notre (mon) père.
3. Ils ouvrent une fenêtre.
4. Il demande une carte.
5. Elles choisissent un drapeau français.
6. Nous regardons (je regarde) un avion.
7. Elle donne une chemise à Pierre.
8. On joue un film policier.
9. Ils écoutent une bande.
10. Je regarde une pièce.
11. Je donne un pull-over à mon père.
12. Elle choisit une robe.

B. Answer the questions according to the pictures, using the plural form of the indefinite determiner. Follow the model.

1. Qu'est-ce qu'on joue?
   On joue des dessins animés.

2. Qu'est-ce qu'elles demandent à leur mère?

3. Qu'est-ce qu'il apporte?

2. Elles demandent des chaussures à leur mère.
3. Il apporte des cartes.

4. Ils écoutent des disques.
5. Je choisis des stylos.
6. Elle porte des bas.
7. Nous finissons (je finis) des livres.
8. Elles apportent des images.
9. Il donne des journaux au professeur.

Ex. C
2. Il y a des garçons sur l'herbe.
3. Il y a des chemises blanches dans votre voiture.
4. Il y a des livres sur ta table.
5. Il y a des stylos rouges là-bas.
6. Il y a des églises près de l'hôtel.
7. Il y a des camions devant l'hôpital.
8. Il y a des autobus verts et blancs au coin de la rue.
9. Il y a des usines loin d'ici.
10. Il y a des agents à l'intérieur du musée.

Ex. D
2. Il y a un garçon sur l'herbe.
3. Il y a une chemise blanche dans votre voiture.
4. Il y a un livre sur ta table.
5. Il y a un stylo rouge là-bas.
6. Il y a une église près de l'hôtel.
7. Il y a un camion devant l'hôpital.
8. Il y a un autobus vert et blanc au coin de la rue.
9. Il y a une usine loin d'ici.
10. Il y a un agent à l'intérieur du musée.

Ex. E
2. Non, il n'a pas de chapeau.
3. Non, il n'y a pas de drapeaux devant la banque.
4. Non, nous n'avons pas (je n'ai pas) de voiture.
(Answers to Ex. E cont'd. at bottom of p. 111.)

Septième
Leçon

4. Qu'est-ce qu'ils écoutent?

5. Qu'est-ce que tu choisis?

6. Qu'est-ce qu'elle porte?

7. Qu'est-ce que vous finissez?

8. Qu'est-ce qu'elles apportent?

9. Qu'est-ce qu'il donne au professeur?

C. Change the definite statements to indefinite statements by using *il y a* and the plural indefinite determiner. Follow the model.

1. Les fleurs jaunes sont sous l'arbre.
   Il y a des fleurs jaunes sous l'arbre.

2. Les garçons sont sur l'herbe.
3. Les chemises blanches sont dans votre voiture.
4. Les livres sont sur ta table.
5. Les stylos rouges sont là-bas.
6. Les églises sont près de l'hôtel.
7. Les camions sont devant l'hôpital.
8. Les autobus verts et blancs sont au coin de la rue.
9. Les usines sont loin d'ici.
10. Les agents sont à l'intérieur du musée.

D. Redo the above exercise in the singular. Follow the model.

1. La fleur jaune est sous l'arbre.
   Il y a une fleur jaune sous l'arbre.

E. Answer the following questions in the negative. Follow the model.

1. Est-ce que tu as des frères?
   Non, je n'ai pas de frères.

2. Est-ce qu'il a un chapeau?
3. Est-ce qu'il y a des drapeaux devant la banque?
4. Est-ce que vous avez une voiture?
5. Est-ce qu'il y a des arbres près de la maison?
6. Est-ce qu'ils ont un magnétophone?
7. Est-ce que Paul et Mireille ont des cousins?
8. Est-ce qu'elles portent des jupes?
9. Est-ce que nous regardons des documentaires à la télé?
10. Est-ce qu'il y a des journaux dans la salle de classe?
11. Est-ce que tu as des images de Paris?
12. Est-ce qu'il apporte une radio à la villa?

Vérifiez vos progrès

Rewrite the sentences using the appropriate form of the verb *avoir* and the indefinite determiner. Be careful! Some are singular, some plural; some are affirmative, some negative. Follow the model.

1. Son pantalon est bleu et ses chaussures sont noires.
   Il (Elle) a un pantalon bleu et des chaussures noires.

2. Votre moto est grise.
3. Mon frère est paresseux.
4. Leurs livres sont difficiles.
5. Ton maillot n'est pas noir.
6. Leurs cousins ne sont pas riches.
7. Notre tante est avare et notre oncle est généreux.
8. Sa jupe est verte et sa chemise est blanche.

5. Non, il n'y a pas d'arbres près de la maison.
6. Non, ils n'ont pas de magnétophone.
7. Non, ils (Paul et Mireille) n'ont pas de cousins.
8. Non, elles ne portent pas de jupes.
9. Non, vous ne regardez pas (nous ne regardons pas) de documentaires à la télé.
10. Non, il n'y a pas de journaux dans la salle de classe.
11. Non, je n'ai pas d'images de Paris.
12. Non, il n'apporte pas de radio à la villa.

RÉVISION ET THÈME

See Teacher's Section for answers to the *révision* and *thème*.

Review of:
1. dates
2. seasons
   weather expressions
3. -er verbs
   indefinite determiners
4. days of the week
   negative + indefinite determiners
5. -ir/-iss- verbs
   possessive determiners
6. -er verbs
   use of definite determiner

Consult the model sentences, then put the English cues into French and use them to form new sentences based on the models.

1. C'est aujourd'hui *vendredi le vingt-cinq septembre.*
   (Tuesday, July 1)
   (Thursday, August 31)

2. C'est l'automne. Il fait frais et il pleut.
   (It's spring.)   (It's sunny out but it's freezing.)
   (It's summer.)   (It's windy and cold out.)

3. Mathieu et Danielle regardent un film policier.
   (I'm listening to a play.)
   (We're preparing some documentaries.)

4. Parce que c'est lundi nous n'avons pas de match.
   (it's Saturday there are no cartoons)
   (it's Sunday she doesn't have a newspaper)

5. Quand je choisis mon livre, je rentre à la maison.
   (we finish our lessons, we go outside)
   (he finishes his lunch, he stays inside)

6. Tu aimes le vent.
   (She likes the sun.)
   (You (pl.) like rain.)

Now that you have done the *Révision*, you are ready to write a composition. Put the English captions describing each cartoon panel into French to form a paragraph.

Today is Wednesday, January 20.

It's winter. It's cold and snowing.

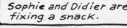

Sophie and Didier are fixing a snack.

Because it's Wednesday, they don't have any homework.

So when they finish their snack, they go outdoors.

They like the snow.

Septième
Leçon

112

AUTO-TEST

A. Describe the weather according to the pictures. Follow the model.

1.

Il fait chaud.

2.

3.

4.

5.

6.

7.

8.

9.

B. Many French phone numbers are written like this: 20-34-02. They are said like this: *vingt trente-quatre zéro deux.* Look at the following phone numbers and write them in French. Then practice saying them aloud.

See Cultural Supplement.

1. 46-50-21   3. 48-11-55   5. 32-30-27
2. 33-07-63   4. 62-49-19   6. 64-04-14

C. Answer the questions using the appropriate pronoun. Follow the model.

1. Il choisit un livre difficile. Et toi?
   Moi, je choisis un livre difficile aussi.

2. Tu maigris avant les vacances. Et tes copains?
3. Vous choisissez toujours des chemises bleues. Et lui?
4. Je finis mes devoirs. Et vous?
5. Elle grossit. Et moi?
6. Les garçons rougissent quelquefois. Et les jeunes filles?
7. Il finit souvent ses devoirs avant neuf heures. Et toi?
8. Je choisis une robe rouge. Et sa cousine?
9. Elles finissent leur déjeuner vers une heure. Et nous?

Proverbe

Après la pluie, le beau temps.

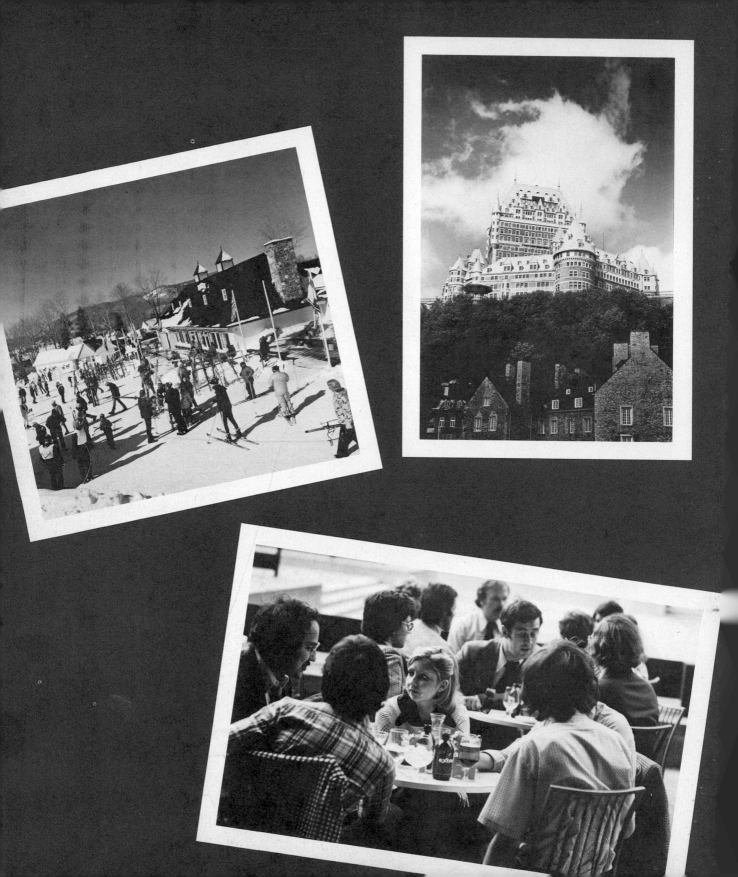

Huitième Leçon

A la montagne

Monsieur et Mme Pelletier et leurs enfants habitent Sherbrooke.[1] Aujour-
d'hui les Pelletier sont au Mont Tremblant,[2] où ils font du ski.

MME PELLETIER	Tu n'as pas ton anorak, Julien?
M. PELLETIER	Non, il est à la maison.
5 MME PELLETIER	Tu n'as pas froid?
M. PELLETIER	Si, j'ai froid, mais mon anorak est trop laid.
MME PELLETIER	Mais non, tu as tort. Il est beau, ton anorak . . . et toi aussi!
M. PELLETIER	Bof . . .
10 MME PELLETIER	Mais ne rougis pas!

[1]Sherbrooke is a French-speaking university city in Quebec, located approximately 120 kilometers east of Montreal.
[2]Mont Tremblant is the highest peak in the Laurentian Mountains (*les Laurentides*). The Laurentians extend from the St. Lawrence River to Hudson Bay.

See Cultural Supplement.

Though *le mont* is not
treated as a vocabulary
item to be learned, you
may want to point out that
it is *à la montagne* but *au
Mont Tremblant.*

In the mountains

Monsieur and Mme Pelletier and their children live in Sherbrooke. Today the Pelletiers are at Mont Tremblant, where they are skiing.

MME PELLETIER   Don't you have your ski jacket, Julien?
M. PELLETIER   No, it's at home.
MME PELLETIER   Aren't you cold?
M. PELLETIER   Yes, I'm cold. But my ski jacket's too ugly.
MME PELLETIER   Oh no, you're wrong. Your ski jacket's good-looking . . . and so are you!
M. PELLETIER   Aw . . .
MME PELLETIER   Don't blush.

Questionnaire

1. Où habitent les Pelletier?   2. Où est-ce qu'ils sont maintenant? Qu'est-ce qu'ils font là?   3. Est-ce que M. Pelletier a son anorak? Où est l'anorak?   4. Est-ce que M. Pelletier n'a pas froid?   5. Est-ce qu'il aime son anorak? Pourquoi?   6. Est-ce que Mme Pelletier aime l'anorak de M. Pelletier?   7. D'après ("according to") Mme Pelletier est-ce que M. Pelletier est beau?

PRONONCIATION

The French sound [y] is not like any English vowel. It is produced with the lips tightly rounded and the tongue in the same position as for the [i] sound. Round your lips and try to say [i]; the result will be the [y] sound.

Exercices

A. Listen, then say the following words aloud.

| tu | une | sur | la jupe |
| le pupitre | l'usine | la voiture | les chaussures |

B. Listen to these pairs, then say them aloud.

| [i]/[y] | si/su | sire/sur | la vie/la vue |
| [u]/[y] | tout/tu | vous/vu | nous/nu |

C. Listen, then say the following sentences aloud.

Il fait du vent.
Tu vas chez Suzanne.
Bruno et Luc étudient.
Tu portes une jupe.
Les pupitres sont près du bureau.
L'autobus est au coin de la rue.

MOTS NOUVEAUX I

1. Look at the following:

En été, il fait chaud.	*In the summer, **it's warm.***
C'est la saison chaude.	*It's **the warm** season.*
Nous avons chaud en été.	*We're warm in the summer.*
En hiver, il fait froid.	*In the winter, **it's cold.***
La neige est froide.	*The snow is cold.*
J'ai froid.	***I'm cold.***
Alors, porte ton anorak *(m.).*	*So wear your **ski jacket.***

Il fait froid and *il fait chaud* are used only to describe weather or temperature in a room. If an inanimate object—a thing—is being described, the French use a form of the verb *être,* and the words *froid* and *chaud* agree with the noun. If a person or animal feels warm or cold, the French use a form of the verb *avoir,* and *froid* and *chaud* do not agree with the noun.

2. The verb *avoir* is also used in certain expressions to show emotional or physical states:

Tu as peur du dragon, toi?	*Are you afraid of the dragon?*
Mais oui! Il est laid, le dragon.	*Of course! The dragon's **ugly.***
Alors, tu as peur de la nuit aussi?	*Then **are you afraid of the dark,** too?*
Mais non! La nuit n'est pas laide!	*No! The dark isn't **ugly.***

Exercices de vocabulaire

1. Ils ont faim.
2. Tu as froid.
3. Le dîner est chaud.
4. Nous avons tort.
5. Le soleil est chaud.
6. Vous avez raison.
7. Les nuits sont froides.
8. Tu as sommeil.

A. Complete the sentences using the appropriate form of *avoir* or *être*.

1. Ils _____ faim.
2. Tu _____ froid.
3. Le dîner _____ chaud.
4. Nous _____ tort.
5. Le soleil _____ chaud.
6. Vous _____ raison.
7. Les nuits _____ froides.
8. Tu _____ sommeil.

B. Answer the questions according to the pictures. Follow the model.

2. Non, il a sommeil.
3. Non, ils ont soif.
4. Non, ils ont peur.
5. Non, il a raison.
6. Non, il a tort.
7. Non, il a chaud.
8. Non, ils ont faim.

1. Est-ce que ta grand-mère a chaud?
Non, elle a froid.

2. Est-ce que le garçon a faim?

3. Est-ce que vos amis ont peur?

4. Est-ce qu'ils ont soif?

5. Est-ce que l'élève a tort?

6. Est-ce qu'il a raison?

7. Est-ce que votre oncle a froid?

8. Est-ce que votre frère et votre sœur ont sommeil?

4. Tu as raison.
5. Vous avez peur.
6. Il a tort.
7. Le vent est chaud.
8. Il fait du soleil.
9. Nous avons sommeil.
10. Les nuits sont chaudes.
11. Il fait frais.
12. Les agents ont froid.
13. Tu as soif.

C. Form sentences using the correct verb: *avoir*, *être*, or *faire*. Follow the models.

1. ma mère / froid   *Ma mère a froid.*
2. la glace / froid   *La glace est froide.*
3. il / du vent   *Il fait du vent.*

4. tu / raison
5. vous / peur
6. il / tort
7. le vent / chaud
8. il / du soleil

9. nous / sommeil
10. les nuits / chaud
11. il / frais
12. les agents / froid
13. tu / soif

Huitième
Leçon

118

MOTS NOUVEAUX II

le jour

le soleil   le ciel   le nuage

le lac

le fleuve   l'eau (f.)

la terre

Il fait jour

On p. 117, the English equivalent of *la nuit* was "the dark." Explain to students that the more usual equivalents of *la nuit* and *le jour* are "night" and "day." *Il fait nuit* means "it's night(time)" or "it's dark out"; *Il fait jour* is "it's day(time)" or "it's light out."

You might want to ask students what the plural of *l'eau* would be.

You might point out the four *fleuves* on a map: la Seine, la Loire, la Garonne, and le Rhône. You may also want to explain the difference between *un fleuve*, which flows into the sea, and *une rivière*, a tributary.

Students might enjoy figuring out what the *-ir/-iss-* verbs *atterrir* and the more recent *alunir* mean.

to land
to land on the moon

la nuit

l'étoile (f.)   la lune

le sable   la mer   l'eau (f.)

Il fait nuit

Exercice de vocabulaire

Choose the word that best completes each sentence. Follow the model.

1. Les nuages sont dans (*le lac*/*le ciel*/*la terre*).
   Les nuages sont dans le ciel.

2. Quand il fait nuit, il y a souvent (*des fleuves*/*des mers*/*des étoiles*) dans le ciel.

3. La plage est près de (*la mer*/*la lune*/*la corbeille*).

4. Quand il neige, (*la lune*/*l'étoile*/*la terre*) est blanche.

5. Leur bateau à voiles est sur (*le stade*/*le lac*/*le ciel*).

6. Quand il fait (*beau*/*jour*/*nuit*), le ciel n'est pas bleu.

7. Le soleil et (*le fleuve*/*le sable*/*la terre*) sont jaunes.

8. Quand ils sont à la plage, ils vont dans (*l'eau*/*l'étoile*/*l'école*).

9. Quand il pleut, (*le ciel*/*le soleil*/*le sable*) est gris.

2. des étoiles
3. la mer
4. la terre
5. le lac
6. nuit
7. le sable
8. l'eau
9. le ciel

EXPLICATIONS I

Le verbe <u>faire</u>

SINGULAR	PLURAL
1 je fais	nous faisons
2 tu fais	vous faites
3 il elle on } fait	ils elles } font

IMPERATIVE: fais! faisons! faites!

1. All three singular forms are pronounced the same: [fe]. In *nous faisons* the *ai* is pronounced like the letter *e* in *le;* in *vous faites* it is pronounced [ε].

2. *Faire* is used in many common expressions:

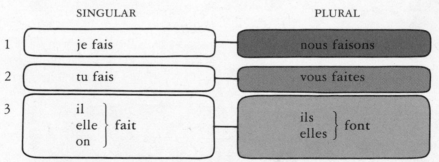

faire du ski   faire la vaisselle   faire des achats   faire de l'alpinisme

faire du ski nautique   faire de l'auto-stop

faire une faute   faire un voyage   faire ses devoirs

See Cultural Supplement.

Students will probably grasp the subtle distinction between *faire une faute* and *avoir tort.* If they do not, it is of minor importance.

Huitième
Leçon

120

The main English equivalents of the verb *faire* are "to do" or "to make":

Nous faisons nos devoirs.　　　*We're doing our homework.*
Ils font des fautes.　　　　　 *They make mistakes.*

However, *faire* also has many special meanings:

Vous faites du ski, n'est-ce pas?　　*You ski, don't you?*
Tu fais un voyage, n'est-ce pas?　　*You're taking a trip, aren't you?*
Ils font des achats, n'est-ce pas?　　*They're shopping, aren't they?*
Il fait mauvais, n'est-ce pas?　　　*It's bad out, isn't it?*
Il fait du soleil, n'est-ce pas?　　　*It's sunny, isn't it?*

Another common use of *faire* is in arithmetic:

Combien font deux et deux?　　　*How much are two and two?*
Deux et deux font quatre.　　　　*Two and two are four.*
Combien font quatre moins deux?　*How much is four minus two?*
Quatre moins deux font deux.　　*Four minus two is two.*

The plural form, *font*, is used in both addition and subtraction.

Exercices

A. Complete the sentences according to the pictures, using the appropriate form of the verb *faire*. Follow the model.

1. J'ai peur quand
je . . .
*J'ai peur quand
je fais du ski.*

2. Tu n'as pas tou-
jours raison.
Quelquefois tu . . .

3. Au printemps,
quand il fait
beau, nous . . .

4. Porte tes habits
chauds! Il . . .

5. Le soir, après
le dîner, je . . .

6. Je n'aime pas aller
dehors quand il . . .

7. Luc! Suzanne! . . . !

8. En automne
nous . . .

9. Elles aiment . . . .

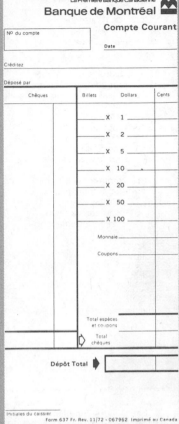

2. . . . tu fais une faute.
3. . . . nous faisons de
l'alpinisme.
4. Il fait froid.
5. . . . je fais la vaisselle.
6. . . . il fait du vent.
7. Faites vos devoirs!
8. . . . nous faisons un
voyage.
9. . . . faire de l'auto-
stop.

10. . . . elles font du ski
    nautique?
11. . . . il fait frais.
12. . . . vous faites des
    (vos) achats.

1. Quatorze et quarante
   font cinquante-quatre.
2. Soixante-huit moins
   trente-deux font
   trente-six.
3. Cinquante et un moins
   vingt font trente et un.
4. Vingt-neuf et vingt-
   sept font cinquante-
   six.
5. Trente-trois et trente-
   quatre font soixante-
   sept.
6. Quarante-six moins
   onze font trente-cinq.

font

fait

faites

fais

fais

fais

faisons

See Cultural Supplement.

faire

10. Est-ce qu'elles . . . 11. On joue au tennis
                               quand il . . . 12. L'après-midi
                                                   vous . . .

B. Answer the following questions.

1. Combien font quatorze et quarante?
2. Combien font soixante-huit moins trente-deux?
3. Combien font cinquante et un moins vingt?
4. Combien font vingt-neuf et vingt-sept?
5. Combien font trente-trois et trente-quatre?
6. Combien font quarante-six moins onze?

C. Complete the passage using the appropriate forms of the verb *faire*.

Il est quatre heures. Hugues et Bruno Pasteur _____ leurs devoirs pendant que leur mère _____ des achats. Monsieur Pasteur entre et parle
aux garçons:

—Qu'est-ce que vous _____, mes enfants?
5 —Je _____ mes devoirs, papa.
—Et toi, Bruno? Qu'est-ce que tu _____?
—Moi aussi, je _____ mes devoirs.
—Mais nous sommes samedi après-midi.
—Oui, mais demain ("tomorrow") nous _____ un voyage à Chamonix
10   avec les Lejeune.
—Ah, oui?
—Oui, eux aussi ils aiment _____ du ski.

Trois adjectifs irréguliers

VOCABULAIRE		
beau, belle	*beautiful, handsome*	vieux, vieille *old*
nouveau, nouvelle	*new*	

Beau, nouveau, and *vieux* have very different masculine and feminine forms:

Le lac est beau.	La fleur est belle.
Les lacs sont beaux.	Les fleurs sont belles.
Le théâtre est nouveau.	La pièce est nouvelle.
Les théâtres sont nouveaux.	Les pièces sont nouvelles.
Le camion est vieux.	La voiture est vieille.
Les camions sont vieux.	Les voitures sont vieilles.

Note that since *beau* and *nouveau* end in -*eau,* their plural is formed by adding an *x.* The singular form *vieux* ends in an *x,* so it remains the same in the
plural.

Exercice

Answer the questions using the adjective that means the opposite of the one given. Follow the model.

1. Est-ce que l'arbre est beau?
   Non, il est laid.
   Et la fleur? Est-ce qu'elle est belle?
   Non, elle est laide aussi.

2. Est-ce que le jardin est laid?
   Et la maison? Est-ce qu'elle est laide?
3. Est-ce que le bateau est vieux?
   Et la voile? Est-ce qu'elle est vieille?
4. Est-ce que l'anorak est nouveau?
   Et la chemise? Est-ce qu'elle est nouvelle?
5. Est-ce que ses neveux sont laids?
   Et ses nièces? Est-ce qu'elles sont laides?
6. Est-ce que les bas sont nouveaux?
   Et les chaussures? Est-ce qu'elles sont nouvelles?
7. Est-ce que les lycées sont vieux?
   Et les écoles? Est-ce qu'elles sont vieilles?

2. Non, il est beau. Non, elle est belle aussi.
3. Non, il est nouveau. Non, elle est nouvelle aussi.
4. Non, il est vieux. Non, elle est vieille aussi.
5. Non, ils sont beaux. Non, elles sont belles aussi.
6. Non, ils sont vieux. Non, elles sont vieilles aussi.
7. Non, ils sont nouveaux. Non, elles sont nouvelles aussi.

Vérifiez vos progrès

A. Complete the sentences with the appropriate form of *avoir*, *être*, or *faire*.

1. En hiver, quand il _____ froid, l'eau _____ froide aussi.
2. Pourquoi est-ce que tu _____ peur de l'eau?
3. Quand est-ce que vous _____ des achats?
4. Quand ils ne révisent pas leurs leçons, ils _____ toujours des fautes.
5. En été, les nuits _____ chaudes, mais il _____ souvent du vent.
6. Quand il _____ mauvais, Georges n'aime pas _____ de l'auto-stop.

B. Answer the questions using the cue in parentheses. Follow the model.

1. Est-ce que leur moto est nouvelle? (les vélos)
   Oui, et leurs vélos sont nouveaux aussi.

2. Est-ce que la lune est belle? (le sable)
3. Est-ce que les motos sont laides? (le camion)
4. Est-ce que ses oncles sont vieux? (les tantes)
5. Est-ce que les nuages sont beaux? (la mer)
6. Est-ce que ses chaussures sont nouvelles? (le jean)
7. Est-ce que leur villa est vieille? (les voitures)

CONVERSATION ET LECTURE

Parlons de vous

1. Est-ce qu'il y a des nuages dans le ciel aujourd'hui? Est-ce que le ciel est bleu? gris? noir?   2. Est-ce qu'il fait froid? Est-ce que vous avez froid? chaud?   3. A quelle heure est-ce que vous déjeunez? Est-ce que vous aimez mieux les déjeuners chauds ou froids?   4. Est-ce que vous habitez près de la mer? d'un lac? des montagnes?   5. Est-ce que vous faites de l'alpinisme? du ski? du ski nautique? des voyages avec votre famille?   6. Est-ce que vous faites de l'auto-stop?   7. Qui prépare le dîner chez vous? Qui fait la vaisselle après le dîner?   8. Qu'est-ce que vous aimez faire après les classes? pendant ("during") vos vacances?   9. Est-ce que vous aimez faire des achats?

A Sainte-Agathe-des-Monts

See Cultural Supplement.

En hiver les Caron, qui habitent Montréal, louent° un châlet près de Sainte-Agathe-des-Monts. Les Caron ont deux enfants, Serge et Suzanne.

louer: *to rent*

Sainte-Agathe est une ville° à soixante-cinq kilo-
5 mètres de Montréal. On connaît° Sainte-Agathe pour° ses très belles pistes de ski° et pour le Festival des Neiges.[1] De décembre à avril il neige beaucoup à Sainte-Agathe, et il fait très froid. Les Caron aiment les sports d'hiver. Ils font du ski et ils pati-
10 nent.° Serge aime jouer au hockey aussi.

la ville: *town*
connaître: *to know*
pour: *for; in order to*
la piste de ski: *ski run*

patiner: *to skate*

SUZANNE	Je vais gagner° le concours° de ski, moi!	gagner: *to win* le concours: *contest*
SERGE	Et notre équipe° va gagner le match de hockey.	l'équipe (f.): *team*
15 SUZANNE	Mais tu es fou!° Toi et tes copains, vous êtes trop jeunes.	fou, folle: *crazy*
MME CARON	Doucement, doucement!° Ce ne sont pas les Jeux° Olympiques, mes enfants. Ce sont les vacances.	doucement: *hold it!* le jeu: *game*
20 SERGE	Oui, mais c'est amusant,° les concours.	amusant, -e: *fun*
M. CARON	Moi, j'aime mieux faire des excursions en traîneau.° Je ne suis pas énergique comme° vous. Et la neige et les arbres et les montagnes sont très beaux.	l'excursion (f.) en traîneau: *sleigh ride* comme: *like*
25 SERGE	Oh, il radote.°	radoter: *to be "out of it"*
SUZANNE	On n'est pas ici pour rester à l'intérieur. Allons, Serge. On va faire du ski.	

Point out the use of *êtes* to agree with *toi et tes copains*.

la neige . . . très beaux (ll. 23–24): Point out that if an adjective modifies more than one noun, it must be in the masculine form if any of the nouns is masculine.

Huitième
Leçon

[1]*Le Festival des Neiges* is a winter carnival that begins in the middle of January and continues through Mardi Gras. In addition to athletic events, there are also ice sculpture contests, costume parties, and fireworks.

À propos...

1. Où habitent les Caron? 2. Où est-ce qu'ils louent un châlet? 3. Pourquoi est-ce qu'on connaît Sainte-Agathe? 4. Est-ce que Sainte-Agathe est près ou loin de Montréal? Quel temps fait-il là-bas en hiver? 5. Qu'est-ce que les Caron aiment faire? 6. Qui aime jouer au hockey? 7. Qui veut ("wants") gagner le concours de ski? le match de hockey? 8. Qu'est-ce que M. Caron aime faire? 9. Et vous, est-ce que vous aimez aller à la montagne? En quelle saison? Pourquoi? Qu'est-ce que vous faites quand vous êtes à la montagne? 10. Est-ce que vous faites du ski? Est-ce que vous patinez? Est-ce que vous jouez au hockey? Est-ce que vous aimez les excursions en traîneau? 11. Est-ce que vous regardez les Jeux Olympiques à la télé tous les quatre ans ("every four years")?

EXPLICATIONS II

Phrases et questions négatives

1. You have learned how to form negative sentences:

Nous faisons nos devoirs.   Nous ne faisons pas nos devoirs.
Ils aiment l'eau froide.   Ils n'aiment pas l'eau froide.

You have learned, too, that *un, une,* and *des* often become *de* or *d'* after a negative:

Elles ont un frère.   Elles n'ont pas de frère.
Tu fais des fautes.   Tu ne fais pas de fautes.

2. Look at the following:

Fais la vaisselle, s'il te plaît!   Ne fais pas la vaisselle!
Restez, s'il vous plaît!   Ne restez pas!
Regardons la télé!   Ne regardons pas la télé!

To give a negative command, the French put *ne* before the imperative form, and *pas* after. Remember that when the 2 sing. form of *aller* and of *-er* verbs is used as a command, the *s* is dropped:

tu vas → va!   tu entres → entre!

3. When there is no verb, *pas* is used without *ne:*

Pas moi.   *Not I.*
Pas toujours.   *Not always.*
Pas de devoirs aujourd'hui.   *No homework for today.*

4. Look at these questions and answers:

Vous avez froid?   { Non, je n'ai pas froid.
or: Vous avez froid, n'est-ce pas?   { Oui, j'ai froid.

Vous n'avez pas froid?   { Non, je n'ai pas froid.
    { Si, j'ai froid.

There are two ways of saying "yes" in French. *Oui* is used to answer an affirmative question, *si* to answer a negative question. *N'est-ce pas* almost implies a "yes" answer, so *oui* is used to answer "yes" to a question that includes *n'est-ce pas*.

Exercices

A. Change the statements to negative commands. Follow the model.

1. Tu arrives à minuit.
   N'arrive pas à minuit!

2. Nous allons au Mont Tremblant.
3. Vous faites vos achats aujour-d'hui.
4. Nous faisons la vaisselle.
5. Vous écoutez, mes fils.
6. Tu vas à la porte.
7. Nous faisons nos devoirs maintenant.
8. Tu portes ton jean.
9. Tu rougis.

B. Answer by saying that the first part of the "this or that" question is correct and that the second part is incorrect. Follow the models.

1. Où est-ce qu'il va? Au cinéma ou au match de football?
   Il va au cinéma—pas au match de football.

2. Quand est-ce qu'elle arrive? Vendredi soir ou samedi matin?
   Elle arrive vendredi soir—pas samedi matin.

3. A quelle heure est-ce qu'ils finissent leurs devoirs? A 10 h. ou à 11 h.?
4. Combien font dix moins zéro? Dix ou zéro?
5. Qui a raison? Monique ou Yvette?
6. Comment est-ce qu'elles vont au théâtre? A pied ou en voiture?
7. Quand est-ce qu'elle fait des voyages? En été ou en automne?
8. Qu'est-ce qu'ils aiment? Les documentaires ou les films policiers?
9. Où est-ce qu'il va? A l'aéroport ou à la gare?
10. Quand est-ce qu'on porte des habits chauds? En hiver ou au prin-temps?
11. Qui a sommeil? Le professeur ou les élèves?
12. Quand est-ce qu'elle aime faire des achats? Le matin ou l'après-midi?

C. Answer the questions in the affirmative. Follow the models.

1. Nous faisons de l'auto-stop aujourd'hui, n'est-ce pas?
   Oui, nous faisons de l'auto-stop aujourd'hui.

2. Le sable n'est pas chaud?
   Si, il est chaud.

3. Est-ce qu'elles ne font pas de voyages?
4. Est-ce qu'elle ne finit pas son petit déjeuner?
5. Est-ce qu'elles ne vont pas aux matchs?
6. Est-ce qu'ils déjeunent vers midi?
7. Elle grossit, n'est-ce pas?
8. Est-ce qu'il fait du vent aujourd'hui?
9. Est-ce qu'il n'y a pas de piscine ici?
10. Est-ce qu'ils ne rentrent pas à la maison?

2. N'allons pas au Mont Tremblant!
3. Ne faites pas vos achats aujourd'hui!
4. Ne faisons pas la vaisselle!
5. N'écoutez pas, mes fils!
6. Ne va pas à la porte!
7. Ne faisons pas nos devoirs maintenant!
8. Ne porte pas ton jean!
9. Ne rougis pas!

Ex. B
Although liaison was once very common after *pas* (*pas au match*), younger speakers today do not tend to use liaison here.

3. Ils finissent leurs devoirs à 10 h.—pas à 11 h.
4. Dix moins zéro font dix—pas zéro.
5. Monique a raison—pas Yvette.
6. Elles vont au théâtre à pied—pas en voiture.
7. Elle fait des voyages en été—pas en automne.
8. Ils aiment les docu-mentaires—pas les films policiers.
9. Il va à l'aéroport—pas à la gare.
10. On porte des habits chauds en hiver—pas au printemps.
11. Le professeur a som-meil—pas les élèves.
12. Elle aime faire des achats le matin—pas l'après-midi.

3. Si, elles font des voyages.
4. Si, elle finit son petit déjeuner.
5. Si, elles vont aux matchs.
6. Oui, ils déjeunent vers midi.
7. Oui, elle grossit.
8. Oui, il fait du vent aujourd'hui.
9. Si, il y a une piscine ici.
10. Si, ils rentrent à la maison.

Vérifiez vos progrès

Write true, full-sentence answers to the questions.

1. Vous ne faites pas la vaisselle après le dîner?
2. Est-ce que vous avez une moto?
3. Est-ce que vous faites toujours vos devoirs?
4. Vous ne révisez pas vos leçons?

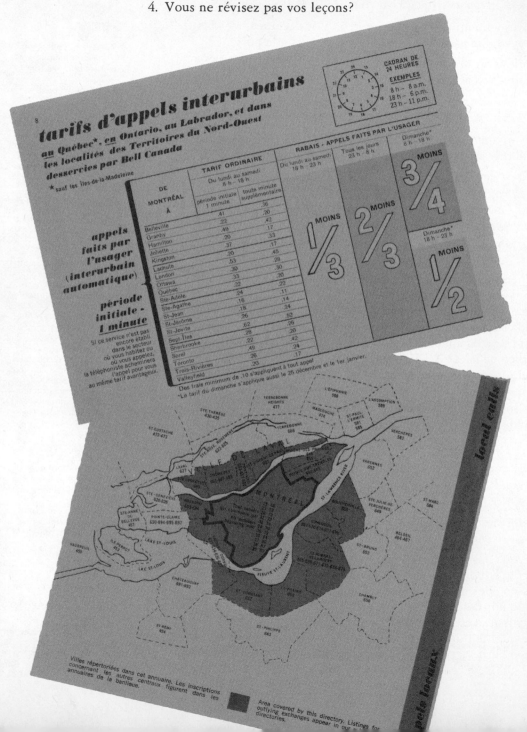

RÉVISION ET THÈME

Consult the model sentences, then put the English cues into French and use them to form new sentences.

1. Elles sont *à la plage. Il fait nuit.*
   (at the lake) (It's daytime.)
   (near the sea) (It's windy.)

2. *Il y a des étoiles, mais pas de lune.*
   (There are rivers, but no mountains.)
   (There are lakes, but no sand.)

3. *La terre est jaune et laide.*
   (The sky is blue and beautiful.)
   (The cars are old and white.)

4. *Martin est à la maison, mais il n'a pas faim.*
   (We're inside, but we're not sleepy.)
   (I'm outside, but I'm not afraid.)

5. *Il fait ses achats.*
   (They're doing the dishes.)
   (We're hitchhiking.)

Now that you have done the *Révision*, you are ready to write a composition. Put the English captions describing each cartoon panel into French to form a paragraph.

See Teacher's Section for answers to the *révision* and *thème*.

Review of:
1. prepositions
   expressions with *faire*
2. plural indefinite determiners
   pas de + noun
3. agreement of adjectives
4. negative expressions with *avoir*
5. expressions with *faire*

We're in the mountains. It's daytime.

There are clouds, but no sun.

The snow is beautiful and white.

Huguette is outside, but she isn't cold.

She's skiing.

Lesson
8

AUTO-TEST

A. Write answers to the questions according to the pictures. Follow the models.

1. Vous n'avez pas sommeil?
   Si, nous avons sommeil.

2. Ils n'ont pas froid?
   Non, ils ont chaud.

3. Tu n'as pas faim?

4. Elle n'a pas peur?

5. Vous n'avez pas chaud?

6. Je n'ai pas raison?

B. Write negative answers to the questions. Follow the model.

1. La lune est belle. Et le ciel?
   Le ciel n'est pas beau.

2. L'appartement est nouveau. Et la maison?
3. Les montagnes sont belles. Et les lacs?
4. Monsieur Lenoir est vieux. Et ses nièces?
5. Les jours sont chauds. Et les nuits?

C. Write answers to the questions using the cues in parentheses. Follow the model.

1. Quand est-ce que vous faites vos devoirs? (le soir)
   Nous faisons nos devoirs le soir.

2. Où est-ce que nous faisons du ski nautique? (près de la villa)
3. Quand est-ce que je fais la vaisselle? (le matin)
4. Quand est-ce que tu fais un voyage? (au printemps)
5. Quand est-ce qu'elle fait des achats? (lundi)

D. Write complete answers to the questions. Follow the model.

1. Combien font seize et trois?
   Seize et trois font dix-neuf.

2. Combien font quarante moins onze?
3. Combien font seize et dix-huit?
4. Combien font soixante-cinq moins quatorze?

Poème

REFRAINS ENFANTINS°

. . . Il pleut Il pleut
Il fait beau
Il fait du soleil
Il est tôt°
5   Il se fait tard°
Il
Il
Il
Il
10   toujours Il
Toujours Il qui pleut et qui neige
Toujours Il qui fait du soleil
Toujours Il
Pourquoi pas Elle
15   Jamais° Elle
Pourtant° Elle aussi
souvent se fait° belle!

enfantin, -e: *chil-
dren's*

tôt: *early*
il se fait tard: *it's
getting late*

jamais: *never*
pourtant: *however*
se fait: *makes herself*

See "Description of a Lesson" for suggestions on
how to present the
poèmes.

See Cultural Supplement.

Jacques Prévert, *Spectacle*
(© Editions Gallimard, 1951)

Proverbe

Tout est bien qui finit bien.

MARDI 22 JUIN
20 h 30

une nuit
à l'opéra

(A Night at the Opera), 1935
Réalisation : Sam Wood
Production : Metro-Goldwyn-Mayer
Durée : 93 minutes
Interprétation : Groucho, Harpo,
Chico et Margaret Dumont,
Siegfried Rumann, Kitty Carlisle,
Allan Jones, etc.

Après un voyage animé sur un transatlantique, les frères Marx mettent leur talent au service du monde du spectacle.

un jour
aux courses

(A Day at the Races), 1937
Réalisation : Sam Wood
Production : Metro-Goldwyn-Mayer
Durée : 109 minutes
Interprétation : Groucho, Chico,
Harpo et Margaret Dumont,
Siegfried Rumann, Allan Jones,
Maureen O'Sullivan, etc.

Un univers encore différent : celui des courses de chevaux, que Groucho, vétérinaire énergique, connaît parfaitement.

« Une nuit à l'opéra » : M. Dumont et Groucho.

MARS 25 et 26
LES DIABLES
Britannique 1971
Drame historique de Ken Russel
avec VANESSA REDGRAVE
OLIVER REED, DUDLEY SUTTON
"Vision délirante d'une histoire vraie" (18 ans)

AVRIL 1 et 2
LA TETE DE NORMANDE ST-ONGE
112 minutes
Québécois 1975
Drame psychologique de Gilles Carle
avec CAROLE LAURE, RENE GIRARD
RAYMOND CLOUTIER
*Jeudi: Une seule représentation (7h.30) suivie
d'une discussion

AVRIL 8 et 9
AMERICAN GRAFFITI [s. titré]
110 minutes
Américain 1973
Comédie de Georges Lucas
avec RICK DREYFUS, RONNY HOWARD
PAUL LE MAT
"Intéressante approche documentaire à la fois
drôle et nostalgique"

014723
SAINT-MICHEL
PARIS
ENTRÉE
13 F
Timbre en cpte Trésor
Paris

JEUDI VENDREDI
8, 9 avril
19 h 30/
21 h 30

Salle Maurice O'Bready
CINÉMAFEUS: "American Graffiti" film américain
(1973) du réalisateur Georges Lucas avec, entre autres, Rick Dreyfus, Ronny Howard et Paul Le Mat.

VENDREDI SAM. ET DIM.
9, 10, 11 avril
20 h 30

Petite salle, Pavillon central
LA BÉBELLE présente "Z'avez vu nos clowns?" Il
y aura une représentation pour les enfants à 14 h le
11 avril.

SAMEDI
10 avril
20 h 30

Salle Maurice O'Bready
LE CHOEUR HÉRITAGE présente "Fantaisie, rêve,
alléluia" sous la direction de Marc Bernier.

LUNDI
12 avril
20 h 30

Salle Maurice O'Bready
"LA NEF DES SORCIÈRES" d'un groupe d'auteurs
féminins québécois, dont Marthe Blackburn, Marie-
Claire Blais et Nicole Brossard, dans une mise en
scène de Luce Guilbeault avec, entre autres, Michelle
Magny et Luce Guilbeault.

JEUDI VENDREDI
15
Salle Maurice O'Bready

Neuvième Leçon

Le choix d'un film

Alain téléphone à Delphine. Plus tard il va sortir avec elle et sa cousine.
Ils vont au cinéma. Mais d'abord il faut choisir un film.

ALAIN   Allô, Delphine. Ici Alain.[1] On sort toujours avec ta cousine?
DELPHINE   Bien sûr.
5 ALAIN   Il y a *Mon Colt 45, mon cheval et moi*[2] à Epernay.[3]
DELPHINE   Pas de westerns, s'il te plaît. Qu'est-ce qu'on joue à Reims?
ALAIN   Eh bien, si tu n'aimes pas les westerns, à Reims il y a un film
            italien et aussi un film policier . . .
DELPHINE   Bon, allons à Reims. J'aime bien les films policiers.

---

[1]The French say *bonjour* or *bonsoir* when they greet someone in person. Over the phone, they
say *allô*. Note how they identify themselves on the phone: *Ici Alain*.
[2]French film and book titles are usually capitalized only up to and including the first noun or
pronoun. Proper names are always capitalized.
[3]Epernay, 140 kilometers northeast of Paris, is located in the champagne-producing region of
France. Nearby, Reims, the capital of Champagne, is an industrial city with a population of
160,000. French kings were traditionally crowned in the magnificent cathedral there because
Clovis, the first Christian king, converted and was baptized at Reims in 496.

See Cultural Supplement.

Point out that *téléphoner* always requires à.

le cheval: This does not become a part of the active vocabulary until Lesson 12.

You might point out Reims and Epernay on a map.

Choosing a movie

Alain is phoning Delphine. Later he's going to go out with her and her cousin. They are going to the movies. But first they have to choose a film.

	ALAIN	Hello, Delphine. This is Alain. Are we still going out with your cousin?
5	DELPHINE	Sure.
	ALAIN	There's *My Colt 45, My Horse and Me* in Epernay.
	DELPHINE	No westerns, please! What's playing in Reims?
	ALAIN	Well, if you don't like westerns, there's an Italian movie in Reims and also a detective film . . .
10	DELPHINE	Good. Let's go to Reims. I really like detective films.

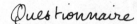

Questionnaire

1. Pourquoi est-ce qu'Alain téléphone à Delphine? 2. Qu'est-ce qu'il demande à Delphine? 3. Qu'est-ce qu'on joue à Epernay? 4. Est-ce que Delphine aime les westerns? 5. Qu'est-ce qu'on joue à Reims? 6. Est-ce que Delphine aime les films policiers? Alors, où est-ce que les trois amis vont aller plus tard?

PRONONCIATION

The nasal vowel sound [ɛ̃] is somewhat like the vowel sound in the English word *sang,* but it is shorter, more nasal, and pronounced with greater tension.

Exercices

A. In the following pairs, the first word contains the [i] sound plus a clearly released final [n] sound. The second word contains the nasal vowel sound [ɛ̃]. Practice saying them aloud.

[in]/[ɛ̃]   voisine/voisin   cousine/cousin   copine/copain

B. In the following pairs, the first word contains the [ɛ] sound plus a clearly released final [n] sound. The second word contains the nasal vowel sound [ɛ̃]. Practice saying them.

[ɛn]/[ɛ̃]   américaine/américain   mexicaine/mexicain
italienne/italien   canadienne/canadien

C. Listen, then say the following sentences aloud.

Alain arrive le quinze juin.
Jacqueline, ma voisine, a une piscine.
Martin, mon voisin, va au jardin.

Son cousin arrive par le train.
Hélène et Germaine sont canadiennes.
Alain et Lucien sont canadiens.

MOTS NOUVEAUX I

Où est-ce que tu vas pendant les vacances?	*Where are you going **during** vacation?*
Le choix est très difficile.	***The choice** is very difficult.*
Pas pour moi. Il faut aller à Epernay.[1]	*Not for me. **I have to go** to Epernay.*
Pour aller à Epernay je fais de l'auto-stop.	***(In order)** to go to Epernay, I hitchhike.*
Où est-ce que vous allez?	*Where are you going?*
Il faut aller en ville.[2]	***I have to go** to town.*
Aujourd'hui?	*Today?*
Oui, malheureusement!	*Yes, **unfortunately**.*
Si on va à Reims, est-ce qu'il ne faut pas téléphoner à la gare?	*If we're going to Reims, **don't we have to phone** the train station?*
Si, mais d'abord il faut téléphoner à maman et à papa.	*Yes, but **first** we have to call **Mom** and **Dad**.*
S'il faut téléphoner, allons-y![3] Il est 5 h.	*If we have to call, let's get going. It's 5:00.*

la ville: Point out the pronounced final *l*: [vil]

Point out the repetition of à in *téléphoner à maman et à papa.*

Je vais à **Paris**. C'est une ville française. On parle français là-bas.[4]

Londres	anglaise	anglais
Tokyo	japonaise	japonais
Lisbonne	portugaise	portugais
Dakar	sénégalaise	wolof et français
Pékin	chinoise	chinois
Washington	américaine	anglais
Mexico[5]	mexicaine	espagnol
Rome	italienne	italien
Montréal	canadienne	français et anglais
Madrid	espagnole	espagnol
Bonn	allemande	allemand

le wolof: Though French is the official language of Senegal, Wolof is one of several important native languages.

---

[1]Though *il faut* literally means "it is necessary," its best English equivalent always depends on the context.

[2]*La ville* can mean either "city" or "town."

[3]*Si* means both "yes" and "if." When it means "if," it elides with *il* and *ils (s'il, s'ils).* When it means "yes," it does not elide.

[4]The names of languages are the same as the masculine form of the adjective and are not capitalized.

[5]The French name for Mexico City is *Mexico.*

2. Ah, tu parles chinois?
3. Ah, tu parles anglais?
4. Ah, tu parles japonais?
5. Ah, tu parles italien?
6. Ah, tu parles espagnol?
7. Ah, tu parles portugais?
8. Ah, tu parles allemand?
9. Ah, tu parles espagnol?
10. Ah, tu parles wolof (français)?
11. Ah, tu parles français (anglais)?

Ex. B
2. Parce qu'elle est française.
3. Parce qu'elle est anglaise (américaine, canadienne).
4. Parce qu'elle est portugaise.
5. Parce qu'elle est chinoise.
6. Parce qu'elle est espagnole (mexicaine).
7. Parce qu'elle est sénégalaise.
8. Parce qu'elle est japonaise.

Ex. C
3. S'ils arrivent à minuit, il faut aller à l'aéroport vers 11 h.
4. Si elles habitent New York, il ne faut pas avoir une voiture.
5. Si tu aimes le football, il faut regarder les matchs dimanche.
6. Si vous travaillez, il faut aller au bureau le matin.
7. S'il fait très chaud le soir, il faut apporter ton maillot.
8. Si je téléphone à Marie, il faut téléphoner aussi à Georges.
9. Si tu n'aimes pas faire de l'auto-stop, il faut aller en ville par le train.
10. Si nous sommes pauvres, il faut rester chez nous pendant les vacances.
11. Si les devoirs sont très difficiles, il faut réviser la leçon.

Exercices de vocabulaire

A. Your neighbor is going to go to another city. Ask if he or she speaks the language or languages that they speak there. Follow the model.

1. Je vais à Paris.   *Ah, tu parles français?*

2. Je vais à Pékin.
3. Je vais à Londres.
4. Je vais à Tokyo.
5. Je vais à Rome.
6. Je vais à Madrid.
7. Je vais à Lisbonne.
8. Je vais à Bonn.
9. Je vais à Mexico.
10. Je vais à Dakar.
11. Je vais à Montréal.

B. Answer the questions. Follow the model.

1. La jeune fille parle allemand. Pourquoi?
   Parce qu'elle est allemande.

2. Sa mère parle français. Pourquoi?
3. Sa cousine parle anglais. Pourquoi?
4. Leur voisine parle portugais. Pourquoi?
5. Sa copine parle chinois. Pourquoi?
6. Ma tante parle espagnol. Pourquoi?
7. Leur grand-mère parle wolof. Pourquoi?
8. Son amie parle japonais. Pourquoi?

C. Combine the sentences by making the first one an "if" clause and the second a "have to" clause. Follow the models.

1. On va au cinéma. Choisissons un film!
   Si on va au cinéma, il faut choisir un film.
2. Nous allons au théâtre. Nous ne dînons pas au restaurant.
   Si nous allons au théâtre, il ne faut pas dîner au restaurant.

3. Ils arrivent à minuit. Allons à l'aéroport vers 11 h.!
4. Elles habitent New York. Elles n'ont pas de voiture.
5. Tu aimes le football. Regarde les matchs dimanche!
6. Vous travaillez. Allez au bureau le matin!
7. Il fait très chaud le soir. Apporte ton maillot!
8. Je téléphone à Marie. Je téléphone aussi à Georges.
9. Tu n'aimes pas faire de l'auto-stop. Va en ville par le train!
10. Nous sommes pauvres. Nous restons chez nous pendant les vacances.
11. Les devoirs sont très difficiles. Révisons la leçon!

MOTS NOUVEAUX II

See Cultural Supplement.

l'auteur: You might point out that, like *le professeur*, this noun is masculine even if the author is a woman.

le concert

le roman

le poème

le poète

l'auteur (m.)

l'histoire (f.)

jouer au basketball

le grand magasin

le gymnase

le western

jouer au hockey

la bibliothèque

le marché

le supermarché

jouer au volleyball

The *h* in *le hockey* is called an "aspirate *h*." When a determiner appears before it, there is no elision: *aller à l'hôpital.* but *jouer au hockey; un jour d'hiver.* but *un match de hockey.*

The plural of *le grand magasin* is *les grands magasins.* The French use *dans* rather than *à* with *le grand magasin.* For example: *Je vais dans le grand magasin aujourd'hui.*

Exercice de vocabulaire

Answer the questions according to the pictures. Follow the models.

1. Où est-ce qu'il faut aller?
   Il faut aller au concert.

2. Qu'est-ce que vous faites?
   Nous jouons au volleyball.

3. Je vais d'abord au supermarché.
4. Il fait ses achats dans le grand magasin.
5. Ils jouent au hockey.
6. Vous étudiez (nous étudions) le (un) poème.
7. Il y a un marché là.
8. Elles finissent une (l') histoire.
9. Je regarde le (un) western.
10. Elles jouent au basketball.
11. On va à la bibliothèque pour choisir un roman.
12. (Pour maigrir), il faut aller au gymnase.
13. Les auteurs aiment les livres.

3. Où est-ce que tu vas d'abord?

4. Où est-ce qu'il fait ses achats?

5. Qu'est-ce qu'ils font?

6. Qu'est-ce que nous étudions?

7. Qu'est-ce qu'il y a là?

8. Qu'est-ce qu'elles finissent?

9. Qu'est-ce que tu regardes?

10. Qu'est-ce qu'elles font?

11. Où est-ce qu'on va pour choisir un roman?

12. Pour maigrir, où est-ce qu'il faut aller?

13. Qui aime les livres?

EXPLICATIONS I

Les verbes en -ir

VOCABULAIRE			
dormir	*to sleep, to be asleep*	servir	*to serve, to wait on*
partir¹	*to leave*	sortir¹	*to go out*

It might help students remember the difference between *partir* and *sortir* if you present the following pairs as opposites: *partir (de)/arriver (à) sortir (de)/entrer (dans)*

You have learned the present tense of the most common type of verbs whose infinitives end in -*ir*. Those are the -*ir/-iss-* type. Here is the second important type—the simple -*ir* verbs:

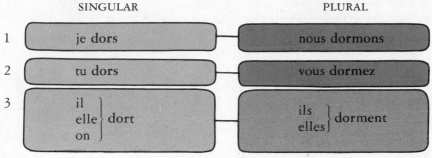

SINGULAR — PLURAL

1 je dors — nous dormons

2 tu dors — vous dormez

3 il / elle / on } dort — ils / elles } dorment

IMPERATIVE: **dors! dormons! dormez!**

1. The plural forms of simple -*ir* verbs are like those of -*er* verbs, with the endings -*ons*, -*ez*, and -*ent* added to the stem: *dorm-*.

2. For the singular forms, the last consonant of the plural stem is dropped (*dorm-* → *dor-*) and the endings -*s*, -*s*, -*t* are added. All three singular forms are pronounced the same.

Exercices

A. Replace the words in italics with the appropriate form of the cue in parentheses. Some are simple -*ir* verbs; others are -*ir/-iss-*. Follow the model.

1. Ils *font un voyage* avec Dominique. (sortir)
   Ils sortent avec Dominique.

2. Elles *rentrent avant* le dîner. (servir)
3. Tu *portes* un maillot blanc? (choisir)
4. Ils *font* leurs devoirs vers 9 h. du soir. (finir)
5. On *prépare* le petit déjeuner à 8 h. du matin. (servir)

2. Elles servent le dîner.
3. Tu choisis un maillot blanc?
4. Ils finissent leurs devoirs vers 9 h. du soir.
5. On sert le petit déjeuner à 8 h. du matin.

¹When the French speak of "leaving" or "going out of" a place, the word *de* is included. Try to think of these words as *partir de* and *sortir de*. Of course, when the place you are leaving is not mentioned, the *de* does not appear:

Je *pars de* la ville avec papa.   Je *pars* avec papa.
Il *sort du* théâtre maintenant.   Il *sort* maintenant.

6. Je pars du gymnase avec des copains.
7. Est-ce que vous maigrissez ou est-ce que vous grossissez?
8. Le train part de la gare de Lyon à midi.
9. Ne dors pas toujours!
10. Nous sortons pendant qu'elles dorment.

2. Je choisis des livres à la bibliothèque aussi.
3. Vous servez (nous servons) le déjeuner à 1 h. aussi.
4. Ils dorment l'après-midi aussi.
5. Nous partons (je pars) après le dîner aussi.
6. Il choisit des poèmes aussi.
7. Elles sortent du grand magasin aussi.
8. Quand elle joue au basketball, elle maigrit aussi.
9. Je sors souvent aussi.
10. Tu pars pour l'aéroport à 5 h. aussi.

6. Je *rentre* du gymnase avec des copains. (partir)
7. Est-ce que vous *restez* ou est-ce que vous *partez?* (maigrir/grossir)
8. Le train *arrive à* la gare de Lyon à midi. (partir de)
9. Ne *rougis* pas toujours! (dormir)
10. Nous *restons ici* pendant qu'elles *regardent la télé.* (sortir/dormir)

B. Answer the questions using the appropriate pronoun. Again note that some are simple -*ir* verbs; others are -*ir*/-*iss*-. Follow the model.

1. Après le concert, ils sortent du théâtre. Et vous?
   Après le concert, nous sortons du théâtre aussi.
2. Ils choisissent des livres à la bibliothèque. Et toi?
3. Elles servent le déjeuner à 1 h. Et nous?
4. Leur mère dort l'après-midi. Et eux?
5. Nos parents partent après le dîner. Et vous?
6. Je choisis des poèmes. Et lui?
7. Il sort du grand magasin. Et elles?
8. Quand je joue au basketball, je maigris. Et elle?
9. Nous sortons souvent. Et toi?
10. Tes sœurs partent pour l'aéroport à 5 h. Et moi?

Les adjectifs

Help students see that *grossir* and *maigrir* are derived from *gros* and *maigre*.

You may need to help students see the distinction between *gros* and *large* and *maigre* and *étroit*.

VOCABULAIRE			
blond, -e	*blond*	gros, grosse	*fat, large*
brun, -e	*brown; a brunette*	maigre	*skinny, thin*
roux, rousse	*redheaded; a redhead*	court, -e*	*short*
bon, bonne	*good*	long, longue	*long*
mauvais, -e	*bad*	étroit, -e	*narrow*
célèbre	*famous*	large	*wide*
inconnu, -e	*unknown*		

*Court is used for things, *petit* for people.

1. Note the pronunciation of the adjectives in these sentences:

Le roman est bon.   La bibliothèque est bonne.
Alain est brun.   Hélène est brune.
Le garçon est canadien.   La jeune fille est canadienne.
Son voisin est américain.   Sa voisine est américaine.

The vowel letters + *n* at the end of these adjectives represent a nasal vowel sound. In the feminine forms, the addition of the letter *e* causes the *n* to be pronounced and the vowel sound is no longer nasal. In spelling, masculine adjectives that end in -*on* or -*ien* double the *n* before adding the *e* for the feminine form.

Neuvième
Leçon

2. Note the pronunciation of the adjectives in these sentences:

Le bateau est **grand**.   La voile est **grande**.
Le roman est **allemand**.   La pièce est **allemande**.
Son frère est **blond**.   Sa sœur est **blonde**.
Le poème est **long**.   L'histoire est **longue**.

These masculine adjectives all end in a nasal vowel sound followed by an unpronounced consonant. In the feminine forms, the addition of the letter *e* causes the last consonant to be pronounced, but the nasal vowel sound remains.

Exercices

A. A brother and sister are returning home. According to the cities mentioned, indicate their nationality. Follow the model.

1. Ils rentrent à New York.
   Il est américain. Elle est américaine. Ils sont américains.

2. Ils rentrent à Montréal.
3. Ils rentrent à Londres.
4. Ils rentrent à Rome.
5. Ils rentrent à Tokyo.
6. Ils rentrent à Bonn.
7. Ils rentrent à Dakar.
8. Ils rentrent à Mexico.
9. Ils rentrent à Lisbonne.
10. Ils rentrent à Madrid.
11. Ils rentrent à Pékin.

B. Answer the questions using the adjective that means the opposite of the one given. Follow the model.

1. Est-ce que ses neveux sont énergiques? Et ses nièces?
   Non, ils sont paresseux. Et ses nièces sont paresseuses aussi.

2. Est-ce que leurs fils sont maigres? Et leurs filles?
3. Est-ce que les romans sont célèbres? Et les pièces?
4. Est-ce que les bureaux sont étroits? Et les chaises?
5. Est-ce que les poèmes sont longs? Et les histoires?
6. Est-ce que les crayons sont bons? Et les gommes?
7. Est-ce que les fleuves sont larges? Et les plages?
8. Est-ce que les auteurs sont inconnus? Et les histoires?
9. Est-ce que les concerts sont mauvais? Et les bandes?
10. Est-ce que les films sont courts? Et les pièces?

C. Choose the appropriate adjective to complete each sentence. Pay close attention to the meaning and agreement of nouns or pronouns and adjectives. Then read the sentences aloud.

1. Tu es blond, mais tes parents sont (*bruns, brunes, blondes*).
2. Le roman est bon, mais il est trop (*large, long, célèbre*).
3. Pas de westerns! Ils sont presque toujours (*étroits, mauvais, grands*).
4. Mon frère maigrit parce qu'il est trop (*gris, large, gros*).
5. La rue est longue et (*maigre, étroite, courte*).
6. Elles parlent espagnol parce qu'elles sont (*mexicaines, espagnols, mexicains*).

7. Je suis brun mais ma sœur est *(rouge, roux, rousse)*.
8. Il dort toujours? Il est très *(avare, inconnu, paresseux)*.
9. Sa voisine est grande et *(gros, grosse, large)*.
10. L'auteur n'est pas célèbre, mais son histoire est *(brune, bonne, bon)*.
11. Ma cousine est blonde, belle et très *(courte, longue, petite)*.

Vérifiez vos progrès

Rewrite the sentences using the appropriate form of each verb and adjective in parentheses.

1. Pourquoi est-ce qu'il *(dormir)*? Parce que les histoires sont trop *(long)*.
2. Qu'est-ce qu'on *(servir)*? Il faut *(servir)* un dîner *(italien)*.
3. Pourquoi est-ce qu'elle *(maigrir)*? Parce qu'elle est trop *(gros)*.
4. Qui *(partir)*? Les auteurs *(célèbre)*.
5. Nous *(finir)* une pièce *(allemand)*. J'aime mieux les pièces *(anglais)* ou *(américain)*.
6. Pourquoi est-ce que tu *(choisir)* toujours des rues *(étroit)*?
7. Quand est-ce que tu *(sortir)* avec tes parents? Nous *(sortir)* samedi parce qu'on joue trois pièces *(canadien)* en ville. Les pièces sont presque *(inconnu)*, mais elles sont très *(bon)*.

CONVERSATION ET LECTURE

Parlons de vous

1. Est-ce que vous sortez souvent? Avec qui? votre famille? des copains? 2. Où est-ce que vous aimez aller quand vous sortez? au cinéma? à un match? dans un musée? au concert? au concert de rock? 3. Est-ce que vous allez souvent en ville pour faire des achats? au marché? au supermarché? dans un grand magasin? 4. Est-ce que vous jouez au volleyball? au basketball? au hockey? En quelle saison? Est-ce que vous allez souvent au gymnase? Qu'est-ce que vous aimez faire là-bas? 5. Au lycée, est-ce que vous étudiez des romans? des poèmes? des auteurs et des poètes célèbres? Des auteurs anglais? américains? français? allemands? Quels auteurs est-ce que vous aimez? 6. Est-ce que vous allez quelquefois à la bibliothèque? Pourquoi? 7. Est-ce que vous aimez mieux étudier chez vous ou à la bibliothèque?

Au cinéma

Deux amis, Martin et Sabine, sortent ce° soir. Ils
vont aller au cinéma en ville. Bien sûr, il faut
d'abord choisir un film, mais le choix n'est pas du
tout facile. Martin aime surtout° les films d'aven-
5 tures.° Sabine aime mieux les films d'épouvante.°

Martin regarde le journal du soir. Chouette! On
joue un film de Cousteau.[1] Vite il téléphone à
Sabine.

SABINE   Allô.
10 MARTIN   Allô, Sabine. Ici Martin. Je regarde le
          journal et il y a . . .
SABINE   Moi aussi. Au Plaza il y a *Le Loup-garou*°
          de Paris. C'est chic, n'est-ce pas?

Alors, comment faire un choix? Après une très
15 longue discussion, ils choisissent un vieux western.
A 7 h. 30[2] ils partent de chez eux et à 8 h. ils arrivent au cinéma. Ils entrent et l'ouvreuse[3] demande
leurs billets.°

L'OUVREUSE   Vos billets, s'il vous plaît.
20 MARTIN   Voici, madame. Pas trop près de
            l'écran,° s'il vous plaît.

Martin donne un pourboire° à l'ouvreuse. Martin
et Sabine sont heureux parce que leurs places° sont
bonnes. Mais avant le grand film,° il y a un long
25 documentaire américain sur les grenouilles.°

SABINE   Il est ennuyeux,° le documentaire,
          n'est-ce pas, Martin?
MARTIN   Rrrrrrrrrr . . .
SABINE   Martin! Est-ce que tu dors?
30 MARTIN   Euh . . . Un esquimau,° s'il vous plaît.[4]
SABINE   Mais non, ce n'est pas l'entracte.°
MARTIN   Ah bon! J'ai sommeil . . . et si on a
          sommeil, il faut dormir, n'est-ce pas?
          Bon courage° avec les grenouilles, Sa-
35   bine.

ce, cette: this

surtout: especially
l'aventure (f.): ad-
venture
l'épouvante (f.):
horror

le loup-garou:
werewolf

le billet: ticket

l'écran (m.): screen

le pourboire: tip   See Cultural Supplement.
la place: seat
le grand film: main
feature
la grenouille: frog
ennuyeux, -euse:
boring

l'esquimau (m.): ice
cream bar
l'entracte (m.): in-
termission
le courage: (here)
luck

---

[1] Jacques-Yves Cousteau, born in 1910, is a well-known French oceanographer who has made
   many films about marine life.
[2] This can be said either as *sept heures trente* or *sept heures et demie.*
[3] An *ouvreuse* is an usher. All ushers in France are women. In both movies and theaters, one is
   seated by an usher and, unless a notice is posted, the patron is expected to give a tip. Where
   tipping is permitted, the ushers do not receive a salary and earn money only from their tips.
[4] Between the short features (documentaries, cartoons, and even commercial ads) and the main
   film, there is usually a brief intermission, during which the ushers sell ice cream and candy.

À propos...

1. Où est-ce que Martin et Sabine vont aller plus tard? 2. Pourquoi est-ce que le choix d'un film est difficile pour eux? 3. Est-ce que Sabine téléphone à Martin? 4. Qu'est-ce qu'il y a au Plaza? 5. Après leur discussion, qu'est-ce qu'ils choisissent? 6. Quand ils entrent dans le cinéma, avec qui est-ce que Martin parle? 7. Qu'est-ce que l'ouvreuse demande à Martin? 8. Décrivez ("describe") les places que Martin demande. 9. Qu'est-ce qu'on joue avant le grand film? 10. Est-ce que Martin et Sabine aiment le documentaire? 11. Qu'est-ce que Martin fait? 12. Et vous, est-ce que vous aimez les documentaires? 13. Est-ce que vous aimez les films d'aventures? les films d'épouvante? 14. Est-ce que vous aimez aussi les westerns? les films policiers? 15. Quand vous ne sortez pas, est-ce que vous regardez des films à la télé? Quels films? 16. Est-ce que Jacques-Yves Cousteau est célèbre? 17. Est-ce que vous regardez quelquefois Cousteau à la télé?

EXPLICATIONS II

Le futur formé avec <u>aller</u>

geler	*to freeze*	demain	*tomorrow*
neiger	*to snow*	plus tard	*later*
pleuvoir	*to rain*		

geler: Remind students that the 3 sing. form that they know has an *accent grave*. Help them hear the difference in pronunciation: [ʒəle] vs. [ʒɛl].

1. Look at the following:

Il neige aujourd'hui.	*It's snowing today.*
Il va neiger plus tard.	*It's going to snow later.*
Je reste chez moi.	*I'm staying home.*
Je vais rester chez moi.	*I'm going to stay home.*

Just as in English, one way to speak of the future in French is to use a form of the verb "to go" *(aller)* followed by the infinitive form of another verb.

2. Note how the negative is formed in the future:

On va sortir du gymnase.	On ne va pas sortir du gymnase.
Nous allons partir demain.	Nous n'allons pas partir demain.

The *ne* and *pas* appear with the form of *aller*.

Exercices

A. Put the sentences in the future according to the model.

1. Papa ouvre la porte.   *Papa va ouvrir la porte.*

2. Nous parlons à l'agent.
3. Je donne mon livre à Guy.
4. Tu travailles au bureau.
5. L'enfant a peur.
6. Ils vont au supermarché.
7. Vous faites vos achats en ville?
8. Elle est très heureuse.
9. Elles portent leurs robes rouges.
10. Je sers le dîner.
11. Tu joues au hockey?

B. Redo the above exercise in the negative. Follow the model.

1. Papa n'ouvre pas la porte.
   Papa ne va pas ouvrir la porte.

C. Answer the questions according to the statements. Always use the appropriate pronoun in your response. Follow the models.

1. Il va pleuvoir demain.
   (a) Quel temps est-ce qu'il va faire?   *Il va pleuvoir.*
   (b) Quand est-ce qu'il va pleuvoir?   *Il va pleuvoir demain.*

2. Les garçons vont servir le dîner vers 7 h.
   (a) Qui va servir le dîner?
   (b) A quelle heure est-ce qu'ils vont servir le dîner?

Ex. A
2. Nous allons parler à l'agent.
3. Je vais donner mon livre à Guy.
4. Tu vas travailler au bureau.
5. L'enfant va avoir peur.
6. Ils vont aller au supermarché.
7. Vous allez faire vos achats en ville?
8. Elle va être très heureuse.
9. Elles vont porter leurs robes rouges.
10. Je vais servir le dîner.
11. Tu vas jouer au hockey?

Ex. B
2. Nous n'allons pas parler à l'agent.
3. Je ne vais pas donner mon livre à Guy.
4. Tu ne vas pas travailler au bureau.
5. L'enfant ne va pas avoir peur.
6. Ils ne vont pas aller au supermarché.
7. Vous n'allez pas faire vos achats en ville?
8. Elle ne va pas être très heureuse.
9. Elles ne vont pas porter leurs robes rouges.
10. Je ne vais pas servir le dîner.
11. Tu ne vas pas jouer au hockey?

Ex. C
2. (a) Les garçons vont servir le dîner.
   (b) Ils vont servir le dîner vers 7 h.

3. (a) On va faire du ski.
   (b) On va faire du ski mercredi.
4. (a) Je vais aller dans les grands magasins.
   (b) Je vais faire mes achats là-bas.
5. (a) Nous allons au théâtre.
   (b) Nous allons porter nos robes blanches.
6. (a) Vous allez faire la vaisselle.
   (b) Vous allez faire la vaisselle après le déjeuner.
7. (a) Je vais aller au gymnase.
   (b) Je vais (là pour) jouer au basketball.
8. (a) Elles vont aller à la bibliothèque.
   (b) Parce qu'elles vont (Pour) faire leurs devoirs (là).

3. On va faire du ski mercredi.
   (a) Qu'est-ce qu'on va faire?
   (b) Quand est-ce qu'on va faire du ski?
4. Plus tard je vais faire mes achats dans les grands magasins.
   (a) Où est-ce que tu vas aller plus tard?
   (b) Qu'est-ce que tu vas faire là-bas?
5. Nous allons porter nos robes blanches au théâtre.
   (a) Où est-ce que vous allez?
   (b) Qu'est-ce que vous allez porter?
6. Vous allez faire la vaisselle après le déjeuner.
   (a) Qu'est-ce que nous allons faire?
   (b) Quand est-ce que nous allons faire la vaisselle?
7. Je vais aller au gymnase pour jouer au basketball.
   (a) Où est-ce que tu vas aller?
   (b) Pourquoi est-ce que tu vas là?
8. Elles vont faire leurs devoirs à la bibliothèque.
   (a) Où est-ce qu'elles vont aller?
   (b) Pourquoi?

Quelle heure est-il?

A couple of times per class, you might ask individuals what time it is.

You might also want to bring French railroad or airline timetables to class so that students can practice these very precise times in a real-life context.

Although *demie* is preferred in its masculine form *(demi)* following *midi* and *minuit*, either is acceptable. Since eleven times out of twelve the feminine form is the only one possible, we teach only that form.

VOCABULAIRE

| et quart *quarter past* | et demie *half past* | moins le quart *quarter to* |

Il est trois heures et quart.

Il est trois heures et demie.

Il est quatre heures moins le quart.

Il est neuf heures cinq.

Il est midi vingt-sept.

Il est dix heures moins vingt-sept.

Il est minuit moins cinq.

Exercice

Answer the questions. Follow the model.

1. Vers quelle heure est-ce qu'il part?
   Il part vers sept heures et demie.

2. Vers quelle heure est-ce que maman sort du bureau?

3. A quelle heure est-ce que tu rentres chez toi?

4. A quelle heure est-ce qu'il faut être au gymnase?

5. Vers quelle heure est-ce que tu finis tes devoirs?

6. Vers quelle heure est-ce qu'ils servent le déjeuner?

7. Quand est-ce que nous partons?

8. Quand est-ce qu'elle va au match de volleyball?

2. Elle sort du bureau vers cinq heures dix.
3. Je rentre chez moi à six heures moins le quart.
4. Il faut être au gymnase à deux heures et quart.
5. Je finis mes devoirs vers huit heures et demie.
6. Ils servent le déjeuner vers onze heures vingt-cinq.
7. Vous partez (nous partons) à dix heures moins dix.
8. Elle va au match de volleyball à quatre heures moins vingt-cinq.

Vérifiez vos progrès

Rewrite the dialogue, putting the italicized verbs in the future.

PAPA   Qu'est-ce que tu *fais?*

MADELEINE   Je *prépare* le déjeuner. Mes amies *arrivent* à 11 h. 30.

PAPA   Qu'est-ce que vous *faites* plus tard, toi et tes amies? Vous *sortez?*

5   MADELEINE   Non, nous *ne sortons pas.* Nous *restons* ici pour regarder un match de basketball à la télé. Tu *restes* à la maison aussi, papa?

PAPA   Non, je *sors* avec ta maman. Nous *partons* vers 1 h. 15.

RÉVISION ET THÈME

See Teacher's Section for answers to the *révision* and *thème*.

Review of:
1. *-ir* verbs
   expressions of time
2. future with *aller*
3. *il faut*
4. future with *aller*
   adjectives of nationality
5. negative
   agreement of adjectives
6. expressions of time
   -ir verbs

Consult the model sentences, then put the English cues into French and use them to form new sentences based on the models.

1. *Robert part du cinéma à quatre heures dix.*
   (I'm going out of the house at 8:35.)
   (You (pl.) are leaving for the airport at 11:05.)

2. *Il va jouer au basketball au gymnase.*
   (They're going shopping at the supermarket.)
   (We're going to eat lunch in the department store.)

3. *Après le dîner, il faut finir l'histoire.*
   (I have to choose a novel)
   (she has to go to the concert)

4. *On va jouer un western italien.*
   (You (sing.) are going to serve a German dinner.)
   (They're going to finish a Spanish poem.)

5. *Le fleuve n'est pas grand, mais il est très large.*
   (The stories aren't good, but they're very short.)
   (The girl isn't short, but she's very fat.)

6. *Maintenant il est midi vingt-cinq. Nous partons.*
   (it's 9:15)   *(They're going out.)*
   (it's 10:30)   *(You (sing.) are sleeping.)*

Now that you have done the *Révision*, you are ready to write a composition. Put the English captions describing each cartoon panel into French to form a paragraph.

Dominique and Madeleine go out of the house at 7:15.

They're going to have dinner at the restaurant.

After dinner, they have to go to the theater.

They're going to put on (*jouer*) an English play.

The play isn't bad, but it's very long.

It's now 11:45. Dominique and Madeleine are asleep.

Neuvième
Leçon

148

AUTO-TEST

A. According to the cities mentioned, indicate where the city is and tell what language has to be spoken. Follow the model.

1. Il va à Pékin.   *C'est une ville chinoise. Il faut parler chinois.*

2. Nous allons à Mexico.   5. Je vais à Rome.
3. Elles vont à Bonn.   6. Tu vas à Lisbonne.
4. Vous allez à Washington.   7. Elle va à Dakar.

B. Rewrite the sentences in the affirmative, using the adjective that means the opposite of the one given. Follow the model.

1. Alain n'est pas maigre.   5. Le roman n'est pas court.
   Il est gros.   6. Ils ne sont pas célèbres.
                        7. Elles ne sont pas blondes.
2. Le bateau n'est pas étroit.   8. L'histoire n'est pas mauvaise.
3. Sa jupe n'est pas longue.   9. Leurs amies ne sont pas grosses.
4. Marie n'est pas grande.

C. Write complete sentences using the correct form of the words given. Convert the hours to the way in which you would say them and write out the numbers. Follow the model.

1. Je/arriver/à/le stade/vers 7 h. 55
   J'arrive au stade vers huit heures moins cinq.

2. Les poètes/partir/à 11 h. 30
3. Tu/servir/le dîner/à 7 h. 15
4. Nous/finir/nos leçons/vers 9 h. 45
5. Vous/dormir/pendant le concert?
6. Je/partir/pour le marché/à 8 h. 40
7. Nous/sortir/de/le grand magasin/avant 5 h. 20
8. Elles/dormir/à/la bibliothèque!
9. Est-ce qu'il/partir/ou est-ce qu'il/choisir/un livre?

D. Redo the above exercise using the future. Follow the model.

1. Je/arriver/à/le stade/vers 7 h. 55
   Je vais arriver au stade vers huit heures moins cinq.

La nuit, tous les chats sont gris.

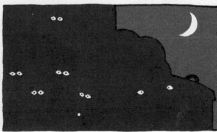

Dixième Leçon

A la terrasse d'un café

Après la classe, Claire, Roger et Maryse vont à la terrasse d'un café. Roger et Maryse commandent des cafés; Claire commande une grenadine.[1] Pendant qu'ils attendent leurs boissons, Roger demande:

See Cultural Supplement.

	ROGER	Qu'est-ce que vous faites ce soir, les filles?[2]
5	CLAIRE	Moi, je finis un roman policier, un Maigret.[3]
	MARYSE	Moi aussi, je reste à la maison. Mais c'est pour faire mes devoirs d'anglais.
	ROGER	Comment est ton prof?
	MARYSE	Pas mauvais.
10	ROGER	Tu parles bien cette langue, alors?
	MARYSE	Mais *of course!*[4]

If any students have read any of Simenon's books— or, perhaps, Agatha Christie's Belgian detective, Hercule Poirot— they may enjoy discussing them. (You might want to point out Christie's regular use of French in her books. A knowledge of the language can make even such very light reading more enjoyable.)

---

[1] *La grenadine*, made from pomegranate juice, is a popular drink in France.

[2] When speaking of more than one girl, the French usually say *les filles* rather than *les jeunes filles*. When speaking directly to them or when speaking of girls and boys together, the French also use *les filles* or *les garçons et les filles*.

[3] Inspector Maigret, a detective created by Belgian-born writer Georges Simenon, is one of the world's most popular fictional policemen.

[4] French students who intend to go to college usually study two foreign languages. Most select English as their "first" language, so it is not unusual to hear them insert simple English words into their conversation—as a joke or to impress their friends.

At a sidewalk café

Note that the English equivalent of *après la classe* is "after school." *Le cours,* the more common term for "course" or "class session," is presented in Lesson 11.

After school, Claire, Roger, and Maryse go to a sidewalk café. Roger and Maryse order coffee; Claire orders a grenadine. While they are waiting for their drinks, Roger asks:

ROGER   What are you doing tonight, girls?

5   CLAIRE   I'm finishing a detective novel, a Maigret.

MARYSE   I'm staying home too—but to do my English homework.

ROGER   How's your teacher?

MARYSE   Not bad.

ROGER   You speak the language well, then?

10   MARYSE   But "of course!"

Questionnaire

1. Où vont Claire, Roger et Maryse après la classe? 2. Qu'est-ce qu'ils commandent? 3. Qu'est-ce que Claire va faire ce soir? Et Maryse? 4. Comment est le professeur d'anglais de Maryse? 5. Est-ce que Maryse parle bien anglais?

PRONONCIATION

The French [r] sound has no equivalent in English. It is pronounced with the tongue in more or less the same position as for the English sound [g]. When you pronounce the [r] sound, the back of your tongue does not quite touch the roof of your mouth.

Exercices

A. Practice the [r] sound in the middle of words.

garage   arriver   parents   pardon   merci   arbre

B. At the end of a word, the [r] sound is very soft. In the following pairs, the first word ends in a vowel sound; the second contains the same vowel, but ends in the [r] sound.

pou/pour   fou/four   lit/lire   soi/soir   pas/par

C. Now practice the [r] sound at the beginning of words.

rue   rouge   robe   rentrer   regarder   restaurant

D. Listen, then say the following sentences aloud.

Richard regarde le roman.   Le professeur regarde leurs devoirs.
Marie rentre du bureau.   Il dort? Alors, je pars pour l'aéroport.

MOTS NOUVEAUX I

l'esquimau: Point out that the plural is *les esquimaux.*

un café
une glace
un esquimau
un Coca
le garçon
la serveuse
une bière
une orangeade
une grenadine
un citron pressé
l'argent (m.)
le billet

On va à la terrasse d'un café.	*We're going to a sidewalk cafe.*
Qu'est-ce que vous allez **commander**?	*What are you going to order?*
Eric commande toujours une glace et un café.	*Eric always orders a dish of ice cream and a cup of coffee.*
Moi, je vais commander une boisson.	*I'm going to order a drink.*
Une orangeade peut-être — ou un citron pressé.[1]	*An orangeade perhaps — or a lemonade.*
Elle travaille bien.	*She works well.*
Oui, et très vite.	*Yes, and very quickly.*
Mais lui, il travaille mal.	*But he works badly.*
Oui, et beaucoup trop lentement.	*Yes, and much too slowly.*
Combien coûte un billet?	*How much does a ticket cost?*
Il coûte peu. Cinq francs.[2]	*It's inexpensive. Five francs.*
Combien coûtent les billets?	*How much do the tickets cost?*
Ils coûtent cher. Quarante francs.	*They're expensive. Forty francs.*

You might want to point out that monetary exchange rates are apt to vary slightly from day to day. We have used a rate of 22 cents to one franc.

[1]In France, lemonade is a kind of do-it-yourself drink. You are served a glass, half a lemon, sugar, and a pitcher of cold water, and you mix the ingredients to your own taste.

[2]The *franc* is worth between twenty and twenty-five cents.

Lesson
10

153

Exercices de vocabulaire

A. Answer the question according to the pictures. Follow the model.

Qu'est-ce que tu commandes?

2. Je commande un es-
   quimau.
3. Je commande un café.
4. Je commande une
   bière.
5. Je commande un citron
   pressé.
6. Je commande un Coca.
7. Je commande une
   orangeade.
8. Je commande une
   glace.

1.

Je commande une grenadine.

2.

3.

4.

5.

6.

7.

8.

1. son billet
2. d'argent
3. la terrasse / des
   boissons / soif
4. les billets / cher
5. lentement
6. une serveuse

B. Choose the word or words that best complete each sentence.

1. Georges part à 7 h. 15. Mais quand il arrive au
   théâtre, il n'a pas *(son vélo / son billet / son café)*.
   Pauvre Georges!
2. Tu ne fais pas tes achats maintenant parce que
   tu n'as pas *(d'argent / d'agent / d'ami)*.
3. Nous allons à *(la terrasse / la terre / la serveuse)* d'un
   café. Nous allons commander *(des corbeilles /
   des dragons / des boissons)* parce que nous avons
   (peur / soif / faim).
4. Ils ne vont pas au cinéma, peut-être parce que
   (les maillots / les billets / les chaises) coûtent
   très *(peu / cher)* — soixante-cinq francs.
5. Il faut être à Reims à 5 h. 30. Mais c'est impossible!
   Le train va trop *(vite / bien / lentement)*.
6. Une fille est quelquefois *(une serveuse / une glace /
   une boisson)*, mais un garçon n'est pas toujours
   un garçon.

Dixième
Leçon

MOTS NOUVEAUX II

Le monsieur là-bas est étranger.	*The gentleman over there is foreign.*	See Cultural Supplement.
La dame[1] est étrangère.	*The lady is foreign.*	
Ils parlent une langue étrangère.	*They're speaking a foreign language.*	
Je vais étudier le français.	*I'm going to study French.*	Although the determiner is often used when an adverb comes between *parler* and the name of the language *(Il parle bien le français),* for simplicity's sake we do not use the determiner in that instance.
L'anglais est une belle langue.	*English is a nice language.*	
Je parle français et anglais.[2]	*I speak French and English.*	
Les gens à côté parlent grec.	*The people nearby speak Greek.*	
L'homme est grec.	*The man is Greek.*	
La femme est grecque aussi.	*The woman is Greek too.*	
Ils habitent Athènes.	*They live in Athens.*	
A Moscou on parle russe.	*In Moscow they speak Russian.*	
Il est russe; elle est russe.	*He's Russian; she's Russian.*	
A Amsterdam on parle hollandais.[3]	*In Amsterdam they speak Dutch.*	
Il est hollandais, n'est-ce pas?	*He's Dutch, isn't he?*	
Non, mais elle est hollandaise.	*No, but she's Dutch.*	
Il est belge; elle est belge.	*He's Belgian; she's Belgian.*	
A Bruxelles on parle français et flamand.	*In Brussels they speak French and Flemish.*	*Bruxelles:* Point out that the *x* is pronounced [s].
A Montréal on parle français.	*In Montreal they speak French.*	
Il est québécois; elle est québécoise.	*He's Quebecois; she's Quebecois.*	
A Stockholm on parle suédois.	*In Stockholm they speak Swedish.*	
Il est suédois; elle est suédoise.	*He's Swedish; she's Swedish.*	
A Copenhague on parle danois.	*In Copenhagen they speak Danish.*	
Il est danois; elle est danoise.	*He's Danish; she's Danish.*	
A Oslo on parle norvégien.	*In Oslo they speak Norwegian.*	
Il est norvégien; elle est norvégienne.	*He's Norwegian; she's Norwegian.*	

C'est le seul garçon.	C'est la seule serveuse.	*only*
C'est le même monsieur.	C'est la même dame.	*same*
C'est l'autre monsieur.	C'est l'autre dame.	*other*
C'est un autre homme.	C'est une autre femme.	*another, a different*
Le garçon est occupé.	La serveuse est occupée.	*busy*
L'appartement est occupé.	La table est occupée.	*occupied*
L'appartement est libre.	La table est libre.	*unoccupied*

---

[1]In pointing someone out, the French almost never say *l'homme,* "the man," or *la femme,* "the woman." They use *le monsieur,* "the gentleman," or *la dame,* "the lady."

[2]The names of languages are masculine, but the definite determiner *le* is not used after the verb *parler.*

[3]The *h* in *hollandais* is an aspirate *h: J'étudie le hollandais.*

See notes at top of p. 157.

Le jeune homme est	La jeune femme est	
fatigué.	fatiguée.	*tired*
inquiet.	inquiète.	*worried*
aimable.	aimable.	*nice*
calé.	calée.	*smart*
Il est sage.	Elle est sage.	*well-behaved*
bête.	bête.	*dumb, stupid*
vraiment bête.	vraiment bête.	*really*

Exercices de vocabulaire

A. Your neighbor is going to a foreign city. Ask if he or she speaks the language used there and express your own liking for it. Follow the model.

1. Je vais à Paris.
   Ah, tu parles français?
   J'aime le français.
2. Je vais à Copenhague.
3. Je vais à Moscou.
4. Je vais à Athènes.
5. Je vais à Amsterdam.
6. Je vais à Pékin.
7. Je vais à Bruxelles.
8. Je vais à Dakar.
9. Je vais à Mexico.
10. Je vais à Oslo.
11. Je vais à Bonn.
12. Je vais à Stockholm.
13. Je vais à Londres.
14. Je vais à Tokyo.

B. Tell the nationality of the people mentioned. Follow the model.

1. Tu habites Paris?
   Oui, je suis français. or *Oui, je suis française.*
2. Vous habitez Athènes, mesdames?
3. Ils habitent Stockholm?
4. Vous habitez Moscou, messieurs?
5. Elles habitent Copenhague?
6. Elles habitent Amsterdam?
7. Elle habite Oslo?
8. Elles habitent Madrid?
9. Il habite Québec?
10. Tu habites Bruxelles?
11. Ils habitent Athènes?

C. Choose the adjective that best completes each sentence. Then make any necessary changes so that it agrees with the noun it is modifying.

1. Patricia a sommeil. Elle est toujours *(fatigué/occupé)*.
2. C'est lui, le garçon qui sert notre dîner? Non, c'est *(un autre/le même)* garçon.
3. J'aime leur enfant. Il est toujours *(bête/sage)*.
4. Notre voiture est très vieille et nous allons faire un long voyage. Maman est vraiment *(calé/inquiet)*.
5. Tu aimes les enfants de tes voisins? Bien sûr. Ils sont très *(aimable/bête)*.
6. J'aime être près de la fenêtre. Est-ce que la table là-bas est *(inquiet/libre)*? Non, madame. Malheureusement les tables près de la fenêtre sont *(libre/occupé)*.
7. Combien de serveuses travaillent ici? Moi, je suis la *(même/seul)* serveuse aujourd'hui.

EXPLICATIONS I

Les verbes réguliers en -re

calé: Note that this word means "smart" as teenagers use it, meaning "well-informed," "knowledgeable."

sage: Though this word means "wise," we use it only in its more limited sense of "well-behaved."

	VOCABULAIRE		
attendre[1]	*to wait, to wait for*	répondre à[2]	*to answer*
entendre	*to hear*	vendre	*to sell*
perdre	*to lose*		

The last main type of regular verbs has infinitives ending in *-re.*

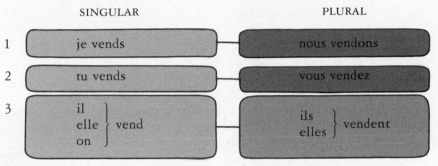

	SINGULAR		PLURAL
1	je vends		nous vendons
2	tu vends		vous vendez
3	il elle } vend on		ils elles } vendent

IMPERATIVE: vends! vendons! vendez!

1. The stem is the infinitive form, minus the *-re* ending.

2. In the plural, the pattern is the same as with *-er* verbs. The plural endings are added and the final consonant of the stem is pronounced.

3. In the singular, the final consonant of the stem is not pronounced. An *s* is added for the 1 and 2 sing. forms, and all three forms are pronounced the same.

Exercice

Replace the verbs in italics with the appropriate form of the verbs in parentheses. Follow the model.

1. Nous *dînons* au restaurant. (attendre)   *Nous attendons au restaurant.*

2. Ils *finissent* le match de hockey. (perdre)

3. Je *téléphone* à Blanche. (répondre)

4. Tu *donnes* tes romans policiers à Frédéric? (vendre)

5. Nous *écoutons* le garçon. (entendre)

6. Vous *arrivez* chez Jacqueline. (attendre)

7. Qu'est-ce que tu *demandes* à Patrick? (vendre)

8. Gabrielle *apporte* les billets. (perdre)

9. *Téléphone* à ta maman, s'il te plaît! (répondre)

10. Je *regarde* les enfants qui *jouent* dans le jardin. (entendre/attendre)

[1]Like *écouter,* "to listen to," *attendre,* "to wait for," is not followed by a preposition.
[2]Like *téléphoner, répondre* is followed by a form of *à.*

You might want to present a simple oral drill using disjunctives before doing the exercise in the book. E.g., *Je réponds au professeur. Et eux? Ils répondent au professeur aussi.*

2. Ils perdent le match de hockey.
3. Je réponds à Blanche.
4. Tu vends tes romans policiers à Frédéric?
5. Nous entendons le garçon.
6. Vous attendez chez Jacqueline.
7. Qu'est-ce que tu vends à Patrick?
8. Gabrielle perd les billets.
9. Réponds à ta maman, s'il te plait!
10. J'entends les enfants qui attendent dans le jardin.

Plural prenominal adjectives are presented in Lesson 13.

Les adjectifs singuliers placés avant le nom

In French, most adjectives come after the noun. For example: *une robe blanche, un garçon français, des femmes avares.* Some common adjectives, however, usually come before the noun.

1. Look at the following:

C'est un **joli** jardin.   C'est une **jolie** bibliothèque.
C'est un **joli** arbre.   C'est une **jolie** histoire.
C'est le **seul** jardin.   C'est la **seule** bibliothèque.
C'est le **seul** arbre.   C'est la **seule** histoire.

Adjectives that end in a vowel or in a pronounced consonant do not change pronunciation when they are used before nouns.

2. Now look at the following:

Voilà un **petit** camion.   Voilà une **petite** carte.
Voilà un **petit** avion.   Voilà une **petite** affiche.
          [t]

When a masculine adjective ending in an unpronounced consonant comes before a noun beginning with a vowel sound, the final consonant is pronounced. In the feminine forms, this consonant is always pronounced.

3. Look at *grand* and *gros:*

C'est un **grand** château.   C'est une **grande** maison.
C'est un **grand** hôtel.   C'est une **grande** église.
          [t]

C'est un **gros** nuage.   C'est une **grosse** voiture.
C'est un **gros** avion.   C'est une **grosse** étoile.
          [z]

Before a masculine noun beginning with a vowel sound, the *d* of *grand* is pronounced [t], and the *s* of *gros* is pronounced [z]. The corresponding feminine forms end in a [d] and an [s] sound.

4. Here are some adjectives that may come before the noun:

TYPE 1: autre, jeune, joli, large, même, pauvre,[1] seul
TYPE 2: long, mauvais, petit
TYPE 3: grand, gros

With the exception of *pauvre,* we do not use any of these adjectives postnominally.

---

[1]When *pauvre* is used before a noun, it means "unlucky" or "pitiful." After a noun it means "without money."

Exercices

A. Put the adjective in parentheses before the noun. Follow the model.

1. Le professeur porte un chapeau *(grand)*.
   Le professeur porte un grand chapeau.

2. Le monsieur *(gros)* parle à son ami.
3. Il y a un hôtel *(grand)* en face du théâtre.
4. Il y a un enfant *(petit)* là-bas, avec un vélo.
5. L'auteur finit un roman *(mauvais)*.
6. L'élève *(autre)* porte un pull-over.
7. C'est le train *(seul)* aujourd'hui.

B. Redo the sentences using the adjectives in parentheses. Pay close attention to the position of the adjectives. Follow the model.

1. On joue une pièce en ville. (autre / étranger)
   On joue une autre pièce étrangère en ville.

2. Ils étudient un poème. (danois / long)
3. Ils ont une villa. (blanche / jolie)
4. Vous attendez toujours le garçon? (même / paresseux)
5. Malheureusement, c'est la table. (libre / seule)
6. Elle vend un roman. (autre / policier)
7. C'est un auteur. (célèbre / jeune)
8. Le chapeau coûte cher. (grand / rouge)

Vérifiez vos progrès

Write complete sentences using the correct form of the words given and putting the adjectives in their appropriate form and position. Follow the model.

1. La dame *(fatigué, pauvre)* / demander / son argent
   La pauvre dame fatiguée demande son argent.

2. Je / vendre / ma jupe *(joli, norvégien)*
3. Une dame *(grec, jeune)* / attendre / le train *(même)*
4. Nous / répondre / à / la fille *(aimable, petit)*
5. Elle / commander / une boisson *(autre, froid)*
6. Elles / entendre / une langue *(autre, étranger)*

CONVERSATION ET LECTURE

Parlons de vous

1. Quelle heure est-il? 2. Quel temps fait-il aujourd'hui? 3. Quelle est
la date? 4. Est-ce que vous êtes souvent occupé? Est-ce que vous travaillez
beaucoup? Qu'est-ce que vous faites? Est-ce que vous travaillez vite ou lentement? 5. Est-ce que vous êtes quelquefois inquiet? Quand et pourquoi?
6. Combien de langues est-ce que vous parlez? Vous connaissez ("know")
des gens qui parlent une langue étrangère? Si "oui," quelle langue est-ce
qu'ils parlent?

Au café

See Cultural Supplement.

Il est midi et demie et M. Germain entre dans le
café tabac des Sports,[1] avenue de la République.[2] Il
s'installe° à une petite table près de la fenêtre,
parce qu'il aime regarder les gens dans la rue. Il
5 commande une bière et un sandwich au jambon.°
"Tout de suite,° monsieur," répond le garçon.

Monsieur Germain déjeune souvent à ce café. C'est
un habitué.° D'habitude° il arrive à la même heure
avec son journal et s'installe à la même table. Il
10 habite loin de son bureau, trop loin pour rentrer
chez lui à l'heure du déjeuner.[3] Voilà pourquoi il va
si° souvent au café.

Aujourd'hui, la table derrière lui n'est pas occupée.
Mais à côté il y a une jeune fille blonde. Devant
15 elle, il y a un café crème[4] et des livres. Près de la
porte, des garçons et des filles jouent à la machine
à sous.° Ce sont des élèves du lycée d'en face.° Eux
aussi, ils ont des sandwichs et des boissons. Et
voici une jeune fille, une brune, qui arrive. Elle va
20 à la table près de M. Germain où l'autre jeune fille
attend. Monsieur Germain ne peut° pas entendre
leur conversation, mais la jeune fille blonde donne
un petit cadeau° à son amie. C'est peut-être son anni-
versaire° aujourd'hui.

s'installer: *to sit
down*
le jambon: *ham*
tout de suite: *right
away*

l'habitué, -e: *regular
customer*
d'habitude: *usually*

si: *(here) so*

la machine à sous:
pinball machine
d'en face: *across the
street*
pouvoir: *to be able*

le cadeau: *gift*
l'anniversaire *(m.)*:
birthday

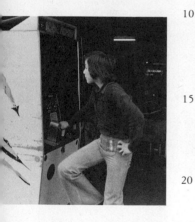

---

[1]A license is required to sell tobacco products. Certain stores, called *les bureaux de tabac,* spe-
cialize in tobacco. Some cafés, called *les cafés tabac,* also hold such a license.

[2]This avenue in Paris runs into the Place de la République, a large square where there is a
monument commemorating the birth of the French Republic in 1792.

[3]Until very recently almost all working people in France had a two-hour lunch break and went
home at noon. This was often the big meal of the day, with the evening meal being more of a
light supper.

[4]A *café crème* is a cup of coffee with cream; a *café au lait,* usually served in a bowl and only at
breakfast, is half coffee and half steamed milk.

25 Monsieur Germain finit sa bière et son sandwich et
il regarde sa montre.° Il faut rentrer au bureau. Il   la montre: *watch*
demande l'addition.° "Voilà, monsieur," répond le   l'addition (*f.*): *check*
garçon. "Au revoir et merci."

À propos ...

1. Quelle heure est-il quand M. Germain entre dans le café?   2. Pourquoi
est-ce qu'il choisit la table près de la fenêtre?   3. Qu'est-ce qu'il commande?
4. Pourquoi est-ce que M. Germain déjeune si souvent au café?   5. Qui est
à la table à côté? Qu'est-ce qu'elle a devant elle?   6. Que font les jeunes
gens qui sont près de la porte? Qu'est-ce qu'ils ont?   7. Qu'est-ce que la
jeune fille blonde donne à son amie? Est-ce que M. Germain entend leur
conversation?   8. Pourquoi est-ce que M. Germain demande tout de suite
l'addition?   9. Et vous, est-ce que vous allez quelquefois au café? Est-ce
qu'il y a un café près de votre lycée? Est-ce que vous allez là-bas pendant
l'heure du déjeuner ou après la classe? Qu'est-ce que vous commandez?
10. Est-ce que vous aimez jouer aux machines à sous? Ça coûte cher?

EXPLICATIONS II

Les déterminants démonstratifs: ce, cet, cette, ces

The demonstrative determiners *ce, cet,* and *cette* mean "this" or "that." *Ces* means "these" or "those." Note how they are used:

Ce monsieur va à cet hôtel.　　Ces messieurs vont à ces hôtels.
Cette dame vend cette image.　　Ces dames vendent ces images.

Ce and *cet* are used before masculine singular nouns—*ce* before a consonant sound and *cet* before a vowel sound. *Cette* is used before all feminine singular nouns. *Ces* is used before all plural nouns. Before a vowel sound, the final *s* is a liaison consonant, pronounced [z].

Exercices

A.　Answer the questions according to the pictures. Use the appropriate demonstrative determiner *ce* or *cette.* Follow the models.

3. Je ferme cette fenêtre (s'il fait froid).
4. Ce café est chaud.
5. Ce supermarché est nouveau.
6. Elles écoutent cette radio.
7. Ce nuage est beau.
8. Ce roman est court.
9. Elles vendent cette robe.
10. Cette bière est mauvaise.
11. Cette étoile est belle.
12. Elles attendent ce train.

1. Qu'est-ce qui est grand?
   Ce bateau est grand.

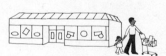

2. Qu'est-ce que tu vends?
   Je vends cette moto.

3. Qu'est-ce que tu fermes s'il fait froid?

4. Qu'est-ce qui est chaud?

5. Qu'est-ce qui est nouveau?

6. Qu'est-ce qu'elles écoutent?

7. Qu'est-ce qui est beau?

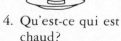

8. Qu'est-ce qui est court?

9. Qu'est-ce qu'elles vendent?

10. Qu'est-ce qui est mauvais?

11. Qu'est-ce qui est beau?

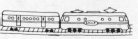

12. Qu'est-ce qu'elles attendent?

B. Redo the above exercise in the plural. Follow the models.

1. Qu'est-ce qui est grand? *Ces bateaux sont grands.*
2. Qu'est-ce que tu vends? *Je vends ces motos.*

C. Answer the questions using the cues in parentheses and the appropriate demonstrative determiner *cet* or *cette*. Follow the models.

1. Quand est-ce qu'ils font leur voyage? (l'hiver)
   Ils font leur voyage cet hiver.
2. Qu'est-ce que Charles aime? (l'orangeade)
   Il aime cette orangeade.
3. Qui est aimable? (l'auteur)
4. Qu'est-ce qu'il faut finir? (l'histoire)
5. Quand est-ce que Marc rentre chez lui? (l'après-midi)
6. Qu'est-ce qu'elles écoutent? (l'opéra)
7. Qu'est-ce que tu choisis? (l'affiche)
8. Qu'est-ce que vous regardez dans le ciel? (l'étoile)
9. Qu'est-ce qu'ils perdent? (l'argent)
10. Qu'est-ce que tu vends? (l'image)
11. Qu'est-ce qui est très grand? (l'hôpital)
12. Qui sert nos boissons? (l'autre serveuse)

Vérifiez vos progrès

Rewrite the sentences, changing the words in italics to the singular. Follow the model.

1. Il répond lentement à *ces jeunes femmes.*
   Il répond lentement à cette jeune femme.
2. Samedi elles vont à *ces marchés.*
3. Donnez *ces journaux* à papa, s'il vous plaît.
4. Arnaud regarde *ces étoiles.*
5. Son père joue quelquefois aux cartes avec *ces messieurs.*
6. Je n'aime pas *ces hôtels.*
7. Est-ce que vous entendez *ces avions* dans le ciel?
8. Il va perdre *ces stylos.*
9. Je ne révise pas *ces histoires.*
10. En automne il y a des feuilles jaunes sur *ces arbres.*

3. Je ferme ces fenêtres (s'il fait froid).
4. Ces cafés sont chauds.
5. Ces supermarchés sont nouveaux.
6. Elles écoutent ces radios.
7. Ces nuages sont beaux.
8. Ces romans sont courts.
9. Elles vendent ces robes.
10. Ces bières sont mauvaises.
11. Ces étoiles sont belles.
12. Elles attendent ces trains.

3. Cet auteur est aimable.
4. Il faut finir cette histoire.
5. Il rentre chez lui cet après-midi.
6. Elles écoutent cet opéra.
7. Je choisis cette affiche.
8. Nous regardons (Je regarde) cette étoile (dans le ciel).
9. Ils perdent cet argent.
10. Je vends cette image.
11. Cet hôpital est très grand.
12. Cette autre serveuse sert vos (nos) boissons.

BIÈRES
Beers

Pression

Kronenbourg Export
le demi .. 3.00
le baron .. 6.00
la chope .. 2.00

Kronenbourg 1664
Thomas Brau
le demi .. 3.50
le baron .. 7.00
la chope .. 1.40

Bouteilles
Kanterbräu 4.00
Kronenbourg
Kronenbourg 1664
Pelforth brune
Tuborg
Paulaner ... 4.50
Guiness
Bass Pale Ale
Heineken ...

BOISSONS FROIDES
Cold drinks

Lait froid .. 3.00
Lait froid aromatisé .. 3.50
Vittel, Perrier, Vichy, Limonade .. 3.00
avec sirop (1/4) - Gini .. 3.50
Bitter San Pellegrino - Gini .. 3.00
Schweppes " Indian Tonic " .. 3.50
Schweppes dry Ginger Ale .. 3.50
Orangina, Ricqlès, Tobler, Sodas, Gini .. 3.50
Pepsi-Cola
Pepsi-Cola à la pression
Pschitt orange-citron à la pression
Tonic à la pression .. 3.00
Jus de fruits - Jus de tomate .. 3.00
Orange ou citron pressé .. 3.50
Cidre .. 4.00
Thé glacé .. 3.50
Café glacé .. 4.00
Pippermint à l'eau .. 3.50
Marie Brizard à l'eau .. 3.50

RÉVISION ET THÈME

See Teacher's Section for
answers to the *révision*
and *thème*.

Review of:
1. demonstrative determiners
   agreement and position
   of adjectives
   adjectives of nation-
   ality
2. demonstrative determiners
   prepositions
   position of adjectives
3. agreement and position
   of adjectives
4. -re verbs
5. adverbs
   -re verbs vs. a similar-
   sounding -er verb
   (commander)

Consult the model sentences, then put the English cues into French and use them to form new sentences based on the models.

1. *Ce soir*, les Dufort vont à *un petit théâtre espagnol* à New York.
   (This week)   *(a large Greek restaurant)*
   (This morning)   *(a small German library)*

2. *Cette maison est en face d'un château célèbre.*
   (Those flowers are under a big tree.)
   (That hospital is near a pretty park.)

3. *Il écoute un long opéra français.*
   (He's watching the same stupid western.)
   (He's looking at another cartoon.)

4. *Là, nous vendons les disques.*
   (she hears the wind)
   (you (sing.) *wait for the waitress)*

5. *Je travaille lentement, et le professeur attend mes devoirs.*
   (He plays badly, and they lose the game.)
   (The drinks aren't expensive, and we order a lemonade and a beer.)

Now that you have done the *Révision*, you are ready to write a composition. Put the English captions describing each cartoon panel into French to form a paragraph.

This afternoon, the Ballards are having lunch at a small Dutch café in London.

This café is next to a large hotel.

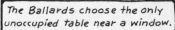

The Ballards choose the only unoccupied table near a window.

There they wait for the waiter.

The waiter arrives quickly and they order Cokes.

AUTO-TEST

A. Replace the italicized determiners with the correct form of the demonstrative determiner and use the appropriate form of the verb in parentheses. Follow the model.

1. Ils ne *(perdre)* pas *l'*argent.
   Ils ne perdent pas cet argent.

2. Je *(vendre)* *la* grande maison rouge.
3. *Le* garçon et *la* serveuse *(servir)* le déjeuner.
4. *Le* professeur ne *(répondre)* pas à *un* élève.
5. Elles *(commander)* le bon citron pressé.
6. Tu *(attendre)* *une* amie à *l'*hôtel?
7. Nous ne *(répondre)* pas à *la* porte après 7 h. 30.
8. Vous *(entendre)* *les* langues étrangères souvent en ville?

B. From the column on the right, choose the most logical response to each statement on the left.

1. Ces dames sont étrangères.
2. C'est un enfant aimable.
3. Cinquante-six pages.
4. Elle parle grec et danois.
5. Les hommes sont fatigués.
6. Soixante francs, madame.

a. Ces billets coûtent trop cher.
b. C'est une très longue histoire!
c. Deux langues étrangères?
d. Il faut travailler lentement.
e. Oui, et très sage aussi.
f. Oui, norvégiennes peut-être.

C. Rewrite the sentences using the cues in parentheses. Be careful to put the adjectives in the correct position. Follow the model.

1. Ce roman est difficile. (la pièce)
   C'est une pièce difficile.

2. Ce monsieur est gros. (la dame)
3. Cet homme est fatigué. (la fille)
4. Ce café est froid. (la boisson)
5. Cet enfant est étranger. (la langue)
6. Cet hôtel est petit. (la bibliothèque)
7. Cet autre garçon est aimable. (la serveuse)
8. Ce jeune homme est calé. (la femme)

Proverbe

Qui va à la chasse perd sa place.

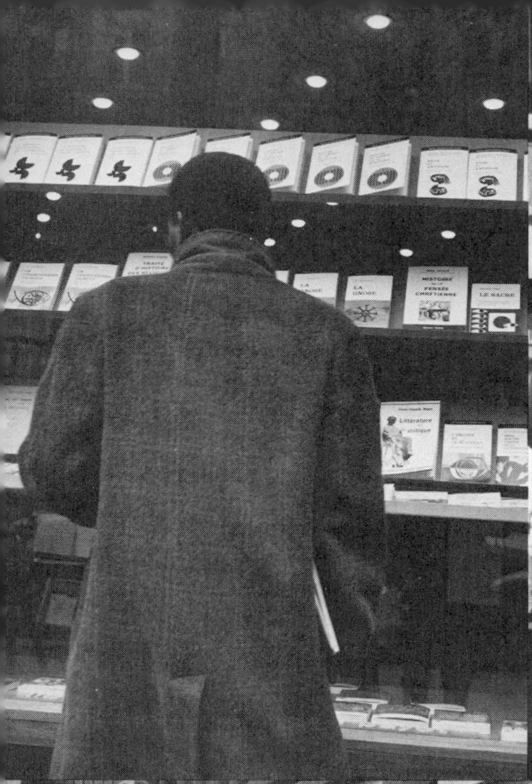

HISTOIRE
PENSÉE CHRÉTIENNE
LA GNOSE
LE SACRÉ
Littérature

POP ART
JOSEPH KESSEL
LES FILS DE L'IMPOSSIBLE

Homéopathie
Orthopédie
Acoustique
CALES
RASOIR
l'efficacité, c'est sa grille en acier au
le confort, c'est sa tête inclinée
PHILIPS
PHILIPS
Prix spécial
r la "Fête des Pères"

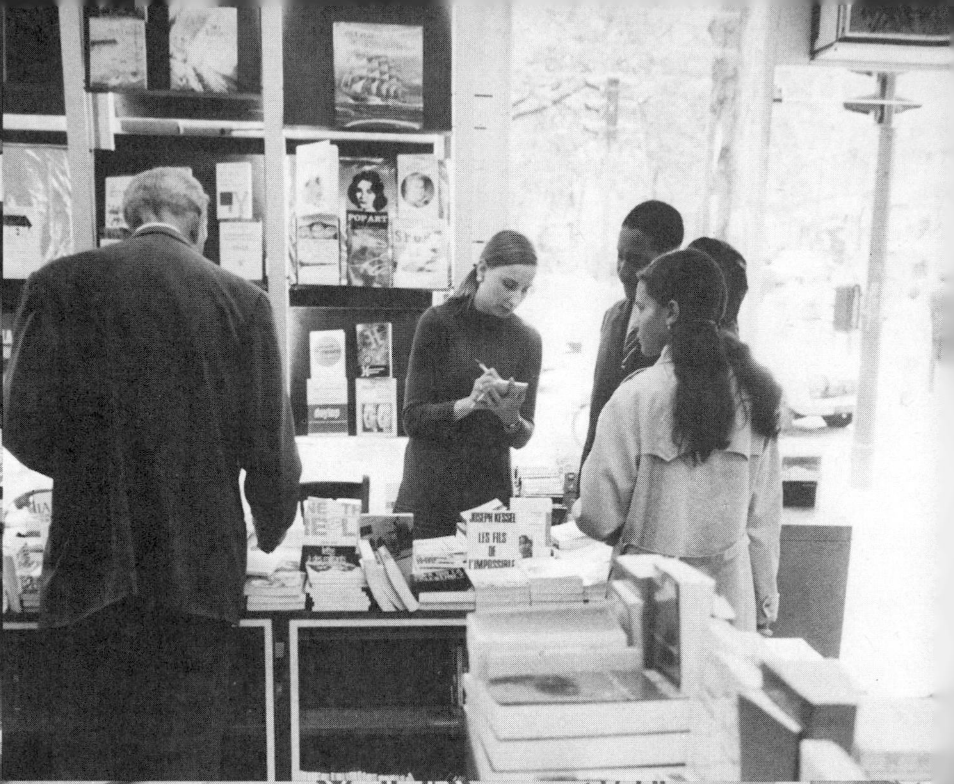

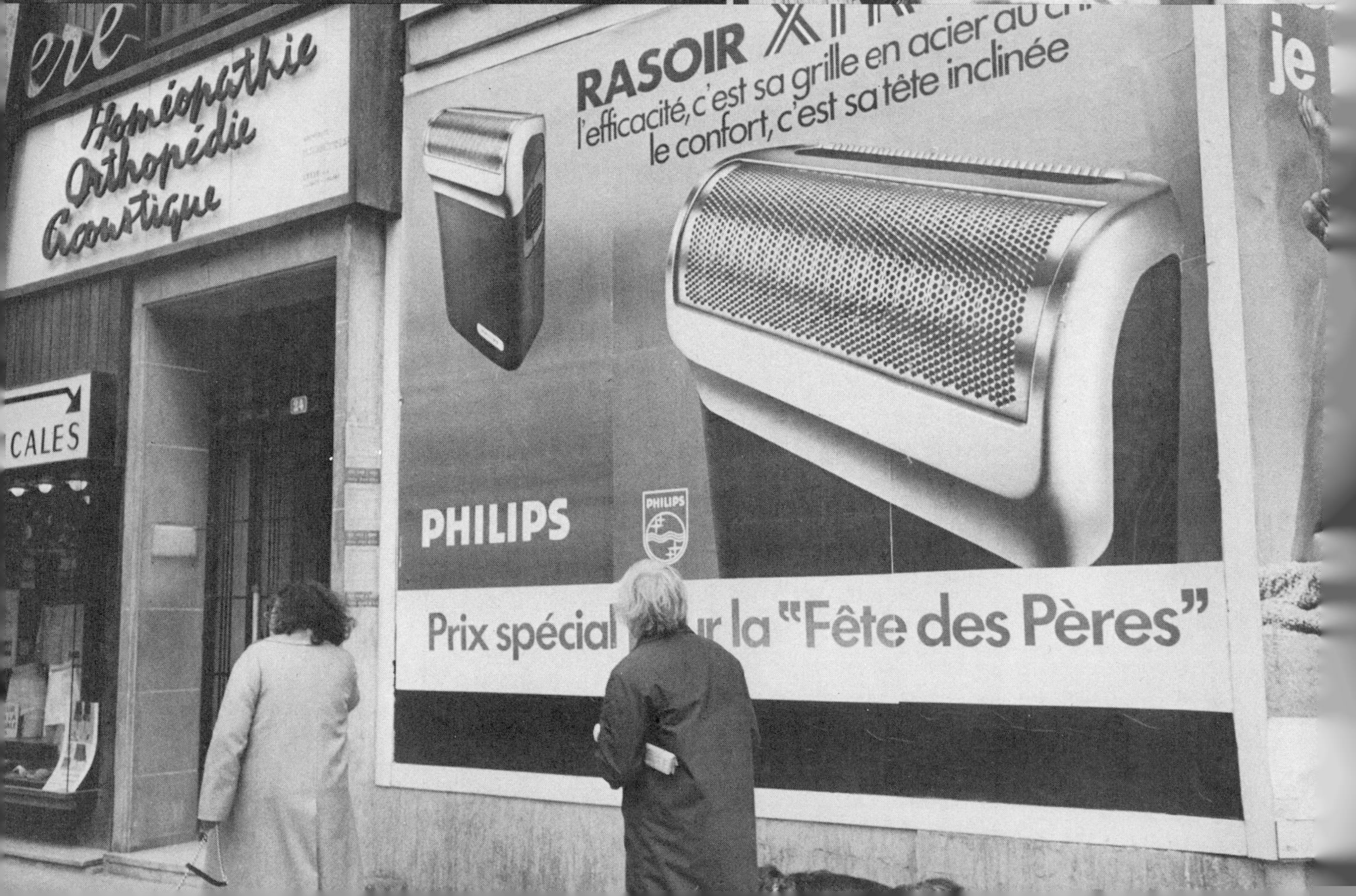

Onzième Leçon

A la librairie

Dimanche prochain, c'est la Fête des Pères.[1] Hier matin, Claude a cherché un cadeau pour offrir à son père. Il a regardé des livres dans une grande librairie.

See Cultural Supplement.

LE VENDEUR	Qu'est-ce qu'il aime, votre père?
5 CLAUDE	Les livres!
LE VENDEUR	Euh . . . bien sûr. Mais qu'est-ce qu'il fait, par exemple?
CLAUDE	Il est professeur. Il enseigne la biologie.
LE VENDEUR	Eh bien, j'ai ce très joli livre d'histoire naturelle. Les photos sont vraiment belles.
10 CLAUDE	Humm . . . Mais ça coûte très cher, n'est-ce pas?
LE VENDEUR	Soixante-huit francs, monsieur.
CLAUDE	Oui, c'est cher. Et ce petit livre?
LE VENDEUR	Trois francs cinquante.[2] Mais c'est un livre de poche!
CLAUDE	Oui, mais c'est le geste qui compte, n'est-ce pas?

l'histoire naturelle: This is not made part of the active vocabulary of the book.

---

[1]Father's Day is in June, but not always on the same day in France as in the U.S. and Canada.
[2]Three francs, fifty centimes, is equivalent to about 80 cents. (There are 100 centimes to a franc.) The rate of monetary exchange changes constantly according to world economic conditions.

At the bookstore

Next Sunday is Father's Day. Yesterday morning Claude looked for a gift to give his father. He looked at some books in a large bookstore.

	SALESPERSON	What does your father like?
	CLAUDE	Books!
5	SALESPERSON	Um, yes, of course. But what does he do, for example?
	CLAUDE	He's a teacher. He teaches biology.
	SALESPERSON	Well, I have this very nice book on natural history. The photos are really lovely.
	CLAUDE	Hmm . . . But it's very expensive, isn't it?
10	SALESPERSON	Sixty-eight francs.
	CLAUDE	Yes, that's expensive! What about this little book?
	SALESPERSON	Three francs fifty. But that's a paperback!
	CLAUDE	Yes, but it's the thought that counts, right?[1]

Questionnaire

1. Pourquoi est-ce que Claude cherche un cadeau pour son père? 2. Quand est-ce que Claude a cherché le cadeau? Où est-ce qu'il a cherché le cadeau? 3. Qu'est-ce que le père de Claude fait? Qu'est-ce qu'il enseigne? 4. Qu'est-ce que le vendeur montre à Claude d'abord? Comment sont les photos? 5. Est-ce que Claude aime ce livre? Combien coûte ce livre? 6. Qu'est-ce que Claude choisit pour offrir à son père? Est-ce que c'est cher? Combien? 7. Est-ce que le vendeur est aimable? Est-ce que Claude est généreux?

PRONONCIATION

Listen carefully and compare how the letter *o* is pronounced in the following words: *poste, école; maillot, stylo*. The sound in *poste* and *école* is an [ɔ] sound. In French, this sound is always followed by a pronounced consonant. The sound in *maillot* and *stylo* is an [o] sound. The lips are much more rounded for the [o] sound than for the [ɔ] sound.

Exercices

A. Listen carefully, then say the following words aloud.

la porte	la poste	l'école	Nicole
le stylo	le maillot	le drapeau	le cadeau

B. Practice the [ɔ] sound. Round your lips before pronouncing the vowel, then release the final consonant sound clearly.

Elle va à Lisbonne.	Le prof de Simone va à Bonn.
Il va à Moscou.	Olivier demande un livre de poche.
Nous allons à Stockholm.	Nicole va offrir un roman à Roger.

[1]In French, the expression is, "It's the gesture that counts."

C. Now practice the [o] sound. Round your lips more than you did for the
[ɔ] sound.

C'est le vélo de Gauthier.   Au revoir, Bruno.
C'est sa radio aussi.   Au revoir, Claude.
C'est le stylo d'Aude.   Au revoir, Pauline.

MOTS NOUVEAUX I

Elle aime faire la grasse matinée.   *She likes to sleep late.*
Elle dort toujours jusqu'à 10 h.   *She always sleeps until 10:00.*
Elle va passer la journée chez elle.   *She's going to spend the day at home.*
Je passe la matinée à la maison.   *I spend the (whole) morning at home.*
    la soirée   *the (whole) evening*
    la journée   *the (whole) day*

Il va offrir un cadeau à maman?[1]   *Is he going to give Mom a gift?*
Oui, c'est la Fête des Mères.   *Yes, it's Mother's Day.*
Et pour la Fête des Pères?   *And for Father's Day?*
Il offre un livre de poche à papa.[2]   *He's giving Dad a paperback.*

Il travaille à la librairie.   *He works at the bookstore.*
C'est un vendeur. Et elle?   *He's a salesperson. What about her?*
C'est une vendeuse.   *She's a salesperson.*
Quelquefois il faut compter les   *Sometimes they have to count the*
   livres.   *books.*

Il faut trouver un cadeau.   *I have to find a gift.*
Qu'est-ce que tu vas chercher,   *What are you going to look for,*
   par exemple?   *for example?*

Le livre est cher.   *The book's expensive.*
La photo est très chère.[3]   *The photograph is very expensive.*
C'est le geste qui compte!   *It's the thought that counts!*

Help students see that *la matinée, la soirée,* and *la journée* represent duration and are used with such words as *passer* and *pendant,* which imply the passing of time.

---

[1]Like *ouvrir, offrir* follows the pattern of *-er* verbs in the present tense: *j'offre, tu offres,* etc. Note, too, that like *donner, téléphoner, répondre,* etc., *offrir* requires the use of *à: Nous offrons des cadeaux à papa.*

[2]The plural of *le livre de poche* is *les livres de poche.*

[3]When it is used with *coûter,* the word *cher* is an adverb. When it is used with *être,* it is an adjective, so it must agree with the noun:

    Les photos coûtent cher.

but: Les photos sont chères.

Exercice de vocabulaire

From the column on the right, choose the most logical response to each statement or question on the left. The answers to 1–6 will be found in a–f; the answers to 7–12 will be found in g–l.

1. a
2. c
3. d
4. b
5. f
6. e

1. Ça coûte 62 F 50, madame.
2. Elle travaille en ville?
3. Il vend des livres?
4. Pourquoi est-ce que tu cherches un cadeau pour maman?
5. Qu'est-ce que tu offres à Dominique?
6. Tu vas à la bibliothèque?

a. Cette affiche est beaucoup trop chère.
b. Dimanche, c'est la Fête des Mères.
c. Oui, c'est une vendeuse au grand magasin.
d. Oui, il travaille dans une librairie.
e. Oui, il faut aller chercher un livre de biologie.
f. Un livre de poche peut-être.

7. h
8. j
9. k
10. l
11. g
12. i

7. Elle est au bureau de 9 h. jusqu'à 6 h. 45.
8. Elle dort toujours?
9. Il faut trouver un bon restaurant.
10. Maintenant, mes enfants, comptons jusqu'à vingt.
11. Qui est cette jolie jeune femme, papa?
12. Tu vas au théâtre ce soir?

g. C'est une photo de grand-maman.
h. C'est une très longue journée.
i. Non, je passe la soirée chez moi.
j. Oui, elle fait la grasse matinée aujourd'hui.
k. Oui, j'ai faim aussi.
l. Un, deux, trois, quatre, . . .

Onzième
Leçon

170

MOTS NOUVEAUX II

Elle est professeur.[1]	She's a teacher.	See Cultural Supplement.
Elle va enseigner l'anglais.	She's going *to teach* English.	
Il est étudiant.	He's *a student.*	The professions are presented in Lesson 13.
Elle est étudiante.	She's *a student.*	
Ils vont faire de l'anglais.	They're going *to take* English.	

Il enseigne la biologie.	He teaches *biology.*
la chimie	*chemistry*
la physique	*physics*
les mathématiques *(f. pl.)*	*mathematics*
l'algèbre *(f.)*	*algebra*
la géométrie	*geometry*

Je fais de la géographie.	I *take* geography.
de l'histoire *(f.)*	*history*
des sciences sociales *(f. pl.)*	*social studies*
du français	*French*
de l'espagnol	*Spanish*

J'ai un cours de français ce matin.	I have *a* French *class* this morning.
Elle va assister à ce cours?	Is she going *to attend* that class?
Oui, il faut passer un **examen.**	Yes, we have *to take a test.*
Elle va **réussir à** l'examen.[2]	She'll **pass** the exam.
Elle ne va pas **rater** l'examen.	She won't **fail** the exam.

Ils vont à l'université *(f.)*.	They go to *the university.*
Il est **nul en** espagnol mais **fort en** maths.[3]	He's **no good in** Spanish but **good in** math.
Elle est **nulle en** français mais **forte en** chimie.	She's **no good in** French but **good in** chemistry.

Il va **poser une question.**	He's going **to ask a question.**	Help students see the difference between *poser une question* "to pose a question" and *demander (à),* "to ask (someone)" or "to ask for."
La réponse est **correcte.**	The answer's **right.**	
La réponse n'est pas **correcte.**	The answer's **wrong.**	

Le mot est **correct.**	The word is correct.
La phrase est **correcte.**	The sentence is correct.
Le chapitre est **difficile.**	The chapter is difficult.

Le **mois prochain** il va au lycée.	*Next month* he's going to school.
L'**année prochaine**	*Next year*
Lundi prochain	*Next Monday*

Je suis **sur la route.**	I'm *on the road.*
Je suis **en route** pour Paris.	I'm *on the way to Paris.*

---

[1]After a personal subject pronoun (*je, tu, il, elle,* etc.) + *être,* the French do not use the definite determiner with professions. Compare: *C'est un professeur,* but *Il est professeur; C'est une étudiante,* but *Elle est étudiante.*

[2]*Réussir à* is an *-ir/-iss-* verb.

[3]*Les mathématiques* is often shortened to *les maths.*

Exercices de vocabulaire

A. Use the appropriate form of the verb in parentheses which best completes each sentence. Follow the model.

1. Elle *(rater/réussir à)* ces examens parce qu'elle est nulle en géométrie.
   Elle rate ces examens parce qu'elle est nulle en géométrie.

2. Samedi prochain, nous *(poser/passer)* un examen au lycée.

3. Quand les étudiants sont forts, les professeurs aiment bien *(étudier/enseigner)*.

4. Parce qu'ils sont sages, Jean-Paul et Didier *(attendre toujours/assister toujours à)* leurs cours.

5. Vous êtes très calés. Alors vous *(réussir/répondre)* toujours aux examens.

6. Il ne faut pas *(porter/poser)* vos questions quand le professeur parle aux étudiants.

7. Nous sommes étudiants. L'année prochaine nous allons *(enseigner les/faire des)* maths à l'université.

8. Tu *(ouvrir/offrir)* un joli cadeau à ta sœur.

2. passons
3. enseigner
4. assistent toujours à
5. réussissez
6. poser
7. faire des
8. offres

B. Answer the question *Qu'est-ce qu'il fait?* or *Qu'est-ce qu'elle fait?* according to the pictures. Follow the models.

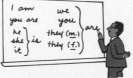

1. *Il enseigne l'anglais.*

2. *Elle fait de l'espagnol.*

3.

4.

5.

6.

7.

8.

9.

10.

3. Il fait de la géographie.
4. Elle enseigne la biologie.
5. Elle fait des sciences sociales.
6. Il enseigne la physique.
7. Il enseigne l'histoire.
8. Il fait du français.
9. Elle fait de la chimie.
10. Elle enseigne l'algèbre.

11.   12.

11. Il fait des mathématiques (maths).
12. Elle fait de la géométrie.

EXPLICATIONS I

Les verbes <u>pouvoir</u> et <u>vouloir</u>

Two very common French verbs, *pouvoir*, "to be able, can," and *vouloir*, "to want," follow the same pattern in the present tense:

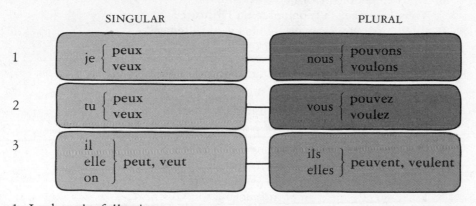

	SINGULAR		PLURAL
1	je { peux / veux	nous	{ pouvons / voulons
2	tu { peux / veux	vous	{ pouvez / voulez
3	il / elle / on } peut, veut	ils / elles	} peuvent, veulent

You may want to teaoh the
imperative forms: *veuille*
and *veuillez,* meaning
"please." We have reserved them until Level II.

1. Look at the following:

   Je veux offrir un cadeau à papa.   *I want to give a present to Dad.*
   Je ne peux pas trouver ce livre   *I can't find that paperback.*
   de poche.

   A verb that comes immediately after *vouloir* and *pouvoir* is always in the infinitive.

2. More polite first person forms of the verb *vouloir* are very often used. They are called "conditional" and are the equivalent of "I'd like" and "we'd like":

   Je voudrais une glace.   *I'd like a dish of ice cream.*
   Nous voudrions commander une glace.   *We'd like to order ice cream.*

3. Another very common use of the verb *vouloir* is in the expression *vouloir dire*, "to mean":

   Qu'est-ce que tu veux dire?   *What do you mean?*
   Qu'est-ce que ces phrases veulent   *What do those sentences mean?*
   dire?

The verb *dire* is presented
in Lesson 14. It is used
here only in the expression *vouloir dire.*

2. Vous pouvez passer l'examen maintenant.
3. Je peux trouver ces livres à la librairie.
4. Elles peuvent finir le chapitre cet après-midi.
5. Tu peux rester à l'intérieur aujourd'hui.
6. Nous pouvons entendre le disque à la radio.
7. Vous pouvez enseigner la géographie ou l'histoire?
8. Elle peut réussir aux examens de maths et d'allemand.
9. Ils peuvent assister au match de hockey.

2. Est-ce qu'ils veulent aller à l'université?
3. Est-ce que vous voulez faire la grasse matinée demain?
4. Est-ce que nous voulons faire un voyage cet été?
5. Est-ce qu'elle veut offrir un petit cadeau à son voisin?
6. Est-ce que tu veux faire du russe ou de l'italien?
7. Est-ce que vous voulez passer la journée ici?
8. Est-ce qu'elles veulent aller chercher des livres de poche aujourd'hui?
9. Est-ce qu'il veut finir la leçon ce matin?

3. Non, il ne veut pas enseigner les sciences sociales.
4. Non, ils ne veulent pas choisir les cadeaux de Noël.
5. Non, tu ne peux pas rentrer plus tard.
6. Non, nous ne voudrions pas parler à cet auteur célèbre.
7. Non, vous ne pouvez pas (nous ne pouvons pas) faire la grasse matinée pendant l'été.
(Answers to Ex. C cont'd. at top of p. 175.)

Exercices

A. Redo the sentences by adding the appropriate form of the verb *pouvoir*. Follow the model.

1. Il répond à la question.
   Il peut répondre à la question.

2. Vous passez l'examen maintenant.
3. Je trouve ces livres à la librairie.
4. Elles finissent le chapitre cet après-midi.
5. Tu restes à l'intérieur aujourd'hui.
6. Nous entendons le disque à la radio.
7. Vous enseignez la géographie ou l'histoire?
8. Elle réussit aux examens de maths et d'allemand.
9. Ils assistent au match de hockey.

B. Redo the sentences by adding the appropriate form of the verb *vouloir*. Follow the model.

1. Est-ce que tu enseignes la biologie?
   Est-ce que tu veux enseigner la biologie?

2. Est-ce qu'ils vont à l'université?
3. Est-ce que vous faites la grasse matinée demain?
4. Est-ce que nous faisons un voyage cet été?
5. Est-ce qu'elle offre un petit cadeau à son voisin?
6. Est-ce que tu fais du russe ou de l'italien?
7. Est-ce que vous passez la journée ici?
8. Est-ce qu'elles vont chercher des livres de poche aujourd'hui?
9. Est-ce qu'il finit la leçon ce matin?

C. Answer the questions in the negative. Follow the models.

1. Nous voudrions aller à l'université. Et toi? *(cond.)*
   Non, je ne voudrais pas aller à l'université.
2. Ils peuvent aller au cinéma samedi. Et vous?
   Non, nous ne pouvons pas aller au cinéma samedi.

3. Je veux enseigner les sciences sociales. Et lui?
4. Tu veux choisir les cadeaux de Noël. Et tes parents?
5. Mon frère peut rentrer plus tard. Et moi?
6. Je voudrais parler à cet auteur célèbre. Et vous? *(cond.)*
7. Nos amies peuvent faire la grasse matinée pendant l'été. Et nous?
8. Nous voulons poser les questions à l'agent. Et eux?
9. Tu peux étudier à la bibliothèque ce soir. Et elles?
10. Nous voudrions passer l'examen demain. Et toi? *(cond.)*

Le passé composé des verbes réguliers en -er

8. Non, ils ne veulent pas poser les questions à l'agent.
9. Non, elles ne peuvent pas étudier à la bibliothèque ce soir.
10. Non, je ne voudrais pas passer l'examen demain.

VOCABULAIRE

déjà	*already*	l'année dernière	*last year*
hier	*yesterday*	le mois dernier	*last month*
hier matin	*yesterday morning*	la semaine dernière	*last week*
hier soir	*last evening, last night*	samedi dernier	*last Saturday*

1. The passé composé is used to talk about an action that has been completed. To form the passé composé of most verbs, you use the present tense of *avoir* and the "past participle" of the verb that is being put into the past tense. The past participle of regular *-er* verbs is formed by replacing the *-er* of the infinitive with *é: regarder → regardé:*

j'ai		nous avons	
tu as		vous avez	
il a	regardé	ils ont	regardé
elle a		elles ont	
on a			

2. The passé composé has two English equivalents:

J'ai **étudié** la leçon.
- *I **studied** the lesson.*
- *I've **studied** the lesson.*

Il a **commandé** un café.
- *He **ordered** coffee.*
- *He's **ordered** coffee.*

3. Now look at the following:

Nous n'avons pas **préparé** le goûter.
- *We **didn't prepare** the snack.*
- *We **haven't prepared** the snack.*

Tu n'as pas **raté** l'examen.
- *You **didn't fail** the exam.*
- *You **haven't failed** the exam.*

In negative sentences with the passé composé, *ne (n')* comes before the form of *avoir* and *pas* after it.

4. Note how adverbs of time are used with the passé composé:

J'ai **regardé** la télé hier.	*I watched TV yesterday.*
Jeudi dernier j'ai **joué** dehors.	*Last Thursday I played outside.*
Il a déjà **écouté** ce disque.	*He's already listened to that record.*

Most adverbs of time come at the beginning or end of the sentence. Some, such as *déjà, vite, souvent,* and *toujours,* come after the form of *avoir* but before the past participle.

Exercices

2. (a) Ils ont passé un de
leurs examens.
(b) Ils ont passé cet
examen hier matin.
3. (a) Viviane et Made-
leine ont étudié la
leçon de chimie.
(b) Elles ont étudié
cette leçon lundi.
4. (a) Non, tu as posé
une question diffi-
cile.
(b) Oui, on (cet étu-
diant) a donné la ré-
ponse correcte.
5. (a) Il a révisé deux
chapitres.
(b) Il a révisé ces cha-
pitres la semaine
dernière.
6. (a) Non, nous avons
déjà trouvé des
cadeaux pour nos
grands-parents.
(b) Nous allons offrir
des livres de poche
à nos grands-
parents.

2. Oui, elles ont regardé
la phrase.
3. Oui, il a apporté six
fleurs jaunes.
4. Oui, nous avons (j'ai) passé l'examen ce matin.
5. Oui, ils ont souvent
passé la soirée en
ville.
6. Oui, j'ai posé mes questions.
7. Oui, nous avons (j'ai) joué
au hockey hier soir.
8. Oui, tu as raté l'examen
de physique.

2. Non, elles n'ont pas
regardé la phrase.
3. Non, il n'a pas apporté
six fleurs jaunes.
4. Non, nous n'avons pas
(je n'ai pas) passé l'examen ce matin.
5. Non, ils n'ont pas souvent passé la soirée en
ville.
6. Non, je n'ai pas posé
mes questions.
7. Non, nous n'avons pas
(je n'ai pas) joué au
hockey hier soir.
8. Non, tu n'as pas raté
l'examen de physique.

A. Answer the questions according to the statements. Follow the model.

1. Hier soir, Lucien et son frère ont joué aux échecs.
   (a) Qui a joué aux échecs?
   Lucien et son frère ont joué aux échecs.
   (b) Quand est-ce qu'ils ont joué aux échecs?
   Ils ont joué aux échecs hier soir.

2. Hier matin, ils ont passé un de leurs examens.
   (a) Qu'est-ce qu'ils ont passé?
   (b) Quand est-ce qu'ils ont passé cet examen?

3. Lundi, Viviane et Madeleine ont étudié la leçon de chimie.
   (a) Qui a étudié la leçon de chimie?
   (b) Quand est-ce qu'elles ont étudié cette leçon?

4. Tu as posé une question difficile, mais cet étudiant a donné la réponse correcte.
   (a) Est-ce que j'ai posé une question facile?
   (b) Est-ce qu'on a donné la réponse correcte?

5. La semaine dernière, Alain a révisé deux chapitres de son livre d'algèbre.
   (a) Alain a révisé combien de chapitres?
   (b) Quand est-ce qu'il a révisé ces chapitres?

6. Nous avons déjà trouvé des cadeaux pour nos grands-parents—des livres de poche.
   (a) Vous allez chercher des cadeaux pour vos grands-parents?
   (b) Qu'est-ce que vous allez offrir à vos grands-parents?

B. Answer the questions according to the model.

1. Ils ont parlé à Suzanne. Et toi?
   Oui, j'ai parlé à Suzanne.

2. J'ai regardé la phrase. Et elles?
3. Nous avons apporté six fleurs jaunes. Et lui?
4. J'ai passé l'examen ce matin. Et vous?
5. Vous avez souvent passé la soirée en ville. Et eux?
6. Elles ont posé leurs questions. Et toi?
7. J'ai joué au hockey hier soir. Et vous?
8. Paul a raté l'examen de physique. Et moi?

C. Redo the above exercise in the negative.
Follow the model.

1. Ils ont parlé à Suzanne. Et toi?
   Non, je n'ai pas parlé à Suzanne.

ÉCOLE MONT NOTRE-DAME
Sherbrooke
DEGRÉ   FOYER
IV L   L
Patricia Fisch
NOM
1363 Amherst
ADRESSE
9/5/60   567 1226
DATE DE NAISSANCE   TÉLÉPHONE
Marie Granger, c.n.d.
1974-1975
700-4   PHOTO ART

Vérifiez vos progrès

Using the cues in parentheses, rewrite the sentences in the passé composé. Be sure to put the adverbs in the correct position. Follow the model.

1. Ces bonnes étudiantes révisent leurs leçons. (hier)
   Hier ces bonnes étudiantes ont révisé leurs leçons.

2. Ils passent l'après-midi à la bibliothèque. (mercredi)
3. J'assiste au concert. (hier soir)
4. Nous montrons les photos à Andrée. (le mois dernier)
5. On trouve ces livres à la librairie au coin de la rue. (vite)
6. Tu comptes jusqu'à soixante? (déjà)
7. Maman n'enseigne pas la chimie à l'université. (l'année dernière)
8. Vous ne jouez pas dehors? (ce matin)

Meilleurs Vœux

CONVERSATION ET LECTURE

Parlons de vous

1. Est-ce que vous offrez des cadeaux à vos parents pour la Fête des Mères et la Fête des Pères? Quoi ("what"), par exemple? Qu'est-ce qu'ils aiment, vous êtes fort? nul? Est-ce que vous êtes fort en langues étrangères? 8. Est-Pères? 3. Est-ce que vous aimez offrir des cadeaux ou est-ce que vous aimez mieux recevoir ("to receive") des cadeaux? Quoi, par exemple?
4. Est-ce que vous passez souvent la soirée chez vous? Qu'est-ce que vous faites? Hier soir, par exemple, est-ce que vous avez étudié? 5. Est-ce que vous aimez faire la grasse matinée? Quels jours est-ce que vous pouvez faire la grasse matinée? 6. Combien de matières ("subjects") est-ce que vous faites cette année? Quelles matières? 7. En quelles matières est-ce que vous êtes fort? nul? Est-ce que vous êtes fort en langues étrangères? 8. Est-ce que vous réussissez toujours à vos examens? Est-ce que vous ratez quelquefois les examens? 9. Est-ce que vous voulez aller à l'université? Quelle université? une université française peut-être?

Au poste de police°

Hier, vers minuit, un agent a arrêté° un homme dans la rue près de la porte de la Banque Nationale de Paris.[1] Il a trouvé beaucoup d'argent° sur cet homme. Ce matin le gérant° de la banque a téléphoné au
5 poste de police pour signaler° un vol° de quinze mille° francs. C'est la même somme° qui est maintenant sur la table devant l'inspecteur Maussade et le suspect!

le poste de police:	*police station*
arrêter:	*to arrest*
beaucoup de:	*a lot of*
le gérant:	*manager*
signaler:	*to report*
le vol:	*theft*
mille:	*thousand*
la somme:	*amount*

---

[1]Often called *la BNP*, this is one of France's largest banks, which has branches throughout the country and abroad.

Students might enjoy acting out this mild parody.

L'INSPECTEUR C'est ton argent, ça?[1]

L'HOMME Oui, monsieur l'inspecteur.

Remind students of the use of the definite determiner when addressing someone by title: *Monsieur l'inspecteur (l'agent, etc.)*.

L'INSPECTEUR Ouais . . .° Qui es-tu?

ouais: *unhuh*

L'HOMME Euh, je m'appelle Jean Dupont.[2]

L'INSPECTEUR Où est-ce que tu habites, "Dupont"?

L'HOMME J'habite 18 rue de la Gare, monsieur.

See Cultural Supplement.

L'INSPECTEUR Et tes papiers, où sont-ils?

L'HOMME Je . . . J'ai perdu° mes papiers.

perdu: *past participle of* perdre

L'INSPECTEUR Tu travailles, toi?

L'HOMME Je suis étudiant. Je fais de l'allemand à l'université. Je voudrais être traducteur.°

le traducteur: *translator*

L'INSPECTEUR Etudiant? Tu n'es pas un peu° vieux pour ça? Où est ta carte d'étudiant,° alors?

un peu: *a bit*

la carte d'étudiant: *student I.D.*

L'HOMME J'ai perdu ma carte d'étudiant aussi, monsieur. Avec mes papiers.

L'INSPECTEUR Ecoute, cette histoire n'est pas vraie.° Tu n'es pas "Jean Dupont"—tu es Paul Rigaud, le célèbre gangster. Nous avons tes empreintes digitales.°

vrai, -e: *true*

les empreintes digitales: *fingerprints*

L'HOMME Mais . . . mais je ne veux pas aller en prison!

le gangster: Point out that, because this is a borrowed word, the *r* is pronounced: [gɑ̃gstɛr].

L'INSPECTEUR C'est toujours la même histoire! A la fin, les grands gangsters pleurent° comme les petits enfants!

pleurer: *to cry*

A propos . . .

1. A quelle heure est-ce qu'on a arrêté le suspect? Qu'est-ce qu'on a trouvé sur lui? 2. Pourquoi est-ce que le gérant de la banque a téléphoné au poste de police ce matin? 3. L'inspecteur Maussade pose beaucoup de questions. Est-ce qu'il aime les réponses? 4. Par exemple, qu'est-ce que l'homme répond quand l'inspecteur demande son nom ("name") et son adresse? Est-ce que ces réponses sont vraies? Quel est son vrai nom? 5. Qu'est-ce qu'il répond quand on demande s'il travaille? C'est vrai? 6. D'après ("according to") le suspect, où sont ses papiers, sa carte d'étudiant, etc.? 7. Si Paul Rigaud n'est pas vraiment étudiant, qu'est-ce qu'il est? Est-ce qu'il est courageux ("brave")? 8. Et vous, est-ce que vous avez une carte d'étudiant? Qu'est-ce qu'il y a sur cette carte? Votre nom, par exemple? 9. Est-ce que vous aimez les films ou les romans policiers? Quels auteurs de romans policiers est-ce que vous aimez?

[1]The inspector uses *tu* and *ton* to show his contempt for the suspect.

[2]Jean Dupont is a name so common in France that it is suspicious.

50 FRANCS

10 FRANCS

5 FRANCS

1 FRANC

1/2 FRANC

20 CENTIMES

10 CENTIMES

5 CENTIMES

2 CENTIMES

1 CENTIME

MONNAIE FRANÇAISE
FRENCH COINS
FRANZÖSISCHE MÜNZEN

ATTENTION : en France, les bureaux de poste n'acceptent que la monnaie et les billets de banque français.

IMPORTANT : French Post Offices only accept French coins and bank-notes.

ACHTUNG : in Frankreich nehmen die Postämter nur französisches Kleingeld und französische Banknoten an.

15

PREFECTURE DE POLICE

POLICE

EXPLICATIONS II

Le passé composé des verbes en -ir/-iss-, -ir et -re

1. You have already learned how to form the passé composé of regular *-er* verbs. Now look at the following:

Il a fini le roman.
{ *He **finished** the novel.*
{ *He's **finished** the novel.*

Elle a servi le dîner.
{ *She **served** dinner.*
{ *She's **served** dinner.*

The past participle of *-ir/-iss-* and *-ir* verbs is formed by replacing the *ir* of the infinitive with *i: finir → fini, servir → servi*.

2. Now look at the following:

Nous avons perdu le match.
{ *We **lost** the game.*
{ *We've **lost** the game.*

Vous avez répondu à la question.
{ *You **answered** the question.*
{ *You've **answered** the question.*

The past participle of regular *-re* verbs is formed by replacing the *re* of the infinitive with *u: perdre → perdu*.

Exercices

A. Change the sentences to the passé composé. Follow the models.

1. Je choisis un film sénégalais.
   J'ai choisi un film sénégalais.
2. Nous ne choisissons pas cette route.
   Nous n'avons pas choisi cette route.
3. Tu maigris, Georges!
4. Claude ne dort pas pendant la matinée.
5. Elle grossit, n'est-ce pas?
6. Luc et Olivier ne finissent pas leurs devoirs.
7. Vous choisissez un roman très difficile.
8. Tu finis cette phrase?
9. Il ne finit pas cette longue pièce espagnole.
10. Ils servent un dîner français.
11. Paul réussit toujours à ses examens de maths.

B. Change the sentences to the passé composé. Follow the models.

1. Luc répond vite au professeur.
   Luc a vite répondu au professeur.
2. Cette étudiante et sa voisine ne répondent pas aux questions.
   Cette étudiante et sa voisine n'ont pas répondu aux questions.
3. En route, Jean perd son livre d'histoire.
4. Nous attendons l'autobus au coin de la rue.
5. Mes parents ne vendent pas leur bateau à voiles.

---

3. Tu as maigri, Georges!
4. Claude n'a pas dormi pendant la matinée.
5. Elle a grossi, n'est-ce pas?
6. Luc et Olivier n'ont pas fini leurs devoirs.
7. Vous avez choisi un roman très difficile.
8. Tu as fini cette phrase?
9. Il n'a pas fini cette longue pièce espagnole.
10. Ils ont servi un dîner français.
11. Paul a toujours réussi à ses examens de maths.

3. En route, Jean a perdu son livre d'histoire.
4. Nous avons attendu l'autobus au coin de la rue.
5. Mes parents n'ont pas vendu leur bateau à voiles.

6. J'entends un camion dans la rue.
7. Pauline ne répond pas à sa grand-mère.
8. Tu ne vends pas un de ces vélos?
9. J'attends mon père près de l'hôpital.
10. Ces dames n'entendent pas tes réponses.

C. Redo the paragraph, changing the italicized verbs or phrases to the passé composé.

Mercredi Thomas et Laurent *passent* la matinée à la maison. Ils *dorment* jusqu'à midi. A 12 h. 45 ils *déjeunent*. L'après-midi ils *jouent* au basketball et à 4 h. ils *préparent* un goûter. Ils *finissent* le goûter à 4 h. 35. Après, ils *attendent* un copain pour regarder le journal télévisé. Après le dîner, ils 5 *choisissent* un film à la télé. A 9 h. 30 leur mère *demande:* "Vous *ne travaillez pas* ce soir, mes enfants?" Ils *ne répondent pas*. Est-ce qu'ils *n'entendent pas* la question? Si, et ils *ferment vite* la télé. Ils *trouvent* leurs livres et leurs cahiers, et ils *révisent* leurs leçons jusqu'à minuit.

Vérifiez vos progrès

Write answers to each question saying that the person has already done the thing being asked about. Follow the model.

1. Tu ne vas pas finir ce poème?
   J'ai déjà fini ce poème.

2. Elle va répondre aux étudiants?
3. Vous maigrissez?
4. La serveuse ne va pas servir les gens à côté?
5. Les feuilles ne vont pas jaunir cet automne?
6. Il perd sa route?
7. Ils vendent leurs billets?
8. Tu ne vas pas choisir une de ces photos?

6. J'ai entendu un camion dans la rue.
7. Pauline n'a pas répondu à sa grand-mère.
8. Tu n'as pas vendu un de ces vélos?
9. J'ai attendu mon père près de l'hôpital.
10. Ces dames n'ont pas entendu tes réponses.

Ex. C
You may want to remind students that *fermer* can mean "to turn off."

ont passé
ont dormi
ont déjeuné
ont joué
ont préparé
ont fini
ont attendu
ont choisi
a demandé
n'avez pas travaillé
n'ont pas répondu
n'ont pas entendu
ont vite fermé
ont trouvé
ont révisé

RÉVISION ET THÈME

See Teacher's Section for answers to the *révision* and *thème*.

Review of:
1. negative passé composé of -*er* verbs
   verbs + *à*
   adverbs of time
2. passé composé of -*re* and -*er* verbs
3. *il faut*
   adverbs of time
   compound nouns
4. negative passé composé of -*ir*/-*iss*- and simple -*ir* verbs
   vouloir/*pouvoir*
   plural nouns ending in *x*
5. class subjects (after *en* and *faire de*)
   negative future with *aller*
   double infinitives

Before doing the *thème*, you might want to remind students of the use of *passer* meaning both "to spend (time)" and "to take (an exam)" and of *réussir à* meaning "to pass (an exam)."

Consult the model sentences, then put the English cues into French and use them to form new sentences.

1. *Il n'a pas parlé aux étudiants la semaine dernière.*
   (*You* (sing.) *didn't phone the bookstore last night.*)
   (*We didn't play soccer last month.*)

2. *Elle a perdu les photos à l'université.*
   (*We waited for the salespeople* (f.) *at the sidewalk café.*)
   (*They* (f.) *spent the evening in the gym.*)

3. *Demain matin, il faut aller au cours de géométrie.*
   (*This evening, we have to find those paperbacks.*)
   (*This afternoon, I have to review the history lesson.*)

4. *Mais je n'ai pas dormi et je ne veux pas regarder les journaux.*
   (*they* (m.) *haven't finished and they can't look for the gifts*)
   (*we didn't lose weight and we don't want to order ice cream bars*)

5. *Il est nul en biologie et il ne va pas vouloir faire de la physique.*
   (*She's good in math but isn't going to be able to take algebra.*)
   (*They* (f.) *are no good in history and won't want to take geography.*)

Now that you have done the *Révision*, you are ready to write a composition. Put the English captions describing each cartoon panel into French to form a paragraph.

Simone didn't attend classes yesterday.

She spent the day at home.

This morning she has to take a chemistry exam.

But she hasn't studied and she can't answer the questions.

She's no good in chemistry, and she's not going to be able to pass the exam.

AUTO-TEST

A. In complete sentences, write the courses that you are taking and tell who teaches each course. Since it is your class schedule, the answers are not in the back of the book. Ask your teacher to go over your answers with you. Follow the model.

1. *Je fais du français. Madame Dupont enseigne le français.*

B. Answer the questions using the pronouns given. Follow the models.

1. Elles peuvent étudier des langues étrangères. Et nous?
   Vous pouvez étudier des langues étrangères aussi.
2. Je veux aller au théâtre avec Georges. Et elle?
   Elle veut aller au théâtre avec Georges aussi.
3. Vous voulez offrir un cadeau à Guillaume. Et lui?
4. Nous pouvons réussir à l'examen. Et toi?
5. Je voudrais passer la matinée à la maison. Et vous? *(cond.)*
6. Il veut aller à l'université. Et eux?
7. Nous pouvons assister au cours de chimie. Et elles?
8. Ils veulent poser une autre question. Et nous?
9. Je voudrais faire des sciences sociales. Et vous? *(cond.)*
10. Elles peuvent sortir dimanche. Et moi?

C. Using the correct form of the words given, write complete sentences in the passé composé. Follow the model.

1. Samedi/dernier/je/ne pas passer/la soirée/à/le cinéma
   Samedi dernier je n'ai pas passé la soirée au cinéma.

2. Hier/nous/attendre/l'autobus/jusqu'à/7 h./de/le soir
3. Le professeur/ne pas répondre/à/les questions/de/les étudiants
4. Nous/réussir/à/l'examen de biologie
5. Tu/perdre/l'argent/à/le supermarché
6. Sa sœur/choisir/deux/livre de poche/dans/la librairie
7. Tu/rater/l'examen/parce que/tu/ne pas réviser/tes leçons

Proverbe

Vouloir, c'est pouvoir.

Collège d'Enseignement Secondaire
Nationalisé - Mixte
76220 - GOURNAY-EN-BRAY

NOM : GRES

Prénom : Florence

Classe : 3ᵉ Tℓ

Qualité : DP

Nom et adresse des parents : Mᵐ Grès
St Aubin 76220 Gournay en Bray

Tél. _____

LE PRINCIPAL,

Douzième Leçon

Le gros chien méchant

See Cultural Supplement.

Sophie Beaulieu, qui a treize ans, et son frère cadet Eugène, qui a neuf ans,[1] vont assez souvent chez leur grand-père. Un après-midi, ils frappent à la porte de son nouvel appartement, mais il n'y a pas de réponse.

You might want to mention that "Beware of the dog" signs read simply *Chien méchant.*

EUGÈNE	Je ne comprends pas. Pourquoi est-ce qu'il n'est pas chez lui?
5	
SOPHIE	Allons demander à la concierge.[2]

Toc! toc! toc! De l'intérieur, on entend: "Ouah, ouah, ouah! Grrr . . ."

EUGÈNE	Oh, là là! C'est un gros chien méchant, ça. Je pars, moi!
LA CONCIERGE	Qui est là?
SOPHIE	C'est Sophie et Eugène Beaulieu.
LA CONCIERGE	Ah, bonjour les enfants! Votre grand-père n'est pas là?
SOPHIE	Non, madame. Est-ce qu'il va rentrer bientôt?
LA CONCIERGE	Malheureusement, je ne sais pas, mademoiselle Sophie. Mais entrez. Voulez-vous prendre quelque chose?
EUGÈNE	Euh . . . mais le chien?
LA CONCIERGE	Oh, je n'ai pas de chien! Ça, c'est un disque! Quand je suis seule, je n'aime pas répondre à la porte. C'est pour faire peur aux inconnus . . .
SOPHIE	Ça a bien réussi,[3] n'est-ce pas, Eugène?

Point out that although Sophie is only 13, the concierge shows her respect for the tenant's grand-daughter by addressing her as "mademoiselle Sophie."

---

[1]The letter *f* of *neuf* is pronounced as a [v] sound before the words *heures* and *ans*.

[2]*Le* or *la concierge* is a custodian, who usually occupies the apartment on the ground floor of the building. The concierge in this dialogue is not typical, because usually they are not at all timid. It is in fact their job to keep an eye on things—to stop strangers, take in mail, answer the building phone, and generally keep a close watch on the building.

[3]Used in this way, the verb *réussir (à)* means "to succeed." For example: *J'ai réussi à trouver un cadeau,* "I succeeded in finding a gift."

The big mean dog

Sophie Beaulieu, who is thirteen years old, and her younger brother Eugène, who is nine, go to their grandfather's quite often. One afternoon, they knock on the door of his new apartment, but there is no answer.

EUGÈNE   I don't understand. Why isn't he home?

5 SOPHIE   Let's go ask the concierge.

Knock! Knock! Knock! From inside is heard: "Woof, woof, woof! Grrr . . ."

EUGÈNE   Uh-oh! That's a big mean dog! I'm getting out of here!

LA CONCIERGE   Who's there?

SOPHIE   It's Sophie and Eugène Beaulieu.

Note the English equivalent here of *Votre grand-père n'est pas là* ("at home").

10 LA CONCIERGE Oh, hello, children. Isn't your grandfather home?

SOPHIE   No. Will he be back soon?

LA CONCIERGE   Unfortunately, I don't know, Sophie. But come in. Would you like something to eat?

EUGÈNE   Uh . . . but what about the dog?

15 LA CONCIERGE Why, I haven't got a dog! That's a record! When I'm alone I don't like to answer the door. That's just to frighten strangers . . .

SOPHIE   It sure succeeded, didn't it, Eugène?

Questionnaire

1. Quel âge a Sophie? et son frère cadet? 2. Où est-ce qu'ils vont cet après-midi? 3. Quand ils frappent à la porte de leur grand-père est-ce qu'il y a une réponse? 4. Quand ils frappent à la porte de la concierge, qu'est-ce qu'ils entendent? 5. Quand la concierge répond à sa porte, où est le chien? 6. Est-ce que la concierge est aimable? Est-ce qu'elle a peur des inconnus? 7. D'abord, Eugène ne veut pas prendre quelque chose chez la concierge. Pourquoi? 8. Est-ce que le disque réussit à faire peur aux inconnus? Est-ce qu'il fait peur à Sophie, par exemple? à Eugène?

PRONONCIATION

Two French vowel sounds that are very much alike are the [œ] sound, as in *leur* and *neuf,* and the [ø] sound, as in *eux* and *deux.*

Exercices

A. These words all contain the [œ] sound followed by a final pronounced consonant. Listen, then repeat.

s<u>eu</u>l   fl<u>eu</u>ve   fl<u>eu</u>r   coul<u>eu</u>r   profess<u>eu</u>r

B. Now listen, then repeat these sentences containing the [œ] sound.

C'est le s<u>eu</u>l vend<u>eu</u>r.   L'aut<u>eu</u>r déj<u>eu</u>ne à n<u>eu</u>f h<u>eu</u>res.

L<u>eu</u>r s<u>œu</u>r a n<u>eu</u>f fl<u>eu</u>rs.   Le profess<u>eu</u>r est à l'intéri<u>eu</u>r.

C. For the [ø] sound, the lips are more rounded than for the [œ] sound. Listen, then repeat these sentences containing the [ø] sound.

Eux, ils sont bleus.   Ses deux neveux sont généreux.
Ces messieurs sont vieux.   Eux, ils ont deux neveux paresseux.

D. Now contrast the [œ] and [ø] sounds. Listen, then repeat.

[œ]/[ø]   heure/eux   pleure/pleut   peur/peu   sœur/ceux

MOTS NOUVEAUX I

L'affiche est au-dessus de la carte.   *The poster is **above** the map.*
La carte est au-dessous de l'affiche.   *The map is **below** the poster.*
Le vélo est au milieu de la route.   *The bike's **in the middle of** the road.*
La voiture est au bord de la route.   *The car's **by the roadside.***
La route est au bord de la mer.   *The road is **by the sea.***

Quel âge avez-vous? ⎫   *How old are you?*
Quel âge as-tu?   ⎭
J'ai seize ans.   *I'm sixteen.*
Tu es enfant unique?[1]   *Are you an **only** child?*
Mais non! J'ai un frère aîné et une   *No! I have an **older** brother and an*
    sœur aînée.   ***older** sister.*
J'ai aussi un frère cadet et une   *I have a **younger** brother and a*
    sœur cadette.   ***younger** sister, too.*

C'est un garçon très méchant.   *That's a very **naughty** boy.*
Sa sœur est assez méchante aussi.   *His sister's **pretty naughty,** too.*

Il est marié. Voilà sa femme.   *He's **married.** There's **his wife.***
    fiancé   sa fiancée   *engaged   his fiancée*
Elle est mariée. Voilà son mari.   *married   her husband*
    fiancée   son fiancé   *engaged   her fiancé*

Tu vas frapper à la porte?   *Are you going **to knock on** the door?*
Tout à coup j'ai peur.   ***Suddenly** I'm afraid.*
Est-ce que le chien est méchant?   *Is the dog **mean?***
Je ne sais pas.   *I **don't know.***

Le concierge habite seul.   *The concierge lives **alone.***
Il est assez vieux.   *He's **pretty old.***
La concierge habite seule.   *The concierge lives **alone.***
Elle est assez aimable.   *She's **rather nice.***
Elle rentre bientôt.   *She returns **soon.***
        tout de suite   *right away*
        enfin   *at last*
Puis elle sort.[2]   ***Then** she goes out.*

Help students be alert to the difference in vowel sounds in *au-dessus* [y] and *au-dessous* [u]. Through placement of classroom objects, help them, too, to understand the difference between *au-dessus de* ("over," "above") and *sur* ("on," "on top of") and *au-dessous de* ("below," "beneath") and *sous* ("under," "underneath").

You might practice telling how old people are, as well as *unique, cadet,* and *aîné,* in a personalized context.

---

[1]Note that the indefinite determiner is not used in such expressions as *enfant unique, fils unique, fille unique.*
[2]Though *bientôt, tout de suite, enfin,* and *tout à coup* can be used either at the beginning or end of a phrase, *puis* can be used only at the beginning.

Exercices de vocabulaire

A. Answer the questions according to the picture.

1. Il y a une maison (un arbre/un vélo) au milieu de cette image.
2. Le soleil est au-dessus des nuages.
3. Il y a des arbres au-dessous des nuages.
4. Non, le jardin est à gauche de la maison.
5. Il y a un bateau au bord du lac.
6. Oui, le vélo est devant la maison.
7. Il y a un arbre derrière la maison.

You might want to expand upon Ex. A by asking questions using other prepositions (*Les fleurs sont loin de la maison? Le bateau est sur le lac?* etc.)

1. Qu'est-ce qu'il y a au milieu de cette image?
2. Qu'est-ce qui est au-dessus des nuages?
3. Qu'est-ce qu'il y a au-dessous des nuages?
4. Est-ce que le jardin est à droite de la maison?
5. Qu'est-ce qu'il y a au bord du lac?
6. Est-ce que le vélo est devant la maison?
7. Qu'est-ce qu'il y a derrière la maison?

B. Choose the word or phrase that best completes the sentence or fits the situation.

1. Est-ce qu'il est marié? Oui, voilà (*sa femme/son mari*).
2. J'ai dix-neuf ans et ma sœur cadette a (*douze ans/vingt ans*).
3. Pourquoi est-ce qu'ils ne répondent pas à la porte? (*C'est une bonne réponse./Je ne sais pas.*)
4. Vite! Il faut partir (*assez lentement/tout de suite*).
5. Je n'ai pas de frères. Je suis fils (*méchant/unique*).
6. Qui est là? (*Je frappe à la porte./C'est moi. Mathieu.*)
7. Quel temps fait-il? (*Je ne sais pas./Midi.*)
8. Elle rentre bientôt? (*Oui, l'année prochaine./Oui, vers 9 h.*)
9. J'attends la concierge. Elle arrive (*enfin/puis*).
10. Jeanne travaille chez elle parce qu'elle aime travailler (*bientôt/seule*).
11. Quel âge avez-vous, mademoiselle? (*Sa fille aînée./J'ai 22 ans.*)

1. sa femme
2. douze ans
3. Je ne sais pas.
4. tout de suite
5. unique
6. C'est moi. Mathieu.
7. Je ne sais pas.
8. Oui, vers 9 h.
9. enfin
10. seule
11. J'ai 22 ans.

Douzième
Leçon

188

MOTS NOUVEAUX II

l'oiseau (m.)

l'agriculteur (m.)

meuh

hii-hii

la vache

le cheval

gron-gron

miaou

ouah-ouah

glou-glou-glou

le cochon

cocorico

le chat

le chien

le dindon

couin-couin

bëëe-bëëe

cot-cot-cot-codèt

le coq

la poule

le canard

le mouton

Est-ce que vous avez un chat?	*Do you have a cat?*	You might need to remind students of the omission of the indefinite determiner after the personal pronoun + être + profession (*il est agriculteur*).
Non, j'ai deux oiseaux—et un chien pour faire peur aux inconnus.	*No. I have two birds—and a dog* ***to*** ***frighten*** *strangers.*	
Ce monsieur a une ferme.	*This man has* ***a*** *farm.*	
Il est agriculteur.	*He's* ***a*** *farmer.*	
Du matin jusqu'au soir il faut penser à la ferme.	*From morning 'til night he has* ***to*** ***think about*** *the farm.*	

Le Zoo

le tigre

le singe

le léopard

la girafe

l'ours (m.)

le lion

l'hippopotame (m.)

le rhinocéros

la souris

l'éléphant (m.)

le zoo: Point out that it is not pronounced like the English word [zu], but is pronounced [zo], as an abbreviated form of *le jardin zoologique.*

l'ours: Point out the pronounced final consonant: [urs].

You might want to present the poem, p. 203, at this time.

Douzième
Leçon

Qui est l'inconnu *(m.)* là-bas?
Il pense à **quelque chose.**
Qui est l'inconnue *(f.)?*
Elle regarde cet animal.
Elle aime les animaux, mais pas le zoo.
Elle aime les vaches et les chevaux, pas
    les ours et les girafes.

*Who's **the stranger** over there?*
*He's thinking about **something.***
*Who's **the stranger?***
*She's looking at that **animal.***
*She likes **animals,** but not **the zoo.***
She likes cows and horses, not
    bears and giraffes.

Exercice de vocabulaire

Identify the animals in the picture. Follow the model. Then answer the questions at the bottom of the page.

1. *C'est un oiseau.*

2. C'est une vache.
3. C'est un cheval.
4. C'est un cochon.
5. C'est un chat.
6. C'est un chien.
7. C'est un dindon.
8. C'est un coq.
9. C'est une poule.
10. C'est un canard.
11. C'est un mouton.
12. Non, ils ne font pas peur à l'agriculteur.
13. Ils habitent la ferme.
14. On peut trouver des léopards, des lions et des tigres au zoo.
15. Il y a une girafe au milieu de l'image du zoo.
16. Il y a un rhinocéros au-dessous de l'ours. Il y a un singe à gauche du léopard. Il y a un éléphant à droite de la souris. Il y a une girafe au-dessus de l'hippopotame.

12. Est-ce que les animaux font peur à l'agriculteur?
13. Où habitent ces animaux?
14. On peut trouver trois grands chats au zoo. Quels chats?
15. Quel animal est-ce qu'il y a au milieu de l'image du zoo (page 190)?
16. Quel animal est-ce qu'il y a au-dessous de l'ours? à gauche du léopard? à droite de la souris? au-dessus de l'hippopotame?

Lesson
12

191

EXPLICATIONS I

Les verbes comme **prendre**

VOCABULAIRE			
prendre	*to take; to have*[1]	apprendre par cœur[2]	*to memorize*
apprendre (à)	*to learn (how)*	comprendre	*to understand*

Prendre, and all verbs ending in *-prendre*, follow this pattern:

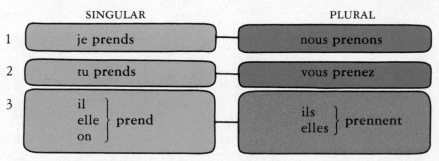

SINGULAR	PLURAL
1 je prends	nous prenons
2 tu prends	vous prenez
3 il / elle / on prend	ils / elles prennent

IMPERATIVE: prends! prenons! prenez!

1. The singular pattern is like that of regular *-re* verbs, and all three forms are pronounced alike.

2. In the 1 and 2 pl. forms, the *d* is dropped and the pronunciation of the stem vowel *e* changes from [ɑ̃], as in *dans*, to [ə] as in *le*.

3. In the 3 pl. form, too, the *d* is dropped, but in spelling another *n* is added. The pronunciation of the stem vowel becomes [ɛ] as in *mère*, and the [n] sound is strongly released.

Exercices

A. Answer the questions using the present tense. Follow the model.

1. Quand est-ce que tu vas apprendre ce poème allemand?
   J'apprends ce poème allemand maintenant.

2. Est-ce que vous allez comprendre cette leçon?
3. Quand est-ce qu'ils vont apprendre le poème par cœur?
4. Est-ce que vous allez apprendre à jouer au tennis?
5. Quand est-ce qu'Alain va prendre quelque chose?
6. Quand est-ce que tu vas comprendre le français?
7. Est-ce que vous allez prendre le petit déjeuner?
8. Est-ce qu'elles vont apprendre l'histoire?
9. Est-ce que tu vas comprendre les questions?

2. Nous comprenons (Je comprends) cette leçon maintenant.
3. Ils apprennent le poème par cœur maintenant.
4. Nous apprenons (J'apprends) à jouer au tennis maintenant.
5. Il prend quelque chose maintenant.
6. Je comprends le français maintenant.
7. Nous prenons (Je prends) le petit déjeuner maintenant.
8. Elles apprennent l'histoire maintenant.
9. Je comprends les questions maintenant.

[1]The expression *prendre quelque chose* means "to have something to eat or drink." Similarly, *il prend un café* means "He's having coffee."
[2]Note how the expression is used: *Elle apprend les mots par cœur*, "She's memorizing the words."

B. Complete the paragraph, using the correct form of the italicized verbs. Be careful! There are regular *-re* verbs as well as *prendre*-type verbs.

A la gare deux garçons *(prendre)* une boisson pendant qu'ils *(attendre)* le train. Tout à coup, ils *(entendre)* deux jeunes filles qui parlent une langue étrangère.

prennent
attendent
entendent

| JEAN-PATRICK | Tu *(comprendre)* cette langue? |
| 5   CHRISTOPHE | Oui. Elles parlent allemand. |

comprends

Bientôt, une des jeunes filles demande en français: "Pardon, messieurs. Où est-ce qu'on *(vendre)* les billets?" Christophe, qui *(apprendre)* l'allemand au lycée, *(répondre)* lentement en allemand. Mais les jeunes filles ne *(comprendre)* pas.

vend
apprend
répond
comprennent

10 UNE JEUNE FILLE	Vous ne *(comprendre)* pas le français, monsieur?
CHRISTOPHE	Si, mademoiselle. Mais je *(comprendre)* aussi votre langue. Nous *(apprendre)* l'allemand au lycée.
LA JEUNE FILLE	Ma sœur et moi, nous ne *(comprendre)* pas du tout l'allemand. Nous sommes belges.
15 CHRISTOPHE	Ah, vous parlez flamand, n'est-ce pas?
LA JEUNE FILLE	Oui, monsieur. Nous *(attendre)* le train pour Bruxelles. Nous *(prendre)* le train qui part à 9 h. 25.

comprenez
comprends
apprenons
comprenons
attendons
prenons

After students have done this exercise they might enjoy acting it out. Note that it can serve as an excellent opportunity for you to check pronunciation of nasal vowel sounds.
[ɑ̃] *prendre, pendant, attendre, entendre, langue, étrangère, allemand, demander, en, français, vendre, apprendre, lentemont, flamand*
[ɔ̃] *garçons, boisson, pardon, on, répondre*
[ɛ̃] *train, bientôt, vingt-cinq*

Les adjectifs **bon**, **premier**, **dernier**; **beau**, **nouveau**, **vieux**

1. When *bon*, *premier*, and *dernier* are used before a masculine noun beginning with a vowel sound they are pronounced like their corresponding feminine form. Their final consonant is pronounced and the vowel sound changes. In these examples, all except the first one in each set is pronounced the same:

un **bon** prof	le **premier** lycée	le **dernier** chapitre
une **bonne** classe	la **première** maison	la **dernière** leçon
un **bon** étudiant	le **premier** hôtel	le **dernier** examen
une **bonne** étudiante	la **première** église	la **dernière** histoire

2. There are special forms for *beau*, *nouveau*, and *vieux* when they occur before a masculine noun beginning with a vowel sound: *beau → bel, nouveau → nouvel*, and *vieux → vieil*. These special forms are pronounced the same as the corresponding feminine forms:

un **beau** jardin	un **nouveau** copain	un **vieux** roman
une **belle** fleur	une **nouvelle** copine	une **vieille** librairie
un **bel** inconnu	un **nouvel** ami	un **vieil** auteur
une **belle** inconnue	une **nouvelle** amie	une **vieille** histoire

3. The meaning of some adjectives may change depending on whether they are used before or after the noun. For example, when *dernier* is used before the noun, it means "very last" or "final." After the noun, it implies "most recent." Compare the two uses of *dernier* in this sentence: **Samedi *dernier* j'ai passé le *dernier* examen.**

In Point 3, we once again limit our attention to those adjectives that we actively use both pre- and postnominally. Should students have noticed the postnominal position of *nouveau* in the recurrent heading *Mots Nouveaux*, you may want to explain that after the noun, *nouveau* means that something is appearing or being seen for the first time; before the noun it means "recent." We do not teach *neuf, neuve* meaning "brand new."

Exercices

Exs. A–B should be done both orally and in writing.

2. Il y a un bel arbre près du beau fleuve.
3. Le zoo attend son premier léopard et son premier hippopotame.
4. Le nouvel étudiant et le nouveau professeur sont en route pour l'université.
5. Le dernier chapitre et le dernier examen sont très difficiles.
6. Le vieil hôtel est à gauche du vieux théâtre.
7. Je vais prendre un bon café et un bon esquimau.
8. Le dernier train et le dernier autobus partent avant minuit.
9. Le vieil agriculteur pense à son vieux cheval.
10. Ce beau monsieur regarde un bel oiseau dans le ciel.

2. Je prends toujours le premier autobus vert.
3. Ils ont dîné avec leur nouvel ami belge.
4. Est-ce que tu as regardé ce bel enfant blond?
5. Vous enseignez à cette nouvelle université canadienne?
6. J'ai perdu ma belle affiche mexicaine.
7. Elle a regardé la belle eau bleue.
8. Enfin ils ont vendu leur vieil ours noir.
9. Apprenez cette première phrase russe tout de suite!
10. Je pense à notre nouveau mouton blanc.

A. Put the appropriate form of the adjective before the italicized masculine nouns. Follow the model.

1. Ce *monsieur* habite un *appartement*. (vieux)
   Ce vieux monsieur habite un vieil appartement.

2. Il y a un *arbre* près du *fleuve*. (beau)
3. Le zoo attend son *léopard* et son *hippopotame*. (premier)
4. *L'étudiant* et le *professeur* sont en route pour l'université. (nouveau)
5. Le *chapitre* et l'*examen* sont très difficiles. (dernier)
6. L'*hôtel* est à gauche du *théâtre*. (vieux)
7. Je vais prendre un *café* et un *esquimau*. (bon)
8. Le *train* et l'*autobus* partent avant minuit. (dernier)
9. L'*agriculteur* pense à son *cheval*. (vieux)
10. Ce *monsieur* regarde un *oiseau* dans le ciel. (beau)

B. Redo the sentences using the adjectives in parentheses. Pay attention to the position of the adjectives. Follow the model.

1. Nous avons parlé à l'auteur. (italien/vieil)
   Nous avons parlé au vieil auteur italien.

2. Je prends toujours l'autobus. (premier/vert)
3. Ils ont dîné avec leur ami. (belge/nouvel)
4. Est-ce que tu as regardé cet enfant? (bel/blond)
5. Vous enseignez à cette université? (canadienne/nouvelle)
6. J'ai perdu mon affiche. (belle/mexicaine)
7. Elle a regardé l'eau. (belle/bleue)
8. Enfin ils ont vendu leur ours. (noir/vieil)
9. Apprenez cette phrase tout de suite! (première/russe)
10. Je pense à notre mouton. (blanc/nouveau)

Vérifiez vos progrès

Complete the sentences using the present tense form of the verb and the appropriate form of the adjective in parentheses. Be careful! Some are regular *-re* verbs and others are *prendre*-type verbs.

1. Le *(nouveau)* étudiant ne va pas apprendre le chinois.
   Le nouvel étudiant n'apprend pas le chinois.

2. Ils ne vont pas comprendre cette *(dernier)* question.
3. Le *(vieux)* agriculteur ne va pas vendre ses cochons.
4. Nous n'allons pas prendre le *(premier)* avion.
5. Une *(bon)* étudiante ne va pas répondre toujours aux mêmes questions.
6. Vous n'allez pas prendre le *(dernier)* autobus?
7. Ils ne vont pas apprendre ce *(beau)* poème par cœur.
8. Nous n'allons pas comprendre cette *(vieux)* histoire.
9. Cet enfant ne va pas prendre ce *(beau)* oiseau.
10. Tu ne vas pas prendre cette *(nouveau)* route pour aller au bureau?

CONVERSATION ET LECTURE

Parlons de vous

1. Quel âge avez-vous? Est-ce que vous avez des frères? des sœurs? aînés ou cadets? Quel âge ont-ils? Est-ce qu'ils sont mariés ou fiancés? Est-ce qu'ils vont au lycée? à l'université?   2. Qu'est-ce qu'il y a qui fait peur aux enfants? aux adultes? Est-ce que vous avez peur de quelque chose? des animaux?   3. Est-ce que vous avez un chien? un chat? Combien?   4. Est-ce que vous habitez une ferme? Est-ce que vous avez visité une ferme?   5. Est-ce que vous aimez aller au zoo? Quels animaux est-ce que vous aimez regarder? Pourquoi?   6. Quand vous allez au café qu'est-ce que vous prenez?   7. Vous apprenez le français cette année. Qu'est-ce que vous apprenez à faire dans votre classe de français? Vous êtes fort en français?

See Cultural Supplement.

La ferme des animaux

Odile et sa sœur cadette Pascale passent la soirée à la maison. Pascale écrit° une lettre à leur frère aîné, Mathieu, qui a vingt et un ans et qui est étudiant à Clermont-Ferrand.[1] Pendant que Pascale écrit la 5 lettre, Odile lit° un roman.

écrire: *to write*

lire: *to read*

—Qu'est-ce que tu lis, Odile? demande Pascale.
—*Animal Farm.*[2] répond Odile.
—C'est en anglais?
—Oui, mais ce livre n'est pas très difficile.
10 —Qu'est-ce que ça veut dire—*Animal Farm?*
—La "ferme des animaux." C'est l'histoire d'une ferme où les animaux ne veulent plus° travailler pour le maître.° Alors ils se révoltent.°
—Les animaux se révoltent?

ne . . . plus: *no longer*
le maître: *master*
se révolter: *to revolt*

15 —Oui. C'est un vieux cochon qui organise la révolte. Dans cette histoire les cochons sont très intelligents. Ce sont les seuls animaux qui savent° lire et écrire. Après la révolte, ils deviennent° les maîtres et les autres animaux travaillent pour eux.

savoir: *to know how*
devenir: *to become*

20 —C'est vraiment bizarre. Qui est l'auteur de ce roman?
—George Orwell, l'écrivain° anglais.
—Ah, oui. L'année dernière nous avons étudié un de ses romans, *1984*[3]—mais en français, pas en anglais!
25 —Je voudrais bien le° lire, moi aussi.
—Ça vaut la peine°—c'est vraiment un très bon livre.

l'écrivain (*m.*): *writer*

le: *(here) it*
ça vaut la peine: *it's worth it*

---

[1]Clermont-Ferrand is a major industrial city in central France. It is the center of the very large French tire industry. There is also a university located there.
[2]In French, the title of the novel is *La République des animaux.*
[3]This is said as *mil neuf cent quatre-vingt-quatre.*

À propos ...

1. Où sont les sœurs? Qui est la sœur aînée?   2. Que font les sœurs?
3. Qui est Mathieu? Où est-il? Qu'est-ce qu'il fait?   4. Quel roman est-ce
qu'Odile lit? Est-ce que le livre est en français? C'est un roman difficile?
5. Dans l'histoire, qu'est-ce que les animaux ne veulent plus faire? Qu'est-ce
qu'ils font enfin?   6. Qui organise la révolte? Qu'est-ce que les cochons
peuvent faire que les autres animaux ne peuvent pas faire?   7. Est-ce qu'il y
a des maîtres après la révolte? Qui sont les nouveaux maîtres?   8. Qui est
l'auteur d'*Animal Farm?*   9. Quand est-ce que Pascale a étudié un livre de
cet auteur? Quel livre? Est-ce que Pascale a aimé ce livre? Est-ce qu'Odile
veut le lire aussi?   10. Et vous, est-ce que vous avez étudié *Animal Farm?*
et *1984?* Est-ce que avez vu ("seen") le dessin animé *Animal Farm?* Si "oui,"
est-ce que vous avèz aimé ce film?   11. Est-ce que vous aimez la science-
fiction? Quels auteurs de science-fiction est-ce que vous aimez?   12. Un
célèbre auteur français, Jules Verne, a écrit ("wrote") des livres de science-
fiction. Est-ce que vous avez lu ("read") ses livres? *Le Tour du monde en
quatre-vingts jours,* peut-être? ou *Vingt Mille Lieues sous les mers?*

EXPLICATIONS II

Comment poser des questions

Exs. A–B can be done after Points 1 and 3.

1. You know that in French the most common ways of asking a question are to use the same word order as for a statement, but (a) to raise the pitch of your voice on the last syllable or (b) to put *est-ce que* (or *est-ce qu'*) at the beginning. There is also a third way:

Il font des fautes.	**Font-ils** des fautes?
Il prend un citron pressé.	**Prend-il** un citron pressé?
Elle aime les chats.	**Aime-t-elle** les chats?

This is called "inversion." It is used much less frequently in spoken French, except in certain common questions such as *quel âge a-t-il?, quel temps fait-il?,* and *quelle heure est-il?* However, it is the most common form in written French.[1]

In inversion, the final *t* in the 3 sing. and 3 pl. forms is always pronounced: *fait-elle, font-ils.* If the 3 sing. form ends in the letter *d,* it is pronounced as a [t] sound: *prend-il.* If the 3 sing. form does not end in the letter *t* or *d,* the letter *t* is inserted: *aime-t-elle, regarde-t-il.*

2. The question words *où, quand, comment,* and *pourquoi* are also used with inversion:

Ex. C can be done after Point 2.

Point out that there is liaison after *quand* and *comment* and that the *d* of *quand* is pronounced [t].

Où allons-nous ce soir?	**Comment allez-vous,** madame?
Quand sort ton ami?	**Pourquoi prennent-elles** le train?

3. Negative questions are formed in the same way as negative statements. *Ne* (or *n'*) is placed before the verb; *pas* is placed after:

Il travaille en ville?	Il ne travaille pas en ville?
Est-ce que tu réponds?	Est-ce que tu ne réponds pas?
Allez-vous au cinéma?	N'allez-vous pas au cinéma?

4. Questions in the passé composé follow the same pattern:

Exs. D–E can be done after Point 4.

Il a attendu sa femme?	Il n'a pas attendu sa femme?
Est-ce que tu as répondu?	Est-ce que tu n'as pas répondu?
A-t-il posé la question?	N'a-t-il pas posé la question?

5. Questions in which "who" is the subject:

Nous sommes au bord de la mer.	Qui est au bord de la mer?
Ils n'ont pas fini l'histoire.	Qui n'a pas fini l'histoire?

In a "who" question, *qui* is followed by the 3 sing. form of the verb.

6. When a person ("who," "whom") is the object of a question, use *qui est-ce que* (or *qui est-ce qu'*):

Ex. F can be done after Points 6–7.

Alain attend l'agriculteur.	Qui est-ce qu'il attend?
Nous écoutons le concierge.	Qui est-ce que vous écoutez?

[1]Do not use inversion with the 1 sing. form, *je.*

7. When a thing ("what") is the object of a question, use *qu'est-ce que* (or *qu'est-ce qu'*):

Ils apprennent le japonais.   **Qu'est-ce qu'ils apprennent?**
Je fais des achats.   **Qu'est-ce que tu fais?**

Before inversion, *qu'est-ce que* becomes *que:*

Qu'est-ce qu'elle fait?   **Que fait-elle?**
Qu'est-ce que les garçons prennent?   **Que prennent les garçons?**

8. For questions that have "which" or "what" plus a noun, use the adjective *quel.* Like all adjectives, it agrees with the noun:

Quel mot est-ce que tu cherches?   **Quelle robe** porte-t-elle?
Quels messieurs vont à Paris?   **Quelles leçons** est-ce qu'il révise?

Exercices

A. Change to questions using *est-ce que.* Follow the models.

  1. Tu peux sortir plus tard?
     Est-ce que tu peux sortir plus tard?
  2. Tu ne veux pas assister au match de hockey?
     Est-ce que tu ne veux pas assister au match de hockey?

  3. Vous attendez Viviane?
  4. Ils font de la physique?
  5. Nous ne prenons pas notre goûter à 4 h.?
  6. Tu vas au supermarché?
  7. Il enseigne les mathématiques?
  8. Elle ne parle pas wolof?

B. Redo the above exercise using inversion. Follow the models.

  1. Tu peux sortir plus tard?
     Peux-tu sortir plus tard?
  2. Tu ne veux pas assister au match de hockey?
     Ne veux-tu pas assister au match de hockey?

C. Form questions using inversion and the appropriate word: *quand, comment,* or *où.* Follow the models.

  1. Elles arrivent *demain.*   *Quand arrivent-elles?*
  2. Il va *à son cours de biologie.*   *Où va-t-il?*
  3. Ils travaillent *bien.*   *Comment travaillent-ils?*

  4. Il a dormi *l'après-midi.*
  5. Ils ont passé la matinée *à la terrasse d'un café.*
  6. Ils ont vendu leur maison *la semaine dernière.*
  7. Elle a parlé *trop vite.*
  8. Il a attendu *au coin de la rue.*
  9. Ils ont joué aux échecs *vendredi dernier.*
  10. Vous avez répondu *très lentement.*

Ex. G can be done after Point 8.

Ex. A
3. Est-ce que vous attendez Viviane?
4. Est-ce qu'ils font de la physique?
5. Est-ce que nous ne prenons pas notre goûter à 4 h.?
6. Est-ce que tu vas au supermarché?
7. Est-ce qu'il enseigne les mathématiques?
8. Est-ce qu'elle ne parle pas wolof?

Ex. B
3. Attendez-vous Viviane?
4. Font-ils de la physique?
5. Ne prenons-nous pas notre goûter à 4 h.?
6. Vas-tu au supermarché?
7. Enseigne-t-il les mathématiques?
8. Ne parle-t-elle pas wolof?

Before doing Ex. C, you might want to review the question words by doing this exercise using *est-ce que.*

4. Quand a-t-il dormi?
5. Où ont-ils passé la matinée?
6. Quand ont-ils vendu leur maison?
7. Comment a-t-elle parlé?
8. Où a-t-il attendu?
9. Quand ont-ils joué aux échecs?
10. Comment avons-nous (est-ce que j'ai) répondu?

D. Form questions in the passé composé using *est-ce que*. Follow the models.

1. Nous avons choisi les réponses correctes.
   Est-ce que nous avons choisi les réponses correctes?
2. Tu n'as pas porté ta nouvelle robe.
   Est-ce que tu n'as pas porté ta nouvelle robe?

3. Ils ont enseigné les sciences sociales au lycée.
4. Vous n'avez pas assisté au concert hier soir.
5. Ils n'ont pas cherché l'argent.
6. Tu as téléphoné à Germaine le mois dernier.
7. Elle a aimé son cours d'anglais.
8. Vous n'avez pas fini vos boissons.

E. Redo the above exercise using inversion. Follow the models.

1. Nous avons choisi les réponses correctes.
   Avons-nous choisi les réponses correctes?
2. Tu n'as pas porté ta nouvelle robe.
   N'as-tu pas porté ta nouvelle robe?

3. Est-ce qu'ils ont enseigné les sciences sociales au lycée?
4. Est-ce que vous n'avez pas assisté au concert hier soir?
5. Est-ce qu'ils n'ont pas cherché l'argent?
6. Est-ce que tu as téléphoné à Germaine le mois dernier?
7. Est-ce qu'elle a aimé son cours d'anglais?
8. Est-ce que vous n'avez pas fini vos boissons?

3. Ont-ils enseigné les sciences sociales au lycée?
4. N'avez-vous pas assisté au concert hier soir?
5. N'ont-ils pas cherché l'argent?
6. As-tu téléphoné à Germaine le mois dernier?
7. A-t-elle aimé son cours d'anglais?
8. N'avez-vous pas fini vos boissons?

3. Qu'est-ce qu'elles regardent?
4. Qui est-ce que vous entendez?
5. Qu'est-ce que tu as trouvé?
6. Qui est-ce qu'ils ont écouté?
7. Qui est-ce qu'ils ont regardé?
8. Qui est-ce que vous n'aimez pas?
9. Qu'est-ce que tu n'as pas fini?

F. Form questions using *qu'est-ce que* or *qui est-ce que.* Follow the models.

1. Ils attendent *leurs copains.*
   Qui est-ce qu'ils attendent?
2. Nous avons aimé *ces dessins animés.*
   Qu'est-ce que nous avons aimé?

3. Elles regardent *ce beau nuage blanc.*
4. Vous entendez *les gens à côté.*
5. Tu as trouvé *les billets.*
6. Ils ont écouté *l'auteur célèbre.*
7. Ils ont regardé *les belles jeunes filles grecques.*
8. Vous n'aimez pas *votre nouvelle voisine.*
9. Tu n'as pas fini *tes devoirs.*

G. Form questions using *est-ce que* and the correct form of the adjective *quel.* Follow the model.

2. Quelles chaussures est-ce que je veux porter?
3. Quels étudiants est-ce qu'ils n'aiment pas?
4. Quelle table est-ce qu'ils vont prendre?
5. Quel chapitre est-ce que tu as étudié?
6. Quels livres de poche est-ce qu'elle choisit?
7. Quelle affiche est-ce qu'il donne à Vincent?
8. Quel disque est-ce qu'elles ont déjà entendu?
9. Quelles langues est-ce qu'ils comprennent?
10. Quel poème est-ce que tu apprends par cœur?

1. Ils regardent *cette belle dame à côté.*
   Quelle dame est-ce qu'ils regardent?

2. Je veux porter *mes vieilles chaussures noires.*
3. Ils n'aiment pas *ces étudiants paresseux.*
4. Ils vont prendre *la dernière table libre.*
5. Tu as étudié *le dernier chapitre du roman.*
6. Elle choisit *des livres de poche.*
7. Il donne *cette grande affiche* à Vincent.
8. Elles ont déjà entendu *cet autre disque.*
9. Ils comprennent *deux langues étrangères.*
10. Tu apprends *ce long poème portugais* par cœur.

Vérifiez vos progrès

Rewrite the questions in the negative. Follow the model.

1. Pourquoi est-ce qu'il va au zoo?
   Pourquoi est-ce qu'il ne va pas au zoo?

2. A-t-il assisté à votre cours de sciences sociales?
3. Où veulent-ils aller pendant leurs vacances?
4. Qui travaille vite?
5. Avez-vous entendu le nouveau disque?
6. Pourquoi est-ce que nous vendons la vieille voiture?
7. Est-ce que tu as réussi à trouver un bon cadeau?
8. Quel chapitre est-ce que tu comprends?
9. Qui est-ce que vous aimez?
10. Où peux-tu aller?

RÉVISION ET THÈME

Consult the model sentences, then put the English cues into French and use them to form new sentences based on the models.

1. Anne et *son frère aîné* sont *au bord de la mer, avec leurs parents.*
   (her younger brothers) (on the corner, next to the bookstore)
   (her young husband)   (by the roadside, near the farm)

2. Nous demandons: *"Quels cochons vendez-vous bientôt?"*
   ("Which poem are you (pl.) *finally learning?")*
   ("Which languages do they (f.) *already understand?")*

3. Tu réponds: "Il y a *un vieux chien anglais.*"
   (an old Dutch cow)
   (an old Senegalese hippopotamus)

4. Vous demandez: *"Où trouve-t-on ces léopards noirs?"*
   ("Why is he looking for that nice farmer?")
   ("When is she bringing those white mice?")

5. Va regarder *ce nouveau coq rouge* là-bas!
   (that new white hen)
   (that new gray elephant)

Now that you have done the *Révision,* you are ready to write a composition. Put the English captions describing each cartoon panel into French to form a paragraph.

See Teacher's Section for answers to the *révision* and *thème.*

Review of:
1. *cadet* vs. *jeune* prepositions
2. *quel* + inversion *prendre*-type verbs vs. regular *-re* verbs position of adverbs
3. forms of *vieux* adjectives of nationality ending in *-ais*
4. question words + inversion insertion of *t* in inversion
5. forms of *nouveau* position of adjectives

Mathieu and his younger sister are in the middle of the zoo, in front of the monkeys.

She asks: "Which animals do you want to look at now?"

Mathieu answers: "There's a new Russian bear."

She asks: "Why do you like those mean animals?"

"Let's go look at that beautiful white bird over there."

AUTO-TEST

A. Write what animal the person hears. Follow the model.

1. J'entends "ouah-ouah." *C'est un chien.*

2. J'entends "glou-glou-glou."
3. J'entends "cot-cot-cot-codèt."
4. J'entends "meuh."
5. J'entends "bèèè-bèèè."
6. J'entends "miaou."

7. J'entends "couin-couin."
8. J'entends "hii-hii."
9. J'entends "cocorico."
10. J'entends "gron-gron."

B. Identify the animals, using the determiners given and the appropriate form of each adjective. Make sure the adjectives are in the correct position. Follow the model.

1. une/blanc/grand
   C'est une grande vache blanche.
2. notre/beau/russe
3. un/petit/jaune et noir

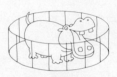

4. notre/maigre/premier
5. un/paresseux/vieux
6. leur/noir/nouveau

7. un/méchant/petit
8. une/gris/vieux
9. un/beau/bleu

C. Write answers to the questions using the cues in parentheses. Follow the model.

1. Qui apprend à travailler seul? (moi)
   J'apprends à travailler seul.

2. Qui comprend le flamand? (ces jeunes gens)
3. Qui apprend l'espagnol? (nous)
4. Qui prend une bière? (toi)
5. Qui comprend les animaux? (l'agriculteur)
6. Qui prend quelque chose? (vous)
7. Qui apprend à jouer aux cartes? (ce petit enfant)
8. Qui comprend cet oiseau? (la concierge et son mari)

D. Write questions based on the statements, asking "who" or "what" — whichever is appropriate. Remember that you will be replacing the italicized words with the interrogative word. Follow the models.

1. Je n'ai pas trouvé *le petit zoo au milieu de la ville*.
   Qu'est-ce que tu n'as pas trouvé?
2. Il attend *cette jeune dame aimable*.
   Qui est-ce qu'il attend?

3. Ils prennent *l'avion qui part à 11 h. 27*.
4. Nous pouvons regarder *ces nouveaux dessins animés canadiens*.
5. Vous n'avez pas étudié *l'autre chapitre*.
6. Elle a cherché *ce nouvel agent*.
7. Ils vendent *une vieille villa au bord de la mer*.
8. Elle aime *les vendeuses qui travaillent dans le grand magasin près de la bibliothèque*.

E. Redo the above exercise, asking "which" questions and using inversion. Follow the models.

1. Je n'ai pas trouvé *le petit zoo au milieu de la ville*.
   Quel zoo n'as-tu pas trouvé?
2. Il attend *cette jeune dame aimable*.
   Quelle dame attend-il?

Du 25 Mai au 15 Juin

*Pour
la première fois
dans
les Tuileries*

Le Cirque Bouglione

Poème

MEA CULPA°

C'est ma faute
C'est ma faute
C'est ma très grande faute d'orthographe°
Voilà comment j'écris°
Giraffe.

mea culpa *(Latin)* = ma
faute

l'orthographe *(f.):*
spelling

écrire: *to write*

Ask students to point out
the misspelling of *la girafe*.

Jacques Prévert, *Histoires*
© Editions Gallimard, 1963

Proverbe

On apprend à tout âge.

LE RELAIS DES GOURMETS
HOTEL - RESTAURANT ★★★★NN
SALONS PARTICULIERS
15, Rue de Geôle · 14000 CAEN

M. GRIFFITH

27/26

S.A. "LES GOURMETS"
au Capital de 192 000 Frs
J. LEGRAS
Président - Directeur Général

Téléphone - 86 - 06 - 01 (lignes groupées)
C. C. P. ROUEN 652.68 X
R. Commerce CAEN 58 B 46
Telex 17 353

14.10.75		
15.10.75	chambre	
	P. déj.	
16.10.75	chambre	40.—
	p. déj.	8
17.10.75	chambre	80
	p. déj.	8
	chambre	80
	p. déj.	8.
	chambre	80.
	p. déj.	8
	S.S.	312
		46.80
	Tel.	358.80
		17 40
		376.20

7.70
Tel : 9.00
0.70

CARON-OZANNE 93197

OIR *Hôtel*

DATE .... 19 ....

NOM .... CHAMBRE ....

INSTRUCTIONS SPÉCIALES .... MARQUE DE BUANDERIE ....

Le linge reçu avant 9:00 a.m. sera retourné le même jour, excepté les samedis, dimanches et jours de fête.

COMPTE DU CLIENT	COMPTE DE L'HÔTEL	HOMMES		MONTANT	COMPTE DU CLIENT	COMPTE DE L'HÔTEL			MONTANT
		Chemises ord.	.60				Jupes ou pant. sport	1.50	
		" du soir	1.00				Jupons longs	.80	
		" (soie, laine)	.85				" à la taille	.65	
		" sport	.75				Mouchoirs	.15	
		Faux cols	.15				Pyjamas	.75	
							" (soie)	1.00	
		Complets lav. (2 pces)	2.50				Robes	2.00/3.00	
		Gilet du soir	.85				Robes de nuit (coton)	.90	
		Mouchoirs	.15				" " " (soie)	1.50	
		Pant. sport Bermuda	1.00				Tailleurs lav. (2 pces)	3.00	
		Pant. ou pant. sport	1.75						
		Pyjamas	.65				Bas	.30 la paire	
		" de soie	.80				Chandails	1.25	
		Robes de ch. 1.50 et plus					Culottes	.50	
		Salopettes (coton)	.60				Gaines	.70	
		" (soie ou laine	.85				Soutien-gorge	.50	
		Caleçons courts (coton)	.40				ENFANTS		
		" longs (coton)	.40				Blouses	.65	
		Cal. longs (soie, laine)	.45						
		Camisoles (coton)	.45				Chemises de nuit	.50	
		" (soie ou laine)	.50				Costumes de garçon	1.00	
		Chaussettes .30 la paire					Gilets de dessous	.30	
							Jupes	.75	
		DAMES					Pyjamas	.50	
		Chemisiers, blouses	.80				Robes	1.00 et plus	
		Chem., blouses (soie)	1.00						
							Chaussettes	.15	
		Crinolines	.80 et plus				Culottes	.30	
		Déshabillés	1.35 et plus				Salopettes	.60	

TOTAL

L'hôtel n'est pas responsable de la décoloration des vêtements ou de la perte causée par le feu. L'hôtel n'est pas responsable des vêtements laissés en sa possession plus de trois mois. Les articles requérant plus de soins seront facturés en conséquence. A moins qu'une liste des articles n'accompagne le paquet, notre compte doit être accepté comme tel.

CL 19-2-69-5000

(English on reverse side)

Treizième Leçon

A Boston

Hamidou va travailler pour Air Mali.[1] Il fait un stage de six mois à Boston pour apprendre l'anglais. Un jour, après ses cours, il rencontre Thierry, un autre jeune Noir.

	HAMIDOU	Tu fais des progrès en anglais!
5	THIERRY	Oui, je crois que ça va assez bien.
	HAMIDOU	Tu aimes le livre?
	THIERRY	Oui, mais je le trouve difficile.
	HAMIDOU	Tu vas rester à Boston?
	THIERRY	Non, je suis de la Guadeloupe.[2] Je suis dans le tourisme, moi.
10		Mon père a un hôtel près de Pointe-à-Pitre.[3]
	HAMIDOU	Ah, je vois. Moi, je suis malien. Je veux être pilote et pour les professions comme pilote, steward et hôtesse de l'air, il faut pouvoir parler anglais.

---

[1] Air Mali is the national airline of the Republic of Mali, a former French colony in West Africa.

[2] Guadeloupe, in the Caribbean Sea, is actually two small islands, Grande-Terre and Basse-Terre, separated by a thin arm of the sea called *la rivière Salée*. Along with the nearby island of Martinique, Guyane Française in South America, and the island of Réunion in the Indian Ocean, Guadeloupe is a *département* of France. In a sense, they are to France what the Hawaiian Islands are to the United States—distant regions that are legally as much a part of the country as if they were on the mainland.

[3] Pointe-à-Pitre, with a population of about 30,000, is the principal city of Guadeloupe.

In Boston

Hamidou is going to work for Air Mali. He is training for six months in Boston in order to learn English. One day, after his classes, he runs into Thierry, another young black.

HAMIDOU   You're making progress in English!
5 THIERRY   Yeah, I think it's going pretty well.
HAMIDOU   Do you like the book?
THIERRY   Yes, but I find it difficult.
HAMIDOU   Are you going to stay in Boston?
THIERRY   No, I'm from Guadeloupe. I'm in the tourist business. My father
10   has a hotel near Pointe-à-Pitre.
HAMIDOU   Oh, I see. I'm from Mali. I want to be a pilot, and for professions like pilot, steward, and stewardess you have to be able to speak English.

Questionnaire

1. Que fait Hamidou à Boston?   2. Qui est-ce qu'il rencontre?   3. Est-ce que Thierry fait des progrès en anglais?   4. Est-ce qu'il n'aime pas le livre?
5. Qu'est-ce que Thierry fait comme profession? Que fait son père?
6. Qu'est-ce que Hamidou veut faire comme profession? Pourquoi est-ce qu'il apprend l'anglais?

PRONONCIATION

The [j] sound is very much like the first sound in the English word "yes," but it is pronounced with greater tension.

Exercices

A. Listen carefully, then say these words aloud. Be careful to pronounce a distinct [j] sound at the end of each word.

fille   feuille   vieille   famille   soleil   sommeil

B. In these words, the [j] sound comes between two vowel sounds. Note that the [j] sound is always part of the second syllable.

maillot   cahier   papier   juillet   crayon   travailler

C. Now say these one-syllable words aloud. Be careful not to insert an [i] sound before the [j] sound.

bien   pied   ciel   pièce   nièce   mieux   vieux

D. Now say these sentences containing the [j] sound.

Hier j'ai travaillé à Lyon.   La fille italienne est inquiète.
Le chien du concierge a sommeil.   Il y a une vieille pièce canadienne.
Sa fiancée travaille à Marseille.   Le premier monsieur est au milieu.

MOTS NOUVEAUX I

le pilote   l'hôtesse de l'air (f.)   le steward   le médecin   l'infirmière (f.)   l'infirmier (m.)

le dentiste   la dentiste   le pharmacien   la pharmacie   la pharmacienne

le juge

l'avocate (f.)   l'avocat (m.)   le vendeur   le magasin   la vendeuse   la boutique

Que fait votre frère? Est-ce
   qu'il a **un emploi?**
Oui, il est **ingénieur** (m.).[1]
Est-ce qu'il aime **le travail?**
Il est vraiment **passionné par** son
   travail.

Quelle est la **profession** de ton père?
Il est médecin.
Que fait ta mère?
Elle est médecin aussi.[2]

*What does your brother do? Does he
   have* **a job?**
Yes, he's **an engineer.**
Does he like **the work?**
He's really **enthusiastic about** *his
   work.*

What's your father's **profession?**
He's a doctor.
What does your mother do?
She's a doctor, too.

le magasin: Point out that
this means "store," where-
as le grand magasin means
"department store." Une
boutique is a specialty
shop.

Remind students that le
professeur is also used for
both males and females.

[1]Remember that when a noun or subject pronoun and the verb *être* are immediately followed by
certain types of nouns, such as professions, the French do not use the indefinite determiner
(*un, une, des*).

[2]Though *l'ingénieur, le pilote, le médecin,* and *le juge* are masculine nouns, they are also used in
speaking of women. Thus *Voilà le juge* would be used even if the judge were a woman.

Exercice de vocabulaire

Answer the questions according to the pictures. Follow the model.

2. Il est juge.
3. Elle est médecin.
4. Elle est pharmacienne.
5. Il est avocat.
6. Il est dentiste.
7. Elle est hôtesse de l'air.
8. Elle est avocate.
9. Il est pilote.
10. Il est infirmier.
11. Elle est infirmière.
12. Il est pharmacien.

1. Quel est son emploi?
Elle est vendeuse.

2. Que fait son mari?

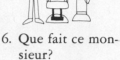 

3. Que fait sa fille?

4. Quelle est sa profession?

5. Que fait ton oncle?

6. Que fait ce monsieur?

7. Que fait ta sœur aînée?

8. Que fait-elle?

9. Qu'est-ce qu'il fait?

10. Quelle est sa profession?

11. Que fait ton amie?

12. Que fait leur neveu?

MOTS NOUVEAUX II

l'acteur (m.)   l'actrice (f.)

On va jouer une pièce.   *We're going to **put on a play.***
Moi, je vais jouer un rôle.   *I'm going to **play a part.***
Qui va jouer le rôle principal?   *Who's going to play **the lead**?*
            les rôles principaux?   *the leads?*

la secrétaire l'homme d'affaires (m.) la femme d'affaires l'employé (de bureau) l'employée (de bureau)

la ménagère le soldat le marin l'artiste (m.) l'artiste (f.)

le facteur la lettre l'ouvrier (m.) l'ouvrière (f.)

Que font leurs sœurs comme profession?	What do their sisters do *for a living?*
Comme vous, elles sont femmes d'affaires.	*Like you, they are business-women.*
Tu vas peut-être **rencontrer** Eric.	*Maybe you'll **run into** Eric.*
Il a toujours le même emploi?	*Does he still have the same job?*
Oui, il est **employé de bureau.**	*Yes, he's a **clerk.***
Dans un bureau de tourisme?	*In a tourist office?*
Oui, il aime le travail.	*Yes, he likes the work.*
Mon amie **malienne** veut être ingénieur comme son père.	*My **Malian** friend wants to be an engineer like her father.*
Elle va **faire un stage** dans une usine.	*She's going **to be in a training program** in a factory.*
Mon ami **malien** fait un stage à Paris.	*My **Malian** friend is training in Paris.*
Il est passionné par le travail et il **fait des progrès** (m. pl.).	*He's enthusiastic about the work and he's **making progress.***

l'employé(e): Point out that this term can be used with or without the addition of *de bureau. Un(e) employé(e)* is any salaried office worker, differing from *un(e) ouvrier(ière)* in that the latter is used exclusively for manual laborers. The closest English equivalent for *employé(e)* would be "clerk."

Exercices de vocabulaire

A. Answer the questions according to the pictures. Follow the models.

1. Qui travaille dans un café?
   Une serveuse travaille dans un café.

2. Qu'est-ce qu'ils font?
   Ils sont employés de bureau.

3. Qui travaille dans une usine?

4. Qu'est-ce qu'ils font?

5. Qui apporte les lettres?

6. Qu'est-ce qu'elles font?

7. Qui travaille à la maison, va au marché, prépare le dîner, fait la vaisselle, etc.?

8. Qu'est-ce qu'ils font?

3. Un ouvrier travaille dans une usine.
4. Ils sont artistes.
5. Un facteur apporte les lettres.
6. Elles sont femmes d'affaires.
7. Une ménagère travaille à la maison, etc.
8. Ils sont soldats.

B. According to the statements, tell what the people want to be. Follow the model.

1. Son frère fait un stage dans un grand hôpital à Lyon.
   Il veut être médecin.   or: *Il veut être infirmier.*

2. Nous sommes passionnés par le théâtre.
3. Mes cousines veulent vendre des habits dans un magasin ou une boutique comme ma tante.
4. Christian et Daniel aiment la mer.
5. Tu aimes beaucoup les avions, Olivier.
6. Je veux travailler à la poste comme mon frère.
7. Ma cousine aime son travail. Elle fait un stage à Air France.
8. Thierry et son frère aîné aiment travailler dans un bureau.
9. Ma sœur cadette fait un stage dans une usine.
10. Ses nièces font des progrès. Aujourd'hui elles sont inconnues peut-être. Mais un jour elles vont jouer des rôles principaux.
11. Elles aiment bien travailler dans la pharmacie de leur oncle.

2. Nous voulons être acteurs.
3. Elles veulent être vendeuses.
4. Ils veulent être marins.
5. Tu veux être pilote (steward).
6. Je veux être facteur (employé de poste).
7. Elle veut être pilote (hôtesse de l'air).
8. Ils veulent être employés de bureau (hommes d'affaires).
9. Elle veut être ingénieur (ouvrière).
10. Elles veulent être actrices.
11. Elles veulent être pharmaciennes.

Treizième
Leçon

EXPLICATIONS I

Les verbes <u>voir</u> et <u>croire</u>

The two verbs *voir,* "to see," and *croire,* "to believe, to think" follow the same pattern in the present tense:

	SINGULAR		PLURAL
1	je { vois / crois		nous { voyons / croyons
2	tu { vois / crois		vous { voyez / croyez
3	il / elle / on } voit, croit		ils / elles } voient, croient

IMPERATIVE: vois! voyons! voyez!
crois! croyons! croyez!

1. The 1 and 2 pl. stem of these two verbs ends in *-oy-.* For all other forms the stem ends in *-oi-.* The endings are regular.

2. Look at the following:

Je **vois que** tu as maigri. { *I see that you've lost weight.* / *I see you've lost weight.* }

Ils **croient qu'**il a fini? { *Do they think that he's finished?* / *Do they think he's finished?* }

In English we often omit the word "that," but *que* can never be omitted.

Exercices

A. Replace the verb *regarder* with the appropriate form of the verb *voir.* Follow the model.

1. Je regarde les animaux.
   Je vois les animaux.

2. Tu regardes ce gros mouton?
3. Ils regardent le beau cheval noir.
4. Nous regardons le petit chat gris.
5. Il regarde les oiseaux bruns.
6. Vous regardez le facteur là-bas?
7. Nous regardons la pharmacie en face.
8. Je regarde le vendeur maintenant.
9. Elles regardent les canards sur le lac.

2. Tu vois ce gros mouton?
3. Ils voient le beau cheval noir.
4. Nous voyons le petit chat gris.
5. Il voit les oiseaux bruns.
6. Vous voyez le facteur là-bas?
7. Nous voyons la pharmacie en face.
8. Je vois le vendeur maintenant.
9. Elles voient les canards sur le lac.

B. Redo the sentences using the cues in parentheses and the appropriate form of the verb *croire*. Follow the model.

1. Cette actrice joue le rôle principal. (je)
   Je crois que cette actrice joue le rôle principal.

2. La ferme est loin d'ici. (elle)
3. La réponse est correcte. (tu)
4. Marianne veut être avocate. (nous)
5. Le père de Mireille est homme d'affaires. (je)
6. Cette leçon est trop difficile. (elles)
7. Votre mère a téléphoné à la boutique. (vous)
8. Ces garçons étudient beaucoup. (ils)

A qui, à quoi

You have seen that questions in which "who" and "what" are the objects are formed with *qui est-ce que* and *qu'est-ce que: Qui est-ce que je vois? Qu'est-ce qu'il croit?* Now look at the following:

Il pense au médecin.   A qui est-ce qu'il pense?
Il pense aux animaux.   A quoi est-ce qu'il pense?

When verbs that are followed by *à* are used in "who" questions, the *à* is simply placed before the *qui est-ce que*. But in "what" questions, *qu'est-ce que* becomes *à quoi est-ce que*. These questions can also be formed using inversion: *A qui pense-t-elle? A quoi pense-t-elle?*

Exercice

Form questions based on the statements. In each case replace the italicized words with the appropriate construction, *à qui* or *à quoi*. Follow the models.

1. J'ai donné l'argent *à la vendeuse.*
   A qui est-ce que tu as donné l'argent?
2. Nous jouons *au volleyball.*
   A quoi est-ce que vous jouez?

3. Ils ont parlé *aux avocats.*
4. Le facteur a donné les lettres *à la concierge.*
5. Je pense *à la ferme de mon oncle.*
6. Le professeur a posé des questions faciles *aux élèves.*
7. Nous avons répondu *à ces questions.*
8. Ils ont vendu le vieil avion *au pilote.*
9. Les tigres font peur *aux enfants.*
10. Ils pensent *à l'examen d'histoire.*
11. Elles jouent *au basketball.*
12. Elles téléphonent *à leurs secrétaires.*
13. Je pense *au printemps—aux fleurs, aux feuilles vertes, aux matinées dans le parc, etc.*

Les adjectifs pluriels placés avant le nom

1. Look at the following:

Voici les **jeunes** médecins.   Voici les **jeunes** ménagères.
Voici les **jeunes** ouvriers.   Voici les **jeunes** ouvrières.

J'aime les **grands** rôles.   J'aime les **grandes** pièces.
J'aime les **grands** acteurs.   J'aime les **grandes** actrices.

Où sont les **bons** dentistes?   Où sont les **bonnes** dentistes?
Où sont les **bons** infirmiers?   Où sont les **bonnes** infirmières?

Voilà les **nouveaux** pharmaciens. Voilà les **nouvelles** pharmaciennes.
Voilà les **nouveaux** avocats.   Voilà les **nouvelles** avocates.

Before a noun beginning with a vowel sound, the *s* or *x* of a plural adjective is a liaison consonant, pronounced [z].

2. When a plural adjective comes before a noun, the indefinite determiner *des* becomes *de:*

J'ai des moutons blancs.   *but:* J'ai de beaux moutons.
Je joue des rôles principaux.   Je joue de bons rôles.

Exercices

A. Answer the questions according to the model.

1. Cette actrice a un beau mari. Et les autres actrices?
   Elles ont de beaux maris aussi.
2. Ce soldat veut avoir un gros chien. Et les autres soldats?
   Ils veulent avoir de gros chiens aussi.
3. Cet enfant a une bonne radio. Et les autres enfants?
4. Cet agriculteur vend une grosse vache. Et les autres agriculteurs?
5. Ce médecin travaille dans un grand hôpital. Et les autres médecins?
6. Ce lycée a une vieille bibliothèque. Et les autres lycées?
7. Ce professeur attend un nouvel étudiant. Et les autres professeurs?
8. Cette vieille dame a un bel oiseau. Et les autres vieilles dames?
9. Ce monsieur voit un vieux film anglais. Et les autres messieurs?

B. Redo the sentences entirely in the plural, inserting the adjective in parentheses before the second noun. Follow the model.

1. Cet autre agriculteur a des canards blancs. (gros)
   Ces autres agriculteurs ont de gros canards blancs.
2. Dans cette petite boutique on vend des habits chers. (beaux)
3. La jeune femme d'affaires cherche des employés de bureau. (nouveaux)
4. Le bon élève a révisé des leçons difficiles. (longues)
5. Notre nouvel ami aime faire des voyages. (longs)
6. Cette petite fille fait des fautes. (grosses)
7. Ce bel acteur croit que ce sont des bureaux de tourisme. (bons)
8. Ce vieil hôpital a des infirmières. (bonnes)

Exs A–B should be done orally.

3. Ils ont de bonnes radios aussi.
4. Ils vendent de grosses vaches aussi.
5. Ils travaillent dans de grands hôpitaux aussi.
6. Ils ont de vieilles bibliothèques aussi.
7. Ils attendent de nouveaux étudiants aussi.
8. Elles ont de beaux oiseaux aussi.
9. Ils voient de vieux films anglais aussi.

2. Dans ces petites boutiques on vend de beaux habits chers.
3. Les jeunes femmes d'affaires cherchent de nouveaux employés de bureau.
4. Les bons élèves ont révisé de longues leçons difficiles.
5. Nos nouveaux amis aiment faire de longs voyages.
6. Ces petites filles font de grosses fautes.
7. Ces beaux acteurs croient que ce sont de bons bureaux de tourisme.
8. Ces vieux hôpitaux ont de bonnes infirmières.

Vérifiez vos progrès

Write complete sentences using the correct form of the words given. Follow the model.

1. Je / voir / des / actrices (beau)
   Je vois de belles actrices.

2. Nous / croire que / ces pharmaciennes (nouveau) / être / passionné par / le travail
3. Tu / croire que / les avocates (jeune) / faire un stage
4. Je / voir / des oiseaux (grand) / dans le ciel
5. Ils / croire que / ce sont / des infirmières (mauvais)
6. Nous / croire que / ils / vouloir / être / des marins (bon)
7. Est-ce que / on / voir / des hôtesses de l'air (jeune)
8. Il / croire que / ce sont / des hommes d'affaires (vieux)
9. Vous / croire que / elles / pouvoir / être / des artistes (bon)
10. Elles / voir / des hippopotames (gros)

CONVERSATION ET LECTURE

Parlons de vous

1. Qu'est-ce que vous croyez que vous allez choisir comme profession? Pourquoi? Est-ce qu'il faut aller à l'université? Est-ce qu'il faut faire un stage? Où fait-on le stage?   2. Qu'est-ce que vous étudiez maintenant qui ("which") va être important pour cette profession?   3. Est-ce que vous avez un emploi? Si "oui," où est-ce que vous travaillez? Quand? l'après-midi? la soirée? le weekend? en été? Vous êtes passionné par le travail?   4. Que fait votre père? Où est-ce qu'il travaille? Est-ce qu'il aime son emploi? Et votre mère, que fait-elle? Où est-ce qu'elle travaille?   5. Si vous avez des frères ou des sœurs aînés, que font-ils? S'ils n'ont pas d'emploi, que veulent-ils faire comme profession?

Les amis sénégalais

Les parents de Christian et de Mireille Villon ont loué° une villa à Deauville en Normandie,[1] où ils passent le mois d'août. Christian et Mireille ont des amis à Deauville et ils sortent souvent avec eux pendant leurs vacances. Cet après-midi, par exemple, ils vont jouer aux boules[2] avec Olivier Diop.

Olivier est sénégalais. Lui et sa sœur cadette, La-mine, passent leurs vacances chez un oncle. Leur

louer: *to rent*

See Cultural Supplement.

---

[1]*La Normandie* (Normandy) is a region in northwestern France, bordered on one side by the English Channel *(La Manche)*. Deauville is a fashionable resort town noted for its racecourse and gambling casino.

[2]*Les boules* is a popular game in France, much like lawn bowling. Players roll a heavy ball toward a smaller ball *(le cochonnet)*. The player or team to come closest to the smaller ball wins.

oncle, qui travaille à Paris pour l'UNESCO,[1] est in-
10 génieur agronome.° Cet été, lui aussi, il a loué une
villa à Deauville.

Olivier, qui a dix-huit ans, est un copain de lycée de
Christian. Ils vont au lycée Saint-Louis[2] à Paris où
Olivier prépare le concours d'entrée° à l'Ecole
15 Polytechnique.[3] Beaucoup de° jeunes gens africains
passent trois ou quatre années dans les écoles françaises, surtout° pour faire des études supérieures.°
Après, ils rentrent d'habitude° chez eux pour travailler.

20 Lamine, la sœur d'Olivier, passe les mois d'été avec
son frère et son oncle. Mais elle attend toujours des

agronome: *agricul-
tural*

le concours d'entrée:
   entrance exam
beaucoup de: *a lot of*
surtout: *especially*
les études supérieu-
   res *(f.pl.): advanced
   studies*
d'habitude: *usually*

---

[1]UNESCO, the United Nations Educational, Scientific, and Cultural Organization, has its headquarters in Paris.
[2]Saint-Louis (Louis IX) was king of France from 1226 to 1270. He is remembered as a very fair
and honest king, who insisted upon equal justice for all people, rich and poor. It is said that he
used to sit under a large oak tree in the Bois de Vincennes, now a large park in Paris, and
people would come to him personally to plead their cause.
[3]In order to attend a *Grande Ecole*, French students must take a very difficult entrance exam, the
concours. After completing the regular course at the *lycée*, a student may spend an additional
year or more just preparing for the *concours* at the school of his or her choice. There are about
fifty *Grandes Ecoles*, each having its own specialty: chemistry and physics, fine arts, teacher-
training, diplomacy and political science, and so forth. There is even a special school to train
future high-level government employees. The Ecole Polytechnique, one of the *Grandes Ecoles*,
trains civil and military engineers.

lettres de ses parents, et elle leur° écrit° souvent.
Elle a vraiment le mal du pays.° Plus tard, Olivier va
rentrer à Paris, mais Lamine, qui a seulement° seize
25 ans, va rentrer à Dakar. Elle, elle ne veut pas rester
en France. Après ses études de lycée, elle veut aller à
l'université de Dakar. Son père a une grande pharmacie là-bas et Lamine veut devenir° pharmacienne
comme lui.

leur: *(here) to them*
écrire: *to write*
avoir le mal du pays:
   to be homesick
seulement: *only*

devenir: *to become*

À propos ...

1. Où est-ce que les Villon passent le mois d'août? Vous croyez que Christian et Mireille aiment passer leurs vacances là-bas? Pourquoi? Qu'est-ce
qu'ils font cet après-midi, par exemple?   2. Avec qui est-ce que les Diop
passent leurs vacances? Que fait ce monsieur comme profession? Où tra-
vaille-t-il?   3. Quel âge a Olivier? A quel lycée est-ce qu'il va? Que fait-il
là?   4. Est-ce qu'il y a d'autres jeunes gens africains dans les lycées français?
Après leurs études, est-ce qu'ils restent d'habitude en France?   5. Quel âge
a la sœur cadette d'Olivier? Pourquoi est-elle un peu ("a little") triste? A
qui est-ce qu'elle écrit quand elle est triste? Est-ce qu'elle va rester en
France?   6. Que fait le père de Lamine et d'Olivier comme profession? Est-
ce que vous croyez que Lamine aime le travail de son père?   7. Et vous, où
est-ce que vous passez vos vacances? Vous avez des amis là?   8. Est-ce que
vous avez des amis qui sont étrangers? Quelle langue est-ce qu'ils parlent?
Est-ce qu'ils font leurs études en Amérique? Qu'est-ce qu'ils font—ou veulent faire—comme profession?

EXPLICATIONS II

Les pronoms compléments d'objet direct: <u>le</u>, <u>la</u>, <u>l'</u>, <u>les</u>

1. Look at the following:

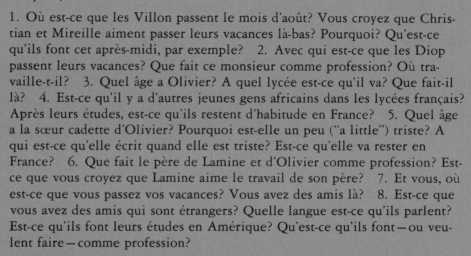

The French equivalents of the direct object pronouns "him," "her," and
"it" are *le* and *la,* depending upon the gender of the noun they are replacing. The equivalent of "them" is *les.* Note that these pronouns are placed
between the subject and the verb.

2. Before a vowel sound, there is elision and liaison:

Elles l'écoutent.   *They're listening to **him** (her, it).*
Elles les écoutent.   *They're listening to **them**.*

3. *Le. la. l'.* and *les* replace the entire object of the verb:

Tu vois **cet avion** dans le ciel?   Tu **le** vois?
Tu vends **ta vieille voiture bleue?**   Tu **la** vends?

Exs. A, C, and E can be done after covering Point 3.

4. The direct object pronoun comes between *ne* and the verb:

Elles **le** regardent.   Elles **ne le** regardent **pas.**
Vous **l'**apportez.   Vous **ne l'**apportez **pas.**
Nous **les** attendons.   Nous **ne les** attendons **pas.**

Exs. B and D can be done after covering Point 4.

5. A pronoun that is the object of a verb in the infinitive comes immediately before the infinitive:

Ils veulent **faire ce travail.**   Ils veulent **le faire.**
Tu peux **apprendre cette phrase?**   Tu peux **l'apprendre?**
Tu ne vas pas **rater ces examens.**   Tu ne vas pas **les rater.**

Ex. F can be done after covering Point 5.

You may want to present the poem (p. 223) now.

6. Verbs that do not require a preposition in French take a direct object:
attendre. chercher. demander. écouter. regarder:

Je **les** attends.   *I'm waiting for them.*
Je **le** demande.   *I'm asking for it.*
Je **la** regarde.   *I'm looking at it (her).*

Exercices

A. Replace the object of the verb with the direct object pronoun *le.* Follow the model.

1. Nous vendons *notre vieux cheval gris* aujourd'hui.
Nous le vendons aujourd'hui.

2. On regarde *le juge.*
3. Tu comprends *le russe* peut-être.
4. Elle joue *le rôle principal* ce soir.
5. Nous prenons *ton stylo jaune.*
6. Tout à coup ils voient *le pilote.*
7. Vous demandez *mon argent.*
8. Ils choisissent *ce gros chat.*
9. Je prépare *le dîner* tout de suite.

B. Redo the above exercise in the negative. Follow the model.

1. Nous ne vendons pas *notre vieux cheval gris* aujourd'hui.
Nous ne le vendons pas aujourd'hui.

C. Answer the questions using the direct object pronoun *la.* Follow the model.

1. Tu choisis *cette actrice* pour le rôle?
Oui, je la choisis pour le rôle.

2. Tu fermes *la porte?*
3. Tu crois *cette histoire?*

2. On le regarde.
3. Tu le comprends peut-être.
4. Elle le joue ce soir.
5. Nous le prenons.
6. Tout à coup ils le voient.
7. Vous le demandez.
8. Ils le choisissent.
9. Je le prépare tout de suite.

2. On ne le regarde pas.
3. Tu ne le comprends pas peut-être.
4. Elle ne le joue pas ce soir.
5. Nous ne le prenons pas.
6. Tout à coup ils ne le voient pas.
7. Vous ne le demandez pas.
8. Ils ne le choisissent pas.
9. Je ne le prépare pas tout de suite.

2. Oui, je la ferme.
3. Oui, je la crois.

4. Oui, je la porte.
5. Oui, je la regarde.
6. Oui, je la comprends.
7. Oui, je la vends au marché.
8. Oui, je la vois.
9. Oui, je la finis.

4. Tu portes *ta nouvelle robe?*
5. Tu regardes *la secrétaire?*
6. Tu comprends *la leçon de chinois?*
7. Tu vends *ta vache* au marché?
8. Tu vois *l'ouvrière là-bas?*
9. Tu finis *la pièce?*

D. Answer in the negative, using the direct object pronoun *l'*. Follow the model.

1. Tu habites *la maison en face de l'hôpital?*
   Non, je ne l'habite pas.

2. Non, ils ne l'attendent pas.
3. Non, elle ne l'enseigne pas.
4. Non, je ne l'étudie pas.
5. Non, il ne l'aime pas.
6. Non, nous ne l'écoutons (je ne l'écoute) pas.
7. Non, elle ne l'apprend pas par cœur.
8. Non, ils ne l'apportent pas à la banque.

2. Ils attendent *le facteur?*
3. Elle enseigne *l'espagnol?*
4. Tu étudies *la biologie?*
5. Il aime *son emploi?*
6. Vous écoutez *ce bel oiseau?*
7. Elle apprend *le rôle* par cœur?
8. Ils apportent *leur argent* à la banque?

E. Answer using the direct object pronoun *les*. Follow the model.

1. Nous voyons *l'avocat et le juge?*
   Bien sûr, vous les voyez.

2. Bien sûr, ils les regardent.
3. Bien sûr, je les vois.
4. Bien sûr, nous les voyons (je les vois).
5. Bien sûr, elle les attend.
6. Bien sûr, ils les aiment.
7. Bien sûr, il les apporte demain.
8. Bien sûr, elles les attendent.

2. Ils regardent *les montagnes?*
3. Tu vois *ces beaux nuages blancs?*
4. Vous voyez *cette infirmière et son mari?*
5. Elle attend *les nouvelles employées?*
6. Ils aiment *les matchs de basketball?*
7. Il apporte *les billets* demain?
8. Ces belles dames attendent *les deux vendeuses occupées?*

F. Answer using the appropriate direct object pronoun. Follow the model.

1. Tu vas montrer *ta nouvelle blouse* à Julie?
   Oui, je vais la montrer à Julie.

2. Oui, elle veut le voir.
3. Oui, je peux les faire.
4. Oui, il faut l'apprendre.
5. Oui, elles veulent la prendre.
6. Oui, elle aime le préparer.
7. Oui, ils peuvent le choisir (ce soir).
8. Oui, nous allons (je vais) les écouter.

2. Elle veut voir *le médecin?*
3. Tu peux faire *ces devoirs?*
4. Il faut apprendre *le rôle?*
5. Ces femmes d'affaires veulent prendre *cette petite table?*
6. Cette ménagère aime préparer *le dîner?*
7. Ils peuvent choisir *le film* ce soir?
8. Vous allez écouter *vos nouveaux disques?*

Treizième
Leçon

Les nombres et les dates

---

cent *hundred*   fois *times (in multiplication)*   mille *thousand*

Numbers above 69 are formed differently from the lower numbers.

1. For 70 to 79, add the numbers 10 to 19 to the word *soixante: soixante-dix* (70), *soixante et onze* (71), *soixante-douze* (72), etc.

2. The French equivalent of 80 is *quatre-vingts*. For 81 to 99, add the numbers 1 to 19: *quatre-vingts, quatre-vingt-un* (81), *quatre-vingt-deux* (82) . . . *quatre-vingt-dix* (90), *quatre-vingt-onze* (91), *quatre-vingt-douze* (92), etc. The final *s*, which appears only in the word for 80, is a liaison consonant before a vowel sound: *quatre-vingts animaux*. Note, too, that the word *et* does not appear in 81 or 91.

3. The number 100 is *cent*.[1] It is never preceded by *un*. To form the numbers 101 to 199, simply add 1 to 99 after the word *cent: cent un, cent deux . . . cent quatre-vingt-dix-neuf*.

4. Numbers above 199 follow the same pattern: *deux cents, deux cent un . . . neuf cent quatre-vingt-dix-neuf*. Note that there is an *s* on *cent* only in the round numbers: 200, 300, etc. *Mille* does not add an *s: deux mille*.

5. What would the following mean?

   quatorze cent quatre-vingt douze   dix-sept cent soixante-seize

   They are famous dates. Another way of saying dates after the year 1000 is to use the word *mille*:[2]

   mil quatre cent quatre-vingt-douze   mil sept cent soixante-seize

Exercices

A. Read the problems aloud. Then give the solution. Follow the model.

   1. 60 + 24 = ?   *Combien font 60 et 24? 60 et 24 font 84.*
   2. 78 − 3 = ?   *Combien font 78 moins 3? 78 moins 3 font 75.*
   3. 2 × 46 = ?   *Combien font 2 fois 46? 2 fois 46 font 92.*

   4. 60 + 11 = ?   6. 9 × 9 = ?   8. 72 + 27 = ?   10. 60 + 21 = ?
   5. 3 × 25 = ?   7. 89 − 3 = ?   9. 86 − 4 = ?   11. 7 × 14 = ?

---

[1] The *t* is silent, except in the expressions *cent ans* and *cent hommes*.
[2] When it is written out in dates, *mille* is spelled *mil*.

Ex. A can be presented after covering Point 2.

We present no exercises on dates. You might want to omit Point 5, or perhaps merely ask students to be able to respond when asked the year of their birth or the present year.

4. Combien font soixante et onze? Soixante et onze font soixante et onze.
5. Combien font trois fois vingt-cinq? Trois fois vingt-cinq font soixante-quinze.
6. Combien font neuf fois neuf? Neuf fois neuf font quatre-vingt-un.
7. Combien font quatre-vingt-neuf moins trois? Quatre-vingt-neuf moins trois font quatre-vingt-six.
8. Combien font soixante-douze et vingt-sept? Soixante-douze et vingt-sept font quatre-vingt-dix-neuf.
9. Combien font quatre-vingt-six moins quatre? Quatre-vingt-six moins quatre font quatre-vingt-deux.
10. Combien font soixante et vingt et un? Soixante et vingt et un font quatre-vingt-un.
11. Combien font sept fois quatorze? Sept fois quatorze font quatre-vingt-dix-huit.

1. Il faut réviser quatre-vingt-quinze pages.
2. Il a cinq cent soixante et un animaux.
3. Ils vendent quatre-vingt-quatorze journaux.
4. Il y a cent un enfants dans le stade.
5. Il a quatre-vingt-seize lettres.
6. Elle a vendu cent dix-huit maillots.

B. Read the math problems aloud, then give the solution.

1. Cette semaine il faut réviser 50 pages d'anglais et 45 pages d'histoire. Combien de pages est-ce qu'il faut réviser?
2. Cet agriculteur a 132 vaches, 27 moutons, 280 poules, 90 canards, 18 chevaux, 10 chats et 4 chiens. Combien d'animaux est-ce qu'il a?
3. Si Jean vend 51 journaux et Pierre vend 43 journaux, combien de journaux est-ce que les deux garçons vendent?
4. S'il y a 80 garçons et 21 petites filles dans le stade, combien d'enfants est-ce qu'il y a dans le stade?
5. Le facteur a 99 lettres. Il donne 3 lettres au concierge. Maintenant combien de lettres est-ce qu'il a?
6. Le mois dernier, cette vendeuse a vendu 30 maillots noirs, 22 maillots jaunes, 25 maillots rouges et 41 maillots blancs. Elle a vendu combien de maillots?

Vérifiez vos progrès

Tell how much the items cost, then answer the questions in the negative using the appropriate direct object pronoun. Follow the models.

1. Tu aimes cette robe?
   Elle coûte cent quarante francs.
   Je ne l'aime pas.

2. Vous allez prendre ces billets?
   Ils coûtent quatre-vingt-un francs.
   Nous n'allons pas les prendre.

3. Tu veux cet oiseau?

4. Ils veulent cette télé?

5. Tu vas demander ce vélo?

6. Vous allez prendre ces chaussures?

7. On veut voir la photo?

8. Vous aimez ces voitures?

RÉVISION ET THÈME

Consult the model sentences, then put the English cues into French and use them to form new sentences.

See Teacher's Section for answers to the *révision* and *thème*.

Review of:
1. *être* + professions singular prenominal adjectives
2. *croire que* direct object pronouns + negative
3. verbs like *prendre de* + plural prenominal adjectives
4. numbers
5. *voir*

1. *Monsieur Bertaud est pharmacien dans une nouvelle pharmacie.*
   (Anne and Monique are doctors in a small hospital.)
   (Adèle is a clerk in a large tourist office.)

2. *Je crois que le jean est laid, et je ne le porte pas.*
   (They think the shoes are expensive, and they don't take them.)
   (We think the books are hard, and we don't like them.)

3. *Un jour vous apprenez qu'on cherche de jeunes vendeurs.*
   (they learn)   (handsome actors)
   (you (sing.) learn)   (good poets)

4. *Il y a déjà cent cinquante élèves qui veulent apprendre l'anglais.*
   (75 engineers who want to take the test)
   (80 lawyers who want to see the judge)

5. *Tu vois que tu ne vas pas faire de progrès.*
   (We see)
   (They see)

Now that you have done the *Révision*, you are ready to write a composition. Put the English captions describing each cartoon panel into French to form a paragraph.

Marion is a saleswoman in a small boutique.

She thinks the work is easy, but she doesn't like it.

One day she learns that they're looking for unknown young actresses.

But there are already 91 girls who want to play the lead.

She sees that she isn't going to succeed.

Lesson 13

221

AUTO-TEST

A. Tell who the people or what the buildings are, and describe them using the correct form of the adjective given. Follow the model.

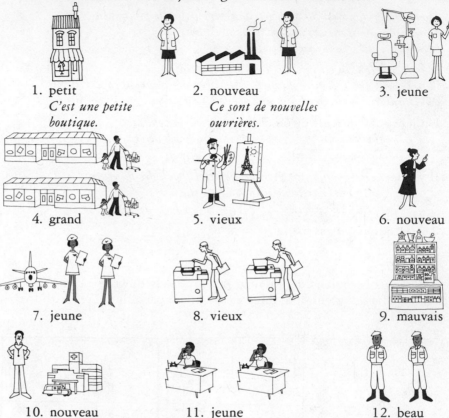

1. petit
C'est une petite boutique.

2. nouveau
Ce sont de nouvelles ouvrières.

3. jeune

4. grand

5. vieux

6. nouveau

7. jeune

8. vieux

9. mauvais

10. nouveau

11. jeune

12. beau

B. Write the answers to the questions using the appropriate direct object pronoun. Follow the models.

1. Nous allons jouer *les rôles principaux?* (Oui . . .)
Oui, vous allez les jouer.
2. Cette ménagère aime *son travail?* (Non . . .)
Non, elle ne l'aime pas.
3. Cette infirmière malienne habite *ce grand appartement?* (Oui . . .)
4. Ce jeune employé va faire *son stage* à Clermont-Ferrand? (Non . . .)
5. Tu rencontres *le facteur* devant la maison? (Non . . .)
6. Vous voyez *ces jeunes marins portugais?* (Oui . . .)
7. Ils vont vendre *ces deux mille livres de poche?* (Oui . . .)
8. Tu vois *ce gros homme d'affaires?* (Oui . . .)
9. On sert *le petit déjeuner* dans ce café? (Non . . .)
10. Ils croient *cette vieille histoire?* (Non . . .)
11. L'agriculteur va chercher *ses animaux?* (Oui . . .)
12. Vous offrez *ces beaux cadeaux* à grand-maman? (Non . . .)

Poème

PAGE D'ÉCRITURE°

Deux et deux quatre
quatre et quatre huit
huit et huit font seize . . .
Répétez!° dit le maître°
5 Deux et deux quatre
quatre et quatre huit
huit et huit font seize.
Mais voilà l'oiseau-lyre°
qui passe° dans le ciel
10 l'enfant le voit
l'enfant l'entend
l'enfant l'appelle:°
Sauve-moi°
joue avec moi
15 oiseau!
Alors l'oiseau descend°
et joue avec l'enfant. . . .

> Jacques Prévert, *Paroles*
> © Editions Gallimard, 1949

l'écriture *(f.): writing*

répéter: *to repeat*
le maître: *(here) teacher*

l'oiseau-lyre *(m.): lyre-bird*
passer: *(here) to go by*

appeler: *to call*
sauver: *to save*

descendre: *to come down*

Voir, c'est croire.

Quatorzième Leçon

Une surprise-party

Samedi prochain c'est l'anniversaire de Jeanne-Marie, et son amie Denise
organise une surprise-party.[1] D'abord elle a invité Christophe et Madeleine,
et maintenant elle téléphone à René pour l'inviter. Elle veut aussi lui emprunter un électrophone et quelques disques.

See Cultural Supplement.

5 RENÉ   Tu invites ta nouvelle voisine? Madeleine me dit qu'elle est sympa.

DENISE Oui, je la trouve très intéressante. Et son frère aussi. Il joue bien
          de la guitare, lui. Je vais leur téléphoner ce soir. Il y a aussi Jac-
          queline.

RENÉ   Qui donc?[2]

10 DENISE L'étudiante américaine. Sa famille passe l'année en France pour le
          travail de son père. Sa société a un bureau à Paris. J'ai joué au
          tennis avec elle dimanche dernier.

RENÉ   Je crois qu'il va y avoir beaucoup de monde à cette petite fête!

il va y avoir: Help students recognize this as the immediate future form of *il y a.*

la fête: Students already know the word in the expression *la Fête des Mères (Pères).* Help them to understand that it means both holiday and party—in general, any *festive* occasion.

---

[1] *Une surprise-party* is any informal party—not a surprise party as we think of it.
[2] *Donc* has no real English equivalent here. It makes the question sound a little less abrupt.

A party

Next Saturday is Jeanne-Marie's birthday, and her friend Denise is organizing a small party. First she invited Christophe and Madeleine, and now she is calling René to invite him. She also wants to borrow a record player and some records from him.

5   RENÉ   Are you inviting your new neighbor? Madeleine tells me she's nice.

DENISE Yes, I find her very interesting. And her brother, too. He really plays the guitar well. I'm going to call them tonight. There's also Jacqueline.

10 RENÉ   Who??

DENISE The American student. Her family's spending the year in France for her father's business. His company has an office in Paris. I played tennis with her last Sunday.

RENÉ   I think there are going to be a lot of people at this little party!

Questionnaire

1. Quel jour est l'anniversaire de Jeanne-Marie?   2. Que fait Denise?
3. Qui est-ce qu'elle a invité d'abord? Et maintenant?   4. Qu'est-ce qu'elle veut emprunter à René?   5. Qu'est-ce que René demande à Denise?
6. Qui pense que la voisine de Denise est sympa? Et Denise, qu'est-ce qu'elle pense de sa voisine?[1] Qu'est-ce qu'elle pense du frère de sa voisine?
7. Qui est l'autre jeune fille que Denise va inviter?   8. Pourquoi est-ce que Jacqueline passe l'année en France?   9. Ça va être vraiment une petite fête?

PRONONCIATION

The [ə] sound in one-syllable words is pronounced when it comes after a word ending in a consonant sound but is often not pronounced when it comes after a word ending in a vowel sound. Listen to the words *le, de,* and *ne* in the following sentences.

Il le fait.   *but:* Je le fais.
La salle de classe.   Pas de westerns.
Ils ne sont pas français.   Nous ne sommes pas français.

In the left-hand column, *le, de,* and *ne* come after words ending in the pronounced consonant *l,* so the letter *e* is pronounced [ə]. In the right-hand column, they come after words ending in a vowel sound, so the letter *e* is not pronounced.

Exercices

A. Practice pronouncing and dropping the [ə] sound in the word *le.*

Il le fait.   Ils le croient.   Il le voit?
Vous le faites.   Nous le croyons.   Qui le voit?

[1] *Penser à* means "to think about"; *penser de* means "to think of" or "to have an opinion about."

B. Practice pronouncing and dropping the [ə] sound in the word *ne*.

Il ne va pas.   Il ne parle pas.   Il ne grossit pas.
Tu n∉ vas pas.   Je n∉ parle pas.   Tu n∉ grossis pas.

C. Listen to these sentences, then say them aloud.

Je n∉ vois pas l∉ stade.   Vous n∉ jouez pas d∉ matchs.
Vous n∉ faites pas d∉ fautes.   Nous n∉ prenons pas d∉ café.
On n∉ sort pas d∉ l'école.   Je n∉ comprends pas l∉ français.

MOTS NOUVEAUX I

You might ask what the plural form of *le manteau* would be.

le timbre   l'enveloppe (f.)   le paquet   la carte postale

le parapluie   l'imperméable (m.)   le manteau   la veste   le complet

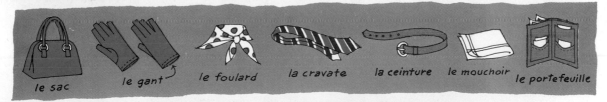

le sac   le gant   le foulard   la cravate   la ceinture   le mouchoir   le portefeuille

l'électrophone (m.)   le réveil   la montre   la bague   le bracelet   le collier

Il va avoir besoin d'un imperméable.   *He'll **need a raincoat**.*
　　　　　　　du parapluie.   　　　***the umbrella**.*
　　　　　　　des gants.   　　　***the gloves**.*
De quoi est-ce qu'il a besoin?[1]   ***What** does he **need**?*
Il a surtout besoin de gants.   *He **especially needs** gloves.*

---

[1]When verbs that are followed by *de* are used in "what" questions, *qu'est-ce que* becomes *de quoi est-ce que*. Thus they follow the same pattern as verbs that are followed by *à*. For example: *De quoi est-ce que tu parles? De quoi parles-tu?*

Exercices de vocabulaire

A. Answer the question according to the pictures. Follow the model.

De quoi est-ce que tu as besoin?

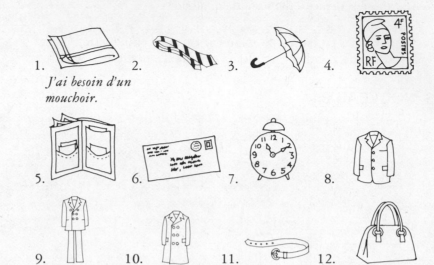

1. *J'ai besoin d'un mouchoir.*

2.

3.

4.

5.

6.

7.

8.

9.

10.

11.

12.

2. J'ai besoin d'une cravate.
3. J'ai besoin d'un parapluie.
4. J'ai besoin d'un timbre.
5. J'ai besoin d'un portefeuille.
6. J'ai besoin d'une enveloppe.
7. J'ai besoin d'un réveil.
8. J'ai besoin d'une veste.
9. J'ai besoin d'un complet.
10. J'ai besoin d'un manteau.
11. J'ai besoin d'une ceinture.
12. J'ai besoin d'un sac.

B. Answer the questions according to the pictures. Follow the model.

2. Je donne un électrophone à Jean.
3. Je vais chercher une bague (en ville).
4. Il a trouvé un collier.
5. Nous regardons (Je regarde) une carte postale.
6. Tu peux offrir des gants à Eve.
7. Je vois un paquet.
8. Elle veut un foulard.
9. Ils ont trouvé un portefeuille.

1. Qu'est-ce que vous offrez à Marie?
Nous offrons un bracelet à Marie.

2. Qu'est-ce que tu donnes à Jean?

3. Qu'est-ce que tu vas chercher en ville?

4. Qu'est-ce qu'il a trouvé?

5. Qu'est-ce que vous regardez?

6. Qu'est-ce que je peux offrir à Eve?

7. Qu'est-ce que tu vois?

8. Qu'est-ce qu'elle veut?

9. Qu'est-ce qu'ils ont trouvé?

MOTS NOUVEAUX II

Jeudi c'est ton **anniversaire** (*m.*).	*Thursday is your **birthday***.
François va **organiser une surprise-party**.[1]	*François is going **to organize a party***.
Qui est-ce qu'il va **inviter**?	*Whom is he going **to invite***?
Il va inviter **beaucoup de monde**.	*He's going to invite **a lot of people***.
Ça va être une **assez** grande **fête**.	*It will be a pretty large **party***.
Il faut **emprunter** des disques **à** Anne.	*He has **to borrow** some records **from** Anne.*
Et Guy va **prêter** son électrophone **à** François.	*And Guy is going **to lend** François his record player.*
Il ne faut pas **oublier** les **cadeaux**.	*We mustn't **forget** the **presents***.
Je ne veux pas les **laisser** ici.	*I don't want **to leave** them here.*

emprunter à / prêter à:
This is a difficult pair. With younger students, you might let them try to monitor each other, awarding "stars" to those who catch their classmates using *de* after *emprunter*.

Jean a **de la chance**.	*Jean is **lucky***.
Son **voisin** est **sympa**.	*His **neighbor** is **nice***.
intéressant	*interesting*
Sa **voisine** est sympa **aussi**.[2]	*His neighbor is nice, too.*
intéressante	*interesting*
Marie n'a pas de chance.	*Marie is **unlucky***.
Son voisin est **ennuyeux**.	*Her neighbor is **boring***.
Sa voisine est **ennuyeuse**.	
Quelques amis vont **l'accompagner**.	*A few friends are going **to go with** her.*
Quelques amies aussi.	*A few girl friends, too.*
Plusieurs filles vont **faire une visite à** Marie.	*Several girls are going **to visit** Marie.*
Plusieurs garçons aussi.	*Several boys, too.*
Chaque fille et **chaque** garçon va **dire**:	*Each girl and each boy is going to say:*
"**Félicitations**!"	*"Congratulations!"*
"**Bon anniversaire**!"	*"Happy Birthday!"*
"**Bon courage**!"	*"Good luck!"*
Il faut **remercier** ses amis.	*She has **to thank** her friends.*
C'est M. Petit.	*That's Mr. Petit.*
Qui donc?	*Who??*
Il travaille pour une **société danoise**.	*He works for a Danish **company***.
Il aime **jouer de la guitare**.	*He likes **to play the guitar**.*
jouer du piano	*to play the piano*
chanter et danser	*to sing and dance*
la danse	*dancing*
la chanson	*the song*
la musique	*(the) music*

---

[1]The plural form is *les surprises-parties.*

[2]*Sympa* is short for *sympathique.* Even in the plural its form does not change: *Ses voisines sont sympa.*

Exercice de vocabulaire

From the column on the right, choose the most logical response to each statement or question on the left. The answers to 1–6 will be found in a–f; the answers to 7–12 will be found in g–l.

1. a
2. f
3. b
4. c
5. d
6. e

1. Aujourd'hui j'ai quinze ans.
2. Il va y avoir beaucoup de monde?
3. Nous avons réussi à nos examens.
4. Pourquoi est-ce que tu remercies ce monsieur?
5. Tu as laissé ton portefeuille? Où donc?
6. Tu peux prêter cinq francs à Jean?

a. Bon anniversaire!
b. Félicitations!
c. Il a prêté cet électrophone à mon petit frère.
d. Je ne sais pas, mais je ne peux pas le trouver.
e. Non. Malheureusement, j'ai oublié mon argent.
f. On a invité plusieurs amis, je crois.

---

7. k
8. i
9. g
10. h
11. l
12. j

7. Est-ce qu'elle joue du piano?
8. Est-ce qu'elle va être seule?
9. Je n'aime pas du tout ce livre d'histoire.
10. Pierre n'a pas de chance!
11. Qu'est-ce qu'on va faire à la surprise-party?
12. Sa société est très grande, n'est-ce pas?

g. Tu le trouves ennuyeux?
h. Il a raté son examen?
i. Non, quelques copains l'accompagnent.
j. Oh oui, et son travail est très intéressant.
k. Oui, et elle chante très bien aussi.
l. Si on a de bons disques, on peut danser, par exemple.

EXPLICATIONS I

Les verbes <u>écrire</u>, <u>lire</u>, <u>dire</u>

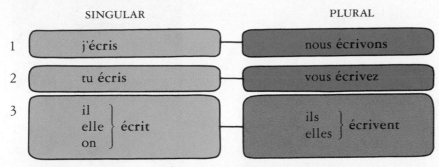

	SINGULAR		PLURAL
1	j'écris		nous écrivons
2	tu écris		vous écrivez
3	il / elle / on écrit		ils / elles écrivent

IMPERATIVE: écris! écrivons! écrivez!

The verb *écrire* means "to write." The plural stem is *écriv-*. In the singular, the *v* is dropped from the stem, and the endings *-s, -s, -t* are added.

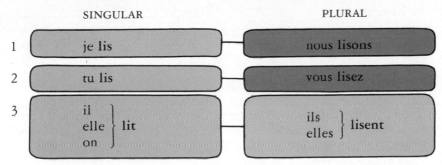

	SINGULAR		PLURAL
1	je lis		nous lisons
2	tu lis		vous lisez
3	il / elle / on lit		ils / elles lisent

IMPERATIVE: lis! lisons! lisez!

The verb *lire* means "to read." The plural stem is *lis-*. In the singular, the *s* is dropped from the stem, and the endings *-s, -s, -t* are added.

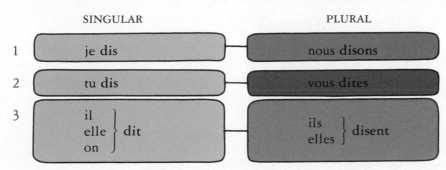

	SINGULAR		PLURAL
1	je dis		nous disons
2	tu dis		vous dites
3	il / elle / on dit		ils / elles disent

IMPERATIVE: dis! disons! dites!

The verb *dire* means "to say, to tell." The plural stem is *dis-*. In the singular, the *s* is dropped from the stem, and the endings *-s, -s, -t* are added. Note that the 2 pl. form is irregular. It has the ending *-tes*, which also occurs in *vous êtes* and *vous faites*.

You might want to do simple pattern drills for each verb separately before doing the exercises in the book.

Exs. A–B require use of the singular forms only.

2. Non, je n'écris pas la carte postale.
3. Non, il ne dit pas "bon courage."
4. Non, tu n'écris pas ces lettres aujourd'hui.
5. Non, je ne dis pas "bonjour" chaque matin.
6. Non, tu ne lis pas ces livres de poche.
7. Non, il n'écrit pas l'histoire.
8. Non, tu ne dis pas "bon anniversaire."
9. Non, elle ne lit pas le journal du soir.

Ex. B
2. Oui, je l'écris.
3. Oui, il le dit.
4. Oui, tu les écris aujourd'hui.
5. Oui, je le dis chaque matin.
6. Oui, tu les lis.
7. Oui, il l'écrit.
8. Oui, tu la dis.
9. Oui, elle le lit.

Ex. C
2. J'écris ces phrases en anglais aussi.
3. Ils lisent trop lentement aussi.
4. Nous lisons (Je lis) la leçon d'espagnol aussi.
5. Vous dites (Nous disons) "au revoir" aussi.
6. Elles disent "bon courage" à l'étudiante aussi.
7. Vous écrivez (Nous écrivons) des poèmes aussi.
8. Elles lisent des romans anglais aussi.
9. Ils écrivent les réponses correctes aussi.

l. 1: lisons
l. 3: lit / lisent
l. 5: écrire
l. 6: écrivons / disent
l. 7: disons
l. 9: lisez
l. 10: écrivez / dites
l. 11: écrit
l. 12: écrivent

Quatorzième
Leçon

232

Exercices

A. Answer the questions in the negative. Follow the model.

1. Tu lis le roman?
   Non, je ne lis pas le roman.

2. Tu écris la carte postale?
3. Il dit "bon courage"?
4. J'écris ces lettres aujourd'hui?
5. Tu dis "bonjour" chaque matin?
6. Je lis ces livres de poche?
7. Il écrit l'histoire?
8. Je dis "bon anniversaire"?
9. Elle lit le journal du soir?

B. Redo the above exercise in the affirmative, using the appropriate direct object pronoun *(le, la, l', les)*. Follow the model.

1. Tu lis le roman?
   Oui, je le lis.

C. Answer the questions using the appropriate pronoun. Follow the model.

1. Ils lisent bien le français. Et nous?
   Vous lisez bien le français aussi.

2. Nous écrivons ces phrases en anglais. Et toi?
3. Vous lisez trop lentement. Et eux?
4. Je lis la leçon d'espagnol. Et vous?
5. Elles disent "au revoir." Et nous?
6. Il dit "bon courage" à l'étudiante. Et elles?
7. Tu écris des poèmes. Et nous?
8. Elle lit des romans anglais. Et elles?
9. J'écris les réponses correctes. Et eux?

D. Complete the paragraph, using the correct form of the italicized verbs.

Cette semaine dans ma classe de français nous *(lire)* quelques poèmes de Prévert. Ils sont intéressants, mais je les trouve difficiles. Chaque jour en classe on *(lire)* pendant cinq ou dix minutes. Les autres élèves *(lire)* bien le français, mais pas moi. La semaine prochaine je crois que nous allons
5 *(écrire)* un thème sur ces poèmes.

Nous *(écrire)* toujours des thèmes! Les professeurs *(dire)* que c'est un bon exercice. Et ils croient que c'est facile. Mes amis et moi, nous *(dire)* que c'est un exercice très difficile!

Est-ce que vous *(lire)* des poèmes français dans votre classe? Est-ce que
10 vous *(écrire)* un thème chaque semaine? Quoi donc? Vous *(dire)* qu'on n'*(écrire)* pas de thèmes dans votre lycée? Je voudrais bien aller à un lycée où les élèves n'*(écrire)* pas de thèmes.

Les pronoms compléments d'objet indirect: <u>lui</u>, <u>leur</u>

1. Look at the following:

Je téléphone **à Jean.**	Je **lui** téléphone.
Je donne le paquet **au facteur.**	Je **lui** donne le paquet.
Je réponds **à Jean et à Louis.**	Je **leur** réponds.
Je prête mon parapluie **aux facteurs.**	Je **leur** prête mon parapluie.

The construction *à* + person is often replaced by an *indirect* object pronoun. The French equivalent of the English indirect object pronouns "him" and "her" is *lui*. The equivalent of "them" is *leur*.

2. Like direct object pronouns, indirect object pronouns replace the entire object of the verb, not just a noun:

Nous empruntons un crayon **à la nouvelle secrétaire belge.**	Nous **lui** empruntons un crayon.
Elle parle **aux jeunes agents qui travaillent là-bas.**	Elle **leur** parle.

3. Indirect object pronouns have the same position in a sentence as direct object pronouns:

DIRECT	INDIRECT
Elles ne **l'**invitent pas.	Elles ne **lui** parlent pas.
Je vais **les** inviter.	Je vais **leur** parler.

Exercices

A. Redo the sentences, replacing the italicized words with the appropriate indirect object pronoun: *lui* or *leur*. Follow the models.

   1. Le professeur répond *à un élève.*
     Le professeur lui répond.
   2. Tu écris des lettres *à tes grands-parents.*
     Tu leur écris des lettres.

   3. Nous écrivons *à Colette.*
   4. Joseph téléphone *au médecin à Paris.*
   5. Cet homme lit *à sa fille et à ses deux fils.*
   6. L'auteur parle *aux étudiants du cours d'anglais.*
   7. Nicole apporte le journal *à papa.*
   8. La pharmacienne pose des questions *à la nouvelle infirmière.*
   9. Ils disent "bonjour" *au concierge.*
  10. Ces histoires font peur *à nos petits frères.*

B. Redo the above exercise in the negative. Follow the models.

   1. Le professeur répond *à un élève.*
     Le professeur ne lui répond pas.
   2. Tu écris des lettres *à tes grands-parents.*
     Tu ne leur écris pas de lettres.

3. Nous lui écrivons.
4. Joseph lui téléphone.
5. Cet homme leur lit.
6. L'auteur leur parle.
7. Nicole lui apporte le journal.
8. La pharmacienne lui pose des questions.
9. Ils lui disent "bonjour."
10. Ces histoires leur font peur.

3. Nous ne lui écrivons pas.
4. Joseph ne lui téléphone pas.
5. Cet homme ne leur lit pas.
6. L'auteur ne leur parle pas.
7. Nicole ne lui apporte pas le journal.
8. La pharmacienne ne lui pose pas de questions.
9. Ils ne lui disent pas "bonjour."
10. Ces histoires ne leur font pas peur.

C. Answer the questions using the appropriate indirect object pronoun: *lui* or *leur*. Follow the model.

1. Il aime faire des visites *à ses cousins?*
   Oui, il aime leur faire des visites.

2. Elle peut emprunter ce foulard *à ta sœur?*
3. Il veut téléphoner *à Denis?*
4. Elle va offrir ces cadeaux *à ses parents?*
5. Ils veulent écrire *à l'acteur célèbre?*
6. Il peut prêter son réveil *à Charles et à son frère?*
7. Il faut donner ces enveloppes *aux secrétaires?*
8. Il faut répondre *au juge?*
9. Elles veulent montrer leurs bagues *aux autres élèves?*

D. Redo the above exercise in the negative. Follow the model.

1. Il aime faire des visites *à ses cousins?*
   Non, il n'aime pas leur faire de visites.

E. Answer the questions according to the statements. Follow the model.

1. Ils vendent leur bateau à voiles aux Dupont.
   (a) Qu'est-ce qu'ils vendent *aux Dupont?*
       Ils leur vendent leur bateau à voiles.
   (b) A qui est-ce qu'ils vendent *leur bateau à voiles?*
       Ils le vendent aux Dupont.
2. Il prête son livre d'algèbre à Paul.
   (a) Qu'est-ce qu'il prête *à Paul?*
   (b) A qui est-ce qu'il prête *son livre d'algèbre?*
3. Claude apporte quelques cartes postales à ses grands-parents.
   (a) Qu'est-ce qu'il apporte *à ses grands-parents?*
   (b) A qui est-ce qu'il apporte *les cartes postales?*
4. Suzanne emprunte l'imperméable à Mireille.
   (a) Qu'est-ce qu'elle emprunte *à Mireille?*
   (b) A qui est-ce qu'elle emprunte *l'imperméable?*
5. Les professeurs lisent plusieurs poèmes russes aux étudiants.
   (a) Qu'est-ce qu'ils lisent *aux étudiants?*
   (b) A qui est-ce qu'ils lisent *les poèmes?*
6. Paul offre un cadeau à son avocat.
   (a) Qu'est-ce qu'il offre *à son avocat?*
   (b) A qui est-ce qu'il offre *le cadeau?*
7. Ils donnent la guitare à leurs amis.
   (a) Qu'est-ce qu'ils donnent *à leurs amis?*
   (b) A qui est-ce qu'ils donnent *la guitare?*
8. Patrick emprunte la voiture à ses parents.
   (a) Qu'est-ce qu'il emprunte *à ses parents?*
   (b) A qui est-ce qu'il emprunte *la voiture?*

Vérifiez vos progrès

Answer the questions using the cue in parentheses and the appropriate indirect object pronoun. Follow the model.

1. Qu'est-ce que tu prêtes à Anne? (un collier et un bracelet)
   Je lui prête un collier et un bracelet.

2. Qu'est-ce que vous écrivez à vos amis? (une longue lettre)
3. Qu'est-ce que nous empruntons à leurs cousins? (la voiture)
4. Qu'est-ce qu'ils offrent à leur père? (une cravate bleue)
5. Qu'est-ce que tu montres à ton amie? (une belle image)
6. Qu'est-ce qu'il donne à ses sœurs? (des paquets)
7. Qu'est-ce que nous disons à nos amis? (quelques mots)
8. Qu'est-ce que tu offres à Lisette? (une jolie montre)
9. Qu'est-ce qu'elle emprunte à sa mère? (plusieurs timbres)

CONVERSATION ET LECTURE

Parlons de vous

1. Quand est-ce que vous invitez vos amis chez vous? Vous les invitez à des surprises-parties? 2. Est-ce que vous aimez organiser des fêtes? Est-ce que vous aimez aller à des fêtes et à des surprises-parties? Qu'est-ce que vous faites là? 3. Est-ce que vous aimez la musique? Vous aimez danser? chanter? Vous apprenez quelques chansons françaises dans votre classe de français? Quelles chansons? 4. Est-ce que vous jouez du piano? de la guitare? d'un autre instrument? de la flûte, du violon, de la clarinette, du violoncelle ("cello") ou du hautbois ("oboe") peut-être? 5. Est-ce que vous lisez beaucoup? Quand vous avez le choix, qu'est-ce que vous aimez lire? des romans? des romans policiers? des pièces? des poèmes? 6. Est-ce vous aimez écrire les thèmes français? Est-ce que vous écrivez des lettres en français à un correspondant ou à une correspondante ("pen pal") en France ou au Québec, par exemple? 7. Est-ce que vous collectionnez ("collect") les timbres? Si oui, est-ce que vous avez des timbres français? 8. Quelle est la date de votre anniversaire? Qu'est-ce que vous aimez recevoir ("to get") comme cadeau? Qu'est-ce que vous offrez à vos amis? à vos parents? 9. De quoi est-ce que vous avez besoin quand il pleut? Qu'est-ce que vous portez quand il fait très froid?

Pourquoi les langues étrangères?

Souvent les élèves demandent à leurs professeurs pourquoi l'étude° des langues étrangères est importante. Pour répondre à cette question, un professeur de français, qui enseigne à San Francisco, a organisé
5   une petite conférence pour ses élèves. Il a invité des gens qui habitent San Francisco, mais qui ont besoin de parler une langue étrangère au cours de° leur tra-

l'étude *(f.): study*

See Cultural Supplement.

au cours de: *in the course of*

Lesson
14

235

vail: une caissière° de banque, un interprète,° un
avocat, une journaliste, une dactylo° et un homme et
une femme d'affaires. Voici, par exemple, le discours°
10 d'une jeune femme, Mlle Patricia Robinson, qui a
parlé aux élèves.

"Au mois de juin 1972 j'ai fini mes études à l'université. Quatre mois plus tard, j'ai trouvé un em-
15 ploi dans une grande société de transport.° Je travaille toujours pour cette même société. Et je crois
que la petite histoire que je vais raconter° va peut-
être vous° montrer l'importance de l'étude des langues étrangères—même° ici à San Francisco. Alors
20 voilà mon histoire:

"Un matin, le patron° entre dans mon bureau et me
demande: 'Pat, vous avez étudié le français au lycée,
n'est-ce pas?' 'Pendant trois ans seulement,'° je lui
réponds. 'Alors, est-ce que vous pouvez traduire°
25 cette feuille d'expédition?'° me demande-t-il. Je regarde la feuille pendant un moment et puis je lui dis:

le caissier, la cais-
sière: *cashier*
l'interprète *(m.&f.)*:
interpreter
la dactylo: *typist*
le discours: *speech*

la société de transport:
moving company
raconter: *to tell*
vous: *(here) (to) you*
même: *(here) even*

le patron, la patron-
ne: *boss*
seulement: *only*
traduire: *to translate*
la feuille d'expédi-
tion: *packing list*

'Je crois que je peux la traduire, mais je vais avoir besoin d'un dictionnaire.'

"Un mois après, c'est presque la même histoire. Le
30 patron me dit: 'Pat, il y a un monsieur au° télé-   au: *(here) on the*
phone. C'est un attaché du Consulat Général de
France.[1] Parlez avec lui, s'il vous plaît.' Je vais au
téléphone et je vois tout de suite que ce jeune di-
plomate est vraiment très bouleversé.° Il est surtout   bouleversé, -e: *upset*
35 difficile de comprendre une langue étrangère au té-
léphone et ce monsieur me parle beaucoup trop
vite. Mais enfin je comprends qu'il croit qu'on a
perdu ses meubles.° Tout à coup je vois que l'a-   les meubles *(m.pl.):*
dresse sur la feuille d'expédition n'est pas correcte.   *furniture*
40 Bientôt on règle° le problème et les meubles arri-   régler: *to solve*
vent chez le diplomate.

"Maintenant je travaille dans le secteur° international   le secteur: *division*
de la société. Je parle souvent français et chaque an-
née je fais des voyages en° France et en Belgique°   en: *(here) to*
45 pour mon travail.   la Belgique: *Belgium*

"Alors, vous me demandez si l'étude des langues
étrangères est importante. Pour moi, la réponse est
certainement° oui."   certainement: *defi-*
nitely

À propos …

1. Quelle question est-ce que les élèves posent souvent à leurs professeurs?
2. Pourquoi est-ce que le prof à San Francisco a organisé une conférence?
Qui est-ce qu'il a invité à la conférence? Que font ces gens comme travail?
3. Quand est-ce que Mlle Robinson a fini ses études?   4. Quand son patron
lui montre la feuille d'expédition est-ce qu'elle peut la traduire? De quoi
est-ce qu'elle a besoin?   5. Est-ce que Mlle Robinson dit qu'il est difficile
de parler français au téléphone? Pourquoi est-ce que l'attaché n'a pas ses
meubles? Est-ce qu'on peut régler le problème?   6. Est-ce que Mlle Robinson travaille toujours pour la même société? Où est-ce qu'elle va pour son
travail? Vous croyez qu'elle trouve son emploi ennuyeux?   7. Et vous, est-
ce que vous pouvez penser à des emplois ou à des situations où la connaissance ("knowledge") d'une langue étrangère peut être importante?   8. Est-
ce que vous avez—ou est-ce que vos parents ont—des amis qui parlent une
langue étrangère dans leur travail? Quelle langue? Qu'est-ce qu'ils font
comme profession? Font-ils des voyages pour leur société?

---

[1] Many countries have consulates in major foreign cities. For example, if a large number of its
citizens are living in a particular foreign city for business or political reasons, it may open a
consulate to offer any help or services the people may need. Consulates also issue travelers'
visas to citizens of the host country and, in general, help in the exchange of cultural and commercial information between nations. Attachés are diplomats with specialized responsibilities;
for example, business or cultural exchanges.

EXPLICATIONS II

Les pronoms compléments d'objet direct et indirect: <u>me</u>, <u>te</u>, <u>nous</u>, <u>vous</u>

1. Look at the following:

DIRECT   Il $\left\{ \begin{array}{l} le \\ la \\ les \end{array} \right\}$ remercie.   Il $\left\{ \begin{array}{l} me \\ te \\ nous \\ vous \end{array} \right\}$ remercie.

INDIRECT   Il $\left\{ \begin{array}{l} lui \\ leur \end{array} \right\}$ donne le paquet.   Il $\left\{ \begin{array}{l} me \\ te \\ nous \\ vous \end{array} \right\}$ donne le paquet.

Me, te, nous, and *vous* can be used as either direct or indirect objects.

2. As with *le, la,* and *les,* there is elision and liaison before a verb beginning with a vowel sound:

Il $\left\{ \begin{array}{l} l' \\ les \end{array} \right\}$ accompagne.   Il $\left\{ \begin{array}{l} m' \\ t' \\ nous \\ vous \end{array} \right\}$ accompagne.

3. *Me, te, nous,* and *vous* have the same position in the sentence as other object pronouns:

Ils ne vous croient pas.   Elle ne nous écrit pas de lettres.
Je veux te remercier.   Il va m'emprunter des cravates.

Exercices

A. Answer the questions using the pronoun *te*. Follow the model.

1. Il me demande des enveloppes?   *Oui, il te demande des enveloppes.*

2. Ils me parlent?
3. Ils me font une visite en août?
4. Elle me comprend?
5. Le professeur de chimie me regarde?
6. Elle me dit quelque chose?
7. Maman me cherche?
8. On me trouve sympa?
9. Elles me voient?
10. Tu me prêtes cette cravate?

B. Answer the questions in the negative using the pronoun *me*. Follow the model.

1. Gérard te prête l'argent?   *Non, il ne me prête pas l'argent.*

2. Jeanne te demande l'heure?
3. Charles te donne la veste?
4. Ils te comprennent?
5. Elle te donne ce mouchoir?
6. Elle te téléphone à 11 h.?
7. Louise te remercie?
8. Les souris te font peur?
9. Il te prête son manteau?

Margin answer key (left column):

2. Oui, ils te parlent.
3. Oui, ils te font une visite en août.
4. Oui, elle te comprend.
5. Oui, il (le professeur de chimie) te regarde.
6. Oui, elle te dit quelque chose.
7. Oui, elle (maman) te cherche.
8. Oui, on te trouve sympa.
9. Oui, elles te voient.
10. Oui, je te prête cette cravate.

2. Non, elle (Jeanne) ne me demande pas l'heure.
3. Non, il (Charles) ne me donne pas la veste.
4. Non, ils ne me comprennent pas.
5. Non, elle ne me donne pas ce mouchoir.
6. Non, elle ne me téléphone pas à 11 h.
7. Non, elle (Louise) ne me remercie pas.
8. Non, elles (les souris) ne me font pas peur.
9. Non, il ne me prête pas son manteau.

C. Answer the questions using the appropriate pronoun: *me (m')* or *te (t')*. Follow the model.

1. Il t'offre un portefeuille pour ton anniversaire?
   Oui, il m'offre un portefeuille pour mon anniversaire.

2. Vous m'écoutez?
3. Il t'emprunte ton réveil?
4. Tu m'invites à la fête?
5. Elles peuvent m'entendre?
6. Ils t'attendent devant le marché?
7. Il peut t'accompagner demain?
8. Etienne va t'apporter la veste?
9. Tu vas m'écrire quelques lettres?

D. Answer the questions using the appropriate pronoun: *nous* or *vous*. Follow the model.

1. Est-ce qu'on peut vous trouver chez vous ce soir?
   Oui, on peut nous trouver chez nous ce soir.

2. Elles vous vendent leur vieille guitare?
3. Est-ce que votre sœur cadette vous cherche?
4. Est-ce qu'ils veulent nous voir tout de suite?
5. Le professeur d'allemand vous lit plusieurs poèmes?
6. Ils vous posent des questions ennuyeuses?
7. Suzanne va nous téléphoner cet après-midi?
8. Est-ce que cet homme nous regarde?
9. Tu veux nous chanter des chansons italiennes?

E. Answer the questions in the negative using the appropriate pronoun: *nous* or *vous*. Follow the model.

1. Jean veut nous accompagner en ville?
   Non, il ne veut pas vous accompagner en ville.

2. Etienne vous apporte son électrophone?
3. Ils nous écrivent des lettres?
4. Est-ce que ces serveuses nous écoutent?
5. Paul vous attend près de la bibliothèque?
6. Est-ce qu'on peut nous entendre?
7. Est-ce qu'ils peuvent vous emprunter votre parapluie?
8. Est-ce qu'ils nous offrent ces beaux sacs?

Vérifiez vos progrès

Write each sentence using the appropriate pronoun.

1. Nous ne . . . voyons pas. (leur, lui, le)
2. C'est un garçon aimable. Il veut . . . remercier. (te, eux, toi)
3. Tu vas . . . emprunter des gants et un parapluie? (nous, les, l')
4. Malheureusement il ne peut pas . . . prêter cet argent. (la, les, vous)
5. Je . . . offre un cadeau pour son anniversaire. (l', t', lui)
6. Pourquoi est-ce qu'il . . . laisse chez lui? (lui, la, leur)
7. Qu'est-ce que vous . . . dites? (les, leur, elles)
8. Il a oublié ses gants. Il . . . cherche maintenant. (lui, les, leur)

2. Oui, nous t'écoutons (je t'écoute).
3. Oui, il m'emprunte mon réveil.
4. Oui, je t'invite à la fête.
5. Oui, elles peuvent t'entendre.
6. Oui, ils m'attendent devant le marché.
7. Oui, il peut m'accompagner demain.
8. Oui, il (Etienne) va m'apporter la veste.
9. Oui, je vais t'écrire quelques lettres.

2. Oui, elles nous vendent leur vieille guitare.
3. Oui, elle (notre sœur cadette) nous cherche.
4. Oui, ils veulent vous voir tout de suite.
5. Oui, il (le professeur d'allemand) nous lit plusieurs poèmes.
6. Oui, ils nous posent des questions ennuyeuses.
7. Oui, elle (Suzanne) va vous téléphoner cet après-midi.
8. Oui, il (cet homme) vous regarde.
9. Oui, je veux vous chanter des chansons italiennes.

2. Non, il ne nous apporte pas son électrophone.
3. Non, ils ne vous écrivent pas de lettres.
4. Non, elles ne vous écoutent pas.
5. Non, il ne nous attend pas près de la bibliothèque.
6. Non, on ne peut pas vous entendre.
7. Non, ils ne peuvent pas nous emprunter notre parapluie.
8. Non, ils ne vous offrent pas ces beaux sacs.

RÉVISION ET THÈME

See Teacher's Section for answers to the *révision* and *thème.*

Review of:
1. *emprunter à / prêter à*
2. *indirect object pronouns + infinitive*
3. *dire*
   croire
   écrire
   postnominal adjectives
4. *indirect object pronouns + infinitive*
5. *dire*
   avoir besoin de
   adverbs
6. *indirect object pronouns*

Consult the model sentences, then put the English cues into French and use them to form new sentences.

1. *J'ai emprunté une enveloppe à Chantal.*
   (They borrowed ties from Dad.)
   (We lent stamps to several friends.)

2. Nous voulons *vous offrir un foulard.*
   (to give her a wallet)
   (to visit them)

3. *Tu dis: Elle croit que j'écris des poèmes intéressants.*
   (We say: We think they write French songs.)
   (You (pl.) *say: They think we write boring stories.)*

4. Elle peut *te montrer un complet.*
   (give me a jacket)
   (bring us an alarm clock)

5. *Elle dit:* Mais *j'ai toujours besoin d'un manteau.*
   (They say)   (she really needs a raincoat)
   (I say)   (they still need belts)

6. Alors, *tu m'écris une lettre et une carte postale.*
   (I'm giving them a necklace and a ring)
   (we're giving you (pl.) *the record player and the tape recorder)*

Now that you have done the *Révision,* you are ready to write a composition. Put the English captions describing each cartoon panel into French to form a paragraph.

① Yesterday, Solange lent Maryse an umbrella.

② Now Maryse wants to bring her a gift.

③ Maryse's brother says: "I think she likes detective novels. You can give her a book."

④ Maryse answers: "But she especially needs an umbrella!"

⑤ "So you give her a book and her umbrella!"

AUTO-TEST

A. First write answers to the questions using the indirect object pronoun
   (*lui, leur*) and the definite determiner. Afterwards, write another sentence
   using the direct object pronoun (*le, la, l', les*) to replace the noun you
   used in the first sentence. Follow the model.

1. Qu'est-ce que nous pouvons offrir à ton frère?
   Vous pouvez lui offrir l'imperméable.
   Vous pouvez l'offrir à mon frère.

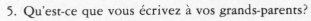
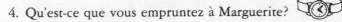

2. Qu'est-ce qu'il prête à Denise?

3. Qu'est-ce que tu montres à Grégoire?

4. Qu'est-ce que vous empruntez à Marguerite?

5. Qu'est-ce que vous écrivez à vos grands-parents?

6. Qu'est-ce qu'il faut emprunter à Roger et à Charles?

7. Qu'est-ce que tes parents vont offrir à grand-maman?

8. Qu'est-ce qu'ils veulent donner à leur fille cadette?

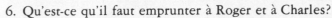 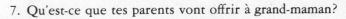 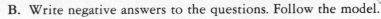

B. Write negative answers to the questions. Follow the model.

1. Est-ce que tu me donnes ce portefeuille?
   Non, je ne te donne pas ce portefeuille.

2. Est-ce que vous nous montrez votre nouveau manteau?
3. Est-ce qu'ils lui posent d'autres questions?
4. Est-ce que tu me vends ces timbres?
5. Est-ce qu'elle leur parle maintenant?
6. Est-ce qu'elles vont te lire sa lettre?
7. Est-ce qu'elles vous prêtent ce foulard aujourd'hui?
8. Est-ce que tu leur empruntes le parapluie?
9. Est-ce que tu veux nous faire une visite?
10. Est-ce qu'il m'offre ce beau collier?

Proverbe

Ne choisit pas qui emprunte.

BRASSERIE DE L'ALMA

5, Place de l'Alma & Avenue Georges V

Tél. : 359-57-11

GARÇON Nº 4   TABLE Nº .... 1 et

1 tomate	5
1 selle avec H.V.	28
1 brie	5
1 café	2
1 ...	10
	50
	750
	57,50

Bar-Restaurant

Menu à .....

Boisson et Service en Sus

Servi de 11³⁰ à 21 hs.

La Carte

Ses Spécialités

SALADES
Salads
Salate
Ensaladas

Salade de saison 3.50
Salad
Salat der Jahreszeit
Ensalada de la estacion

Salade mixte 5.00
Salade, tomate
Mixed salad (salad, tomatoe)
Gemischter Salat (Salat, Tomate)
Ensalada mixta (ensalada, tomate)

Salade du Cloître 8.00
Salade, tomate, gruyère, noix
Cloister salad (salad, tomatoe, gruyere cheese, nuts)
Klostersalat
(Salat, Tomate, Schweizerkäse, Nüsse)
Ensalada del clautro
(ensalada, tomate, queso de gruyère, nuez)

La Parisienne 8.00
Salade, tomate, céleri, jambon
Parisian (salad, tomatoe, cellery, ham)
Die Pariserin (Salat, Tomate, Sellerie, Schinken)
La Parisiana (ensalada, tomate, apio, jamon)

Salade d'Arcole 8.00
Salade, tomate, œuf dur, poulet, riz
Arcole salad
(salad, tomatoe, hard boiled egg, chicken, rice)
Arcoler Salat
(Salat, Tomate, hartes Ei, Hühnchen, Reis)
Ensalada de Arcole
(ensalada, tomate, huevo duro, pollo, arroz)

L'Assiette des Tours, (crudités de saison) ... 8.00
Céleri, tomate, carottes, pommes de terre, riz
Tower salad
(cellery, tomatoes, carots, potatoes, rice)
« L'assiette des Tours » (Sellerie, Tomate, Karotte,
Kartoffel, Reis)
El plato de las torres
(apio, tomate, zanahorias, patatas, arroz)

Salade Niçoise 8.00
Salade, tomate, poivron, thon, céleri,
anchois, œuf dur, olives
Niçoise salad (salad, tomatoe, sweet peppers,
tuny fish, anchovies, hard boiled egg, olives)
Nizza-salat (Salat, Tomate, Paprikaschote,
Thunfisch, Sellerie, Anchovis, hartes Ei, Oliven)
Ensalada de Niza (ensalada, tomate, pimientes, atun,
apio, anchoa, huevo duro, olivas)

Schrimps Salad bowl 9.00
Salade, crevettes, tomate, olives, sauce corail
Schrimps salad bowl
(salad schrimps, tomatoe, olives, pink sauce)
Schrimps salad bowl
(Salat, Krabben, Tomate, Oliven, Korallensosse)
Schrimps salad bowl
(ensalada, camarones, tomates, olivas, salsa coral)

Quinzième Leçon

Au restaurant

Les Valjean déjeunent dans un petit restaurant du Vieux Nice[1] avec leurs
deux filles.

See Cultural Supplement.

	LE GARÇON	Pour commencer, messieurs-dames?[2]
	M. VALJEAN	De la soupe à l'oignon pour tout le monde, s'il vous plaît.
5	LE GARÇON	Oui, et ensuite?
	M. VALJEAN	Une salade niçoise[3] pour ces demoiselles, du jambon pour madame, et moi, je voudrais du coq au vin.
	LE GARÇON	Bien, monsieur.
	MME VALJEAN	Tu oublies ton régime, hein?
10	M. VALJEAN	Chut! j'ai faim.

l'oignon: Point out that the *oi* is pronounced as an open o here: [ɔɲɔ̃].

chut: Point out the final pronounced consonant: [ʃyt].

---

[1]Nice is a city on the *Côte d'Azur. Le Vieux Nice* is the beautiful, very old section of the town.
[2]The expression *messieurs-dames,* like "ladies and gentlemen," is always plural. Note that the man is addressed first in French.
[3]A *salade niçoise* usually contains lettuce, tomatoes, olives, green peppers, radishes, tuna, and anchovies. Note that in English, too, we speak of a New York steak, a Virginia ham, a Maine lobster, and so on. In French, geographical adjectives are far more common, and there is a special adjective form for the name of almost every province, city, and town. Thus: Paris—parisien, parisienne; Nice—niçois, niçoise; Cannes—cannois, cannoise; Marseille—marseillais, marseillaise; Lyon—lyonnais, lyonnaise; Provence—provençal, provençale, etc. We would not normally translate such names as *salade niçoise* into English.

Lesson 15

243

At the restaurant

The Valjeans are having lunch in a little restaurant in the old section of
Nice with their two daughters.

WAITER	Ladies. Sir. What would you like to begin with?
M. VALJEAN	Onion soup for everyone, please.
5 WAITER	Yes, and then?
M. VALJEAN	A salade niçoise for these young women, ham for the lady, and I'd like coq au vin.
WAITER	Very good, sir.
MME VALJEAN	Forgetting your diet, eh?
10 M. VALJEAN	Shhh! I'm hungry.

Questionnaire

1. Où déjeunent les Valjean?   2. Qu'est-ce que M. Valjean commande pour
commencer?   3. Qu'est-ce que les deux filles vont prendre? Et Mme Valjean, que prend-elle? Et M. Valjean?   4. Qu'est-ce que Mme Valjean demande à son mari? Comment est-ce qu'il lui répond? Est-ce que vous croyez
qu'il aime son régime?

PRONONCIATION

The following words all end in the nasal vowel sound [ã].

Jean   quand   vent   blanc   temps   grand

Exercices

A. Listen to these words, then say them aloud. Be careful to pronounce the
[ã] sound quickly and with tension.

flamand   enfant   pendant   lentement   entend

B. Now say these words containing the nasal vowel sound [ã] followed by a
pronounced consonant.

bande   grande   France   banque   tante   prendre

C. Practice the [ã] sound in the following pairs of words. The first word
ends in the [ã] sound; the second ends in a pronounced consonant.

temps / tante   gens / j'entre   vent / vendre   blanc / blanche

D. In the following pairs, the first word ends in the *nonnasal* vowel sound
[a] followed by a pronounced *m* or *n*. The second word ends in the nasal
vowel sound [ã].

[a] / [ã]   Anne / en   dame / dans   Cannes / quand   Jeanne / Jean

E. Now repeat these sentences containing the nasal vowel sound [ã]:

Ces gens sont vraiment grands.   L'agent entre dans la banque.
L'enfant prend son argent.   Grand-maman rentre dimanche.

MOTS NOUVEAUX I

Pour commencer, messieurs-dames?	*Ladies. Gentlemen. What would you like to start with?*
Une salade niçoise pour tout le monde.	*A salade niçoise for everyone.*
Oui, et ensuite?	*Yes, and then?*
Une omelette et des haricots verts *(m.pl.)* pour moi.	*An omelette and green beans for me.*
Et un croque-monsieur pour mademoiselle.[1]	*And a croque-monsieur for the young woman.*
Il va commander des huîtres *(f.pl.)*. des escargots *(m.pl.)*.[2]	*He's going to order oysters. snails.*
Pas de hors-d'œuvre *(m.pl.)* pour moi.[3]	*No first course for me.*
Je suis au régime.	*I'm on a diet.*
Le dessert est excellent.	*The dessert is excellent.*
Les légumes sont excellents.	*The vegetables are excellent.*
La viande est excellente.	*The meat is excellent.*
Les pâtisseries sont excellentes.	*The pastries are excellent.*
La demoiselle demande l'addition *(f)*.	*The young woman asks for the check.*
Elle va laisser un pourboire?	*Is she going to leave a tip?*
Non, le service est compris.[4]	*No, the tip's included.*

tout le monde: Point out the unpronounced mute *e:* [tulmɔ̃d].

If possible, bring to class an *escargot* plate and tongs.

Point out that there is no final *s* on *les hors-d'œuvre*. Students may understand this better if you explain the literal meaning "outside of the work" (i.e., not part of the meal itself).

You might mention that a French person is far less apt to be *au régime* than is an American.

Exercice de vocabulaire

Choose the word or phrase that best completes the sentence or fits the situation.

1. Si tout le monde a fini, demandons *(l'addition/le pourboire)* au garçon.
2. J'aime bien les desserts, surtout *(les parapluies/les pâtisseries)*.
3. On vend d'excellents *(légumes/régimes)* dans ce supermarché.
4. Si tu es au régime, prends *(une salade/une glace)*.
5. Le service n'est pas compris. Il faut laisser *(un café/un pourboire)*.
6. Qu'est-ce que vous voulez comme dessert, *(croque-monsieur/messieurs-dames)*?
7. Si tu veux des légumes, prends *(des escargots/des haricots verts)*.
8. D'abord je prends des huîtres et *(ensuite/pour commencer)* une omelette.

1. l'addition
2. les pâtisseries
3. légumes
4. une salade
5. un pourboire
6. messieurs-dames
7. des haricots verts
8. ensuite

---

[1] *Un croque-monsieur*, a grilled ham and swiss cheese sandwich, is a popular snack or lunch. The plural form is the same: *les croque-monsieur*.

[2] Snails are very popular in France. They are cooked in butter, garlic, and herbs, and served on special plates that have indentations. A long-handled clamp is used to hold the shell while the meat is removed with a thin fork.

[3] The *h* in *haricots* and *hors-d'œuvre* is an "aspirate *h*," and when plural determiners appear before them, there is no liaison: *les huîtres*, but *les haricots verts, des hors-d'œuvre*.

[4] In France the tip is usually already added into the cost of the meal when you receive the check.

l'oeuf: Point out that the final *f* is pronounced: [œf]. In the plural, however, since it is no longer a final consonant, it is not sounded, and the plural form is pronounced: [ø].

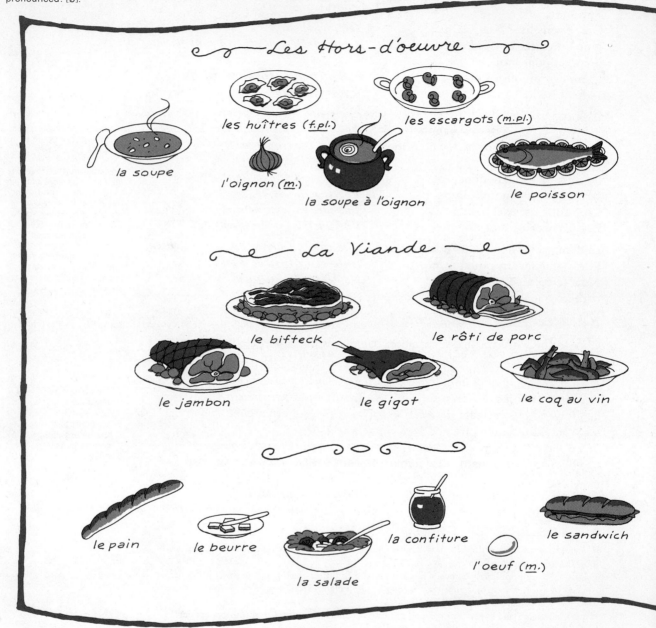

Les Hors-d'oeuvre

la soupe

les huîtres (*f.pl.*)

les escargots (*m.pl.*)

l'oignon (*m.*)

la soupe à l'oignon

le poisson

La Viande

le bifteck

le rôti de porc

le jambon

le gigot

le coq au vin

le pain

le beurre

la salade

la confiture

l'oeuf (*m.*)

le sandwich

The plural of *le sandwich* is *les sandwichs.*
Wine is served regularly in France. White wine is usually served with fish and fowl, red wine with most other meats. Mineral, or spring, water is the main type of drinking water.

Les Légumes (m.pl.)

les haricots verts (m.pl.)   les petits pois (m.pl.)

le riz   la pomme de terre   les pommes frites (f.pl.)

Les Boissons (f.pl.)

l'eau minérale (f.)   le vin   le lait

le café   la crème   le sucre   le thé

Les Desserts (m.pl.)

les pâtisseries (f.pl.)   la tarte aux pommes   la pomme   la crème caramel   la mousse au chocolat

les fruits (m.pl.)   le fromage

Cheese is often served either as dessert or as a separate course before dessert. *Mousse* is a whipped, very rich, pudding-like dessert. *Crème caramel* is baked, molded custard with a rich caramel sauce.
When in English we speak of "fruit" as a singular noun, the French use a plural.

Exercices de vocabulaire

A. Answer the question according to the pictures. Follow the model.

Qu'est-ce qu'il aime?

2. Il aime les pommes de terre.
3. Il aime le bifteck.
4. Il aime la confiture.
5. Il aime le lait.
6. Il aime la crème caramel.
7. Il aime la salade.
8. Il aime le riz.
9. Il aime les fruits.
10. Il aime la soupe à l'oignon.
11. Il aime la tarte aux pommes.
12. Il aime le sucre.

1. *Il aime le poisson.* 2. 3. 4.

5. 6. 7. 8.

9. 10. 11. 12.

B. Answer the question according to the pictures. Follow the model.

Qu'est-ce que tu prends?

2. Je prends du rôti de porc.
3. Je prends du vin.
4. Je prends du fromage.
5. Je prends du thé.
6. Je prends du pain.
7. Je prends du coq au vin.
8. Je prends du jambon.

1. *Je prends du gigot.* 2. 3. 4.

5. 6. 7. 8.

C. Answer the question according to the pictures. Follow the model.

Qu'est-ce qu'ils ont commandé?

2. Ils ont commandé des escargots.
3. Ils ont commandé des pommes frites.
4. Ils ont commandé des œufs.
5. Ils ont commandé des sandwichs.
6. Ils ont commandé des haricots verts.
7. Ils ont commandé des petits pois.
8. Ils ont commandé des pâtisseries.

1. *Ils ont commandé des huîtres.* 2. 3. 4.

5. 6. 7. 8.

EXPLICATIONS I

Les verbes en -cer et -ger

VOCABULAIRE

annoncer	*to announce*	manger	*to eat*
commencer	*to begin, to start*	nager	*to swim*
prononcer	*to pronounce*	plonger	*to dive*

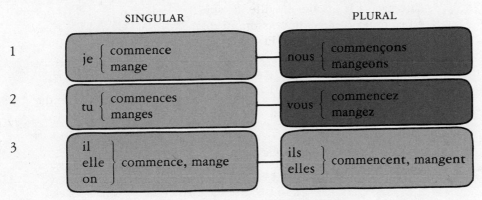

SINGULAR · PLURAL

1 je { commence / mange · nous { commençons / mangeons

2 tu { commences / manges · vous { commencez / mangez

3 il / elle / on } commence, mange · ils / elles } commencent, mangent

IMPERATIVE: commence! commençons! commencez!
mange! mangeons! mangez!

Verbs that end in *-cer* and *-ger* are regular but show a spelling peculiarity. Since *c* is pronounced with a "hard" sound [k] before the letter *o* (c<u>o</u>mme, haric<u>o</u>ts), to maintain the "soft" sound [s], the *c* becomes *ç* in the 1 pl. form. Like *c*, *g* is also pronounced with a "hard" sound [g] before the letter *o* (g<u>o</u>mme, gig<u>o</u>t). So an *e* is inserted in the 1 pl. form to maintain the "soft" sound [ʒ].

Exercices

A. Complete the sentences using the correct form of the appropriate verb: *annoncer, commencer,* or *prononcer.*

1. Mes parents _____ que nous allons faire une visite à mon oncle.
2. Quand nous lisons, nous ne _____ pas chaque mot.
3. La fête _____ tout de suite.
4. Nous _____ bien le français, n'est-ce pas?
5. Après le dîner, nous _____ nos devoirs de chimie.
6. Le professeur de géométrie a _____ un examen.
7. On _____ que l'avion arrive à 11 h. 30.

1. annoncent
2. prononçons
3. commence
4. prononçons
5. commençons
6. annoncé
7. annonce

2. Oui, nous mangeons (je mange) trop.
3. Oui, ils nagent quand il ne pleut pas.
4. Oui, tu plonges très bien.
5. Oui, en été nous nageons (je nage) chaque matin.
6. Oui, il a mangé des pommes frites.
7. Oui, nous nageons (je nage) à la piscine en ville.
8. Oui, elle nage comme un poisson.
9. Oui, nous plongeons (je plonge) dans l'eau.

Ex. A can be done after covering Point 1.

Ex. B can be done after covering Point 2.

Exs. C–D and F can be done after covering Point 3.

Ex. E can be done after covering Point 4.

Quinzième
Leçon

250

B. Answer the questions using the appropriate pronoun. Follow the model.

1. Nous mangeons des pâtisseries. Et elles?
   Oui, elles mangent des pâtisseries.

2. Je mange trop. Et vous?
3. Tu nages quand il ne pleut pas. Et eux?
4. Elle plonge très bien. Et moi?
5. En été, je nage chaque matin. Et vous?
6. Vous avez mangé des pommes frites. Et lui?
7. Elle nage à la piscine en ville. Et vous?
8. Vous nagez comme un poisson. Et elle?
9. Elles plongent dans l'eau. Et vous?

Le partitif

1. In French, when you speak of a thing or things *in general*, you use the definite determiner:

Les œufs sont blancs.	*Eggs are white.*
Les pommes de terre sont blanches.	*Potatoes are white.*
Le sucre est blanc.	*Sugar is white.*
La crème est blanche.	*Cream is white.*

2. To speak of "some," you use *des,* though in English we often omit the word "some":

J'ai commandé des œufs.	*I ordered (some) eggs.*
J'ai commandé des pommes de terre.	*I ordered (some) potatoes.*

3. But many words are rarely, if ever, used in the plural. In that case, the equivalent of "some" is *du, de la,* or *de l'.* This is called the "partitive." Again, "some" is often omitted in English:

Tu veux du sucre?	*Do you want (some) sugar?*
Tu veux de la crème?	*Do you want (some) cream?*
Tu veux de l'eau?	*Do you want (some) water?*

4. You have seen that after a negative the indefinite determiners (*un, une, des*) often become *de,* meaning "any":

Il annonce un examen.	Il n'annonce pas d'examen.
Il porte des gants.	Il ne porte pas de gants.

   The same is true of the partitive forms *du, de la,* and *de l':*

Je veux du sucre.	Je ne veux pas de sucre.
Je veux de l'eau.	Je ne veux pas d'eau.

5. Remember that in such expressions as *avoir besoin de,* the *de* becomes *des* only when specific items are being referred to. When a partitive "some" is meant, it remains *de* (or *d'*):

J'ai besoin des œufs.	*I need the eggs.*
J'ai besoin d'œufs.	*I need (some) eggs.*

Exercices

A. Answer the questions according to the models.

    1. Est-ce qu'ils ont commandé du gigot?   *Oui, ils aiment le gigot.*
    2. Est-ce qu'elle a mangé des escargots?   *Oui, elle aime les escargots.*

    3. Est-ce qu'il a préparé des petits pois?
    4. Est-ce qu'il a commandé de la mousse au chocolat?
    5. Est-ce qu'elles ont mangé du fromage?
    6. Est-ce qu'elle a préparé des pommes de terre?
    7. Est-ce qu'ils ont servi du vin?
    8. Est-ce qu'elles ont commandé de la salade?
    9. Est-ce qu'il a mangé du rôti de porc?
    10. Est-ce qu'elle a commandé de l'eau minérale?

3. Oui, il aime les petits pois.
4. Oui, il aime la mousse au chocolat.
5. Oui, elles aiment le fromage.
6. Oui, elle aime les pommes de terre.
7. Oui, ils aiment le vin.
8. Oui, elles aiment la salade.
9. Oui, il aime le rôti de porc.
10. Oui, elle aime l'eau minérale.

B. Answer the questions using the cues in parentheses. Follow the model.

    1. Qu'est-ce qu'il a commandé? (les huîtres)
        Il a commandé des huîtres.

    2. Qu'est-ce qu'elle a préparé? (les hors-d'œuvre)
    3. Qu'est-ce que les petits enfants ont entendu? (les histoires)
    4. Qu'est-ce qu'elle a commandé? (les haricots verts)
    5. Qu'est-ce qu'ils ont écouté à la radio? (les chansons espagnoles)
    6. Qu'est-ce qu'elle a vendu? (les habits)
    7. Qu'est-ce que le facteur a laissé? (les paquets)
    8. Qu'est-ce qu'ils ont choisi? (les esquimaux)

2. Elle a préparé des hors-d'œuvre.
3. Ils ont entendu des histoires.
4. Elle a commandé des haricots verts.
5. Ils ont écouté des chansons espagnoles (à la radio).
6. Elle a vendu des habits.
7. Il (Le facteur) a laissé des paquets.
8. Ils ont choisi des esquimaux.

C. Answer the questions using the cues in parentheses. Follow the model.

    1. Qu'est-ce que la serveuse leur apporte? (le jambon)
        Elle leur apporte du jambon.

    2. Qu'est-ce que Mme Dupont lui offre? (le thé)
    3. Qu'est-ce qu'elle leur prépare? (le poisson)
    4. Qu'est-ce qu'ils lui demandent? (le café)
    5. Qu'est-ce que le garçon leur apporte? (la crème et le sucre)
    6. Qu'est-ce que papa leur sert? (le coq au vin)
    7. Qu'est-ce que la ménagère lui demande? (le pain et le beurre)
    8. Qu'est-ce que la serveuse leur donne? (le riz)

2. Elle lui offre du thé.
3. Elle leur prépare du poisson.
4. Ils lui demandent du café.
5. Il leur apporte de la crème et du sucre.
6. Il leur sert du coq au vin.
7. Elle lui demande du pain et du beurre.
8. Elle leur donne du riz.

D. Answer the questions using the cues in parentheses. Follow the model.

    1. Qu'est-ce qu'il a commandé? (la soupe à l'oignon)
        Il a commandé de la soupe à l'oignon.

    2. Qu'est-ce qu'ils ont servi comme boisson? (l'eau minérale)
    3. Qu'est-ce qu'il a perdu? (l'argent)
    4. Qu'est-ce qu'on a commandé? (la crème caramel)
    5. Qu'est-ce qu'elle a trouvé? (la confiture)
    6. Qu'est-ce qu'ils ont choisi? (l'orangeade)
    7. Qu'est-ce qu'il a vendu? (la glace)
    8. Qu'est-ce qu'elle a préparé? (la mousse au chocolat)

2. Ils ont servi de l'eau minérale (comme boisson).
3. Il a perdu de l'argent.
4. On a commandé de la crème caramel.
5. Elle a trouvé de la confiture.
6. Ils ont choisi de l'orangeade.
7. Il a vendu de la glace.
8. Elle a préparé de la mousse au chocolat.

2. Non, elles n'ont pas vendu d'esquimaux.
3. Non, elle (la serveuse) n'a pas apporté d'eau minérale.
4. Non, elle ne prépare pas de coq au vin.
5. Non, elles n'ont pas commandé de sandwichs.
6. Non, elle n'a pas servi de crème caramel.
7. Non, elles ne commandent pas de croque-monsieur.
8. Non, il n'a pas apporté de riz.

E. Answer the questions in the negative. Follow the model.

1. Ils ont commandé des haricots verts, n'est-ce pas?
   Non, ils n'ont pas commandé de haricots verts.

2. Elles ont vendu des esquimaux, n'est-ce pas?
3. La serveuse a apporté de l'eau minérale, n'est-ce pas?
4. Elle prépare du coq au vin, n'est-ce pas?
5. Elles ont commandé des sandwichs, n'est-ce pas?
6. Elle a servi de la crème caramel, n'est-ce pas?
7. Elles commandent des croque-monsieur, n'est-ce pas?
8. Il a apporté du riz, n'est-ce pas?

F. Answer the questions according to the pictures. Follow the model.

2. Il veut de la soupe.
3. Elle choisit du gigot.
4. Elles commandent des petits pois.
5. Il prépare du jambon.
6. Ils choisissent de la tarte aux pommes.
7. Elles prennent de l'eau minérale.
8. Elle (La serveuse) apporte des pâtisseries.
9. Ils veulent du pain et du lait.
10. On prend des fruits et du fromage.

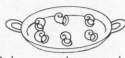

1. Qu'est-ce qu'on prend comme hors-d'œuvre?
   On prend des escargots.

2. Qu'est-ce qu'il veut pour commencer?

3. Qu'est-ce qu'elle choisit comme viande?

4. Qu'est-ce qu'elles commandent comme légume?

5. Qu'est-ce qu'il prépare pour le dîner?

6. Qu'est-ce qu'ils choisissent comme dessert?

7. Qu'est-ce qu'elles prennent comme boisson?

8. Qu'est-ce que la serveuse apporte?

9. Qu'est-ce qu'ils veulent comme goûter?

10. Qu'est-ce qu'on prend après le dîner?

11. Qu'est-ce qu'il cherche?   12. Qu'est-ce qu'ils demandent?

11. Il cherche du sucre.
12. Ils demandent de la crème.

Vérifiez vos progrès

Write sentences in French to express each of the following things (for "want," use the conditional form—*voudrais*—rather than *veux*).

1. Write a sentence saying that you like bread but don't like potatoes.
2. Write a sentence saying that you want a grilled ham and swiss cheese sandwich.
3. Write a sentence saying that you need eggs and milk.
4. Write a sentence saying that you don't like leg of lamb.
5. Write a sentence saying that to begin you want onion soup.
6. Write a sentence saying that for dessert you want pastries and for a drink, mineral water.
7. Write a sentence saying that you don't want a first course.
8. Write a sentence saying that you want fish, rice, and peas.

CONVERSATION ET LECTURE

Parlons de vous

1. Quand vous dînez dans un restaurant, est-ce que vous commandez des hors-d'œuvre? Qu'est-ce que vous aimez commander comme dessert? comme boisson? 2. Est-ce que vous aimez les légumes? les fruits? le riz? les pommes de terre? les pommes frites? 3. Qui prépare votre petit déjeuner? Qu'est-ce que vous aimez prendre comme petit déjeuner? 4. Qu'est-ce que vous prenez comme goûter? 5. Décrivez ("describe") votre dîner d'hier soir.

Une soirée à Genève[1]

See Cultural Supplement.

Françoise et Laurent Mesnard sont un jeune couple suisse.° Ils habitent Genève et parce qu'ils travaillent tous les deux° ils dînent souvent au restaurant. Laurent aime beaucoup la haute cuisine° et les bons

5   vins. C'est aujourd'hui le 15 avril, l'anniversaire de Françoise, et ils sont dans un des excellents restaurants de Genève avec M. et Mme Aubert, les parents de Françoise. C'est une petite fête bien agréable. Ils ont déjà commandé les hors-d'œuvre: des escargots

suisse: *Swiss*
tous (toutes) les
  deux: *both*
la haute cuisine:
  gourmet cooking

---

[1]Geneva is a large, French-speaking city in western Switzerland. It is especially known as the home of many international organizations, such as the International Red Cross and the World Health Organization.

10 pour tout le monde et un bon vin blanc pour les
accompagner.

LAURENT	Je prends le tournedos,° je crois.	le tournedos: *filet mignon*
LE GARÇON	Très bien, monsieur. Vous le prenez comment? Saignant?°	saignant, -e: *rare*
15 LAURENT	Non, à point.° Françoise, tu prends aussi le tournedos?	à point: *medium*
FRANÇOISE	Non, je crois que je vais prendre une escalope de veau.°	l'escalope de veau *(f.): veal cutlet*
M. AUBERT	Et toi, Antoinette? Qu'est-ce que tu prends?	
20		
MME AUBERT	Le tournedos, comme Laurent.	
LE GARÇON	Et pour monsieur?	
M. AUBERT	Voyons, qu'est-ce que je vais prendre, moi?	
25 FRANÇOISE	Du poisson, peut-être? Il est toujours très bon ici.	
M. AUBERT	Pas ce soir. Je crois que je voudrais du gigot avec des pommes frites, s'il vous plaît.	
30 LE GARÇON	Très bien. Et ensuite?	
LAURENT	Une salade verte[1] pour tout le monde, n'est-ce pas?	
FRANÇOISE	Oui, oui.	

---

[1]*Une salade verte* is a lettuce salad. Throughout France, such salads are served after the main
course.

35 Un quart d'heure plus tard, le garçon apporte les escargots et la bouteille° de vin blanc. Il ouvre la bouteille et il verse° le vin. Laurent porte un toast à° sa
femme:

la bouteille: *bottle*
verser: *to pour*
porter un toast à: *to
toast*

LAURENT   Bon anniversaire, Françoise. Et bon
           appétit° à tout le monde.

bon appétit: *enjoy
your meal*

À propos ...

1. Françoise et Laurent sont français? Où est-ce qu'ils habitent?   2. Pourquoi est-ce qu'ils dînent souvent au restaurant? Et ce soir, pourquoi dînent-
ils au restaurant? Avec qui est-ce qu'ils dînent?   3. Qu'est-ce qu'on a déjà
commandé?   4. Qui prend le tournedos? Comment est-ce qu'il l'aime?
5. Que prend Françoise? Et sa mère? Et son père—est-ce qu'il prend du
poisson?   6. Qu'est-ce qu'on prend ensuite?   7. Que dit Laurent quand il
porte le toast à Françoise?   8. Et vous, quelle est la date de votre anniversaire? Comment est-ce que vous aimez passer votre anniversaire? Si c'est
dans un restaurant, qu'est-ce que vous aimez prendre?

EXPLICATIONS II

Les pronoms compléments d'objet y, en

1. In Lesson 14 you saw that *à* + person becomes *lui* or *leur:*

Je parle à Jean.	Je lui parle.
Je parle à Jean et à David.	Je leur parle.

Now look at the following:

Il rentre à Paris.	Il y rentre.	*He's returning there.*
Il répond à la question.	Il y répond.	*He's answering it.*
Je réponds aux lettres.	J'y réponds.	*I'm answering them.*

The construction *à* + place or thing is replaced by *y*. Note that there is
elision in the 1 sing. form *(j'y)*. There is also liaison [z] in all plural
forms *(nous_y, vous_y, ils_y, elles_y)*, and liaison [n] after *on (on_y)*.

2. *Y* is also used to replace expressions of location introduced by such
words as *en, dans, devant, derrière, sur,* etc.:

Je vais en ville.	J'y vais.
Ils entrent dans l'hôtel.	Ils y entrent.

3. Look at the following:

Il prend du jambon.	Il en prend.	*He's having some.*
J'ai peur des chiens.	J'en ai peur.	*I'm afraid of them.*
Vous sortez d'ici?	Vous en sortez?	*Are you leaving here?*

The construction *de* + thing is replaced by *en*. Again, there is elision in
the 1 sing. form *(j'en)* and liaison after *on* and the four plural subject pronouns. The *n* of *en* is also a liaison consonant before a vowel sound:
nous_en_avons.

Exs. A and F can be done
after covering Point 1.

Ex. B can be done after
covering Point 2.

Ex. C can be done after
covering Point 3.

4. Look at the position of *y* and *en* in negative sentences and in sentences where the verb is followed by another verb in the infinitive:

Il n'y rentre pas.	*He isn't returning there.*
Il n'en commande pas.	*He isn't ordering any.*
Il va y rentrer.	*He's going to return there.*
Il veut en commander.	*He wants to order some.*

Y and *en* have the same position as any other object pronoun. In negative sentences, the *e* of *ne* is elided before *y* and *en*.

Exercices

A. Answer the questions using the pronoun *y*. Follow the model.

1. Vous faites un stage *à l'hôpital?*   *Oui, nous y faisons un stage.*

2. Vous téléphonez *à la pharmacie?*
3. Tu assistes *aux matchs?*
4. Tu vas *à l'aéroport?*
5. Tu réponds *aux questions?*
6. Vous rentrez *à Genève?*
7. Vous dînez *au restaurant?*
8. Tu restes *à Paris?*

B. Answer the questions using the pronoun *y*. Follow the model.

1. L'avocate trouve son parapluie *sous le bureau?*
   Oui, elle y trouve son parapluie.
2. Les soldats arrivent *au bord de la mer* demain?
3. Elles déjeunent *au café à côté du théâtre* aujourd'hui?
4. La dentiste habite *en face du supermarché?*
5. Les juges entrent *dans la bibliothèque?*
6. Cette ouvrière laisse sa moto *au garage?*
7. Les femmes d'affaires rentrent *en ville?*
8. Les chaises sont *au milieu de la salle de classe?*

C. Answer the questions using the pronoun *en*. Follow the model.

1. Tu as besoin *de chaussettes?*   *Oui, j'en ai besoin.*

2. Tu veux *du pain?*
3. Tu demandes *de l'argent?*
4. Tu as peur *des animaux?*
5. Tu écoutes *des bandes?*
6. Vous écrivez *des lettres?*
7. Vous avez besoin *du stylo?*
8. Vous parlez *de ce chapitre?*
9. Vous prenez *de la crème?*

D. Answer the questions in the negative, using the appropriate pronoun: *y* or *en*. Follow the models.

1. Ils sont *au coin de la rue?*   *Non, ils n'y sont pas.*
2. Il a besoin *de l'électrophone?*   *Non, il n'en a pas besoin.*

3. Il pleut *sur la Côte d'Azur?*
4. Elle répond *aux lettres?*
5. Elles mangent *des pommes?*
6. Elle a *du vin?*
7. Elles vont *à la banque?*
8. Ils ont peur *de ces avions?*
9. Elle travaille *dans le jardin?*
10. Il prend *du jambon?*

E. Answer the questions using the appropriate pronoun: *y* or *en*. Follow the models.

1. Tu veux parler *de vos cours?*   *Oui, je veux en parler.*
2. Vous voulez dîner *en ville?*   *Oui, nous voulons y dîner.*

3. Tu peux apporter *de la salade?*
4. Vous pouvez assister *à la pièce?*
5. Tu veux prendre *des œufs?*
6. Vous allez rentrer *à Cannes?*
7. Tu veux commander *du rôti de porc?*
8. Vous voulez nager *dans ce fleuve?*

3. Oui, je peux en apporter.
4. Oui, nous pouvons (je peux) y assister.
5. Oui, je veux en prendre.
6. Oui, nous allons (je vais) y rentrer.
7. Oui, je veux en commander.
8. Oui, nous voulons (je veux) y nager.

F. Answer the questions using the appropriate pronoun: *lui, leur,* or *y*. Follow the models.

1. Tu apportes de l'argent *à la banque?*   *Oui, j'y apporte de l'argent.*
2. Tu donnes de l'argent *à ton frère?*   *Oui, je lui donne de l'argent.*
3. Tu prêtes de l'argent *à tes parents?*   *Oui, je leur prête de l'argent.*

4. Tu téléphones *à l'hôpital?*   7. Tu réponds *aux lettres?*
5. Tu téléphones *au médecin?*   8. Tu apportes le paquet *à la poste?*
6. Tu réponds *aux élèves?*   9. Tu apportes le paquet *au facteur?*

4. Oui, j'y téléphone.
5. Oui, je lui téléphone.
6. Oui, je leur réponds.
7. Oui, j'y réponds.
8. Oui, j'y apporte le paquet.
9. Oui, je lui apporte le paquet.

Vérifiez vos progrès

Write answers to the questions using the cues in parentheses and the appropriate pronoun: *y* or *en*. Follow the models.

1. Qui ne plonge pas dans le lac? (Paul)   — *Paul n'y plonge pas.*
2. Qui prend du jambon? (nous)   *Nous en prenons.*

3. Qui cherche des crayons bleus? (elles)
4. Qui a besoin d'un parapluie et d'un imperméable? (moi)
5. Qui va à la ferme cette semaine? (nous)
6. Qui attend Jean dans la boutique? (ils)
7. Qui ne mange pas de haricots verts? (vous)
8. Qui frappe à la porte? (nous)
9. Qui veut des pâtisseries? (on)
10. Qui ne danse pas à la surprise-party? (Martine)

RÉVISION ET THÈME

See Teacher's Section for answers to the *révision* and *thème*.

Review of:
1. forms of *à*
   verb tenses
   adverbs of time
2. *-cer / -ger* verbs
   y
   possessive *de*
   possessive determiners
   prenominal adjectives
3. *prendre*
   partitive
   comme
4. partitive vs. nouns in
   a general sense
   en
5. indefinite determiner
   vs. partitive
6. nouns in a general sense
   coûter cher / peu
   -ger verbs
   negative + *de*

Consult the model sentences, then put the English cues into French and use them to form new sentences based on the models.

1. Les frères Legrand *sont au régime cette semaine.*
   (*attended the play last night*)
   (*are going to play cards tomorrow afternoon*)

2. *J'y rentre* parce que c'est *le dernier jour de mes vacances.*
   (*We swim there*)   (*our neighbors' new swimming pool*)
   (*We begin there*)   (*the first lesson of our book*)

3. *Ils prennent des escargots comme hors-d'œuvre.*
   (*We have wine to drink.*)
   (*I have fruit and cheese for dessert.*)

4. Je prends *du coq au vin. Il n'aime pas le coq au vin.* Alors, *il n'en prend pas.*
   (*beans*)   (*You* (pl.) *don't like beans.*)   (*you don't take any*)
   (*bread and jam*)(*They like bread and jam.*)   (*they want some*)

5. Ensuite je voudrais *une omelette et de l'eau minérale.*
   (*a ham and cheese sandwich and milk*)
   (*a pastry and tea*)

6. *Les pommes coûtent peu, mais il ne mange pas de fruits. Les fruits sont bons!*
   (*Peas are cheap, but you* (sing.) *don't eat vegetables. Potatoes are good.*)
   (*Steak is expensive, so we don't eat meat. Fish is good.*)

Now that you have done the *Révision*, you are ready to write a composition. Put the English captions describing each cartoon panel into French to form a paragraph.

AUTO-TEST

A. Answer the questions using the cues in parentheses. Follow the model.

1. Quand est-ce que vous commencez? (bientôt)
   Nous commençons bientôt.

2. Qu'est-ce que vous mangez? (des sandwichs)
3. Qu'est-ce que vous prononcez? (ces phrases espagnoles)
4. Quand est-ce que vous nagez? (avant le déjeuner)
5. Qu'est-ce que vous commencez? (la nouvelle leçon)
6. Quand est-ce que vous dansez? (ce soir)
7. Où est-ce que vous plongez? (dans le lac)
8. Qui est-ce que vous remerciez? (les employés de bureau)

B. Answer the questions using the cues in parentheses. Follow the model.

1. Tu veux du jambon? (le gigot)   *Non, je veux du gigot.*

2. Vous mangez des pommes de terre? (le riz)
3. Il a besoin de la confiture? (le beurre)
4. Vous voulez des omelettes? (les croque-monsieur)
5. Est-ce qu'il y a des huîtres? (la soupe à l'oignon et les escargots)
6. Elles ont besoin de pain? (les œufs et le fromage)

C. Answer the questions in the negative, using the appropriate pronoun: *y* or *en*. Follow the models.

1. Tu fais des voyages?   *Non, je n'en fais pas.*
2. Nous allons au stade?   *Non, vous n'y allez pas.*

3. Elles choisissent des fruits?
4. On va à la terrasse d'un café?
5. Il sert des petits pois?
6. Ils vont à la librairie?
7. Elles vendent des journaux?
8. Il rentre à son bureau?
9. Elle arrive au zoo?
10. Tu veux des livres de poche?

Proverbe

Il ne faut pas mettre tous ses œufs dans le même panier.

Seizième Leçon

La bouillabaisse[1]

Colette habite Paris, mais cet été, elle passe quelques semaines chez son
oncle et sa tante à Marseille.[2] Ce matin Colette a rencontré son copain
Hugues. Elle lui a parlé de son dîner de la veille.

See Cultural Supplement

HUGUES   Qu'est-ce qui ne va pas, ma vieille? Tu n'as pas bonne mine au
5   jourd'hui.

COLETTE   Hier soir des amis ont voulu me préparer un repas typiquement
            provençal.[3]

HUGUES   Qu'est-ce que tu as mangé? Du poison?

COLETTE   Non, du poisson.[4] Ils ont fait une bouillabaisse.

10 HUGUES   Ah! Mais c'est bon, ça!

COLETTE   Pas la bouillabaisse de mes amis. Ils ont mis trop d'ail, pas assez
            d'huile, et ils ont oublié les tomates. Quel gâchis!

l'ail: Point out the unpronounced final *l*: [aj].

---

[1]*Bouillabaisse*, a thick fish soup, is one of the dishes for which the area around Marseilles is
famous. It was originally a simple fisherman's meal, made by cooking several kinds of fish
together with spices, olive oil, and garlic. It is now a popular dish, and restaurants serve a more
elaborate version of it.

[2]Marseille, on the Mediterranean, was established in the sixth century B.C. and is the oldest city
in France. With a population of roughly 900,000, it is second only to Paris in size and is one
of the principal ports of Europe. Note that it is spelled Marseilles in English.

[3]*Provençal*, the adjective form of the name Provence, is used to describe the area in southeast
France that includes the Mediterranean coast. The name derives from the Latin word *provincia*,
"the province." This area has many Roman ruins, including bridges, aqueducts, and coliseums
dating back to the time of Julius Caesar.

[4]The words *le poison* and *le poisson* differ by only one sound: [z] versus [s]. Try the tongue twister: *Poisson sans boisson, c'est poison.*

The bouillabaisse

Colette lives in Paris, but this summer she is spending a few weeks with her aunt and uncle in Marseilles. This morning Colette ran into her friend Hugues. She talked to him about her dinner the night before.

HUGUES What's wrong, friend? You don't look so hot today.

5 COLETTE Last night some friends wanted to prepare a typically Provençal meal for me.

HUGUES What did you eat? Poison?

COLETTE No, fish. They made a bouillabaisse.

HUGUES Oh! But that's good!

10 COLETTE Not my friends' bouillabaisse. They put in too much garlic, not enough oil, and they forgot the tomatoes. What a mess!

Questionnaire

1. Où habite Colette? 2. Où est-ce qu'elle passe quelques semaines?
3. Qui est-ce qu'elle a rencontré ce matin? 4. De quoi est-ce qu'ils ont parlé? 5. Est-ce que Colette a bonne mine? 6. Qu'est-ce que ses amis ont voulu lui préparer? 7. Qu'est-ce qu'il y a dans une bouillabaisse?
Qu'en pense Hugues? 8. Est-ce que Colette a aimé le repas? Pourquoi?

PRONONCIATION

The [ɥ] sound has no English equivalent. It is pronounced with the lips pursed and the tip of the tongue against the lower front teeth.

Exercices

A. Listen carefully to these words, then say them aloud.

huit   lui   nuit   puis   je suis
juillet   nuage   pluie   suédois   tout de suite

B. In the following pairs, the first word contains the [y] sound, the second contains the [ɥ] sound.

[y]/[ɥ]   lu/lui   su/suis   nu/nuage   pu/puis   plu/pluie

C. In the following pairs, the first word contains the [w] sound, the second contains the [ɥ] sound.

[w]/[ɥ]   oui/huit   Louis/lui   jouer/juillet

D. Listen to the sentences, then say them aloud.

Je suis suédois.   Tu es suédoise. Et lui?
Les nuages apportent la pluie.   Il n'y a pas de pluie en juillet.

MOTS NOUVEAUX I

la cuisine

la cuisinière

l'évier (m.)

le réfrigérateur

la salle à manger

la fourchette

le couteau

la cuillère

la nappe

la serviette

l'assiette (f.)

le verre

la tasse

la soucoupe

le sel

le poivre

Lesson
16

263

Exercices de vocabulaire

A. Answer the questions according to the pictures. Follow the model.

1. Qu'est-ce que j'ai oublié?
   Tu as oublié le poivre.

2. Qu'est-ce que tu as emprunté à Agnès?

3. Qu'est-ce qu'il a perdu?

4. Qu'est-ce qu'elle a trouvé?

5. Qu'est-ce que tu as prêté à Guillaume?

6. Qu'est-ce que vous avez vendu?

7. Qu'est-ce qu'ils ont apporté?

8. Qu'est-ce qu'elles ont choisi?

9. Qu'est-ce qu'ils ont réussi à trouver?

10. Qu'est-ce qu'elle a demandé?

B. Answer the questions according to the picture.

1. Qu'est-ce qu'il y a sur la soucoupe?
2. Qu'est-ce qu'il y a à droite du couteau?
3. Combien de fourchettes est-ce qu'il y a? Combien de couteaux?
4. Qu'est-ce qu'il y a à gauche des fourchettes?
5. Qu'est-ce qu'il y a à droite du sel?
6. Qu'est-ce qu'il y a à côté de la tasse?
7. Qu'est-ce qu'il y a sur l'assiette?

MOTS NOUVEAUX II

Moi, je n'aime pas
    faire le ménage
    faire la cuisine
    mettre le couvert
    débarrasser la table

Pourquoi est-ce que Lydie va **cacher**
    les fourchettes, les cuillères et
    les couteaux?
Parce qu'elle ne veut pas mettre
    le couvert.
Bientôt elle va aussi **casser la**
    vaisselle.

Mon père aime faire la cuisine.
Hier soir, par exemple, il a préparé
    une bouillabaisse.
C'est **typiquement** provençal.
Et la veille il a préparé du
    coq au vin.
La **veille de Noël** il prépare
    toujours **le repas.**

Qu'est-ce que tu prends comme petit
    déjeuner?
Un bol de café au lait.[1]

Où est **l'ail** (m.)?
    l'huile (f.)
    la tomate

Il faut **mettre**
    beaucoup d'ail
    beaucoup de tomates
    assez d'huile
    assez de sel
Quel **gâchis!** Il y a **trop**
    d'oignons et **trop de** poivre.

Qu'est-ce qui ne va pas, mon vieux? }
                ma vieille? }
Je n'ai pas bonne mine?
Non! Tu as mangé du **poison?**

I don't like
    to do housework
    to cook
    to set the table
    to clear the table

*Why is Lydie going to **hide***
    the forks. the spoons. and
    the knives?
Because she doesn't want to set
    the table.
*Pretty soon she's going to **break***
    the dishes, too.

My father likes to cook.
Last night. for example. he
    *made **bouillabaisse.***
*That's **typically** Provencal.*
*And the **night before** he made*
    coq au vin.
***Christmas Eve** he always pre-*
    *pares **the meal.***

What do you have for breakfast?

A bowl of café au lait.

*Where's the **garlic?***
    *the **oil***
    *the **tomato***

*You have to **put in***
    a lot of garlic
    a lot of tomatoes
    enough oil
    enough salt
*What a mess! There are **too***
    *many onions and **too much** pepper.*

*What's wrong, **pal?***

Don't I look good?
*No! Did you eat **poison?***

See Cultural Supplement.

These and other expressions of quantity are explained in Lesson 18. We treat them here solely as lexical items.

ALIMENTATION
GROCERY

Il est plus de 20 h. Tout est fermé. vous ne voulez pas dîner au restaurant. Heureusement, certains magasins d'alimentation sont encore ouverts.

It is past 8 o'clock. everything is closed and, though ravenous. you don't feel like eating in a restaurant. There are fortunately some food shops which are still open at that time.

LE MUNICHE : 27, rue de Buci, 6e. 633-62-09
Jusqu'à 22 h.
De 16 h 30 à 2 h du matin. Fermé le mercredi
From 4.30 p.m. to 2 a.m. Closed Wednesday.

DOMINIQUE : 19, rue Bréa, 6e. 325-28-40.
Jusqu'à 22 h. Produits russes.
Until 10 p.m. Russian food items.

MUTTI : 63, avenue des Ternes, 17e. 754-61-14.
Jusqu'à 22 h 30.
Until 10.30 p.m.

---

[1]*Café au lait.* which is prepared by mixing equal parts of coffee and warm milk, is often served in bowls rather than cups. Note that the French breakfast is a small meal. Generally it consists only of some type of bread and butter or jam and a bowl of *café au lait.*

1. débarrasser la table
2. l'évier
3. la veille
4. mettre le couvert
5. C'est chouette, ça!
6. cache
7. une tomate
8. De l'huile
9. Du poisson
10. Il n'y a pas assez de

Exercice de vocabulaire

Choose the word or phrase that best completes the sentence or fits the situation.

1. Après le dîner il faut *(aller dans la salle à manger/débarrasser la table).*
2. On fait la vaisselle dans *(la cuisinière/l'évier).*
3. Il faut attendre jusqu'à *(la veille/la vieille)* de Noël pour ouvrir les cadeaux.
4. Il est presque sept heures du soir. Il faut *(faire le ménage/mettre le couvert).*
5. Ce soir on sert un bon repas français. *(C'est chouette, ça!/Quel gâchis!)*
6. Qu'est-ce que tu fais avec cet argent? Chut! Je le *(cache/casse).*
7. Tu restes toujours au soleil? Tu es déjà rouge comme *(une cuisine/une tomate).*
8. Qu'est-ce qu'il y a dans ce verre? *(De l'ail/De l'huile)* pour la salade.
9. Qu'est-ce que tu vas mettre dans la bouillabaisse? *(Du poisson/Des boissons),* bien sûr.
10. Onze tasses et douze soucoupes! *(Il n'y a pas assez de/Il y a trop de)* tasses.

EXPLICATIONS I

Le verbe __mettre__

The verb *mettre* means "to put (in), to place, to set; to put on (clothing)."

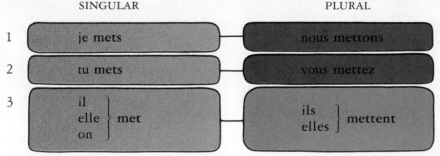

	SINGULAR	PLURAL
1	je mets	nous mettons
2	tu mets	vous mettez
3	il elle } met on	ils elles } mettent

IMPERATIVE: mets! mettons! mettez!

1. The plural forms of *mettre* follow the pattern of other *-re* verbs. The infinitive ending is dropped and the plural endings are added to the stem *mett-.*

2. In the singular, the second *t* is dropped, and the ending *-s* is added to the 1 and 2 sing. forms. All three singular forms are pronounced the same.

Exercices

A. Answer the questions in the negative. Follow the model.

1. Est-ce que tu mets du beurre sur le pain?
   Non, je ne mets pas de beurre sur le pain.

2. Est-ce qu'ils mettent le couvert?
3. Est-ce que je mets assez de sel?
4. Est-ce que tu mets du sucre dans le café?
5. Est-ce que nous mettons trop de poivre dans la soupe?
6. Est-ce que vous mettez la nappe sur la table?
7. Est-ce qu'elle met cette jupe aujourd'hui?

B. Replace the words in italics with the appropriate present-tense form of the verb *mettre*. Follow the model.

1. Elle *va mettre* les cuillères à côté des couteaux.
   Elle met les cuillères à côté des couteaux.

2. Nous *voulons mettre* le thé sur la cuisinière maintenant.
3. Tu *veux mettre* le lait dans le réfrigérateur?
4. Qu'est-ce qu'elles *aiment mettre* dans la salade niçoise?
5. Je *vais mettre* le couvert vers 6 h. 30.
6. Vous *allez mettre* des habits chauds ce matin?
7. Est-ce qu'il *peut mettre* les assiettes dans la salle à manger?
8. Ils *vont mettre* du vin sur la table.

Partioipes passés irréguliers

You know how to form the passé composé of regular verbs, using *avoir* and a past participle. Irregular verbs tend to have irregular past participles:

1. The past participles of verbs like *prendre* end in *-is:*

prendre	il prend	il a **pris**
apprendre	il apprend	il a **appris**
comprendre	il comprend	il a **compris**

2. The past participle of *mettre* is like that of *prendre:*

mettre	il met	il a **mis**

3. The following verbs have past participles ending in *-u:*

voir	il voit	il a **vu**
croire	il croit	il a **cru**
lire	il lit	il a **lu**
pouvoir	il peut	il a **pu**
pleuvoir	il pleut	il a **plu**
vouloir	il veut	il a **voulu**

4. The past participles of *ouvrir* and *offrir* end in *-ert:*

ouvrir	il ouvre	il a **ouvert**
offrir	il offre	il a **offert**

2. Non, ils ne mettent pas le couvert.
3. Non, tu ne mets pas assez de sel.
4. Non, je ne mets pas de sucre dans le café.
5. Non, vous ne mettez (nous ne mettons) pas trop de poivre dans la soupe.
6. Non, nous ne mettons (je ne mets) pas la nappe sur la table.
7. Non, elle ne met pas cette jupe aujourd'hui.

2. Nous mettons le thé sur la cuisinière maintenant.
3. Tu mets le lait dans le réfrigérateur?
4. Qu'est-ce qu'elles mettent dans la salade niçoise?
5. Je mets le couvert vers 6 h. 30.
6. Vous mettez des habits chauds ce matin?
7. Est-ce qu'il met les assiettes dans la salle à manger?
8. Ils mettent du vin sur la table.

5. The past participles of *faire, dire,* and *écrire* are like the 3 sing. form:

faire	il fait	il a fait
dire	il dit	il a dit
écrire	il écrit	il a écrit

6. The past participles of *avoir* and *être* are highly irregular:

avoir	il a	il a eu
être	il est	il a été

Exercices

A. Answer the questions in the affirmative. Follow the model.

1. Est-ce qu'elles n'ont pas pu aller à la fête?
   Si, elles ont pu aller à la fête.

2. Est-ce que tu n'as pas fait la vaisselle ce matin?
3. Est-ce que je n'ai pas écrit les réponses correctes?
4. Est-ce qu'elle n'a pas eu tort?
5. Est-ce que nous n'avons pas mis assez de crème?
6. Est-ce que vous n'avez pas vu la nouvelle bibliothèque?
7. Est-ce que tu n'as pas cru cette vieille histoire?
8. Est-ce qu'il n'a pas ouvert la fenêtre?
9. Est-ce qu'ils n'ont pas pris de thé?

B. Put the sentences in the present tense. Follow the model.

1. Ils ont lu le dernier chapitre.
   Ils lisent le dernier chapitre.

2. Il a plu à la campagne.
3. J'ai pu y assister mercredi.
4. Vous avez dit "félicitations" à l'actrice.
5. Tu as voulu l'accompagner à l'hôpital?
6. Elle a offert du vin avec le repas.
7. Elles ont fait le ménage pour leur mère.
8. Nous avons mis des fruits et du fromage sur une grande assiette.
9. Il a compris plusieurs phrases.

C. Redo the sentences in the passé composé. Follow the model.

1. Elle ne met pas les tasses sur la table.
   Elle n'a pas mis les tasses sur la table.

2. Ils ne peuvent pas finir avant 3 h.
3. Tu n'as pas de chance, mon vieux.
4. Nous n'ouvrons pas la porte de la cuisine.
5. Il ne veut pas faire de l'alpinisme.
6. Vous n'avez pas raison.
7. Je ne vois pas beaucoup de vendeuses.
8. Elle n'offre pas trop de hors-d'œuvre.
9. Je ne lis pas beaucoup de romans policiers.
10. Ils sont très aimables aujourd'hui.

2. Si, j'ai fait la vaisselle ce matin.
3. Si, tu as écrit les réponses correctes.
4. Si, elle a eu tort.
5. Si, vous avez (nous avons) mis assez de crème.
6. Si, nous avons (j'ai) vu la nouvelle bibliothèque.
7. Si, j'ai cru cette vieille histoire.
8. Si, il a ouvert la fenêtre.
9. Si, ils ont pris du thé.

Ex. B
2. Il pleut à la campagne.
3. Je peux y assister mercredi.
4. Vous dites "félicitations" à l'actrice.
5. Tu veux l'accompagner à l'hôpital?
6. Elle offre du vin avec le repas.
7. Elles font le ménage pour leur mère.
8. Nous mettons des fruits et du fromage sur une grande assiette.
9. Il comprend plusieurs phrases.

2. Ils n'ont pas pu finir avant 3 h.
3. Tu n'as pas eu de chance, mon vieux.
4. Nous n'avons pas ouvert la porte de la cuisine.
5. Il n'a pas voulu faire de l'alpinisme.
6. Vous n'avez pas eu raison.
7. Je n'ai pas vu beaucoup de vendeuses.
8. Elle n'a pas offert trop de hors-d'œuvre.
9. Je n'ai pas lu beaucoup de romans policiers.
10. Ils ont été très aimables aujourd'hui.

D. Put the sentences first in the present tense, then in the passé composé. Follow the model.

1. Il va pleuvoir aujourd'hui.
   Il pleut aujourd'hui. Il a plu aujourd'hui.

2. Je vais ouvrir les paquets tout de suite.
3. On va dire "au revoir."
4. Je vais écrire ces phrases en anglais.
5. Ils vont mettre les fourchettes à gauche des assiettes.
6. Tu vas avoir besoin de ton manteau.
7. Elle va lire la leçon de chimie.
8. Nous allons offrir des cadeaux aux petits enfants.
9. Puis elles vont faire un voyage à Bruxelles.
10. Nous allons apprendre l'espagnol.

2. J'ouvre les paquets tout de suite. J'ai ouvert. . .
3. On dit "au revoir." On a dit. . .
4. J'écris ces phrases en anglais. J'ai écrit. . .
5. Ils mettent les fourchettes à gauche des assiettes. Ils ont mis. . .
6. Tu as besoin de ton manteau. Tu as eu. . .
7. Elle lit la leçon de chimie. Elle a lu. . .
8. Nous offrons des cadeaux aux petits enfants. Nous avons offert. . .
9. Puis elles font un voyage à Bruxelles. Puis elles ont fait. . .
10. Nous apprenons l'espagnol. Nous avons appris. . .

Vérifiez vos progrès

Rewrite the sentences in the passé composé. Follow the model.

1. Nous ne voulons pas partir tout de suite.
   Nous n'avons pas voulu partir tout de suite.

2. Je mets mon chapeau gris et je dis "au revoir."
3. Il pleut ce matin, mais Marie ne porte pas son imperméable.
4. Qui voit l'autre gant?
5. Tu ne peux pas aller au marché cette semaine.
6. Nous faisons nos devoirs et ensuite je fais la vaisselle.
7. Elles n'offrent pas beaucoup de cadeaux à leurs cousines.
8. Vous écrivez des cartes postales?
9. Ils prennent des croque-monsieur et des citrons pressés.

CONVERSATION ET LECTURE

Parlons de vous

1. Est-ce que vous avez lu quelques bons livres cette année? Quels livres? Vous avez lu ces livres dans votre cours d'anglais? 2. Vous avez vu quelques bons films? Quels films? Vous avez vu ces films à la télé? 3. Qu'est-ce que vous avez fait hier soir? 4. Qu'est-ce qu'on vous a offert comme cadeaux de Noël l'année dernière? Vous les avez mis sous un arbre de Noël? Vous avez ouvert les paquets la veille de Noël?

Dans la cuisine

Hier, quand Gilles est rentré° à la maison vers cinq   *est rentré: returned*
heures, il a vu son frère aîné, David, dans la cuisine.
Il lui a demandé: "Qu'est-ce que tu fais?" "Ce soir,
c'est nous qui préparons le dîner," lui a répondu
5   David, qui aime bien faire la cuisine.

GILLES   Pourquoi est-ce que tu dis "nous"? Je ne
              veux pas faire la cuisine, moi.

DAVID   Tu peux faire une salade, n'est-ce pas? Et
              d'abord, tu peux mettre le couvert pendant
10   que je prépare la viande et les légumes.

GILLES   D'accord. Où est la nappe?

DAVID   Nous n'avons pas besoin de mettre une
              nappe. Il y a déjà des sets° sur la table.   *le set: place mat*

GILLES   Et les serviettes? Elles y sont aussi?

15   DAVID   Non, je crois qu'elles sont dans le buffet de
              la salle à manger. Regarde dans le troisième
              tiroir° à gauche.   *le tiroir: drawer*

Gilles est allé° chercher les serviettes. Mais il est   *est allé: went*
revenu° bientôt et a demandé: *est revenu: came back*

20   GILLES   Nous sommes cinq, n'est-ce pas?

DAVID   Bien sûr. Papa, maman, Nicole, toi et moi.

GILLES   Alors, je n'ai pas pu trouver assez de four-
              chettes.

DAVID   Est-ce que tu as fait la vaisselle après le
25   déjeuner?

GILLES   Non.

le set: Point out the pronounced final consonant: [sɛt].

DAVID   Alors, regarde dans l'évier.

Gilles est allé à l'évier. Il y a trouvé des fourchettes
et aussi des cuillères, des couteaux, des assiettes,
30   des tasses et des verres. Il a pris seulement° trois   seulement: *only*
fourchettes.

DAVID   Et le reste° de la vaisselle? Pourquoi est-ce   le reste: *rest*
que tu le laisses dans l'évier?

GILLES   Parce que j'ai besoin seulement des four-
35   chettes.

DAVID   Comme° tu es paresseux!   comme: *(here) how*

GILLES   Attends. Je vais faire cette vaisselle. Mais
d'abord je vais apporter les assiettes et les
verres dans la salle à manger.

40   Gilles les prend et il va lentement vers° la salle à   vers: *(here) toward*
manger.

DAVID   Pourquoi est-ce que tu ne les mets pas sur
un plateau?° Gilles, fais attention!°   le plateau: *tray*
                                            faire attention: *to*
PATATRAS!° Et cinq assiettes et cinq verres sont   *watch out*
45   cassés.   patatras!: *crash!*
                  la moitié de: *half*

DAVID   Maintenant que tu as cassé la moitié de° la
vaisselle, qu'est-ce qu'on va faire?

GILLES   On peut aller dîner au restaurant, peut-être?

cassés: Though adjectival
use of the past participle
is not taught in Level One,
students should be able to
understand this with no
difficulty.

À propos ...

1. A quelle heure est-ce que Gilles est rentré hier?   2. Qui est-ce qu'il a vu
dans la cuisine?   3. Est-ce que David aime faire la cuisine? Et Gilles, est-ce
qu'il aime la faire aussi?   4. Qui va faire une salade? Qu'est-ce que David
va faire pendant que Gilles met le couvert?   5. Pourquoi est-ce qu'on n'a
pas besoin de mettre une nappe?   6. Les serviettes sont déjà sur la table?
Où sont-elles?   7. Qu'est-ce que Gilles n'a pas pu trouver? Où est-ce qu'il
les trouve enfin? Pourquoi sont-ils là?   8. Est-ce qu'il trouve seulement des
fourchettes dans l'évier?   9. Pourquoi laisse-t-il le reste de la vaisselle dans
l'évier?   10. Gilles dit qu'il va faire la vaisselle. Est-ce qu'il la fait tout de
suite?   11. Est-ce que Gilles met les assiettes et les verres sur un plateau?
Qu'est-ce qui arrive ("happens")?   12. Où est-ce que la famille va peut-être
dîner ce soir?   13. David dit que son frère cadet est paresseux. A-t-il raison?   14. Et vous, est-ce que vous êtes paresseux? Vraiment paresseux, ou
paresseux seulement chez vous?   15. Est-ce que vous mettez le couvert, par
exemple? Vous l'avez fait hier soir? Vous débarrassez la table? Vous faites
la vaisselle? Qui a fait la vaisselle chez vous hier soir?   16. Est-ce que vous
aimez faire la cuisine? Qu'est-ce que vous aimez préparer?   17. Est-ce que
votre mère ou votre père fait bien la cuisine? Vos frères ou vos sœurs?
18. Vous faites le ménage quelquefois? Vous allez au marché? Quand vous
n'allez pas au lycée, qu'est-ce que vous faites le matin? Vous faites la grasse
matinée peut-être?

Les pronoms compléments d'objet au passé composé

Exs. A–B can be done after covering Point 1.

1. Look at the following:

J'ai téléphoné à Jean.	Je lui ai téléphoné.
Elle a écrit à ses parents.	Elle leur a écrit.
Nous avons assisté au match.	Nous y avons assisté.
Ils ont commandé du gigot.	Ils en ont commandé.

In the passé composé, object pronouns come before the form of *avoir*.

Exs. C and E can be done after covering Point 2.

2. Note what happens with the direct object pronouns *le. la.* and *les:*

Elle a attendu son mari.	Elle l'a attendu.
but: Il a attendu sa femme.	Il l'a attendue.
Elles ont attendu leurs maris.	Elles les ont attendus.
Ils ont attendu leurs femmes.	Ils les ont attendues.

The past participle agrees with the preceding direct object. If the direct object is feminine singular, an *e* is added; if it is masculine plural, an *s* is added; if it is feminine plural, an *es* is added. Note that *le* and *la* are elided to *l'*, and that the *s* of *les* is a liaison consonant. However, if the direct object pronoun is *en*, the past participle does not change, even if *en* replaces a feminine noun: *Tu prends des pâtisseries? → J'en ai déjà pris.*

Ex. F can be done after covering Point 3.

3. When *me. te. nous.* and *vous* are used as *indirect* objects, the past participle does not agree:

Il m'a téléphoné.	Il nous a téléphoné.
Il t'a téléphoné.	Il vous a téléphoné.

When they are used as *direct* objects, the past participle does agree:

Il m'a { regardé. / regardée.	Il nous a { regardés. / regardées.
Il t'a { regardé. / regardée.	Il vous a { regardé, monsieur. / regardée, madame. / regardés, messieurs. / regardées, mesdames.

Note that with the direct object pronoun *vous*, the past participle may have any of the four forms, depending upon who is being spoken to. Again there is elision (*me* and *te → m'. t'*) and the *s* of *nous* and *vous* is a liaison consonant.

Ex. G can be done after covering Point 4.

4. Note the following:

J'ai écrit la lettre.	Je l'ai écrite.
J'ai compris les leçons.	Je les ai comprises.
J'ai pris les couteaux.	Je les ai pris.

When an *e* is added to a past participle that ends in a consonant, the consonant is pronounced. If a past participle already ends in an *s.* no *s* is added to make masculine plural agreement.

5. In the negative, the object pronoun comes between the *ne (n')* and the form of *avoir;* the *pas* comes after the form of *avoir:*

Ils n'ont pas pris d'œufs.   Ils n'en ont pas pris.
Je n'ai pas écrit la réponse.   Je ne l'ai pas écrite.
Tu n'as pas ouvert les lettres.   Tu ne les as pas ouvertes.

Exercices

A. Answer using the appropriate indirect object pronoun, *lui* or *leur*. Follow the model.

1. Ils ont donné l'argent *au vendeur?*
   Oui, ils lui ont donné l'argent.

2. Vous avez téléphoné *au médecin?*
3. Nous avons écrit *aux marins?*
4. Elle a fait une visite *à ses nièces?*
5. Tu as dit "bon anniversaire" *à ta secrétaire?*
6. Elles ont posé des questions *aux hommes et aux femmes d'affaires?*
7. Henri a offert des portefeuilles *à ses sœurs?*
8. Elle a emprunté un foulard *à sa mère?*

B. Answer using the appropriate object pronoun, *y* or *en*. Follow the model.

1. Ils ont joué *au football américain* la semaine dernière?
   Oui, ils y ont joué la semaine dernière.

2. Ils ont réussi *à l'examen de sciences sociales?*
3. Tu as commandé *de la mousse au chocolat?*
4. Nous avons dîné *en ville* mardi?
5. Il a assisté *aux cours de maths?*
6. Vous avez choisi *des tasses et des soucoupes?*
7. Elle a offert *de la tarte aux pommes* à Marcel?
8. Vous avez eu besoin *de l'argent?*
9. Elle a dormi *en classe?*

C. Answer using the direct object pronoun *l'*. Make sure that the past participle agrees with the noun that the object pronoun is replacing. Follow the models.

1. A-t-elle servi *la bouillabaisse?*   *Oui, elle l'a servie.*
2. As-tu fait *le ménage?*   *Oui, je l'ai fait.*

3. A-t-il demandé *l'addition?*   7. Ont-ils trouvé *la confiture?*
4. As-tu caché *le poison?*   8. Avez-vous eu *sa veste?*
5. As-tu remercié *ton oncle?*   9. J'ai oublié *le paquet?*
6. A-t-elle laissé *la cravate?*   10. As-tu cassé *cette assiette?*

D. Redo the above exercise in the negative. Follow the models.

1. A-t-elle servi *la bouillabaisse?*   *Non, elle ne l'a pas servie.*
2. As-tu fait *le ménage?*   *Non, je ne l'ai pas fait.*

Ex. D can be done after covering Point 5.

Due to the difficulty of the structures involved, all exercises should be written. Because of the pronunciation change, Ex. G should also be handled orally.

2. Oui, nous lui avons (je lui ai) téléphoné.
3. Oui, vous leur avez (nous leur avons) écrit.
4. Oui, elle leur a fait une visite.
5. Oui, je lui ai dit "bon anniversaire."
6. Oui, elles leur ont posé des questions.
7. Oui, il leur a offert des portefeuilles.
8. Oui, elle lui a emprunté un foulard.

Ex. B
2. Oui, ils y ont réussi.
3. Oui, j'en ai commandé.
4. Oui, vous y avez (nous y avons) dîné mardi.
5. Oui, Il y a assisté.
6. Oui, nous en avons (j'en ai) choisi.
7. Oui, elle en a offert à Marcel.
8. Oui, nous en avons (j'en ai) eu besoin.
9. Oui, elle y a dormi.

Ex. C
3. Oui, il l'a demandée.
4. Oui, je l'ai caché.
5. Oui, je l'ai remercié.
6. Oui, elle l'a laissée.
7. Oui, ils l'ont trouvée.
8. Oui, nous l'avons (je l'ai) eue.
9. Oui, tu l'as oublié.
10. Oui, je l'ai cassée.

Ex. D
3. Non, il ne l'a pas demandée.
4. Non, je ne l'ai pas caché.
5. Non, je ne l'ai pas remercié.
6. Non, elle ne l'a pas laissée.
7. Non, ils ne l'ont pas trouvée.
8. Non, nous ne l'avons pas (je ne l'ai pas) eue.
9. Non, tu ne l'as pas oublié.
10. Non, je ne l'ai pas cassée.

Lesson
16

E. Answer using the direct object pronoun *les*. Remember that the past participle must agree with the object pronoun. Follow the models.

1. Tu as cherché *tes colliers?*
   Oui, je les ai cherchés.
2. Il a apporté *les cuillères et les fourchettes?*
   Oui, il les a apportées.

3. J'ai bien prononcé *les mots?*
4. Elle a préparé *les tomates?*
5. Ils ont mangé *les pâtisseries?*
6. Tu as perdu *les enveloppes?*
7. Tu as trouvé *tes mouchoirs?*
8. Elles ont fini *les chansons?*
9. Il a lu *ces poèmes sénégalais?*
10. Tu as raté *les examens?*

F. Answer using the appropriate pronoun: *m', t', nous,* or *vous*. Watch for the agreement or nonagreement of the past participle. Follow the model.

1. Papa m'a écoutée? Il m'a répondu?
   Oui, il t'a écoutée. Oui, il t'a répondu.

2. Il t'a compris? Il t'a prêté son parapluie?
3. Nicole nous a attendues? Elle nous a apporté le livre de biologie?
4. Les Robert nous ont invités à une fête? Ils nous ont téléphoné?
5. Le facteur vous a rencontrées? Il vous a donné un grand paquet?
6. Luc vous a vue à la bibliothèque? Il vous a emprunté un stylo?
7. L'hôtesse de l'air t'a remerciée? Elle t'a offert du thé?
8. Le professeur vous a entendus? Elle vous a posé des questions?

G. Answer using the appropriate direct object pronoun, *l'* or *les*. Remember that the past participle must agree with the object pronoun. Follow the model.

1. Tu as mis *les serviettes* sur la table?
   Oui, je les ai mises sur la table.

2. Tu as ouvert *la fenêtre?*
3. Tu as écrit *la lettre?*
4. Tu as bien fait *tes devoirs?*
5. Tu as écrit *ces poèmes?*
6. Tu as compris *la question?*
7. Tu as dit *ces longues phrases?*
8. Tu as appris *ces danses?*
9. Tu as mis *tes bracelets?*

Vérifiez vos progrès

Write true "yes" or "no" answers to the questions, using the appropriate object pronoun—*l', les; lui, leur; y* or *en*. Be sure to make the past participle agree with all direct object pronouns.

1. Vous avez réussi *à votre dernier examen de français?*
2. Vous avez fait *vos devoirs* hier soir?
3. Vous avez donné vos devoirs *au professeur* ce matin?
4. Vous avez regardé *la télé* hier?
5. Vous avez débarrassé *la table* après le dîner hier soir?
6. Vous avez pris *des œufs* ce matin?
7. Vous avez compris *cette leçon?*
8. Vous avez écrit *les réponses aux autres questions?*

RÉVISION ET THÈME

Consult the model sentences, then put the English cues into French and use them to form new sentences.

1. *Nous avons pu prononcer les mots.*
   (I was able to begin my work.)
   (She wanted to put on her raincoat.)

2. *Il l'a ouvert dans la salle à manger et il m'a dit "félicitations!"*
   (We saw her at the movies and said "happy birthday" to her.)
   (She gave them (f.pl.) to the children and they told her "thank you.")

3. *Tu n'as pas apporté ton portefeuille, alors il faut faire de l'auto-stop.*
   (I didn't set the table, so I have to do the housework.)
   (We didn't do the cooking, so we have to do the dishes.)

4. *Il a appris les chansons et il les a chantées à la surprise-party.*
   (She understood the answers and wrote them in her notebook.)
   (I found the salt and pepper and put them in the kitchen.)

5. *"On y met les verres?" m'a demandé le garçon.*
   ("They (m.) put the knives there," the doctor told us.)
   ("I put the spoons and forks there," the housewife answered him.)

6. *Tu as vendu la cuisinière, n'est-ce pas?*
   (He's hidden the napkins and the tablecloth, hasn't he?)
   (We broke the cup and saucer, didn't we?)

Now that you have done the *Révision*, you are ready to write a composition. Put the English captions describing each cartoon panel into French to form a paragraph.

See Teacher's Section for answers to the *révision* and *thème*.

Review of:
1. irregular past participles
2. direct and indirect object pronouns in passé composé
   irregular past participles
3. negative passé composé
   il faut
   expressions with *faire*
4. regular and irregular past participles
   direct object pronouns in passé composé
5. *mettre*
   y
   indirect object pronouns in passé composé
   inversion of noun subject and verb
6. passé composé
   n'est-ce pas

Bruno and Diane wanted to go shopping.

Their father met them at the door and said to them: "Ah, no!"

"You didn't prepare the meal, so you have to clear the table."

They took the dishes and put them in the sink.

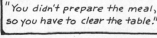
"You're leaving the dishes there?" their father asked them.

"We cleared the table, didn't we?" Bruno answered him.

Lesson
16

275

AUTO-TEST

A. Answer the questions in the present tense, using the appropriate direct object pronoun, *l'* or *les*. Follow the model.

1. Tu as mis *ton manteau?*
   Je le mets maintenant.

2. Elles ont mis *l'eau* sur la cuisinière?
3. Vous avez mis *le couvert*, mes filles?
4. Il a mis *le lait* dans le réfrigérateur?
5. Ils ont mis *les fleurs* dans la salle à manger?
6. Elle a mis *son imperméable?*
7. Tu as mis *ton vélo* dans le garage?

B. Answer in the negative using the appropriate direct object pronoun. Remember that the past participle must agree. Follow the model.

1. Tu as préparé *la bouillabaisse?*
   Non, je ne l'ai pas préparée.

2. Il a oublié *le sel et le poivre?*
3. Ils ont cassé *ces verres?*
4. Tu as ouvert *les lettres?*
5. Vous avez vu *les infirmières?*
6. Nous avons compris *le chapitre?*
7. Les ménagères ont cru *les vendeurs?*
8. Il a remercié *l'avocate?*
9. Elles ont fait *leurs robes?*

C. Answer using the cues in parentheses. Remember that when these pronouns are used as direct objects, the past participle must agree. In each case, assume that *m'* and *t'* represent one female; *nous* and *vous*, several females. Follow the models.

1. Qui as-tu cru? (vous)   *Je vous ai crues.*
2. A qui a-t-elle parlé? (vous)   *Elle vous a parlé.*

3. A qui a-t-il téléphoné? (t')
4. A qui ont-elles répondu? (m')
5. Qui as-tu vu? (vous)
6. A qui a-t-il écrit? (m')
7. Qui as-tu choisi? (t')
8. Qui a-t-elle rencontré? (nous)

D. Answer using the appropriate direct object pronoun, *l'*, *les*, or *en*. Then answer a second time using the appropriate indirect object pronoun, *lui*, *leur*, or *y*. Follow the model.

1. Tu as écrit cette lettre à ta tante?
   Oui, je l'ai écrite à ma tante. Je lui ai écrit cette lettre.

2. Elles ont pris leurs repas en ville?
3. Vous avez dit "bon courage" aux soldats?
4. J'ai montré la nappe et les serviettes à cette jeune femme?
5. Tu as offert cette nouvelle veste à ton frère?
6. Il a mis des cuillères dans l'évier?
7. Ils ont prêté l'électrophone et la radio à leurs neveux?

Poème

DÉJEUNER DU MATIN

Il a mis le café
Dans la tasse
Il a mis le lait
Dans la tasse de café
5 Il a mis le sucre
Dans le café au lait
Avec la petite cuiller°   la cuiller = la cuillère
Il a tourné
Il a bu° le café au lait   il a bu: *he drank*
10 Et il a reposé° la tasse   reposer: *to put back*
Sans me parler°   sans me parler: *without speaking to me*
Il a allumé°   allumer: *to light*
Une cigarette
Il a fait des ronds°   le rond: *ring*
15 Avec la fumée°   la fumée: *smoke*
Il a mis les cendres°   la cendre: *ash*
Dans le cendrier°   le cendrier: *ashtray*
Sans me parler
Sans me regarder
20 Il s'est levé°   il s'est levé: *he got up*
Il a mis
Son chapeau sur sa tête°   la tête: *head*
Il a mis
Son manteau de pluie°   le manteau de pluie = l'imperméable
25 Parce qu'il pleuvait°   il pleuvait: *it was raining*
Et il est parti°   il est parti: *he left*
Sous la pluie
Sans une parole°   la parole = le mot
Sans me regarder
30 Et moi j'ai pris
Ma tête dans ma main°   la main: *hand*
Et j'ai pleuré.°   pleurer: *to cry*

Jacques Prévert, *Paroles*
© Editions Gallimard, 1949

Proverbe

Qui casse les verres les paie.

Dix-Septième Leçon

Un voyage en voiture

Marie-Thérèse et sa sœur, Hélène, ne passent pas leurs vacances en France cet été. Elles sont parties pour la Grèce avec une amie, Gisèle, qui a une deux-chevaux.[1] En route, les filles veulent aussi visiter l'Italie et la Yougoslavie. Pendant le voyage, elles parlent des projets de vacances des parents
5 de Gisèle.

See Cultural Supplement.

la deux-chevaux: CV is an abbreviation of cheval vapeur, a unit of work equal to 75 kilogrammeters (kgm) per second.

MARIE-THÉRÈSE	Tes parents restent à Avignon[2] cet été?
GISÈLE	Non, non, ils sont déjà partis en voyage il y a quinze jours.
MARIE-THÉRÈSE	Ah bon! Où est-ce qu'ils sont allés?
10 GISÈLE	Au Portugal.
HÉLÈNE	Ils font le voyage en voiture?
GISÈLE	Bien sûr. Eux, ils ont leur jolie caravane. Ce n'est pas du tout comme cette deux-chevaux!

[1] The deux-chevaux (2-CV) is a very small, inexpensive French car. Its name comes from the amount of horsepower it has under the French system. Very few French teenagers own cars. Those who do usually have a car such as a 2-CV.

[2] Avignon is a city of 90,000 population in the southeast of France. It is especially well-known as the site of le Palais des Papes, where the Pope lived during the fourteenth century, and for its unfinished stone bridge, le pont Saint-Bénezet, which crosses part way over the Rhône River. Since 1947 there has been an annual summer cultural festival there, with both indoor and street performances.

A car trip

Marie-Thérèse and her sister, Hélène, aren't spending their vacation in France this summer. They have left for Greece with a friend, Gisèle, who has a Citroën 2-CV. On the way, the girls also want to visit Italy and Yugoslavia. During the trip, they talk about Gisèle's parents' vacation plans.

5	MARIE-THÉRÈSE	Are your parents staying in Avignon this summer?
	GISÈLE	No, they already left on a trip two weeks ago.
	MARIE-THÉRÈSE	Oh. Where did they go?
	GISÈLE	To Portugal.
	HÉLÈNE	Are they traveling by car?
10	GISÈLE	You bet! *They've* got their beautiful camper. It's not at all like this *deux-chevaux*.

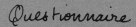

Questionnaire

1. Est-ce que Marie-Thérèse passe ses vacances en France cet été? 2. Où est-ce qu'elle va? Est-ce qu'elle y va seule? 3. Qui a une voiture? C'est une voiture américaine? 4. Quels autres pays ("countries") est-ce que les filles veulent visiter en route? 5. De quoi est-ce qu'elles parlent pendant le voyage? 6. Est-ce que les parents de Gisèle passent l'été à Avignon? Où est-ce qu'ils sont allés? Quand est-ce qu'ils sont partis? 7. Est-ce qu'ils ont pris le train? Comment est-ce qu'ils font le voyage? 8. Est-ce que les parents de Gisèle ont une deux-chevaux aussi? Qu'est-ce qu'ils ont?

PRONONCIATION

To pronounce the [ɛ] sound, start from the position for the [e] sound, but spread your mouth into a more open smile. Always keep your jaws steady.

Exercices

A. Listen, then say the following words aloud.

être	la fenêtre	est-ce que	presque	l'herbe
le verre	la cuillère	l'assiette	la serviette	derrière

B. These words contain both the [e] and the [ɛ] sounds.

Hélène	Thérèse	Etienne	l'élève	énergique

C. Listen, then say the following sentences aloud.

Eve cherche une veste pour Pierre.   C'est la veille de Noël, Adèle.
Ma mère a ouvert la lettre.   Vous êtes à l'hôtel avec elle.

MOTS NOUVEAUX I

L'Atlantique *(f.)* est un océan.
La Yougoslavie est un pays.
L'Europe *(f.)* est un continent.

La Belgique **se trouve au nord**
de la France.
La mer Méditerranée se trouve
au sud de la France.
La Suisse se trouve **à l'est**
de la France.
L'océan Atlantique se trouve **à
l'ouest** de la France.

*The Atlantic is **an ocean.***
*Yugoslavia is **a country.***
*Europe is **a continent.***

*Belgium **is located to the north***
of France.
The Mediterranean Sea is located
***to the south** of France.*
*Switzerland is **east** of France.*

*The Atlantic Ocean is **west** of*
France.

The choice of countries taught in this lesson has, of necessity, been somewhat arbitrary. If you have students whose families or forebears came from countries not taught here, try to add them to the list. Encourage students to talk about those countries that interest them, whether because of their own ethnic heritage or of trips they have made, social studies courses taken, or whatever.

Point out the pronunciation of *le pays* [pei] and of the final pronounced consonant of *le sud* [syd], *l'est* [ɛst], *l'ouest* [wɛst], *le Danemark:* [danmɑrk].

se trouver: We use this only in the 3 sing. and 3 pl. forms. You may want simply to treat it as an "odd" verb for now, cautioning students against using it in any except the third person forms. Pronominal verbs are taught in Level Two.

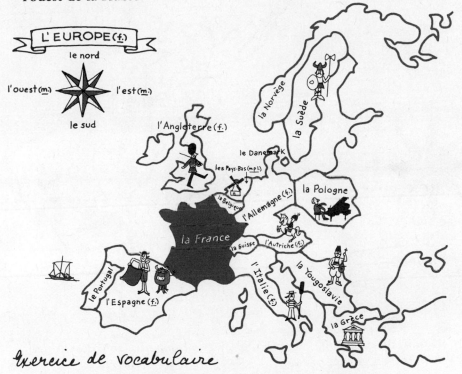

Exercice de vocabulaire

Answer the questions according to the map. Follow the model.

1. Quel pays se trouve au nord de l'Allemagne et de la Pologne?
   La Suède se trouve au nord de l'Allemagne et de la Pologne.

2. Quel pays se trouve à l'ouest de l'Espagne?
3. Quel pays se trouve à l'est de la Suisse?
4. Quel pays se trouve à l'est de l'Allemagne?
5. Quel pays se trouve au sud-ouest de la France?
6. Quel pays se trouve au nord-ouest de la France?
7. Quel pays se trouve au sud-est de la Yougoslavie?
8. Quel pays se trouve au nord de la Suisse et de l'Autriche?
9. Quel pays se trouve au nord-est de l'Angleterre et à l'ouest de la Suède?

2. Le Portugal se trouve à l'ouest de l'Espagne.
3. L'Autriche se trouve à l'est de la Suisse.
4. La Pologne se trouve à l'est de l'Allemagne.
5. L'Espagne se trouve au sud-ouest de la France.
6. L'Angleterre se trouve au nord-ouest de la France.
7. La Grèce se trouve au sud-est de la Yougoslavie.
8. L'Allemagne se trouve au nord de la Suisse et de l'Autriche.
9. La Norvège se trouve au nord-est de l'Angleterre et à l'ouest de la Suède.

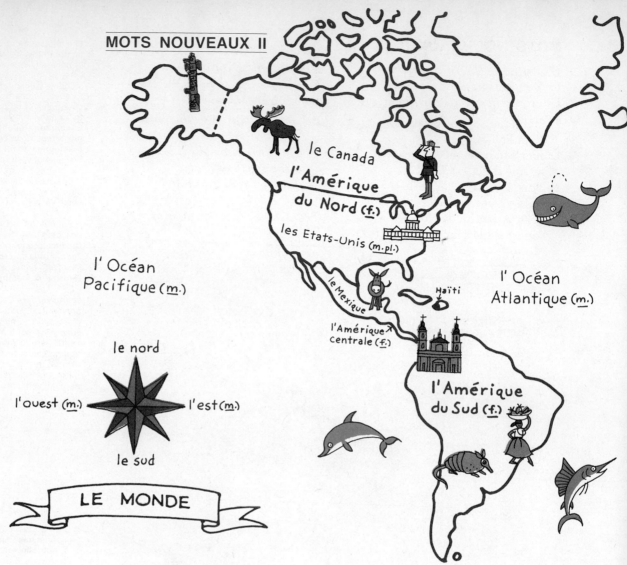

le Canada

l'Amérique du Nord (f.)

les Etats-Unis (m. pl.)

l'Océan Pacifique (m.)

l'Océan Atlantique (m.)

le Mexique

Haïti

l'Amérique centrale (f.)

le nord

l'ouest (m.)   l'est (m.)

le sud

l'Amérique du Sud (f.)

LE MONDE

les Etats-Unis: Point out the liaison: [etazyni].

le camping: Point out the nasal vowel sound: [kɑ̃piŋ].

On va faire du camping.	*We're going to camp out (to go camping).*
partir en voyage	*to leave on a trip*
partir en vacances	*to leave on vacation*
être en vacances	*to be on vacation*
prendre des vacances	*to take a vacation*
passer des vacances en Grèce	*to spend a vacation in Greece*
passer huit jours en Angleterre	*to spend a week in England*
passer quinze jours en Guyane[1]	*to spend two weeks in Guiana*
visiter[2] l'Autriche et la Suisse	*to visit Austria and Switzerland*

[1]La Guyane française, la Guadeloupe, la Martinique, and la Réunion are overseas departments of France (*les départements d'outre-mer*). Departments are administrative districts, much like states in the U.S. or provinces in Canada. They are thus not separate countries, but are legally a part of France.

[2]*Visiter* is used with places; *faire une visite à* is used with people.

Dix-Septième
Leçon

la Russie

l'Asie (f.)

l'Europe (f.)

la Chine

le Japon

le Mali

le Sénégal

l'Afrique (f.)

l'Océan Pacifique (m.)

l'Australie (f.)

Il m'a téléphoné il y a une heure.
                    il y a huit jours
                    il y a un an
                    il y a longtemps
Il a parlé de **ses projets** (*m.pl.*)
   pour l'été.
Ses parents ont **une caravane.**
Ils vont aller à Avignon.

D'où est-ce qu'il a téléphoné?
De Bruxelles.

L'avion arrive **de bonne heure.**
          à l'heure
          en retard

*He called me **an hour ago.***
          a week ago
          a year ago
          a long time ago
*He talked about his summer **plans**.*

*His parents have **a camper**.*
They're going to go to Avignon.

*Where did he call **from**?*
Brussels.

*The plane's arriving **early**.*
          on time
          late

Inasmuch as this is a map of countries and continents, we have not included le Québec or the four *départements d'outre-mer.* If you have not done so on a large map, you might point out their location here. La Guadeloupe and la Martinique, roughly 5/16" ESE of Haiti; la Guyane française on the NE coast of South America above the "i" and "q"; la Réunion, roughly 1/4" east of the center of Madagascar.

Lesson
17

283

Exercice de vocabulaire

Choose the word or phrase that best completes the sentence or fits the situation.

1. A l'est de / Pacifique
2. des continents
3. le Mexique
4. l'Australie
5. Où est-ce qu'ils veulent aller?
6. en retard
7. une caravane
8. Presque deux heures!
9. De Bonn
10. du camping
11. lui faire une visite
12. on part en vacances
13. l'année dernière

1. Où se trouve le Japon? *(A l'est de/A l'ouest de)* la Chine, dans l'océan *(Atlantique/Pacifique)*.
2. L'Asie, l'Afrique, l'Europe, etc., sont *(des continents/des pays)*.
3. Il y a trois pays dans l'Amérique du Nord: le Canada, les Etats-Unis et *(l'Amérique Centrale/le Mexique)*.
4. Il y a un continent qui est aussi un pays—c'est *(l'Australie/l'Autriche)*.
5. Ils font leurs projets de vacances maintenant. *(Ils les ont passées en Belgique, n'est-ce pas?/Où est-ce qu'ils veulent aller?)*
6. Je n'aime pas ce train. Il arrive toujours *(à l'heure/en retard)*.
7. Mes frères, ma sœur cadette et une de mes cousines vont nous accompagner. Alors il faut aller chercher *(une caravane/une deux-chevaux)*.
8. Ce monsieur est vraiment ennuyeux. Est-ce qu'il a parlé longtemps? *(Il y a deux heures!/Presque deux heures!)*
9. D'où est-ce qu'elles arrivent? *(De Bonn./De bonne heure.)*
10. Vous prenez la caravane? Oui, nous voulons faire *(de l'auto-stop/du camping)* cet été.
11. Tu vas en Allemagne? Oui, ma grand-mère y habite. Elle est très vieille et je voudrais *(la visiter/lui faire une visite)*.
12. Tu n'as pas bonne mine, mon vieux! Ah, je suis très fatigué, mais demain—enfin!—*(on part en vacances/je passe mes vacances)*.
13. Il a laissé son emploi il y a longtemps? Oui, *(l'année dernière/il y a huit jours)*.

EXPLICATIONS I

Le verbe venir

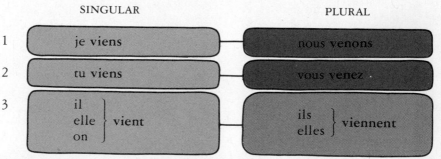

VOCABULAIRE		
venir *to come*	devenir *to become*	revenir *to come back*

	SINGULAR	PLURAL
1	je viens	nous venons
2	tu viens	vous venez
3	il elle on } vient	ils elles } viennent

IMPERATIVE: viens! venons! venez!
PAST PARTICIPLE: venu

1. The 1 and 2 pl. forms are regular. The *-ir* is dropped from the infinitive, and the endings *-ons* and *-ez* are added.

2. The singular stem is *vien-*. to which the regular endings *-s. -s.* and *-t* are added. All three forms are pronounced alike: [vjɛ̃].

3. The 3 pl. form is *viennent*. The *-nn-* is clearly released, and thus there is no nasal vowel sound: [vjɛn].

4. All verbs whose infinitive form ends in *-venir* follow this pattern. Two of the most common are *devenir* and *revenir*. Their past participles are *devenu* and *revenu*.

5. When *venir* is followed by a verb in the infinitive, its English equivalent is just what you would expect:

Je viens manger.   *I'm coming to eat.*
Nous venons les voir demain.   *We're coming to see them tomorrow.*

However, when *venir* is followed by *de* plus a verb in the infinitive, it means "to have just." This is called the "immediate past":

Je viens de manger.   { *I've just eaten.*
                        { *I just ate.*

Nous venons de les voir.   { *We've just seen them.*
                            { *We just saw them.*

Exercices

A. Answer the questions using the appropriate pronoun. Follow the model.

1. Vous venez toujours de bonne heure. Et moi?
   Tu viens toujours de bonne heure aussi.

2. Je reviens lundi matin. Et eux?
3. Yvette et Christine deviennent avocates. Et Julie?
4. Il vient souvent en retard. Et nous?
5. Tu deviens pilote. Et lui?
6. Nous revenons à pied. Et elles?
7. Ils viennent des Etats-Unis. Et vous?

B. Redo the sentences using the appropriate form of *venir de* + infinitive. Follow the model.

1. Nous avons rencontré les ouvriers.
   Nous venons de rencontrer les ouvriers.

2. Il a plu.
3. Ils ont vu le nouvel électrophone.
4. Nous avons fait nos projets de vacances.
5. Elles ont entendu la musique espagnole.
6. Tu as pris un Coca.
7. Je lui ai offert un manteau.
8. Tu m'as emprunté quelques timbres.

2. Ils reviennent lundi matin aussi.
3. Julie (Elle) devient avocate aussi.
4. Vous venez (Nous venons) souvent en retard aussi.
5. Il devient pilote aussi.
6. Elles reviennent à pied aussi.
7. Nous venons (Je viens) des Etats-Unis aussi.

2. Il vient de pleuvoir.
3. Ils viennent de voir le nouvel électrophone.
4. Nous venons de faire nos projets de vacances.
5. Elles viennent d'entendre la musique espagnole.
6. Tu viens de prendre un Coca.
7. Je viens de lui offrir un manteau.
8. Tu viens de m'emprunter quelques timbres.

Note that this is also a review of direct object pronouns in the passé composé and before an infinitive.

2. Je viens de les lire.
3. Ils viennent de le vendre.
4. Il vient de le laisser.
5. Elle vient de la trouver.
6. Nous venons de le passer.
7. Je viens de la perdre.
8. Ils viennent de les ouvrir.
9. Nous venons de les apprendre.

C. Answer the questions using the appropriate form of *venir de.* Follow the model.

1. Elles ont écrit les cartes postales. Quand est-ce qu'elles les ont écrites?
   Elles viennent de les écrire.

2. J'ai lu plusieurs romans allemands. Quand est-ce que tu les as lus?
3. Ils ont vendu ce vieux piano. Quand est-ce qu'ils l'ont vendu?
4. Georges a laissé le pourboire. Quand est-ce qu'il l'a laissé?
5. Elle a trouvé sa montre. Quand est-ce qu'elle l'a trouvée?
6. Nous avons passé l'examen de physique. Quand est-ce que vous l'avez passé?
7. J'ai perdu ma bague. Quand est-ce que tu l'as perdue?
8. Ils ont ouvert ces grands paquets. Quand est-ce qu'ils les ont ouverts?
9. Nous avons appris les nouvelles chansons françaises. Quand est-ce que vous les avez apprises?

Le passé composé avec <u>être</u>

VOCABULAIRE			
descendre[1]	*to come down, to go down*	mourir	*to die*
descendre de	*to get out of, to get off*	naître	*to be born*
monter	*to come up, to go up, to climb*	retourner	*to go back*
monter dans	*to get in, to get on*	tomber	*to fall*

1. The verbs above and those below, which you already know, form their passé composé with *être:*

arriver	*to arrive*	Il est arrivé.
partir	*to leave*	Il est parti.
entrer	*to enter, to come in, to go in*	Il est entré.
sortir	*to go out*	Il est sorti.
aller	*to go*	Il est allé.
venir	*to come*	Il est venu.
rentrer	*to return, to go back, to come back*	Il est rentré.
revenir	*to come back*	Il est revenu.
rester	*to stay*	Il est resté.
devenir	*to become*	Il est devenu.

2. Look at the following:

Jean écrit: "J'y suis allé." Jeanne écrit: "J'y suis allée."
Tu es sorti, Jean? **Tu es sortie, Jeanne?**
Il est devenu médecin. **Elle est devenue médecin.**
Ils écrivent: "**Nous sommes partis** à 2 h." Elles écrivent: "**Nous sommes parties** à 2 h."

[1]*Descendre* is a regular *-re* verb.

Vous êtes tombé, monsieur?
Vous êtes restés à l'hôtel, messieurs?
Ils sont **descendus** à la plage.

Vous êtes tombée, madame?
Vous êtes restées à Paris, mesdames?
Elles y sont **descendues** aussi.

When a verb forms its passé composé with *être,* its past participle agrees with the subject of the verb in gender and number.

3. *Naître* and *mourir* are irregular verbs. For now you need only know their past participles:

Louis Pasteur est **né** en 1822.
Marie Curie est **née** en 1867.

Il est **mort** en 1895.
Elle est **morte** en 1934.

See Cultural Supplement.

Exercices

A. Answer the questions according to the statements. Follow the model.

1. Lisette et Michèle sont venues me voir ce matin.
   (a) Qui est venu te voir?
      Lisette et Michèle sont venues me voir.
   (b) Quand est-ce qu'elles sont venues?
      Elles sont venues ce matin.

2. Nous sommes rentrés de Copenhague il y a huit jours.
   (a) D'où est-ce que vous êtes rentrés?
   (b) Quand est-ce que vous en êtes rentrés?

3. Le pauvre petit garçon! Il est tombé de son vélo.
   (a) Pourquoi est-ce que tu dis "le pauvre petit garçon"?
   (b) D'où est-il tombé?

4. Hier cette secrétaire est arrivée au bureau en retard et elle est partie une heure après.
   (a) Qui est arrivé en retard?
   (b) Elle y est restée longtemps?

5. Estelle m'a dit que Brigitte est devenue actrice.
   (a) Estelle est devenue actrice?
   (b) Qui t'a parlé de Brigitte?

6. Mes parents sont sortis hier soir, mais moi, je suis resté chez nous.
   (a) Qui est sorti hier soir?
   (b) Est-ce que tu les as accompagnés?

7. Jeanne d'Arc est née il y a cinq cents ans et elle est morte à l'âge de 19 ans.
   (a) Est-ce que Jeanne est née il y a longtemps?
   (b) A quel âge est-ce qu'elle est morte?

8. Gaël et moi, nous sommes partis de la fête à minuit.
   (a) A quelle heure est-ce que vous êtes partis?
   (b) Avec qui est-ce que tu es parti?

B. Redo the sentences in the passé composé. Follow the model.

1. Elle va à Cannes cet été. *Elle est allée à Cannes cet été.*

2. Isabelle vient plus tard, vers midi.

2. (a) Nous sommes rentrés de Copenhague.
   (b) Nous (en) sommes rentrés il y a huit jours.
3. (a) Parce qu'il est tombé (de son vélo).
   (b) Il est tombé de son vélo.
4. (a) Cette secrétaire est arrivée en retard.
   (b) Non, elle est partie une heure après.
5. (a) Non, (elle m'a dit que) Brigitte est devenue actrice.
   (b) Estelle m'a parlé de Brigitte.
6. (a) Mes parents sont sortis hier soir.
   (b) Non, je suis resté chez nous (je ne les ai pas accompagnés).
7. (a) Oui, elle est née il y a cinq cents ans (longtemps).
   (b) Elle est morte à l'âge de 19 ans.
8. (a) Nous sommes partis à minuit.
   (b) Je suis parti avec Gaël.

2. Isabelle est venue plus tard, vers midi.

3. Le train de Lyon part à 3 h. 15.
4. Notre chat gris tombe de l'arbre.
5. Marlène reste au gymnase mais Agnès rentre chez elle.
6. Bernard rentre dimanche soir, le deux avril.
7. Leur fils aîné devient steward.
8. Quand est-ce qu'Elisabeth arrive?
9. Le nouvel étudiant entre dans le lycée.
10. La serveuse descend de l'autobus et tout à coup elle tombe.

C. Replace the words in italics with the appropriate past-tense form of the verb in parentheses. When two forms of the past participle are possible, show both. Follow the model.

1. Nous *avons assisté* au cours d'algèbre. (aller)
   Nous sommes allés au cours d'algèbre.
   Nous sommes allées au cours d'algèbre.

2. J'*ai répondu* tout de suite. (venir)
3. Tu *as fait un stage* dans cet hôpital? (naître)
4. Eric *a attendu* dans l'avion. (monter)
5. Nous *avons fait la cuisine* la semaine dernière. (arriver)
6. Les vendeuses *ont parlé* de la librairie. (sortir)
7. J'*ai joué* à la plage. (descendre)
8. Tu *as frappé* à la porte? (aller)

D. Redo the paragraph in the passé composé.

Samedi, *je fais* du camping avec ma famille. Nous *partons* de bonne heure et nous *arrivons* à la campagne vers 2 h. de l'après-midi. Nous *passons* deux jours pas loin d'un joli lac. Mon père et moi, nous *descendons* au lac pour nager, et nous *voyons* deux petites filles. Tout à coup, une des filles *tombe* dans l'eau. Tout de suite, nous *nageons* vers elle et papa *la prend* par la chemise. La mère des enfants *arrive*. Elle *remercie* papa et puis elle *part* avec ses enfants. Nous, nous *rentrons* chez nous.

Vérifiez vos progrès

Write complete sentences, putting the verbs in parentheses in the passé composé. Follow the model.

1. Il *(passer)* huit jours en Afrique et puis il *(rentrer)* en Europe.
   Il a passé huit jours en Afrique et puis il est rentré en Europe.

2. Ils *(sortir)* à 9 h. mais ils *(revenir)* une heure plus tard.
3. Napoléon *(naître)* en 1769; il *(mourir)* en 1821.
4. Les jeunes filles *(descendre)* à la plage et elles *(nager)* jusqu'à 4 h.
5. Elle *(rester)* en Chine et elle *(devenir)* médecin.
6. Elles *(venir)* te voir parce que tu *(vouloir)* leur parler.
7. Edouard et Luc *(monter)* dans le train, mais le train *(ne pas partir)* tout de de suite.
8. Hélène *(partir)* en vacances, mais nous *(rester)* en ville.

CONVERSATION ET LECTURE

Parlons de vous

Note that this a reference list only.

Les états des Etats-Unis sont:

l'Alabama *(m.)*	l'Indiana *(m.)*	l'état de New York
l'Alaska *(m.)*	l'Iowa *(m.)*	le Nouveau Mexique
l'Arizona *(m.)*	le Kansas	l'Ohio *(m.)*
l'Arkansas *(m.)*	le Kentucky	l'Oklahoma *(m.)*
la Californie	la Louisiane	l'Oregon *(m.)*
la Caroline du Nord	le Maine	la Pennsylvanie
la Caroline du Sud	le Maryland	le Rhode Island
le Colorado	le Massachusetts	le Tennessee
le Connecticut	le Michigan	le Texas
le Dakota du Nord	le Minnesota	l'Utah *(m.)*
le Dakota du Sud	le Mississippi	le Vermont
le Delaware	le Missouri	la Virginie
la Floride	le Montana	la Virginie Occidentale
la Georgie	le Nebraska	l'état de Washington
Hawaii	le Nevada	le Wisconsin
l'Idaho *(m.)*	le New Hampshire	le Wyoming
l'Illinois *(m.)*	le New Jersey	

Les provinces du Canada sont:

la Colombie-Britannique	l'Ontario *(m.)*	l'Ile du Prince-
l'Alberta *(m.)*	le Québec	Edouard *(f.)*
la Saskatchewan	le Nouveau-Brunswick	la Terre-Neuve
le Manitoba	la Nouvelle-Ecosse	

Encourage students to discuss any trips they may have taken to French-speaking areas of Canada.

1. Dans quel état est-ce que vous habitez? Dans quelle ville? Quelle est la capitale de l'état? 2. Dans quel état est-ce que vous êtes né? 3. Vous avez fait des voyages dans d'autres états? Quand est-ce que vous y êtes allé? l'été dernier? il y a longtemps? il y a plusieurs années? 4. Vous pouvez nommer ("to name") trois états qui touchent au ("border on") Canada? au Mexique? à l'océan Atlantique? à l'océan Pacifique? au Golfe du Mexique? 5. Où est-ce qu'il y a des montagnes? des plages? 6. Quelles provinces du Canada est-ce que vous avez visitées?

En panne° en Espagne

Une route déserte° en Espagne. Au bord de la route on voit, au clair de lune,° une grande caravane blanche et, devant elle, une grosse voiture. Elle est belle, mais elle ne bouge° pas. Un homme et une femme
5 regardent le moteur. Inquiets, ils ne disent rien.°

Monsieur et Mme Hébert sont en vacances et les voici° à neuf heures du soir en panne dans un pays étranger. Tout à coup M. Hébert dit: "Zut, zut et zut!"

(être) en panne: *(to have a) breakdown*
désert, -e: *deserted*
au clair de lune: *in the moonlight*
bouger: *to move*
ne . . . rien: *nothing*

les voici: *here they are*

See Cultural Supplement.

10 —Qu'est-ce que c'est? C'est grave?° lui demande sa
femme.
—Oui, je crois que c'est le carburateur. Mais je ne
vois pas ce qu'il y a° exactement.°
—Nous n'avons vraiment pas de chance! Qu'est-ce
15 qu'on fait maintenant?
—Je ne sais pas.
—Eh bien, on peut toujours passer la nuit ici. Après
tout,° nous sommes partis pour faire du camping.
—Mais il n'y a pas d'eau, pas d'électricité. Il faut
20 plutôt° trouver un garage ce soir. Nous pouvons y
laisser la voiture et passer la nuit dans un hôtel.
—D'accord! Mais comment est-ce qu'on va trouver
un garage? On ne peut pas y aller à pied! C'est peut-
être très loin.
25 —Geneviève . . .
—Oui?
—Tu as jamais° fait de l'auto-stop?
—Non. Mais je peux vite apprendre.
—Allons-y!
30 —Est-ce que le garagiste° va te comprendre?°
—Qu'est-ce que tu veux dire?!? Bien sûr, il va me
comprendre. Après tout, j'ai étudié l'espagnol il n'y
a pas trop longtemps. Euh . . . . . . Comment dit-on
"carburateur" en espagnol?

grave: *serious*

ce qu'il y a: *what's wrong*
exactement: *exactly*

tout: *all*

plutôt: *instead*

jamais: *ever*

le garagiste: *garage mechanic*

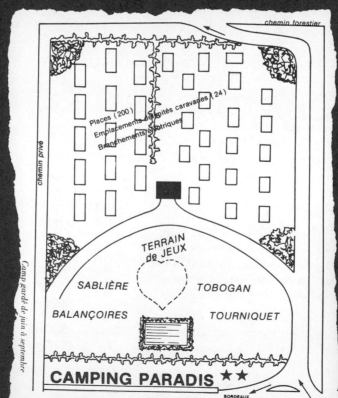

chemin forestier

chemin privé

Places (200)
Emplacements pour mobilités caravanes (24)
Branchements électriques

Camp gardé de juin à septembre

TERRAIN de JEUX

SABLIÈRE   TOBOGAN

BALANÇOIRES   TOURNIQUET

CAMPING PARADIS ★★

BORDEAUX   SOULAC

Lieudit «Fourthon»   Ravitaillement sur place
Saint-Laurent (2.035 habitants) à 3km.   Fermes à proximité

À propos …

1. Où se trouve la caravane? Est-ce que les Hébert sont près de chez eux? Qu'est-ce qu'ils font? Quelle heure est-il?   2. Que dit M. Hébert enfin?   3. Est-ce que la panne est grave? Qu'est-ce que c'est?   4. Est-ce que les Hébert ont de la chance?   5. Qu'est-ce que Mme Hébert veut faire? Et son mari, qu'est-ce qu'il veut faire?   6. Comment est-ce qu'ils vont trouver un garage?   7. Est-ce que vous croyez que le garagiste va comprendre M. Hébert? Pourquoi?   8. Et vous, est-ce que vous avez jamais été en panne sur une route déserte? dans un pays étranger?   9. Est-ce que vous avez jamais fait de l'auto-stop? du camping? Où donc?   10. Est-ce que vos parents ont une caravane? Si "oui," décrivez ("describe") la caravane.   11. Est-ce que vous êtes allé en Europe? au Canada? au Mexique? Si "oui," parlez de votre voyage. Quels pays est-ce que vous avez visités?   12. Où est-ce que vous aimez passer vos vacances? Vous avez fait des projets de vacances pour l'été prochain? Qu'est-ce que vous allez faire?

EXPLICATIONS II

Continents, pays et villes

The prepositions "in," "at," "to," and "from" have several equivalents in French.

1. With cities *à* and *de* are used:

Il a passé ses vacances à Avignon.   *He spent his vacation in Avignon.*
Elle est arrivée d'Avignon hier.   *She arrived from Avignon yesterday.*

2. With *feminine* place names, *en* and *de* are used without the definite determiner:

La France est un beau pays.   *France is a beautiful country.*
Nous sommes allés **en Suède.**   *We went to Sweden.*
Elle vient de rentrer **d'Espagne.**   *She just returned from Spain.*

When *de* is used to mean "of," the definite determiner is usually used:

Il est resté dans le nord **de la France.**   *He stayed in the north of France.*
Il a vu les montagnes **de la Suisse.**   *He saw the mountains of Switzerland.*

3. With *masculine* countries, *à* and *de* + definite determiner are used:

Le Japon est un beau pays.   *Japan is a beautiful country.*
Les Etats-Unis sont grands.   *The United States is big.*
Elle est rentrée **au Mali.**   *She returned to Mali.*
Il a travaillé **aux Etats-Unis.**   *He worked in the United States.*
Il est revenu **du Canada?**   *Did he come back from Canada?*
Ils sont arrivés **des Pays-Bas.**   *They arrived from the Netherlands.*

3. Il est venu d'Amérique.
4. . . . de Chine.
5. . . . d'Autriche.
6. . . . de Pologne.
7. . . . des Pays-Bas.
8. . . . du Canada.
9. . . . de Yougoslavie.
10. . . . des Etats-Unis.
11. . . . d'Angleterre.
12. . . . du Mexique.

3. Je vais à Londres, la capitale de l'Angleterre.
4. . . . à Mexico, . . . du Mexique.
5. . . . à Moscou, . . . de la Russie.
6. . . . à Washington, . . . des Etats-Unis.
7. . . . à Dakar, . . . du Sénégal.
8. . . . à Rome, . . . de l'Italie.
9. . . . à Tokyo, . . . du Japon.
10. . . . à Stockholm, . . . de la Suède.
11. . . . à Madrid, . . . de l'Espagne.
12. . . . à Athènes, . . . de la Grèce.
13. . . . à Oslo, . . . de la Norvège.
14. . . . à Copenhague, . . . du Danemark.

3. Ils sont allés en Australie.
4. . . . au Mexique.
5. . . . en Asie.
6. . . . en Belgique.
7. . . . en Europe.
8. . . . en Suisse.
9. . . . au Japon.
10. . . . aux Pays-Bas.
11. . . . au Danemark.
12. . . . en Allemagne.

Exercices

A. Answer the question. Follow the models.

D'où est-ce qu'il est venu?

1. le Sénégal   *Il est venu du Sénégal.*
2. l'Australie   *Il est venu d'Australie.*

3. l'Amérique   8. le Canada
4. la Chine   9. la Yougoslavie
5. l'Autriche   10. les Etats-Unis
6. la Pologne   11. l'Angleterre
7. les Pays-Bas   12. le Mexique

B. Answer the question according to the models.

Où est-ce que tu vas?

1. Paris   *Je vais à Paris, la capitale de la France.*
2. Lisbonne   *Je vais à Lisbonne, la capitale du Portugal.*

3. Londres   9. Tokyo
4. Mexico   10. Stockholm
5. Moscou   11. Madrid
6. Washington 12. Athènes
7. Dakar   13. Oslo
8. Rome   14. Copenhague

C. Answer the question according to the models.

Où est-ce qu'ils sont allés?

1. l'Afrique   *Ils sont allés en Afrique.*
2. le Portugal *Ils sont allés au Portugal.*

3. l'Australie   8. la Suisse
4. le Mexique   9. le Japon
5. l'Asie   10. les Pays-Bas
6. la Belgique   11. le Danemark
7. l'Europe   12. l'Allemagne

Vérifiez vos progrès

Write complete sentences telling the countries where the languages mentioned are spoken. Then, using the pronoun cues, tell that the person or people come from that country. Follow the models.

1. le suédois/je   *On parle suédois en Suède. Je viens de Suède.*
2. le wolof/tu   *On parle wolof au Sénégal. Tu viens du Sénégal.*

3. le hollandais/vous   8. le russe/je
4. l'allemand/elle   9. le portugais/ils
5. le norvégien/tu   10. le japonais/vous
6. le flamand/elles   11. le grec/elle
7. le danois/nous   12. l'italien/ils

RÉVISION ET THÈME

Consult the model sentences, then put the English cues into French and use them to form new sentences.

See Teacher's Section for answers to the *révision* and *thème*.

1. *Nous venons d'arriver d'Espagne.*
   (*They (m.) have just returned from the Netherlands.*)
   (*I just came back from Norway.*)

2. *J'y ai fait du camping avec des copains.*
   (*They visited their grandparents there.*)
   (*She visited the museums there with her brother.*)

3. *Il est allé au Mexique il y a deux ans. Il aime le Mexique.*
   (*She came to the United States a long time ago. She likes the United States.*)
   (*They (f.) arrived in Switzerland two weeks ago. They like Switzerland.*)

4. *Il fait presque toujours du soleil au bord de la mer.*
   (*It's still raining south of the city.*)
   (*It snows too much in the northwest [part] of the state.*)

5. *Je n'y ai pas plongé.*
   (*We didn't eat any.*)
   (*She didn't swim there.*)

6. *Chaque matin je suis arrivé à la pharmacie à l'heure.*
   (*Every evening we (m.) got on the bus on time.*)
   (*Every year you (f.pl.) left on vacation late.*)

Review of:
1. *venir de*
   de + countries
2. *y* in passé composé
   faire une visite à vs.
   visiter
3. passé composé with
   être
   il y a + time
   à / en + countries
   definite determiner +
   countries
4. weather expressions
   position of adverbs
   cardinal points
5. *y* and *en* in passé
   composé
   -ger verbs
6. passé composé with
   être
   adverbs of time

Now that you have done the *Révision*, you are ready to write a composition. Put the English captions describing each cartoon panel into French to form a paragraph.

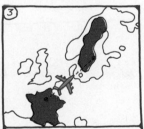

Albert and Yvette have just returned from Portugal.

They visited their cousins there.

They went to Sweden a year ago. They like Sweden.

But it's often cold in the northeast (part) of the country. They didn't swim there, for example.

But in Portugal, every morning they went down to the beach early.

AUTO-TEST

A. Write answers to the questions using the correct form of the verb. Follow the model.

1. Il vient de Pologne. Et eux?
   Ils viennent de Pologne aussi.

2. Elle devient dentiste. Et toi?
3. Vous venez toujours de bonne heure. Et elles?
4. Nous revenons demain soir. Et lui?
5. Je deviens professeur. Et vous?
6. Tu viens du Mali. Et elle?
7. On vient de finir cette leçon. Et vous?

B. Rewrite the following sentences in the passé composé. Be careful! Some of the verbs require *être* and some require *avoir*. Follow the model.

1. Il tombe dans l'eau et il nage.
   Il est tombé dans l'eau et il a nagé.

2. Elle rentre en France et elle cherche un appartement.
3. Nous travaillons à l'hôpital mais nous ne devenons pas infirmiers.
4. Elles vont en Suisse où elles voient les belles montagnes.
5. Ils font un voyage mais ils ne prennent pas le train.
6. Ils descendent de l'avion et ils téléphonent à leurs parents.
7. J'attends l'autobus et il n'arrive pas.
8. Elle passe quinze jours en Chine et puis elle rentre au Canada.
9. Ils visitent la Belgique, la France et l'Allemagne, mais ils ne vont pas en Autriche.
10. Elle perd son portefeuille et elle retourne au cinéma pour le chercher.
11. Quand ils entendent ma réponse ils partent tout de suite.

Deux vieilles chansons

AU CLAIR DE LA LUNE°

Au clair de la lune,
Mon ami Pierrot,
Prête-moi ta plume°
Pour écrire un mot.
5 Ma chandelle° est morte,
Je n'ai plus° de feu;°
Ouvre-moi ta porte,
Pour l'amour° de Dieu.°

Au clair de la lune,
10 Pierrot répondit:°
"Je n'ai pas de plume,
Je suis dans mon lit.°

au clair de (la) lune:
in the moonlight

la plume: *quill pen*

la chandelle: *candle*
ne . . . plus: *no more*
le feu: *fire*
l'amour *(m.): love*
Dieu: *God*

répondit = a répondu

le lit: *bed*

You might want to point out the imperatives + *moi*. This construction is taught in Level Two.

Dix-Septième
Leçon

294

Va chez la voisine,
Je crois qu'elle y est;
15 Car° dans sa cuisine
On bat le briquet."°

car = parce que
battre le briquet: *to light a fire*

SUR LE PONT° D'AVIGNON

le pont: *bridge*

Sur le pont d'Avignon,
l'on° y danse, l'on y danse,
Sur le pont d'Avignon,
L'on y danse tout en rond.°

l'on = on

en rond: *in a circle*

5 Les beaux messieurs font comme ça
Et puis encore° comme ça.
Sur le pont, etc.

encore: *again*

Les belles dames font comme ça
Et puis encore comme ça . . .

10 Les musiciens font comme ça
Et puis encore comme ça . . .

Les couturières° font comme ça
Et puis encore comme ça . . .

la couturière: *seamstress*

Les militaires° font comme ça
15 Et puis encore comme ça . . .

le militaire = le soldat

Proverbe

Quand le chat est parti, les souris dansent.

106012
2E CL. PLACE ENTIERE
GOURNAY-FERRIERES
⌀
PARIS ST.LAZARE
AMIENS
89 Km
VAL. 3 JOURS
PRIX: 18.00
106012

la mi-août en BRETAGNE
229 F
SNCF

Dix-Huitième Leçon

Les vacances d'été

Au mois d'août beaucoup de gens quittent Paris.[1] Mais il y a tant de touristes! Cependant, le jeune Edouard Droit ne part pas. Il reste à Paris avec les touristes, parce que son père et sa mère prennent leurs vacances en hiver.

EDOUARD C'est affreux! Personne ne reste ici—tous mes copains sont
5 partis.
MME DROIT En effet, il n'y a que trois familles dans notre immeuble cette
semaine.
EDOUARD C'est embêtant! Qu'est-ce qu'on peut faire?
MME DROIT Je ne sais pas. Tu ne peux rien faire . . . . Si! Pense aux va-
10 cances que tu vas passer à Barèges[2] l'hiver prochain pendant
que tes copains vont rester ici.

See Cultural Supplement.

---

[1]Under French law, everyone has one month's paid vacation every year. Most Parisians, except
those in the tourist business, take the month of August.
[2]Barèges is a popular resort town in the Pyrénées, the mountain range that separates France and
Spain. It is famous for its thermal baths and winter sports.

Summer vacation

In August, a lot of people leave Paris. But there are so many tourists! However, young Edouard Droit isn't leaving. He's staying in Paris with the tourists, because his father and mother take their vacation in the winter.

EDOUARD	This is awful! Nobody's staying here — all my friends have left.
5 MME DROIT	You're right. There are only three families in our building this week.
EDOUARD	It's annoying. What's there to do?
MME DROIT	I don't know. You can't do anything . . . Yes, you can! Think about the vacation you're going to have in Barèges next winter
10	while your friends stay here.

Questionnaire

1. Au mois d'août, que font les gens qui habitent Paris?   2. Qui se trouve à Paris en août?   3. Edouard quitte Paris? Pourquoi? Son père est dans le tourisme peut-être? Pourquoi le croyez-vous?   4. Edouard est heureux? Qu'est-ce qu'il dit?   5. Combien de familles sont restées dans l'immeuble des Droit?   6. Où vont les Droit cet hiver?

PRONONCIATION

The [w] sound is always followed by a pronounced vowel. It is pronounced with greater tension than its English equivalent.

Exercices

A. These words contain the [w] sound. Listen, then say them aloud.

    moi   toi   quoi   trois   choix   loin   coin

B. Now compare the sounds [u] and [w]. Be careful to pronounce the [w] sound and the vowel that follows it as one syllable.

    [u] / [w]   où / oui   joue / jouer   vous / voir   sous / soif

C. Now compare the sound combinations [wa] and [wɛ̃]. Be careful to pronounce both of the combinations as single syllables.

    [wa] / [wɛ̃]   loi / loin   mois / moins   soi / soin   quoi / coin

D. Say these two-syllable words aloud.

choisir	voiture	western	boisson
suédois	chinois	étroit	pourquoi

E. Listen carefully to the following sentences, then say them aloud.

Moi, je vois François.   Il croit qu'il va jouer avec moi.
Voilà les trois histoires.   Oui, Louis croit qu'on a froid.

MOTS NOUVEAUX I

l'horaire (*m.*)

la malle

la boîte

la valise

faire sa valise

faire ses bagages (*m. pl.*)

fermer à clef

la clef

la clef: Point out the unpronounced final f: [kle].

Voilà un touriste avec beaucoup de
    bagages.
Et une touriste avec sa valise.
Ils vont quitter la Côte d'Azur?
En effet.
Pourquoi?
Parce qu'il y a tant de touristes.

J'ai demandé des renseignements
    (*m.pl.*) à quelqu'un.
"Je regrette, monsieur," il m'a
    répondu, "mais je n'ai pas
    d'horaire."
"Alors, où est le bureau de ren-
    seignements?"
"Je regrette, monsieur. Je ne
    sais pas."
On peut toujours regretter, n'est-ce
    pas? Le train, cependant, ne m'a
    pas attendu.

Quelqu'un vient de vous téléphoner.
Hier il m'a téléphoné une fois.
                deux fois
                cinq fois
C'est embêtant.
En effet.

*There's **a** tourist with a lot of*
    luggage.
*And a tourist with **her** suitcase.*
*Are they going **to leave the Riviera?***
Indeed they are.
Why?
*Because there are **so many** tourists.*

*I asked **someone** for **information**.*

*"**I'm sorry**," he answered, "but I don't*
    *have a **timetable**."*

*"Then where's **the information desk?**"*

"I'm sorry, sir. I don't know."

*One can always **be sorry**, right?*
    *The train, **however**, didn't wait*
    for me.

Someone just phoned you.
Yesterday he called me once.
                twice
                five times
*That's **annoying**.*
You bet!

en effet: You might want
to point this out as an
expression of emphatic
agreement. We offer three
English equivalents: "in-
deed," "you bet," and, in
the English version of the
dialogue, "you're right."

Lesson
18

299

Exercice de vocabulaire

From the column on the right, choose the most logical response to each statement or question on the left. The answers to 1-6 will be found in a-f; the answers to 7-12 will be found in g-l.

1. c
2. a
3. f
4. b
5. e
6. d

1. Elle dit que cette demoiselle est dans le tourisme?
2. Il y a beaucoup de monde ici.
3. Je ne peux pas l'ouvrir.
4. Pourquoi est-ce que vous avez tant de bagages?
5. Tu cherches un horaire?
6. Vous avez fait votre valise?

a. Ce sont des touristes, je crois.
b. Je fais un voyage de six mois.
c. Oui, elle a un bureau pas loin de l'hôtel Carlton.
d. Oui, je l'ai faite hier soir.
e. Oui, mais il n'y en a pas.
f. Quoi? Tu n'as pas apporté ta clef?

7. j
8. i
9. g
10. h
11. l
12. k

7. Elle ne va pas quitter le pays cet été?
8. Monsieur Germont leur a téléphoné?
9. Quelqu'un est à la porte, maman.
10. Qu'est-ce qu'il y a dans cette boîte?
11. Qu'est-ce qu'il y a dans cette grande malle?
12. Tu ne lui as pas posé les questions?

g. C'est embêtant. Tu peux lui répondre?
h. C'est un petit cadeau pour la concierge.
i. En effet! Plusieurs fois! Il veut les voir tout de suite.
j. Non, son neveu lui fait une visite.
k. Si. Cependant, il n'a pas pu me donner de renseignements.
l. Ce sont nos habits. Nous partons en voyage demain matin.

MOTS NOUVEAUX II

Les Cartier habitent un grand immeuble.

The Cartiers live in a large **apartment building.**

D'habitude ils restent chez eux
        tous les jours
        tous les matins
        tous les soirs

They **usually** stay home
        every day
        every morning
        every evening

Ce soir, cependant, ils vont au théâtre.

This evening, however, they're going to the theater.

Monsieur Cartier est pressé.
Sa femme est pressée.
La circulation est affreuse.
Le bruit de la circulation est affreux.

*Monsieur Cartier is **in a hurry.***
*His wife is **in a hurry.***
*The traffic is **terrible.***
*The noise of the traffic is **terrible.***

"On va arriver avant le commencement de la pièce?"
"Si on a de la chance, on va arriver avant la fin!"

*"Will we arrive before **the beginning** of the play?"*
*"If we're lucky, we'll arrive before **the end!"***

Quand ils arrivent enfin, M. Cartier regarde dans son portefeuille.	*When they finally arrive, M. Cartier looks in his wallet.*
Il voit qu'il a son argent, ses papiers, ses cartes—tout **sauf** les billets.	*He sees that he has his money, his papers, his cards—everything **except** the tickets.*
"Nous sommes partis **sans** les billets," dit-il.	*"We left **without** the tickets," he says.*
Le **silence** de sa femme est affreux.	*His wife's **silence** is awful.*

Ils ont vu tout l'argent.	*They saw all the money.*
tous les gens	* all the people*
toute la circulation	* all the traffic*
toutes les cartes	* all the cards*
Mais pas de billets.	*But no tickets.*
C'est un peu embêtant.	*It's a little annoying.*

Exercice de vocabulaire

Choose the word or phrase that best completes the sentence or fits the situation.

1. Nous sommes le 21 mars. C'est (*le commencement*/*la fin*) de l'hiver.
2. Tout le monde parle. Il y a tant (*de bruit*/*de circulation*).
3. Si on est pressé, on travaille (*lentement*/*vite*).
4. A quelle heure part l'avion? Regardez (*l'horaire*/*la malle*).
5. Il est sorti (*avec*/*sans*) la clef? Non, il l'a laissée sur la table.
6. Vous avez vos (*bagages*/*renseignements*)? Oui, mais je ne les ai pas fermés à clef.
7. Tout le monde est parti (*avec*/*sauf*) Benoît. Il reste à la maison pour attendre le facteur.
8. Elle peut aller à pied parce qu'elle (*a tant de*/*n'a pas de*) valises.
9. Quel (*bruit*/*silence*)! C'est toujours comme ça quand toute la classe passe un examen.
10. Ils vont quelquefois au restaurant. Cependant, ils dînent (*d'habitude*/*tous les soirs*) chez eux.
11. Tu aimes ce grand nouvel immeuble au coin? Mais non, il est (*affreux*/*pressé*).
12. "Je regrette, madame," m'a dit l'infirmière, "mais le médecin est un peu (*embêtant*/*en retard*) ce matin."

1. la fin
2. de bruit
3. vite
4. l'horaire
5. avec
6. bagages
7. sauf
8. n'a pas de
9. silence
10. d'habitude
11. affreux
12. en retard

EXPLICATIONS I

Les verbes connaître et savoir

VOCABULAIRE			
connaître	*to know, to be acquainted with*	reconnaître	*to recognize*
		savoir	*to know, to know how*

Connaître means "to know" in the sense of "to be acquainted with": *Je connais Marie; Je connais Paris; Je connais ce disque.*

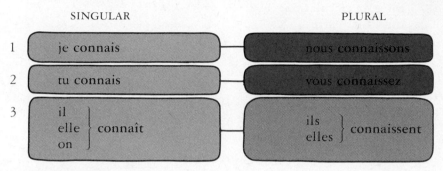

SINGULAR — PLURAL

1. je connais / nous connaissons
2. tu connais / vous connaissez
3. il elle on connaît / ils elles connaissent

PAST PARTICIPLE: **connu**

1. The plural stem of *connaître* is *connaiss-*.
2. In the singular, the *ss* of the plural stem is dropped, and the endings *-s. -s.* and *-t* are added. All three singular forms are pronounced alike. Note that the circumflex appears only in the 3 sing. form: *connaît.*
3. *Reconnaître* also follows this pattern.

Savoir means "to know" in all senses except knowing people or places. For example: *Je sais le mot; Je sais qu'il est calé.* When followed by a verb in the infinitive, *savoir* means "to know how": *Je sais danser; Je sais lire.*

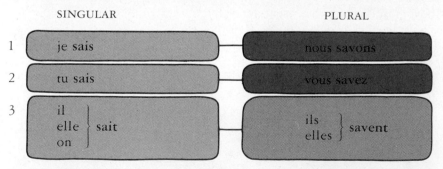

SINGULAR — PLURAL

1. je sais / nous savons
2. tu sais / vous savez
3. il elle on sait / ils elles savent

PAST PARTICIPLE: **su**

1. The plural stem of *savoir* is *sav-*.
2. In the singular, the *v* of the plural stem is dropped, and the *a* becomes *ai*. The endings *-s. -s.* and *-t* are then added to the stem *sai-*. All three singular forms are pronounced alike.

Exercices

A. Answer the questions using the appropriate direct object pronoun. Follow the model.

1. Je reconnais cette chanson. Et vous?
   Nous la reconnaissons aussi.

2. Elle connaît leur ami portugais. Et nous?
3. Nous reconnaissons ce monsieur. Et elles?
4. Je reconnais la vendeuse dans cette boutique. Et vous?
5. Vous connaissez les rues de Paris. Et lui?
6. Ils reconnaissent cette histoire. Et toi?
7. François connaît l'Angleterre. Et vous?
8. Je connais bien ce musée. Et eux?

2. Vous le connaissez (Nous le connaissons) aussi.
3. Elles le reconnaissent aussi.
4. Nous la reconnaissons (Je la reconnais) aussi.
5. Il les connaît aussi.
6. Je la reconnais aussi.
7. Nous la connaissons (Je la connais) aussi.
8. Ils le connaissent bien aussi.

B. Replace the verb in italics with the appropriate form of the verb *savoir*. Follow the model.

1. Je *crois* qu'ils sont partis en voyage hier.
   Je sais qu'ils sont partis en voyage hier.

2. Nous *voulons* jouer du piano.
3. Tu *crois* qu'elle a raison.
4. Ils *vont* parler suédois.
5. Il *croit* qu'Antoinette et son mari sont très sympa.
6. Vous *pouvez* chanter ces chansons grecques?
7. Je *vais* faire la cuisine.
8. Elles *croient* que la dentiste est occupée.

2. Nous savons jouer du piano.
3. Tu sais qu'elle a raison.
4. Ils savent parler suédois.
5. Il sait qu'Antoinette et son mari sont très sympa.
6. Vous savez chanter ces chansons grecques?
7. Je sais faire la cuisine.
8. Elles savent que la dentiste est occupée.

C. Complete the sentences using the appropriate form of the correct verb *connaître* or *savoir*.

1. Je _____ ces gens à côté.
2. Ils _____ bien leur leçon de géographie.
3. Vous _____ ce café en face du cinéma?
4. Il _____ mon frère cadet.
5. Il _____ bien faire ses bagages.
6. Nous _____ que tu n'as pas lu ce chapitre.
7. Tu _____ que c'est embêtant.
8. Nous _____ tous les garçons qui sont à la fête.
9. Elles _____ la Pologne parce qu'elles y sont nées.
10. Vous _____ que Grégoire ne peut pas nous accompagner tous les jours.

1. connais
2. savent
3. connaissez
4. connaît
5. sait
6. savons
7. sais
8. connaissons
9. connaissent
10. savez

Quelques expressions négatives

ne . . . jamais	*never, not ever*	ne . . . plus	*no longer, no more, not*
ne . . . personne	*no one, nobody,*		*anymore*
	not anyone, not	ne . . . que	*only*
	anybody	ne . . . rien	*nothing, not anything*

1. Look at the following constructions:

Tu **ne** comprends **jamais**.	*You **never** understand.*
Tu **ne** comprends **personne**.	*You **don't** understand **anyone**.*
Tu **ne** comprends **plus**.	*You **no longer** understand.*
Tu **ne** comprends **que** l'anglais.	*You **only** understand English.*
Tu **ne** comprends **rien**.	*You **don't** understand **anything**.*

Like *pas*, these words require *ne* before the verb.

2. Note how they are used in the passé composé and in the future:

Il n'a **jamais** compris.	Il ne va **jamais** comprendre.
Il n'a **plus** compris.	Il ne va **plus** comprendre.
Il n'a **rien** compris.	Il ne va **rien** comprendre.
but: Il n'a compris **personne**.	Il ne va comprendre **personne**.
Il n'a compris **qu'**un mot.	Il ne va comprendre **qu'**un mot.

Jamais, plus, and *rien* follow the same pattern as *pas. Personne* and *que* come after the past participle or the infinitive.

3. *Personne* and *rien* can also be used as the subject of the sentence:

Personne ne reste ici.	***Nobody** stays here.*
Rien ne coûte cher ici.	***Nothing**'s expensive here.*

4. Look at the following:

Elle écoute **quelquefois**.	Elle n'écoute **jamais**.
Elle écoute **quelqu'un**.	Elle n'écoute **personne**.
Elle écoute **quelque chose**.	Elle n'écoute **rien**.
Elle écoute **toujours**.	Elle n'écoute **plus**.

The affirmative expressions on the left correspond to the negative expressions on the right:

quelquefois	*sometimes*	ne . . . **jamais**	*never*
quelqu'un	*someone*	ne . . . **personne**	*no one*
quelque chose	*something*	ne . . . **rien**	*nothing*
toujours	*still*	ne . . . **plus**	*no longer*

5. Note how these negative expressions are used with *y* and *en*:

Elle n'y va **plus**.	*She **no longer** goes **there**.*
Tu n'y connais **personne**.	*You **don't** know **anyone there**.*
Il n'en a **jamais**.	*He **never** has **any** (of them).*
Je n'en sais **rien**.	*I **don't** know **anything** (about it).*

Exercices

A. Put the sentences into the present tense. Follow the model.

1. Nous n'avons jamais fait les malles.
   Nous ne faisons jamais les malles.

2. Je n'ai trouvé qu'une valise.
3. Il n'a rien perdu.
4. Ils ne sont jamais arrivés de bonne heure.
5. Je n'ai vu personne dans la rue.
6. Vous n'avez rien mangé.
7. Tu n'as demandé qu'un horaire.
8. Il n'a invité personne à la fête.

B. Put the sentences into the passé composé. Follow the models.

1. Nous ne voyons personne.
   Nous n'avons vu personne.
2. Nous n'arrivons jamais à l'heure.
   Nous ne sommes jamais arrivés à l'heure.

3. Je ne vois que des boîtes sous le bureau.
4. Vous ne dites rien aux employés.
5. Je ne reconnais personne.
6. Nous ne regardons que des documentaires à la télé.
7. Il n'y descend jamais.
8. Je n'écris rien dans mon cahier.
9. Personne ne quitte la maison jusqu'à midi.
10. On ne sert que des boissons et des hors-d'œuvre.

C. Answer in the negative using *jamais, personne, plus,* or *rien*.
Follow the model.

1. Tu en manges quelquefois?
   Non, je n'en mange jamais.

2. Tu lui prêtes quelque chose?
3. Tu oublies les clefs quelquefois?
4. Tu en sais quelque chose?
5. Quelqu'un frappe à la porte?
6. Tu mets quelque chose dans la malle?
7. Tu les attends toujours?
8. Tu lui offres quelque chose?
9. Tu mets toujours le couvert?
10. Tu es pressé quelquefois?

2. Je ne trouve qu'une valise.
3. Il ne perd rien.
4. Ils n'arrivent jamais de bonne heure.
5. Je ne vois personne dans la rue.
6. Vous ne mangez rien.
7. Tu ne demandes qu'un horaire.
8. Il n'invite personne à la fête.

Ex. B
Point out that although *ne . . . que* is considered a "negative expression," *des* does not become *de* following it.

3. Je n'ai vu que des boîtes sous le bureau.
4. Vous n'avez rien dit aux employés.
5. Je n'ai reconnu personne.
6. Nous n'avons regardé que des documentaires à la télé.
7. Il n'y est jamais descendu.
8. Je n'ai rien écrit dans mon cahier.
9. Personne n'a quitté la maison jusqu'à midi.
10. On n'a servi que des boissons et des hors-d'œuvre.

2. Non, je ne lui prête rien.
3. Non, je n'oublie jamais les clefs (je ne les oublie jamais).
4. Non, je n'en sais rien.
5. Non, personne ne frappe à la porte (n'y frappe).
6. Non, je ne mets rien dans la malle (je n'y mets rien).
7. Non, je ne les attends plus.
8. Non, je ne lui offre rien.
9. Non, je ne mets plus le couvert (je ne le mets plus).
10. Non, je ne suis jamais pressé.

Vérifiez vos progrès

Write negative answers, using the expression that means the opposite of the one used in the question. Follow the model.

1. Est-ce que tu connais quelqu'un qui travaille ici?
   Non. je ne connais personne qui travaille ici.

2. Est-ce qu'ils en savent quelque chose?
3. Est-ce qu'elles ont reconnu quelqu'un?
4. Est-ce que j'y vais toujours?
5. Vous avez quelque chose?
6. Est-ce que vous savez toujours toutes les réponses?
7. Est-ce que vous connaissez quelqu'un à Montréal, monsieur?
8. Est-ce que vous êtes sortie quelquefois, madame?
9. Est-ce que tu la fermes toujours à clef?
10. Est-ce que vous faites quelquefois vos bagages?

CONVERSATION ET LECTURE

Parlons de vous

1. Est-ce que vous habitez une maison ou un immeuble? Si c'est un immeuble, combien d'étages ("stories") est-ce qu'il a? 2. Est-ce que vous quittez la maison à la même heure tous les matins? A quelle heure? Vous êtes quelquefois pressé? souvent? toujours? Vous quittez quelquefois la maison sans vos livres ou vos devoirs? 3. Est-ce qu'il y a quelque chose que vous trouvez embêtant le matin? Quoi? 4. Qu'est-ce qu'il y a dans votre ville qui est vraiment beau? affreux? 5. D'habitude, qu'est-ce que vous faites le soir? 6. Quand il ne faut plus étudier le soir—c'est-à-dire ("that's to say"), quand vous avez fini tous vos devoirs—qu'est-ce que vous aimez faire? 7. Qu'est-ce que vous ne savez pas faire que vous voulez apprendre à faire? Par exemple, si vous ne savez pas jouer aux échecs, est-ce que vous voulez apprendre à y jouer? 8. C'est la fin de l'année scolaire ("school year"). Qu'est-ce que vous avez appris cette année?

Une lettre de la Louisiane

See Cultural Supplement.

Louise Boisseau vient de recevoir° une longue lettre de son amie Claude Chambard, qui est hôtesse de l'air à Air France. Claude passe huit jours en Louisiane avec une amie.

recevoir: *to receive*

Lafayette, Louisiane
le 3 juin

Ma chère° Louise,

Je t'écris d'une région des Etats-Unis qui ressemble
beaucoup à° notre vieille France,[1] la Louisiane aca-
dienne.[2] A la campagne et même° dans une grande
ville comme Lafayette, il y a beaucoup de gens qui
parlent français. Ils ont des noms° français et ils servent même du café comme nous le faisons en France.[3]
Ce sont les Acadiens ou "Cajuns."[4] Leurs ancêtres°
sont venus ici vers 1750, quand les Anglais les ont
chassés° de leur pays—de l'Acadie, au Canada. Ils
ont choisi la Louisiane parce qu'elle était° aussi une
colonie française. Plus tard, cependant, Napoléon l'a
vendue aux Etats-Unis.

Je suis venue ici avec mon amie Anne-Marie. Elle a
des cousins à Lafayette, chez qui nous passons le
weekend. Ils sont très aimables.

Demain nous allons voir la Nouvelle Orléans et le
golfe du Mexique. Anne-Marie me dit que ça va
être une excursion° très intéressante pour moi qui
n'ai jamais vu les "bayous." Ce sont des rivières°
très tranquilles avec de grands vieux arbres, des
roseaux° et de la mousse° grise qui tombe des
arbres.

Hier soir on nous a servi un "gombo." C'est une
soupe de poisson avec du riz et des tomates. Mais
ce n'est pas du tout comme notre bouillabaisse. Elle
est très, très épicée.°

La semaine prochaine je vais faire le service des
Antilles: Miami—Fort-de-France, avec escale° à Port
au Prince.[5]

Je connais la Martinique mais je ne suis jamais

cher, chère: (here)
dear
ressembler à: to
resemble
même: (here) even
le nom: name

l'ancêtre (m.): an-
cestor
chasser: to expel
était: was

l'excursion (f.):
short trip
la rivière: small
river
le roseau: reed
la mousse: moss

épicé, -e: spicy

l'escale (f.): stop

---

[1] Claude is referring to old customs, speech patterns, etc., which are still found in small French
towns and villages.
[2] This area in southwestern Louisiana was settled mainly by French people whom the British had
expelled from Acadia (now Nova Scotia).
[3] *Café au lait* is very popular in Louisiana.
[4] The people of Acadian Louisiana, called "Cajuns" (from the local pronunciation of *acadien*),
speak French. Cajun French does not differ too much from the local dialects spoken in small
towns in the northwestern provinces of France.
[5] *Faire le service de* means "to work the route of." Claude is saying that she will be working on
flights going to the West Indies (*les Antilles*). Fort-de-France is the capital of Martinique. Port
au Prince is the capital of Haiti, a former French colony. In 1802, the slaves, led by Toussaint
l'Ouverture and Dessalines, defeated Napoleon's army, and thus Haiti became the second inde-
pendent nation in the Americas—and the first black republic in the world.

allée en Haïti. Je crois que je vais beaucoup l'aimer. C'est un pays où le français est la langue officielle, mais où tout le monde parle créole.[1] Malheureusement je n'ai appris qu'une phrase en créole: *"M ap chaché youn otèl ki pa tro chè."* Tu l'as comprise? Ça veut dire: "Je cherche un hôtel qui n'est pas trop cher."

Je ne rentre à Paris que vers la fin de juillet. Je vais t'apporter un petit paquet de cartes postales et d'autres souvenirs de mes voyages en Louisiane, au Canada et aux Antilles. Comme ça je pourrai° vous donner des renseignements sans fin sur l'Amérique francophone.° (Les photos que je prends, moi, sont affreuses; alors j'ai acheté° beaucoup de cartes postales.) A bientôt.

je pourrai: *I'll be able*
francophone: *French-speaking*
acheter: *to buy*

Je t'embrasse,[2]
Claude

A propos . . .

1. Que fait Claude comme profession? Elle est en vacances maintenant?
2. D'où est-ce qu'elle écrit cette lettre? 3. En quoi est-ce que Lafayette est comme la France? 4. Qui sont les Acadiens? Quand est-ce qu'ils sont arrivés en Louisiane? Pourquoi ont-ils quitté le Canada? 5. Est-ce qu'Anne-Marie connaît quelqu'un à Lafayette? 6. Que vont faire les filles demain? Qu'est-ce que c'est qu'un "bayou"? 7. Qu'est-ce que les filles ont mangé la veille? 8. Quel service est-ce que Claude va faire la semaine prochaine?
9. Est-ce que Claude connaît Haïti? Elle parle créole? Que veut dire la phrase qu'elle a apprise? 10. Pourquoi est-ce que Claude a acheté tant de cartes postales? 11. Et vous, quand vous êtes en voyage, est-ce que vous prenez des photos? Comment sont vos photos? 12. Est-ce que vous connaissez quelques pays étrangers? Quelle langue est-ce qu'on y parle?
13. Quand vous allez faire un voyage, qui fait vos bagages? Qui va chercher les renseignements nécessaires ("necessary")—les horaires ou les cartes routières ("road maps"), par exemple? 14. Qu'est-ce que vous allez faire cet été? Vous avez des projets de vacances? Quels projets?

---

[1]Creole is a language that resulted from the contact of French and West African languages. It is spoken widely in the Antilles and in areas of Louisiana.
[2]*Embrasser* means "to kiss." This is a common way for relatives or close friends to sign a letter. It is equivalent to saying "love."

EXPLICATIONS II

Quelques expressions de quantité

1. You have seen that the indefinite determiners and the partitive often become *de* (or *d'*) after a negative:

J'ai **un** frère.	Je n'ai pas **de** frère.
J'ai **une** malle.	Je n'ai pas **de** malle.
Il a **des** journaux.	Il n'a pas **de** journaux.
Il y a **du** bruit.	Il n'y a pas **de** bruit.
Il y a **de la** circulation.	Il n'y a pas **de** circulation.
Il y a **des** huîtres.	Il n'y a pas **d'**huîtres.

But note the following:

C'est **un** bateau à voiles.	Ce n'est pas **un** bateau à voiles.
Ce sont **des** romans anglais.	Ce ne sont pas **des** romans anglais.
C'est **du** pain.	Ce n'est pas **du** pain.

If the verb is *être,* the indefinite determiners and the partitive do not become *de* after a negative.

2. After expressions of quantity, *de* (or *d'*) is used:

Il mange **beaucoup de** fruits.	*He eats **a lot of** fruit.*
Ils ont **assez d'**argent.	*They have **enough** money.*
La ville a **trop d'**hôtels.	*The city has **too many** hotels.*
Il y a **tant de** bruit.	*There's so **much** noise.*
Elle a **tant d'**amies.	*She has so **many** friends.*
Il y a **peu de** circulation ce soir.	*There's **little** traffic this evening.*
J'ai **peu de** valises.	*I have **few** suitcases.*
J'ai **un peu d'**argent.	*I have **a little** money.*

Exercices

A. Redo the sentences in the negative. Follow the models.

1. Il y a des oignons dans la soupe.
   Il n'y a pas d'oignons dans la soupe.
2. C'est de la crème caramel.
   Ce n'est pas de la crème caramel.
3. Je voudrais de la salade.
4. C'est une tarte aux pommes.
5. Ce sont des huîtres.
6. D'habitude ils commandent des escargots.
7. C'est du rôti de porc.
8. C'est de la confiture.
9. Il y a des assiettes dans l'évier.
10. Il met du lait dans les verres.

3. Je ne voudrais pas de salade.
4. Ce n'est pas une tarte aux pommes.
5. Ce ne sont pas des huîtres.
6. D'habitude ils ne commandent pas d'escargots.
7. Ce n'est pas du rôti de porc.
8. Ce n'est pas de la confiture.
9. Il n'y a pas d'assiettes dans l'évier.
10. Il ne met pas de lait dans les verres.

Dix-Huitième
Leçon

B. Answer the questions using the cues in parentheses. Follow the model.

1. Elle a pris du dessert? (trop)
   Elle a pris trop de dessert.

2. On a eu du vin? (un peu)
3. Il y a des histoires dans ce livre? (peu)
4. Elle a mis de l'ail dans la bouillabaisse? (trop)
5. Elles ont préparé des pommes frites? (assez)
6. Ils ont chanté des chansons? (beaucoup)
7. Il y a de la circulation tous les matins? (trop)
8. Il a des romans policiers? (tant)
9. Elles ont apporté des sandwichs? (beaucoup)

2. On a eu un peu de vin.
3. Il y a peu d'histoires dans ce livre.
4. Elle a mis trop d'ail dans la bouillabaisse.
5. Elles ont préparé assez de pommes frites.
6. Ils ont chanté beaucoup de chansons.
7. Il y a trop de circulation tous les matins.
8. Il a tant de romans policiers.
9. Elles ont apporté beaucoup de sandwichs.

C. Redo the sentences in the affirmative using the cues in parentheses. Follow the model.

1. D'habitude il ne mange pas de tartes. (beaucoup)
   Aujourd'hui il mange beaucoup de tartes!

2. D'habitude elles n'ont pas d'argent (assez)
3. D'habitude nous n'avons pas de bagages. (trop)
4. D'habitude elle ne fait pas de bruit. (tant)
5. D'habitude tu ne me demandes pas de renseignements. (trop)
6. D'habitude je ne pose pas de questions. (beaucoup)
7. D'habitude ils ne prennent pas de pain. (un peu)
8. D'habitude ils n'ont pas d'horaires. (assez)
9. D'habitude il n'y a pas de mauvaises pommes. (beaucoup)
10. D'habitude on ne vend pas d'affiches. (tant)

2. Aujourd'hui elles ont assez d'argent.
3. Aujourd'hui nous avons trop de bagages.
4. Aujourd'hui elle fait tant de bruit.
5. Aujourd'hui tu me demandes trop de renseignements.
6. Aujourd'hui je pose beaucoup de questions.
7. Aujourd'hui ils prennent un peu de pain.
8. Aujourd'hui ils ont assez d'horaires.
9. Aujourd'hui il y a beaucoup de mauvaises pommes.
10. Aujourd'hui on vend tant d'affiches.

Vérifiez vos progrès

Write answers to the questions using the cues in parentheses. Follow the model.

1. Ils ont des valises aujourd'hui? (tant)
   Tant de valises!

2. Elle connaît des gens à Sherbrooke? (peu)
3. Combien d'hôtels est-ce qu'il y a là? (beaucoup)
4. Combien de fois est-ce que nous sommes allés au cinéma? (trop)
5. Combien d'auteurs a-t-il lus? (tant)
6. Elles ont assisté à quelques matchs? (beaucoup)
7. Vous avez pris des fruits? (assez)
8. Il y a d'autres immeubles près de chez toi? (très peu)

RÉVISION ET THÈME

See Teacher's Section for answers to the *révision* and *thème*.

In #2 and in the *thème*, point out the use of *sur* ("to") with *la Côte d'Azur*.

Review of:
1. negative expressions
2. expressions of quantity
   passé composé with
   être
   compound nouns
3. negative expressions
   passé composé with
   être
   seasons
4. *savoir*
   expressions of quantity
5. adverbs of time
   huit jours / journée / tous les jours
   à / en / chez
6. *connaître*
   position of adverbs

Consult the model sentences, then put the English cues into French and use them to form new sentences based on the models.

1. *Pourquoi est-ce qu'il n'y a que des clefs dans la boîte?*
   (isn't there anyone in the apartment building)
   (isn't there anything in the trunk)

2. *Trop de gens sont arrivés sur la Côte d'Azur.*
   (So many students (f.) have entered the classroom.)
   (A lot of workers have gone out of the dining room.)

3. *Bien sûr, rien n'y est arrivé en hiver.*
   (Indeed, no one returned there in the spring.)
   (So nobody went down there in the fall.)

4. *Nous savons qu'il y a beaucoup de bruit là-bas aussi.*
   (They (m.) know)   (enough timetables)
   (I know)   (too much traffic)

5. *Cette année elle passe huit jours au Danemark.*
   (Sometimes we spend the day in town.)
   (This time I'm spending every day at home.)

6. *Je connais bien les renseignements.*
   (He already knows the end.)
   (They (f.) really know the beginning.)

Now that you have done the *Révision*, you are ready to write a composition. Put the English captions describing each cartoon panel into French to form a paragraph.

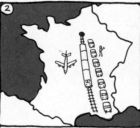

1. Why are there only tourists in Paris?

2. A lot of people have gone to the Riviera.

3. However the Girauds have never gone there in the summer.

4. They know that there are too many tourists there too.

5. Usually they spend their vacation in Austria.

6. They know the country well.

Dix-Huitième
Leçon

312

AUTO-TEST

A. Rewrite each sentence, changing the verb in italics to the appropriate form of the correct verb, *connaître* or *savoir*. Follow the model.

1. Elle *révise* ses leçons.   *Elle sait ses leçons.*
2. Ils *croient* que nous partons vers minuit.
3. Est-ce que vous *aimez* vos voisins?
4. Il *invite* tous ces jeunes gens.
5. Je n'en *dis* rien.
6. Nous n'*attendons* pas le médecin.
7. Tu *visites* la Chine ou le Japon?
8. Nous *voyons* que vous êtes pressés, messieurs.
9. Vous *apprenez à* jouer de la guitare?

B. Write answers to each question using the negative cues in parentheses. Follow the models.

1. Qui connaît Jacques? (personne)   *Personne ne connaît Jacques.*
2. Qui est-ce qu'il attend? (personne)   *Il n'attend personne.*
3. Qu'est-ce qu'ils ont dit? (rien)
4. Qu'est-ce que tu as apporté? (que ce livre de poche)
5. Quand est-ce qu'elle est allée à l'aéroport? (jamais)
6. Quand est-ce qu'elles en parlent? (plus)
7. De quoi est-ce que tu as besoin? (rien)
8. Qu'est-ce qu'il y a au milieu de la route? (rien)

C. Rewrite the sentences using the cues in parentheses. Follow the model.

1. Il n'a pas pris les billets. (assez)   *Il n'a pas pris assez de billets.*
2. Il n'y a pas de touristes. (beaucoup)
3. Nous avons reconnu les gens. (peu)
4. Je n'ai plus besoin de bagages. (tant)
5. Elles ne vous donnent jamais de renseignements. (assez)
6. Tu as des mouchoirs blancs. (tant)
7. Il y a de nouveaux immeubles en ville. (trop)

Proverbe

Qui ne risque rien n'a rien.

Answers to <u>Vérifiez vos progrès</u>

If you have difficulty with any exercises, first check the *Explications* in the book. If you feel that you need further help in order to maintain your progress, be sure to check with your teacher.

Leçon 1, p. 8

1. Bien, merci. Et vous?
2. Bien, merci. Et toi?
3. Bien, merci. Et vous?
4. Bien, merci. Et vous?

Leçon 2, p. 22

2. Vous allez à l'hôtel.
3. Raoul et Denis (*or:* Ils) vont à l'usine.
4. Elle va à la banque.
5. Je vais à la montagne.
6. Nous allons à l'hôpital.

Leçon 2, p. 26

2. Ce sont les bureaux de Jean-Paul.
3. Ce sont les salles de classe d'Alice et de Suzanne.
4. Ce sont les villas de Mme Lebrun et de Mme Lenoir.

Leçon 3, p. 37

2. Tu es chez toi.
3. Il est chez lui.
4. Nous sommes chez nous.
5. Je suis chez moi.
6. Vous êtes chez vous.
7. Elle est chez elle.
8. Ils sont chez eux.

Leçon 3, p. 41

2. Oui, ce sont mes cousins.
3. Oui, c'est mon oncle.
4. Oui, c'est ma cousine.
5. Oui, c'est ma grand-mère.
6. Oui, c'est mon frère.
7. Oui, ce sont mes grands-parents.
8. Oui, ce sont mes neveux.

Leçon 4, p. 53

2. Vos cousines vont à la plage en autobus.
3. Leurs livres sont sous le pupitre.
4. Vos copains sont chez nous.
5. Nos crayons sont avec le cahier.
6. Leurs amis vont à la gare en moto.
7. Nos chaises sont derrière la porte.
8. Leurs bateaux à voiles sont à la plage.
9. Vos sœurs vont à l'église à pied.

Leçon 4, p. 57

2. Non, elle n'a pas dix-sept livres.
3. Non, il (*or:* Jean-Jacques) n'a pas cinq calendriers.
4. Non, vous n'avez pas (*or:* nous n'avons pas) huit fenêtres dans la salle de classe.
5. Non, elles n'ont pas quinze robes.
6. Non, nous n'avons pas (*or:* je n'ai pas) vingt crayons.
7. Non, elle (*or:* Mme Lebeau) n'a pas treize chapeaux.
8. Non, je n'ai pas quatorze cousins.
9. Non, ils n'ont pas neuf stylos.

Leçon 5, p. 69

2. Combien de livres et de cahiers est-ce qu'elle a?
3. De quelle couleur sont les chaussures?
4. Comment est-ce qu'ils vont à Cannes?
5. Qu'est-ce qui est en face de notre (*or:* votre) hôtel?
6. Qu'est-ce qui est à droite de l'opéra?
7. De quelle couleur est l'autobus?
8. Combien d'enfants est-ce qu'ils ont?
9. Comment est-ce que nous allons (*or:* vous allez) à l'aéroport?
10. Qu'est-ce qui est à gauche de l'église?

Leçon 5, p. 73

2. La banque est à gauche de la poste.
3. Je vais au bureau.
4. L'arbre est à côté du garage.
5. Les enfants vont aux lycées en autobus.
6. Nous allons au théâtre.
7. Sa villa est près du port.
8. Nous sommes loin de l'aéroport.
9. L'opéra est à droite des restaurants.
10. Le cinéma est en face des jardins.

Leçon 6, p. 87

1. Les Leclerc ont quatre enfants maintenant. Ils habitent toujours Montréal, où M. Leclerc travaille à l'hôpital.
2. L'après-midi les jeunes filles jouent au tennis. Le soir elles révisent leurs leçons pendant que tu regardes la télé.
3. Notre mère travaille à la banque et nos grands-parents restent à la maison avec nous. Le soir nous dînons chez nous ou au restaurant au coin de la rue.
4. Vous ouvrez la porte et Thomas entre dans la maison. Il porte son pull-over rouge et son jean. Il rentre du lycée.

Leçon 6, p. 93

2. Non, ils sont paresseux.
3. Non, elle est petite.
4. Non, elles sont généreuses.
5. Non, elles sont blanches.
6. Non, il est grand.
7. Non, elle est énergique.
8. Non, ils sont avares.
9. Non, il est noir.
10. Non, ils sont tristes.

Leçon 7, p. 105

A. 1. Il y a cinquante-deux semaines dans une année.
2. Il y a vingt-huit ou vingt-neuf jours dans le mois de février.
3. Il y a trente et un jours dans le mois de juillet.
4. Il y a quarante-huit heures dans deux jours.

B. 1. Quand il fait beau, nous ne finissons pas toujours nos devoirs.
2. Quelquefois les feuilles ne jaunissent pas en automne.
3. Je ne rougis pas souvent.
4. En été elle maigrit parce qu'elle joue au tennis.
5. En hiver tu grossis beaucoup parce que tu n'aimes pas aller dehors.
6. Quand il ne pleut pas, on ouvre les fenêtres.
7. Choisissez les affiches, mes enfants!

Leçon 7, p. 111

2. Vous avez une moto grise.
3. J'ai un frère paresseux.
4. Ils (*or:* Elles) ont des livres difficiles.
5. Tu n'as pas de maillot noir.
6. Ils (*or:* Elles) n'ont pas de cousins riches.
7. Nous avons une tante avare et un oncle généreux.
8. Elle a une jupe verte et une chemise blanche.

Leçon 8, p. 123

A. 1. En hiver, quand il fait froid, l'eau est froide aussi.
2. Pourquoi est-ce que tu as peur de l'eau?
3. Quand est-ce que vous faites des achats?
4. Quand ils ne révisent pas leurs leçons, ils font toujours des fautes.
5. En été, les nuits sont chaudes, mais il fait souvent du vent.
6. Quand il fait mauvais, Georges n'aime pas faire de l'auto-stop.

B. 2. Oui, et le sable est beau aussi.
   3. Oui, et le camion est laid aussi.
   4. Oui, et ses tantes sont vieilles aussi.
   5. Oui, et la mer est belle aussi.
   6. Oui, et son jean est nouveau aussi.
   7. Oui, et leurs voitures sont vieilles aussi.

Leçon 8, p. 128

1. Si, je fais la vaisselle après le dîner. *or:* Non, je ne fais pas la vaisselle après le dîner.
2. Oui, j'ai une moto. *or:* Non, je n'ai pas de moto.
3. Oui, je fais toujours mes devoirs. *or:* Non, je ne fais pas toujours mes devoirs.
4. Si, je révise mes leçons. *or:* Non, je ne révise pas mes leçons.

Leçon 9, p. 142

1. Pourquoi est-ce qu'il dort? Parce que les histoires sont trop longues.
2. Qu'est-ce qu'on sert? Il faut servir un diner italien.
3. Pourquoi est-ce qu'elle maigrit? Parce qu'elle est trop grosse.
4. Qui part? Les auteurs célèbres.
5. Nous finissons une pièce allemande. J'aime mieux les pièces anglaises ou américaines.
6. Pourquoi est-ce que tu choisis toujours des rues étroites?
7. Quand est-ce que tu sors avec tes parents? Nous sortons samedi parce qu'on joue trois pièces canadiennes en ville. Les pièces sont presque inconnues, mais elles sont très bonnes.

Leçon 9, p. 147

PAPA	Qu'est-ce que tu vas faire?
MADELEINE	Je vais préparer le déjeuner. Mes amies vont arriver à 11 h. 30.
PAPA	Qu'est-ce que vous allez faire plus tard, toi et tes amies? Vous allez sortir?
MADELEINE	Non, nous n'allons pas sortir. Nous allons rester ici pour regarder un match

de basketball à la télé. Tu vas rester à la maison aussi, papa?

PAPA	Non, je vais sortir avec ta maman. Nous allons partir vers 1 h. 15.

Leçon 10, p. 159

2. Je vends ma jolie jupe norvégienne.
3. Une jeune dame grecque attend le même train.
4. Nous répondons à la petite fille aimable.
5. Elle commande une autre boisson froide.
6. Elles entendent une autre langue étrangère.

Leçon 10, p. 163

2. Samedi elles vont à ce marché.
3. Donnez ce journal à papa, s'il vous plaît.
4. Arnaud regarde cette étoile.
5. Son père joue quelquefois aux cartes avec ce monsieur.
6. Je n'aime pas cet hôtel.
7. Est-ce que vous entendez cet avion dans le ciel?
8. Il va perdre ce stylo.
9. Je ne révise pas cette histoire.
10. En automne il y a des feuilles jaunes sur cet arbre.

Leçon 11, p. 177

2. Mercredi, ils ont passé l'après-midi à la bibliothèque.
3. Hier soir, j'ai assisté au concert.
4. Le mois dernier, nous avons montré les photos à Andrée.
5. On a vite trouvé ces livres à la librairie au coin de la rue.
6. Tu as déjà compté jusqu'à soixante?
7. L'année dernière, maman n'a pas enseigné la chimie à l'université.
8. Ce matin, vous n'avez pas joué dehors?
(*With the exception of* vite *and* déjà, *all the adverbs of time could go at the beginning or end of the sentence.*)

Leçon 11, p. 181

2. Elle a déjà répondu aux étudiants.
3. Nous avons (*or:* J'ai) déjà maigri.
4. Elle (*or:* La serveuse) a déjà servi les gens à côté.

5. Elles (*or:* Les feuilles) ont déjà jauni.
6. Il a déjà perdu sa route.
7. Ils ont déjà vendu leurs billets.
8. J'ai déjà choisi une de ces photos.

Leçon 12, p. 194

2. Ils ne comprennent pas cette dernière question.
3. Le vieil agriculteur ne vend pas ses cochons.
4. Nous ne prenons pas le premier avion.
5. Une bonne étudiante ne répond pas toujours aux mêmes questions.
6. Vous ne prenez pas le dernier autobus?
7. Ils n'apprennent pas ce beau poème par cœur.
8. Nous ne comprenons pas cette vieille histoire.
9. Cet enfant ne prend pas ce bel oiseau.
10. Tu ne prends pas cette nouvelle route pour aller au bureau?

Leçon 12, p. 200

2. N'a-t-il pas assisté à votre cours de sciences sociales?
3. Où ne veulent-ils pas aller pendant leurs vacances?
4. Qui ne travaille pas vite?
5. N'avez-vous pas entendu le nouveau disque?
6. Pourquoi est-ce que nous ne vendons pas la vieille voiture?
7. Est-ce que tu n'as pas réussi à trouver un bon cadeau?
8. Quel chapitre est-ce que tu ne comprends pas?
9. Qui est-ce que vous n'aimez pas?
10. Où ne peux-tu pas aller?

Leçon 13, p. 214

2. Nous croyons que ces nouvelles pharmaciennes sont passionnées par le travail.
3. Tu crois que les jeunes avocates font un stage.
4. Je vois de grands oiseaux dans le ciel.
5. Ils croient que ce sont de mauvaises infirmières.
6. Nous croyons qu'ils veulent être de bons marins.
7. Est-ce qu'on voit de jeunes hôtesses de l'air?
8. Il croit que ce sont de vieux hommes d'affaires.
9. Vous croyez qu'elles peuvent être de bonnes artistes.
10. Elles voient de gros hippopotames.

Leçon 13, p. 220

3. Il coûte soixante-dix-neuf francs. Je ne le veux pas.
4. Elle coûte mille quatre cents francs. Ils ne la veulent pas.
5. Il coûte deux cent quatre-vingt-quinze francs. Je ne vais pas le demander.
6. Elles coûtent quatre-vingt-dix-huit francs. Nous n'allons pas (*or:* Je ne vais pas) les prendre.
7. Elle coûte soixante et onze francs. On ne veut pas la voir.
8. Elles coûtent seize mille huit cent quatre-vingts francs. Nous ne les aimons pas (*or:* Je ne les aime pas).

Leçon 14, p. 235

2. Nous leur écrivons (*or:* Je leur écris) une longue lettre.
3. Vous leur empruntez (*or:* Nous leur empruntons) la voiture.
4. Ils lui offrent une cravate bleue.
5. Je lui montre une belle image.
6. Il leur donne des paquets.
7. Vous leur dites (*or:* Nous leur disons) quelques mots.
8. Je lui offre une jolie montre.
9. Elle lui emprunte plusieurs timbres.

Leçon 14, p. 239

1. Nous ne le voyons pas.
2. C'est un garçon aimable. Il veut te remercier.
3. Tu vas nous emprunter des gants et un parapluie?
4. Malheureusement il ne peut pas vous prêter cet argent.
5. Je lui offre un cadeau pour son anniversaire.
6. Pourquoi est-ce qu'il la laisse chez lui?
7. Qu'est-ce que vous leur dites?
8. Il a oublié ses gants. Il les cherche maintenant.

(This was a very difficult exercise. If you got most of the sentences right—and understood why they were right and why the others would have been wrong—then you did very well. Be sure to check with your teacher if you have any questions.)

Answers to
Vérifiez vos progrès

Leçon 15, p. 253

1. J'aime le pain, mais je n'aime pas les pommes de terre.
2. Je voudrais un croque-monsieur.
3. J'ai besoin d'œufs et de lait.
4. Je n'aime pas le gigot.
5. Pour commencer, je voudrais de la soupe à l'oignon.
6. Comme dessert, je voudrais des pâtisseries et comme boisson, de l'eau minérale.
7. Je ne voudrais pas de hors-d'œuvre.
8. Je voudrais du poisson, du riz et des petits pois.

Leçon 15, p. 257

3. Elles en cherchent.
4. J'en ai besoin.
5. Nous y allons.
6. Ils y attendent Jean.
7. Vous n'en mangez pas.
8. Nous y frappons.
9. On en veut.
10. Martine n'y danse pas.

Leçon 16, p. 269

2. J'ai mis mon chapeau gris et j'ai dit "au revoir."
3. Il a plu ce matin, mais Marie n'a pas porté son imperméable.
4. Qui a vu l'autre gant?
5. Tu n'as pas pu aller au marché cette semaine.
6. Nous avons fait nos devoirs et ensuite j'ai fait la vaisselle.
7. Elles n'ont pas offert beaucoup de cadeaux à leurs cousines.
8. Vous avez écrit des cartes postales?
9. Ils ont pris des croque-monsieur et des citrons pressés.

Leçon 16, p. 274

1. Oui, j'y ai réussi. *or:* Non, je n'y ai pas réussi.
2. Oui, je les ai faits hier soir. *or:* Non, je ne les ai pas faits hier soir.

3. Oui, je lui ai donné mes devoirs ce matin. *or:* Non, je ne lui ai pas donné mes devoirs ce matin.
4. Oui, je l'ai regardée hier. *or:* Non, je ne l'ai pas regardée hier.
5. Oui, je l'ai débarrassée après le dîner hier soir. *or:* Non, je ne l'ai pas débarrassée après le dîner hier soir.
6. Oui, j'en ai pris ce matin. *or:* Non, je n'en ai pas pris ce matin.
7. Oui, je l'ai comprise. *or:* Non, je ne l'ai pas comprise.
8. Oui, je les ai écrites. *or:* Non, je ne les ai pas écrites.

Leçon 17, p. 288

2. Ils sont sortis à 9 h., mais ils sont revenus une heure plus tard.
3. Napoléon est né en 1769; il est mort en 1821.
4. Les jeunes filles sont descendues à la plage et elles ont nagé jusqu'à 4 h.
5. Elle est restée en Chine et elle est devenue médecin.
6. Elles sont venues te voir parce que tu as voulu leur parler.
7. Edouard et Luc sont montés dans le train, mais le train n'est pas parti tout de suite.
8. Hélène est partie en vacances, mais nous sommes restés (*or:* restées) en ville.

Leçon 17, p. 292

3. On parle hollandais aux Pays-Bas. Vous venez des Pays-Bas.
4. On parle allemand en Allemagne. Elle vient d'Allemagne.
5. On parle norvégien en Norvège. Tu viens de Norvège.
6. On parle flamand en Belgique. Elles viennent de Belgique.
7. On parle danois au Danemark. Nous venons du Danemark.
8. On parle russe en Russie. Je viens de Russie.
9. On parle portugais au Portugal. Ils viennent du Portugal.
10. On parle japonais au Japon. Vous venez du Japon.
11. On parle grec en Grèce. Elle vient de Grèce.
12. On parle italien en Italie. Ils viennent d'Italie.

Answers to
Vérifiez vos progrès

Leçon 18, p. 306

2. Non, ils n'en savent rien.
3. Non, elles n'ont reconnu personne.
4. Non, tu n'y vas plus.
5. Non, nous n'avons rien (*or:* je n'ai rien).
6. Non, nous ne savons plus (*or:* je ne sais plus) toutes les réponses.
7. Non, je ne connais personne à Montréal.
8. Non, je ne suis jamais sortie.
9. Non, je ne la ferme plus à clef.
10. Non, nous ne faisons jamais nos bagages (*or:* je ne fais jamais mes bagages).

Leçon 18, p. 311

2. Peu de gens!
3. Beaucoup d'hôtels!
4. Trop de fois!
5. Tant d'auteurs!
6. Beaucoup de matchs!
7. Assez de fruits!
8. Très peu d'immeubles!

Answers to Auto-Tests

Following each set of answers we point out where you can turn in the book if you
feel that you need further review. Always check with your teacher if you don't
fully understand an exercise or the structures involved.

Leçon 1, p. 11

A. 2. C'est le cahier.
   3. C'est l'affiche.
   4. C'est la porte.
   5. C'est la gomme.
   6. C'est le professeur.
(Did you remember that le professeur *can refer to a man
or a woman?)*

B. 2. Voilà la fenêtre.
   3. Voici le livre.
   4. Voici le papier.
   5. Voilà la corbeille.
   6. Voilà le professeur.
(If you need to review the gender of these nouns, see p. 5.)

C. 3. Comme ci, comme ça. Et toi?
   4. Oui. Et vous?
   5. Bien. Et toi?
   6. Très bien, merci, madame. Et vous?
(To review these responses, see pp. 7–8.)

Leçon 2, p. 27

A. 2. Vous allez à la plage.
   3. Nous allons à la gare.
   4. Tu vas à la montagne.
   5. Jean-Claude et Roger *(or:* Ils) vont à la poste.
   6. Je vais à la maison.
(To review aller, *see p. 21.)*

B. 1. Où sont les drapeaux?
   2. Où sont les hôpitaux?
   3. Où sont les stylos?

   4. Où sont les autobus?
   5. Où sont les salles de classe?
   6. Où sont les cartes?
(If you need to review these plural forms, see pp. 23–24.)

C. 2. C'est la banque de M. Lenoir et de Mme
      Dupont.
   3. C'est le calendrier d'Isabelle.
   4. Ce sont les tables de Marie-Claire.
   5. Ce sont les cahiers d'Olivier et d'Hélène.
   6. Ce sont les villas de Mme Thomas, de Mlle
      Monet et de M. Jeanson.
(Did you remember to repeat the de *with each person's
name? If not, see p. 25.)*

Leçon 3, p. 43.

A. 2. Lui, il est à l'école.
   3. Vous, vous êtes *(or:* Nous, nous sommes) à
      l'appartement.
   4. Elles, elles sont à la plage.
   5. Nous, nous sommes *(or:* Moi, je suis) à la
      montagne.
   6. Eux, ils sont à l'hôpital.
   7. Elle, elle est à la maison.
(To review the pronouns, see p. 35; for the verb être,
see p. 36.)

B. 2. C'est sa jupe.
   3. Ce sont ses bas.
   4. Ce sont ses chaussures.
   5. C'est son pull-over.
   6. C'est son chapeau.
   7. C'est sa chemise.
   8. C'est son pantalon.
   9. Ce sont ses chaussettes.
*(To review the vocabulary for clothing, see p. 33. Did
you remember that* sa, son, *and* ses *agree with the noun?
If not, see pp. 38–39.)*

C. 2. Oui, c'est mon frère, mais où est ma sœur?
   3. Oui, ce sont mes gommes, mais où est mon cahier?
   4. Oui, c'est ma robe, mais où sont mes chaussures?
   5. Oui, ce sont mes bandes, mais où est mon magnétophone?
   6. Oui, c'est mon oncle, mais où est ma tante?
   7. Oui, c'est mon chapeau, mais où est mon pull-over?
   8. Oui, c'est ma table, mais où sont mes chaises?
   9. Oui, c'est mon calendrier, mais où sont mes livres?
   10. Oui, ce sont mes nièces, mais où sont mes grands-parents?
(To review the possessive determiners, see pp. 38–39.)

Leçon 4, p. 59

A. 2. Nous allons à Cannes avec nos oncles.
   3. Vous avez votre robe.
   4. Tu vas à la gare avec ta voisine?
   5. Ils ont leur voiture.
   6. Nous sommes avec nos amies.
   7. Vous avez vos motos.
   8. Voilà leurs jardins.
(To review these possessive determiners, see p. 51.)

B. 1. Georges a trois sœurs, deux frères, dix cousins, treize cousines, quatre oncles et cinq tantes.
   2. Dans la salle de classe, nous avons dix-neuf élèves et vingt pupitres.
   3. Monsieur Dupont a seize crayons, huit stylos, trois gommes et onze cahiers sur son bureau.
(If you had difficulty spelling out the numbers, see p. 55.)

C. 2. Vous n'avez pas vos motos.
   3. Je ne vais pas à l'école à pied.
   4. Nous n'avons pas nos pull-overs.
   5. Tu ne vas pas à Nice en vélo.
   6. Ce ne sont pas mes cousines.
   7. Tu n'as pas ma voiture.
   8. Ils ne vont pas à Paris par le train.
   9. Elles n'ont pas leurs bateaux à voiles.
   10. Les feuilles ne sont pas sur l'herbe.
   11. Nous ne sommes pas en jean.
   12. Vous n'êtes pas en pantalon et en blouse.
(Did you place ne *before and* pas *after the verb to form the negative? If not, review p. 56. To review the forms of* aller, être, *or* avoir, *see pp. 21, 36, and 55.)*

Leçon 5, p. 75

A. 2. Combien de bateaux à voiles est-ce qu'il y a?
   3. De quelle couleur sont leurs chaussettes?
   4. Qui va au restaurant? Où est-ce que Thomas et Frédéric vont? Où vont Thomas et Frédéric?
   5. Qu'est-ce qui est en face du café? Où est le cinéma?
   6. Comment est-ce que vous allez à votre (*or:* nous allons à notre) villa? Qui va à votre (*or:* notre) villa par le train? Où est-ce que vous allez (*or:* nous allons) par le train?
   7. Qui est à l'aéroport? Où est Jean?
   8. Pourquoi est-ce qu'ils ne vont pas à la piscine? Qu'est-ce qu'ils n'ont pas?
(To review the interrogatives, see p. 66.)

B. 2. Mon pull-over est rouge.
   3. Ma moto est bleue.
   4. Mes chemises sont jaunes.
   5. Mes livres sont noirs.
   6. Mes voitures sont bleues.
(To review colors, see pp. 67–68.)

C. 3. Il va au café à côté du cinéma (avec son frère).
   4. Je vais à la plage près du port.
   5. Nous allons (*or:* Je vais) aux jardins en face du château.
   6. Les habits du garçon (*or:* Ses habits) sont sur la chaise à gauche de la table.
   7. Elles vont au restaurant en face du bureau.
   8. L'école est loin des hôtels.
   9. Ils vont à la banque à droite des usines.
   10. Leurs amis (*or:* Ils) vont aux musées près du parc.
(To review à *and* de + *definite determiner, see p. 71.)*

Leçon 6, p. 95

A. 2. Nous, nous regardons (*or:* Moi, je regarde) la télé.
   3. Vous, vous préparez (*or:* Nous, nous préparons) le goûter.
   4. Elles, elles travaillent au bureau.
   5. Nous, nous regardons (*or:* Moi, je regarde) le journal télévisé.

Answers to
Auto-Tests

6. Toi, tu aimes mieux rester ici.

7. Elle, elle demande son cahier à Claude.

8. Moi, je montre les images à Cécile.

(To review regular -er verbs, see pp. 84–85.)

B. 2. Je déjeune à midi.

3. Je joue au tennis à trois heures.

4. Je rentre du bureau à cinq heures.

5. Je dîne à six heures.

(To review telling time, see p. 92.)

C. 1. Martin va toujours au lycée à 8 h. du matin. Il est grand. Il porte son pantalon bleu, sa chemise blanche et son pull-over rouge. Ses chaussettes sont bleues aussi, mais ses chaussures sont noires.

2. Françoise n'est pas du tout paresseuse. Elle travaille à la banque. Aujourd'hui elle porte sa jupe verte, ses bas gris et sa blouse blanche. Ses chaussures sont grises et son chapeau est vert. Ses habits sont jolis, n'est-ce pas?

(To review adjectives, see pp. 67–68 and 90.)

Leçon 7, p. 113

A. 2. Il pleut.

3. Il gèle.

4. Il fait froid.

5. Il fait du vent.

6. Il fait du soleil.

7. Il neige.

8. Il fait frais.

9. Il fait mauvais.

(To review weather expressions, see p. 99.)

B. 1. quarante-six cinquante vingt et un

2. trente-trois zéro sept soixante-trois

3. quarante-huit onze cinquante-cinq

4. soixante-deux quarante-neuf dix-neuf

5. trente-deux trente vingt-sept

6. soixante-quatre zéro quatre quatorze

(To review the numbers 21–69, see p. 104; for the numbers 1–20, see p. 55.)

C. 2. Eux, ils maigrissent avant les vacances aussi.

3. Lui, il choisit toujours des chemises bleues aussi.

4. Nous, nous finissons nos (*or:* Moi, je finis mes) devoirs aussi.

5. Toi, tu grossis aussi.

6. Elles, elles rougissent quelquefois aussi.

7. Moi, je finis souvent mes devoirs avant neuf heures aussi.

8. Elle, elle choisit une robe rouge aussi.

9. Vous, vous finissez votre (*or:* Nous, nous finissons notre) déjeuner vers une heure aussi.

(To review these -ir/-iss- verbs, see p. 103.)

Leçon 8, p. 130

A. 3. Non, j'ai soif.

4. Si, elle a peur.

5. Non, nous avons faim.

6. Si, tu as raison.

(To review these expressions with avoir, *see p. 117; if you need help answering negative questions, see p. 126.)*

B. 2. La maison n'est pas nouvelle.

3. Les lacs ne sont pas beaux.

4. Ses nièces ne sont pas vieilles.

5. Les nuits ne sont pas chaudes.

(To review these irregular adjectives, see p. 122.)

C. 2. Vous faites (*or:* Nous faisons) du ski nautique près de la villa.

3. Tu fais (*or:* Vous faites) la vaisselle le matin.

4. Je fais un voyage au printemps.

5. Elle fait des achats lundi.

(To review the verb faire, *see pp. 120–121.)*

D. 2. Quarante moins onze font vingt-neuf.

3. Seize et dix-huit font trente-quatre.

4. Soixante-cinq moins quatorze font cinquante et un.

(To review the numbers, see pp. 55 and 104.)

Leçon 9, p. 149

A. 2. C'est une ville mexicaine. Il faut parler espagnol.

3. C'est une ville allemande. Il faut parler allemand.

4. C'est une ville américaine. Il faut parler anglais.

5. C'est une ville italienne. Il faut parler italien.

6. C'est une ville portugaise. Il faut parler portugais.

7. C'est une ville sénégalaise. Il faut parler français ou wolof.

(To review the adjectives of nationality and languages, see p. 135.)

B. 2. Il est large.
   3. Elle est courte.
   4. Elle est petite.
   5. Il est long.
   6. Ils sont inconnus.
   7. Elles sont brunes.
   8. Elle est bonne.
   9. Elles sont maigres.

(To review these adjectives, see p. 140.)

C. 2. Les poètes partent à onze heures et demie.
   3. Tu sers le dîner à sept heures et quart.
   4. Nous finissons nos leçons vers dix heures moins le quart.
   5. Vous dormez pendant le concert?
   6. Je pars pour le marché à neuf heures moins vingt.
   7. Nous sortons du grand magasin avant cinq heures vingt.
   8. Elles dorment à la bibliothèque!
   9. Est-ce qu'il part ou est-ce qu'il choisit un livre?

(To review simple -ir verbs, see p. 139. For -ir/-iss- verbs, see p. 103. To review expressions of time, see p. 146.)

D. 2. Les poètes vont partir à onze heures et demie.
   3. Tu vas servir le dîner à sept heures et quart.
   4. Nous allons finir nos leçons vers dix heures moins le quart.
   5. Vous allez dormir pendant le concert?
   6. Je vais partir pour le marché à neuf heures moins vingt.
   7. Nous allons sortir du grand magasin avant cinq heures vingt.
   8. Elles vont dormir à la bibliothèque!
   9. Est-ce qu'il va partir ou est-ce qu'il va choisir un livre?

(To review the future formed with aller, see p. 145.)

Leçon 10, p. 165

A. 2. Je vends cette grande maison rouge.
   3. Ce garçon et cette serveuse servent le déjeuner.
   4. Ce professeur ne répond pas à cet élève.
   5. Elles commandent ce bon citron pressé.
   6. Tu attends cette amie à cet hôtel?
   7. Nous ne répondons pas à cette porte après 7 h. 30.

8. Vous entendez ces langues étrangères souvent en ville?

(To review the regular -re verbs, see p. 157. For demonstrative determiners, see p. 162.)

B. 1. f; 2. e; 3. b; 4. c; 5. d; 6. a.

C. 2. C'est une grosse dame.
   3. C'est une fille fatiguée.
   4. C'est une boisson froide.
   5. C'est une langue étrangère.
   6. C'est une petite bibliothèque.
   7. C'est une autre serveuse aimable.
   8. C'est une jeune femme calée.

(To review these adjectives, see pp. 155–156 and 158.)

Leçon 11, p. 183

A. Check your answers with your teacher.

B. 3. Il veut offrir un cadeau à Guillaume aussi.
   4. Je peux réussir à l'examen aussi.
   5. Nous voudrions (*or:* Je voudrais) passer la matinée à la maison aussi.
   6. Ils veulent aller à l'université aussi.
   7. Elles peuvent assister au cours de chimie aussi.
   8. Vous voulez (*or:* Nous voulons) poser une autre question aussi.
   9. Nous voudrions (*or:* Je voudrais) faire des sciences sociales aussi.
   10. Tu peux (*or:* Vous pouvez) sortir dimanche aussi.

(To review pouvoir and vouloir, see p. 173.)

C. 2. Hier nous avons attendu l'autobus jusqu'à 7 h. du soir.
   3. Le professeur n'a pas répondu aux questions des étudiants.
   4. Nous avons réussi à l'examen de biologie.
   5. Tu as perdu l'argent au supermarché.
   6. Sa sœur a choisi deux livres de poche dans la librairie.
   7. Tu as raté l'examen parce que tu n'as pas révisé tes leçons.

(Did you remember the plural of livre de poche? To review the passé composé, see pp. 175 and 180.)

Leçon 12, p. 202

A. 2. C'est un dindon.
   3. C'est une poule.
   4. C'est une vache.
   5. C'est un mouton.
   6. C'est un chat.
   7. C'est un canard.
   8. C'est un cheval.
   9. C'est un coq.
   10. C'est un cochon.
(To review, see p. 189.)

B. 2. C'est notre bel ours russe.
   3. C'est un petit tigre jaune et noir.
   4. C'est notre première girafe maigre.
   5. C'est un vieil éléphant paresseux.
   6. C'est leur nouvel hippopotame noir.
   7. C'est un petit singe méchant.
   8. C'est une vieille souris grise.
   9. C'est un bel oiseau bleu.
(To review the names of the animals, see p. 190. For the adjectives, see pp. 158 and 193.)

C. 2. Ces jeunes gens comprennent le flamand.
   3. Nous apprenons l'espagnol.
   4. Tu prends une bière.
   5. L'agriculteur comprend les animaux.
   6. Vous prenez quelque chose.
   7. Ce petit enfant apprend à jouer aux cartes.
   8. La concierge et son mari comprennent cet oiseau.
(To review these verbs, see p. 192.)

D. 3. Qu'est-ce qu'ils prennent?
   4. Qu'est-ce que vous pouvez (*or:* nous pouvons) regarder?
   5. Qu'est-ce que nous n'avons pas (*or:* je n'ai pas) étudié?
   6. Qui est-ce qu'elle a cherché?
   7. Qu'est-ce qu'ils vendent?
   8. Qui est-ce qu'elle aime?
(To review, see pp. 197–198.)

E. 3. Quel avion prennent-ils?
   4. Quels dessins animés pouvez-vous (*or:* pouvons-nous) regarder?
   5. Quel chapitre n'avons-nous pas (*or:* est-ce que je n'ai pas) étudié?

   6. Quel agent a-t-elle cherché?
   7. Quelle villa vendent-ils?
   8. Quelles vendeuses aime-t-elle?
(Did you remember to make the form of quel *agree with the noun? If you used* je *in your answer to #5, did you remember not to use inversion? To review, see p. 198.)*

Leçon 13, p. 222

A. 3. C'est une jeune dentiste.
   4. Ce sont de grands marchés.
   5. C'est un vieil artiste.
   6. C'est une nouvelle avocate.
   7. Ce sont de jeunes hôtesses de l'air.
   8. Ce sont de vieilles employées (de bureau).
   9. C'est une mauvaise pharmacie.
   10. C'est un nouvel infirmier.
   11. Ce sont de jeunes femmes d'affaires.
   12. Ce sont de beaux soldats.
(To review the adjectives, see pp. 193 and 213.)

B. 3. Oui, elle l'habite.
   4. Non, il ne va pas le faire à Clermont-Ferrand.
   5. Non, je ne le rencontre pas devant la maison.
   6. Oui, nous les voyons (*or:* je les vois).
   7. Oui, ils vont les vendre.
   8. Oui, je le vois.
   9. Non, on ne le sert pas dans ce café.
   10. Non, ils ne la croient pas.
   11. Oui, il (*or:* l'agriculteur) va les chercher.
   12. Non, nous ne les offrons pas (*or:* je ne les offre pas) à grand-maman.
(To review direct object pronouns, see pp. 216–217.)

Leçon 14, p. 241

A. 2. Il lui prête le mouchoir.
      Il le prête à Denise.
   3. Je lui montre les bagues.
      Je les montre à Grégoire.
   4. Nous lui empruntons (*or:* Je lui emprunte) la montre.
      Nous l'empruntons (*or:* Je l'emprunte) à Marguerite.
   5. Nous leur écrivons (*or:* Je leur écris) la carte postale.
      Nous l'écrivons à nos (*or:* Je l'écris à mes) grands-parents.
   6. Il faut leur emprunter les ceintures.
      Il faut les emprunter à Roger et à Charles.

allée en Haïti. Je crois que je vais beaucoup l'aimer.
C'est un pays où le français est la langue officielle,
40 mais où tout le monde parle créole.¹ Malheureusement je n'ai appris qu'une phrase en créole: *"M ap
chaché youn otèl ki pa tro chè."* Tu l'as comprise? Ça
veut dire: "Je cherche un hôtel qui n'est pas trop
cher."

45 Je ne rentre à Paris que vers la fin de juillet. Je vais
t'apporter un petit paquet de cartes postales et
d'autres souvenirs de mes voyages en Louisiane, au
Canada et aux Antilles. Comme ça je pourrai° vous
donner des renseignements sans fin sur l'Amérique
50 francophone.° (Les photos que je prends, moi, sont
affreuses; alors j'ai acheté° beaucoup de cartes postales.) A bientôt.

je pourrai: *I'll be able*
francophone: *French-speaking*
acheter: *to buy*

> Je t'embrasse,²
> Claude

A propos ...

1. Que fait Claude comme profession? Elle est en vacances maintenant?
2. D'où est-ce qu'elle écrit cette lettre? 3. En quoi est-ce que Lafayette
est comme la France? 4. Qui sont les Acadiens? Quand est-ce qu'ils sont
arrivés en Louisiane? Pourquoi ont-ils quitté le Canada? 5. Est-ce qu'Anne-
Marie connaît quelqu'un à Lafayette? 6. Que vont faire les filles demain?
Qu'est-ce que c'est qu'un "bayou"? 7. Qu'est-ce que les filles ont mangé la
veille? 8. Quel service est-ce que Claude va faire la semaine prochaine?
9. Est-ce que Claude connaît Haïti? Elle parle créole? Que veut dire la
phrase qu'elle a apprise? 10. Pourquoi est-ce que Claude a acheté tant de
cartes postales? 11. Et vous, quand vous êtes en voyage, est-ce que vous
prenez des photos? Comment sont vos photos? 12. Est-ce que vous connaissez quelques pays étrangers? Quelle langue est-ce qu'on y parle?
13. Quand vous allez faire un voyage, qui fait vos bagages? Qui va chercher
les renseignements nécessaires ("necessary") — les horaires ou les cartes routières ("road maps"), par exemple? 14. Qu'est-ce que vous allez faire cet
été? Vous avez des projets de vacances? Quels projets?

---

¹Creole is a language that resulted from the contact of French and West African languages. It is
spoken widely in the Antilles and in areas of Louisiana.
²*Embrasser* means "to kiss." This is a common way for relatives or close friends to sign a letter.
It is equivalent to saying "love."

7. Ils (*or:* Mes parents) vont lui offrir le sac.
   Ils (*or:* Mes parents) vont l'offrir à grand-maman.
8. Ils veulent lui donner les gants.
   Ils veulent les donner à leur fille cadette.

(Did you remember to place the direct and indirect object pronouns before the infinitives in #6–8? To review these object pronouns, see pp. 216–217 and 233.)

B. 2. Non, nous ne vous montrons pas (*or:* Non, je ne vous montre pas) mon nouveau manteau.
   3. Non, ils ne lui posent pas d'autres questions.
   4. Non, je ne te vends pas ces timbres.
   5. Non, elle ne leur parle pas maintenant.
   6. Non, elles ne vont pas me lire sa lettre.
   7. Non, elles ne me prêtent pas ce foulard aujourd'hui.
   8. Non, je ne leur emprunte pas le parapluie.
   9. Non, je ne veux pas vous faire une visite.
   10. Non, il ne vous (*or:* t') offre pas ce beau collier.

(To review, see pp. 233 and 238.)

Leçon 15, p. 259

A. 2. Nous mangeons des sandwichs.
   3. Nous prononçons ces phrases espagnoles.
   4. Nous nageons avant le déjeuner.
   5. Nous commençons la nouvelle leçon.
   6. Nous dansons ce soir.
   7. Nous plongeons dans le lac.
   8. Nous remercions les employés de bureau.

(To review verbs whose infinitives end in -cer or -ger, see p. 249. Did you remember that danser *and* remercier *are regular -er verbs?)*

B. 2. Non, nous mangeons (*or:* je mange) du riz.
   3. Non, il a besoin du beurre.
   4. Non, nous voulons (*or:* je veux) des croque-monsieur.
   5. Non, il y a de la soupe à l'oignon et des escargots.
   6. Non, elles ont besoin d'œufs et de fromage.

(To review the partitive, see p. 250.)

C. 3. Non, elles n'en choisissent pas.
   4. Non, on n'y va pas.
   5. Non, il n'en sert pas.
   6. Non, ils n'y vont pas.
   7. Non, elles n'en vendent pas.
   8. Non, il n'y rentre pas.

9. Non, elle n'y arrive pas.
10. Non, je n'en veux pas.

(To review y *and* en, *see pp. 255–256.)*

Leçon 16, p. 276

A. 2. Elles la mettent sur la cuisinière maintenant.
   3. Nous le mettons maintenant.
   4. Il le met dans le réfrigérateur maintenant.
   5. Ils les mettent dans la salle à manger maintenant.
   6. Elle le met maintenant.
   7. Je le mets dans le garage maintenant.

(To review mettre, *see p. 266.)*

B. 2. Non, il ne les a pas oubliés.
   3. Non, ils ne les ont pas cassés.
   4. Non, je ne les ai pas ouvertes.
   5. Non, nous ne les avons pas (*or:* je ne les ai pas) vues.
   6. Non, vous ne l'avez pas (*or:* nous ne l'avons pas) compris.
   7. Non, elles (*or:* les ménagères) ne les ont pas crus.
   8. Non, il ne l'a pas remerciée.
   9. Non, elles ne les ont pas faites.

(To review the irregular past participles, see pp. 267–268. To review agreement, see pp. 272–273.)

C. 3. Il t'a téléphoné.
   4. Elles m'ont répondu.
   5. Je vous ai vues.
   6. Il m'a écrit.
   7. Je t'ai choisie.
   8. Elle nous a rencontrées.

(Note that the question à qui? *indicates an* indirect *object. Past participles agree only with* direct *object pronouns. To review, see p. 272.)*

D. 2. Oui, elles les ont pris en ville.
   Oui, elles y ont pris leurs repas.
   3. Oui, nous l'avons dit aux soldats.
   Oui, nous leur avons dit "bon courage."
   4. Oui, tu les as montrées à cette jeune femme.
   Oui, tu lui as montré la nappe et les serviettes.
   5. Oui, je l'ai offerte à mon frère.
   Oui, je lui ai offert cette nouvelle veste.

6. Oui, il en a mis dans l'évier.
   Oui, il y a mis des cuillères.
7. Oui, ils les ont prêtés à leurs neveux.
   Oui, ils leur ont prêté l'électrophone et la radio.
(To review, see p. 272.)

10. Elle a perdu son portefeuille et elle est retournée au cinéma pour le chercher.
11. Quand ils ont entendu ma réponse ils sont partis tout de suite.
(To review the passé composé formed with être, *see pp. 286–287.)*

Leçon 17, p. 294

A. 2. Je deviens dentiste aussi.
   3. Elles viennent toujours de bonne heure aussi.
   4. Il revient demain soir aussi.
   5. Nous devenons professeurs (*or:* Je deviens professeur) aussi.
   6. Elle vient du Mali aussi.
   7. Nous venons (*or:* Je viens) de finir cette leçon aussi.
(To review venir, *see pp. 284–285.)*

B. 2. Elle est rentrée en France et elle a cherché un appartement.
   3. Nous avons travaillé à l'hôpital mais nous ne sommes pas devenus infirmiers.
   4. Elles sont allées en Suisse où elles ont vu les belles montagnes.
   5. Ils ont fait un voyage mais ils n'ont pas pris le train.
   6. Ils sont descendus de l'avion et ils ont téléphoné à leurs parents.
   7. J'ai attendu l'autobus et il n'est pas arrivé.
   8. Elle a passé quinze jours en Chine et puis elle est rentrée au Canada.
   9. Ils ont visité la Belgique, la France et l'Allemagne, mais ils ne sont pas allés en Autriche.

Leçon 18, p. 313

A. 2. Ils savent que nous partons vers minuit.
   3. Est-ce que vous connaissez vos voisins?
   4. Il connaît tous ces jeunes gens.
   5. Je n'en sais rien.
   6. Nous ne connaissons pas le médecin.
   7. Tu connais la Chine ou le Japon?
   8. Nous savons que vous êtes pressés, messieurs.
   9. Vous savez jouer de la guitare?
(To review connaître *and* savoir, *see p. 302.)*

B. 3. Ils n'ont rien dit.
   4. Je n'ai apporté que ce livre de poche.
   5. Elle n'est jamais allée à l'aéroport.
   6. Elles n'en parlent plus.
   7. Je n'ai besoin de rien.
   8. Il n'y a rien au milieu de la route.
(To review the negative expressions, see p. 304.)

C. 2. Il n'y a pas beaucoup de touristes.
   3. Nous avons reconnu peu de gens.
   4. Je n'ai plus besoin de tant de bagages.
   5. Elles ne vous donnent jamais assez de renseignements.
   6. Tu as tant de mouchoirs blancs.
   7. Il y a trop de nouveaux immeubles en ville.
(To review the expressions of quantity, see p. 310.)

Vocabulaire Français-Anglais

The *Vocabulaire français-anglais* contains all active vocabulary from the text. In addition, passive vocabulary from the *Conversation et Lecture* sections, the *poèmes,* and the *proverbes* is included.

A dash (—) in a subentry represents the word at the beginning of the main entry; for example, faire des —s following l'achat means faire des achats.

The number following each entry indicates the lesson in which the word or phrase is first introduced. Two numbers indicate that it is introduced in one lesson and elaborated upon in a later lesson.

Passive vocabulary—those words not introduced in the *Mots Nouveaux* sections or a *vocabulaire*—is indicated by the letter P preceding the lesson number. Two numbers indicate that the word is introduced passively in one lesson and made active in a later lesson.

Adjectives are shown in the masculine singular form followed by the appropriate feminine ending.

à to (2); at, in (3); on (4)
abord: d'— first (9)
acadien, -ienne Acadian (P18)
l'accent *m.* accent mark (P2)
   l'— aigu acute accent (´) (P2)
   l'— circonflexe circumflex accent (^) (P2)
   l'— grave grave accent (`) (P2)
accompagner to accompany, to go with (14)
accord: d'— okay (3)
l'achat: faire des —s to shop, to go shopping (8)
acheter to buy (P18)
l'acteur *m.* actor (13)
l'actrice *f.* actress (13)
l'addition *f.* check, bill (P10; 15)
l'adresse *f.* address (P14)
l'adulte *m.&f.* adult (P12)
l'aéroport *m.* airport (5)

les affaires *f.pl.:*
   la femme d'— *f.* businesswoman (13)
   l'homme d'— *m.* businessman (13)
l'affiche *f.* poster (1)
affreux, -euse terrible, awful (18)
l'Afrique *f.* Africa (17)
l'âge *m.* age (12)
   quel — avez-vous? how old are you? (12)
l'agent *m.* policeman (5)
agréable pleasant (P15)
l'agriculteur *m.* farmer (12)
aigu: l'accent — acute accent (´)(P2)
l'ail *m.* garlic (16)
aimable nice, kind (10)
aimer to like, to love (6)
   — mieux to prefer (6)
aîné, -e older (P6;12)
l'air: l'hôtesse de l'— *f.* stewardess (13)

l'algèbre *f.* algebra (11)
l'Allemagne *f.* Germany (17)
allemand, -e German (9)
l'allemand *m.* German (language) (9)
aller to go (2)
   allons-y! let's get going! (4)
allô hello (*on telephone*) (9)
allumer to light (P16)
alors so, in that case, then (P1;3)
l'alpinisme *m.:* faire de l'— to go mountain-climbing (8)
américain, -e American (2;9)
   le football — football (P5; 6)

l'Amérique *f.* America (17)
l' — centrale Central America (17)
l' — du Nord (Sud) North (South) America (17)
l'ami *m.,* l'amie *f.* friend (2)
l'amour *m.* love (P17)
amusant, -e fun (P8)
l'an *m.:* avoir . . . ans to be . . . years old (12)
l'ancêtre *m.* ancestor (P18)
anglais, -e English (9)
l'anglais *m.* English *(language)* (9)
l'Angleterre *f.* England (17)
l'animal, *pl.* les animaux *m.* animal (12)
animé: le dessin — movie cartoon (6)
l'année *f.* year (7)
l' — scolaire school year (P18)
l'anniversaire *m.* birthday (P10;14)
bon —! happy birthday! (14)
annoncer to announce (15)
l'anorak *m.* ski jacket (8)
les Antilles *f.pl.* Antilles (P18)
août *m.* August (7)
l'appartement *m.* apartment (2)
appeler to call (P13)
je m'appelle my name is (1)
il s'appelle his name is (P5)
l'appétit *m.:* bon — enjoy your meal (P15)
apporter to bring (6)
apprendre to learn (12)
— à + *verb* to learn how (12)
— par cœur to memorize, to learn by heart (12)
appris *past participle of* apprendre (16)

après after, afterward (P5;7)
d'— according to (P7)
l'après-midi *m.* afternoon, in the afternoon (6)
de l'— P.M. (6)
l'arbre *m.* tree (4)
l'argent *m.* money (P3;10)
arrêter to stop (P7); to arrest (P11)
arriver to arrive (P3;6); to happen (P16)
l'artiste *m.&f.* artist (P4;13)
l'Asie *f.* Asia (17)
assez (de) enough (16;18)
— + *adj.* quite, pretty, rather + *adj.* (12)
l'assiette *f.* plate (16)
assister à to attend (11)
Athènes Athens (10)
l'Atlantique *f.* Atlantic Ocean (17)
l'attaché *m.* attaché (P14)
attendre to wait, to wait for (10)
attention: faire — (à) to watch out (for) (P16)
au (à + le) (5)
au-dessous de below (12)
au-dessus de above (12)
aujourd'hui today (P3;7)
c'est — today is (P6;7)
au revoir good-by (1)
aussi also, too (P2;4)
l'Australie *f.* Australia (17)
l'auteur *m.* author (9)
l'autobus *m.* bus (2)
l'automne *m.* autumn, fall (7)
l'auto-stop *m.:* faire de l'—to hitchhike (8)
l'auto-test *m.* self-test (P1)
autre other (10)
l'Autriche *f.* Austria (17)
aux (à + les) (5)
avant before (7)
avare stingy, greedy (6)
avec with (3)
l'aventure *f.* adventure (P9)
l'avion *m.* airplane (4)
l'avocat *m.,* l'avocate *f.* lawyer (13)
avoir to have (4)
See also âge, an, besoin,

chance, chaud, faim, froid, mal, mine, peur, raison, soif, sommeil, tort
avril *m.* April (7)

les bagages *m. pl.* luggage, baggage (18)
faire ses — to pack one's bags (18)
la bague ring (14)
le bal masqué costume party (P4)
la bande tape (2)
la banque bank (2)
la barbe beard (P4)
le bas stocking (3)
le basketball basketball (9)
le bateau, *pl.* les bateaux boat (4)
le — à voiles sailboat (4)
battre: — le briquet to light a fire (P17)
beau (bel), belle handsome, beautiful (8;12)
il fait beau it's nice out (7)
beaucoup very much, a lot (5)
— de much, many, a lot of (P7;16;18)
— de monde a lot of people (14)
bel *see* beau
belge Belgian (10)
la Belgique Belgium (P14;17)
belle *see* beau
le béret beret (P4)
le besoin: avoir — de to need (14)
bête dumb, stupid (10)
le beurre butter (15)
la bibliothèque library (9)
bien well (1); good (P1)
— sûr of course, certainly (9)
ça va — things are fine (1)
bientôt soon (12)
à — see you later (P2)
la bière beer (10)

le bifteck steak (15)
le billet ticket (P9;10)
la biologie biology (11)
bizarre strange (P4)
blanc, blanche white (6)
bleu, -e blue (5)
blond, -e blond (9)
la blouse blouse (3)
bof! aw! (7)
la boisson drink, beverage (10)
boire: il a bu he drank (P16)
la boîte box (18)
le bol bowl (16)
bon, bonne good (9)
avoir bonne mine to look
well (16)
bon anniversaire! happy
birthday! (14)
bon appétit enjoy your
meal (P15)
de bonne heure early (17)
bonjour hello (1)
le bord: au — de by (12)
bouger to move (P17)
la bouillabaisse bouillabaisse,
fish stew (16)
les boules f.pl. lawn bowling
(P13)
bouleversé, -e upset (P14)
la bouteille bottle (P15)
la boutique shop, boutique
(13)
le bracelet bracelet (14)
le briquet: battre le — to
light a fire (P17)
le bruit noise (18)
brun, -e brown, brunette (9)
Bruxelles Brussels (10)
bu see boire
le buffet buffet, sideboard (P16)
le bureau, pl. les bureaux desk
(2); office (5)
l'employé m. l'employée f.
de — office clerk (13)

ça that (1)
— va? how are things? (1)
— va bien things are fine
(1)

comme ci, comme ça so-
so (1)
cacher to hide (16)
le cadeau, pl. les cadeaux gift,
present (P10;11)
cadet, -ette younger (12)
le café café (5); coffee (10)
le — au lait café au lait
(16)
le — crème coffee with
cream (P10)
la terrasse d'un — side-
walk café (10)
le cahier notebook (1)
le caissier, la caissière cashier
(P14)
calé, -e smart (10)
le calendrier calendar (2)
le camion truck (4)
la campagne country, countryside (2)
le camping: faire du — to go
camping, to camp out
(17)
le Canada Canada (17)
canadien, -ienne Canadian
(2;9)
le canard duck (12)
il fait un froid de — it's
freezing cold (P7)
la cantine lunchroom (P5)
la capitale capital (city) (P17)
car because (P17)
le caramel: la crème — caramel custard (15)
la caravane van, camper (17)
le carburateur carburetor (P17)
la carte map (2); card (6)
la — d'étudiant student
I.D. (P11)
la — postale post card
(P6;14)
la — routière road map
(P18)
casser to break (16)
ce (cet), cette this, that (P9;
10)
ce qu'il y a what's wrong
(P17)
ce sont these are, those
are, they are (2)

c'est this is, that is, it is (1)
c'est-à-dire that's to say
(P18)
la cédille cedilla (ç) (P2)
la ceinture belt (14)
célèbre famous (9)
le cendre ash (P16)
le cendrier ashtray (P16)
cent hundred (13)
central, -e: l'Amérique —e f.
Central America (17)
cependant however (18)
certainement definitely (P14)
ces these, those (10)
cet, cette see ce
la chaise chair (2)
le châlet chalet (P8)
la chance: avoir de la — to be
lucky (14)
la chandelle candle (P17)
la chanson song (14)
chanter to sing (14)
le chapeau, pl. les chapeaux
hat (3)
le chapitre chapter (11)
chaque each, every (14)
la chasse hunt (P10)
chasser to expel (P18)
le chat cat (P9;12)
le château, pl. les châteaux
château, castle (5)
chaud, -e warm, hot (8)
avoir — to be warm (hot)
(8)
il fait — it's warm (hot)
out (7)
la chaussette sock (3)
la chaussure shoe (3)
la chemise shirt (3)
cher, chère expensive (11);
dear (P18)
coûter cher to be expen-
sive (10)
chercher to look for (11)
le chercheur d'or gold digger
(P3)

le cheval, *pl.* les chevaux horse (12)

chez to (at) someone's house or business (P1;2)

chic! neat! great! (7)

le chien dog (12)

la chimie chemistry (11)

la Chine China (17)

chinois, -e Chinese (9)

le chinois Chinese *(language)* (9)

le chocolat: la mousse au — chocolate mousse (15)

choisir to choose (7)

le choix choice (9)

la chose: quelque — something (12)

chouette! great! neat! (4)

chut! hush! (15)

ci: comme ci, comme ça so-so (1)

le ciel sky, heaven (8)

le cinéma movies; movie theater (5)

cinq five (4)

cinquante fifty (7)

cinquième fifth (P5)

circonflexe: l'accent — circumflex accent (î) (P2)

la circulation traffic (18)

le citron pressé lemonade, citron pressé (10)

clair: au — de (la) lune in the moonlight (P17)

la clarinette clarinet (P14)

la classe class (1)

la salle de — classroom (1)

la clef key (18)

fermer à — to lock (18)

le climat climate (P7)

le Coca Coke (10)

le cochon pig (12)

le cœur: apprendre par — to memorize, to learn by heart (12)

le coin corner (5)

au — (de la rue) on the corner (5)

le collier necklace (14)

collectionner to collect (P14)

la colonie colony (P18)

combien (de) how much? how many? (5)

— font? how much is? *(in math)* (8)

commander to order (10)

comme like, as; for (P4;13)

— ci, — ça so-so (1)

le commencement beginning (18)

commencer to begin, to start (15)

comment how (5)

le complet suit (14)

comprendre to understand (12)

compris *past participle of* comprendre (16)

le service est — the tip is included (15)

compter to count (11)

le concert concert (9)

concierge *m.&f.* concierge, janitor (12)

le concours contest (P8)

le — d'entrée entrance exam (P13)

la conférence conference (P14)

la confiture jam (15)

la connaissance knowledge (P14)

connaître to know, to be acquainted with (P8;18)

connu *past participle of* connaître (18)

le continent continent (17)

la conversation conversation (P4)

le copain, la copine friend (4)

Copenhague Copenhagen (10)

le coq rooster (12)

le — au vin chicken cooked in wine, coq au vin (15)

la corbeille wastebasket (1)

la corde: il pleut des —s it's pouring rain (P7)

correct, -e correct (11)

le correspondant, la correspondante pen pal (P14)

la Côte d'Azur the Riviera (5)

le côté:

à — next door (P5); nearby (10)

à — de next to, beside (5)

la couleur color (5)

de quelle —? what color? (5)

le coup: tout à — suddenly (12)

le couple couple (P15)

le courage: bon —! good luck! (P9;14)

courageux, -euse brave (P11)

le cours class, course (11)

au — de in the course of (P14)

court, -e short (9)

le cousin, la cousine cousin (3)

le couteau, *pl.* les couteaux knife (16)

coûter to cost (10)

— cher to be expensive (10)

— peu to be inexpensive (10)

la couturière seamstress (P17)

le couvert: mettre le — to set the table (16)

la craie chalk (2)

la cravate necktie (14)

le crayon pencil (1)

la crème cream (15)

la — caramel caramel custard (15)

crier to shout (P5)

croire to believe, to think (13)

le croque-monsieur grilled ham and cheese, croquemonsieur (15)

cru *past participle of* croire (16)

la cuillère spoon (16)

la cuisine kitchen (16)

faire la — to cook, to do the cooking (16)

la haute — gourmet cooking (P15)

la cuisinière stove (16)

la dactylo typist (P14)
la dame lady (10)
le Danemark Denmark (17)
danois, -e Danish (10)
le danois Danish (*language*) (10)
dans in, into (P1;4)
la danse dance (14)
danser to dance (14)
la date date (7)
de of (2); from (6); about (14); some, any (7;15)
débarrasser to clear (16)
décembre *m.* December (7)
décrire to describe (P4)
le déguisement costume (P4)
dehors outside, outdoors (7)
déjà already (11)
déjeuner to have breakfast or lunch (6)
le déjeuner lunch (6)
    le petit — breakfast (6)
demain tomorrow (9)
demander to ask, to ask for (6)
    — à to ask (*someone*), to ask (*someone*) for (6)
demie: *time* + et demie half past (9)
la demoiselle young lady (15)
dentiste *m.&f.* dentist (13)
le département department (P13)
    le — d'outre-mer overseas department (P17)
dernier, -ière last (11)
derrière behind (4)
des (de + les) (5)
descendre to come down, to go down (P13;17)
    — de to come down from, to get off (17)
désert, -e deserted (P17)
le dessert dessert (15)
le dessin animé movie cartoon (6)
dessous *see* au-dessous de
dessus *see* au-dessus de

deux two (4)
    tous (toutes) les — both (P15)
la deux-chevaux Citroën 2-CV car (17)
deuxième second (P2)
devant in front of (4)
devenir to become (P13;17)
devenu *past participle of* devenir (17)
les devoirs *m.pl.* homework (6)
le dictionnaire dictionary (P14)
Dieu God (P17)
difficile difficult, hard (5)
dimanche *m.* Sunday (7)
le dindon turkey (12)
dîner to dine, to have dinner (6)
le dîner dinner (6)
le diplomate diplomat (P14)
dire (à) to say (to), to tell (14)
    c'est-à-— that's to say (P18)
    dis! say! (P5)
    vouloir — to mean (11)
le discours speech (P14)
la discussion discussion (P9)
le disque record (6)
dit *past participle of* dire (16)
dix ten (4)
dix-huit eighteen (4)
dix-huitième eighteenth (P18)
dixième tenth (P10)
dix-neuf nineteen (4)
dix-sept seventeen (4)
dix-septième seventeenth (P17)
le documentaire documentary (6)
le dommage: c'est — too bad (P3)
donc! *emphatic exclamation* (14)
donner (à) to give (to) (6)
dormir to sleep (9)
doucement! hold it! (P8)
douze twelve (4)
douzième twelfth (P12)
le dragon dragon (8)

le drapeau, *pl.* les drapeaux flag (2)
droite: à — (de) to the right (of) (5)
drôle funny (P4)
du (de + le) (5)

l'eau, *pl.* les eaux *f.* water (8)
    l' — minérale mineral water (15)
les échecs *m.pl.* chess (6)
l'école *f.* school (2)
écouter to listen (to) (6)
l'écran *m.* screen (P9)
écrire to write (P12;14)
écrit *past participle of* écrire (P12;16)
l'écriture *f.* writing (P13)
l'écrivain *m.* writer (P12)
l'effet *m.:* en — indeed, you bet (18)
l'église *f.* church (2)
l'électrophone *m.* record player (14)
l'électricité *f.* electricity (P17)
l'éléphant *m.* elephant (12)
l'élève *m.&f.* pupil, student (1)
elle she, it (2); her (3)
elles *f.pl.* they (2); them (3)
embêtant, -e annoying (18)
embrasser to kiss (P18)
l'emploi *m.* job (13)
l'employé *m.*, l'employée *f.* employee, clerk (13)
    l' — de bureau office clerk (13)
les empreintes digitales *f.pl.* fingerprints (P11)
emprunter (à) to borrow (from) (14)
en in (3;7); to (9); some, any (15)
    — + *clothing* in (3)
    — + *vehicles* by (4)
    — retard late (17)

encore again (P1)

énergique energetic, lively (6)

l'enfant *m.&f.* child (3)

enfantin, -e children's (P8)

enfin finally, at last (12)

ennuyeux, -euse boring, dull (14)

enseigner to teach (11)

ensemble together (P5)

ensuite next, then (15)

entendre to hear (10)

l'entracte *m.* intermission (P9)

entrer (dans) to enter, to go in, to come in (6)

l'entrée *f.:* le concours d'— entrance exam (P13)

l'enveloppe *f.* envelope (14)

épicé, -e spicy (P18)

l'épouvante *f.* horror (P9)

l'équipe *f.* team (P8)

l'escale *f.* stop (P18)

l'escalope de veau *f.* veal cutlet (P15)

l'escargot *m.* snail (15)

l'Espagne *f.* Spain (17)

espagnol, -e Spanish (9)

l'espagnol *m.* Spanish (language) (9)

l'Esquimau, *pl.* les Esquimaux Eskimo (P6)

l'esquimau, *pl.* les esquimaux *m.* ice cream bar (P9; 10)

l'est *m.* east (17)

est-ce que *introduces a question* (P2;5)

qu'— what? (6)

qui — whom? (12)

et and (1)

l'étage *m.* story (of a building) (P18)

les Etats-Unis *m.pl.* United States (17)

été *past participle of* être (16)

l'été *m.* summer (7)

l'étoile *f.* star (8)

étranger, -ère foreign (10)

être to be (3)

nous sommes lundi, etc. it's Monday, etc. (7)

étroit, -e narrow (9)

l'étude *f.* study (P14)

les —s supérieures advanced studies (P13)

l'étudiant *m..* l'étudiante *f.* student (11)

la carte d'— student I.D. (P11)

étudier to study (6)

eu *past participle of* avoir (16)

euh er, uh (6)

l'Europe *f.* Europe (17)

eux *m.pl.* they, them (3)

l'évier *m.* sink (16)

exactement exactly (P17)

l'examen *m.* exam, test (11)

passer un — to take a test (11)

rater un — to fail a test (11)

réussir à un — to pass a test (11)

excellent, -e excellent (15)

l'exemple *m.:* par — for example (11)

l'exercice *m.* exercise (P1)

l'excursion *f.* trip (P18)

l'— en traîneau sleigh ride (P8)

les explications *f.pl.* explanations (P1)

l'expédition *f.:* la feuille d'— packing list (P14)

la face:

(d')en — across the street (P10)

en — de opposite, across from (5)

facile easy (5)

le facteur postman (P6;13)

la faim: avoir — to be hungry (8)

faire to do, to make (6;8)

— attention (à) to watch out (for) (P16)

— de + *school subjects* to take (11)

— le service de to work the route of (P18)

— peur à to frighten, to scare (12)

il se fait tard it's getting late (P8)

See also achat, alpinisme, auto-stop, bagages, beau, camping, chaud, combien, cuisine, frais, froid, jour, matinée, mauvais, ménage, nuit, progrès, ski, soleil, stage, valise, vent, visite, voyage

fait *past participle of* faire (16)

falloir to be necessary, to have to, must (9)

la famille family (3)

fana *m.&f.* fan (P5)

fatigué, -e tired (P5;10)

il faut *see* falloir

la faute mistake (8)

félicitations! congratulations! (14)

la femme woman (10); wife (12)

la — d'affaires businesswoman (13)

la fenêtre window (1)

la ferme farm (12)

fermer to close (6); to turn off (P7)

— à clef to lock (18)

le festival festival (P5)

la fête party, celebration (14)

la Fête des Mères (des Pères) Mother's (Father's) Day (11)

la — foraine traveling carnival (P7)

le feu fire (P17)

la feuille leaf (4)

la — d'expédition packing list (P14)

février *m.* February (7)

fiancé, -e engaged (12)

le fiancé, la fiancée fiancé, fiancée (12)
la fille daughter (3); girl (10)
  la jeune — girl (3)
le film movie, film (6)
  le — policier detective film (6)
  le grand — main feature (P9)
le fils son (3)
la fin end (18)
  finir to finish (7)
  flamand, -e Flemish (10)
le flamand Flemish (language) (10)
la fleur flower (4)
le fleuve river (8)
la flûte flute (P14)
  fois times (in math) (13)
la fois time (18)
  deux — twice (18)
  quelque — sometimes (7)
  une — once (18)
le football soccer (P5;6)
  le — américain football (P5;6)
  foraine: la fête — traveling carnival (P7)
  fort, -e: — en + school subjects good in (11)
  fou, folle crazy (P8)
le foulard scarf (P4;14)
la fourchette fork (16)
  frais: il fait — it's cool out (7)
le franc franc (10)
  français, -e French (2;9)
le français French (language) (9)
la France France (17)
  francophone French-speaking (P18)
  frapper (à) to knock (on) (12)
le frère brother (3)
  frites: les pommes — f.pl. French fries (15)
  froid, -e cold (8)
  avoir — to be cold (8)
  il fait — it's cold out (7)
  il fait un — de canard it's freezing cold (P7)

le fromage cheese (15)
les fruits m.pl. fruit (15)
la fumée smoke (P16)

le gâchis mess (16)
  gagner to win (P8)
le gangster gangster (P11)
le gant glove (14)
le garage garage (4)
le garagiste garage mechanic (P17)
le garçon boy (3); waiter (10)
la gare railroad station (2)
  gauche: à — (de) to the left (of) (5)
  geler to freeze (9)
  il gèle it's freezing (7)
  généreux, -euse generous (6)
les gens m.pl. people (10)
la géographie geography (11)
la géométrie geometry (11)
le gérant, la gérante manager (P11)
le geste gesture (11)
le gigot leg of lamb (15)
la girafe giraffe (12)
la glace ice (7); ice cream (10)
le golfe du Mexique Gulf of Mexico (P17)
la gomme eraser (1)
le goûter afternoon snack (6)
  grand, -e big, large (6)
  le — film main feature (P9)
  le — magasin department store (9)
la grand-mère grandmother (3)
le grand-père grandfather (3)
les grands-parents m.pl. grandparents (3)
  grasse: faire la — matinée to sleep late (11)
  grave serious (P17)
  l'accent — grave accent (`) (P2)
  grec, grecque Greek (10)
le grec Greek (language) (10)

la Grèce Greece (17)
la grenadine grenadine (10)
la grenouille frog (P9)
  gris, -e gray (6)
  gros, grosse fat, large (9)
  grossir to gain weight, to get fat (7)
la Guadeloupe Guadeloupe (P13)
le Guignol Guignol, Punch and Judy (4)
la guitare guitar (14)
le gymnase gymnasium (9)

  habiter to live, to live in (6)
les habits m.pl. clothes (3)
  habitude: d' — usually (P10; 18)
  l'habitué m., l'habituée f. regular customer (P10)
  Haïti Haiti (17)
les*haricots verts m.pl. green beans (15)
le*hautbois oboe (P14)
  hein eh, huh (P3;15)
  l'herbe f. grass (4)
  l'heure f. hour, o'clock (6)
  à l' — on time (17)
  à quelle —? what time? at what time? (6)
  à une (deux) —(s) at 1:00 (2:00) (6)
  de bonne — early (17)
  quelle — est-il? what time is it? (6)
  heureux, -euse happy (6)
  hier yesterday (11)
  — soir last night, last evening (11)
  l'hippopotame m. hippopotamus (12)
  l'histoire f. story (9); history (11)
  l'hiver m. winter (7)

*Words marked by an asterisk begin with aspirate *h*, so there is no liaison or elision.

le*hockey hockey (9)
*hollandais, -e Dutch (10)
le*hollandais Dutch *(language)*
(10)
l'homme *m.* man (10)
l'— d'affaires businessman
(13)
l'hôpital, *pl.* les hôpitaux *m.*
hospital (2)
l'horaire *m.* timetable (18)
les*hors-d'œuvre *m.pl.* appetizer,
hors d'œuvres (15)
l'hôtesse de l'air *f.* stewardess
(13)
l'hôtel *m.* hotel (2)
l'huile *f.* oil (16)
huit eight (4)
— jours a week (17)
huitième eighth (P8)
l'huître *f.* oyster (15)

l'— agronome agricultural
engineer (P13)
inquiet, -iète worried (10)
l'inspecteur *m.* inspector (P11)
s'installer to sit down (P10)
intelligent, -e intelligent
(P12)
intéressant, -e interesting
(14)
l'intérieur *m.:* à l'— inside, indoors (7)
international, -e; *pl.* inter-
nationaux, -nales in-
ternational (P14)
l'interprète *m.&f.* interpreter
(P14)
inviter to invite (14)
l'Italie *f.* Italy (17)
italien, -ienne Italian (9)
l'italien *m.* Italian *(language)*
(9)

le jour day (P6;7)
huit —s a week (17)
il fait — it's daytime, it's
light out (8)
par — per day (P6)
quel — sommes-nous? what
day is it? (7)
quinze —s two weeks (17)
tous les —s every day (18)
le journal, *pl.* les journaux newspaper (6)
le — télévisé TV news (6)
journaliste *m.&f.* journalist
(P14)
la journée (the whole) day (11)
le juge judge (13)
juillet *m.* July (7)
juin *m.* June (7)
la jupe skirt (3)
jusqu'à until (P6;11)

ici here (5); this is *(on telephone)* (9)
l'idée *f.* idea (P7)
il he, it (2)
il y a there is, there are (P4;
5)
ce qu'— what's wrong (P17)
— + *time* ago (17)
l'île *f.* island (P)
ils *m.pl.* they (2)
l'image *f.* picture (2)
l'immeuble *m.* apartment building (18)
l'imperméable *m.* raincoat (14)
l'importance *f.* importance
(P14)
important, -e important (P14)
impossible impossible (5)
inconnu, -e unknown (9)
l'inconnu *m.,* l'inconnue *f.*
stranger (12)
l'infirmier *m.,* l'infirmière *f.*
nurse (13)
l'ingénieur *m.* engineer (13)

jamais ever (P17)
ne . . . — never (18)
le jambon ham (P10;15)
le sandwich au — ham
sandwich (P10)
janvier *m.* January (7)
le Japon Japan (17)
japonais, -e Japanese (9)
le japonais Japanese *(language)*
(9)
le jardin garden (4)
jaune yellow (5)
jaunir to turn yellow (7)
je I (2)
le jean jeans (P3;4)
le jeu, *pl.* les jeux game (P8)
jeudi *m.* Thursday (7)
jeune young (5)
la — fille girl (3)
joli, -e pretty (5)
jouer to play (6)
— à to play *(games, sports)*
(6)
— de to play *(musical instruments)* (14)
— une pièce to put on a
play (13)

le kilomètre kilometer (P8)

la (l') *f.* the (1); her, it (13)
là here, there (P4;5)
là-bas there, over there (3)
le lac lake (8)
laid, -e ugly (8)
laisser to leave (behind) (14)
le lait milk (15)
le café au — café au lait
(16)
la langue language (10)
large wide (9)
le (l') *m.* the (1); him, it (P12;
13)
la leçon lesson (P1;6)
la lecture reading (P1)
le légume vegetable (15)
lentement slowly (10)
le léopard leopard (12)
les *m.&f.pl.* the (2); them (13)
la lettre letter (13)
leur to (for, from) them (P13;
14)
leur, -s their (4)
se lever to get up (P16)

la librairie bookstore (11)
libre unoccupied, free (10)
le lion lion (12)
lire to read (14)
Lisbonne Lisbon (9)
le lit bed (P17)
le livre book (1)
le — de poche paperback (11)
loin (de) far (from) (5)
les loisirs *m.pl.* leisure-time activities (P)
Londres London (9)
long, longue long (9)
longtemps a long time (17)
louer to rent (P8)
la Louisiane Louisiana (P18)
le loup-garou werewolf (P9)
lu *past participle of* lire (P12; 16)
lui him (3); to (for, from) him (her) (14)
lundi *m.* Monday (7)
la lune moon (8)
au clair de (la) — in the moonlight (P17)
le lycée high school (5)

ma my (3)
la machine à sous pinball machine (P10)
madame, *pl.* mesdames Mrs., ma'am (1;3)
mademoiselle, *pl.* mesdemoiselles Miss (1;3)
le magasin store (13)
le grand — department store (9)
le magnétophone tape recorder (2)
mai *m.* May (7)
maigre thin, skinny (9)
maigrir to lose weight, to get thin (7)
le maillot bathing suit (3)
la main hand (P16)
maintenant now (5)
mais but (3)

— non of course not, heck no (2)
la maison house (2)
le maître master (P12); teacher (P13)
mal bad (1); badly (10)
le mal: avoir le — du pays to be homesick (P13)
malheureusement unfortunately (9)
le Mali Mali (17)
malien, -ienne Malian (13)
la malle trunk (18)
maman *f.* mother, mom (9)
manger to eat (15)
la salle à — dining room (16)
le manteau, *pl.* les manteaux coat, overcoat (14)
le marché market (9)
mardi *m.* Tuesday (7)
le — gras Mardi Gras (P4)
le mari husband (P6;12)
marié, -e married (P6;12)
le marin sailor (13)
mars *m.* March (7)
la Martinique Martinique (P2)
le match, *pl.* les matchs game, match (P5;6)
les mathématiques, les maths *f.pl.* mathematics, math (11)
la matière subject (P11)
le matin morning, in the morning (6)
du — A.M. (6)
tous les —s every morning (18)
la matinée (the whole) morning (11)
faire la grasse — to sleep late (11)
mauvais, -e bad (P7;9)
il fait — it's bad out, it's nasty out (7)
me (m') to (for, from) me (14)
méchant, -e naughty; mean (12)
le médecin doctor (13)
la Méditerranée Mediterranean (17)

même same (10); even (P14)
le ménage: faire le — to do the housework (16)
la ménagère housewife (13)
la mer sea (8)
merci thank you, thanks (1)
mercredi *m.* Wednesday (P6; 7)
la mère mother (3)
mes *pl.* my (3)
messieurs-dames ladies and gentlemen (15)
la météo weather report (P7)
mettre to put, to place, to put on (P15;16)
— le couvert to set the table (16)
les meubles *m.pl.* furniture (P14)
mexicain, -e Mexican (9)
Mexico Mexico City (9)
le Mexique Mexico (17)
le golfe du — Gulf of Mexico (P17)
midi noon (6)
mieux: aimer — to prefer (6)
mil thousand *(in dates)* (P12;13)
le mileu: au — de in the middle of (12)
le militaire soldier (P17)
mille thousand (P11;13)
la mine: avoir bonne — to look well (16)
minérale: l'eau — *f.* mineral water (15)
minuit midnight (6)
mis *past participle of* mettre (16)
la mode: la revue de — fashion magazine (P6)
moi me, I (3)
moins minus (8)
time + — le quart quarter to (9)
le mois month (7)
la moitié: la — de half (P16)
mon my (P1;3)

le monde world (17)

beaucoup de — a lot of people (14)

tout le — everyone, everybody (15)

monsieur, *pl.* messieurs Mr., sir (1;3)

le — man, gentleman (10)

la montagne mountain (2)

à la — to (in) the mountains (2)

monter to go up, to come up, to climb (17)

— dans to get on (17)

la montre (wrist)watch (P10;14)

Montréal Montreal (9)

montrer (à) to show (to) (6)

mort *past participle of* mourir (17)

Moscou Moscow (10)

le mot word (P1;11)

le moteur motor (P17)

la moto motorbike (4)

le mouchoir handkerchief (14)

mourir to die (17)

la mousse moss (P18)

la — au chocolat chocolate mousse (15)

le mouton sheep (12)

le musée museum (5)

le musicien, la musicienne musician (P17)

la musique music (14)

nager to swim (15)

naître to be born (17)

la nappe tablecloth (16)

naturel, -le natural (11)

nautique *see* ski

ne:

— . . . jamais never (18)

— . . . pas not (4)

— . . . personne nobody, no one, not anyone (18)

— . . . plus no longer, not any more (P12;18)

— . . . que only (18)

— . . . rien nothing, not anything (18)

né *past participle of* naître (17)

nécessaire necessary (P18)

la neige snow (7)

neiger to snow (7)

n'est-ce pas? *interrogative tag* aren't I? isn't it? don't we? etc. (5)

neuf nine (4)

neuvième ninth (P9)

le neveu, *pl.* les neveux nephew (3)

le nez nose (P4)

niçoise *see* salade

la nièce niece (3)

Noël Christmas (7)

la veille de — Christmas Eve (16)

noir, -e black (5)

le Noir, la Noire black person (P13)

le nom name (P11)

le nombre number (P4)

nommer to name (P17)

non no (1)

le nord north (17)

l'Amérique du Nord *f.* North America (17)

le nord-est northeast (17)

le nord-ouest northwest (17)

la Norvège Norway (17)

norvégien, -ienne Norwegian (10)

le norvégien Norwegian (*language*) (10)

nos *pl.* our (4)

notre our (4)

nous we (2); us (3); to (for, from) us (14)

nouveau (nouvel), nouvelle new (P1;8;12)

novembre *m.* November (7)

le nuage cloud (8)

la nuit night, the dark (8)

il fait — it's nighttime, it's dark out (8)

nul, nulle: — en + *school subjects* no good in (11)

occupé, -e busy, occupied (10)

l'océan *m.* ocean (17)

octobre *m.* October (7)

l'œuf *m.* egg (15)

offert *past participle of* offrir (16)

officiel, -ielle official (P18)

offrir à to offer (to), to give (to) (11)

l'oignon *m.* onion (15)

la soupe à l'— onion soup (15)

l'oiseau, *pl.* les oiseaux *m.* bird (12)

l'— -lyre *m.* lyre-bird (P13)

l'omelette *f.* omelette (15)

on we, they (2)

l'oncle *m.* uncle (3)

onze eleven (4)

onzième eleventh (P11)

l'opéra *m.* opera, opera house (5)

l'or: le chercheur d'— gold digger (P3)

l'orangeade *f.* orangeade (10)

organiser to organize (P12; 14)

l'orthographe *f.* spelling (P12)

ou or (5)

où where (1)

d'— from where (17)

oublier to forget (14)

l'ouest *m.* west (17)

oui yes (1)

l'ours *m.* bear (12)

ouvert *past participle of* ouvrir (16)

l'ouvreuse *f.* usher (P9)

l'ouvrier *m.*, l'ouvrière *f.* worker, laborer (13)

ouvrir to open (6)

le Pacifique Pacific Ocean (17)

la page page (2)

le pain bread (15)

le palais palace (P5)

la palette palette (P4)

le panier basket (P15)
la panne breakdown (*of a car*) (P17)
   (être) en — (to have a) breakdown (P17)
le pantalon pants, slacks (3)
papa *m.* father, dad (9)
le papier paper (1)
le paquet package (14)
par by (4)
   — exemple for example (11)
   — jour per day (P6)
   regarder — to look out of (7)
le parapluie umbrella (14)
le parc park (4)
parce que because (4)
pardon excuse me, pardon me (5)
les parents *m.pl.* parents (3)
paresseux, -euse lazy (6)
parler to talk, to speak (6)
la parole word (P16)
partir (de) to leave (9)
pas not (1;8)
   ne . . . — not (4)
   — de + *noun* no (8)
   — du tout not at all (5)
le passé composé *past tense* (P10)
passer to spend (*time*) (11); to go by (P13)
   — un examen to take a test (11)
passionné, -e par enthusiastic about (13)
la pâtisserie pastry (15)
patatras! crash! (P16)
patiner to skate (P8)
le patron, la patronne boss (P14)
pauvre poor (5)
payer to pay (P6)
le pays country (17)
   avoir le mal du — to be homesick (P13)
les Pays-Bas *m.pl.* the Netherlands (17)
la peine: ça vaut la — it's worth it (P12)

Pékin Peking (9)
pendant during (P8;9)
   — que while (6)
penser (à) to think (about) (12)
   — de to think of (14)
perdre to lose (10)
le père father (3)
personne . . . ne no one, nobody (18)
petit, -e little, small (6)
   le — déjeuner breakfast (6)
   les —s pois *m.pl.* peas (15)
peu:
   coûter — to be inexpensive (10)
   — de few, little (18)
   un — (de) a little (P11;18)
la peur:
   avoir — (de) to be afraid (of) (8)
   faire — à to scare, to frighten (12)
peut-être perhaps, maybe (10)
la pharmacie pharmacy (13)
le pharmacien, la pharmacienne pharmacist (13)
la photo photo(graph) (11)
la phrase sentence (P4;11)
la physique physics (11)
le piano piano (14)
la pièce play (6)
   jouer une — to put on a play (13)
le pied: à — on foot (4)
le pilote pilot (13)
le pinceau paintbrush (P4)
la piscine swimming pool (2)
la piste: la — de ski ski run (P8)
la place seat (P9); place (P10)
la plage beach (2)
plaît: s'il te (vous) — please (5;9)
le plateau tray (P16)
pleurer to cry (P11)
pleuvoir to rain (P7;9)
   il pleut it's raining (7)
   il pleut des cordes it's pouring rain (P7)

plonger to dive (15)
plu *past participle of* pleuvoir (16)
la pluie rain (7)
la plume quill pen (P17)
plus:
   ne . . . — no longer, not any more (P12;18)
   — tard later (9)
plusieurs several (14)
plutôt instead (P17)
la poche: le livre de — paperback (11)
le poème poem (9)
le poète poet (9)
le point: à — medium (*of meat*) (P15)
le pois: les petits — *m.pl.* peas (15)
le poison poison (16)
le poisson fish (15)
le poivre pepper (16)
la police police (P10)
policier:
   le film — detective film (6)
   le roman — detective novel (10)
la Pologne Poland (17)
la pomme apple (15)
   la — de terre potato (15)
   la tarte aux —s apple pie (15)
   les —s frites French fries (15)
le pont bridge (P17)
le porc: le rôti de — roast pork (15)
le port port (5)
la porte door (1)
le portefeuille wallet, billfold (14)
porter to wear (P5;6)
   — un toast à to toast (P15)
portugais, -e Portuguese (9)
le portugais Portuguese (*language*) (9)
le Portugal Portugal (17)

poser une question to ask a question (11)
possible possible (5)
postal, -e: la carte —e post card (14)
la poste post office (2)
le poste de police police station (P10)
la poule hen (12)
pour for, (in order) to (P6;9); to (11)
le pourboire tip, gratuity (P9; 15)
pourquoi why (P3;4)
pourtant however (P8)
pouvoir can, to be able (P10; 11)
premier, -ière first (P1;12)
le — + *month* the first of (7)
prendre to take, to have (12)
— quelque chose to have something to eat (or drink) (12)
préparer to prepare, to fix (6)
près (de) near (5)
presque almost (7)
pressé, -e in a hurry (18)
le citron — lemonade, citron pressé (10)
prêter (à) to lend (to) (14)
prier: je vous (t')en prie you're welcome (5)
principal, -e; *pl.* principaux, -pales principal (13)
le role — the lead (*in a play*) (13)
le printemps spring (7)
au — in the spring (7)
pris *past participle of* prendre (16)
le prison: aller en—to go to prison (P11)
le problème problem (P14)
prochain, -e next (11)
le professeur, le prof teacher (1)
la profession profession (13)

les progrès *m.pl.* progress (P1;13)
faire des — to make progress (13)
les projets *m.pl.* plans (17)
prononcer to pronounce (15)
la prononciation pronunciation (P1)
le propos: à — by the way (P2)
provençal, -e; *pl.* provençaux, -çales of (from) Provence (16)
le proverbe proverb (P7)
les provisions *f.pl.* food (P)
pu *past participle of* pouvoir (16)
puis then (P2;12)
le pull-over sweater (3)
le pupitre student desk (2)

quand when (P5;6)
la quantité quantity (P18)
quarante forty (7)
le quart:
time + et — quarter past (9)
time + moins le — quarter to (9)
quatorze fourteen (4)
quatorzième fourteenth (P14)
quatre four (4)
quatre-vingt-dix ninety (13)
quatre-vingts eighty (13)
quatrième fourth (P4)
que what (12); that (13)
ne . . . — only (18)
québécois, -e of (from) Quebec, Québecois (10)
quel, quelle what, which (P5; 12)
à — heure? (at) what time (6)
de — couleur? what color? (5)
— âge avez-vous? how old are you? (12)
— heure est-il? what time is it? (6)
— jour sommes-nous? what day is it? (7)

— temps fait-il? what's it like out? (7)
quelque chose something (12)
prendre — to have something (to eat or drink) (12)
quelquefois sometimes (7)
quelques some, a few (14)
quelqu'un someone (18)
qu'est-ce que what? (6)
qu'est-ce qui what? (5)
— ne va pas? what's wrong? (16)
la question question (11)
poser une — to ask a question (11)
le questionnaire questionnaire (P3)
qui who (1); which (P13)
à — to whom (13)
— est-ce que whom? (12)
quinze fifteen (4)
— jours two weeks (17)
quinzième fifteenth (P15)
quitter to leave (18)
quoi what (P7;13)
à — what? (13)
de — what? about what? (14)

raconter to tell (P14)
la radio radio (6)
radoter to be "out of it" (P8)
la raison: avoir — to be right (8)
rater to fail (11)
recevoir to receive, to get (P11)
reconnaître to recognize (18)
reconnu *past participle of* reconnaître (18)
le réfrigérateur refrigerator (16)
regarder to watch, to look (at) (6)
— par to look out of (7)
le régime diet (15)
au — on a diet (15)
la région region (P18)

régler to solve (P14)
regretter to be sorry (18)
remercier to thank (14)
rencontrer to meet, to run into (P2;13)
les renseignements *m.pl.* information (18)
rentrer to come back, to go back, to return (6)
le repas meal (16)
répéter to repeat (P13)
répondre à to answer (10)
la réponse answer, response (11)
reposer to put back (P16)
le restaurant restaurant (5)
le reste rest (P16)
rester to stay, to remain (6)
retard: en — late (17)
retourner to go back (17)
ressembler à to resemble (P18)
réussir (à) + *infinitive* to succeed (in) (12)
— à un examen to pass a test (11)
le réveil alarm clock (14)
revenir to come back (P16; 17)
revenu *past participle of* revenir (17)
réviser to go over, to review (6)
la révision review (P1)
revoir: au — good-by (1)
la révolte revolt (P12)
se révolter to revolt (P12)
la revue magazine (P5)
la — de mode (de sports) fashion (sports) magazine (P6)
le rhinocéros rhinoceros (12)
riche rich (P3;5)
rien . . . ne nothing (P17;18)
risquer to risk (P18)
le riz rice (15)
la robe dress (3)
le rock rock music (P9)
le rôle part, role (13)
le — principal the lead *(in a play)* (13)
le roman novel (9)

le — policier detective novel (10)
le rond smoke ring (P16)
en — in a circle (P17)
le roseau, *pl.* les roseaux reed (P18)
le rôti de porc roast pork (15)
rouge red (P4;5)
rougir to become red, to blush (7)
rousse *see* roux
la route road; way (11)
en — (pour) on the way (to) (P2;11)
routière: la carte — road map (P18)
roux, rousse redheaded, a redhead (9)
la rue street (5)
russe Russian (10)
le russe Russian *(language)* (10)
la Russie Russia (17)

sa his, her, its (3)
le sable sand (8)
le sac purse (14)
sage well-behaved (10)
saignant, -e rare *(of meat)* (P15)
sais *see* savoir
la saison season (7)
la salade salad (15)
la — niçoise Nicoise salad (15)
la salle:
la — à manger dining room (16)
la — de classe classroom (1)
salut hello; good-by (2)
samedi *m.* Saturday (7)
le sandwich, *pl.* les sandwichs sandwich (15)
le — au jambon ham sandwich (P10)
sans without (18)
sauf except, but (18)
sauver to save (P13)
savoir to know, to know how (18)

je ne sais pas I don't know (12)
la science-fiction science fiction (P12)
les sciences sociales *f.pl.* social studies (11)
scolaire: l'année — school year (P18)
secrétaire *m.&f.* secretary (13)
le secteur division (P14)
seize sixteen (4)
seizième sixteenth (P16)
le sel salt (16)
le semaine week (7)
le Sénégal Senegal (17)
sénégalais, -e Senegalese (9)
le sens meaning (P)
sept seven (4)
septembre *m.* September (7)
septième seventh (P7)
la serveuse waitress (10)
le service:
à votre — at your service (5)
faire le — de to work the route of (P18)
le — est compris the tip is included (15)
la serviette napkin (16)
servir to serve, to wait on (9)
ses *pl.* his, her, its (3)
le set place mat (P16)
seul, -e only (10); alone (12)
seulement only (P7)
si if (P5;9); yes (8); so (P10)
s'il vous (te) plaît please (5;9)
signaler to report (P11)
le silence silence (18)
le singe monkey (12)
la situation situation (P14)
six six (4)
sixième sixth (P6)
le ski skiing (8)
faire du — to ski (8)
faire du — nautique to water-ski (8)
la piste de — ski run (P8)

social, -e; *pl.* sociaux, -ciales:
les sciences sociales
f.pl. social studies (11)
la sociéte company, business (14)
la — de transport moving
company (P14)
la sœur sister (3)
la soif: avoir — to be thirsty (8)
le soir evening, in the evening
(P4;6)
du — P.M. (6)
hier — last night, last evening (11)
tous les —s every night
(18)
la soirée (the whole) evening (11)
soixante sixty (7)
soixante-dix seventy (13)
le soldat soldier (13)
le soleil sun (7)
il fait du — it's sunny (7)
la somme amount (P11)
le sommeil: avoir — to be
sleepy (8)
son his, her, its (3)
le son sound (P)
sortir (de) to go out (9)
le sou: la machine à —s pinball
machine (P10)
la soucoupe saucer (16)
la soupe soup (15)
la — à l'oignon onion soup
(15)
la souris mouse (12)
sous under (3)
le souvenir souvenir (P18)
souvent often (7)
les sports *m.pl.* sports (6)
la revue de — sports mag-
azine (P6)
le stade stadium (5)
le stage training period, internship (13)
faire un — to train, to intern (13)
le steward steward (13)
le stylo pen (1)

su *past participle of* savoir (18)
le sucre sugar (15)
le sud south (17)
l'Amérique du Sud *f.*
South America (17)
le sud-est southeast (17)
le sud-ouest southwest (17)
la Suède Sweden (17)
suédois, -e Swedish (10)
le suédois Swedish (*language*)
(10)
suisse Swiss (P15)
la Suisse Switzerland (17)
la suite: tout de — right away
(P10;12)
supérieur, -e: les études —es
advanced studies (P13)
le supermarché supermarket (9)
sur on (3)
sûr: bien — of course, certainly (9)
la surprise-party informal party, get-together (14)
surtout especially (P9;14)
le suspect suspect (P11)
sympa likable, nice (14)

ta your (3)
la table table (2)
le tableau, *pl.* les tableaux
blackboard (2)
tant de so much, so many (18)
la tante aunt (3)
tard: plus — later (9)
il se fait — it's getting late
(P8)
la tarte pie (15)
la — aux pommes apple
pie (15)
la tasse cup (16)
te (t') to (for, from) you (14)
la télé TV (6)
le téléphone: au — on the
phone (P14)
téléphoner à to telephone, to
phone (9)
télévisé: le journal — TV
news (6)

le temps weather (7)
quel — fait-il? what's it
like out? what's the
weather like? (7)
le tennis tennis (6)
la terrasse d'un café sidewalk
café (10)
la terre land, earth (8)
la pomme de — potato
(15)
tes *pl.* your (3)
la tête head (P16)
le thé tea (15)
le théâtre theater (5)
le thème theme, composition
(P1)
le tigre tiger (12)
le timbre stamp (14)
le tiroir drawer (P16)
toast: porter un — à to toast
(P15)
toc! toc! knock! knock! (12)
toi you (1)
la tomate tomato (16)
tomber to fall (17)
ton your (P1;3)
le tort: avoir — to be wrong (8)
tôt early (P8)
toucher à to border on (P17)
toujours always, still (P5;6)
le tourisme tourism (13)
touriste *m.&f.* tourist (18)
le tournedos filet mignon (P15)
tourner to turn, to stir (P16)
tout, -e; *pl.* tous, toutes all;
every (P8;18)
après — after all (P17)
pas du — not at all (5)
tous (toutes) les deux both
(P15)
tous les jours every day
(18)
— à coup suddenly (12)
— de suite right away (P10;
12)
— le monde everyone, ev-
erybody (15)
le traducteur, la traductrice
translator (P11)
traduire to translate (P14)

le train train (4)
le traîneau: l'excursion en —
        f. sleigh ride (P8)
    tranquille tranquil, quiet
        (P18)
le transport transportation, mov-
        ing (P)
le travail, pl. les travaux work,
        job (13)
    travailler to work (6)
    treize thirteen (4)
    treizième thirteenth (P13)
    tréma diaeresis (¨) (P2)
    trente thirty (7)
    très very (1)
    triste sad, unhappy (6)
    trois three (P2;4)
    troisième third (P3)
    trop too (7)
        — de too much, too many
            (16;18)
    trouver to find (11)
        se — to be, to be located
            (17)
    tu you (2)
    typiquement typically (16)

    un, une one (4); a, an (P5;7)
    unique only (12)
    l'université f. university (11)
    l'usine f. factory (2)

les vacances f.pl. vacation (7)
    en — on vacation (7)
    passer des — to spend a
        vacation (17)
    prendre des — to take a
        vacation (17)
la vache cow (12)
la vaisselle dishes (8)
la valise suitcase (18)
    faire sa — to pack one's
        suitcase (18)

vaut; ça — la peine it's worth
    it (P12)
le veau: l'escalope de — f. veal
    cutlet (P15)
la veille (de) night before, eve
    (16)
    la — de Noël Christmas
        Eve (16)
le vélo bike (4)
le vendeur, la vendeuse sales-
        person (11)
    vendre to sell (10)
    vendredi m. Friday (7)
    venir to come (17)
        — de + infinitive to have
            just (17)
le vent wind (7)
    il fait du — it's windy (7)
    venu past participle of venir
        (17)
    vérifier to check (P1)
le verre glass (16)
    vers around, about (7); toward
        (P16)
    verser to pour (P15)
    vert, -e green (6)
la veste jacket (14)
la viande meat (15)
    vieux (vieil), vieille old (8;
        12)
        mon vieux, ma vieille old
            pal (16)
la villa villa (2)
la ville city, town (9)
    en — in(to) town (9)
le vin wine (15)
    le coq au — chicken cook-
        ed in wine (15)
    vingt twenty (4)
le violon violin (P14)
le violoncelle cello (P14)
la visite: faire une — à to visit
    (someone) (14)
    visiter to visit (a place) (17)
    vite quick! hurry! (4); quick-
        ly, fast (10)
le vocabulaire vocabulary (P1)

voici here is, here are (1)
voilà there is, there are (1)
la voile: le bateau à —s sail-
        boat (4)
    voir to see (13)
le voisin, la voisine neighbor (4)
la voiture car (4)
le vol theft (P11)
le volleyball volleyball (9)
    vos pl. your (4)
    votre your (4)
    vouloir to want (P8;11)
        je voudrais I'd like (11)
        nous voudrions we'd like
            (11)
        — dire to mean (11)
    voulu past participle of vou-
        loir (16)
    vous you (1;2); to (for, from)
        you (14)
le voyage trip (17)
    en — on a trip (17)
    faire un — to take a trip
        (8)
    vrai, -e real (P5); true (P11)
    vraiment really, truly (10)
    vu past participle of voir (P12;
        16)

le weekend weekend (P13)
le western western (movie) (9)
le wolof Wolof (a Senegalese
        language) (9)

    y there; it (15)
        il y a there is, there are (5)
        il y a + time ago (17)
la Yougoslavie Yugoslavia (17)

    zéro zero (7)
le zoo zoo (12)
    zut! darn! (7)

English-French Vocabulary

The *English-French Vocabulary* contains active vocabulary only.

a, an un, une (7)
able: to be — pouvoir (11)
about de (6); vers (7)
 — what de quoi (14)
above au-dessus de (12)
to accompany accompagner (14)
acquainted: to be — with
  connaître (18)
across from en face de (5)
actor l'acteur *m.* (13)
actress l'actrice *f.* (13)
afraid: to be — (of) avoir
  peur (de) (8)
Africa l'Afrique *f.* (17)
after, afterward après (7)
afternoon l'après-midi *m.* (6)
 in the — l'après-midi *m.*
  (6); *time* + de l'après-
  midi (6)
ago il y a + *time* (17)
airplane l'avion *m.* (4)
airport l'aéroport *m.* (5)
alarm clock le réveil (14)
algebra l'algèbre *f.* (11)
all tout, -e; *pl.* tous, toutes
  (18)
 not at — pas du tout (5)
almost presque (7)
alone seul, -e (12)
already déjà (11)
also aussi (4)
always toujours (6)
a.m. du matin (6)
America l'Amérique *f.* (17)
 Central — l'Amérique centrale (17)

North — l'Amérique du
  Nord (17)
 South — l'Amérique du
  Sud (17)
American américain, -e (2; 9)
and et (1)
animal l'animal, *pl.* les animaux *m.* (12)
to announce annoncer (15)
annoying embêtant, -e (18)
answer la réponse (11)
to answer répondre à (10)
any des (7); *(after negative)* de
  (7;15); en (15)
 not — more ne . . . plus
  (18)
anybody, anyone; not — ne
  . . . personne (18)
anything: not — ne . . . rien
  (18)
apartment l'appartement *m.*
  (2)
 — building l'immeuble *m.*
  (18)
appetizer les hors-d'œuvre
  m.pl. (15)
apple la pomme (15)
 — pie la tarte aux pommés
  (15)
April avril *m.* (7)
around vers (7)
to arrive arriver (6)
artist l'artiste *m.&f.* (13)
as comme (13)
Asia l'Asie *f.* (17)
to ask, to ask for demander (6)
 to — a question poser une
  question (11)
 to — (someone), to — (someone) for demander à (6)
Athens Athènes (10)

Atlantic Ocean l'Atlantique
  f. (17)
at à (3); chez (3)
 — last enfin (12)
to attend assister à (11)
August août *m.* (7)
aunt la tante (3)
Australia l'Australie *f.* (17)
Austria l'Autriche *f.* (17)
author l'auteur *m.* (9)
autumn l'automne *m.* (7)
awful affreux, -euse (18)

bad mal (1); mauvais, -e (9)
 it's — out il fait mauvais
  (7)
badly mal (10)
baggage les bagages *m.pl.*
  (18)
bank la banque (2)
basketball le basketball (9)
 to play — jouer au basketball (9)
bathing suit le maillot (3)
to be être (3); se trouver (17)
beach la plage (2)
beans les haricots verts *m.pl.*
  (15)
bear l'ours *m.* (12)
beautiful beau (bel), belle
  (8;12)
because parce que (4)
to become devenir (17)
beer la bière (10)
before avant (7)
 the night — la veille (de)
  (16)
to begin commencer (15)

beginning le commencement (18)

behind derrière (4)

Belgian belge (10)

Belgium la Belgique (17)

to believe croire (13)

below au-dessous de (12)

belt la ceinture (14)

beside à côté de (5)

bet: you — en effet (18)

beverage la boisson (10)

big grand, -e (6)

bike le vélo (4)

bill l'addition f. (15)

billfold le portefeuille (14)

biology la biologie (11)

bird l'oiseau, pl. les oiseaux (12)

birthday l'anniversaire m. (14)

black noir, -e (5)

blackboard le tableau, pl. les tableaux (2)

blond blond, -e (9)

blouse la blouse (3)

blue bleu, -e (5)

to blush rougir (7)

boat le bateau, pl. les bateaux (4)

sail — le bateau à voiles (4)

book le livre (1)

bookstore la librairie (11)

boring ennuyeux, -euse (14)

born né, -e (17)

to be — naître (17)

to borrow (from) emprunter (à) (14)

bouillabaisse la bouillabaisse (16)

boutique la boutique (13)

bowl le bol (16)

box la boîte (18)

boy le garçon (3)

bracelet le bracelet (14)

bread le pain (15)

to break casser (16)

breakfast le petit déjeuner (6)

to have — déjeuner (6)

to bring apporter (6)

brother le frère (3)

brown brun, -e (9)

brunette brun, -e (9)

Brussels Bruxelles (10)

building: apartment — l'immeuble m. (18)

bus l'autobus m. (2)

business la société (14)

businessman l'homme d'affaires m. (13)

businesswoman la femme d'affaires f. (13)

busy occupé, -e (10)

but mais (3); sauf (18)

butter le beurre (15)

by en (4); par (4); au bord de (12)

café le café (5)

sidewalk — la terrasse d'un café (10)

café au lait le café au lait (16)

calendar le calendrier (2)

camper la caravane (17)

to camp out faire du camping (17)

can see able

Canada le Canada (17)

Canadian canadien, -ienne (2;9)

car la voiture (4)

caramel custard la crème caramel (15)

card la carte (6)

to play —s jouer aux cartes (6)

post — la carte postale (14)

cartoon: movie — le dessin animé (6)

castle le château (5)

cat le chat (12)

celebration la fête (14)

Central America l'Amérique centrale f. (17)

certainly bien sûr (9)

chair la chaise (2)

chalk la craie (2)

chapter le chapitre (11)

château le château, pl. les châteaux (5)

check l'addition f. (15)

cheese le fromage (15)

grilled ham and — le croque-monsieur (15)

chemistry la chimie (11)

chess les échecs m.pl. (6)

to play — jouer aux échecs (6)

chicken la poule (12)

— cooked in wine le coq au vin (15)

child l'enfant m.&f. (3)

China la Chine (17)

Chinese chinois, -e (9); le chinois (9)

chocolate mousse la mousse au chocolat (15)

choice le choix (9)

to choose choisir (7)

Christmas Noël (7)

— Eve la veille de Noël (16)

church l'église f. (2)

Citroën 2-CV car la deux-chevaux (17)

citron pressé le citron pressé (10)

city la ville (9)

to (in) the — en ville (9)

class la classe (1); le cours (11)

classroom la salle de classe (1)

to clear débarrasser (16)

clerk l'employé m., l'employée f. (de bureau) (13)

to climb monter (17)

climbing: to go mountain- — faire de l'alpinisme m. (8)

clock: alarm — le réveil (14)

to close fermer (6)

cloud le nuage (8)

clothes les habits m.pl. (3)

coat le manteau, pl. les manteaux (14)

rain — l'imperméable m. (14)

coffee le café (10)

a cup of — un café (10)

Coke le Coca (10)

cold froid, -e (8)
   it's — out il fait froid (7)
   to be — *(of people)* avoir froid (8)
color la couleur (5)
   what —? de quelle couleur? (5)
to come venir (17)
   to — back rentrer (6); revenir (17)
   to — down descendre (17)
   to — in entrer (dans) (6)
   to — up monter (17)
company la société (14)
concert le concert (9)
concierge le/la concierge (12)
congratulations! félicitations! (14)
continent le continent (17)
to cook faire la cuisine (16)
cool: it's — out il fait frais (7)
Copenhagen Copenhague (10)
coq au vin le coq au vin (15)
corner le coin (5)
   on the — au coin de la rue (5)
correct correct, -e (11)
to cost coûter (10)
to count compter (11)
country la campagne (2); le pays (17)
course:
   of — bien sûr (9)
   of — not mais non (2)
cousin le cousin, la cousine (3)
cow la vache (12)
cream la crème (15)
cup la tasse (16)
   — of coffee un café (10)

dad papa *m.* (9)
dance la danse (14)
to dance danser (14)

Danish danois, -e (10); le danois (10)
dark: it's — out il fait nuit (8)
date la date (7)
daughter la fille (3)
day le jour (7); la journée (11)
   Father's (Mother's) Day la Fête des Pères (des Mères) (11)
   it's —time il fait jour (8)
   what — is it? quel jour sommes-nous? (7)
December décembre *m.* (7)
Denmark le Danemark (17)
dentist le/la dentiste (13)
department store le grand magasin (9)
desk le bureau, *pl.* les bureaux (2); le pupitre (2)
dessert le dessert (15)
detective:
   — film le film policier (6)
   — novel le roman policier (10)
to die mourir (17)
diet le régime (15)
   on a — au régime (15)
difficult difficile (5)
to dine dîner (6)
dining room la salle à manger (16)
dinner le dîner (6)
   to have — dîner (6)
dishes la vaisselle (8)
to dive plonger (15)
to do faire (6;8)
doctor le médecin (13)
documentary le documentaire (6)
dog le chien (12)
door la porte (1)
down: to come (go) — descendre (17)
dragon le dragon (8)
dress la robe (3)
drink la boisson (10)
to drink: to have something to — prendre quelque chose (12)

duck le canard (12)
dull ennuyeux, -euse (14)
dumb bête (10)
during pendant (9)
Dutch hollandais, -e (10); le hollandais (10)

each chaque (14)
early de bonne heure (17)
earth la terre (8)
east l'est *m.* (17)
easy facile (5)
to eat manger (15)
   to have something to — prendre quelque chose (12)
egg l'œuf *m.* (15)
eight huit (4)
eighteen dix-huit (4)
eighty quatre-vingts (13)
elephant l'éléphant *m.* (12)
eleven onze (4)
employee l'employé *m.*, l'employée *f.* (13)
end la fin (18)
energetic énergique (6)
engaged fiancé, -e (12)
engineer l'ingénieur *m.* (13)
England l'Angleterre *f.* (17)
English anglais, -e (9); l'anglais *m.* (9)
enough assez (de) (16)
to enter entrer (dans) (6)
enthusiastic (about) passionné, -e (par) (13)
envelope l'enveloppe *f.* (14)
eraser la gomme (1)
especially surtout (14)
Europe l'Europe *f.* (17)
eve la veille (de) (16)
   Christmas Eve la veille de Noël (16)
evening le soir (6); la soirée (11)
   in the — le soir (6); *time* + du soir (6)
   last — hier soir (11)
every chaque (14); tous les, toutes les (18)

everybody, everyone tout le monde (15)
exam l'examen *m.* (11)
   to fail an — rater un examen (11)
   to pass an — réussir à un examen (11)
   to take an — passer un examen (11)
example: for — par exemple (11)
excellent excellent, -e (15)
except sauf (18)
excuse me pardon (5)
expensive cher, chère (11)
   to be — coûter cher (10)
   to be in — coûter peu (10)

factory l'usine *f.* (2)
to fail rater (11)
fall l'automne *m.* (7)
to fall tomber (17)
family la famille (3)
famous célèbre (9)
far (from) loin (de) (5)
farm la ferme (12)
farmer l'agriculteur *m.* (12)
fast vite (10)
fat gros, grosse (9)
   to get — grossir (7)
father le père (3)
   Father's Day la Fête des Pères (11)
February février *m.* (7)
few peu de (18)
   a — quelques (14)
fiancé(e) le fiancé, la fiancée (12)
fifteen quinze (4)
   6:15 six heures et quart (9)
fifty cinquante (7)
film le film (6)
   detective — le film policier (6)
finally enfin (12)
to find trouver (11)
fine: things are — ça va bien (1)
to finish finir (7)

first premier, -ière (12)
   (at) — d'abord (9)
   the — of le premier + *month* (7)
fish le poisson (15)
   — stew la bouillabaisse (16)
five cinq (4)
to fix préparer (6)
flag le drapeau, *pl.* les drapeaux (2)
Flemish flamand, -e (10); le flamand (10)
flower la fleur (4)
foot: on — à pied (4)
football le football américain (6)
   to play — jouer au football américain (6)
for pour (9)
foreign étranger, -ère (10)
to forget oublier (14)
fork la fourchette (16)
forty quarante (7)
   —-five quarante-cinq (7)
   5:45 six heures moins le quart (9)
four quatre (4)
fourteen quatorze (4)
franc le franc (10)
France la France (17)
free libre (10)
to freeze geler (9)
   it's freezing il gèle (7)
French français, -e (2;9); le français (9)
French fries les pommes frites *f.pl.* (15)
Friday vendredi *m.* (7)
friend l'ami *m.,* l'amie *f.* (2); le copain, la copine (4)
to frighten faire peur à (12)
from de (6)
   across — en face de (5)
front: in — of devant (4)
fruit les fruits *m.pl.* (15)

to gain weight grossir (7)

game le match, *pl.* les matchs (6)
garage le garage (4)
garden le jardin (4)
garlic l'ail *m.* (16)
generous généreux, -euse (6)
gentleman le monsieur, *pl.* les messieurs (10)
   ladies and gentlemen messieurs-dames (15)
geography la géographie (11)
geometry la géométrie (11)
German allemand, -e (9); l'allemand *m.* (9)
Germany l'Allemagne *f.* (17)
gesture le geste (11)
to get:
   — fat grossir (7)
   — off (out of) descendre (de) (17)
   — on (in) monter (dans) (17)
   let's — going allons-y! (4)
gift le cadeau, *pl.* les cadeaux (11)
giraffe la girafe (12)
girl la jeune fille (3); la fille (10)
to give (to) donner à (6); offrir à (11)
glass le verre (16)
glove le gant (14)
to go aller (2)
   to — back rentrer (6); retourner (17)
   to — camping faire du camping (17)
   to — down descendre (17)
   to — in entrer (dans) (6)
   to — out sortir (de) (9)
   to — over réviser (6)
   to — shopping faire des achats (8)
   to — up monter (17)
   to — with accompagner (14)

good bon, bonne (9)
— in (+ *school subjects*) fort,
-e en (11)
no — in (+ *school subjects*)
nul, nulle en (11)
good-by au revoir (1); salut
(2)
grandfather le grand-père (3)
grandmother la grand-mère
(3)
grandparents les grands-parents *m.pl.* (3)
grass l'herbe *f.* (4)
gratuity le pourboire (15)
gray gris, -e (6)
great! chouette! (4); chic! (7)
Greece la Grèce (17)
greedy avare (6)
Greek grec, grecque (10); le
grec (10)
green vert, -e (6)
— beans les haricots verts
m.pl. (15)
grenadine la grenadine (10)
grilled ham and cheese le
croque-monsieur (15)
Guignol le Guignol (4)
guitar la guitare (14)
to play the — jouer de la
guitare (14)
gymnasium le gymnase (9)

Haiti Haïti (17)
half past *time* + et demie (9)
ham le jambon (15)
grilled — and cheese le
croque-monsieur (15)
handkerchief le mouchoir
(14)
handsome beau (bel), belle
(8;12)
happy heureux, -euse (6)
— birthday bon anniver-
saire (14)
hard difficile (5)

hat le chapeau, *pl.* les chapeaux (3)
to have avoir (4); prendre (12)
— to il faut (9)
he il (2)
to hear entendre (10)
heaven le ciel (8)
heck no mais non (2)
hello bonjour (1); salut (2);
(on telephone) allô (9)
hen la poule (12)
her elle (3); sa, son, ses (3);
la (l') (13)
to (for, from) — lui (14)
here ici (5); là (5)
— is, — are voici (1)
to hide cacher (16)
high school le lycée (5)
him lui (3); le (l') (13)
to (for, from) — lui (14)
hippopotamus l'hippopotame
m. (12)
his sa, son, ses (3)
history l'histoire *f.* (11)
to hitchhike faire de l'auto-stop
m. (8)
hockey le hockey (9)
to play — jouer au hockey
(9)
home: at — chez + moi, toi,
etc. (2)
homework les devoirs *m.pl.*
(6)
hors d'œuvres les hors-d'œuvre *m.pl.* (15)
horse le cheval, *pl.* les chevaux (12)
hospital l'hôpital, *pl.* les hôpitaux *m.* (2)
hot chaud, -e (8)
it's — out il fait chaud (7)
to be — *(of people)* avoir
chaud (8)
hotel l'hôtel *m.* (2)
hour l'heure *f.* (6)
house la maison (2)
at (to) the — of chez (2)
housewife la ménagère (13)
housework: to do the —
faire le ménage (16)
how comment (5)
— are things? ça va? (1)

— many, — much com-
bien de (5)
— much is? *(in math)* combien font (8)
— old are you? quel âge
avez-vous? (12)
to know — savoir (18)
however cependant (18)
hundred cent (13)
hungry: to be — avoir faim
(8)
hurry! vite! (4)
in a — pressé, -e (18)
husband le mari (12)

I je (2); moi (3)
ice la glace (7)
ice cream la glace (10)
— bar l'esquimau, *pl.* les
esquimaux *m.* (10)
if si (9)
impossible impossible (5)
in à (3); dans (4); en (3)
included: tip — le service
est compris (15)
indeed en effet (18)
indoors à l'intérieur (7)
inexpensive: to be — coûter
peu (10)
information les renseignements *m.pl.* (18)
inside à l'intérieur (7)
interesting intéressant, -e (14)
to intern faire un stage (13)
internship le stage (13)
into dans (4)
to invite inviter (14)
it elle, il (2); le, la, l' (13); y
(15)
— is c'est (1); il (elle) est
(3)
its sa, son, ses (3)
Italian italien, -ienne (9); l'italien *m.* (9)
Italy l'Italie *f.* (17)

jacket la veste (14)
ski — l'anorak *m.* (8)

jam la confiture (15)
janitor le/la concierge (12)
January janvier *m.* (7)
Japan le Japon (17)
Japanese japonais, -e (9); le japonais (9)
jeans le jean (4)
job l'emploi *m.* (13)
judge le juge (13)
July juillet *m.* (7)
June juin *m.* (7)
just: to have — venir de + *infinitive* (17)

key la clef (18)
kind aimable (10)
kitchen la cuisine (16)
knife le couteau, *pl.* les couteaux (16)
to knock (on) frapper (à) (12)
to know connaître (18); savoir (18)
    I don't — je ne sais pas (12)
    to — how savoir (18)

laborer l'ouvrier *m.*, l'ouvrière *f.* (13)
ladies and gentlemen messieurs-dames (15)
lady la dame (10)
    young — mademoiselle, *pl.* mesdemoiselles (1;3); la demoiselle (15)
lake le lac (8)
lamb: leg of — le gigot (15)
land la terre (8)
language la langue (10)
large grand, -e (6); gros, grosse (9)
last dernier, -ière (11)
    at — enfin (12)
    — evening hier soir (11)
    — night hier soir (11)
late en retard (17)
    to sleep — faire la grasse matinée (11)
later plus tard (9)

lawyer l'avocat *m.*, l'avocate *f.* (13)
lazy paresseux, -euse (6)
lead *(in a play)* le rôle principal, *pl.* les rôles principaux (13)
leaf la feuille (4)
to learn apprendre (12)
    to — by heart apprendre par cœur (8)
    to — how apprendre à + *infinitive* (12)
to leave partir (de) (9); quitter (18)
    to — (something) behind laisser (14)
left: to the — (of) à gauche (de) (5)
leg of lamb le gigot (15)
lemonade le citron pressé (10)
to lend (to) prêter (à) (14)
leopard le léopard (12)
lesson la leçon (6)
let's *1 pl. form of any verb* (2)
letter la lettre (13)
library la bibliothèque (9)
light: it's — out il fait jour (8)
likable sympa (14)
to like aimer (6)
    I'd — je voudrais (11)
    we'd — nous voudrions (11)
lion le lion (12)
Lisbon Lisbonne (9)
to listen (to) écouter (6)
little petit, -e (6)
    a — un peu (de) (18)
to live (in) habiter (6)
lively énergique (6)
located: to be — se trouver (17)
to lock fermer à clef (18)
London Londres (9)
long long, longue (9)
    a — time longtemps (17)
longer: no — ne . . . plus (18)
to look (at) regarder (6)
    to — for chercher (11)
    to — out of regarder par (7)

to — well avoir bonne mine (16)
to lose perdre (10)
    to — weight maigrir (7)
lot:
    a — beaucoup (5)
    a — of beaucoup de (16)
    a — of people beaucoup de monde (14)
to love aimer (6)
luck:
    good —! bon courage! (14)
    to be lucky avoir de la chance (14)
luggage les bagages *m.pl.* (18)
lunch le déjeuner (6)
    to have — déjeuner (6)

ma'am, madam madame, *pl.* mesdames (1;3)
mailman le facteur (13)
to make faire (8)
Mali le Mali (17)
Malian malien, -ienne (13)
man l'homme *m.* (10); le monsieur, *pl.* les messieurs (10)
many beaucoup de (16)
    how — combien de (5)
    so — tant de (18)
    too — trop de (16)
map la carte (2)
March mars *m.* (7)
market le marché (9)
    super— le supermarché (9)
married marié, -e (12)
match le match, *pl.* les matchs (6)
math(ematics) les mathématiques, les maths *f.pl.* (11)
May mai *m.* (7)
maybe peut-être (10)

me moi (3)

   to (for, from) — me (m')
(14)

meal le repas (16)

mean méchant, -e (12)

to mean vouloir dire (11)

meat la viande (15)

Mediterranean la Méditer-
ranée (17)

to meet rencontrer (13)

to memorize apprendre par
cœur (12)

mess le gâchis (16)

Mexican mexicain, -e (9)

Mexico le Mexique (17)

Mexico City Mexico (9)

middle: in the — of au milieu de (12)

midnight minuit (6)

milk le lait (15)

mineral water l'eau minérale
f. (15)

minus moins (8)

Miss mademoiselle (1)

mistake la faute (8)

mom maman f. (9)

Monday lundi m. (7)

money l'argent m. (10)

monkey le singe (12)

month le mois (7)

Montreal Montréal (9)

moon la lune (8)

more: no — ne . . . plus (18)

morning le matin (6); la matinée (11)

   every — tous les matins
(18)

in the — le matin (6); time
+ du matin (6)

Moscow Moscou (10)

mother la mère (3); maman
f. (9)

   Mother's Day la Fête des
Mères (11)

motorbike la moto (4)

mountain la montagne (2)

to go —-climbing faire
de l'alpinisme m. (8)

to (in) the —s à la mon-
tagne (2)

mouse la souris (12)

mousse: chocolate — la
mousse au chocolat
(15)

movie le film (6)

   — cartoon le dessin animé (6)

   —s le cinéma (5)

   — theater le cinéma (5)

Mr. Monsieur (1)

Mrs. Madame (1)

much beaucoup de (16)

   how — combien (de) (5)

   so — tant (de) (18)

   too — trop (de) (16)

   very — beaucoup (5)

museum le musée (5)

music la musique (14)

must il faut (9)

my ma, mon, mes (3)

name: my — is je m'appelle
(1)

napkin la serviette (16)

narrow étroit, -e (9)

natural naturel, -le (11)

naughty méchant, -e (12)

near près (de) (5)

nearby à côté (10)

neat! chic! (7)

necessary: it's — il faut (9)

necklace le collier (14)

necktie la cravate (14)

to need avoir besoin de (14)

neighbor le voisin, la voisine
(4)

nephew le neveu, pl. les neveux (3)

the Netherlands les Pays-Bas
m.pl. (17)

never ne . . . jamais (18)

new nouveau (nouvel), nouvelle (8;12)

news: TV — le journal télévisé (6)

newspaper le journal, pl. les
journaux (6)

next (adj.) prochain, -e (11);
(adv.) ensuite (15)

   — to à côté de (5)

nice aimable (10); sympa (14)

   it's — out il fait beau (7)

Niçoise salad la salade niçoise (15)

niece la nièce (3)

night la nuit (8)

   every — tous les soirs (18)

   it's —time il fait nuit (8)

   last — hier soir (11)

   the — before la veille (de)
(16)

nine neuf (4)

nineteen dix-neuf (4)

ninety quatre-vingt-dix (13)

no non (1); pas de + noun (8)

   heck — mais non (2)

   — good in + school subjects nul, nulle en (11)

   — longer ne . . . plus (18)

   — one personne . . . ne
(18)

nobody personne . . . ne (18)

noise le bruit (18)

noon midi (6)

north le nord (17)

North America l'Amérique
du Nord f. (17)

northeast le nord-est (17)

northwest le nord-ouest (17)

Norway la Norvège (17)

Norwegian norvégien, -ienne
(10); le norvégien (10)

not pas (1;8); ne . . . pas (4)

   — any more ne . . . plus
(18)

   — anyone ne . . . personne (18)

   — anything ne . . . rien
(18)

   — at all pas du tout (5)

   of course — mais non (2)

notebook le cahier (1)

nothing rien . . . ne (18)

novel le roman (9)

   detective — le roman policier (10)

November novembre *m.* (7)
now maintenant (5)
nurse l'infirmier *m.*, l'infirmière *f.* (13)

occupation la profession (13)
occupied occupé, -e (10)
ocean l'océan *m.* (17)
o'clock une heure, deux heures, etc. (6)
October octobre *m.* (7)
of de (2;5)
off: to get — descendre (de) (17)
to offer (to) offrir à (11)
office le bureau, *pl.* les bureaux (5)
— clerk l'employé *m.*, l'employée *f.* de bureau (13)
post — la poste (2)
often souvent (7)
oil l'huile *f.* (16)
okay d'accord (3)
old vieux (vieil), vieille (8;12)
how — are you? quel âge avez-vous? (12)
— pal mon vieux, ma vieille (16)
older aîné, -e (12)
omelette l'omelette *f.* (15)
on sur (3); à (4)
to get — monter (dans) (17)
once une fois (18)
one un, une (4)
onion l'oignon (15)
— soup la soupe à l'oignon (15)
only seul, -e (10); unique (12); ne . . . que (18)
to open ouvrir (6)
opera (house) l'opéra *m.* (5)
opposite en face de (5)
or ou (5)
orangeade l'orangeade *f.* (10)
order: in — to pour (9)
to order commander (10)
to organize organiser (14)
other autre (10)
our notre, nos (4)

out:
to get — of descendre (de) (17)
to go — sortir (de) (9)
outdoors dehors (7)
outside dehors (7)
over:
— there là-bas (3)
to go — réviser (6)
overcoat le manteau, *pl.* les manteaux (14)
oyster l'huître *f.* (15)

Pacific Ocean le Pacifique (17)
to pack (one's bags) faire ses bagages *m.pl.* (18)
package le paquet (14)
page la page (2)
pal: old — mon vieux, ma vieille (16)
pants le pantalon (3)
paper le papier (1)
(news) — le journal, *pl.* les journaux (6)
paperback le livre de poche (11)
pardon me pardon (5)
parents les parents *m.pl.* (3)
park le parc (4)
part (*in a play*) le rôle (13)
party la fête (14); la surprise-party (14)
to pass (a test) réussir à (un examen) (11)
pastry la pâtisserie (15)
peas les petits pois *m.pl.* (15)
Peking Pékin (9)
pen le stylo (1)
pencil le crayon (1)
people les gens *m.pl.* (10)
a lot of — beaucoup de monde (14)
pepper le poivre (16)
perhaps peut-être (10)
pharmacist le pharmacien, la pharmacienne (13)
pharmacy la pharmacie (13)
to phone téléphoner à (9)
photo(graph) la photo (11)

physics la physique (11)
piano le piano (14)
to play the — jouer du piano (14)
picture l'image *f.* (2); la photo (11)
pie la tarte (15)
apple — la tarte aux pommes (15)
pig le cochon (12)
pilot le pilote (13)
to place mettre (16)
plane l'avion *m.* (4)
plans les projets *m.pl.* (17)
plate l'assiette *f.* (16)
play la pièce (6)
to put on a — jouer une pièce (13)
to play jouer (6)
to — (*musical instruments*) jouer de (14)
to — (*sports & games*) jouer à (6)
please s'il vous (te) plaît (5; 9)
p.m. de l'après-midi (6); du soir (6)
poem le poème (9)
poet le poète (9)
poison le poison (16)
Poland la Pologne (17)
policeman l'agent *m.* (5)
pool: swimming — la piscine (2)
poor pauvre (5)
pork roast le rôti de porc (15)
port le port (5)
Portugal le Portugal (17)
Portuguese portugais, -e (9); le portugais (9)
possible possible (5)
post card la carte postale (14)
poster l'affiche *f.* (1)
postman le facteur (13)
post office la poste (2)
potato la pomme de terre (15)

to prefer aimer mieux (6)
to prepare préparer (6)
present le cadeau, *pl.* les cadeaux (11)
pretty joli, -e (5)
— + *adj.* assez (12)
profession la profession (13)
progress: to make — faire des progrès *m.pl.* (13)
to pronounce prononcer (15)
Provence: of (from) — provençal, -e; *pl.* provençaux, -çales (16)
Punch and Judy le Guignol (4)
pupil l'élève *m.&f.* (1)
purse le sac (14)
to put (in, on) mettre (16)
to — on a play jouer une pièce (13)

quarter:
— past (six) (six) heures et quart (9)
— to (six) (six) heures moins le quart (9)
québecois québécois, -e (10)
question la question (11)
to ask a — poser une question (11)
quick! vite! (4)
quickly vite (10)
quite assez (12)

radio la radio (6)
railroad station la gare (2)
rain la pluie (7)
to rain pleuvoir (9)
it's —ing il pleut (7)
raincoat l'imperméable *m.* (14)
rather assez + *adj.* (12)
to read lire (14)

really vraiment (10)
to recognize reconnaître (18)
record le disque (6)
— player l'électrophone *m.* (14)
recorder: tape — le magnétophone (2)
red rouge (5)
to turn — rougir (7)
redheaded, a redhead roux, rousse (9)
refrigerator le réfrigérateur (16)
to remain rester (6)
response la réponse (11)
restaurant le restaurant (5)
to return rentrer (6)
to review réviser (6)
rhinoceros le rhinocéros (12)
rice le riz (15)
rich riche (5)
right:
— away tout de suite (12)
to be — avoir raison (8)
to the — (of) à droite (de) (5)
ring la bague (14)
river le fleuve (8)
the Riviera la Côte d'Azur (5)
road la route (11)
roast pork le rôti de porc (15)
role le rôle (13)
lead — le rôle principal, *pl.* les rôles principaux (13)
room:
class — la salle de classe (1)
dining — la salle à manger (16)
rooster le coq (12)
to run into rencontrer (13)
Russia la Russie (17)
Russian russe (10); le russe (10)

sad triste (6)
sailboat le bateau à voiles (4)
sailor le marin (13)

salad la salade (15)
salesperson le vendeur, la vendeuse (11)
salt le sel (16)
same même (10)
sand le sable (8)
sandwich le sandwich, *pl.* les sandwichs (15)
Saturday samedi *m.* (7)
saucer la soucoupe (16)
to say (to) dire (à) (14)
to scare faire peur à (12)
scarf le foulard (14)
school l'école *f.* (2)
high — le lycée (5)
sea la mer (8)
season la saison (7)
secretary le/la secrétaire (13)
to see voir (13)
to sell vendre (10)
Senegal le Sénégal (17)
Senegalese sénégalais, -e (9)
sentence la phrase (11)
September septembre *m.* (7)
to serve servir (9)
service: at your — à votre service (5)
to set the table mettre le couvert (16)
seven sept (4)
seventeen dix-sept (4)
seventy soixante-dix (13)
several plusieurs (14)
she elle (2)
sheep le mouton (12)
shirt la chemise (3)
shoe la chaussure (3)
shop la boutique (13)
to shop faire des achats (8)
short petit, -e (6); court, -e (9)
to show (to) montrer à (6)
sidewalk café la terrasse d'un café (10)
silence le silence (18)
to sing chanter (14)
sink l'évier *m.* (16)
sir monsieur, *pl.* messieurs (1;3)
sister la sœur (3)
six six (4)
sixteen seize (4)

sixty soixante (7)
to ski faire du ski (8)
   to water- — faire du ski nautique (8)
ski jacket l'anorak *m.* (8)
skiing le ski (8)
skinny maigre (9)
skirt la jupe (3)
sky le ciel (8)
slacks le pantalon (3)
to sleep dormir (9)
   to — late faire la grasse matinée (11)
sleepy: to be — avoir sommeil (8)
slowly lentement (10)
small petit, -e (6)
smart calé, -e (10)
snack le goûter (6)
snail l'escargot *m.* (15)
snow la neige (7)
to snow neiger (7)
so alors (3)
   — much, — many tant de (18)
soccer le football (6)
   to play — jouer au football (6)
social studies les sciences sociales *f.pl.* (11)
sock la chaussette (3)
soldier le soldat (13)
some des (7;15); quelques (14); de la (l'), du (15); en (15)
someone quelqu'un (18)
something quelque chose (12)
   to have — (to eat or drink) prendre quelque chose (12)
sometimes quelquefois (7)
son le fils (3)
song la chanson (14)
soon bientôt (12)
sorry: to be — regretter (18)
so-so comme ci, comme ça (1)
soup la soupe (15)
   onion — la soupe à l'oignon (15)
south le sud (17)

South America l'Amérique du Sud *f.* (17)
southeast le sud-est (17)
southwest le sud-ouest (17)
Spain l'Espagne *f.* (17)
Spanish espagnol, -e (9); l'espagnol *m.* (9)
to speak parler (6)
to spend *(time)* passer (11)
spoon la cuillère (16)
sports les sports *m.pl.* (6)
spring le printemps (7)
   in the — au printemps (7)
stadium le stade (5)
stamp le timbre (14)
star l'étoile *f.* (8)
to start commencer (15)
station: railroad — la gare (2)
to stay rester (6)
steak le bifteck (15)
steward le steward (13)
stewardess l'hôtesse de l'air (13)
still toujours (6)
stingy avare (6)
stocking le bas (3)
store le magasin (13)
   book — la librairie (11)
   department — le grand magasin (9)
story l'histoire *f.* (11)
stove la cuisinière (16)
stranger l'inconnu *m.*, l'inconnue *f.* (12)
street la rue (5)
student l'élève *m.&f.* (1); l'étudiant *m.*, l'étudiante *f.* (11)
studies: social — les sciences sociales *f.pl.* (11)
to study étudier (6)
stupid bête (10)
to succeed (in) réussir à + *infinitive* (12)
suddenly tout à coup (12)
sugar le sucre (15)
suit le complet (14)
   bathing — le maillot (3)
suitcase la valise (18)

to pack one's — faire sa valise (18)
summer l'été *m.* (7)
sun le soleil (7)
   it's sunny il fait du soleil (7)
Sunday dimanche *m.* (7)
supermarket le supermarché (9)
sweater le pull-over (3)
Sweden la Suède (17)
Swedish suédois, -e (10); le suédois (10)
to swim nager (15)
swimming pool la piscine (2)
Switzerland la Suisse (17)

table la table (2)
   to set the — mettre le couvert (16)
tablecloth la nappe (16)
to take prendre (12)
   to — *(courses)* faire de + *course* (11)
   to — a test passer un examen (11)
   to — a trip faire un voyage (8)
to talk parler (6)
tape la bande (2)
   — recorder le magnétophone (2)
tea le thé (15)
to teach enseigner (11)
teacher le professeur, le prof (1)
to telephone téléphoner à (9)
television la télé (6)
to tell dire (à) (14)
ten dix (4)
tennis le tennis (6)
   to play — jouer au tennis (6)
terrible affreux, -euse (18)

test l'examen *m.* (11)
    to fail a — rater un examen (11)
    to pass a — réussir à un examen (11)
    to take a — passer un examen (11)
to thank remercier (14)
    thank you, thanks merci (1)
    that ça (1); ce (cet), cette (10); que (13)
    — is c'est (1)
the le, la, l' (1); les (2)
theater le théâtre (5)
    movie — le cinéma (5)
their leur, -s (4)
them elles, eux (3); les (13)
    to (for, from) — leur (14)
then alors (3); puis (12); ensuite (15)
there là (5); y (15)
    over — là-bas (3)
    — is, — are voilà (1); il y a (5)
these ces (10)
    — are ce sont (2)
they elles, ils, on (2); eux (3)
    — are ce (ils, elles) sont (2; 3)
thin maigre (9)
    to get — maigrir (7)
things: how are — ? ça va? (1)
to think penser (12); croire (13)
    to — about penser à (12)
    to — of penser de (14)
thirsty: to be — avoir soif (8)
thirteen treize (4)
thirty trente (7)
    6:30 six heures et demie (9)
this ce (cet), cette (10)
    — is c'est (1); (on telephone) ici (9)
those ces (10)
    — are ce sont (2)

thousand mille (13); (in dates) mil (13)
three trois (4)
Thursday jeudi *m.* (7)
ticket le billet (10)
tie la cravate (14)
tiger le tigre (12)
time la fois (18)
    a long — longtemps (18)
    (at) what —? à quelle heure? (6)
    on — à l'heure (17)
    —s (in math) fois (13)
    what — is it? quelle heure est-il? (6)
timetable l'horaire *m.* (18)
tip le pourboire (15)
    — included le service est compris (15)
tired fatigué, -e (10)
to à (2;5); chez (2); en (9)
today aujourd'hui (7)
    — is c'est aujourd'hui (7); nous sommes (7)
tomato la tomate (16)
tomorrow demain (9)
too aussi (4); trop (7)
    — much, — many trop de (16)
tourism le tourisme (13)
tourist le/la touriste (18)
town la ville (9)
    to (in) — en ville (9)
traffic la circulation (18)
train le train (4)
    — station la gare (2)
to train faire un stage (13)
training period le stage (13)
tree l'arbre *m.* (4)
trip le voyage (17)
    on a — en voyage (17)
    to take a — faire un voyage (8)
truck le camion (4)
truly vraiment (10)
trunk la malle (18)
Tuesday mardi *m.* (7)
turkey le dindon (12)
to turn:
    — red rougir (7)
    — yellow jaunir (7)

TV la télé (6)
    — news le journal télévisé (6)
twelve douze (4)
twenty vingt (4)
twice deux fois (18)
two deux (4)
typically typiquement (16)

ugly laid, -e (8)
umbrella le parapluie (14)
uncle l'oncle *m.* (3)
under sous (3)
to understand comprendre (12)
unfortunately malheureusement (9)
unhappy triste (6)
United States les Etats-Unis *m.pl.* (17)
university l'université *f.* (11)
unknown inconnu, -e (9)
unoccupied libre (10)
until jusqu'à (11)
up: to go — monter (17)
us nous (3)
    to (for, from) — nous (14)
vacation les vacances *f.pl.* (7)
    on — en vacances (7)
    to spend a — passer des vacances (17)
    to take a — prendre des vacances (17)
van la caravane (17)
vegetable le légume (15)
very très (1)
    — much beaucoup (5)
villa la villa (2)
to visit (someone) faire une visite à (14); (a place) visiter (17)
volleyball le volleyball (9)
    to play — jouer au volleyball (9)

to wait (for) attendre (10)
    to — on servir (9)
waiter le garçon (10)

waitress la serveuse (10)
wallet le portefeuille (14)
to want vouloir (11)
warm chaud, -e (8)
  it's — out il fait chaud (7)
  to be — (of people) avoir
    chaud (8)
wastebasket la corbeille (1)
watch la montre (14)
to watch regarder (6)
water l'eau, pl. les eaux f. (8)
  mineral — l'eau minérale
    f. (15)
to water-ski faire du ski nautique (8)
way: on the — (to) en route
  (pour) (11)
we nous, on (2)
to wear porter (6)
weather le temps (7)
Wednesday mercredi m. (7)
week la semaine (7); huit
  jours (17)
  two —s quinze jours (17)
weight:
  to gain — grossir (7)
  to lose — maigrir (7)
welcome: you're — je vous
  (t') en prie (5)
well bien (1)
  to look — avoir bonne
    mine (16)
well-behaved sage (10)
west l'ouest m. (17)
western (movie) le western (9)

what? qu'est-ce qui? (5);
  qu'est-ce que? (6);
  quel?, quelle? (6;7;
  12); que? (12); quoi?
  (13)
when quand (6)
where où (1)
  from — d'où (17)
which? quel?, quelle? (12)
while pendant que (6)
white blanc, blanche (6)
who qui (1)
whom? qui est-ce que? (12)
  to — à qui (13)
why pourquoi (4)
wide large (9)
wife la femme (12)
wind le vent (7)
  it's windy il fait du vent
  (7)
window la fenêtre (1)
wine le vin (15)
winter l'hiver m. (7)
with avec (3)
  to go — accompagner (14)
without sans (18)
Wolof le wolof (9)
woman la femme (10)
word le mot (11)
work le travail, pl. les travaux
  (13)
to work travailler (6)
worker l'ouvrier m., l'ouvrière
  f. (13)
world le monde (17)

worried inquiet, -iète (10)
wristwatch la montre (14)
to write écrire (14)
wrong:
  to be — avoir tort (8)
  what's —? qu'est-ce qui ne
    va pas? (16)

year l'année f. (7); l'an m. (12)
  to be . . . —s old avoir
    . . . ans (12)
yellow jaune (5)
  to turn — jaunir (7)
yes oui (1); si (8)
yesterday hier (11)
you toi (1); tu (2); vous (1;2)
  to (for, from) — te (t'),
    vous (14)
young jeune (5)
  — lady mademoiselle, pl.
    mesdemoiselles (1;3);
    la demoiselle (15)
younger cadet, -ette (12)
your ta, ton, tes (3); votre,
  vos (4)
Yugoslavia la Yougoslavie
  (17)

zero zéro (7)
zoo le zoo (12)

Index

à:
+ determiner 64, 71, 291
+ qui and quoi 212
replaced by indirect object
pronoun 233, 238, 272
uses of 33, 71
vs. chez 17
with geographical terms 135,
155, 281, 291
accents 15
adjectives 67–68, 90, 122, 140–
141, 158, 193, 213
beau, nouveau, vieux 122,
193
ending in a nasal vowel 140–
141, 193
interrogative 198
of nationality 135, 155
position of 68, 158, 193, 213
possessive *see* determiners
adverbs, position of 175, 187
age 187
aller 21
future formed with 145, 304
articles *see* determiners
aspirate *h* 137, 155, 245
auxiliary verbs *see* passé composé
and verbs + infinitive
avoir 55
expressions with 117; *see also*
Vocabulaire
in telling age 187
passé composé formed with
175
past participle of 268

chez 9, 17
commands *see* imperative

connaître 302
past participle of 302
croire 211
past participle of 267

dates 101
days of the week 101
months 101
years 219
de:
after negative 108, 126
before plural adjectives 213
+ determiner 71
in expressions of quantity 310
partitive 250, 310
possessive 25
+ quoi 227
used with venir 285
uses of 71
with geographical terms 291
determiners:
definite 5, 23, 250
demonstrative 162
indefinite 108, 126, 213, 250,
310
partitive 250, 310
possessive 31, 38, 51
with languages 155
with professions 171, 185, 207
dire 231
past participle of 268
direct object pronouns *see* pronouns

écrire 231
past participle of 268
elision:
with definite determiner 5
with est-ce que 66
with je 55, 84
with ne 56
with nonaspirate *h* 137
with object pronouns 216,
233, 238, 272
with si 135
en:
as object pronoun 255–256,
272, 304

with articles of clothing 33,
47
with geographical terms 291
with passé composé 272
with vehicles 48
-er verbs 84
passé composé of 175
être 36
passé composé formed with
286
past participle of 268

faire 120
expressions with 99, 120–121;
see also Vocabulaire
past participle of 268
falloir (il faut) 135
future formed with aller 145, 304

gender 5, 21
geographical terms:
cities, 135, 155, 291
countries 281–283, 291

immediate future 145, 304
immediate past 285
imperative 21, 84
negative 126
see also individual verb listings
indirect object pronouns *see* pronouns
infinitive 23
see also verbs + infinitive
interrogative:
adjectives 198
est-ce que 23, 66, 197–198
inversion 197–198, 212
negative 126, 197
question words 64, 66, 83, 101,
197–198, 212, 227
intonation 14
inversion 197–198, 212
-ir verbs 139
passé composé of 180
-ir/-iss- verbs 103
passé composé of 180